The Generals of
Gettysburg

The Leaders of
America's Greatest Battle

Larry Tagg

- For Mariel & Eric -

Savas Publishing Company
1475 S. Bascom Ave., Suite 204, Campbell, California 95008

The General of Gettysburg:
The Leaders of America's Greatest Battle
by Larry Tagg

Printing Number
10 9 8 7 6 5 4 3 2 1
First Edition

ISBN 1-882810-30-9

Copyright © 1998 Larry Tagg
Maps copyright © 1998 Morningside Books

Includes bibliographic references

Savas Publishing Company
1475 S. Bascom Avenue, Suite 204,
Campbell, California 95008   (800) 732-3669

This book is printed on 50-lb. Natural acid-free paper

The paper in this book meets or exceeds the guidelines for permanence and durability
of the Committee on Production Guidelines for Book Longevity of the Council on Library Resources

Table of Contents

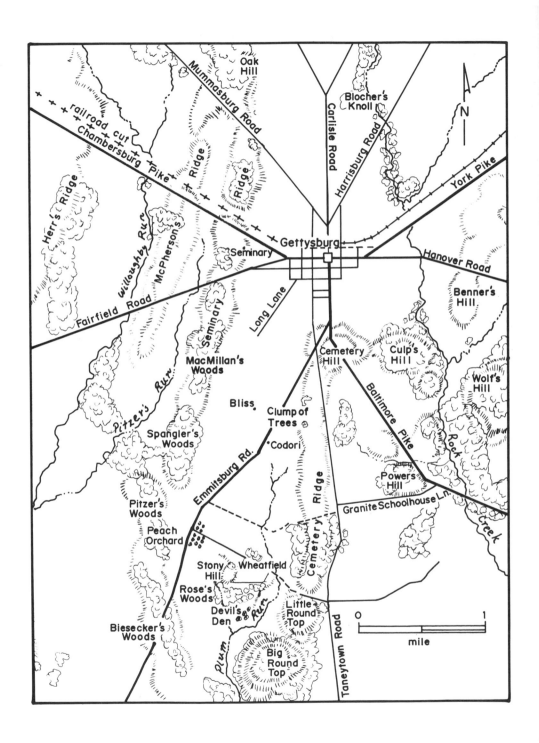

Introduction

"Character is destiny."

Twenty-five-hundred-years ago, Greek philosopher Heraclitus wrote a text that has since been lost to history. His students, however, remembered his theories and ideas and preserved them for scholars as a series of epigrams. The terse but sage three words that open this introduction constitute Heraclitus' most famous and ingenious turn of mind. "Character," which may be defined as "the attributes or features that make up and distinguish the individual," is a powerful thing. Writers of fiction have long recognized this, and thus the character of protagonists and antagonists is a central engine in every great work of literature. Writers of military history, on the other hand, often stress strategy and tactics at the expense of the character of their subjects.

The traditional recounting of battles and strategy will never lose its appeal. The mythic attraction of the American Civil War will not diminish; indeed, in our anti-heroic society, the intrigue of a war where opponents stood and fired at each other while only a few paces apart may be greater than ever. But as the Army of Northern Virginia's preeminent historian, Douglas Southall Freeman, noted more than a half-century ago, "Further study. . .may prove both more profitable and more interesting where it deals with men and morale than where it merely describes in new terms the familiar strategy and battles." Certainly Freeman, better than any other historian of his age, appreciated the impact of character on Robert E. Lee's judgments and actions

The Battle of Gettysburg, in particular, is ripe for the approach suggested by Freeman, especially since the main events of the engagement (indeed, nearly all aspects of it) are well established. New insight into the fight might best be gained by examining the lives of the leaders who served on that field. What can be learned by studying these men? What "attributes or features" distinguished them as individuals and as army officers? What role did their pre-Gettysburg experiences have on the way in which they conducted themselves in Pennsylvania during those several fateful days in July 1863? Did officers who methodically worked their way through the ranks perform better at Gettysburg? How did the "civilian" generals, i.e., those without professional military training, fair under the pressure of mid-1863 combat? It is hoped that my examination of the character and military development of the leaders at Gettysburg will shed some new light on why the battle turned out as it did, and why a particular officer acted a certain way in a certain situation.

But I did not write *The Generals of Gettysburg* to illustrate the obvious wisdom of Heraclitus or Freeman; I wrote it because I became intrigued with the men who found themselves in one of the most horrific battles in history. To many of us, they seem exotic warriors from a more romantic time, an era that appears to have tolerated eccentricity much more easily than our own. In some respects the men who fought at Gettysburg were more sentimental than we are, and their biblically-inspired forms of written expression appear quite foreign to people of the post-modern era. These men were plunged into the cruelest of man's occupations—and set about producing some of the highest drama in our nation's history.

Unfortunately, it is sometime difficult (especially for the lay reader) to readily uncover the background, the "attributes or features" of these men. Most of the reference books on Civil War generals tend to read like dictionaries—dry listings of dates and events, of ranks and battles fought—and thus are mainly useful to other historians. Such studies usually do not possess the power to stir one's imagination. It is my hope the present volume will add color, depth, and breadth to the portrait of the actors in this central American drama.

As I began devouring Civil War literature many years ago, my mind formed indelible images and certain conceptions (and misconceptions) of these generals, and thus the genesis of this book came about. As time passed and my interest in the subject grew more serious, I resolved to set about the task of profiling the generals of Gettysburg—more for my own use than anything else. Every time I read an account that mentioned some interesting trait, foible, or anecdote about such men, I faithfully scribbled down the information and eventually entered these snippets of material into my computer. After years of voraciously reading scholarly book-length studies, magazine and journal articles, and to a lesser degree, manuscript materials, and walking about on the field of Gettysburg, I had catalogued a good bit of information on these officers. I discovered that the sketches of the generals uncover a kaleidoscopic variation of colorful backgrounds and produce a lively pastiche portrait of broader American society in the Civil War era.

One of the best sources on these Gettysburg generals are the words that flowed from their pens immediately before and after the campaign: their letters, telegrams and battle reports. I thus had a stroke of luck when a friend lent me his 128 volumes of *The War of the Rebellion: The Official Records of the Union and Confederate Armies*. Plunging into the *Official Records*, or simply *OR*, added a new dimension to my understanding of what had transpired in Pennsylvania. The twelve months prior to Gettysburg, from June 1862 to June 1863, witnessed a level of fighting between the opposing armies in the East unprecedented in the annals of warfare. Mechanicsville, Gaines' Mill, Savage's Station, Glendale, Malvern Hill, Cedar Mountain, Second Bull Run, South Mountain, Sharpsburg, Fredericksburg, Chancellorsville, Brandy Station, plus the dozens—hundreds—of skirmishes and smaller engagements, claimed the lives of tens of thousands of Americans and provided officers with harsh practical experience of leading men in the unforgiving cauldron of combat. The detailed reports of these engagements provide a wealth of evidence as to how these officers acted when the bullets flew thick and fast. Some grew timid and listless, while others rose to the occasion and did their duty as they understood it; others had a tendency toward rashness, a trait often exacerbated by the thunder of discharging weapons. Additionally, a thorough examination of the *OR* frequently yielded interesting tales of lesser-known leaders, many of whom, to my earlier amazement and fascination, were. . .amateurs.

When Fort Sumter fell in 1861, the U.S. Army numbered a mere 16,000 soldiers. By the summer of 1863, hundreds of thousands of men had enlisted in the Union and Confederate armies. To lead these huge numbers of new recruits, both Union and Confederate governments were at pains to produce legions of new officers. The "Minute-men" tradition developed during America's Revolutionary period held that military skills were easily learned, and "anybody" could lead men into combat. In a similar democratic vein, the rank and file demanded and received the right to elect their officers. After all, they had elected their political representatives, why not elect their captains and colonels as well? Political interests often determined who would wear a general's stars. Both Jefferson Davis and Abraham Lincoln nominated their respective generals, and political allegiance was often paramount in the consideration of candidates for promotion. Politicians from every state campaigned energetically for high rank either for themselves or another. The result was that thousands of new military officers were appointed and elected from the pool of politicians, lawyers, landed gentry, railroad executives, and businessmen. By July 1863, many of these amateurs had risen to high rank.

Though most of the Old Army officers had been schooled at West Point, the Virginia Military Institute, or some other military academy, they were nearly as unprepared as their amateur comrades for fighting on the scale presented by the Civil War. In 1861, when he was commissioned into Confederate service after two decades in the Regular Army, Brig. Gen. Richard "Dick" Ewell candidly remarked that he had learned everything about commanding fifty dragoons and had forgotten everything else. Every professional officer, if he were honest, would have had to make a similar admission, for they all were inexperienced in the business of commanding large formations of soldiers in combat. They learned on the job, and by the third year of the war, almost all those who had risen to the rank of general were experienced veterans of large-scale, desperately fought battles. Most, in fact, had seen as many battles in the previous year as their European counterparts saw in a lifetime. By virtue of this experience, many of the leaders who fought in the fields, wood lots, rocky slopes, and streets of Gettysburg were among the finest combat commanders in the world.

Despite the experience of some, however, there were novel factors that added to the uncertainty of the leadership situation in both armies that summer. Lt. Gen. Thomas "Stonewall" Jackson's mortal wounding at Chancellorsville had catalyzed the reorganization of Gen. Robert E. Lee's Army of Northern Virginia from two corps into three. Richard Ewell and Ambrose P. Hill were newly-minted lieutenant generals and leading corps for the first time when they clashed with the enemy at Gettysburg. Five of Lee's nine division commanders had little or no experience in their present positions, and recently promoted generals commanded six of Lee's thirty-seven brigades, with another half dozen under colonels who had yet to show they deserved a wreath around their colonel's stars.

Major General George Meade's Army of the Potomac had undergone perhaps an even more profound shake-up in the composition of its regiments and command structure preceding Gettysburg. Some 40,000 men had left the army through May and June (about half were casualties at Chancellorsville, and the remaining half were men who had gone home when their enlistments expired). Meade became the Army of the Potomac's commander only three days before the battle in a move that smacked of desperation on the part of Washington. None of the Union army's seven corps commanders and only two of the nineteen division commanders had been in place at Antietam nine months before. In fact, fully one third of these men had been assigned to their units in the eight weeks leading up to Gettysburg.

This volume seeks to explore the ramifications these sweeping changes had on the central battle of the Civil War by examining the backgrounds, personalities, and performances of both the neophyte and veteran commanders. Instead of trying to reach some sweeping conclusion for each officer, it seemed appropriate to fully set forth the background of the subject, together with a succinct yet sufficiently detailed discussion of his service at Gettysburg—and let the reader reach his own conclusions.

One common thread that runs through many of the accounts that follow is the mayhem bullets and shells caused to the bodies and minds of these men. Officers in the Civil War were often required to gain the loyalty of their troops by proving their bravery and contempt for danger in battle, and commanders often rode at the head of their men in order to rally and inspire them in desperate times. The natural result of such a tactic was that the casualty rate for generals was fifty percent higher than for privates. In the year before Gettysburg, large numbers of generals were laid low for long periods while they recuperated from hideous injuries. Where possible, I tried to be as specific as I could about their wounds, tracing the paths of the bullets and the damage they caused. This is not from some morbid fascination, but out of a respect for the bravery and sacrifice of those maimed and as an antidote to the romantic idealization of war.

I did not set out to write a battle history of Gettysburg, for others have already capably performed that service. Nor is *The Generals of Gettysburg* intended to be a definitive accounting of what each of these men did there. My main purpose was to produce a book which would illuminate *who* these remarkable men were, while at the same time offering something enjoyable to read and consider on several simultaneous levels. These men had much to do with determining the fate of our nation, and they acted and reacted in the only way they knew how.

Character *is* destiny.

LRT

February 1998

Note on Numbers and Sources

As one might imagine, the size of the armies that fought at Gettysburg is in dispute. I believe the best source on this subject is John Busey and David Martin, *Regimental Strengths at Gettysburg* (Baltimore, 1982), and I have relied on this work for the figures provided herein. Any errors of course, are mine.

Concluding each entry in this study is a brief listing of suggested further readings. The nearly endless ocean of sources and source material on Gettysburg makes it impossible to do little more than scratch at the surface.

I have tried to send readers to a few specific sources tailored to each subject, as opposed to generalized campaign or Civil War histories. (This is not always possible, for many of these men have little or nothing written about them.) Thus, Edwin B. Coddington's *The Gettysburg Campaign: A Study in Command* (New York, 1968), perhaps the best single volume on the subject, is not listed after each entry, nor are citations to the *Official Records*. Similarly, Douglas Southall Freeman's *Lee's Lieutenants: A Study in Command*, vol. 3 (New York, 1944) provides insightful information on almost every Southern officer found within the pages of my book, although I utilized it sparingly and usually when other more specific sources were not available. The same holds true for the *Official Records*; readers are encouraged, if they wish to read and study at that level, to seek out the set themselves. All 128 volumes are now available on a single CD-Rom by Broadfoot Publishing Company, which makes researching with the cumbersome and poorly indexed collection much easier.

The best Gettysburg research has been churned out in the last ten years, and much of it is found in *The Gettysburg Magazine*, published bi-annually by Robert Younger of Morningside Press. This magnificent periodical has been setting the standard for scholarship on this campaign for almost a decade, and is required reading for professionals and general readers alike. It was indispensable to me in writing this book.

Acknowledgments:

During the course of working on this book, I became indebted to many people for their inspiration, advice, and help. It is impossible to thank everyone, and I apologize in advance if I inadvertently left out anyone.

I would first like to thank Russ Rider, who regaled me with tales of Civil War generals and so planted the seeds of inspiration for this project. I would also like to thank Jody Caldarulo, who loaned me his mammoth set of *The War of the Rebellion: The Official Records of the Union and Confederate Armies,* without which this book would not have been possible. John J. Hennessy, one of the true scholars of the Army of the Potomac, corresponded with me and helped formulate my approach to my topic.

Others who offered information about particular generals or sources were: D. Scott Hartwig and Alan Gaff, who helped examine the performance of Brig. Gen. Solomon Meredith; Helen A. Shaw and Marshall D. Krolick helped clear up an ambiguity in the existing literature concerning Col. William Gamble; Richard Rollins on Pickett's Charge and some queries on Col. John Brockenbrough's whereabouts on July 3; Bob Huddleston and John Leo helped search for new sources; Bradley Eide shared his considerable knowledge about Brig. Gen. Samuel Zook; Norm Stevens gave information on Col. Joseph Fisher; Ken Woolley shared material on Brig. Gen. Francis Barlow; Doug Cubbison provided information on Brig. Gen. John Geary; John M. Kelly helped with material on Brig. Gen. Alexander Webb; Tom Shay shared facts regarding Brig. Gen. John Caldwell; Kevin S. Coy shared information on Col. Edward Cross; and R. D. Winthrop provided facts on Brig. Gen. Judson Kilpatrick. I am indebted to each of you and to all the others that assisted me in this project, including editor Dana B. Shoaf, whose timely exertions and helpful suggestions strengthened the text significantly.

Many of these ladies and gentlemen may be found regularly exchanging information on the Internet's Gettysburg Discussion Group. The indefatigable Dennis and Bob Lawrence moderate this excellent source of information about the battle, and the group's web site may be found at: www.arthes.com/gdg/.

I would be remiss if I did not thank John Heiser for his excellent maps, and the wonderful gang at Prussia Graphics in Santa Clara, California—Monalisa, Susan, and Dave—who went above and beyond the call helping with this book. To all of them a mighty "Huzzah!"

Throughout the project, I have been assisted and advised by my publisher and general editor, Theodore P. Savas, without whose gentle urgings I would have gone to considerably less trouble in the research and scope of this book.

ARMY OF THE POTOMAC

(93,514 MEN / 372 GUNS)

MAJOR GENERAL
GEORGE GORDON MEADE

Before sunrise on June 28, 1863, three days before the opening shots of the crucial battle of the war, a messenger woke George Meade in his tent and informed him that he was now commander of the Army of the Potomac. Meade was so surprised by the visit that when he first awoke to find the man in his tent, his first thought was that he was being placed under arrest. He tried to decline the promotion, but was told that it was impossible—the army was now his whether he liked it or not.

The common response among the men, when they heard the news, was "What's Meade ever done?" On horseback, he was not a figure who brought forth wild waves of cheering. He was utterly lacking in charisma and was incapable of arousing anyone's enthusiasm by his mere presence—as McClellan and Hooker had; even the incompetent Burnside looked downright Napoleonic next to Meade. He gave more the impression of a dried-up professor than the leader of a volunteer army. Tall and thin, near-sighted and rather ungainly, at age forty-seven he looked considerably older. He was thin-faced with a "small and compact" balding head, a grizzled beard, large pouches under bespectacled blue eyes that were "serious, almost sad," a great hawkish nose, and a broad high forehead. The total effect was thoughtful and patrician.

And Meade was a patrician, in a nineteenth-century Philadelphia sort of way. Born in Cadiz, Spain of a prominent Philadelphia family with international mercantile interests, he graduated from West Point in 1832 in the upper third of his class. On his twenty-fifth birthday he married Margaretta Sergeant, daughter of John Sergeant, running mate of Henry Clay in the 1832 presidential election. Meade was,

however, a completely unassuming man. Colonel Philip de Trobriand, a brigade commander in the III Corps, wrote that he "was more reserved than audacious, more modest than presumptuous, on which account he treated his corps commanders more as friends than as inferiors." His chief of artillery Henry J. Hunt, though never his close friend, was pleased to have him as a commander because, in Hunt's opinion, Meade was a gentleman. There was no trace of self-seeking in Meade's letters to his wife. In a letter written shortly before his promotion to command of the army he soberly analyzed his chances for the appointment and concluded:

I do not. . .stand any chance, because I have no friends, political or others, who press or advance my claims or pretensions, and there are so many others who are pressed by influential politicians that it is folly to think I stand any chance upon mere merit alone. Besides, I have not the vanity to think my capacity so pre-eminent, and I know there are plenty of others equally competent with myself, though their names may not have been so much mentioned.

One of Meade's qualifications was coolness under fire. On one occasion, mounted with his staff, he surveyed the situation through field glasses while Rebel bullets whizzed and buzzed all around. His staffers wished he would find what he was looking for so they could all scramble back to safety. He lowered his glasses slowly and looked around at his nervous cadre of officers. "This is pretty hot," he remarked, "it may kill some of our horses." His fearlessness had resulted in his being wounded twice by bullets almost simultaneously at the Battle of Glendale during the Peninsula Campaign; the first hit him in the fleshy part of the forearm, but the other entered his right side and exited an inch from his spine, just above the hip. At Fredericksburg two bullets pierced his hat, while at South Mountain, a spent piece of canister badly bruised his thigh. His horse, "Old Baldy," was wounded under him at Second Bull Run and again at Antietam.

In his letters to his wife Meade showed a willingness to comment frankly on every facet of the war effort. This love of truth and dedication to duty may help explain an element of his nature which was universally remarked upon by his contemporaries—his temper. An energetic and exacting man, Meade was well-known for his violent impatience with what he deemed stupidity, negligence, or laziness. He would erupt quickly in outbursts of rage or annoyance, especially under the stress of active campaigning or a pitched battle. As his aide Theodore Lyman expressed it: "I don't know any thin old gentleman...who, when he is wrathy, exercises less of Christian charity than my well-beloved chief!" Another who worked with him put it this way: "I never saw a man in my life who was so characterized by straightforward truthfulness as he is...and woe to those, no matter who they are, who do not do it right!" Though irritable and peppery under stress, his decisions were "always founded in good reason," and while his manner was hard on people, it brought about results. Lyman wrote that Meade was "always stirring up somebody. But by worrying, and flaring out unexpectedly on various offi-

cers, he does manage to have things pretty shipshape.

"Though too sparing in his praise of the work of his subordinates—partly out of a reluctance to show his feelings and partly out of an Old Army sense that total effort was each man's duty—he exhibited signs of a more pleasant side. When not absorbed with his work, Meade was a different person, telling funny stories with "great fluency and . . . elegant language," and on occasion would sit by the campfire "talking familiarly with the aides." Such was not the norm however, and he usually kept himself apart and made no effort to make himself popular. He made it a rule not to speak to members of the press, and in retaliation journalists agreed among themselves not to mention him in dispatches except in reference to setbacks. Soldiers depended on the newspapers for news as much as anybody, so his blacklisting by the reporters probably explains why Meade's ascension to command came as such a surprise to the rank and file. Their superior officers, however, were better acquainted with Meade's record.

In the first months of the war he was named brigadier general of volunteers and given a brigade in the Pennsylvania Reserve division. In the Army of the Potomac's first action on the Peninsula in the summer of 1862, his Pennsylvania Reserves saw more action than any other division in the army, and he rendered heroic service and was twice wounded amid the hottest of the fighting. Meade returned to duty forty-two days later before he had fully recovered his strength. At the end of that summer of 1862, he was again commanding his brigade at Second Bull Run, where the Pennsylvania Reserves were one of the few formations to keep their discipline in the disastrous loss; the men also made a heroic stand on Henry Hill to protect the retreating army against Confederate pursuit.

Meade was in command of the division when it stormed the heights at South Mountain, so exciting the admiration of his corps commander that the man was heard to exclaim, "Look at Meade! Why, with troops like those, led in that way, I can whip anything!" A few days later at the Battle of Antietam, General McClellan himself selected Meade—in preference to others his superior in rank—to replace the wounded Joe Hooker a the head of the First Corps. After the battle, President Lincoln and his entourage rode over the field with a dozen generals, including Meade. While they rode, General McClellan described the battle for Lincoln. According to Meade in a letter to his wife, McClellan stated, "it was here that Meade did this and here that Meade did that. It was very gratifying." The review of the field acquainted the Commander in Chief with Meade, probably for the first time.

It was Meade's division at the Battle of Fredericksburg in December 1862 that provided the only success of the day for the army, briefly breaking through the Confederate line before he was forced back for want of reinforcements. This famous exploit on the worst day in the history of the Army of the Potomac certainly further recommended Meade to Lincoln. After the Army of the Potomac had suffered the brunt of Jackson's flank assault at the Battle of Chancellorsville in May 1863, Hooker convened a meeting of his generals to discuss strategy. Meade argued vigorously for an attack against the enemy. "I have never known anyone so vehemently to advise an attack on the field of battle," exclaimed Col. Alexander Webb, one of Meade's staff officers. Meade was very assertive (as Reynolds put it) "in favor of an advance in the direction of Fredericksburg at daylight the next morning. . . ." Meade thought the issue of Washington's safety had become a cliche for this army, and "threw that out of the question altogether." Unfortunately for Federal arms, General Hooker lacked the nerve or judgment to go over to the offensive, and thus subsequently forfeited the battle.

Much of the talk in the officers' tents after the disappointment at Chancellorsville, then, revolved around Meade. Three corps commanders who were senior to Meade in rank—Generals Couch, Slocum, and Sedgwick—all sent word to him that they were willing to serve under his leadership. Couch, who was actively seeking the replacement of Hooker, mentioned only Meade for the post when questioned by an official from Washington. Sedgwick was also heard to say, when interviewed, "Why, Meade is the proper one to command this army." Finally, the able General John Reynolds, also an early commander of the Pennsylvania Reserves, when asked after Chancellorsville if he would command the army, declined and suggested Meade as the best suited for the task. After the failure of a prima donna like Joe Hooker, Meade's gritty personality and lack of flamboyance were undoubtedly viewed as positive traits. President Lincoln was also swayed by the fact that Meade made his home in Philadelphia, thinking that as a Pennsylvanian he would "fight well on his own dunghill." Thus it was that the early-morning messenger from Washington appeared suddenly in Meade's tent on June 28.

Through it all, George Meade was very much a family man, devoted to his wife and seven children. If he was known as "a damned old goggle-eyed snapping turtle" to his men, his temper never appeared in his letters home. "I think a great deal about you, and all the other dear children," he wrote in one letter home to a daughter in the spring of 1862. "I often picture to myself as I last saw you—yourself, Sarah, and Willie lying in bed, crying, because I had to go way, and while I was scolding you for crying, I felt like crying myself." The old general continued, writing, "It is very hard to be kept away from you, because there is no man on earth that loves his children more dearly than I do, or whose happiness is more dependent on being with his family. Duty, however, requires me to be here, to do the little I can to defend our old flag, and whatever duty requires us to do, we should all, old and young, do cheerfully, however disagreeable it may be."

Having been in command of the army for only three days when Gettysburg opened, Meade was handicapped by his uncertainty as to what it could be realistically called upon to do. This consideration affected his style of command. In stark contrast to his opponent, Robert E. Lee, Meade was actively and directly involved in the events on the battlefield. He had been a division and a corps commander too long and too recently to stand aloof at headquarters while others moved the army's huge formations across the landscape, and his nervous energy required that he be active. He was constantly in the saddle, issuing orders and seeing that they were obeyed. One of those carrying his directives was his second son George, who had joined his staff one month earlier and who was with him as an aide throughout Gettysburg. Lt. Frank Haskell, in his Gettysburg sketch of Meade, wrote, "His habitual personal appearance is quite careless, and it would be rather difficult to make him look well dressed." At Gettysburg his dress was perfectly in keeping with his personal lack of airs—he wore the familiar dark blue flannel blouse with two-star shoulder straps, field cap, light blue pantaloons tucked into his high-top boots, an officer's leather belt and the regulation sword. Meade was ready for army command, and he was about to prove it.

GETTYSBURG: From his headquarters at Taneytown, Meade sent out the day's marching orders for the Army of the Potomac a little after midnight on July 1. These directives moved the army forward on a broad front, to prevent Lee from slipping around either flank and threatening Washington or Baltimore. On the left, Reynolds advanced his First Corps to Gettysburg, followed closely by the Eleventh, with the Third Corps within supporting distance at Emmitsburg. In the center, the Twelfth Corps would advance to Two Taverns (also within supporting distance of Gettysburg), while the Second Corps would remain in reserve at Taneytown. On the right, the Fifth Corps would move to Hanover, supported by the Sixth Corps moving to Manchester. Thinking that Lee slightly outnumbered him, Meade also sent out a second, conditional plan calling for a defensive fall-back to Pipe Creek in northern Maryland. The general blueprint for this strategy was set forth in an order called the "Pipe Creek Circular."

Meade remained at Taneytown on July 1, and his first news from the front came about 11:30 a.m. when Reynolds informed him that the Confederates were advancing in strong force, and he (Reynolds) would do everything possible to keep them from seizing "the heights beyond the town." Meade's initial fear was that Reynolds would fail to hold the town, retreat toward Emmitsburg, and uncover the road to Taneytown, thus exposing the army's center. Meade responded by ordering Winfield Hancock to begin marching his Second Corps from Taneytown toward Gettysburg.

About 1:00 p.m., Meade received word of Reynolds' death. Rather than go to the front himself, he preferred to remain in the rear and send his trusted friend Hancock to take command of the fighting. Since this involved placing Hancock over two officers who outranked him—Generals Dan Sickles and Oliver Howard, both of whose corps Meade assumed to be on or near the scene—Meade gave Hancock written authority and set him on his way by 1:30 p.m. By 6:00 that evening Meade announced in a telegram to Washington his decision to concentrate the army and fight at Gettysburg. His reasoning was sound: two corps (the First and Eleventh) were already there on good ground, two more (the Third and Twelfth) were close by, and two others (the Second and Fifth) would reach the field by the next day. In addition, Meade also believed the fighting on July 1 had caught the enemy without Lt. Gen. James Longstreet's First Corps. A flurry of orders followed: at 7:00 p.m. he ordered George Sykes to march his Fifth Corps to Gettysburg and at 7:30 p.m. sent John Sedgwick's Sixth Corps and Dan Sickles' Third Corps similar orders. Meade's only exhibition of negligence on July 1 consisted in his believing Slocum would be governed by events and move his Twelfth Corps forward the short distance to Gettysburg to reinforce the embattled defenders (Meade should have ordered him to do so). In fact, Slocum refused to march his corps toward Gettysburg until after the day's fighting was over. Meade arranged the movements of the supply train and the artillery reserve during the evening, then headed toward the battlefield at 10:00 p.m. with a small party of officers.

After an hour of riding along the Taneytown Road, the party reached the bivouac of the Second Corps, where Meade stopped briefly and gave orders to push it forward at daylight. Continuing, Meade arrived on Cemetery Hill about 11:30 p.m., greeted the assembled generals, and informed them that the rest of the army was moving up and that it would fight there. He then made a walking survey of the Union position in the moonlight. Just before dawn, he mounted and rode south along the line of Cemetery Ridge, then to Culp's Hill, making sketches of the terrain and indicating the positions he wished each corps to take. He then established his headquarters in a farmhouse centrally located on the Taneytown Road, eight hundred feet in the rear of Cemetery Hill.

All morning of July 2 there was a flow of orderlies and aides through the farmhouse, "dashing up with reports and off with orders" in preparation of the resumption of the battle. Despite his lack of sleep, Meade was alert and firm, even pleasant in his manner. By noon all of his corps were present except for the Sixth Corps, which was still marching hard to reach the field. His army was deployed, from left to right, as follows: Sickles' Third Corps, on the southern half of Cemetery Ridge with its left near Little Round Top; Hancock's Second Corps, extending the line north along Cemetery Ridge to Cemetery Hill; Howard's Eleventh Corps, on Cemetery Hill with remnants of the First Corps immediately behind in reserve; Slocum's Twelfth Corps, dug in on Culp's Hill. Sykes Fifth Corps had just arrived and was resting in the rear near Power's Hill. It was a powerful position from which to receive an attack.

Although Meade was expecting an attack on his right, where the enemy was visible, it was General Sickles and the unseen enemy on his left that would cause him trouble that day. Early that afternoon, Sickles' expressed agitation about where, exactly, he should put his corps. Staff members had shuttled back and forth—at one point Sickles himself appeared at headquarters for clarification. Meade's attention, however, was drawn to the other flank around Culp's Hill. In mid-afternoon, as soon as received word that Sedgwick's Sixth Corps was approaching the field, he dispatched orders to Sykes' Fifth Corps to move to the left to support Sickles. It was not until around 4:00 p.m. that Meade rode to the left to examine Sickles' position for himself, where he made a jaw-dropping discovery: Sickles had, without Meade's permission, advanced his line almost one mile westward to the high ground along the Emmitsburg Road. In addition to exposing the high hills behind his left, his right flank was now uncovered and well in advance of Hancock's Second Corps. Before anything could be done about this, the boom of cannon announced the opening of James Longstreet's massive attack against Sickles' front.

Recognizing Little Round Top as the key to the Union left, Meade sent his chief engineer, Maj. Gen. Gouverneur Warren, to investigate its status. When Warren sent back word that there were no troops there, Meade ordered Sykes to send troops from his Fifth Corps to occupy it. His order to Sykes was but the first in a series of improvisations Meade made involving several corps on the afternoon of July 2. He was near the battle line the whole afternoon, so near that his horse was badly wounded. At one point he rode forward with the skirmish line, waving his hat and yelling "Come on, gentlemen!" He timed his orders for reinforcements precisely, and hard-pressed units consistently received support at just the right moment. In the end, Longstreet's assault ground its way forward up the southern end of Cemetery Ridge and the slope of Little Round Top, but was turned back. The defense of the left flank cost Meade thirteen shattered brigades—some so completely used up they could not again be relied upon as effective fighting organizations.

One of Meade's questionable decisions—and one that came as close to disaster as any—was the order pulling Slocum's

Twelfth Corps off Culp's Hill to reinforce the left. An earlier misunderstanding between Meade and Slocum arising out of the "Pipe Creek Circular" caused Slocum to believe he was the commander of the army's "Right Wing" (the Fifth and Twelfth Corps) throughout the battle at Gettysburg. This awkward situation led to organizational chaos within his corps—especially when most of the Twelfth Corps withdrew off Culp's Hill in the darkness to reinforce the embattled left flank.

A single brigade was left behind and the Confederates moved into the void, capturing abandoned lines late on the evening of July 2. At the end of the day, however, even with his left battered and his right partially in enemy hands, Meade could take satisfaction in the first tangible success the Army of the Potomac had enjoyed against Lee since Malvern Hill a year earlier. From about 9:00 that evening until midnight Meade met in his cramped headquarters with eleven of his top generals, who echoed Meade's resolve to "stay and fight it out."

Meade rose before dawn on July 3. Just before daybreak heavy fighting broke out on Culp's Hill, where the Twelfth Corps had returned to reclaim its abandoned lines. Meade had confidence in the ability of Twelfth Corps leaders Henry Slocum and Alpheus Williams, and he did not go in person to supervise their conduct of the battle. Instead, he sent a fresh Sixth Corps brigade to Culp's Hill as a reinforcement and advised Maj. Gen. Oliver Howard on nearby Cemetery Hill to have his men stand by to be ready to move there if needed. The battle raged all morning until 11:00 a.m., when the last of the Confederates on the hill were successfully driven off. The entire episode on that front—another tactical victory for the army—provided a backdrop to Meade's activities that morning. Witnesses described Meade as appearing confident, "more the General, less the student" than before, but retaining his "quick and nervous" manner. After the fighting ceased on Culp's Hill, Meade accepted Brig. Gen. John Gibbon's invitation for lunch, which he ate while seated on an empty cracker box in the company of some of his fellow generals. About noon, he rode along the length of Cemetery Ridge to Little Round Top, then returned to headquarters.

Meade's headquarters in the Widow Leister house was situated directly behind Cemetery Ridge, which was the target of the 150-gun Confederate cannonade that began around 1:00 p.m. The headquarters became a very dangerous place, and shells hit the house numerous times (one fragment wounded Maj. Gen. Dan Butterfield, Meade's chief of staff). Sixteen horses were killed while tied to the fence rail in the yard. Nevertheless, Meade was reluctant to move, afraid couriers with important news would be unable to locate him if he shifted his location. He eventually relented and briefly rode to Slocum's headquarters on Power's Hill, then changed his mind and returned to the center of his army. He received disturbing reports that his own artillery was inflicting but little harm in return, and Meade ordered his guns to cease fire, hoping the Rebels would follow suit and let the smoke clear so that enemy infantry could not approach unseen.

When the long ranks of three divisions of Confederate infantry appeared out of the woods on Seminary Ridge around 3:00 p.m. and headed toward the right center of the Union line on Cemetery Ridge, Meade did not react quickly to the danger. Although he eventually busied himself by sending for supporting columns from other parts of the line, they arrived too late to be of assistance in beating back Pickett's Charge. That task fell mainly on General Hancock's Second Corps, which was stretched out rather thinly on the ridge and outnumbered perhaps two to one. However, within about one hour the Army of the Potomac had beaten back one of the grandest attacks in history. Meade rode up to the ridge line in the swirling smoke and, when told the enemy had been turned back said simply, "Thank God." A second later he made a motion as if to take off his hat and wave it in the air, but he caught himself and merely waved his hand and cried, "Hurrah." He spurred his horse and made a triumphal ride along the ridge all the way to Little Round Top.

The battle was now in Meade's hands; would he go over to the offensive with a counterattack or remain in position, content with a defensive victory? The lateness in the day, the absence of the wounded Hancock, the fatigue of the men, the disorganized patchwork quilt of command that existed after three days of carnage, the long casualty lists, and the still-fearsome reputation of Lee all militated against a bold move at that hour. Recent and as yet unpublished scholarship also points to the fact that the army was desperately low on ammunition. Meade had won the crucial contest in Pennsylvania, and he now prudently refused to jeopardize that victory.

Although it is difficult to know for sure, President Lincoln may never have forgiven Meade for not destroying Lee north of the Potomac River. In addition to his opportunity at Gettysburg, Meade also trapped Lee's army against the swollen Potomac near Falling Waters ten days later, where he again declined to attack his wounded foe. His generals were also leery of attacking Lee, for his position was strong and his flanks were well anchored.

George Meade continued to command the Army of the Potomac until the end of the war, although his success in that position has been overshadowed by the presence of Ulysses S. Grant, who in March of 1864 had been made the commander-in-chief of all the Union armies.

General Meade died in 1872.

For further reading:

Cleaves, Freeman. *Meade of Gettysburg.* Norman, 1960.

Downs, David. "'His Left was Worth a Glance:' Meade and the Union Left on July 2, 1863." *Gettysburg Magazine*, #7, 1992.

Meade, George, Jr. *The Life and Letters of George Gordon Meade*, 2 vols. New York, 1913.

Pfanz, Harry W. *Gettysburg: Culp's Hill and Cemetery Hill.* Chapel Hill. 1993.

———. *Gettysburg: The Second Day.* Chapel Hill, 1987.

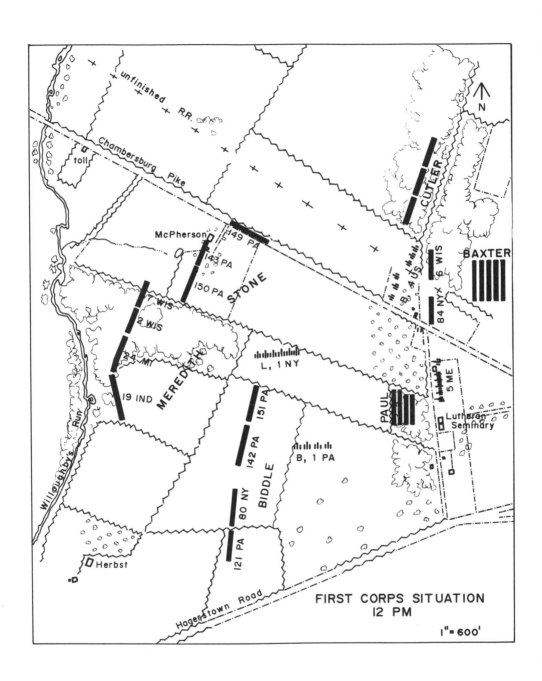

FIRST CORPS SITUATION
12 PM

1" = 600'

FIRST CORPS

(12,222 MEN / 28 GUNS)

MAJOR GENERAL
JOHN FULTON REYNOLDS

By the summer of 1863, John Reynolds, commander of the First Corps, was among the most respected men in the Army of the Potomac; not one negative comment about him from his contemporaries is recorded. After the Union debacle at Chancellorsville in May, President Lincoln, aware of the fact that Reynolds was the one universally admired major general his Eastern army possessed, invited him to the White House for a conference. What happened in the meeting was never recorded, but it is believed that Lincoln offered command of the army to Reynolds. Reynolds supposedly replied that he would accept this post only if he was promised a free hand in running the army and was shielded from the political interference that had plagued his predecessors. Lincoln was unable meet his terms. Reynolds thus returned to the head of the First Corps, and three weeks later, just before the crucial clash in Pennsylvania, command of the army was thrust on Maj. Gen. George Meade. When Reynolds heard the news, he put on his dress uniform and made a formal visit to the new army commander, who was wearing an old field-worn uniform and muddy boots. Meade rose to greet Reynolds, and began groping for words to express his discomfort at the awkward situation of being promoted over the man who had the day before been his superior. Reynolds gently stopped Meade and assured him that the job had gone to the right man.

Both meetings illustrate the respect John Reynolds had earned from his peers. "General Reynolds obeys orders literally himself, and expects all under him to do the same," wrote First Corps chief of artillery Col. Charles Wainwright. Maj. Gen. George McClellan had called him "remarkably brave and intelligent, an honest, true gentleman." Lt. Frank Haskell, Brig. Gen. John Gibbon's observant aide-de-camp, called Reynolds "one of the soldier generals of the army, a man whose soul was in his country's work." Admiration for him thus derived in part from his direct and unpretentious—even Spartan—manner. But he possessed other natural gifts as well. A handsome man of forty-two, Reynolds was a picture-perfect general in uniform—six feet tall, narrow-waisted, erect, with dark hair and eyes, beard neatly groomed, and a deep tan gained from years of outdoor life. He was magnificent to watch as he rode the battlefield, rated by consensus as one of the army's best horsemen.

Like many of the other corps commanders, Reynolds was considered a conservative Democrat of the McClellan mold, which made him suspect in the eyes of the radical members of the Joint Committee on the Conduct of the War. Senator Benjamin Wade, the chairman of the Joint Committee, had even declared that he wanted Reynolds removed from the army. But Reynolds was a quiet man about his politics, just as he was quiet about most everything else. This reserve regarding political matters disappointed some officers. "General Reynolds is very different from

[Maj. Gen. Joseph] Hooker," wrote one colonel, "in that he never expresses an opinion about other officers. . .I can get nothing out of him." It was his silence on matters regarding politics that made Reynolds untouchable to men like Wade.

Reynolds, a native of Lancaster, Pennsylvania (located fifty miles from the Gettysburg battlefield), received his early schooling in a nearby Moravian village. He attended the Lancaster County Academy and eventually found himself at West Point, where he graduated 26th among the 52 cadets of the class of 1841. Assigned to the artillery, he served for the next eighteen years against the Seminoles, in the Mexican War (where he was cited for bravery at Monterrey and Buena Vista), on the frontier, and in the Mormon Expedition in the late 1850s. In 1860, he was brought east and made Commandant of Cadets at West Point, where he also served as instructor of artillery, cavalry, and infantry tactics.

Reynolds' Civil War career is remarkable in that he was highly regarded despite a record with so few battlefield accomplishments. In August 1861 he was made brigadier general of volunteers and assigned to a brigade of the Pennsylvania Reserve Division, an "overflow" division of three brigades formed when Pennsylvania volunteers enlisted in numbers greater than the quota Lincoln initially requested. His brigade trained in the defenses of Washington until the following spring, when the Pennsylvania Reserves marched south to Fredericksburg as part of Maj. Gen. Irvin McDowell's First Corps, while the bulk of the Army of the Potomac fought with McClellan on the Peninsula. On June 10, 1862, McClellan persuaded Lincoln to release the Pennsylvania Reserve Division to him for the expected fighting around Richmond, and Reynolds' brigade was thus present for the Seven Days' Battles in late June.

Reynolds' Pennsylvanians first came under fire at Mechanicsville. They performed quite well and repulsed Maj. Gen. A. P. Hill's Light Division, a feat that earned Reynolds a postbattle commendation from Brig. Gen. George McCall. After the Battle of Gaines' Mill the next day, however, Reynolds—exhausted after two days of continuous fighting—fell asleep and was overlooked in the army's

retreat. It was a bad time to take nap. Reynolds was shaken awake by Rebel pickets the next morning, and he spent the next six weeks in Richmond's Libby Prison, mortified at being captured in such an ignominious manner.

Exchanged in early August, he returned to the Pennsylvania Reserves, and this time was assigned to command the entire division, since McCall had himself been captured only two days after Reynolds. Reynolds' Division joined Maj. Gen. John Pope's Army of Virginia in time for the Battle of Second Bull Run, where Reynolds' performance stood out—especially when compared against the plethora of miserable Federal efforts on that field. On the evening of the second day of the battle, when the Federal left had been crushed and Pope's entire army was fleeing the field, Reynolds marched his brigades onto Henry Hill for a last-ditch stand. He grabbed the flag of the 2nd Reserves regiment, waved it and yelled, "Now boys, give them the steel, charge bayonets, double quick!" Reynolds' counterattack stalled the Rebel advance and gained precious moments for the Union cause. He reformed his lines, clutched the banner of the 6th Reserves by its bullet-splintered staff, and rode the length of his line waving the flag overhead. His actions, said one of his awed men, "infus[ing] into the men a spirit anything else than one to run." Pope's retreating army owed its survival in large measure to Reynolds' powers of inspiration.

In the ensuing raid of Maryland by Robert E. Lee's victorious army, Pennsylvania governor Andrew Curtin, frantic in the belief that his state was about to be invaded, called out the local militia forces and pulled every string he had in Washington to obtain Reynolds as their commander. Both McClellan and Hooker complained that "a scared governor ought not to be permitted to destroy the usefulness of an entire division." Curtin prevailed, however, and Reynolds spent two weeks in Pennsylvania drilling old men and farm boys while the soldiers of his Reserve Division fought and died at the Battle of Antietam under the command of George G. Meade.

When he returned to the army at the end of September, Reynolds was promoted to the head of the First Corps (Joseph Hooker having been moved up to lead one of the "Grand Divisions created by Maj. Gen. Ambrose Burnside—the new commander of the Army of the Potomac.) At the December 13 Battle of Fredericksburg, it was Reynolds' old Pennsylvania Reserve Division—still led by Meade—that succeeded in making the only break in the Confederate line. However, Meade's men were unsupported by Reynolds' remaining two divisions, a failure most likely due to the fact that Reynolds' superiors, Maj. Gens. William Franklin and Ambrose Burnside, did not give the Pennsylvanian a clear idea of how his attack should proceed.

The Battle of Chancellorsville in May 1863 was the culmination of a week of high frustration for Reynolds. Originally posted on the extreme left flank of the Union army, Reynolds' First Corps had made several bridgeheads across the Rappahannock River when it was recalled and marched nearly twenty miles to the opposite end of the Federal line. Faulty communications slowed his countermarch. The delay left the Eleventh Corps, which was guarding the army's extreme right, unsupported and with its own right flank "in the air." The Eleventh Corps' was attacked end-on and nearly destroyed by Thomas J. "Stonewall" Jackson's Corps, a success which set in motion a series of setbacks that drained army commander Hooker's desire for offensive action. Once Reynolds' corps was finally in place, Hooker took a vote among the corps commanders on how to proceed with the battle. Reynolds, Meade, and Maj. Gen. Oliver Howard voted for advancing against the Rebels. Maj. Gens. Darius Couch and Daniel Sickles voted to retreat. Even though the vote was three to two favoring attack, Hooker decided to pull out and forfeit the battle. Leaving the meeting, Reynolds muttered loud enough for Hooker to hear, "What was the use of calling us together at this time of night when he intended to retreat anyhow?" Reynolds' 17,000-man corps was not engaged at Chancellorsville and suffered less than 300 casualties in the entire campaign. The disgusted Reynolds joined a chorus of voices urging Hooker's removal, which finally came about on June 28, just three days before Gettysburg.

It can be argued that John Reynolds achieved universal respect only by virtue of being the best of the mediocre cast of corps commanders in the Army of the Potomac. More likely, however, he had never really had a chance to show what he could do. By this third summer of the war, Reynolds had been in corps command longer than any other officer in the army.

As he rode toward the familiar landscape of Pennsylvania at the end of June, Reynolds wore a gold ring in the shape of two clasped hands on a chain about his neck. Engraved inside this treasured keepsake was the inscription "Dear Kate." Four years previously he had met Katherine "Kate" Hewitt as he returned from an assignment on the West Coast. If time permitted within the next few weeks, they had hoped to have a reunion in Philadelphia, so Kate could meet his family. The two planned to marry as soon as the war ended.

GETTYSBURG: For the final approach to Lee's army, Reynolds was entrusted by General George Meade with the advanced (left) wing of the Army of the Potomac—comprised of the First, Third, and Eleventh Corps. On July 1, riding north toward Gettysburg with Brig. Gen. James Wadsworth at the head of his First Division, Reynolds heard the boom of artillery ahead and received word from cavalryman Brig. Gen. John Buford of an enemy advance on the town along the Chambersburg Pike. He galloped toward the sounds of combat with his staff and, at a little after 10:00 a.m., found Buford's men doggedly slowing the Rebel advance toward McPherson's Ridge. Commending Buford on his choice of ground, Reynolds sent a message urging Howard to hurry the Eleventh Corps forward, and informed Meade that he would fight the Confederates " inch by inch, and if driven into the town I will barricade the streets and hold them as long as possible."

Having thus gone a long way toward choosing the ground over which the developing battle would be fought, he rode back to wait for Wadsworth's column. When Brig. Gen. Lysander Cutler's brigade arrived with Capt. James Hall's 2nd Maine Battery, Reynolds hurried them at the "double-quick" across the fields west of town to McPherson's Ridge, where Buford's cavalry had just started to give way before the attack of the brigades of Brig. Gens. James Archer and Joseph Davis.

After deploying Hall's battery and the regiments of Cutler's brigade, Reynolds hurried back to guide the Iron Brigade to the front. Alarmed at the headway Archer's Confederates were making south of the Chambersburg Pike, Reynolds exhorted the 2nd Wisconsin, the Iron Brigade's lead regiment, to hurry forward and meet the Confederates head on, shouting "Forward men, forward for God's sake and drive those fellows out of those woods." As the mid-westerners ran up the slope loading their muskets in the face of Archer's opening volleys, Reynolds rode at their rear. He turned in his saddle to look for supports, and was hit behind the right ear by a musket ball. He swayed in the saddle before falling to the ground, dying in the arms of his staff a few moments later.

With only a fraction of his corps available, the Pennsylvania general had placed himself at the head of his troops confronting an enemy of unknown size. Dedicated to an aggressive forward defense in the vanguard of the entire Army of the Potomac, Reynolds, at the cost of his own life, had blunted the Rebel thrust and bought valuable time that permitted the balance of Meade's army to take possession of the coveted high ground southeast of Gettysburg.

For further reading:

Hartwig, D. Scott, "The Defense of McPherson's Ridge." *Gettysburg Magazine*, # 1, 1989.

Nichols, Edward J. *Toward Gettysburg: A Biography of General John F. Reynolds.* Gaithersburg, 1987.

Riley, Michael A. *"For God's Sake, Forward": General John F. Reynolds, USA.* Gettysburg, 1995.

MAJOR GENERAL
JOHN NEWTON

Forty-year-old John Newton was the newest of the eight Union corps commanders present for duty on July 2. He had, in fact, been named to his post by Major General Meade only the night before, following Maj. Gen. John Reynolds' untimely death during the opening hours of the first day's fighting. Newton had no experience leading a corps, nor was he regarded as daring or brilliant, but Meade had only four major generals from which to choose as a replacement. These were Newton, Maj. Gen. Abner Doubleday (who had done a good job on July 1 as the acting commander of First Corps), Maj. Gen. David Birney (who had just received his commission the previous month), and Maj. Gen. Carl Schurz, a political appointee without extensive military education or experience. Schurz was out of the question for an Old Army man like Meade, who disdained political generals—especially from the Eleventh Corps. Birney had been too recently promoted. Of the two remaining candidates, Meade preferred Newton to Doubleday, who actually outranked Newton by date of commission, but in whom Meade had little confidence. The First Corps men themselves, however, who had witnessed Doubleday's skill and courage in the desperate afternoon hours of July 1 after Reynolds' death, grumbled in annoyance at the announcement of Newton's promotion. They felt that Doubleday, a true "First Corps man," deserved to command the corps.

In appearance, said Lt. Frank Haskell, Brig. Gen. John Gibbon's aide-de-camp, Newton was "a well-sized, shapely, muscular, well dressed man, with brown hair, with a very ruddy, clean-shaved, full face, blue eyes, blunt, round features, [who] walks very erect, curbs in his chin, and has somewhat of that smart sort of swagger, that people are apt to suppose characterizes soldiers." If Newton lacked Reynolds' military flair, he was considered competent by most of his fellow officers. Even Col. Charles Wainwright, Newton's new chief of artillery, who thought him "intensely lazy" and a lover of creature comforts when compared to the Spartan Reynolds, admitted that Newton was intelligent and competent. In 1842, he had graduated 2nd in a class of 56 at West Point and was assigned to the Engineers. His pre-war service included routine engineering duties, a stint as an instructor at the Academy, and the post of chief engineer on the 1858 expedition against the Mormons.

Although he began the war as an engineer, Newton was promoted to brigadier general of volunteers in the fall of 1861 and stationed with his brigade in Washington D.C., where he helped design the defenses until March 1862. With his brigade on the Peninsula in Maj. Gen. William B. Franklin's Sixth Corps, Newton led his men in action for the first time at Gaines' Mill, where he performed well in heavy fighting, and at Malvern Hill. He was praised for his actions at both engagements by his division commander, Brig. Gen. Henry Slocum.

In September 1862, after the fighting at Crampton's Gap on South Mountain, where his troops helped to overwhelm the Rebel defenders, Newton was recommended by Franklin for a promotion to major general "for his conspicuous gallantry and important services during the entire engagement." A few days later at the climactic Battle of Antietam, Newton's corps was held out of the action in a reserve position. Newton's Crampton's Gap performance, however, was still fresh in Franklin's mind when, in mid-October,

Slocum was promoted to the command of the Twelfth Corps. Franklin chose Newton to take Slocum's place at the head of Third Division, Sixth Corps. Newton led the division for eight months until he was summoned to Meade's headquarters on the evening of July 1 to replace Reynolds.

In the disaster at Fredericksburg in December 1862, Newton was again held in reserve and missed the fighting. The following week, Newton and Brig. Gen. John Cochrane traveled to Washington and met with President Lincoln to level complaints against army commander Maj. Gen. Ambrose Burnside. General Franklin and a number of other high-placed officers were removed in the recriminations that followed; Burnside eventually resigned.

Newton's most distinguished moment came in May 1863 at the Battle of Chancellorsville, when his division successfully stormed Marye's Heights, the bastion above Fredericksburg from which the Confederates had hammered back successive Union charges the previous December. His triumph there—one of the few Federal victories during the campaign—was fresh in his and others' minds when the Gettysburg Campaign began. Though he was a competent division commander and had the confidence of General Meade, Gettysburg would be Newton's first opportunity to lead a corps in battle. It did not help matters that he was completely unfamiliar with his new command.

GETTYSBURG: When he reached the battlefield early on the morning of July 2, Newton found the battered First Corps had been withdrawn and most of it placed in reserve behind Cemetery Hill. As the sun set that day, the tremendous battle that had begun on the Union left flank had begun working its way toward the center. Meade ordered Newton to rush forward Doubleday's and Brig. Gen. John Robinson's divisions from the reverse slope of Cemetery Hill to the threatened Second Corps front on Cemetery Ridge. Newton galloped at the head of his two divisions to the ridge crest, where he met Meade for a short conversation. Newton had just pulled out a flask and held it out to the army commander when a shell exploded nearby, showering them with dirt. The explosion did not, according to an observer, "interfere in any way with the important duty under consideration." The battle-scarred First Corps, meanwhile, rushed past the imbibing major generals toward the threat posed by Brig. Gen. A. R. Wright's Confederate brigade, which proved to be the last Rebel effort of the day. Within moments, the Southerners were observed to be falling back, and Meade halted Newton's men on Cemetery Ridge.

That night, at the gathering of generals at Meade's headquarters, Newton—whose opinion as an engineer was esteemed by the others—pronounced the town of Gettysburg to be "no place to fight a battle in," citing the possible danger of Lee shifting his forces around the left. Newton did approve, though of the Army of the Potomac's current dispositions, confidently stating that the Rebels "have hammered us into a solid position they cannot whip us out of." It was agreed that the army should stay and fight a defensive battle.

Early on the morning of July 3, Newton, with his sharp eye for ground, personally made the dispositions of all Union troops between Maj. Gen. Winfield Hancock's Second Corps on Cemetery Ridge and Maj. Gen. George Sykes' Fifth Corps men on Little Round Top. At the climax of Pickett's Charge, he ordered Robinson's Division from behind Cemetery Hill to fill in on the right of the embattled Second Corps, but—as on the previous day—the Rebels were falling back just as Robinson arrived. A few minutes later, after Hancock was wounded, Meade demonstrated his confidence in Newton by placing him in command of the entire battle line between Sykes and Maj. Gen. Oliver Howard's Eleventh Corps. The battle ended, however, before Newton could be tested in this role.

Newton continued in command of the First Corps through the fall campaigning. When the corps was eliminated in the March 1864 reorganization, however, he was left without a command. The political fallout from his anti-Burnside scheming caught up with him. Viewed as a potential troublemaker by many in the army's high command and in Washington, Newton's commission to major general was revoked in April and he was transferred west, where he served as a brigadier general for the rest of the conflict.

After the war Newton resumed his career with the Corps of Engineers. He was promoted to brigadier general in 1884 and retired two years later. Involved thereafter in railroading and public works, he died in New York from acute rheumatism in 1895.

For further reading:

Hartwig, D. Scott. "The Defense of McPherson's Ridge." *Gettysburg Magazine,* # 1, 1989.

Nichols, Edward J. *Toward Gettysburg: A Biography of General John F. Reynolds.* Gaithersburg, 1987.

Riley, Michael A. *"For God's Sake, Forward":* General John F. Reynolds, USA. Gettysburg, 1995.

FIRST DIVISION

(3,857 MEN)

BRIGADIER GENERAL
JAMES SAMUEL WADSWORTH

James Wadsworth was a trim, vigorous fifty-six years old at the time of Gettysburg. Topped by snow-white hair with striking white mutton-chop sideburns, he led his division with a Revolutionary War saber in his hand. Yet Wadsworth was not a military man at all. His father had been one of the largest landowners in New York state, and young James was raised with the expectation of inheriting his public responsibilities. He spent two years at Harvard and studied law, though he had no real intentions of entering into a legal practice. By the Civil War, James had taken his father's place at the head of the wealthy family estate and, out of a well-developed sense of noblesse oblige, had in addition become a philanthropist and Republican politician. In this same spirit of public service he volunteered for duty when Fort Sumter fell. He had no illusions about his military acumen, and was content to serve as a volunteer aide on the staff of Union army commander Irvin McDowell at Bull Run. McDowell recommended Wadsworth for command and he was jumped in rank all the way from volunteer aide-de-camp to brigadier general in August 1861. He was given a brigade in McDowell's corps, and then in March 1862—before the end of his first year in uniform—was made commander of the Washington defenses.

This last responsibility seemed to overwhelm the inexperienced Wadsworth, and the Union war effort suffered the consequences. It was Wadsworth who complained to Lincoln during the Peninsula Campaign that the capital had been left unprotected by McClellan, resulting in Lincoln's decision to withhold the entire First Corps from joining McClellan in his drive on Richmond. Wadsworth quickly fell out of favor with "Little Mac," and in the fall of 1862, seeing no prospect of serving in McClellan's army, Wadsworth allowed his supporters to run him for governor of New York against the anti-war Democrat Horatio Seymour. He was so intent on being a good soldier, however, that he declined to leave the army to campaign. As a result, he lost the election.

In late December 1862, after McClellan had departed the army for the last time, Wadsworth joined the Army of the Potomac as commander of the First Division, First Corps. He became much admired and liked by his new division, who was impressed by a man so devoted to the Union cause that he had given up a comfortable life and was serving without pay. The men were also won over by his attention to their well-being. Wadsworth was a stickler about things like adequate rations and decent housing, and the concerned general would often arise before dawn on frigid winter mornings in order to personally inspect the quarters of his men and determine if they were warm and decently ventilated. (On the rigorous march to Gettysburg, for example, he "requisitioned" shoes from civilians for his men to wear.)

Wadsworth's inexperience on the field of battle became painfully obvious at Chancellorsville, his first engagement with his new division. He waffled when ordered to cross the Rappahannock River below Fredericksburg, ordering the Iron Brigade to cross the river in boats and then countermanding the command when Rebel marksmen on the opposite bank opened fire. Wadsworth changed his mind again and the Westerners rowed across with only light casualties. Army commander Joseph Hooker eventually ordered the division to retrace its steps to the north bank, ending Wadsworth's participation in the battle.

By July 1863, Wadsworth had been at the head of the division for about six months, and only been lightly engaged at Chancellorsville. His abilities as a field commander were still undetermined, although he was recognized by his superiors for his administrative talents.

GETTYSBURG: Wadsworth's Division was in the vanguard of Maj. Gen. John Reynolds' First Corps as it marched toward Gettysburg on the morning of July 1, and was the first contingent of Union infantry to reach the field. From about 11:00 a.m. until the general retreat later that afternoon, Wadsworth's men performed some of the bloodiest, most heroic defensive fighting of the war on the ridges west of town.

Attacked on McPherson's Ridge by Maj. Gen. Henry Heth's Confederate division, Wadsworth's inexperience became evident when he hastily withdrew part of Brig. Gen. Lysander Cutler's brigade and left Capt. James Hall's 2nd Maine Battery exposed. The artillerymen hurriedly harnessed up and pulled out, leaving behind one of their six field pieces in their precipitate flight. Wadsworth rookie mistake enraged Hall.

After this misstep, however, Wadsworth did a good job, swinging the right of his line back to defend against Maj. Gen. Robert Rodes' Division, which was sweeping off Oak Ridge from the north. He pulled back in good order to Seminary Ridge when the McPherson's Ridge line was overlapped by the enemy.

Wadsworth's gallant effort to buy the time necessary for the rest of the Federal army to gather on the formidable hills to the east cost him almost half of his division. Hundreds of First Division Unionists were killed, wounded, or taken prisoner. When the entire corps gave way that afternoon, Wadsworth and the remaining men of his pair of brigades withdrew to the north face of Culp's Hill, where the disorganized units prepared to resist an expected attack that was never delivered.

Wadsworth was distraught at the mauling of his beloved regiments. A messenger on the evening of July 1 found him "sitting on a stone fence by the roadside, his head bowed in grief, the most dejected woe-begone person one would likely find on a world-around voyage—a live picture of Despair: General Reynolds killed, the first corps decimated a full half, and its first division almost wiped out of existence. The General greeted us warmly, adding, 'I am glad you were not with us this afternoon.'"

On the evening of July 2, just as the defenses of Culp's Hill were being stripped to provide reinforcements for the left flank, Maj. Gen. Edward Johnson's Division rushed up the hill toward Brig. Gen. George Greene's outnumbered brigade. Wadsworth, though fighting off Rebels on his front, sent two regiments to bolster Greene, and the thin Union force held through the night. An attack drove away the Rebels early the next morning.

Wadsworth left the army less than two weeks after Gettysburg. After an absence of eight months, he returned in March 1864 to command a division in the Fifth Corps. On May 6, in the Wilderness, an enemy round pierced his forehead and lodged in his brain. Wadsworth lingered without regaining conscience until he expired on May 8.

For further reading:

Allen, Louis F. *Memorial of the Late Gen. James S. Wadsworth*. Buffalo, 1864.

Hartwig, D. Scott. "The Defense of McPherson's Ridge." *Gettysburg Magazine*, # 1, 1989.

Mahood, Wayne, "General James S. Wadsworth" (unpublished manuscript), Geneseo, NY.

Pearson, Henry G. *James S. Wadsworth of Geneseo: Brevet Major-General of United States Volunteers*. New York, 1913.

FIRST BRIGADE

THE "IRON BRIGADE"

(1,829 MEN)

BRIGADIER GENERAL SOLOMON MEREDITH

Nicknamed "Long Sol" because of his towering, ramrod straight 6'7" frame, Meredith was an ambitious man who had spent the antebellum years honing political skills. Born into a poor North Carolina Quaker family, and facing little or no educational and financial prospects, Meredith left the South when he was a young man and walked to Indiana. Once settled in the Hoosier state, he entered into county politics. He had the natural politician's uncanny ability to remember names and faces. During the next twenty years he prospered as a farmer while serving as a county sheriff, legislator, and a United States marshal for the district of Indiana. This last position was a political plum that resulted from his loyal service to the Republican party and his close personal and professional friendship with the famous "war governor" of Indiana, fellow Republican Oliver P. Morton.

When the Civil War broke out, Meredith used his political connections to secure an assignment as colonel of the 19th Indiana regiment. This regiment became part of John Gibbon's famous "Iron Brigade." Meredith's lack of military ability caused some grumbling in the ranks. Even one of the most generous early opinions of him, by a man in the 19th, is rather tepid: "Colonel Meredith talks right, acts right, and in fact does the very best that he knows how. I think he means well." In October 1861, the regimental surgeon reported to Governor Morton, "Our Col. has no practical sense. The officers have all found it out. Lt. Col. is a good man, or we would have all gone to sticks before now. Bad administration is seen and felt throughout all the Regt. Our Col. unfortunately wants to attend to all departments down to the smallest minutiae. Of course he fails of necessity." The surgeon wrote again 18 days later: "You would be startled to hear how the officers and soldiers talk about 'Old Sol.' It seems that he is about being promoted to a Brigadier. If he is not, there will soon be a petition signed by the whole Regt. for him to resign." Another man wrote that Meredith was "notoriously unfit to command." There was a conspiracy among the men of the regiment to help Meredith get promoted to brigadier general so he would be taken away. In January 1862, an inspection of Meredith's regiment showed muskets "indifferently cleaned," accouterments in "bad condition," and the regiment generally the least well disciplined in the brigade.

Meredith suffered a fall from his horse during the Iron Brigade's first engagement at Brawner's Farm, the opening act of the Second Battle of Bull Run. He recovered quickly, rejoining the brigade on its march through Maryland a couple of weeks later, and commanded his regiment in a tough fight at South Mountain on September 14. When the Iron Brigade spearheaded the Union army's opening attack at Antietam three days later, Meredith was absent. Citing his recent fall and exhaustion, he had reported himself unfit

for duty and had traveled to Washington to recuperate and campaign for a promotion (possibly even at the White House, trading on his acquaintance with President Lincoln). For Gibbon, a tough professional soldier, this absence on the eve of a great battle was tantamount to desertion—especially since Meredith's replacement was killed in action. Gibbon, however, was promoted in October to command a division in another corps, and lost his chance for retribution against Meredith. "Long Sol," who by October was back in Indiana trying to drum up political support for an all-Indiana brigade, heard that Gibbon's promotion had left the Iron Brigade without a brigadier, and he began a campaign for Gibbon's old post. Meredith's political connections obtained army commander and Indiana native Maj. Gen. Burnside's recommendation for the position, and corps commander Joe Hooker—himself angling for advancement and eager to cultivate Governor Morton as a patron—installed Meredith at the head of the Iron Brigade with the new rank of brigadier general. Gibbon, who was still intensely interested in his old command, was outraged that the army would "relieve a competent colonel [Lysander Cutler, who was in temporary command] and put that fine body of men in charge of an incompetent Brig. General [Meredith]."

Meredith's first battle as commander of the Iron Brigade was at Fredericksburg in December 1862. The brigade was not heavily engaged and lost just 65 men. However, Meredith failed to execute an order given toward the end of the day by Brig. Gen. Abner Doubleday, his division commander, to have the brigade put out skirmishers and retire to a safer position. While there is a possibility Meredith never received the order, Doubleday was incensed to find that after two hours his directive had not been carried out. He relieved Meredith of command on the spot and replaced him with Colonel Cutler.

The demotion was only temporary, however, and Meredith headed the Iron Brigade at the Battle of Chancellorsville in May 1863. Two of his regiments had the demanding task of crossing the Rappahannock in pontoon boats under fire. They did so with the loss of about 60 men, and established a bridgehead on the opposite bank. Meredith came across soon after, standing in one of the boats swinging his hat and hurrahing. A change of orders pulled Meredith and his men back across the river and ended their participation at Chancellorsville. As the Mid-Westerners marched toward Gettysburg, the fifty-three-year-old Meredith had still not proven himself competent as a brigade leader.

GETTYSBURG: The morning of July 1 found the Iron Brigade marching toward Gettysburg on the Emmitsburg Road. The brigade broke into a double-quick step when within about one mile of the McPherson's Ridge fight and arrived there around 10:30 a.m., with Meredith riding at the rear of the column. Meredith's men deployed south of the Chambersburg Pike facing west near Willoughby Run, where they met the attack of Archer's Brigade. The Iron Brigade was aligned, from left to right, as follows: 19th Indiana, 24th Michigan, 2nd Wisconsin, and 7th Wisconsin. The 6th Wisconsin came up thereafter and moved to the right of the brigade, assisting in the fight at the Railroad Cut. Meredith's regiments enveloped and routed the Confederates, inflicting heavy casualties. Among the captured was General Archer himself, the first general officer from Lee's army ever to be taken prisoner.

Meredith pulled his brigade back after its successful pummeling of the surprised Confederates and was reforming his line when a shell exploded near him. According to an account in the August 28 Richmond [Indiana] *Palladium* newspaper, Meredith: "was stuck in the head by a fragment of the shell and stunned, at the same moment, and by the same fire, that his horse was struck by four balls and a shell, and fell dead, his body crushing the general's leg and side frightfully. The wound in the head fractured the skull and affected the brain very seriously. The fall broke several ribs and tore them loose from the breastbone at the same time, and so seriously injured the right leg that it is yet after nearly two months, greatly discolored." The battle was over for "Long Sol" Meredith. The Iron Brigade's regimental commanders said little about Meredith in their battle reports. Brig. Gen. James Wadsworth did not even mention Meredith in his divisional report,

and temporary commander of the First Corps, Maj. Gen. Abner Doubleday, only discussed him in connection with his injury. Meredith never wrote a report of the battle.

The injuries he received from the fall at Gettysburg were the reason given for Meredith's relative inactivity for the rest of the war. He returned from sick leave in October 1863, and in November commanded the division for one day before being transferred west to a much quieter command—the garrison at Cairo, Illinois. In January and February 1864, he went home to Indiana due to "general nervous prostration," the lingering effects of his Gettysburg injury. He finished out the war in the serene backwaters of West Kentucky. Meredith served as surveyor general of the Montana Territory after the war for two years before returning to his Indiana farm to raise livestock. He died there in 1875.

For further reading:

Beaudot, W., and Herdegen, L. *In the Bloody Railroad Cut at Gettysburg.* Dayton, 1991.

Gaff, Alan D. *On Many a Bloody Field: Four Years in the Iron Brigade.* Bloomington, 1996.

Hartwig, D. Scott. "The Defense of McPherson's Ridge." *Gettysburg Magazine,* # 1, 1989.

Nolan, Alan T. *The Iron Brigade: A Military History.* Bloomington, 1994.

SECOND BRIGADE
(2,000 MEN)

BRIGADIER GENERAL
LYSANDER CUTLER

Born in Worcester County, Massachusetts, grizzled and tough-looking Lysander Cutler lived much of his life in Maine and Wisconsin. Brought up on a farm, he also learned the clothier's trade, surveyed, and taught school as a young man. Though he gained some military experience in the 1830s fighting Indians as an officer in the Maine militia, Cutler spent the majority of his time in business pursuits. In 1843, he founded his own woolen mill, a venture that in less than ten years made him a

fortune. Unfortunately, however, the mill burned down and Cutler's wealth disappeared with it.

Undaunted, he built another woolen mill and enlarged his operations to include other factories, tenements, a foundry, a gristmill, and a sawmill. As a successful businessman, Cutler was elected to the Maine senate, college trusteeships, and a railroad directorship. He was financially ruined for the second time by the panic of 1856, however, and decided to leave Maine and move to Milwaukee to restart his career yet again. In Wisconsin, Cutler worked as a claims investigator for a mining company even though it required him to venture into Indian territory, where he was constantly threatened with ambush and death. He remained with the mining company until its operations became financially unstable. By the outbreak of the war, the enterprising Cutler had his own grain business in Milwaukee.

Commanding respect as an influential businessman and old Indian fighter, Cutler received a commission as colonel of Milwaukee's 6th Wisconsin regiment in the first summer of the Civil War. He immediately showed an unfortunate capacity to irritate. Arbitrary and overbearing in his treatment of junior officers, he subjected officers he found unacceptable to a system of "examinations" which soon resulted in their removal. This caused bitter feelings not only among the officers but especially among the troops of the "foreign" companies, whose immigrant leaders were removed and replaced by men of different ethnic stock. Despite such harsh policies, Cutler rose to temporary command of the brigade until he was replaced by artilleryman John Gibbon in the summer of 1862. Cutler's long-suffering junior officers rejoiced at this change in command.

However, no one could deny that Cutler—described by one soldier under his command as being as "rugged as a wolf"—was a tenacious fighter, a trait that endeared him to the tough-minded Gibbon. During the bloody fight with Stonewall Jackson's men at Brawner's Farm, Cutler was severely wounded in the right thigh. When Gibbon was promoted away from the brigade in October, he recommended that the recuperating Cutler take his place at the head of the Iron Brigade. As it turned out, the 19th Indiana's Solomon Meredith exercised his superior political connections and was awarded the position instead, much to Gibbon's dismay.

Still hobbling on two canes as a result of his Brawner's Farm injury, Cutler returned to the Army of the Potomac in October 1862, and was commissioned brigadier general on November 29. At the Battle of Fredericksburg, divisional commander Abner Doubleday—acting in a fit of pique—placed him in command of the Iron Brigade after Doubleday judged Brig. Gen. Solomon Meredith was tardy in executing an order. The assignment was only temporary, however, as Meredith was back at the head of the brigade within a few hours. The following March Cutler was given command of the Second Brigade, First Division, First Corps. He led it in May at Chancellorsville, where it was only lightly engaged. Gettysburg would be the fifty-six-year-old Cutler's first real chance to show what he could do with a brigade, although he was already known as a competent officer and a hard fighter. He was expected to give a good account of himself.

GETTYSBURG: Arriving on McPherson's Ridge to relieve Brig. Gen. John Buford's embattled troopers at 10:15 a.m. on July 1, Cutler positioned his men—the first infantry brigade from the Army of the Potomac to reach the field—astride the Chambersburg Pike facing west. The 84th and 95th New York regiments were south of the road, and the balance of the brigade was deployed north of it. For some reason, division commander Brig. Gen. James Wadsworth confused matters when he ordered Cutler's two right regiments to withdraw in the face of Joe Davis' Confederate brigade. When Brig. Gen. John Robinson's division came up on Cutler's right and formed on the north end of Seminary Ridge, Cutler's riflemen formed a line facing northwest between McPherson's Ridge at the Pike and Robinson's position. Cutler's regiments were thus vulnerable to fire from Maj. Gen. Robert Rodes' Confederate artillery on Oak Hill. When Rodes attacked with Brig. Gens. Daniel's and Iverson's brigades around 2:30 p.m., Cutler wheeled north and blazed away at them, initially repulsing the assault. Repeated enemy attacks, however, inflicted casualties approaching 50% in Cutler's brigade, and the whole Federal First Corps position gave way around 4:00 p.m. During the chaotic Union flight to Cemetery Hill, Cutler had two horses shot out from under him.

Cutler reported that on July 2 and 3, when his regiments were posted facing north between Cemetery and Culp's Hills, "most of the time we were immediately under the eye of the division commander," and the fighting was mostly from trenches, with little loss.

In the year following Gettysburg, the battle-scarred Cutler was a fixture in the division, serving as division commander in Wadsworth's absence between July 15 and the army reorganization the following March, when he was given command of the remnants of the Iron Brigade. After Wadsworth was mortally wounded at the Battle of the Wilderness in May, Cutler took command of the division and led it through the spring and early summer battles to Petersburg. He was struck in the face and badly disfigured by a shell fragment in August 1864, and left the army for administrating duties in Michigan for the remainder of the war.

Cutler returned to Milwaukee an invalid as a result of his injuries. His health continued to deteriorate, and he died of a stroke in 1866.

For further reading:

Beaudot, W., and Herdegen, L. *In the Bloody Railroad Cut at Gettysburg.* Dayton, 1991.

Gaff, Alan D. *On Many a Bloody Field: Four Years in the Iron Brigade.* Bloomington, 1996.

Hartwig, D. Scott. "The Defense of McPherson's Ridge." *Gettysburg Magazine,* # 1, 1989.

Nolan, Alan T. *The Iron Brigade: A Military History.* Bloomington, 1994.

SECOND DIVISION

(2,997 MEN)

BRIGADIER GENERAL JOHN CLEVELAND ROBINSON

By the outbreak of the Civil War, John Robinson was a salty old regular, having spent practically his whole adult life in dusty Army outposts. Solid and dependable, he was not the sort of man around whom colorful stories proliferated. He was remarkable mainly for the volume of his beard—"In a much-bearded army," wrote one army wag, "he was the hairiest general I ever saw"—and for the violence of his temper.

Sent to West Point from his native New York, his formal military education was interrupted in 1835 when he was expelled in his third year for a breach of regulations. He briefly studied law but soon decided to reenter the army. He was commissioned directly into the 5th Infantry as a second lieutenant and served with that regiment in the Mexican

War. He was still associated with the 5th fifteen years later when the Civil War began.

In April 1861, Robinson (by then a captain) was the commander of Baltimore's Fort McHenry and the 5th was garrisoning the stronghold. The war was only a few weeks old when circumstances gave Robinson a chance to show his ability to react decisively to a crisis. When rioting citizens attacked the 6th Massachusetts in Baltimore as it made their way south to defend Washington, Robinson quickly and secretly prepared the men of the 5th for a siege at Fort McHenry. He also aggressively turned McHenry's guns toward the city, persuading local officials to leave his post alone.

Robinson spent much of the war's first year on recruiting duty, but in the spring of 1862 he was promoted to brigadier general. Shortly thereafter, when Brig. Gen. Charles Jameson fell sick after the Battle of Seven Pines, Robinson was given Jameson's brigade in Brig. Gen. Philip Kearny's Third Corps division. (At Gettysburg, Brig. Gen. Charles Graham commanded this brigade). Robinson performed brilliantly at Glendale during the Seven Days' Battles, his first engagement as a brigadier. After his gritty performance, Third Corps commander Brig. Gen. Samuel Heintzleman called Robinson "particularly distinguished," and Kearny, who was closer to the action, wrote at the end of his official report: "I have reserved General Robinson for the last. To him this day is due, above all others in this division, the honors of this battle. The attack was on his wing. Everywhere present, by personal supervision and noble example he secured for us the honor of victory." Just two months later, however, Robinson turned in an uncharacteristically tentative and ineffectual performance during the first day of fighting at Second Bull Run. Only in the final Northern attack of the afternoon, when Kearny's division nearly broke Jackson's line at the Railroad Cut, did Robinson make a determined effort with his brigade. Even then he failed to engage all his regiments.

Stationed near Washington, Robinson's brigade missed the Battle of Antietam. At Fredericksburg, while the division helped repulse a Confederate counterattack, Robinson's brigade was the last to be deployed and had little chance to affect the engagement's outcome. Despite his mediocre post-Peninsula performances, on December 30 he was promoted to the command of the Second Division, First Corps, replacing the wounded Brig. Gen. John Gibbon. Robinson's first engagement as a division leader came at Chancellorsville in May 1863, where his division was but lightly engaged, losing just 55 men. He was still untested in division command as his brigades marched toward Gettysburg six weeks later.

GETTYSBURG: Last in the First Corps line of march on the morning of July 1, Robinson's division did not break its camp north of Emmitsburg until after 9:00 a.m. After about a seven-mile march, his brigades began to arrive at the Lutheran Seminary at 11:30 a.m., just as the morning fighting was drawing to a close. Robinson's men were initially held in reserve. Brig. Gen. Gabriel Paul's brigade arrived first and was employed throwing up barricades on the western side of the Seminary. Paul's efforts would provide a fall-back position for the First Corps brigades then defending McPherson's Ridge a few hundred yards to the west. Brig. Gen. Henry Baxter's brigade began to arrive one half-hour after Paul, at the same time Maj. Gen. Robert Rodes' Confederate division appeared on Oak Hill to the north, menacing the First Corps' right flank. Robinson immediately sent Baxter north along Seminary Ridge to meet the threat. His regiments advanced to the Mummasburg Road, dangerously near Rodes' massing brigades, and formed an unusual V-shaped line with the apex facing the Rebels.

About 2:00 p.m. Col. Edward O'Neal's Brigade attacked the right wing of Baxter's line, and was quickly repulsed. When Brig. Gen. Alfred Iverson's Tarheel brigade started forward a few minutes later, the left extension of Baxter's line, hidden behind a stone wall, surprised the Rebels. Baxter's shattering volleys felled scores of the North Carolinians and dozens more were brought into the Union lines as prisoners. Robinson arrived in time to witness this Confederate debacle before ordering forward Paul's brigade to reinforce this position. Brig. Gen. Stephen Ramseur's fresh Southern brigade attacked from the north soon thereafter, testing the newly-strengthened line. The Union men's mettle proved strong, and Ramseur's Confederates were also repulsed. About 3:00 p.m., however, Baxter's men were running low on ammunition and Robinson permitted them to withdraw, leaving Paul's regiments to face the continued (but piecemeal) assaults of Rodes' Division. Paul's regiments resisted until they too emptied their cartridge boxes. They retreated when they saw the other units of the First Corps falling back toward Gettysburg. Paul's brave men, standing alone to cover the withdrawal of the rest of the First Corps, lost heavily in prisoners. Robinson's remnants fell back to the extreme northern end of Cemetery Ridge. That night, only half the 3,000 men that started the day with the division answered roll call. Almost 1,000 of those absent were marching toward the Confederate rear as prisoners. On July 2 and again on July 3, Robinson and his men, posted on the reverse slope of Cemetery Hill, were called up to repulse Confederate attacks, but in both cases arrived too late to do any fighting.

Robinson handled his two brigades masterfully on the first day, repelling furious attacks by a foe that outnumbered him. One colonel took the unusual step of commending his superiors in his report: "I wish to say one word outside of my regiment in regard to Generals Baxter and Robinson. They were on every part of the field, encouraging and stimulating the men by their presence and bravery." Robinson was also commended by his superior that afternoon, Maj. Gen. Abner Doubleday. At Gettysburg, Robinson proved he could lead large numbers of men in combat, and he was retained in division command when the army was reorganized in the spring of 1864—an incontrovertible sign of respect for his ability. In May 1864, in the opening hours of the Battle of Spotsylvania, Robinson personally led a desperate attack by his division and his left knee was shattered by a bullet. His leg was amputated at mid-thigh, and Robinson never returned to field duty.

The crippled officer commanded various departments after the war and retired in 1869 from disability due to his war wounds. He served as lieutenant governor of New York from 1872 to 1874, then served at the head of veterans' organizations. He received the Congressional Medal of Honor in 1894 for his service at Spotsylvania, and died three years later of chronic Bright's disease.

For further reading:

Gaff, Alan D. *On Many a Bloody Field: Four Years in the Iron Brigade.* Bloomington, 1996.

Nolan, Alan T. *The Iron Brigade: A Military History.* Bloomington, 1994.

FIRST BRIGADE
(1,537 MEN)

BRIGADIER GENERAL
GABRIEL RENE PAUL

Gabriel Paul was a fifty-year-old Regular Army man with a neat white goatee and mustache, the grandson of one of Napoleon's officers who had emigrated and settled in St. Louis. Paul was a career soldier, a West Point graduate who ranked 18th in the class of 1834. After he left the Academy he served as an infantry officer in the Seminole and Mexican Wars and against the Indians in the Southwest. His pre-war record does not reflect any particular distinction or ambition—he rose only to the rank of major in twenty-five years.

Paul's Civil War career began when he was put in command of a regiment at Fort Union in New Mexico in late 1861. Things were quiet until the spring of 1862, when he pursued a beaten Confederate invasion force. After his regiment was mustered out in May, he had nothing to do for several months, until his wife made a personal visit to President Lincoln in August. Citing his long service record, she urged the president to promote her husband to brigadier general. Her efforts were successful, and Paul was commissioned brigadier in a matter of days. In October he was given a brigade of New Yorkers in the First Corps, whose former commander, Marsena Patrick, had just been reassigned as the Army's provost marshal. General Paul missed his brigade's first battle at Fredericksburg because he was in Washington with what was officially reported as a "severe domestic affliction."

In the spring of 1863 there was a constant reshuffling of Paul's responsibilities. His appointment to brigadier general expired without Senate confirmation in March, but he was reappointed to this rank in April. His New York regiments were mustered out and replaced by five regiments—four of which were from New Jersey—composed of nine-month men who had yet to experience battle. At the Battle of Chancellorsville in May 1863, Paul's regiments did not directly encounter any Confederates, but were so skittish they fired into each other by accident and inflicted seven casualties. In June these men were mustered out, and in the reorganization of the First Corps Paul was again put in charge of a new group of regiments, this time a veteran brigade in the Second Division. He was doubtless struggling to familiarize himself with his new situation as he marched toward Gettysburg. He had yet to see combat in the Civil War on the scale that the impending battle presented, and he was at the head of a new brigade, in a new division.

GETTYSBURG: Paul's brigade broke its bivouac on Marsh Creek—some seven miles south of Gettysburg—a little after 9:00 a.m. on July 1, and led the advance of the division toward the town. It arrived at the Lutheran Seminary about 11:30 a.m., just as Brig. Gen. James Wadsworth's division was repulsing Henry Heth's two Confederate brigades on McPherson's Ridge. Paul's men marched around to the western face of the building, where they were ordered to throw up a fence rail barricade as a fall back position for the First Corps. About 3:00 p.m., Paul's brigade, the First Corps' last reserve, marched nearly a mile north to meet the threat of Maj. Gen. Robert Rodes' Confederate Division, which was making its presence felt on Oak Ridge. Paul's men reinforced Robinson's other brigade under Brig. Gen. Henry Baxter, which had just thrown back assaults by two Confederate brigades. Paul joined Baxter's line where Seminary Ridge meets the Mummasburg Road. The position represented the right flank of the First Corps line. Paul and his 1,500 men were filing into position when Brig. Gen. Stephen Ramseur's fresh Rebel brigade advanced toward them. His line was bent in a V-shaped salient, held from left to right by the 94th New York, 107th New York, 16th Maine, 104th New York, and 13th Massachusetts. As Paul rode up behind one of his regiments to get it into position to meet the attack, he was shot in the head. The bullet entered his right temple and emerged through the left eye socket, tearing out both of his eyes.

Taken immediately to the rear with this ghastly wound, Paul lay in a coma for several days. The blinded general spent the remainder of his life suffering from violent headaches and increasingly frequent epilepsy attacks (up to six a day), all the result of his crippling Gettysburg wound. He died from a severe seizure in 1886.

For further reading:

Gaff, Alan D. *On Many a Bloody Field: Four Years in the Iron Brigade.* Bloomington, 1996.

Nolan, Alan T. *The Iron Brigade: A Military History.* Bloomington, 1994.

Paul, J. B. *Paul's Brigade at Gettysburg.* (np), 1966.

SECOND BRIGADE

(1,452 MEN)

BRIGADIER GENERAL
HENRY BAXTER

Henry Baxter was a forty-two-year-old storekeeper and miller from Michigan. Though without a military education, he did have fighting antecedents—both grandfathers were veterans of the Revolutionary War—and he had organized his own militia unit called the Jonesville "Light Guards." On the basis of his militia experience, he entered the Civil War as a captain in the 7th Michigan infantry. He received a severe abdominal wound while leading his company in the Seven Days' Battles, and was promoted to lieutenant colonel a week later. Baxter recovered in time to rejoin the 7th Michigan for the Battle of Antietam, and was stricken again during the Rebel ambush of John Sedgwick's division in the West Woods by a bullet that entered his right leg and passed into his abdomen.

He went home to Michigan to heal, and was back with his regiment before the Battle of Fredericksburg in December 1862, though he still found walking painful. During Baxter's absence, the 7th's colonel, Norman Hall, had been promoted to brigade leader, so at Fredericksburg Baxter found himself in command of the regiment for the first time.

Baxter's exploits at that battle marked a highpoint of his career. Hall chose his old 7th Michigan to make a desperate amphibious assault under fire across the Rappahannock River to seize the town from Rebels dug into rifle pits and the cellars of buildings along the waterfront. The crossing resulted in a successful lodgment, though not before Baxter was shot yet again, this time through the body. When Baxter returned to the army in the spring after recovering from his third wound, he was promoted from lieutenant colonel to brigadier general and given command of a brigade of New Yorkers and Pennsylvanians.

Baxter's first battle as a brigade commander was at Chancellorsville, where his brigade was only lightly engaged and suffered the loss of just 22 men. However, his swift rise from captain to brigadier general in the year preceding Gettysburg indicates that his fellow officers were impressed with his gritty up-front style of leadership.

GETTYSBURG: Baxter's brigade, second in the line of march of John Robinson's two-brigade division, made the seven-mile march to Gettysburg on the morning of July 1. It arrived at the Lutheran Seminary about noon, during a lull in the battle. Since Maj. Gen. Robert Rodes' 8,000-man enemy division had just started to appear on Oak Hill about a mile north, menacing the right of the First Corps line, Baxter's brigade was dispatched to guard that flank. Advancing a full four hundred yards beyond the nearest friendly brigade, Baxter posted his men close to the massing Rebels in a tight V-line formation facing generally northwest. His right wing ran along the Mummasburg Road, while his left faced west and looked out over open fields. Baxter's left flank did not connect with Lysander Cutler's brigade, which was deployed on his left.

At about 2:00 p.m. Rodes' Southerners began their attack in piecemeal fashion. The first to advance was Col. Edward O'Neal's brigade, which moved generally south and was quickly and boldly repulsed by the Pennsylvanians and New Yorkers deployed there to meet him. At 2:30 p.m. Alfred Iverson's Brigade left Oak Ridge and headed straight for the gap between Baxter and Cutler. Division commander John Robinson ordered Baxter to change front to the left, and Baxter's regiments took position behind a low stone wall facing west. His left now connected with Cutler, while his right rested on the Mummasburg Road. His men were in line, left to right, as follows: 97th New York, 11th Pennsylvania, 83rd New York, 88th Pennsylvania, 12th Massachusetts, and 90th Pennsylvania. Iverson's men, meanwhile, advanced without skirmishers to reconnoiter what lay before them. They approached to within point-blank range as Baxter's men crouched unseen behind the piled stones. Without warning the Federals rose up and poured a devastating volley into Iverson's surprised North Carolinians, dropping scores of them on the spot. A protracted exchange followed, and Baxter's men soon ran low on ammunition. Baxter personally led a charge against the shattered remnants of Iverson's Brigade, capturing four flags and rounding up hundreds of dazed Confederates.

In the process of beating back Iverson, Baxter's men received welcome reinforcements in the form of Brig. Gen. Gabriel Paul's Brigade. Out of ammunition and thoroughly exhausted, Baxter withdrew his regiments southward. Some of his men moved to the railroad cut, where they supported Stewart's Battery B, 4th U.S. Artillery. Eventually Baxter pulled back to the north end of Cemetery Ridge late in the afternoon. He had lost fully half of his brigade in his magnificent defense of the First Corps' right flank. Baxter's brigade spent most of the rest of the battle in reserve behind Cemetery Hill, where it suffered occasionally from enemy shells and sharpshooters.

After the battle, Baxter received deserved praise from his division commander, John Robinson. He also received an unusual commendation from a subordinate in one of his colonel's reports: "I wish to say one word outside of my regiment in regard to Generals Baxter and Robinson. They were on every part of the field, encouraging and stimulating the men by their presence and bravery."

Baxter continued in command of his brigade in the following months and survived the reorganization of the army during the spring of 1864. At the Battle of the Wilderness in May 1864, he was shot in the left thigh—his fourth serious wound—but returned yet again to lead a brigade during the siege of Richmond and Petersburg until war's end. Baxter returned to Michigan and served two years as Register of Deeds before being appointed minister to Honduras by President Grant in 1869. He returned home to go into the lumber business in 1872, and died from pneumonia the following year.

For further reading:

Lash, Gary G. "Brig. Gen. Henry Baxter's Brigade at Gettysburg, July 1." *Gettysburg Magazine*, #10, 1994.

Martin, David. *Gettysburg, July 1, 1863.* Conshohocken, 1996.

THIRD DIVISION

(4,701 MEN)

MAJOR GENERAL ABNER DOUBLEDAY

Although Abner Doubleday was the highest ranking division commander in the Army of the Potomac at Gettysburg, he was a strictly average general, never making any momentous mistakes or enjoying extraordinary battlefield success. Fellow troops sarcastically nicknamed him "Old Forty-Eight Hours" for his deliberate, even slothful, style. The portly Doubleday inspired no one with his appearance; and he could be quarrelsome, stiff, and a shade pompous. He also liked to cast himself as the "hero of Sumter," because he had sighted the cannon that fired the first Union shot of the war. The lack of respect he received from other officers must have irked him. Army commander Maj. Gen. George Meade, who had spent much of 1862 with him as a fellow division commander in the First Corps, held Doubleday's leadership abilities in low esteem. Upon learning, early in 1863, that Doubleday was to lead his old division, Meade wrote to his wife that he was glad because the division "will think a great deal more of me than before." Brig. Gen. John Buford also did not care much for Doubleday, and made his own dispositions on Gettysburg's first day without consulting his superior. Col. Charles Wainwright, First Corps artillery chief, wrote in his diary that he "had no confidence" in Doubleday and thought he would be a "weak reed to lean upon" in an emergency.

Despite his peers' poor opinion of him, the forty-four-year-old Doubleday was an experienced officer. He came from a prominent family in upstate New York. His grandfather had fought in the Revolutionary War and his father had served four years in Congress. Abner had already worked as a civil engineer for two years before entering West Point, from which he graduated 24th out of 56 in the Class of 1942. He was a career artilleryman and served in that branch for twenty years throughout the Mexican and Seminole Wars and the tedium of the peacetime army. That tedium was ended in April 1861, when he found himself under bombardment at Fort Sumter.

After uneventful duty during the remainder of 1861, Doubleday became a brigadier general of volunteers early in February 1862. Assigned to Irvin McDowell's corps, his brigade missed the Peninsula fighting and did not go into action until the Battle of Brawner's Farm at the end of August 1862. He displayed some initiative in his combat debut, throwing two of his regiments into line to bolster Brig. Gen. John Gibbon's brigade against a larger Confederate force. Doubleday did this on his own hook, since the division commander, Brig. Gen. Rufus King, was incapac-

itated by an epileptic seizure at the time. Together the two brigades fought a superior force to a standstill. The next evening at the end of the first day of the Battle of Second Bull Run, however, Doubleday's fortunes took a turn for the worse. His men were routed when they stumbled onto Maj. Gen. General James Longstreet's Corps, which was just arriving on the battlefield in the gathering darkness. On the battle's second day, Doubleday's men regained their poise and helped cover the retreat of the army.

Doubleday was given command of the First Division of the First Corps just prior to Antietam, replacing Brig. Gen. John Hatch (who had just replaced Rufus King), who was wounded at South Mountain. Doubleday led his men into the carnage of the Cornfield and West Woods, and one colonel described him as a "gallant officer . . . remarkably cool and at the very front of battle." At Fredericksburg in December, Doubleday's division, due to a confusion of orders, did little more than spar with enemy artillery. In January 1863 there was a reorganization of the First Corps and Doubleday was appointed to command the newly-formed Third Division. He led this division at Chancellorsville, but was not seriously engaged there. Although he had been in command of his division for six months by the time the Gettysburg Campaign got underway, Doubleday still had not led it in combat.

GETTYSBURG: Doubleday was thrust into command of the First Corps upon the death of Maj. Gen. John Reynolds about 11:00 a.m. on July 1. As he saw it, his duty was to hold McPherson's Ridge as long as possible. While shepherding Brig. Gen. James Wadsworth's division into position, he had the satisfaction of seeing them rout the first of the Rebel assaults from the west—two brigades of Maj. Gen. Henry Heth's Division—at about 11:30.

Doubleday posted Wadsworth and two brigades of his own Third Division before noon, and wisely ordered the building of breastworks as a fall-back line on Seminary Ridge. When a new threat appeared on his right on Oak Hill in the form of Maj. Gen. Robert Rodes' 8,000-man division, he directed General Paul's brigade to the imperiled flank. Until about 4:00 p.m. he constantly shifted troops, moving divisions, brigades, even regiments to derive the best advantages of terrain against an enemy that not only outnumbered him but was coming at him from two directions—Rodes from the north, and A. P. Hill's Corps from the west. The five hours Doubleday spent leading his 9,500 men through the bitter combat on McPherson's Ridge and Seminary Ridge was his best performance of the war. Ten Southern brigades numbering more than 16,000 men attacked the First Corps throughout much of July 1, and seven of these brigades incurred crippling casualties ranging from 35 to 50 percent. The outflanked Unionists finally give way late in the afternoon, and Doubleday supervised as orderly a retreat as possible through Gettysburg to the hills beyond.

As the First Corps limped onto Culp's Hill and Cemetery Hill to reform after the day's savage fighting, only about one-third of it was present and ready for duty. It would never recover from the first day at Gettysburg. Under Reynolds' and Doubleday's direction, it had bought time for the rest of the army to concentrate on the defensive terrain south and east of the town. Aware that he had performed well, Doubleday was hurt and angered when Meade—who heard disparaging remarks about his performance from General O. O. Howard—replaced him as the head of the First Corps with John Newton.

Doubleday justifiably bore a grudge against both Howard and Meade for being demoted after what he judged was his best performance. As it turned out, he would never fight another battle. A few days after Gettysburg the unassigned general left the army, unwanted by Meade and unprotected by Maj. Gen. Henry Halleck or Secretary of War Edwin Stanton. In the end, however, he ended up one of the most famous generals of all—not for his military record, but for being mistakenly identified as "The Inventor of Baseball."

Doubleday remained in the army until 1873 and wrote two books on his Civil War experiences after he retired. He died from heart disease in New Jersey in 1893.

For further reading:

Doubleday, Abner. *Chancellorsville and Gettysburg.* New York, 1994.

Doubleday, Abner. *Gettysburg Made Plain.* New York, 1888.

Hartwig, D. Scott. "The Defense of McPherson's Ridge." *Gettysburg Magazine,* # 1, 1989.

Martin, David. *Gettysburg, July 1, 1863.* Conshohocken, 1996.

Ramsey, David M. "The 'Old Sumter Hero': A Biography of Major-General Abner Doubleday." Thesis, Florida State University, 1980.

FIRST BRIGADE

(1,361 MEN)

BRIGADIER GENERAL
THOMAS ALGEO ROWLEY

Thomas Rowley was a fifty-five-year-old cabinetmaker-turned-court clerk from Pittsburgh. An active political operator of long standing, he had served as captain of a company of volunteers in the Mexican War. With plenty of ambition and this credential, he enlisted when the Civil War broke out and was appointed to the colonelcy of the 13th Pennsylvania, a three-month regiment. The 13th was mustered out in August 1861 without seeing action, but most of the men reenlisted under the new 102nd Pennsylvania, retaining Rowley as their leader.

Assigned to the Fourth Corps, the regiment fought under Rowley for the first time the next summer in the Peninsula Campaign at the battles of Williamsburg and Seven Pines. In the latter battle, a bullet struck Rowley in the back of the head, stunning him severely and fracturing his skull, but he remained on the field to encourage the men. His bravery earned him a commendation after the battle from his commander, Brig. Gen. John Peck. Despite his head injury, Rowley went on to lead the 102nd at Malvern Hill.

Though Rowley's regiment didn't fight at Second Bull Run or Antietam, he was promoted to brigadier general on November 29, 1862, and placed in the Sixth Corps. He led his brigade into the fight at Fredericksburg, where it lost just twelve men, but was replaced during the fight by Brig. Gen. Frank Wheaton. This change occurred primarily because Wheaton had been without a command and was ahead of Rowley on the list of promotions.

By March 1863, Rowley was given a newly-organized First Corps brigade—three regiments of green Pennsylvanians. They remained green after Chancellorsville in May, where the corps was little used and only one man in the brigade was killed, though a reshuffling of regiments in May and June leavened the brigade with some veterans. Considering his slight military knowledge and minimal battle experience, Rowley must have been grateful for the addition of these experienced troops to his brigade as he led his men into Pennsylvania.

GETTYSBURG: Rowley arrived in good condition with the lead elements of his division at 11:30 a.m. on the morning of July 1. As the day wore on and the First Corps found itself in desperate straits, Rowley proceeded to get drunk. In an inebriated fog, he became convinced he was the acting corps commander—even though all the division commanders clearly outranked him. Rowley rode blindly through the whirling chaos of the retreat from Seminary Ridge, cursing his troops and ordering them to stay and fight. Fortunately, his men could make no sense of his commands. When he gave up trying to rally the soldiers and rode toward town, he toppled from his horse into a ditch, and had to be helped to his feet by his staff. By the time he reached Cemetery Hill, a subordinate

reported that Rowley "was raving and storming, and giving wild and crazy orders," and "had become positively insane [adding to] the confusion and peril." According to the First Corps provost marshal, "General Rowley, in great excitement, had lost his own third division, and was giving General Wadsworth's troops contradictory orders, calling them cowards, and whose conduct was so unbecoming a division commander and unfortunately stimulated with poor commissary [whiskey]." The provost marshal was forced to call on men of the 6th Wisconsin to arrest Rowley at bayonet point.

Rowley sobered up enough to command his brigade as it remained in reserve on the second and third days of the battle. Within a week, Rowley found himself manning a draft office in Maine, and he never returned to the field. He was a Pittsburgh lawyer and peace officer after the war until his death from heart disease in 1892.

For further reading:

Hartwig, D. Scott. "The Defense of McPherson's Ridge." *Gettysburg Magazine*, # 1, 1989.

Herdegen, Lance. "The Lieutenant who Arrested a General. *Gettysburg Magazine*, #4, 1991.

Martin, David. *Gettysburg, July 1, 1863*. Conshohocken, 1996.

SECOND BRIGADE

THE "BUCKTAIL BRIGADE"

(1,317 MEN)

COLONEL
ROY STONE

For the first year and a half of the war, Roy Stone was associated with the 13th Pennsylvania Reserves. This outfit had become famous as the "Pennsylvania Bucktails," rugged woodsmen and lumbermen from the wilds of northwestern Pennsylvania, who learned early in childhood to shoot for food and work hard to survive. The organizer of the regiment, Colonel Thomas L. Kane, had

disqualified himself from field command due to inexperience, and Stone, the 13th's major, found himself leading the regiment in all its early battles.

As part of the Pennsylvania Reserve Division, Stone and the Bucktails distinguished themselves in almost constant combat during the Seven Days' Battles on the Peninsula in the summer of 1862, losing 247 men in fighting at Mechanicsville (after which Stone received "particular thanks" for his distinguished conduct from division commander Brig. Gen. George McCall), Gaines' Mill, and Glendale. In the latter battle, Stone was riding through the swampy woodland with McCall when they came upon the enemy. In the ensuing melee, McCall was captured and Stone fled, escaping with a slight wound from a parting enemy volley. In his report after the Seven Days, acting division commander Brig. Gen. Truman Seymour singled out Stone, writing, "Major Roy Stone deserves the highest praise on all occasions."

The War Department was so impressed with the straight-shooting Bucktails and their skirmish tactics that they detached Stone from his regiment and sent him back into the Pennsylvania mountains with instructions to bring back a whole brigade's worth of bucktailed warriors. Stone successfully recruited one regiment, designated the 149th Pennsylvania, and at the end of August 1862 was promoted to colonel. His regiment, however, languished in the Washington defenses for the rest of the year. In February 1863, two more regiments of Pennsylvanians were added to Stone's command. These soldiers attached bucktails from white-tailed deer onto their forage caps and dubbed themselves the "Bucktail Brigade." The original Bucktails were outraged. They claimed the Secretary of War had authorized them alone to wear bucktails as distinctive badges, and they contemptuously called Stone's new brigade the "Bogus Bucktails." At Chancellorsville, the brigade's first battle, Stone's men had no chance to prove themselves, and except for a brief tangle with some pickets, never saw the enemy.

Stone was eager to prove his brigade was the equal of his former command and wanted nothing better than to dispel the disparaging tag of "Bogus Bucktails." While he had distinguished himself as a regimental commander, he was completely without battle experience as a brigade leader, and had not seen action since the Seven Days' Battles. His main asset was his long association with his three regiments of Pennsylvanians.

GETTYSBURG: Stone's brigade started its seven-mile march from Marsh Creek on the Emmitsburg Road to Gettysburg about 9:00 a.m. on July 1. The Pennsylvanians arrived at the Lutheran Seminary a couple of hours later, just as Brig. Gen. James Wadsworth's division had finished throwing back Maj. Gen. Henry Heth's attack on McPherson's Ridge. During the following lull in the battle, Stone put his men into line on the right of the Iron Brigade. His Pennsylvania regiments were deployed, from left to right, as follows: the 150th, 143rd, and 149th. All three faced west and were just south of the Chambersburg Pike. About 1:30 p.m. Stone saw Rodes' attack developing to the north (his right) and shifted the 149th Pennsylvania to face in that direction along the pike, forming a V-shaped line to fend off an attack from two directions. His men were thus exposed in a dangerous salient. "I relied greatly upon Stone's brigade to hold the post assigned them," reported acting corps commander Maj. Gen. Abner Doubleday, who considered the brigade's fight to be "in truth the key-point of the first day's battle."

About 3:00 p.m., Brig. Gen. Junius Daniel's Confederate brigade approached from the north, and Stone's men delivered two volleys in succession at close range, followed by a charge which repulsed Daniel's men. During a second attack by the Southerners, Stone went down with a wound in the hip and arm near the McPherson barn. He was captured when the Confederates finally swept over the position a short time later.

Paroled by the Confederates, Stone returned to the brigade the following spring. At the Battle of the Wilderness in May 1864, he was injured when his horse fell on him, and was unable to return to field duty for the remainder of the war. Stone was commissioned as brigadier general of volunteers more than thirty years later, in the Spanish-American War. He died in 1901.

For Further Reading:

Hartwig, D. Scott. "The Defense of McPherson's Ridge." *Gettysburg Magazine,* # 1, 1989.

Martin, David. *Gettysburg, July 1, 1863.* Conshohocken, 1996.

Thomson, O. R. Howard, & William Rauch. *History of the Bucktails.* Dayton, 1988.

THIRD BRIGADE
THE "PAPER COLLAR BRIGADE"

(1,950 MEN)

BRIGADIER GENERAL
GEORGE JERRISON STANNARD

Forty-three-year-old George Stannard had been a foundry operator in the sleepy town of St. Albans near the Canadian border when the war broke out. A native of Vermont, Stannard had served as a colonel in the state militia, and on that basis was elected lieutenant colonel of the 2nd Vermont volunteer regiment when Fort Sumter fell. Local lore claimed he was the first Vermonter to volunteer for duty in 1861.

He fought with the 2nd Vermont at Bull Run in the summer of 1861, impressing his regimental commander who cited him for being "square up to the work." Stannard was offered the colonelcy of the new 3rd Vermont but turned it down because he thought he had not served long enough to qualify for the position. During the 1862 Peninsula Campaign, Brig. Gen. Winfield Hancock credited Stannard with securing a crucial bridge at the Battle of Williamsburg. A week after the campaign concluded, Stannard was made colonel and given his own regiment, the 9th Vermont. While stationed in Harpers Ferry during the September 1862 Antietam Campaign, the 9th surrendered with the rest of the garrison to Thomas J. "Stonewall" Jackson.

Stannard was subsequently exchanged following this ignominious episode, and returned to Vermont. In March 1863, he was given a brigadier general's star, and the following month was put at the head of a brigade composed of three nine-month Vermont regiments (the 13th, 14th, and 16th). Stannard joined the brigade while it was camped in the defenses of Washington, its post since mustering in the previous fall. (The brigade's previous commander had been captured in his bed at Fairfax Court House by John Mosby's Rebel raiders). Stannard's "quiet but effective" command style earned him immediate respect from his men. He drilled his new brigade five hours a day until late June, when it became one of four brigades sent from the capital's garrison to join the Army of the Potomac as it headed for Pennsylvania. The Vermonters' uniforms were still a tell-tale bright blue, and the hardened campaigners of the army took one look at these mint-condition reinforcements and derisively dubbed them the "Paper Collar Brigade."

GETTYSBURG: Stannard, who had last seen combat experience on the Peninsula, and his untested brigade of nine-month men, performed far above expectations during the fight in Pennsylvania. After a grueling seven-day march from Washington, Stannard's nearly 2,000-strong brigade arrived at twilight on the evening of July 1, too late to participate in the day's fighting. It was placed on Cemetery Ridge near a small copse of trees. Stannard remained on watch that night and described the situation on his frontto the newly-arrived Maj. Gen. George Meade when the commanding officer rode down the line about 2:00 a.m.

On July 2 the Vermonters were withdrawn behind Cemetery Hill. Stannard watched the battle from Cemetery Ridge with his binoculars. In the waning moments of daylight, his Vermonters were called upon to repulse the attack of Brig. Gen. Ambrose Wright's Confederate brigade on Cemetery Ridge, but the enemy onslaught was pushed back before they were needed.

Stannard won his share of eternal glory on July 3 on Cemetery Ridge during the repulse of Pickett's Charge. The Southern attack initially headed straight for the Vermonters, but veered to the left during its final approach to the main Union line—either to shy away from the Union shelling from the direction of Little Round Top, or to target the copse of trees further north on the ridge. Stannard had enough presence of mind and belief in his men to swing two of his regiments (the 13th and 16th) out at a 90 degree angle, and they proceeded to rake the exposed right flank of Brig. Gen. James Kemper's Brigade. Stannard's deadly envelopment was one of the critical factors that helped doom the Confederate attack. Many Southerners who were not mowed down by the Vermonters' flanking fire surrendered to Stannard's men.

As Pickett's men staggered away from their beating, the brigades of Brig. Gen. Cadmus Wilcox and Col. David Lang appeared heading toward the Union line on the south side of Stannard's brigade. Seeing the gray lines advancing over the Emmitsburg Road, Stannard wheeled two regiments (the 16th and 14th) and once again used an enfilade fire to force back the enemy (Lang's Floridians). A few moments later Stannard was wounded in the right thigh by a shell fragment. Despite the pain, he stayed on the field until nightfall.

Second Corps commander Hancock praised Stannard and his men saying, "The troops of General Stannard behaved with spirit at the Battle of Gettysburg. They were well ordered and well and vigorously handled by General Stannard and his subordinate officers, who did not hesitate to put them in front of the fight, and to keep them there until the battle was decided." The First Corps' Maj. Gen. Abner Doubleday was even more effusive: "I can only say that they performed perhaps the most brilliant feat during the war. For they broke the desperate charge of Pickett, saved the day and with it, the whole North from invasion and devastation."

Stannard's painful wound would not allow him to remain with his infantrymen, and he went back to Vermont to recover. When he returned to duty in September, it was with General Ben Butler's Army of the James. Stannard spent the next year with that army, rising to division command before he lost an arm in front of Richmond in September 1864. He was assigned to duty back home in Vermont for the last seven months of the war. He resigned from the army in 1867 to become a customs official in his home state, and was the doorkeeper of the House of Representatives for the last four years of his life. Stannard died in 1886.

For further reading:

Buena, Anthony. "The First Vermonter to Enlist in the War, Union General George Stannard Helped Turn the Tide at Gettysburg." *America's Civil War*, 9, July 1996.

Coffin, Howard. *Full Duty: Vermonters in the Civil War.* Dayton, 1995.

———. *Nine Months to Gettysburg.* Woodstock, 1997.

Dickson, Christopher C. "The Flying Brigade: Brig. Gen. George Stannard and the Road to Gettysburg." *Gettysburg Magazine*, #16, 1997.

Trimble, Tony. "Paper Collars: Stannard's Brigade at Gettysburg." *Gettysburg Magazine*, #2, 1990.

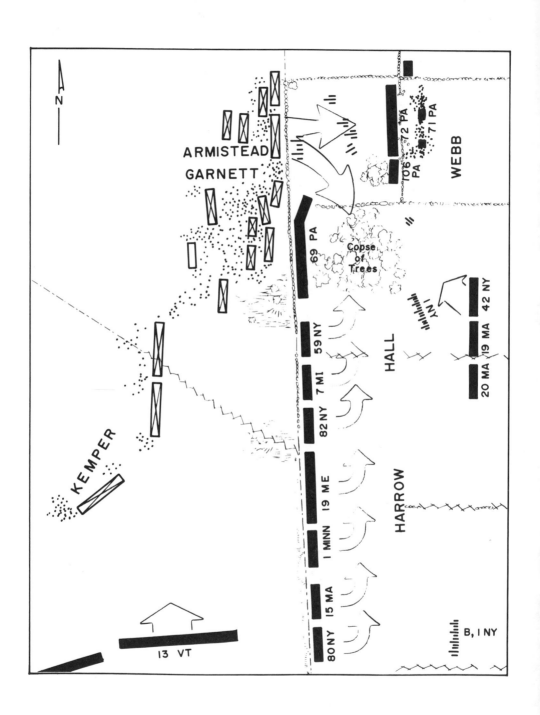

SECOND CORPS

(11,247 MEN / 28 GUNS)

MAJOR GENERAL
WINFIELD SCOTT HANCOCK

Winfield Hancock certainly looked the part of a high-ranking officer. The observant staffer Frank Haskell saved his highest superlatives for the 6' 2" Second Corps chief. Of all the army's officers, Haskell believed "Hancock was. . .in many respects the best-looking, dignified, gentlemanly and commanding. He was tall and well proportioned, had a ruddy complexion, brown hair, and he wore a mustache and a tuft of hair upon his chin . . . . Had General Hancock worn citizen's clothes, and given commands in the army to those who did not know him, he would be likely to be obeyed at once, for he had the appearance of a man born to command." Another officer wrote that "one felt safe to be near him." Others were impressed with his sartorial splendor; a Maine artilleryman wrote that "his very atmosphere was strong and invigorating. . . . I remember (how refreshing to note!) even his linen clean and white, his collar wide and free, and his broad wrist bands showing large and rolling back

from his firm, finely molded hands." Grant himself recalled him as having been "tall, well-formed and. . .young and fresh-looking, he presented an appearance that would attract the attention of an army as he passed. His genial disposition made him friends, and his personal courage and his presence with his command in the thickest of the fight won for him the confidence of troops serving under him. No matter how hard the fight, the Second Corps always felt that their commander was looking after them."

Hancock was born and raised in Norristown, Pennsylvania, less than 100 miles from Gettysburg. As a schoolboy he showed a fondness for things military and organized a military company among his schoolmates. He entered West Point at sixteen and graduated in 1844, 18th out of 25 cadets. After a two-year hitch in Texas, he acquired battle experience in the Mexican War. When the endless routine of army posts drove many other officers back into civilian life, he stayed in the army and accumulated additional experience while serving in the Mormon Expedition and the Seminole War. One observer wrote, "he loved 'papers,' rejoicing in forms and regulations and requisitions." Thus in the years between 1850 and 1861, Hancock developed another laudable trait when he learned to appreciate attention to detail. He ended his pre-war career as a captain in command of the quartermaster's depot in Los Angeles. There, he presided at a legendary farewell dinner for his friends Albert S. Johnston, Lewis Armistead, and other officers who had resigned to "go South" after Fort Sumter

The War Department made Hancock a brigadier general in the first fall of the conflict. He differed from most Regular Army officers in that he liked volunteer soldiers and did his best to make them feel equal in importance to Regular troops, and his men repaid him for that attitude. His mixed brigade of Pennsylvania, New York, Wisconsin, and Maine soldiers fought so well during the Peninsula Campaign's fight at Williamsburg that Maj. Gen. George McClellan telegraphed, "Hancock was superb today." The adjective stuck in the public mind and he would later campaign for president as "Hancock the Superb" nearly thirty years later.

At Antietam in September 1862, Hancock's brigade was held in reserve with the rest of the Sixth Corps. While the battle was raging, Hancock was chosen to replace the fatally wounded Maj. Gen. Israel Richardson in command of the First Division, Second Corps. Hancock arrived after the division's attack on the enemy center had lost its momentum, and he merely presided over the men while they held their position in the Sunken Road. Promoted to major general on November 29, 1862, Hancock led Richardson's old division into battle for the first time at Fredericksburg, where he was ordered to make a futile attack into the teeth of the Confederate defenses on Marye's Heights. A bullet went through his coat and grazed his abdomen, and two thousand of his men were shot down in the slaughter before the stone wall lining the base of the heights.

The following spring at Chancellorsville, Hancock and his division performed brilliantly while covering the withdrawal of the army on May 2. He was struck with several small spent shell fragments although he remained on the field. When Maj. Gen. Darius Couch, the leader of the Second Corps, refused to continue serving under army commander Joe Hooker, the thirty-nine-year-old Hancock was the obvious choice to replace Couch at the head of the corps. He was officially given command on May 22, just six weeks before Gettysburg.

Hancock looked, acted, and sounded like a soldier. He had a loud bull voice, and in an army of expert swearers, multiple witnesses testified that Hancock had an unrivaled command of the profane idiom—he was the champion of precise cursing, used effectively and with vigor. His men liked to relate that "the air was blue all around him" as he galloped along his lines while ordering his troops to charge at Williamsburg. One colonel said Hancock "always swore at everybody, above all on the battlefield." At Chancellorsville, Hancock had started a habit of placing regiments in important positions in person. He would vault from his horse, grab the first man at one end of the regiment's front line, physically plant the soldier firmly on the desired spot and roar, "Will you stay here?" Hancock would then align the regimental colors on the shaken and often dumbstruck enlistee, order the rest of the unit into line, remount, and ride off.

While it is true that he had commanded the corps for only a few weeks at Gettysburg, "Hancock's men" were already familiar with him as the major general of their First Division. In addition to being a great natural leader of troops, Hancock was an excellent tactician. General Grant later remarked that he knew of no blunder Hancock had made on the battlefield. Although outranked by all the other infantry corps commanders except the Fifth Corps' Maj. Gen. George Sykes, Hancock was Major General Meade's most highly trusted friend and subordinate. At Gettysburg Hancock wore a black felt slouch hat "stiff enough for the brim and crown to hold their shapes," an officer's undress uniform coat buttoned at the top and open at the waist, a sword belt under the coat, and a field and staff officer's sword.

GETTYSBURG: Hancock was at the top of his game in early July 1863, and no other Union general at Gettysburg dominated men by the sheer force of their presence more completely than Hancock. His presence and direction were crucial on all three days of the battle. Rarely in warfare has the arrival of one man on a battlefield been more timely and consequential than Hancock's arrival at Gettysburg on July 1. Maj. Gen. Carl Schurz of the Eleventh Corps saw Hancock arrive with Meade's orders and testified, "The appearance of General Hancock at the front was a most fortunate event. . .It gave the troops a new inspiration. . .His mere presence was a reinforcement, and everybody on the field felt stronger for his being there." Abner Doubleday, another major general at the scene, agreed: "Hancock was our genius, for he at once brought order out of confusion and made such admirable dispositions that he secured the ridge and held it." One of Hancock's subordinates painted the same picture. Before he came, "wreck, disaster, disorder, almost the panic that precedes disorganization, defeat and retreat were everywhere." After he appeared on Cemetery Hill, "soldiers retreating stopped, skulkers appeared from under their cover, lines were reformed." An artilleryman could never forget the "inspiration of his commanding, controlling presence, nor the fresh courage he imparted. . . ."

Meade arrived to assume control in the middle of the night, and on the morning of July 2, Hancock's Second Corps arrived and was posted in the Union center, from Cemetery Hill a mile or so south to where Maj. Gen. Daniel Sickles's Third Corps took over. At the climax of the afternoon fighting, when Lt. Gen. James Longstreet's attack rolled forward toward the Round Tops, Meade learned that Sickles had been wounded. He immediately put Hancock in command of the Third Corps, placing him effectively in control of all the Union troops from Cemetery Hill to Little Round Top. Hancock set about improvising a defense which held back the enemy throughout the late afternoon and early evening. He seemed to be everywhere at once, placing regiments by hand as he had done at Chancellorsville, and directing desperate charges by individual regiments—such as the heroic self-destruction of the 1st Minnesota.

Much to the South's misfortune, Pickett's Charge, which was launched on the afternoon of the battle's third day, was aimed squarely at Hancock's line. The general was constantly in view of his men during the attack, inspecting his lines and remaining close at hand to respond as quickly as possible to any emergencies. Even as the war's most famous assault headed directly toward his command, Hancock still managed to exceed his authority, giving orders to Maj. Gen. Newton's troops and Brig. Gen. Henry Hunt's cannoneers. In the final stages of the fighting, while riding over to Brig. Gen. George Stannard's First Corps brigade to give it an order, Hancock was severely wounded in the front of the right thigh. Although the injury put him out of action, the last of the Confederate attackers were turned back only a few minutes later, ending the battle.

At first Hancock thought he had been shot with a ten-penny nail. It was, in fact, a bullet, which had hit the pommel of his saddle and carried splintered pieces of wood and the nail

into the wound. A tourniquet was made from a handkerchief and twisted with a pistol barrel to stop the flow of blood. A surgeon on the field probed the wound with his finger and removed the nail and bits of wood. Hancock would never be the same again. After a lengthy and painful recuperation, he returned to the Second Corps in December 1863. Riding a horse, however, aggravated and reopened the wound. It continued to seep blood and fluid for the next year, forcing him from the field for weeks at a time. He finally retired from active duty during the Petersburg siege in November 1864.

Hancock was promoted to major general in in 1866 and remained in various departmental commands until he ran for president in 1880, an election he lost narrowly to James Garfield. He died six years later of an infected boil, complicated by diabetes, while still in command of the Department of the East.

For further reading:

Hancock, Mrs. W. S., ed. *Reminiscences of Winfield Scott Hancock*. New York, 1887.

Jordan, David. *Winfield Scott Hancock: A Soldier's Life*. Indianapolis, 1988.

Pfanz, Harry. *Gettysburg: The Second Day*. Chapel Hill, 1987.

Tucker, Glenn. *Hancock the Superb*, Indianapolis. 1960.

Walker, Francis A. *General Hancock*. New York, 1894.

Wright, Steven. "'Don't Let me Bleed to Death': The Wounding of Maj. Gen. Winfield Scott Hancock." *Gettysburg Magazine*, #6, 1992.

FIRST DIVISION

(3,320 MEN)

BRIGADIER GENERAL
JOHN C. CALDWELL

John Caldwell, a young man of thirty at Gettysburg, was one of those rare individuals who rose to divisional command despite having no acquaintance with military affairs before the war. Nor did he have much battle experience leading a division prior to the Get-

tysburg Campaign, for he had only been promoted when Maj. Gen. Winfield S. Hancock, the previous division commander, left to head the Second Corps on May 22, 1863.

Born in Vermont, the scholarly Caldwell graduated from Amherst and served as teacher and principal at the Washington Academy at East Machias, Maine, for five years preceding the onset of the war. Several months after the outbreak of hostilities, in November 1861, he was elected colonel of the 11th Maine, a contingent assigned to the Army of the Potomac. Caldwell received a rapid series of promotions thereafter. In April 1862, just as the Peninsula Campaign was getting under way, he was bumped to brigadier general., and in June received command of the First Brigade, First Division, Second Corps (commanded at Gettysburg by Col. Edward Cross) after Brig. Gen. Oliver O. Howard was wounded at Seven Pines.

Caldwell led his brigade with some success through the army's battles of 1862. He was personally thanked for his "gallantry" in coming to the aid of Maj. Gen. Philip Kearny's division in the crucial action at Glendale during the Seven Days' Battles, and at Antietam briefly directed the division after Maj. Gen. Israel Richardson was wounded. After the battle, however, it was whispered that Caldwell had hidden himself in the rear behind a haystack. His handling of the brigade in the assault on the Bloody Lane was criticized as lax and uninspired. At Fred-

icksburg, while preparing his men to charge Marye's Heights, he was struck in the left side but remained on the field. A few minutes later he was hit again, this time in the left shoulder, although he was able to direct one of his regiments. Here again, however, there was a small stain on Caldwell's record—another of his regiments broke and ran to the rear. At Chancellorsville in May 1863, Caldwell performed well in difficult circumstances when the division was forced to face in opposite directions and cover the retreat of the army around the Chancellor House on May 3.

By the time of Gettysburg, Caldwell was one of the Federal army's most experienced brigade commanders. Despite his civilian background, he evidently enjoyed the confidence of Hancock, who otherwise would have suggested someone other than Caldwell to command the First Division when he was promoted. The men under him spoke well of him, too. "Caldwell is an agreeable man and well liked," wrote one man of his brigade who served with him before Gettysburg. "There is none of the assumed dignity and importance so common among officers . . . He is much more familiar with his officers than General Meagher [of the Irish Brigade] and is much better liked by them than M[eagher] by his." However, when Hancock left the Second Corps to go personally to Gettysburg on July 1, army commander Meade ordered Brig. Gen. John Gibbon of the Second Division take command of the corps—in spite of the fact that Caldwell outranked him. Given Meade's preference for West Pointers, the move was probably a reflection of Caldwell's lack of training as a professional soldier.

GETTYSBURG: Arriving early in the morning of the July 2 by way of the Taneytown Road, Caldwell's division was initially placed in the middle of Cemetery Ridge as a reserve, in a formation that enabled it to move quickly. Around 5:00 p.m., when the call for help came from Maj. Gen. Dan Sickles's front, Caldwell had all four of his brigades moving within minutes. Approaching the Wheatfield from the north, he delivered the only coordinated division-sized Federal assault at Gettysburg. The attack was handled expertly. Within ten minutes, in unfamiliar terrain with nothing to guide them but the sound of the heaviest fighting, three of Caldwell's brigades were surging in unison toward the enemy. The sudden attack threw three Confederate brigades back in disorder and gained ground beyond the original Union line. A short time later, however, Maj. Gen. Lafayette McLaws' Confederate division rushed forward, bearing down on Caldwell's exposed right flank.

When his attack stalled, Caldwell continued to be active and alert, riding in person (essentially acting as his own staff) to ask for the support of nearby brigades when it became evident that no higher officer was overseeing or coordinating the Union effort on this critical part of the battlefield. While he was thus occupied, he couldn't see that McLaws' brigades had sent his division tumbling back from the Wheatfield. An aide finally got his attention and pointed out that his men were running away in confusion. Caldwell's division, outflanked and exhausted, raced to the rear and couldn't be rallied until after dark.

Caldwell was unjustly criticized by Maj. Gen. George Sykes, the Fifth Corps chief, who reported to Hancock that the division had "done badly." As a result, Caldwell lost Hancock's confidence—this was Hancock's old division, after all. He withheld praise from Caldwell after the battle, and ordered an investigation of the July 2 conduct by the First Division. The investigation vindicated Caldwell. Lieutenant Colonel C. H. Morgan of Hancock's staff, who himself had come upon Caldwell's division in full flight to the rear, wrote "[the investigation] showed that no troops on the field had done better." Despite Caldwell's vindication, Hancock replaced him less than a year later, when the Army of the Potomac was consolidated from five corps to three in March 1864.

Caldwell practiced law after the war and served in several diplomatic positions. He died in 1912.

For further reading:

Campbell, Eric. "Caldwell Clears the Wheatfield." *Gettysburg Magazine*, #3, July 1990.

Hartwig, D. Scott. "John C. Caldwell's Division in the Wheatfield." in Gary Gallagher, ed. *The Second Day at Gettysburg*, Kent, 1993.

Pfanz, Harry. *Gettysburg: The Second Day.* Chapel Hill, 1987.

FIRST BRIGADE

(853 MEN)

COLONEL
EDWARD E. CROSS

Thirty-one-year-old Edward Cross was as fearless and tough a fighter as there was in either army. He was an imposing figure, tall, rangy, and erect "like an Indian," one man observed—with a full reddish beard and balding head. Cross was known for habitually pacing "in his quick, nervous, way, his hands clasped behind his back," and was possessed by "a sharp, impulsive manner" on the battlefield. He always had a lieutenant tie a red silk bandanna around his head when he was about to go into a fight. He'd worn it at the head of his regiment, the 5th New Hampshire, on the Peninsula, at Antietam, Fredericksburg, and Chancellorsville.

In the Battle of Seven Pines a year earlier, he'd shouted "Charge 'em like hell, boys—show them you are damned Yankees!" Then, as his regiment advanced, Cross fell wounded. When some of his men came over to help him off the field, he lifted himself up on an elbow and told them, "Never mind me—

whip the enemy first and take care of me afterward." He recovered from his Seven Pines wound in time to lead the bloody attack on the Sunken Lane at Antietam, where he was again wounded. He was struck a third time at Fredericksburg in front of the stone wall on Marye's Heights. "If all the colonels in the army had been like him we should never have lost a battle,"remarked one of his men.

Born in Lancaster, New Hampshire, Cross was well educated and well traveled. He served a stint as a printer, then as a reporter and editor for the Cincinnati Atlas. City life was too placid for a young man with his abundant energy, so he headed for Arizona, where he worked in the mining business and as a trapper, buffalo hunter, explorer, and part-time Indian fighter. In Arizona he fought a duel—with rifles—then went to Mexico and fought another, this time with swords. Surviving both, he became an officer in the army of Mexico's liberal party, just as war was about to break out in the United States.

When the Civil War began he returned to New Hampshire. Even though he had no formal military education, as an experienced fighter he was a natural choice to lead the state's 5th Regiment. "He taught us to aim in battle," wrote one of his soldiers, "and above all things he ignored and made us ignore the idea of retreating. Besides this he clothed us and fed us well, taught us to build good quarters, and camped us on good ground."

But Cross was a controversial officer. His men knew him as a grim warrior. At Antietam he had taken them in with the words: "If any man runs I want the file closers to shoot him. If they don't, I shall myself." He had a critical nature, jumped to conclusions, and was so outspoken that his friends believed his advancement had been slowed by his criticism of certain politicians and policies—how else, they argued, could such a fighter always be overlooked for promotion? He had even made enemies in his own brigade. The day before the Battle of Gettysburg opened, Cross replaced the colonel of the untried recruits of the 148th Pennsylvania, the brigade's newest and biggest regiment, with someone more experienced from another regiment. As a result, the men of the 148th, which represent-ed about one-half of the strength of his brigade, considered him a tyrant.

GETTYSBURG: Colonel Cross arrived on the battlefield on the morning of July 2 a troubled man. He had had a premonition of his own death, and in his pocket was an ominous black bandanna instead of the red silk one he customarily wore. He had a lieutenant tie it around his head as the sounds of General Sickles' Third Corps battle with James Longstreet drifted ever closer. About 5:00 p.m., as orderlies came dashing along the lines and the division prepared to move south to succor the embattled Third Corps, Hancock himself rode up in front of Cross. "Colonel Cross, this day will bring you a star," he shouted. Cross shook his head and replied calmly, "No, General, this is my last battle." The colonel vaulted into the saddle to lead his men toward the sound of the fighting.

Cross' brigade was the first in the division to be deployed, forming up hurriedly in the northeast corner of the Wheatfield, facing south. His brigade was aligned, from left to right, as follows: 5th New Hampshire, 148th Pennsylvania, 81st Pennsylvania, and 61st New York. Once deployed, Cross ordered the men forward in his usual sharp and animated manner, with his sword drawn and the morbid black bandanna wrapped around his forehead.

As they neared the middle of the field, Cross' regiments received their first heavy fire from Confederates crouching behind a stone wall at the southern end of the field. Cross was on the exposed right flank of his brigade, on a knoll in the middle of the Wheatfield, when he dismounted, "eagerly scanning the ground in the front." He stepped back from the line and shouted "Boys—instruct the commanders to be ready to charge when the order is given. Wait here for the command, or, if you hear the bugles of the 5th New Hampshire on the left, move forward on the run!" He strode over to the 5th Regiment, which was almost in contact with Brig. Gen. George Anderson's Confederates on the east side of the field. As he reached his old regiment—"the hottest place on the line," according to Cross' lieutenant—he fell mortally wounded with a bullet in the stomach before he could give the order to charge.

Cross was taken to a field hospital where he died the next day. His last words were, "I think the boys will miss me."

For further reading:

Campbell, Eric. "Caldwell Clears the Wheatfield." *Gettysburg Magazine*, #3, July, 1990.

Hartwig, D. Scott. "John C. Caldwell's Division in the Wheatfield," in Gary Gallagher, ed. *The Second Day at Gettysburg*, Kent, 1993.

Pfanz, Harry. *Gettysburg: The Second Day.* Chapel Hill, 1987.

SECOND BRIGADE

THE "IRISH BRIGADE"

(532 MEN)

COLONEL
PATRICK KELLY

A native of Ireland with no military education, Kelly began the war as captain of a company in the legendary all-Irish 69th New York Militia, which fought at First Bull Run. When the 69th, a ninety-day unit, was mustered out in the fall of 1861, Kelly was commissioned at the same rank in one of the new Regular Army units, the 16th United States Infantry. With this regiment he fought in the Western Theater at the Battle of Shiloh in April 1862,

where he won a brevet promotion for bravery. Soon after Shiloh, he returned to Virginia and accepted a commission as lieutenant colonel of the 88th New York, one of the regiments in the colorful Irish Brigade. Kelly commanded the regiment at Fair Oaks on June 1. The brigade's commander, Brig. Gen. Thomas F. Meagher, commended the 88th in his report but failed to mention Kelly personally. He was not present at the Seven Days' Battles.

Kelly led the 88th at Antietam in September 1862, and was mentioned after that battle in Winfield Hancock's omnibus commendation of the field officers serving in his division. He was promoted to colonel on October 20, 1862, and after the slaughter of the division in front of the stone wall at Fredericksburg on December 13, Kelly received a perfunctory commendation from Hancock: "active and resolute, as he always is, and with his regiment, performed their usual good service." At Chancellorsville, the Irish Brigade was used mainly to support batteries around the Chancellor House, and Kelly's regiment was spared from the heavy casualties they had suffered in previous battles. Kelly assumed command of the Irish Brigade as its senior colonel when Meagher resigned in despair over, among other things, the brigade's decimated condition. Although Kelly was elevated to brigade command on the eve of the Gettysburg Campaign, he was experienced and led one of the hardest-fighting and most celebrated brigades in the Union army. One of his men later wrote, "He was a father to the brigade, as he was always to his own regiment, a brave, gentle, splendid soldier."

GETTYSBURG: Kelly and the Irish Brigade arrived on Cemetery Ridge with the rest of Caldwell's division on the morning of July 2. About 5:00 p.m. that afternoon, word came down that the division was preparing to move toward the fight roaring to the south. Father William Corby, chaplain of one of the Irish regiments, stood on a boulder and offered absolution to the entire brigade as its members knelt with heads bowed in prayer. A major in the Second Corps reported that the rest of the division, as well as corps leader Hancock, solemnly watched this "scene [that] was more than impressive, it was awe-inspiring."

After a short march Caldwell's three brigades were formed for battle at the northern end of the Wheatfield; Kelly's regiments held the center of the line, deployed from right to left as follows: the 116th Pennsylvania, 28th Massachusetts, and the 63rd, 69th, and 88th New York regiments stacked up on the left. The brigades of Brig. Gens. Edward Cross and Samuel Zook covered Kelly's flanks and moved out first, attracting most of the enemy fire, thereby enabling Kelly's men to cross the field with little loss. As the Irish Brigade drew within twenty paces of the tree line at far end of the field, Brig. Gen. James Kershaw's South Carolinians suddenly became visible. One Union veteran remembered that "Someone in the ranks cried out, 'There they are!,'" and the muskets of the Irish Brigade poured forth a thunderous volley. The Irishmen drove Kershaw's Confederates back up the wooded hill immediately south of the Wheatfield, loading and firing within a few feet of the enemy lines. Mounting losses, Kershaw's stubborn resistance, and the confusion brought about by the intermingling of the brigade with Zook's command in the smoky woods slowly brought the advance to a halt. A renewed Confederate onslaught from the west collapsed Caldwell's division, and Kelly's battle-fatigued Irishmen went streaming to the rear. Kelly left 198 men on the field, or 37 percent of the brigade. Kelly himself, however, was the only one of Caldwell's brigade leaders who emerged unscathed from the withering fire of the Wheatfield. "Kelly behaved with his wonted gallantry," said Caldwell after the battle.

The Irish colonel continued to lead the decimated Irish Brigade as a colonel through the fall months until he was replaced by Col. Richard Byrnes in February 1864. Kelly regained the reins of command when Byrnes was wounded at Cold Harbor in early June 1864, but was killed two weeks later, on June 16, at Petersburg.

For further reading:

Campbell, Eric. "Caldwell Clears the Wheatfield." *Gettysburg Magazine*, #3, 1990.

Cavanaugh, Michael. *Memoirs of Gen. Thomas Francis Meagher.* Dayton, 1991.

Conyngham, D. P. *The Irish Brigade and Its Campaigns.* New York, 1994.

Hartwig, D. Scott. "John C. Caldwell's Division in the Wheatfield," in Gary Gallagher, ed. *The Second Day at Gettysburg*, Kent, 1993.

Jones, Paul. *The Irish Brigade.* Washington and New York, 1969.

Pfanz, Harry. *Gettysburg: The Second Day.* Chapel Hill, 1987.

THIRD BRIGADE
(975 MEN)

BRIGADIER GENERAL
SAMUEL KOSCIUSKO ZOOK

Samuel Zook, forty-two-years-old at the start of the Gettysburg Campaign, was one of the many volunteer generals who had militia experience but no formal military schooling. He grew up in the rich historical milieu of Valley Forge, Pennsylvania, and was infatuated with the military from his early childhood. As a boy he enjoyed commanding his schoolmates on the fortifications around his home (even to the point of "arresting" his sister for failure to obey orders). As soon as he could carry a musket, Zook became involved in local militia activity.

Professionally, Zook gravitated toward the new science of telegraphy, and was one of its pioneers, helping to string telegraphic wire as far west as the Mississippi River. By the time he was forty he had established himself as superintendent of the Washington and New York Telegraph Company and was living in New York City. He also joined the 6th New York Militia and had worked his way up to the rank of lieutenant colonel by the time the Civil War broke out.

The 6th New York Militia volunteered as a ninety-day unit in the first summer of the war. During these months, while the First Bull Run Campaign was being fought, Zook served as military governor in Annapolis. He used this time to solicit friendships and politic for the command of his own regiment. He was not a man to be denied, for when the 6th New York was mustered out in October 1861, Zook quickly became the colonel of the new 57th New York Volunteers. During this period, Zook sent a letter stating his principles on the matter of regimental command to a captain named William Clark, in response to Clark's inquiry about joining the 57th. "I am determined to have none but gentlemen for my officers & no amount of men will induce me to depart from this determination," explained Zook. "Some Colonels are so eager to get men they will receive the most ignorant & vulgar loafers."

The 57th first saw action on the Peninsula. During the Seven Days' Battles, Zook demonstrated his enterprise. Scouting far out in front of his men, he rode behind enemy lines and discovered a ruse employed by Confederate Maj. Gen. John Magruder, who was shifting troops back and forth in view of the Union lines to make his numbers appear larger than they actually were. Zook reported the deception and begged permission to personally lead an assault, but corps commander Brig. Gen. Edwin "Bull" Sumner was afraid to give such an order on his own responsibility. Sumner referred Zook's observation to army headquarters, but General McClellan overlooked the report.

Zook was on medical leave and missed the Battle of Antietam, probably as a result of his ongoing bout with rheumatism, an affliction so severe he occasionally had trouble moving.

The standard remedy of the day was poisonous alkaloid colchicine, which only exacerbated Zook's suffering by adding intestinal disorders to his woes. When he returned to the army in October 1862, he stepped back in as the new leader of his brigade, though he still only held a colonel's rank. As senior colonel, he inherited command from Brig. Gen. William H. French, who had been promoted to divisional command just before the Maryland Campaign.

In mid-November, Zook's brigade was one of the first in the Army of the Potomac to arrive at Fredericksburg. Although he wanted to cross the Rappahannock River immediately, the pontoons did not arrive until weeks later, by which time the Confederates were dug in and prepared for an assault. On December 10, Zook wrote prophetically, "If we had had the pontoons promised when we arrived here we could have the hills on the other side of the river without costing over 50 men—Now it will cost at least ten thousand if not more."

Three days later the army lost over twelve thousand men trying to take "the hills," and 527 of the casualties were from Zook's brigade. Leading the heartbreaking attack on Marye's Heights, Colonel Zook had his horse shot from under him and was momentarily stunned by the fall, but managed to lead his men to within sixty yards of the stone wall, one of the deepest Union advances of the day. After the battle, division leader Winfield S. Hancock praised Zook's attack for its "spirit." "Now by God!" wrote Zook afterward, "if I don't get my [brigadier-general's] star, I'm coming home."

Zook was not disappointed, for he received his commission to brigadier general early in 1863. In the fighting around the Chancellor House at the Battle of Chancellorsville later in the spring, his brigade faced east while the brigades facing west and south did most of the heavy fighting. As a consequence, Zook's men suffered only 188 casualties, far less than others that fought that day. After the battle, Zook again went on medical leave for his rheumatism, returning to his regiments as they moved towards Gettysburg at the end of June. Morale in his brigade was high, according to Zook's letter to his father on June 28:

"The men are in good spirits, and will fight splendidly."

Zook was a blunt and firm disciplinarian who despised cowardice. He often expressed his sentiments with a towering mastery of profanity. In this, he was even able to hold his own with the redoubtable Winfield Hancock, according to an enlisted man's description of an incident on the road to Chancellorsville: "It was the greatest cursing match I ever listened to; Zook took advantage of Hancock, by waiting until the latter got out of breath, and then he opened his pipe organ, and the air was very blue." For all that, his men also knew him to be a good-hearted man.

GETTYSBURG: General Zook and his brigade arrived on Cemetery Ridge with the rest of Caldwell's division on the morning of July 2. Late that afternoon, the division prepared to move south to support General Sickles' Third Corps, which was attempting to arrest a Confederate assault aimed at the rolling up the Union left flank. As Zook moved south toward the sound of battle with Caldwell's other brigades, he was intercepted by Maj. Henry Tremain from General Sickles' staff. Tremain urgently asked him to detach his brigade and move into action immediately.

As Tremain recalled later, General Zook replied, "with a calm, firm look, inspiring me with its significance, 'If you will give me the order of General Sickles I will obey it.'" Tremain obliged, and Zook left his division and followed the staffer, deploying for battle, as chance would have it, directly on the right end of the line Caldwell was preparing to send into the Wheatfield fighting. Zook's regiments were deployed, from right to left, as follows: 140th Pennsylvania, 52nd New York, and 66th New York; the 57th New York was positioned behind the Pennsylvanians.

Zook's men plunged forward with their general mounted in their midst. He made an easy target on horseback, and was one of the first to fall when an enemy bullet slammed into his stomach. Supported in the saddle by two members of his staff, Zook made his way to the rear, where he told aide Lt. Josiah Favill, "It's all up for me." The general was car-

ried to a field hospital on the Baltimore Pike, and died there the next day around 5:00 p.m.

For further reading:

Campbell, Eric. "Caldwell Clears the Wheatfield." *Gettysburg Magazine*, #3, 1990.

Favill, Josiah M. *The Diary of a Young Officer.* Chicago, 1909.

Gambone, Al. *The Life of General Samuel K. Zook.* Dayton, 1995.

Hartwig, D. Scott. "John C. Caldwell's Division in the Wheatfield," in Gary Gallagher, ed. *The Second Day at Gettysburg,* Kent, 1993.

Pfanz, Harry. *Gettysburg: The Second Day.* Chapel Hill, 1987.

FOURTH BRIGADE
(851 MEN)
COLONEL
JOHN RUTTER BROOKE

John Brooke, a native of Montgomery County, Pennsylvania, was only twenty-five years old in the summer of 1863. His photographs reveal a spit-and-polish officer with a neatly groomed beard and oiled, wavy hair. His service record indicates that he was an ambitious young man with substantial military industry and talent. Brooke entered the war as a company captain in the 4th Pennsylvania Volunteers, a ninety-day regiment mustered in during the patriotic frenzy following Fort Sumter's shelling on April 12, 1861. The first important campaign of the war was beginning to take shape in July—and the regiment's enlistment was due to expire on the 20th of the month. On the day before the Battle of Bull Run, the regiment refused the appeals of Secretary of War Simon Cameron and commanding Maj. Gen. Irvin McDowell and voted to head back to Washington while the rest of the Union army continued marching toward the enemy. Captain Brooke must have been mightily disgusted.

Eager for a chance to get into action, he set to work raising his own regiment. On November 7, 1861, he was commissioned colonel of the 53rd Pennsylvania Volunteers. This accomplishment is even more impressive when one realizes that the youthful Brooke had no military education (in fact, he had been schooled at a seminary).

The 53rd Pennsylvania was transferred to the Virginia Peninsula in the spring of 1862 as part General French's brigade, Hancock's division, Second Corps. Brooke won praise for his actions at Fair Oaks (where his right index finger was shot off), and Savage's Station. When French was promoted to divisional command a few days before the Battle of Antietam, Brooke took over command of the brigade. His fine performance in helping drive the enemy out of the Sunken Road earned him a mention in Winfield Hancock's list of officers whose battlefield conduct was of "the highest distinction."

Soon however, Col. Samuel Zook, Brooke's senior in rank, returned from sick leave and command of the brigade passed to him. Brooke returned to his regiment and led it in the futile assault against Marye's Heights at Fredericksburg on December 13, 1862, where the Pennsylvanians lost heavily. When the division added another brigade in April 1863, Brooke was plucked out of regimental command and placed at its head—without being promoted to brigadier general.

At Chancellorsville on May 3, while his Fourth Brigade fell back from the vicinity of the Chancellor House, Brooke watched in horror as the advancing Confederates captured the 27th Connecticut virtually en masse (nearly 300 men). In all, Brooke lost 527 men killed, wounded, and captured on May 3. Hancock made an enigmatic entry in his report concerning Brooke's performance: "The commanders of brigades—Brig. Gens. Meagher, Caldwell, and Zook performed their duties faithfully and well. Col. J. R. Brooke, commanding Fourth Brigade, was of great assistance to me by his promptness and efficiency." The ignominy of Chancellorsville may very well have been the reason Brooke was still a colonel when the Gettysburg Campaign got underway; the jury was still out as to whether he was fit for brigade command.

GETTYSBURG: Brooke's brigade was held in reserve as the other three brigades of Brig. Gen. John Caldwell's division plunged into the Wheatfield after 5:00 p.m. on July 2. Brooke ordered his men lie down as they waited to go in, steadying their nerves with patriotic talk: "Boys—remember the enemy has invaded our own soil! The eyes of the world [are] upon us! [and] we are expected to stand up bravely to our duty!"

After only a few minutes, Caldwell called for Brooke to go forward in relief of Col. Edward Cross' brigade. Brooke's line stretched across nearly the entire field, and it advanced on a diagonal from northeast to southwest, overlapping Cross' regiments on the left and Col. Patrick Kelly's on the right. Brooke's regiments were aligned, from right to left, as follows: 145th Pennsylvania, 27th Connecticut, 53th Pennsylvania, 64th New York, and 2nd Delaware.

For a few moments, the brigade stalled on a crest in the middle of the Wheatfield. "Fix bayonets!" Brooke yelled above the deafening roar—"the right thing at the right time," recalled one of his soldiers. It took a few minutes to get the line started forward again, but finally Brooke's brigade pitched ahead with a cheer, and the impetus of the charge carried into the exhausted enemy brigades of Brig. Gens. George Anderson and Joseph Kershaw. Brooke himself seized a regimental flag and led the way forward, and his men triumphantly drove the Rebel line back to the crest of the Stony Hill, south and west of the Wheatfield. The Federals went "right over the Johnnies [in] some of the most severe fighting our division had ever done," wrote one lieutenant. Brooke realized, though, that his men had outrun their supports, and he sent back to Caldwell for help.

From the crest of the Stony Hill, Brooke could see the advance of the brigades of Brig. Gens. William Barksdale and William Wofford as they swarmed over the Peach Orchard salient. Although Brooke did not immediately realize it, the attack threatened to overwhelm the right flank of Caldwell's division. Within a short while all four of Caldwell's brigades were racing to the rear. Brooke realized the extent of the danger just before the collapse, and attempted to get his men out as fast as he could— even though he had become painfully disabled when his ankle was severely bruised by a spent piece of iron; he hobbled from the field with an aide under each arm. Brooke's regiments were scattered far and wide in their hasty retreat, and the brigade could not be rallied until after nightfall.

Caldwell lavished elaborate praise upon Brooke in his report of the battle and recommended the Pennsylvanian for promotion. The army's command machinery, however, worked very slowly. Brooke retained command of his brigade when the army was reorganized during the spring of 1864, but he had to wait until May to receive his brigadier's star. He received a wound at Cold Harbor in June that required a ten-month period of recuperation. Brooke returned to duty just before the end of the war in command of a division in the (then) quiet backwater of the Shenandoah Valley.

Appointed to the U.S. Army after the war, Brooke served through the Spanish-American War. He retired in 1902, having attained the rank of major general. He was the next to last Union general to die, in 1926.

For further reading:

Campbell, Eric. "Caldwell Clears the Wheatfield." *Gettysburg Magazine*, #3, 1990.

Hartwig, D. Scott. "John C. Caldwell's Division in the Wheatfield," in Gary Gallagher, ed. *The Second Day at Gettysburg*, Kent, 1993.

Pfanz, Harry. *Gettysburg: The Second Day*. Chapel Hill, 1987.

SECOND DIVISION
(3,608 MEN)

BRIGADIER GENERAL JOHN GIBBON

John Gibbon was a lean thirty-six year old in 1863, keenly intelligent, blunt in speech, and one of the most able division commanders in the Union army. A soldier of the 19th Maine described him as having "brown hair and a reddish mustache. He was, upon the whole, a good looking officer, and never appeared nervous or excited." "Gibbon is compactly made with ruddy complexion, full jaws and chin, with an air of calm firmness of manner," wrote one of the general's aides. His manner was cold and restrained on the field of battle. Col. Theodore Lyman, General Meade's aide, wrote that Gibbon was "the most American of Americans, with his sharp nose and up-and-down manner of telling the truth, no matter whom it hurts." To Lyman, he was "a tower of strength, cool as a steel knife, always, and unmoved by anything and everything." While he had the strength of character to admit privately that he was afraid, Gibbon went about his duty showing only calm. His experience had something to do with it—he'd seen plenty of combat and had already proven his courage to the extent that he didn't need to prove it further by recklessly endangering himself. He was a man who commanded the respect, rather then the emotions, of his officers and men. Colonel Rufus Dawes of the Iron Brigade described him in action at the Battle of South Mountain as "always on the highest ground, where he could see the whole line, giving his orders in a voice so loud and clear as to be heard throughout."

Though he was born in Philadelphia, Gibbon was raised in North Carolina. He was held back a year from entering West Point when he failed to answer correctly a question on the date of Independence Day. He eventually graduated in the bottom half of his class of 1847, which also produced future Confederate generals Ambrose P. Hill and lifelong friend Henry Heth—both of who would oppose Gibbon at Gettysburg. After graduation, he served in the Mexican and Seminole Wars and on the plains against the Indians before putting in five years as artillery instructor and quartermaster at West Point. It was while at West Point that he wrote *The Artillerist's Manual*, which demonstrated the force of his intellect. It was a highly scientific work, replete with mathematical formulae. The manual was adopted as an official text by the War Department in 1859, and was used as "The Book" by artillerists on both sides during the Civil War.

Since he had lived for so long in North Carolina, many expected Gibbon to "go South" to find a command when the war began. Gibbon, though, saw the matter in an uncomplicated way: he had taken an oath of loyalty as an officer of the United States Army, and that stood above all else. His three brothers all served in the Confederate Army (one was brigade surgeon for Brig. Gen. James Lane's Confederate brigade at Gettysburg), and they disowned him as a traitor.

Gibbon began his Civil War service as chief of artillery for Irvin McDowell's division during the first fall and winter of the war. Promotions in the artillery were slow, however, so he left his familiar batteries for infantry regiments in the spring of 1862. The move resulted in a promotion to brigadier general and he was given command of the only all-Western brigade in the Army of the Potomac.

To his surprise, he found that he liked his new command. Although a strict disciplinarian and Regular Army man, Gibbon appreciated the qualities of volunteer soldiers. He recognized, as many Regular Army officers refused to, their quick intelligence, initiative, and ingenuity. He also realized that they must be led, because they could not be driven. He admired their courage and realized that they were not susceptible to punishment as a motivator; praise was more effective. Tempering his discipline and drill with understanding, he forged his Wisconsin and Indiana troops into fighters as good as either army ever possessed. To heighten their morale he saw to it that they were outfitted in uniforms with white gaiters and black Hardee Hats—hence their nickname, the "Black Hat Brigade." At Brawner's Farm on August 28, 1862, the neophyte brigade stood toe-to-toe against a larger force of Stonewall Jackson's veterans. Gibbon's regiments went on to impress Maj. Gen. George McClellan with their gritty uphill attack at South Mountain two weeks later, where they reportedly acquired their famous moniker "Iron Brigade." (Another brigade also claimed to have earned this nickname at South Mountain; the controversy is still being debated by some.) Gibbon led his men through the Maryland Campaign and at Antietam where, a brigadier in full uniform, he took time out to serve as gunner and No. 3 man for several rounds among the cannoneers along the Hagerstown Road. Afterward he wrote his wife, "I am as tired of this horrible war as you are, and would be perfectly willing never to see another battle field."

On November 5, 1862, Gibbon was rewarded for his excellent service and promoted to command the Second Division, First Corps. While leading the Second Division in the Battle of Fredericksburg, a piece of shell injured his right wrist and broke a bone in the same hand. Taken to Baltimore to recover, his wound healed slowly but he was able to rejoin the army in March 1863, when he was appointed to lead the Second Division, Second Corps, a command he held for the next year and a half. At Chancellorsville, his men were held across the Rappahannock in reserve. If Gibbon had some degree of uncertainty about his new division as the Gettysburg Campaign got underway, the arrest of two of his brigadiers—Alfred Sully and Joshua Thomas "Paddy" Owen—did not help matters. Gibbon's decision meant two of his three brigades would fight the battle under new and untried commanders.

GETTYSBURG: Commanding general George G. Meade, a good friend who had great trust in Gibbon, gave him command of the Second Corps twice in the first two days of the battle—despite the fact that Brig. Gen. John Caldwell was superior in rank. The first incident occurred on the afternoon of July 1, when Second Corps commander Maj. Gen. Winfield Hancock was sent ahead to act as commanding officer on the battlefield. The second was on July 2, when Third Corps commander Maj. Gen. Daniel Sickles fell severely wounded. Sickles' injury prompted Meade to expand Winfield Hancock's authority to include the Third Corps and part of the First Corps, while Gibbon led the Second.

A decisive meeting was held at Meade's headquarters on the evening of July 2 to discuss the army's next move. As the gathering broke, Meade took Gibbon aside and predicted, "If Lee attacks tomorrow, it will be on your front." Through noon on July 3, it looked like there would be no attack at all. Gibbon lounged through the sultry morning, his brigades deployed on Cemetery Ridge, holding the army's center. In the midst of the carnage at Gettysburg, he wrote to his wife, his "Darling Mama," to tell her that he was still well, that God had been good to him, and that she should kiss the children for him and write often.

At noon he threw a luncheon behind the ridge for all the generals near his position. When an intense Confederate cannonade started around 1:00 p.m., he sat down on the reverse slope of the hill in a comparatively safe place, then returned to his lines and chatted with his men while shells exploded nearby. Until the shelling stopped and the long gray lines of enemy infantry hove into view, he believed the enemy would retreat rather than attack. As three Confederate divisions rolled toward him, Gibbon paid last-minute attention to his troop dispositions. His three brigades were deployed, from left to right, as follows: Harrow-Hall-Webb (with the latter's regiments holding the "Angle.") For twenty minutes or so, as the musketry began to rattle and the great roar of the battle rose, there was little for Gibbon to do other than observe the action and exhort his men to stand firm. As the Southern lines bunched together and paused before the wall in his front, Gibbon rushed to the left end of his line and ordered Brig. Gen. William Harrow to wheel his brigade and enfilade the massed Confederates. Just then a bullet tore into the middle of his left arm, near the shoulder, and passed backward through his body, fracturing the shoulder blade. He grew faint and was helped from the field.

The severe wound took a long time to heal, and Gibbon did not rejoin the army for eight months. Hancock, meanwhile, praised his conduct at Gettysburg, as "all that could be desired in division commanders." There was no question that Gibbon would remain in command of his Second Corps division as the Army of the Potomac was reorganized in the spring of 1864. After serving through the relentless combat of Lt. Gen. Ulysses S. Grant's 1864 Overland Campaign, Gibbon was promoted to major general in June 1864, and given a corps in the Army of the James in the final stages of the war.

After the war, Gibbon fought Indians for most of the rest of his career. He retired from the U.S. Army in 1891 and died from pneumonia in 1896.

For further reading:

Gibbon, John. *Personal Recollections of the Civil War.* New York, 1928.

Lavery, Dennis and Mark Jordan. *Iron Brigade General: John Gibbon, A Rebel in Blue.* Dayton, 1993.

Longacre, Edward G. "The Fighting Life of John Gibbon: Cool as a Steel Knife." *Civil War Times Illustrated,* 36, Nov., 1987.

Pfanz, Harry. *Gettysburg: The Second Day.* Chapel Hill, 1987.

Wright, Steven and Blake Magner, "John Gibbon: The Man and the Monument." *Gettysburg Magazine,* #13, July, 1995.

First Brigade

(1,366 MEN)

Brigadier General
William Harrow

Harrow was a misfit in the command structure of the Second Corps' Second Division. He had no military education, which set him apart from divisional leader Brig. Gen. John Gibbon, as well as fellow brigade commanders Brig. Gen. Alexander Webb and Col. Norman Hall. In addition, at forty-years-old, Harrow was the oldest brigade commander in the division. He seemed by nature to be a troublemaker and was never popular with his superiors. Indeed, he would resign his command three times during the course of the war. However, he outranked both Webb and Hall and unofficially commanded the division on July 1 while Gibbon acted as corps commander in Maj. Gen. Winfield Hancock's stead.

Harrow's pre-war life paralleled that of President Lincoln's. He was a native of Kentucky and had practiced law in Illinois (where he actually traveled the Eighth Judicial Circuit with Lincoln) and Indiana. Harrow began the war as captain of the "Knox County Invincibles" in the 14th Indiana, and was colonel of the regiment by the Shenandoah Valley Campaign of 1862. Brigadier General Nathan Kimball commended Harrow, along with all of his regimental commanders, after the victory in the Valley at Kernstown. By the end of July 1862, however, Harrow—whose health had never been strong—had become too feeble to stay in the field. He was coughing up blood, and his doctor suspected tuberculosis. After he resigned, however, his health rebounded, and he was re-appointed in time for Antietam, where he lost more than half his regiment while slugging it out with the Confederates in the Bloody Lane.

In the next few months, Harrow fought one health problem after another. He was sick in his quarters in November with bronchitis which, together with neuralgia and a facial abscess, kept him from taking the field at Fredericksburg in December. By January 1863, he was on sick leave in Washington,

D.C. When his health finally stabilized, Harrow received a promotion to brigadier general in April 1863. He replaced Brig. Gen. Alfred Sully in the command of a brigade in the Second Division, Second Corps in early June. Sully had been relieved of his duties by divisional commander John Gibbon just before the Battle of Chancellorsville, when he balked at Gibbon's order to summarily execute members of a mutinous regiment. (Although a court later found Gibbon unjustified, Sully never again served with the Army of the Potomac.)

Harrow had proven himself to be a brave and competent regimental commander, but he lacked military schooling and experience that would have increased his odds of success at brigade-level command. The Kentucky native was so new to the brigade that many of his men would not have recognized him as their brigade leader. The sickly Harrow remained ill as his brigade tromped the dusty roads leading into Gettysburg, but he refused to leave his command, stating he would not "play safe" during a fight.

GETTYSBURG: On the morning of July 2, Harrow's brigade came up from the south on the Taneytown Road and was posted on Cemetery Hill in a mobile reserve formation with the rest of Gibbon's division. The morning passed peacefully, but in the afternoon the battle raged on the left flank near the Peach Orchard and Round Tops, inching ever closer to Cemetery Ridge. General Hancock dispatched Caldwell's division to the threatened sector, which left a gap in the Union center on Cemetery Ridge. Parts of Harrow's and Hall's brigades were shifted left to plug the chasm. Hancock employed one of Harrow's regiments, the 1st Minnesota, in a heroic sacrificial charge into the teeth of the last Confederate surge of the day on Cemetery Ridge, but Harrow was on another part of the field and was not a player in the drama.

July 3 started much like the previous day, and the Second Corps rested peacefully on Cemetery Ridge. When the earthshaking Confederate cannonade erupted around 1:00 p.m. as a prelude to Pickett's Charge, Harrow immediately made himself conspicuous, utilizing the opportunity to let his men see him and learn to recognize him. According to the description of a captain in a nearby unit, Harrow:

with folded arms and in cool dignity walked up and down in front of the line, apparently indifferent to the rain of shot and shell. . . .I thought as I saw him that the force of his example might be lost and it would prove disheartening if, as seemed probable, he should be struck down while teaching us to despise the danger. Fortunately for him and perhaps for the men, nothing of the kind happened and he paraded slowly back and forth along the line several times, uninjured and admired.

When the artillery barrage began, Harrow's position in the Union defensive line on Cemetery Ridge was about two hundred yards south of the small copse of trees—the target of the attack. His regiments were deployed, right to left, as follows: 15th Massachusetts, 1st Minnesota, 19th Maine, and 82nd New York. Hall's brigade was in position on Harrow's right flank, and Webb's brigade continued the line north beyond Hall. Thus Harrow held the left of Gibbon's divisional line. Colonel Theodore Gates (First Corps) commanded two regiments on Harrow's left flank. When the Southern infantry moved out to attack, Brig. Gen. James Kemper's Virginia Brigade turned toward the copse of trees as it approached the crest of Cemetery Ridge. Harrow's men delivered a savage fire into Kemper's front and passing flank. Within a few minutes masses of Confederates were pouring over the wall and threatening to overrun

Alexander Webb's line. Harrow ordered his regiments to Webb's assistance, but in their haste to attack the units became so intertwined one historian described the mass as "practically immobile." Their musketry, however, together with assistance from Hall's soldiers, helped dissolve the spearhead of Pickett's attack.

Harrow appears to have given few combat orders during the two days of fighting (July 2-3). Gibbon and Hancock personally directed Harrow's regiments, one by one, on July 2, and on July 3, the movements of the regiments were largely a spontaneous mob-like surge of men toward the melee raging at the copse of trees during the battle's high-water mark. Although both Webb and Hall were mentioned by Gibbon in his battle report for their "great gallantry and conspicuous qualities," Harrow was not included in the praise. He also may have hurt his image by managing to walk away from the battle physically unharmed—one of the few generals in the area to do so. Ironically, Harrow took over command of the division (he was senior brigadier) when Gibbon was wounded in the last minutes of the battle. He led the division for the rest of the summer. When Alexander Webb, his junior in rank, replaced him on August 15, the fractious Harrow resigned his commission and left the Army of the Potomac for good.

Harrow returned to Indiana to practice law and enter politics. While campaigning for Horace Greeley in the 1872 presidential election, he was killed in a train wreck.

For further reading:

Gibbon, John. *Personal Recollections of the Civil War.* New York, 1928.

Hartwig, D. Scott. It Struck Horror to Us All." *Gettysburg Magazine,* # 4, 1991.

Pfanz, Harry. *Gettysburg: The Second Day.* Chapel Hill, 1987.

Stewart, George. *Pickett's Charge.* Boston, 1959.

Second Brigade
The "Philadelphia Brigade"
(1,224 men)

Brigadier General
Alexander Stewart Webb

In the summer of 1863, twenty-eight-year-old Alexander Webb was known as a rising young officer of talent and ability. Webb was the progeny of a prominent family. His grandfather had been on George Washington's staff during the Revolutionary War, and his father, James Watson Webb, had been a Regular Army officer, an influential New York newspaper owner and editor, and a minister to Brazil. After graduating 13th out of 34 cadets in his West Point class of 1855, he was appointed to the artillery and served in the Seminole War and then as a professor of mathematics at West Point before the Civil War began.

Webb was a good-looking, meticulously groomed officer with a compact build, bronzed complexion, dark hair and goatee. Colonel Charles S. Wainwright, chief of artillery of the First Corps, a friend and social peer of Webb, wrote that he was one of the "most conscientious, hard working and fearless young officers that we have." General Meade's aide Theodore Lyman considered him "jolly and pleasant," although he was put off by Webb's "way of suddenly laughing

in a convulsive manner, by drawing in his breath, instead of letting it out—the way which goes to my bones." But despite this annoying quirk, Lyman regarded Webb as a "thorough soldier, wide-awake, quick, and attentive to detail."

Most of Webb's duty in the first two years of the Civil War consisted of staff work, and his service was rewarded with the rapid promotion that came frequently to efficient staff officers. When the war began, he assisted the army's chief of artillery, with whom he served throughout the Peninsula Campaign. During the Maryland Campaign of September 1862, Webb acted as chief of staff for the Fifth Corps. For the rest of the year he was assigned to Washington D.C., as an inspector of artillery. In January 1863, Webb returned to the George Meade's Fifth Corps as Meade's chief of staff. At Chancellorsville, Meade thrust Webb into combat by having him lead detachments of infantry into the confused fighting of May 3. He performed well, for Meade called "particular attention" to Webb's "intelligence and zeal" in his battle report.

Webb was rising rapidly on Meade's coattails in the days before Gettysburg and an opportunity soon arose for him to secure a permanent combat command. Just three days before the battle, Brig. Gen. Joshua Thomas "Paddy" Owen, the commander of the predominantly Irish "Philadelphia Brigade," was clapped under arrest by John Gibbon for an offense committed on the march into Pennsylvania. Gibbon chose Webb to take over Owen's regiments.

Webb, a non-Irish New Yorker, was thrust into an uncomfortable situation. To the hard-bitten veterans he looked dandified in his spit-and-polish staff officer's uniform. Discipline problems had been eroding the effectiveness of the Philadelphia Brigade for some time. High straggling rates, absenteeism, arrests, and even a shootout between two officers that resulted in the death of a captain, dragged down the morale of the Keystone natives. The new brigadier may have felt pressure from Gibbon to enforce much stricter standards of discipline. The tense situation came to a head on Webb's second day of command when the brigade was fording Monocacy Creek near

Frederick, Maryland. The water was knee-deep, and the men hoped to take their shoes and socks off, since marching in wet brogans invariably resulted in painful blisters. Webb, however, aware of the urgency of the situation, would not allow them to halt and remove their shoes. To set an example, he dismounted and waded as well, but everybody saw his high boots and knew that he could ride comfortably afterward. He was showered with boos and catcalls, and resentment continued to fester among his men as their feet began to ache. To make matters worse, Webb called together his officers, who had been dressing like privates, and ordered them to wear their insignia. This was an unpopular idea, since shoulder straps made ready targets for enemy sharpshooters. Further, he told them to bring all stragglers to brigade headquarters, where they would be summarily shot. Though the field officers undoubtedly left the meeting muttering among themselves, straggling in the brigade was drastically reduced.

Webb's greatest challenge was that he had never formally commanded so much as a company of infantry before Gettysburg. Moreover, his recent arrival in the Philadelphia Brigade meant that many of his soldiers would not know him if they saw him, and he would have a hard time being obeyed in a moment of crisis.

GETTYSBURG: Webb marched his four Pennsylvania regiments up to Cemetery Ridge with the rest of the Second Corps on the morning of July 2. His brigade did not participate in the day's fighting until near dark, when the Confederate attack that began on the Union left approached the center en echelon. Webb utilized his 69th Pennsylvania regiment and engaged Brig. Gen. Ambrose Wright's Confederate brigade as it topped the ridge and marched in his direction. Webb's regiments, deployed on high ground and behind long and low stone walls with artillery support, occupied a strong defensive position. He ordered his remaining three regiments forward at the "double-quick" to support the 69th. The 106th Pennsylvania moved up on the right of the 69th, while the 71st and 72nd advanced behind it. Wright's men fell back in some disorder, and Webb's brigade chased

them as far as the Emmitsburg Road, where they captured about 300 Confederates and reclaimed three abandoned Union artillery pieces. Soon after, Webb sent two of his regiments to answer a call for help on Cemetery Hill, but they were not needed.

On July 3, Webb's brigade held essentially the same position as it did on the afternoon of the previous day. Despite the close call he had experienced the previous day, Webb did not attempt to improve his position by ordering his men to dig in. The copse of trees on Cemetery Ridge—the target for Maj. Gen. George Pickett's massing columns—sat squarely behind Webb's left regiment (69th Pennsylvania). In the middle of the tremendous bombardment which preceded the assault, Webb stood conspicuously exposed in front of his line and leaned on his sword, puffing leisurely on a cigar while cannonballs whistled by and shells exploded around him. The men yelled at him to take shelter, but as one man wrote, "He stood like a statue watching the movement of the enemy"; Webb's bravery was now manifest to his soldiers. Later Webb said he felt that 110 guns had been sighting on him. "This was awful," he remembered. "I lost fifty of my men lying down, and . . . excellent officers, [while I] was struck three or four times with stones, etc. I knew then that we were to have a fierce attack. . ."

After the Southern artillery ceased fire, Webb made a few adjustments in his line, perhaps more than was good for those nervous troops in his command on the cusp of their first big engagement. As Pickett's Virginia division bore down on Webb's troops, two companies of the 71st Pennsylvania positioned along the front stone wall on the right of the 69th turned and ran away, causing Webb to fear a breakthrough and personal disgrace. He approached his reserve regiment, the 72nd Pennsylvania, as screaming enemy infantry swarmed up to the stone wall just yards behind him. He shouted to the regiment to charge, but its members refused to budge. He walked over to the standard bearer so he could take the colors and personally lead an attack. Evidently the standard bearer didn't recognize him, because he fought Webb for the colors before he went down, shot numerous times. Webb ultimately gave up on the

72nd and strode—in front of the seething mass of Confederates blasting away inside the wall—over to his 69th Pennsylvania regiment, which was still firing defiantly into the Rebels even though their line was slowly being forced back. A bullet clipped Webb on the inside of his thigh on the walk over, but he kept going. With the help of two of Col. Norman Hall's regiments and Brig. Gen. William Harrow's men, Webb's infantrymen slaughtered the Southerners in heaps. Eventually, most of the Confederates began to turn and head back toward Seminary Ridge, while hundreds of others threw down their arms and surrendered. One of the mortally wounded inside the angle was Confederate Brig. Gen. Lewis Armistead.

Hancock later toasted that, "In every battle and on every important field there is one spot to which every army [officer] would wish to be assigned—the spot upon which centers the fortunes of the field. There was but one such spot at Gettysburg and it fell to the lot of Gen'l Webb to have it and hold it and for holding it he must receive the credit due him."

In the surge of adulation after Gettysburg, Webb replaced the wounded Gibbon in command of the Second Division and led it through the fall campaigns. When Gibbon returned to command in the spring of 1864, Webb went back to brigade command. At the Battle of Spotsylvania in May 1864, a bullet passed through the corner of his right eye and came out his ear, but luckily he was not fatally injured. He returned to the army in the last months of the war as the Army of the Potomac's chief of staff. General Webb remained in the U.S. Army until 1870, then spent thirty-three of his remaining years as president of the College of the City of New York. He died in 1911.

For further reading:

Hartwig, D. Scott. It Struck Horror to Us All." *Gettysburg Magazine*, #4, 1991.

Lash, Gary G. "The Philadelphia Brigade at Gettysburg." *Gettysburg Magazine*, #7, 1992.

Pfanz, Harry. *Gettysburg: The Second Day.* Chapel Hill, 1987.

Sword, Wiley. "Alexander Webb and his Colt Navy Revolver: In the 'Pinch of the Fight' During 'Pickett's Charge' at Gettysburg." *Gettysburg Magazine*, # 15, 1996.

——. "Facing the Gray Wave: Alexander Webb at Gettysburg." *Civil War Times Illustrated*, 19, Jan. 1981.

THIRD BRIGADE
(922 MEN)

COLONEL
NORMAN JONATHAN HALL

Norman Hall was an unusually capable twenty-six-year-old Regular Army officer with muttonchop sideburns and a thin brown mustache. He was a young man of whom great things were expected. A native of New York who had entered West Point from Michigan, he had received a commission in the artillery after his graduation in 1858. He was placed at Fort Sumter, where he was the youngest officer in the garrison during the bombardment that signaled the beginning of the Civil War. After the fort's surrender, Hall was in charge of the detail that fired the salute as the American flag was lowered.

After his experience at Sumter, Hall distinguished himself as chief of artillery for Joseph Hooker's division, and served on the staff of the chief of engineers during the Peninsula

Campaign. His performance as a staff officer led to his promotion to the head of the 7th Michigan regiment in July 1862. Although wounded at Antietam when Maj. Gen. John Sedgwick's division was ambushed in the West Woods, Hall stayed on the field and took command of the entire brigade when its commander, Brig. Gen. Napoleon T. Dana, was also wounded.

His most famous exploit came in the army's next battle, at Fredericksburg. There, he and his brigade crossed the Rappahannock River in pontoon boats under fire from Brig. Gen. William Barksdale's Mississippians, who were dug into rifle pits and cellars in the riverfront buildings of the town. In bloody street fighting, Hall's men rooted out the Rebels out of the city house by house. Colonel Hall, who as a Regular Army man had a very unsentimental attitude about the business of war, saw and admired the same attitude in his regiments. Describing the action of the 20th Massachusetts in the streets of Fredericksburg to fellow officers, he said proudly, "The 20th has no poetry in a fight." The next day, Hall led the brigade in the futile assault on Marye's Heights. His brigade lost 515 men in the two days of fighting.

At the Battle of Chancellorsville, Hall's brigade was kept out of the fighting by an impassable canal on the westward side of Fredericksburg, and thus spent most of the battle in reserve, losing 67 men during the entire campaign. By the time of the Gettysburg Campaign, Hall had been in more or less continuous command of his brigade since Antietam the previous September, a remarkably long stretch in the Army of the Potomac—especially for an officer so young.

GETTYSBURG: Hall arrived at Cemetery Hill just south of the copse of trees on the morning of July 2, and went into position with the rest of Brig. Gen. John Gibbon's Second Division. In the Confederate attack late that afternoon, Hall parceled out two regiments (42nd New York and 19th Massachusetts) to help Brig. Gen. Andrew Humphreys stabilize his divisional front to the south. A short time later, however, Brig. Gen. Ambrose Wright's Georgia brigade lapped up against Hall's remaining regiments. The Confederates were able to push back Hall's men for a brief time, but they were soon repulsed with the aid of additional troops.

On July 3, Hall had three regiments deployed behind the low stone wall at the crest of Cemetery Ridge, aligned left to right as follows: 20th Massachusetts, 7th Michigan, and 59th New York. He held his remaining pair of units, the 19th Massachusetts and 42nd New York, in reserve behind the right rear of his line. Pickett's Charge pierced the line on Brig. Gen. Alexander Webb's brigade front just north of Hall near the copse of trees. Although he had his hands full fighting Kemper's Virginians in front of him, Hall peeled off two regiments to go to the aid of Webb. They arrived in time to help shoot down or capture most of the Southern infantrymen who had swarmed over the stone wall.

After the battle, division commander Gibbon praised the "great gallantry and conspicuous qualities" of both Webb and Hall. Although Webb was lionized for his brave performance on July 3, he always believed half of his glory rightfully belonged to Colonel Hall, who acted with initiative and skill in coming to Webb's aid and beating back the attack. Hall deserved more credit than he received for the repulse of Pickett's Charge. Despite the respect and good wishes of both Gibbon and Webb, Hall failed to rise in rank or responsibility, and was back with his regiment by November 1863. He retired from the army in February 1865, two months before the end of the war. He died soon after the war's end, in 1867.

For further reading:

Hartwig, D. Scott. It Struck Horror to Us All." *Gettysburg Magazine*, # 4, 1991.

Pfanz, Harry. *Gettysburg: The Second Day*. Chapel Hill, 1987.

Stewart, George. *Pickett's Charge*. Boston, 1959.

THIRD DIVISION
(3,644 MEN)

BRIGADIER GENERAL
ALEXANDER HAYS

Alexander Hays was a hot-headed and hard-drinking forty-four-year-old Pennsylvanian who was most at home in a fight. He reviled "scientific leaders" and called strategy "a humbug. Next thing to cowardice." His appearance fitted his fiery personality: he was six feet tall and husky, with sandy red hair. As one of his soldiers admiringly described him, he was "a princely soldier; brave as a lion. . . one of those dashing, reckless, enthusiastic generals. . . .His old brigade, the Third of his division, idolized him, and we would have followed him to the death."

Born north of Pittsburgh in Venango County, Hays was the son of a member of Congress and a general in the Pennsylvania militia. Developing a military bent himself, Alexander left Allegheny College in his senior year to enter West Point. He proved he was no scholar by graduating 20th out of 25 in the Class of 1844. Once out of school, he showed a restless soul. After two years of frontier duty he returned to Pittsburgh to get married, then served in the Mexican War. Thereafter, Hays resigned from army service and joined an iron business that failed. California beckoned, and

he traveled west to join in the Gold Rush. In 1851, he returned to western Pennsylvania yet again and accepted employment in the bridge-building industry.

Hays reentered the army when the Civil War broke out, and was made captain of a company of Regulars. In October 1861, however, he raised the 63rd Pennsylvania Volunteers and become its colonel. He led the regiment for the first time in combat at Seven Pines, where both he and his men performed well, although his brigadier did not single Hays out for praise. A month later, at Glendale during the Seven Days' Battles, Hays' regiment made a gritty bayonet charge into the enemy line to cover the retreat of a friendly battery. He was singled out for distinction in reports filed by his brigadier, Brig. Gen. John Robinson, and his division commander, Maj. Gen. Phil Kearny, who called it a "heroic action."

Hays went on sick leave a month later. A surgeon reported that he suffered from blindness in his right eye and partial paralysis of his left arm, from which he had suffered since the Seven Days' Battles. Hays was out of action for about a month, but was back in the thick of the fighting at Second Bull Run in August 1862, where his regiment spearheaded Kearny's divisional attack against Stonewall Jackson's men on the Railroad Cut. A bullet shattered Hays' leg during the assault, knocking him back out of action for many months.

Hays was promoted to brigadier general while he convalesced, and he returned to duty in the spring of 1863. He patiently commanded a brigade in the Washington defenses until the Confederate army raided Pennsylvania in June. When Maj. Gen. William French of the Third Division, Second Corps, was transferred to an improvised reserve division on June 28, three days before Gettysburg, Hays' brigade was added to French's former command, and Hays took over as commander of the Third Division by virtue of his seniority.

Hays was both new to division-level command as the Gettysburg Campaign opened and completely unfamiliar with two of his three brigades. He quickly established himself with his men, however, demonstrating that he respected and loved volunteer troops. Hays called them his "'Bluebirds' whose badge is the 'Shamrock,'" and they in turn loved him for his brave and vigorous leadership.

GETTYSBURG: Always an emotional fighter, Hays had a special intensity at Gettysburg. "I was fighting for my native state," he explained, "and before I went in thought of those at home I so dearly love. If Gettysburg was lost all was lost for them, and I only interposed a life that would be otherwise worthless." Only skirmishing disturbed his Cemetery Ridge sector of the Second Corps line on July 2. His old Third Brigade, however, led by Col. George Willard, was directed into the spreading late-afternoon battle by corps commander Maj. Gen. Winfield S. Hancock, and was thrown into the fierce combat to the south (where Willard was killed).

True to his nature, when his men were cowering under the terrific cannonade preceding Pickett's Charge on July 3, Hays stepped into the open and ordered his men gather up all discarded rifles, clean them, load them and have them handy. This kept the men busy during the barrage, and some of the men had as many as four to six loaded rifles at hand for the upcoming infantry assault. His brigades were deployed immediately to the right of John Gibbon's division, with Smyth's brigade deployed behind the stone wall on the crest of the ridge, Willard's behind him, and Carroll's right on the right end of the line. Hays sensed what was coming. "Now, boys, you will see some fun!" he shouted to his men when the artillery went silent. The Confederate lines came into view as Hays predicted, and as they approached he drilled his men in the manual of arms to keep them steady. "He was riding up and down the lines in front of us," one of his soldiers later reported, "exhorting the 'boys' to stand fast and fight like men. . . .Once he rode by and said, 'Boys, don't let 'em touch these pieces,' and in a few minutes he rode back again laughing, sung out, 'Hurrah, boys, we're giving them hell,' and he dashed up to the brow of the hill and cheered our skirmishers." The men evidently took heart from his performance.

Hays made some last-minute adjustments to the line and waited until the Southerners got entangled with the fence bordering the Emmitsburg Road about two hundred yards away. "Fire!" he shouted, and his entire line erupted in sheets of flame. Though outnumbered, Hays' division—with the help of a converging fire from friendly infantry and artillery to its right—slaughtered the enemy infantry moving against its front. Hays threw out another regiment to pour fire into the flank of the massed Confederates, and after a few minutes the Rebel lines melted away.

When the smoke cleared, Hays, who was unhurt but had lost two horses shot out from under him, kissed his aide in the exhilaration of the moment, grabbed a captured battle flag and rode down the division's line, dragging it in the dirt behind his horse while waving his hat and exhorting the men to cheer. The moment was so exciting, his aide wrote later, "My horse seemed to be off the ground traveling through the air." General Hancock praised Hays' conduct as "all that could be desired in a division commander."

Hays continued in command of the Third Division during the fall campaigning, but in the army reorganization of March 1864, he was reduced to the command of a brigade to make room at the divisional level for his senior in rank, Maj. Gen. David Birney.

On May 5, 1864, the first day of the Battle of the Wilderness, General Hays was felled by a bullet which passed through his head, killing him instantly.

For further reading:

Fleming, George T. *General Alexander Hays at the Battle of Gettysburg*. Pittsburgh, 1913.

———, ed., *Life and Letters of Alexander Hays*. Pittsburgh, 1919.

Pfanz, Harry. *Gettysburg: The Second Day*. Chapel Hill, 1987.

———

First Brigade

(977 men)

Colonel
Samuel Sprigg Carroll

Sam Carroll's nickname was "Old Brick Top," because of his thinning red hair (which was accented by a huge pair of side-whiskers). He was a fearless and vigorous brigade leader, and one who would attack "wherever [he] got a chance, and of [his] own accord." Eleventh Corps commander Maj. Gen. Oliver O. Howard described him in 1863 as being "a young man of quickness and dash," and "for fearless and energetic action Colonel Carroll had not a superior." He was admired not only by those who commanded him, but also by those he commanded. One of his subordinates described him as "a thorough soldier and unsurpassed commander of men," while another remembered Carroll as "a splendid commander to lead a forlorn hope," for his voice was like the blast of a trumpet, and to hear it ordering a charge was "worth a whole regiment itself as a reinforcement."

Carroll came from a prominent District of Columbia family. His father was for many years clerk of the Supreme Court. Young Carroll's years as a student at West Point were a disaster, and he graduated 44th out of 49 cadets in the Class of 1856. After serving four years on the frontier, he became the Military Academy's quartermaster, and he and his family shared a double house with Oliver Howard's wife and children. The families became close, and when Howard fell seriously ill in Washington in 1861, Carroll's mother took him into her home and nursed him back to health.

Although the Civil War began in April of 1861, West Point did not release Carroll for field duty until the fall. By December he was the colonel of the 8th Ohio regiment, and he joined this command in Romney, West Virginia. He performed well in his first battle at Kernstown during the opening of Thomas J. "Stonewall" Jackson's Valley Campaign in March of 1862, and was commended for his actions by division commander Brig. Gen.

James Shields. On the basis of his performance at Kernstown, he was given command of a brigade in May, and on June 9 led it into a fight for the first time at Port Republic, where the Union forces were defeated by Jackson. This time General Shields sharply condemned the young officer: "Colonel Carroll neglected to burn the bridge at Port Republic. . . .He held it three-quarters of an hour and wanted the good sense to burn it. They took up an indefensible position afterward instead of a defensible one." (Shields neglected to mention that five days earlier he had expressly ordered Carroll to "go forward at once with the cavalry and guns to save the bridge at Port Republic.") To add injury to insult, Carroll was hurt during the battle when his wounded horse fell on him.

Transferred to Maj. Gen. John Pope's Army of Virginia in the summer of 1862, Carroll's brigade was only lightly engaged at Cedar Mountain on August 9. However, he was included in a short list of those praised by Pope after the battle. A week later, Carroll was wounded in a skirmish with Rebel cavalry while inspecting his pickets near the Rapidan River, receiving a painful flesh wound in the chest that incapacitated him for the next month and kept him out of the battles of Second Bull Run and Antietam.

He recovered by late September and was briefly assigned to the Washington defenses before returning to the field in time to command a Third Corps brigade at Fredericksburg. There, although his brigade was used only in a supporting role and was thus unable to influence the battle, Carroll was singled out for praise by division commander Brig. Gen. Amiel Whipple, who wrote of his "bravery and skill."

"Old Brick Top"—who was only thirty at Gettysburg—requested in early 1863 that he and the 8th Ohio be transferred to the Second Corps. While he waited for the change of assignment, he went on sick leave because his lung was hemorrhaging from his wound of the previous summer, he suffered from an intermittent fever, and he had rheumatism in his left hip and knee. His request for transfer was granted on March 25, 1863. He returned to the army and took command of a veteran Second Corps brigade, to which his 8th Ohio had been newly assigned. Its previous brigadier, Brig. Gen. Nathan Kimball, had been severely wounded by a canister ball in the thigh at Fredericksburg. Carroll commanded this brigade at Chancellorsville where, after a fine performance on May 3, division commander Maj. Gen. William French termed him "dashing and gallant," in his official report of the battle.

Despite having led brigades in several battles (Port Republic, Fredericksburg, and Chancellorsville), and earning the commendation of his superiors, Sam Carroll was still a colonel by the time the Gettysburg Campaign opened. Perhaps his lack of promotion was due to the black mark of Shields' scathing Port Republic report. Whatever the reason, it is no credit to the promotional machinery of the Army of the Potomac that a West Point-trained veteran brigade commander like Carroll was still a colonel in the summer of 1863. He was a man possessed with dash and gallantry, and his soldiers liked to identify themselves as "Sam Carroll's men," which says much about his leadership.

GETTYSBURG: Posted just south of Cemetery Hill upon arriving on the battlefield on the morning of July 2, Carroll listened to the battle near the Round Tops draw closer. He wasn't called on until dark, when Maj. Gen. Jubal Early's Division struck Howard's Eleventh Corps lines on Cemetery Hill form the north. Hearing the sounds of fighting resounding to the north, Second Corps commander Maj. Gen. Winfield S. Hancock dis-

patched Carroll's brigade as a reinforcement. With little direction, Carroll trotted his men in column and deployed his regiments exactly where they were most needed by marching toward sound of the heaviest gunfire. He skillfully positioned his men in the dark for an attack, facing obliquely to the left and uphill. The debris of the earlier fighting made it difficult to advance with a wide front, so Carroll placed the 14th Indiana in the advance and stacked up two other regiments (7th West Virginia and 4th Ohio) behind it. Carroll ordered his men to "Charge bayonets!". . .Give them —!" and his men dashed forward over dead and wounded bodies with a cheer. His narrow and deep counter-charge proved irresistible. It drove through Ricketts' captured guns and quickly pushed Brig. Gen. Harry Hays' Louisianans off the crest they had captured and back down the hillside. After remaining for a while in an advanced position with no flank support, Carroll sought permission to retire. His old friend and Eleventh Corps commander Howard refused to allow this, and Carroll and three of his four regiments stayed to defend Cemetery Hill.

Carroll's fourth regiment, his old 8th Ohio, had been left behind at Cemetery Ridge on the right of Hays' division. When the Confederates launched Pickett's Charge on the afternoon of July 3, the Ohioans wheeled out from their position between the Sunken Road and Emmitsburg Road and devastated the left flank of Joe Davis' Brigade. After the battle, Carroll's division commander, Alexander Hays, wrote, "Too much credit cannot be given to Carroll and his command for the gallant manner in which they went to the relief of the troops on our right." To his report of the battle Howard appended a personal "hearty thanks" to Carroll.

"Old Brick Top" commanded his brigade through the fall campaign and retained command when the Army of the Potomac was reduced from five corps to three in March 1864. Surprisingly, he still had not received a much-deserved promotion to brigadier general. On May 12, 1864, his arm was splintered by a bullet at Spotsylvania, ending his military career. Carroll belatedly received his brigadier's star, effective from the date of his wound.

In 1869, Carroll was retired from the U.S. Army at the rank of major general for disability arising from his war wounds. He lived in or near his native Washington, D.C., until his death from pneumonia in 1893.

For further reading:

Pfanz, Harry. *Gettysburg: The Second Day.* Chapel Hill, 1987.

Fleming, George T. *General Alexander Hays at the Battle of Gettysburg.* Pittsburgh, 1913.

SECOND BRIGADE

(1,069 MEN)

COLONEL
THOMAS ALFRED SMYTH

Thirty-one-year-old Thomas Smyth was an Irishman who emigrated from the family farm in County Cork and settled in Philadelphia. He worked as a carver until he joined William Walker's filibustering expedition to Nicaragua in 1855. When he returned to America, he took up coach making in Delaware.

Smyth began the war in October 1861 as a major in the 1st Delaware volunteer regiment. His history henceforth was that of his regiment, which did not see action until it joined the Army of the Potomac just before the

Maryland Campaign in September 1862. Smyth fought with the regiment at Antietam, where the entire brigade was repulsed in front of the Sunken Road. Afterward, the acting commander of the regiment cited him for his "exemplary coolness and bravery." Smyth's regiment was also involved in the futile assault against Marye's Heights at Fredericksburg, where he was once again mentioned by other officers for his "skill and gallantry" and "coolness and ability." He was promoted twice within the next two months, first to lieutenant colonel, and then to full colonel. Smyth led his Delaware troops again at Chancellorsville, but he was only lightly engaged. The 1st Delaware was transferred to another brigade just after the battle. Smyth, as its senior colonel (and despite having come from a civilian background), was placed in command, since its previous leader, Brig. Gen. William Hays, had been captured at Chancellorsville. As the Gettysburg Campaign opened, Smyth was new to brigade-level command and was almost completely unfamiliar with his regiments.

GETTYSBURG: Smyth's brigade consisted of the 14th Connecticut, 1st Delaware, 12th New Jersey, 10th New York Battalion, and 108th New York. On July 2, these regiments were positioned since the morning at the northernmost end of the Second Corps line on Cemetery Ridge. Parts of two of Smyth's regiments, his old 1st Delaware and the 12th New Jersey, skirmished briskly for much of the afternoon on the ground of the Bliss farm, about midway between the opposing lines. The Federals eventually were forced out of the position by a contingent of Mississippians.

On July 3, Smyth's division commander, Brig. Gen. Alexander Hays, intermingled Smyth's regiments with the Third Brigade regiments to double the thickness of his line, fighting them essentially as one unit. Smyth's regiments were deployed along a low stone wall just north of the Angle, aligned left to right as follows: 14th Connecticut, 1st Delaware, 12th New Jersey, 10th New York Battalion, and 108th New York. During the cannonade which preceded Pickett's Charge, Smyth was wounded in the head and face by a shell, which knocked him out of the fighting. His men fought well and assisted in repulsing the massive assault, and Smyth returned to duty the next day.

Smyth's performance at Gettysburg evidently convinced his superiors that he deserved to continue in command at the brigade level. Although he did not receive his promotion to brigadier general until October 1864, he commanded brigades through most of the rest of the Civil War (and at times, he also led his division). Unfortunately, he was destined for a tragic end.

On April 7, 1865, a Confederate shot him through the mouth at Farmville during Lee's retreat to Appomattox. The unfortunate general died two days later, the same day Lee surrendered at Appomattox. Smyth was the last Union general to die from his battle wounds.

For further reading:

Maull, D. W. *The Life and Military Services of the Late Brigadier General Thomas A. Smyth*. Washington, D. C., 1870.

Pfanz, Harry. *Gettysburg: The Second Day*. Chapel Hill, 1987.

THIRD BRIGADE

THE "HARPERS FERRY BRIGADE"

(1,508 MEN)

COLONEL
GEORGE LAMB WILLARD

George Willard, thirty-five, was a New Yorker and descendant of Revolutionary War and War of 1812 generals. His family had wanted him to pursue a less dangerous profession, and sent him to Ohio at a young age to "become a practical business man." Instead, he enlisted in the 15th Infantry at the onset of the Mexican War at the age of eighteen, and became a first sergeant. He received an officer's commission in the Regular Army in 1848. Willard did remarkably well in the Regular Army for an officer without a West Point education, rising to the rank of captain by the time of the Civil War.

When President Lincoln called for two-year volunteers in 1861, Captain Willard responded by raising an entire regiment, the 2nd New York, fully expecting to be named its colonel. At the time, however, regulations prohibited Regular Army officers from commanding volunteer troops while retaining their old commissions. Unwilling to part with his captaincy in the U.S. Army, Willard gave up his chance to lead his regiment. Staying with the Regulars, the goatee-sporting officer with dark hair and a sad face was promoted to major and fought with the 19th United States in the Peninsula Campaign in the spring and early summer of 1862, on several occasions commanding the regiment. In August 1862, as the volunteer ranks swelled and qualified officers were desperately needed to lead them, the earlier regulation was relaxed. Willard was allowed to keep his Regular rank and he joined the volunteer army as colonel of the new 125th New York Volunteers. The regimental historian waxed eloquent on the new colonel, commenting on his "striking personal appearance" and "rare soldierly accomplishments."

The regiment was shipped to West Virginia and one month later, in September 1862, Willard and his men were captured at Harpers Ferry during the Maryland Campaign. His career appeared stalled in its tracks. For seven months, from the fall of 1862 to the spring of 1863, he marked time the best way he could, drilling his paroled and demoralized regiment in a Chicago camp.

When the men were exchanged, they were transferred to the defenses of Washington and brigaded with other New York regiments, all bitter veterans of the Harpers Ferry humiliation. They remained in the Washington "outer" defenses near Bull Run, until June. Less than a week before the Battle of Gettysburg, the brigade was attached to the Third Division, Second Corps of the Army of the Potomac as reinforcements. The transfer took place so quickly the New Yorkers did not even have time to fasten the blue trefoil badges of the division on their caps before the fighting started. Willard, as senior colonel, took command of the brigade on the march north toward Pennsylvania when its previous commander, Brig. Gen. Alexander Hays, was put at the head of the division.

As Willard's men swung into the moving column, the veterans of the Second Corps immediately disparaged his men as the "Harpers Ferry Brigade," calling them "band-box soldiers." Although Willard was only in command by virtue of the date of his commission—and was completely inexperienced as a brigade commander—he seemed to be the right man to lead the Harpers Ferry men into battle. He shared their feelings, had the expertise of a career soldier, and seemed to be an officer of promise. In addition, both Willard and his New Yorkers were itching to erase the stain of their earlier surrender.

GETTYSBURG: Willard, like the other men of his division, spent the late afternoon hours of July 2 behind Cemetery Hill listening to the spreading battle far to the south near the Round Tops. A few minutes before dark on the evening of July 2, as the battle was creeping its way north, Second Corps commander Maj. Gen. Winfield S. Hancock accompanied Willard's brigade from its position near Cemetery Hill south down Cemetery Ridge. Brig. Gen. William Barksdale's Mississippians were surging forward through a gap in the Union line, and someone needed to plug it. Hancock appeared with Willard and ordered him to attack Barksdale and blunt the charge.

The men of the "Harpers Ferry Brigade" recognized this as their chance to erase the shame of their infamous surrender. Willard formed his lines carefully near the George Weikert farm north of Weikert's woods during a terrific hail of enemy fire. His New York regiments were aligned, left to right, as follows: 39th, 125th, and 126th; the 111th was initially positioned in the second line. Willard ordered the men to fix bayonets. Someone shouted "Remember Harpers Ferry!" and hundreds of other voices took up the cry. Willard yelled "Forward!" and the brigade marched slowly and deliberately at the advancing Mississippians, firing as they moved west. When they hit the Confederate line, in the low ground along Plum Run, it was the Southerners who broke and retreated. Some claim Barksdale went down in front of the 126th New York, hit with several wounds. Willard's men pursued the enemy, recapturing Union guns as they advanced toward the Emmitsburg Road. Thus redeemed and at the height of his glory, Willard had just crossed Plum Run when a shell fragment tore away his face and part of his head, killing him instantly.

For further reading:

Campbell, Eric. "'Remember Harpers Ferry': The Degradation, Humiliation, and Redemption of George L. Willard's Brigade." *Gettysburg Magazine*, #7-8, 1992 and 1993.

Pfanz, Harry. *Gettysburg: The Second Day.* Chapel Hill, 1987.

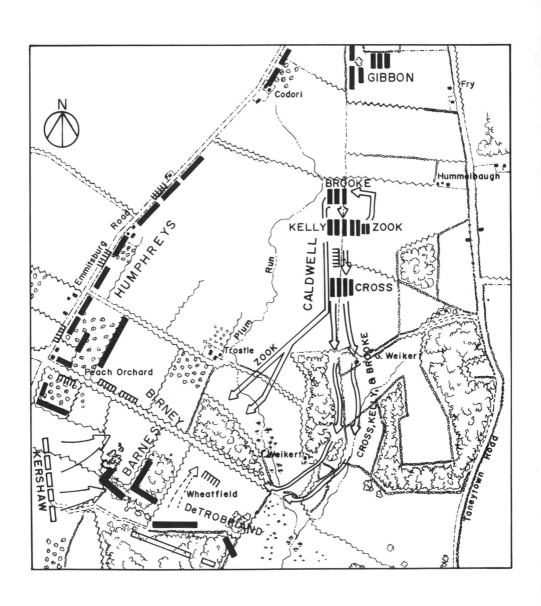

THIRD CORPS
(10,626 MEN / 30 GUNS)

MAJOR GENERAL
DANIEL EDGAR SICKLES

In neither army was there another man with a past as garish as Dan Sickles. He was not a trained soldier—he had "graduated" from the rigors of New York City's Tammany politics rather than those of West Point—but by sheer audacity and aggressiveness, this heavy drinking, womanizing, and scheming soldier had risen farther than any other political general in the Army of the Potomac.

Despite his controversial nature, his legions of detractors, who included General Meade, could not deny Sickles possessed some talent and immense personal courage. Colonel Regis de Trobriand, one of Sickles' brigadiers, called attention in his memoirs to his other admirable qualities:

He was gifted in a high degree with that multiplicity of faculties which has given rise to the saying that a Yankee is ready for everything. He has a quick perception, an energetic will, prompt and supple intelligence, an active temperament. Naturally ambitious, he brings to

the service of his ambitions a clear view, a practical judgment and a deep knowledge of political tactics. When he has determined on anything, he prepares the way, assembles his forces, and marches directly to the assault. Obstacles do not discourage him. . .he has many strings in his bow, if one breaks he will replace it by another. In him, ability does not exclude frankness. He likes, on the contrary, to play with his cards on the table with his friends and against his enemies.

Sickles was born on October 20, 1819, in New York City, the son of a well-to-do patent lawyer. He showed his swaggering self-confidence and contrary nature at a young age by repeatedly running away from home. His dissolute lifestyle of hanging out with prostitutes and other unsavory characters—habits which would stay with him throughout his life—began at a young age. Sickles eventually entered New York University, but later left to study law. About this time he began his long association with Tammany Hall's Democratic politics in New York City. In 1843, at the age of twenty-four, he was admitted to the bar and was elected to the New York State Assembly in 1847, where he was known to escort prostitutes into the legislative chambers. He married in 1852, and true to his irascible nature, the union was tinged with controversy: his bride was sixteen and Sickles was twice her age.

Sickles' political career rose to the national level, and he spent a year abroad as secretary to the minister to Great Britain, where he scandalized the host country by refusing to toast the health of Queen Victoria at an Independence Day banquet. Returning to America, Sickles became a militia officer and was elected a state senator in 1855, and then became a member of Congress in 1856. Sickles, was a states' rights Democrat with a prosperous law practice, set his sights on nothing less than the presidency. For someone of such high ambition, he made no effort to curb his excessive lifestyle. He lived far beyond his means, continued his lecherous indiscretions, and made himself a notorious figure in D. C. society. Then, in 1859, he shot and killed Philip Barton Key.

Key was the son of the author of "The Star-Spangled Banner," a militia captain, political dabbler, and man-about-town in the capital, where he was known as "the handsomest man in all Washington society." Key had legal business with Sickles, and after a while began trysting with Sickles' wife in a shabby apartment. Sickles found out about the affair and shot Key dead in Lafayette Park—just across the street from the White House. After the shooting, Sickles calmly walked down the street and surrendered himself to the Attorney General of the United States. At his murder trial, Sickles was defended by a phalanx of lawyers, including the future Secretary of War Edwin Stanton. His defense, for the first time in recorded history, was the plea of "temporary insanity." Sickles was triumphantly acquitted. Sickles finally committed the scandal that ruined his future in Washington when he publicly forgave his wife. Mary Chesnut, the famous Southern diarist, watched him from the House gallery one day and described a man totally ostracized, carefully avoided by every other man on the floor, "left alone as if he had the smallpox."

Sickles returned to New York and had just resumed practicing law when the war broke out in April 1861. He realized that the war offered him a chance to retrieve his prominence by becoming a military hero, and so he decided to raise a regiment. Recruiting handbills were printed and volunteers began to appear. Sickles realized that a man who mustered in the most soldiers stood the best chance of getting a brigadier general's star from Congress, and so he raised an entire brigade, dubbing it the "Excelsior Brigade."

With characteristic impudence, Sickles considered it his brigade, independent of New York state authority. As an independent military organization, however, it was supposed to pay its own way, and debts began piling up immediately. Sickles, an old hand at high-level mooching from his Tammany days, got permission to move part of the brigade to Staten Island, and managed to shelter his Excelsiors in a circus tent loaned by none other than P. T. Barnum. Another fourteen hundred men were quartered in a vacant hall on lower Broadway. Sickles contracted with a bathhouse to give them all a wash and shave at ten cents each. After seeing to these arrangements, he began pestering Lincoln and everyone he knew in Washington to swear his troops in as United States volunteers. The governor of New York was outraged at Sickles' attempt to place New York volunteers beyond his authority and he tried to disband the brigade. It required a general order from the Secretary of War to force Sickles to place the Excelsior Brigade under the governor's control, and the regiments were mustered in as the 70th, 71st, 72nd, 73rd, and 74th New York Volunteers. After First Bull Run, as the embattled Lincoln administration began crying out for more troops, Sickles' brigade was put on a train for the capital, where it would eventually join the Army of the Potomac. The maneuvering politico was sworn in as a brigadier general.

Sickles had the immediate good fortune of finding himself in Brig. Gen. Joseph Hooker's division. Hooker, a grand attention-seeker himself, rose through the ranks, and Sickles' star rose as well. Sickles was absent (characteristically pulling strings in Washington) during his brigade's first fight in the spring of 1862 at Williamsburg—its heaviest combat on the Virginia Peninsula. He was also absent during the Second Battle of Bull Run in August 1862. In the army reorganization following that battle, Hooker rose to command the First Corps, and Sickles took charge of Hooker's old division in the Third Corps. On November 29, 1862, the New Yorker was promoted to major general.

It was a testament to Sickles' political talents that in an army rife with backbiting, he risen from being a civilian to the rank of major general and command of a corps within two short years. As shown, he often left his troops in the field to hurry to Washington to curry favor in person, and he had assiduously courted the friendship of the President and Mrs. Lincoln. However adept he had proven himself to be at functioning within the army's political environment, however, he was always under scrutiny because of his lack of military knowledge. Brigadier General Gouverneur Warren, chief engineer of the Army of the Potomac, believed that Sickles was not as good a soldier as others of his rank, and would be a poor choice to fight an independent battle— as corps commanders sometimes were called upon to do. Warren later admitted that Sickles did the "best he could, and with the corps he had managed very well."

At the Battle of Fredericksburg the next month, Sickles' division remained in reserve and saw little action. When Hooker was named as the new commander of the Army of the Potomac in January 1863, Sickles' heyday had finally arrived. Despite his lack of substantive combat experience, Hooker liked Sickles' aggressive nature and attitude and he placed him in command of the Third Corps on February 5, 1863. Many of the regular army officers expressed dismay at his advancement, for Sickles was the only non-West Pointer among the seven corps chiefs, a sour mood spread over the officer corps. Others complained that Sickles' undisciplined personal impulses (together with Hooker's and Dan Butterfield's) were quickly imbuing army headquarters with the air of a combination bar and brothel.

It wasn't until Chancellorsville in May 1863 that Sickles finally saw heavy combat. He had moved his corps aggressively forward to punish the tail end of what appeared to be Stonewall Jackson's retreating column. Instead, Jackson was marching to crush the right flank of the army, which he did in magnificent style. Sickles found himself in control of important high ground at Hazel Grove and a fierce round of combat ensued. Hooker eventually ordered him to abandon the position, a tactical mistake which cost the Third Corps substantial losses. Sickles' experience in the tangled thickets at Chancellorsville seemed to vindicate his aggressive behavior, taught him the value of holding high ground, and jaundiced his view of higher authority. All three of these factors would color his actions at Gettysburg.

When Hooker was suddenly replaced with Maj. Gen. George Meade as the army's new commander just a few days before Gettys-

burg, a new faction of officers took control of the reins of power. Meade detested Sickles' personal habits and distrusted his lack of military education. The New Yorker was near the top of Meade's enemy's list. To make matters worse for Sickles, the march toward the battlefield was full of frustrating starts, stops, and delays, and Meade blamed him for more than his share of those problems. Sickles also resented the autonomy he lost when Meade empowered First Corps commander John Reynolds to oversee the First, Third, and the Eleventh Corps. By the time Sickles reached the field, relations between himself and Meade were acutely uncomfortable.

GETTYSBURG: While the battle of July 1 was being fought on the ridges west of Gettysburg, Sickles was with his Third Corps at Emmitsburg, ten miles to the south. He received two sets of orders there, one from Meade (to remain in Emmitsburg and guard the left flank of the army), and another from John Reynolds (to hurry north to Gettysburg). Though Sickles' irritation with Meade increased with this discrepancy in orders, he handled the situation well. He notified headquarters of the incongruity of the directives and detached one brigade from each of his two divisions to stay in Emmitsburg. With the balance of his corps (four brigades), Sickles marched to Gettysburg. Major General David Birney, the commander of the Third Corps' First Division, started two brigades of his division northward in mid-afternoon and arrived on the lower end of Cemetery Ridge a little after 6:00 p.m. Second Division leader Brig. Gen. Andrew A. Humphreys arrived at Gettysburg with two more brigades about midnight. Sickles spent the evening of July 1 encamped near his men.

On the morning of July 2, Sickles' last two brigades rejoined him on the southern end of the field, and his corps took up its assigned position south of Winfield Hancock's Second Corps on Cemetery Ridge. Sickles' men extended the Union army's left flank all the way to Little Round Top. Sickles rode to army headquarters at about 11:00 a.m., still unsure about the exact ground his infantry should occupy. Meade, however, was seemingly preoccupied with the Union army's right, and Sickles—justifiably concerned about the left flank—received the impression he was being ignored or slighted.

The politician-turned-general had learned the hard way about the importance of high ground at Chancellorsville, and he disliked the fact that the position assigned to him by Meade was forty feet lower than the Emmitsburg Road, a thoroughfare about a mile west of his present position that ran in a line roughly parallel to his front. He also didn't like the fact that the continuity of his present position was broken up by woods and rock formations. As a result, he made one of the most controversial decisions of the entire war: he abandoned the position assigned to him by Meade and moved his entire corps forward to the high ground. His alignment was a giant, wide V-shaped front with the point of the V aiming west from a small peach orchard along the Emmitsburg Road. Humphrey's division was deployed along the road on the right of the corps, with Birney's divisional line angling off to the southeast.

Grave problems with this new position became immediately apparent. Both of Sickles' flanks were now in the air, since the Second Corps had remained on Cemetery Ridge, hundreds of yards behind his right rear, and the commanding position of Little Round Top was too far to the east (behind him) to provide a topographical anchor for his left. Compounding these problems was the fact that Sickles' elongated new line bulged out in a salient at the Peach Orchard, where it could be struck from three directions (west, southwest, and northwest). Although Sickles sought approval for his new dispositions, the enemy attacked before he could be either withdrawn or reinforced.

The assault was launched late on the afternoon of July 2 when James Longstreet's charging Confederate brigades moved forward against Sickles thinly-spread troops. Within an hour the Peach Orchard salient was demolished, the Third Corps was overwhelmed and falling back, and the massive Confederate assault was moving east toward the Round Tops. At about 6:00 p.m., Sickles abandoned his threatened headquarters.

During the evacuation his right knee was grazed by a cannonball, too lightly to spook his horse but hard enough to shatter his leg. He was carried off in a stretcher with his cap over his eyes. To let the men know that he was alive, he puffed ostentatiously on a cigar as aides bore him to the rear.

Sickles' right leg was amputated just above the knee a few hours later, and his days as a field commander were over. Some would say the loss of his leg helped cast him a hero for the cause of Union, despite the fact his decision to move to the Emmitsburg Road had led to the virtual destruction of the Third Corps. Others contend the movement helped absorb Longstreet's attack well in advance of the Round Tops, allowing reinforcements to hold the heights while Sickles' men bore the brunt of the attack.

Sickles retired from U.S. Army in 1869 with the rank of major general, whereupon President Grant appointed him minister to Spain. There, true to form, he became a lover of Queen Isabella. After a return to Congress in 1893-1895, he was removed from the New York Monuments Commission in 1912 for alleged embezzlement. He died of a stroke in 1914, separated from his family, "irresponsible, and cantankerous."

For further reading:

Pfanz, Harry W. *Gettysburg: The Second Day.* Chapel Hill, 1987.

Pinchon, Edgcumb. *Dan Sickles: Hero of Gettysburg, "Yankee King of Spain."* New York, 1945.

Robertson, William Glenn. "The Peach Orchard Revisited: Daniel E. Sickles and the Third Corps on July 2, 1863," in Gary Gallagher, ed. *The Second Day at Gettysburg.* Kent, 1993.

Sauers, Richard Allen. *A Caspian Sea of Ink: The Meade-Sickles Controversy.*" Baltimore, 1989.

Stevenson, James. *History of the Excelsior or Sickles' Brigade.* Paterson, 1863.

Swanberg, W. A. *Sickles the Incredible.* New York, 1956.

FIRST DIVISION
(5,095 MEN)

MAJOR GENERAL
DAVID BELL BIRNEY

David Birney "reminds me of a graven image," wrote one of his men, "and could act as a bust for his own tomb, being utterly destitute of color" and "as expressionless as Dutch cheese." Theodore Lyman of Meade's staff wrote later of Birney,

He was a pale, Puritanical figure, with a demeanor of unmovable coldness; only he would smile politely when you spoke to him. He was spare in person, with a thin face, light-blue eye, and sandy hair. As a General he took very good care of his Staff and saw they got due promotion. He was a man, too, who looked out for his own interests sharply and knew the mainspring of military advancement. His unpopularity among some persons arose partly from his own promotion, which, however, he deserved, and partly from his cold covert manner.

While he may have appeared colorless, Birney's procession through Frederick, Maryland, on the march to Gettysburg while acting as corps commander in Sickles' absence, indicates he had a flair for the trappings of military life. A line or two of mounted cavalrymen led the way with drawn sabers, fol-

lowed by a band, General Birney with his neatly-arrayed staff, and the soldiers of the Third Corps bringing up the rear. Birney's little parade gave the officers something to gossip about, and prompted artilleryman Charles Wainwright to comment that "he certainly means to have all the 'pomp and circumstance of war' he can get. Such feats are not common in this army, and do not take." Despite Birney's coldness and pomposity, he was a capable leader. Lyman was very clear about that. "In my belief," he wrote, "we had few officers who could command 10,000 men as well as he. . .I always felt safe when he had the division; it was always well put in and safely handled."

The thirty-eight year old Birney was the son of James B. Birney, a Kentuckian who had once owned slaves but who had become one of the country's most vehement abolitionists (he had run twice for president on the Liberty Party ticket). David also showed an intellectual bent by attending Andover Academy, studying law in Cincinnati, and practicing law in Philadelphia. By the outbreak of the Civil War he had a very successful practice with many influential friends.

Birney foresaw the coming of the Civil War. In 1860, he began an intensive study of military subjects and received an appointment as lieutenant colonel of a Pennsylvania militia regiment. With this meager preparation he obtained appointments to colonel of the 23rd Pennsylvania in August 1861 and a promotion to brigadier general in February 1862. Though the appointments were politically motivated, he proved to be competent and dependable in command. His first taste of combat came at the head of a Third Corps brigade (Brig. Gen. Hobart Ward's brigade at Gettysburg) at Seven Pines, where he was mistakenly removed from command because of a misunderstanding that arose during the heavy fighting on the first day of the battle. Cleared of charges of disobedience (and commended by fiery division commander Brig. Gen. Philip Kearny), he was restored to duty in time for the Seven Days' Battles a month later, where his brigade repulsed superior numbers at Glendale. Kearny again praised Birney, this time for his "coolness and judicious arrangements."

At Second Bull Run, Birney's brigade lost over 600 men in intense fighting. Two days later, he replaced Kearny in command of the division when that officer was killed at Chantilly on September 1, 1862. Stationed in Washington during the Maryland Campaign, Birney missed the bloodbath of Antietam. His division was back with the army at Fredericksburg, where he again got into some trouble, this time for allegedly balking when asked to support George Meade's division in its attack against Stonewall Jackson's front. Oddly, he was complimented in General George Stoneman's official report for "the handsome manner in which he handled his division." Birney led his brigades well in the heavy and confused fighting at Chancellorsville, where his division lost a horrendous 1,607 casualties—more than any other division in the army. As a result of his distinguished service in that battle, he received a promotion to major general to date from May 20, just a few weeks before the opening of the Gettysburg Campaign.

Despite his lack of a military background, by the summer of 1863 Birney was a seasoned and capable combat leader. He knew his division and its leaders well, having been associated with the unit and its members since its inception in early 1862.

GETTYSBURG: Birney received his marching orders in Emmitsburg in mid-afternoon on July 1 and made a three-hour tramp to Gettysburg. At dusk, with two brigades of his division, he arrived and went into camp on Cemetery Ridge, just north of Little Round Top. The third brigade, Col. Regis de Trobriand's, arrived at 10:00 a.m. on July 2, and Birney's division went into position along Cemetery Ridge facing west, its left resting on Little Round Top. Birney's men comprised the far left of the Army of the Potomac. At 11:00 a.m. Birney sent out a detachment to scout the woods on Seminary Ridge about one and one-half miles west of his position. The reconnaissance discovered large numbers of Confederates in the area, which convinced Maj. Gen. Dan Sickles, the Third Corps commander, that he was about to be attacked. Birney's probe

prompted Sickles to move his entire Third Corps forward nearly a mile to higher ground along the Emmitsburg Road.

Birney soon found himself responsible for a line that extended east and south from the Peach Orchard (where he placed Graham's brigade), across Stony Hill (where De Trobriand deployed), and along Houck's Ridge (where Ward's men were aligned). Ward's left was on the ridge's terminus at Devil's Den. There were two immediate problems with the new position. First, he didn't have enough men to cover that distance; and second, the Peach Orchard position was a salient which could be pressed from several directions at one time. The woods housing the enemy opposite the Peach Orchard were only a few hundred yards away to the west, which further compounded Birney's anxiety.

About 4:30 that afternoon, Maj. Gen. John Bell Hood's Confederate division marched out of the tree line and slammed into Birney's line. The far left of Birney's position, from Stony Hill to Devil's Den, was immediately in danger of being overwhelmed. Little Round Top—the key to the Union defensive line—was immediately east of Devil's Den, and Birney had failed to post any defenders there. While Sickles sent out calls for assistance, Birney pulled regiments from de Trobriand's brigade and sent them to shore up his flanks, but these units had no time to establish their new positions before they were struck by the onrushing Rebel attack. Birney's fragmented regimental dispositions made coordination and communication nearly impossible, and he began to give orders to any units in the vicinity, whether or not they were under his authority. His interference created additional confusion among the Fifth and Second Corps units rushing to his assistance.

As Hood's Division crushed and drove back Birney's brigades, 3,000 more Confederates in the brigades of Brig. Gens. William Barksdale and William Wofford boiled out of the woods directly in front of the Peach Orchard around 5:30 p.m. The attack, delivered by Lafayette McLaw's Division, overran the salient and large segments of the Emmitsburg Road defensive line.

After the Peach Orchard position collapsed, Sickles went off the field with his leg mangled by a cannonball, and command of the Third Corps passed to Birney. For Birney, the timing could not have been worse. His own division was being routed off the field, and Humphreys' division was fighting for its life near the Emmitsburg Road. A short while later, when George Meade learned that Sickles had been wounded, he extended Maj. Gen. Winfield Hancock's authority to include both his own Second Corps and that of the Third Corps. Thus, Birney's tenure as the head of the Third Corps effectively ended.

The battle continued to ebb and flow until nightfall. Hancock's skillful defensive tactics, coupled with outstanding efforts by the men in the ranks and their officers, managed to beat back Longstreet's attack just short of Little Round Top. One story has it that as Birney watched the survivors of his mangled division gather in the twilight, he whispered to one of his lieutenants, "I wish I were already dead."

That night, a meeting of general officers was held at Meade's headquarters to determine the following day's course of action. Birney considered the Third Corps as "used up," and he did not believe the army was capable of continuing the fight. He was a defeated man. Meade, though, decided to remain in position on July 3, and the remnants of the Third Corps were placed behind Cemetery Ridge and were not used on the final day of the battle.

However questionable his performance in the Battle of Gettysburg, Birney stayed at the helm of the decimated Third Corps through the fall campaigns of Bristoe and Mine Run. In the spring reorganization of the army in 1864, the corps was broken up and Birney was reduced in the army hierarchy, replacing Brig. Gen. Alexander Hays at the head of the Third Division, Second Corps. He took command of the Second Corps when Hancock's Gettysburg wound broke open in June 1864, and then was given a corps in the Army of the James when Hancock returned to duty.

Birney's health deteriorated that summer, and by October he had to leave the army. He died of typhoid fever on October 18, 1864.

For further reading:

Davis, Oliver W. *Life of David Bell Birney, Major General, United States Volunteers.* Gaithersburg, 1987.

Pfanz, Harry W. *Gettysburg: The Second Day.* Chapel Hill, 1987.

Sauers, Richard Allen. *A Caspian Sea of Ink: The Meade-Sickles Controversy."* Baltimore, 1989.

FIRST BRIGADE
(1,516 MEN)

BRIGADIER GENERAL
CHARLES KINNAIRD GRAHAM

Thirty-nine year old Charles Graham, a patrician-looking New York City native with a long curly brown beard, evinced a martial disposition early in life when he entered the navy as a midshipman at the age of seventeen. After seven years at sea—which included duty in the Gulf of Mexico during the Mexican War—he resigned in 1848 to study both law and engineering. While maintaining a law practice, the ambitious and energetic Graham worked as a civil engineer at the Brooklyn Naval Yard constructing dry docks and assisted in planning New York's Central Park.

Graham's affiliation with the Third Corps was the result of his long friendship with Dan Sickles, the future commander of the corps. They had both been active in Tammany Hall politics, where patronage was an accepted part of doing business, and Sickles arranged to have Graham's predecessor at the Navy Yard fired so Graham could have his job (the displaced engineer attacked Sickles in a rage after losing his position). When the war came, Graham volunteered for what promised to be glamorous duty in Sickles' Excelsior Brigade, and brought 400 of his dock workers with him. These men became the nucleus of the 74th New York Infantry and Graham became their colonel.

Throughout the year preceding Gettysburg, Graham fought disease more than the enemy. While he went to the Peninsula in the spring of 1862 with the Excelsior Brigade, he was almost immediately stricken with fever and forced to resign on April 10 to go home and recover. He returned the next month to lead his regiment at the Battle of Seven Pines, but by the Seven Days' Battles Graham had caught camp dysentery. He remained with his regiment through the week of nearly continual fighting, although his regiment saw little service and lost only 54 men in two engagements. Once the Union army had retreated to Harrison's Landing, a surgeon reported that Graham's dysentery was "approaching the typhoid form." Weak and frequently delirious, he was assigned to recruiting duty in New York to regain his health. A promotion to brigadier general arrived in November 1862—due largely to his friend Sickles' influence, since Graham had yet to illustrate prowess on the battlefield. His illness lingered for some time and prevented him from returning to field duty until February 1863.

In March, Graham was given command of Brig. Gen. John Robinson's Pennsylvania brigade when that officer was promoted to command the Second Division, First Corps. He led his brigade in combat for the first time at Chancellorsville that May, where 756 of his men fell in the fighting around the Chancellor House. He received plaudits for his conduct from his division commander, Maj. Gen. David Birney. Graham was still learning the intricate business of leading a brigade as he marched his Pennsylvanians toward Gettysburg.

GETTYSBURG: Graham's men arrived on the battlefield at dusk on July 1 in company with Brig. Gen. Henry H. Ward's regiments; both brigades bivouacked on Cemetery Ridge. Graham was sent by his old friend and Third Corps commander, Maj. Gen. Daniel Sickles, to make the 10-mile ride back to Emmitsburg to bring up two brigades—one from each of Sickles' divisions—which had been left behind. At 7:30 that evening, George Meade sent an order to Graham requesting he immediately bring the brigades to Gettysburg. Although Graham received the message sometime before 1:30 a.m., he waited several hours before rousing the men for the march—an unwarranted delay in an emergency situation.

Even when Graham did get the two brigades (plus two batteries and their attendant wagons) on the road, the column moved slowly and straggled badly, taking five or six hours to march 10 miles. In addition to his poor marching discipline, Graham's approach to the battlefield was reckless. He ignored Meade's warning to turn off the road at Marsh Creek in order to avoid possibly running into enemy troops, marching instead on the Emmitsburg Road all the way up to the Peach Orchard, where he turned west toward the Union lines.

Graham's brigade took its position on Cemetery Ridge just north of Little Round Top, but during the middle of the afternoon of July 2, Sickles advanced his entire corps almost a mile west to take advantage of higher—and what he believed was more defensible—ground. By 4:00 p.m., Graham's division commander, Maj. Gen. David Birney, had placed Graham and his brigade in the Peach Orchard, facing west. Graham's Pennsylvania regiments occupied a front five hundred yards wide along the Emmitsburg Road from the southern edge of the Peach Orchard to the Trostle farm lane. The regiments were aligned, from left to right, as follows: 68th, 114th (a Zouave unit), 57th, and 105th; the 63rd was sent west and was skirmishing in front of the brigade. Graham knew his position was weak and that he did not have enough men to hold it against a determined enemy. He was seeking reinforcements when the storm broke loose.

Within an hour James Longstreet unleashed a sweeping en echelon assault against the left flank of the army. Graham's men watched as Maj. Gen. John Hood's Southern division battled its was into their left-rear against Colonel de Trobriand's brigade. Within a short while Brig. Gen. William Barksdale's Mississippians exploded out of the trees only 600 yards away and headed straight for Graham's line. The momentum of Barksdale's attack crashed into the Pennsylvanians and broke through the line at the Wentz farm, sweeping through the Peach Orchard. In the ensuing melee, a shell fragment hit Graham in the hip, and a musket ball tore through both his shoulders. Somehow he still managed to walk without assistance, but he was captured a short time later, along with about 250 of his men.

Graham was sent to a Richmond prison camp. Though he was exchanged in September, he never again held an active field command. After the war, Graham returned to civil engineering—he was especially concerned with New York Harbor projects—until his death from pneumonia in 1889.

For further reading:

Pfanz, Harry. *Gettysburg: The Second Day.* Chapel Hill, 1987.

Sauers, Richard Allen. *A Caspian Sea of Ink: The Meade-Sickles Controversy."* Baltimore, 1989.

SECOND BRIGADE

(2,188 MEN)

BRIGADIER GENERAL HENRY HOBART WARD

By the time of the Civil War, Ward had accumulated a lifetime of military experience in both field and administrative positions. Like fellow brigadier Graham, Ward was a

native of New York City. He left Trinity Collegiate School at the age of eighteen and enlisted as a private in the Regular Army. He fought in the Mexican War, was wounded at Monterrey, and won promotions up to the rank of sergeant major. Ward left the army in 1851, but not the military. He became assistant commissary general for New York state that same year, and four years later was the Empire State's commissary general, a post he held until 1859. Ward's military knowledge and abundant political connections helped him become the colonel of the 38th New York regiment when the Civil War broke out.

Ward led the 38th at First Bull Run and succeeded temporarily to command of the entire brigade when its leader, Col. Orlando Willcox, fell wounded. Willcox went on to praise Ward in his battle report. Ward rose to prominence on the Virginia Peninsula in 1862, where his solid performances in several battles were roundly praised by his superiors. He received a particularly ringing endorsement for his role at Williamsburg from Brig. Gen. Phil Kearny, his division commander. "I ordered Col. Hobart Ward, with the Thirty-eighth New York (Scott Life Guard), to charge down the road and take the rifle pits in the center of the abatis by their flank," wrote Kearny. "This duty Colonel Ward performed with great gallantry, and by his martial demeanor imparted all confidence in the attack."

At Seven Pines, Ward again inherited brigade command on the second day of the battle when Brig. Gen. David Birney was wrongfully relieved for disobeying an order. Third Corps commander Brig. Gen. Samuel P. Heintzelman, and Second Division commander Brig. Gen. Joe Hooker, joined in singing Ward's praises, calling his performance "gallant." Kearny again mentioned his name in reference to a "brilliant charge." Ward and his men saw little action during either the Seven Days' Battles or the Second Bull Run Campaign. Following Kearny's death at the Battle of Chantilly, Ward took permanent command of the brigade when General Birney was bumped up to replace the slain Kearny. The next month, October 1862, Ward was promoted to the appropriate rank of brigadier general.

Ward led the brigade in combat for the first time at Fredericksburg, where his men suffered heavy losses opposite Stonewall Jackson's front in a desperate counterattack to blunt enemy pursuit. At Chancellorsville, the brigade participated in heavy fighting as well as one of the war's rare night attacks. The nighttime maneuver did not go well once the firing started in the darkness, and one of Ward's men claimed, "The scare wasn't confined to the privates; officers dodged hither and thither, some of them so frightened that they couldn't have told their names." Ward was among those who panicked, galloping to the rear in such a hurry that he rode down two of his own men. This embarrassing moment, however, did not permanently stain his hard-won reputation as a solid combat leader.

As he approached Gettysburg, the forty year old Ward had seen about as much fighting as had any Union brigadier. He had been in command of the same brigade for ten months, and had fought with it in a half-dozen engagements. He was a veteran fighter who could be depended on.

GETTYSBURG: Ward and his brigade (which included the 1st and 2nd U.S. Sharpshooters, which operated as a demi-brigade under the command of Col. Hiram Berdan) came onto the field and bivouacked on Cemetery Ridge with Brig. Gen. Charles Graham's infantry at dusk on July 1 after a hot, muddy march from Emmitsburg.

On the morning of July 2, his regiments were deployed north of Little Round Top and in the Peach Orchard. Birney ordered Ward to dispatch the 3rd Maine to the Peach Orchard, and Berdan's pair of regiments were sent forward on a scouting mission. In mid-afternoon, Birney obeyed Third Corps commander Maj. Gen. Dan Sickles' order to move the line forward, and Ward's soldiers soon comprised the extreme left of the Army of the Potomac. His brigade was formed in a shallow crescent facing generally west from the Wheatfield on his right flank to Devil's Den on his left. Ward's five remaining regiments were aligned, from left to right, as follows: 99th Pennsylvania, 4th Maine, 124th New York, 86th New York, and 20th Indiana.

When Maj. Gen. John Hood's Division attacked from the west and south about 4:30 p.m., three of its four brigades pounded against Ward's line. The New Yorker expertly juggled his regiments and held back the furious Confederate assault for an hour and a half in fighting that frequently became hand-to-hand. As Ward's men were being pushed back and outflanked, reinforcements from the Second and Fifth Corps arrived to assist in stemming the onslaught with something closer to equal numbers. Ward's brigade was withdrawn beyond the Wheatfield, and he praised his remaining men— 50% of the brigade was dead or wounded— as they wearily came off the field. They camped that night east of the Taneytown Road. The fought-out brigade was put in reserve behind Cemetery Ridge on July 3, and was not used again in the battle. In his report of the battle, David Birney mentioned Ward's "cordial co-operation" in his report, faint praise for the New Yorker's gritty and pressure-packed performance defending the critical ground in front of Little Round Top.

Ward retained his brigadier's post in the army's consolidation in March 1864, an indication his reputation was in good standing among the Army of the Potomac's high command. At the Wilderness in May 1864, however, his career collapsed in shame when he inexplicably got drunk and fled the fighting. He was relieved of command, placed under arrest, and mustered out of the service in July 1864.

For thirty-two years after the war, General Ward served as clerk of the superior and supreme courts of New York. He was run over by a train and killed in 1903.

For further reading:

Pfanz, Harry. *Gettysburg: The Second Day.* Chapel Hill, 1987.

Sauers, Richard Allen. *A Caspian Sea of Ink: The Meade-Sickles Controversy."* Baltimore, 1989.

THIRD BRIGADE

(1,387 MEN)

COLONEL PHILIPPE RÉGIS DÉNIS DE KEREDERN DE TROBRIAND

Colonel de Trobriand was unique among the officers of the Army of the Potomac. Photographs taken of him during the Civil War show a relaxed, romantic, cosmopolitan man of letters—an abrupt departure from the usually stiff and stoic poses of that era. Colonel de Trobriand was even distinguishable from other volunteer generals who were the progeny of the upper-class families of Boston, New York, and Philadelphia. He was an aristocratic Frenchman, the son of a baron of ancient lineage who had been one of Napoleon's generals. Born in a chateau near Tours, he spent his youth fighting duels, studying law, and writing poetry and prose, and even published a novel in 1840. The Frenchman came to the United States on a dare in 1841 at the age of twenty-five. He mingled with the social elite of New York City, where he married an heiress named Mary Jones. The couple were wed in Paris and lived in Venice for a time, hobnobbing with the available nobility in that historic city. They returned to the United States to take up permanent residence in New York. Colonel de Trobriand became one of the city's literati during the 1850s, earning a living writing and editing for French language publications.

When the Civil War broke out in 1861, de Trobriand became a citizen of the United States and in August 1861, was given command of the predominantly French 55th New York regiment, the "Gardes Lafayette." De Trobriand and the 55th experienced their first combat in early May 1862 on the Virginia Peninsula at Williamsburg. He fought well there, but by mid-May was left prostrate in a shanty with "swamp fever." He missed the rest of the campaign and was unable to return to the army until July. That fall, his regiment was placed with Brig. Gen. Hobart Ward's brigade in the Third Corps and sent to Fredericksburg, where it was held in reserve and thus escaped the winter bloodbath.

Just before Christmas 1862, the 55th and the 38th New York (Ward's old command) merged, and Colonel de Trobriand was placed in charge of the combined regiment. He led the outfit at Chancellorsville in May 1863, though it was not heavily engaged in that campaign. When the Third Corps was reorganized after its terrible losses at Chancellorsville, Colonel de Trobriand was given command of a new brigade—even though he had not yet participated in any heavy action (his losses at Williamsburg, Fredericksburg, and Chancellorsville were 17, eight, and 37, respectively).

GETTYSBURG: On July 1, Colonel de Trobriand's brigade was one of two left in Emmitsburg to guard the left rear of the army when the rest of Maj. Gen. Dan Sickles' Third Corps marched toward the battlefield. It eventually followed in the footsteps of its fellow units and arrived at the battlefield about 10:00 a.m. on July 2. That afternoon, when the Third Corps was advanced west to take up a new position, de Trobriand's regiments were deployed in a wooded and rocky area facing generally southwest, midway between Brig. Gen. Charles Graham's brigade at the Peach Orchard and Brig. Gen. Hobart Ward's brigade near Devil's Den. The colonel eventually aligned his regiments in the Stony Hill sector in roughly a T-shaped deployment (the bottom of the T facing southwest) to take advantage of the terrain. The 17th Maine held the far right facing the Peach Orchard, while the 40th New York extended the line southwest toward Plum Run. The 5th Michigan and 110th Pennsylvania (six companies) crossed the "T" and faced to the southwest, overlooking Plum Run itself, with much of the 5th on skirmish duty on the Rose farm grounds. Colonel de Trobriand's fifth regiment, the 3rd Michigan, had been pulled by Birney for skirmish duty between the Rose farm and the Emmitsburg Road.

About 4:30 that afternoon, Maj. Gen. John Bell Hood's Division assaulted out of the woods to the southwest Maj. Gen. David Birney's attenuated First Division line. The initial weight of the attack fell on the Devil's Den sector and Ward's brigade, which required assistance to hold its ground. On Birney's order, De Trobriand dispatched the 40th New York for the task, which marched into Plum Run Valley northeast of the hotly-contested pile of rocks. Birney also directed the Frenchman to send the 17th Maine to hold a stone wall between the Wheatfield and the Rose Woods, effectively stripping the right flank of the brigade and opening it up to an assault from the west.

De Trobriand stoutly defended his position, even after supports on both sides had fallen back, holding off numerous attacks by Brig. Gen. George Anderson's Georgia brigade, and Brig. Gen. Joseph Kershaw's South Carolina brigade. When Brig. Gen. John Caldwell's Second Corps division arrived as reinforcements, Birney ordered de Trobriand to withdraw. The brigade's sur-

vivors moved to the rear and bivouacked east of the Taneytown Road. Colonel de Trobriand's brigade had been in the maelstrom of the battle, and every third man had become a casualty. Colonel de Trobriand, along with the rest of Birney's shattered division, was put in reserve on July 3. Although it was called upon to support some artillery batteries, it did not see any additional fighting at Gettysburg.

After the battle, Birney wrote:

Colonel de Trobriand deserves my heartiest thanks for his skillful disposition of his command by gallantly holding his advanced position until relieved by other troops. This officer is one of the oldest in commission as colonel in the volunteer service [and] has been distinguished in nearly every engagement of the Army of the Potomac, and certainly deserves the rank of brigadier-general of volunteers, to which he has been recommended.

Colonel de Trobriand demonstrated at Gettysburg that he deserved a brigadier's star and permanent command of a brigade, but there was no immediate official response to Birney's recommendation. He continued to lead his brigade as a colonel through the fall of 1863 until his regiments were mustered out in November. His promotion came in January 1864, but he had to wait seven months for a command.

When Hobart Ward was drummed out of the army for intoxication, de Trobriand took over his brigade and commanded it until Appomattox. Before the end of the War he was trusted with even higher responsibilities, and occasionally led a division during the Petersburg and Appomattox campaigns.

After the war, De Trobriand continued his service with U. S. Army on the frontier and on Reconstruction duty until 1879. He spent his retirement years in New Orleans and New York, and died in 1897 of pneumonia.

For further reading:

de Trobriand, P. Regis. *Four Years with the Army of the Potomac.* Boston, 1889.

Pfanz, Harry W. *Gettysburg: The Second Day.* Chapel Hill, 1987.

Sauers, Richard Allen. *A Caspian Sea of Ink: The Meade-Sickles Controversy.*" Baltimore, 1989.

SECOND DIVISION

(4,924 MEN)

BRIGADIER GENERAL ANDREW ATKINSON HUMPHREYS

Andrew A. Humphreys had none of the charisma of Maj. Gen. Dan Sickles, his corps commander. His troops sarcastically called him "Old Goggle Eyes" behind his back because of his reading spectacles. At the age of fifty-three, though he was tall and slim and not yet gray, they considered him an old man. He was new to his division, and his men considered him to be a strict, exacting disciplinarian, an unfeeling, bow-legged tyrant.

Humphreys was indeed one of the most demanding officers in the army. When he advanced into a fight, he left no one behind. At the Battle of Fredericksburg, one colonel had detached six of his youngest and most frail boy-soldiers to stay behind and guard the regiment's knapsacks, but Humphreys, swearing mightily, ordered them back into line. Two were killed. Charles Anderson Dana, the Assistant Secretary of War, thought him "one of the loudest swearers" he had ever known, a man of "distinguished and brilliant profanity," much like Maj.

Gen. Winfield Hancock of the Second Corps. But Dana also found Humphreys to be completely without vanity in a profession swarming with prima donnas. Theodore Lyman, of Maj. Gen. George Meade's staff, served with Humphreys after Gettysburg, and described him as a boyish-acting old gentleman, with quick peppery ways, and a habit for fastidiousness, "continually washing himself and putting on paper dickeys." Another of his peers considered him "eminent both as a scientist and a soldier, a man of broad and liberal views, of commanding intellect, and of the highest personal honor." After meals, Humphreys liked to discourse with his staff on a wide range of various intellectual topics. He regarded the military profession as a "godlike occupation," and expressed a fondness for combat, once observing that war was a "very bad thing in the sequel, but before and during a battle it is a damn fine thing!"

Humphreys often personally led his men into battle, writing later that "for certain good reasons connected with the effect of what I did upon the spirit of the men and from an invincible repugnance to ride anywhere else, I always rode at the head of my troops." Lt. Adolphus Cavada of the general's staff recalled that just before he rode at the head of his men toward Marye's Heights at Fredericksburg, Humphreys bowed to his staff, "and in the blandest manner remarked, 'Young gentlemen, I intend to lead this assault; I presume, of course, you will wish to ride with me?'" They did so, and five of the seven staff officers fell injured or dead from their mounts. During the charge, his two brigades faltered in the face of incredible Rebel gunfire, but Humphreys remained sitting on his horse as hostile fire cut the air about him. Another brigade assailing the same position saw Humphreys in this position and began cheering his bravery. Humphreys gave them a wave of his cap and a grim smile, and then went riding off into the twilight. It was his personal fortitude and disregard for danger that eventually served to earn his soldiers' admiration and respect.

Humphreys came from a respected Philadelphia family, and he counted the naval architects that designed the *USS Constitution* and *USS Constellation*—and many other ships of the Old Navy—in his lineage. Humphreys graduated from West Point 13th out of 33 students in the class of 1831 and served in the artillery in the Seminole War. His interest shifted quickly to engineering, however, and by 1838 he was serving in the Corps of Topographical Engineers, conducting hydrographic surveys on the Mississippi River, a vocation also practiced by future generals Robert E. Lee and George Meade. His *Report on the Physics and Hydraulics of the Mississippi River* was published the year the Civil War began, a valuable and respected text which was translated into foreign languages and permanently established Humphreys' scientific reputation.

When the Civil War began, Humphreys' health, which had never been good, prevented him from joining the army until late 1861. He was appointed as chief engineer on Maj. Gen. George B. McClellan's staff, a post he held through the Peninsula Campaign. Just before the Battle of Antietam, he was given command of a new Fifth Corps division of nine-month men, which were held in reserve in that battle. It was three months later, at Fredericksburg, that his rookie division won fame for driving closer to the Confederate position behind the stone wall than any other Federal unit. "He behaved with distinguished gallantry at Fredericksburg," wrote Maj. Gen. George Meade, the new commander of the Fifth Corps. Meade sympathized with Humphreys when he was omitted from a long list for promotion while, claimed Meade, other men "such [as] Sickles . . .who have really done nothing," rose in rank.

After the Battle of Chancellorsville, where Humphreys' division was not heavily engaged, the term of service of his nine month regiments expired; most of the men failed to reenlist. Other units similarly situated followed suit, and nearly an entire division evaporated from the Fifth Corps. On May 23, about five weeks before Gettysburg, Humphreys was transferred to a division in Maj. Gen. Daniel Sickles' Third Corps to replace Maj. Gen. Hiram Berry, who had been killed at Chancellorsville. Humphreys

was the only West Point-trained general officer in the new corps, and thus a valuable addition to Sickles.

Humphreys, although unfamiliar with his new division, was developing into a fine field officer. Meade considered him a "splendid man," and when he became commander of the Army of the Potomac three days before Gettysburg, he asked Humphreys to be his chief of staff. The Philadelphia native refused the offer, since accepting it meant giving up combat duty for a desk job.

GETTYSBURG: Moving toward Gettysburg from Emmitsburg on the afternoon of July 1, Humphreys's division finally arrived after nightfall. He had followed a guide down a wrong road and nearly blundered headlong into a column of Confederates at Black Horse Tavern, several miles to the west of the nearest friendly troops. Humphreys discovered his predicament and quietly shuffled his division away from the peril. By midnight, he was camped with the other Third Corps units on the southern end of Cemetery Ridge.

In mid-afternoon of July 2, Humphreys' division moved forward, by Sickles' order, to an exposed position, stretched out in a line running generally north and south along the Emmitsburg Road, facing west. His left flank abutted Maj. Gen. David Birney's division at the Peach Orchard, a dangerous salient in Sickles' new line. Humphreys' right flank, much to his dismay, dangled dangerously one half-mile in front of the Second Corps supports on Cemetery Ridge.

The initial punch of James Longstreet's Confederate attack late that afternoon fell upon Maj. Gen. David Birney's men near Devil's Den and Stony Hill, well beyond Humphreys' left-rear. To his displeasure, Humphreys' reserve brigade under Col. George Burling was drawn away to the southeast to reinforce Birney. This left Humphreys with only two brigades under Cols. William Brewster (on the left) and Joseph Carr (on the right), when the Confederate brigades of Brig. Gens. William Barksdale, Cadmus Wilcox, and Col. David Lang stepped out of the woods in his front. "Had my Division been left intact," Humphreys later claimed, "I would have driven the enemy back, but this ruinous habit (it doesn't deserve the name of system) of putting troops in position & then drawing off its reserves & second line to help others, who if similarly disposed would need no such help, is disgusting."

At the zenith of the Southern assault, Sickles went down with a severe leg wound. Command of the corps fell on General Birney's shoulders, who ordered Humphreys to form a new line to the rear. Despite the immense difficulty of retreating in good order while under intense attack by superior numbers, Humphreys managed to execute Birney's directive. According to his subordinates, Humphreys placed himself "at the most exposed positions in the extreme front, giving personal attention to all the movements of the Division [with] conspicuous courage and remarkable coolness" during the retrograde movement. At one point, a shell struck Humphreys' already-wounded horse, and the poor animal sprang in the air, pitching the general violently to the ground. Humphreys remounted an aide's horse without fanfare and continued directing his division.

Humphreys managed to withdraw his soldiers, in reasonably good order, all the way to Cemetery Ridge—despite leaving 1,500 men dead or wounded on the half-mile of ground over which he had made his fighting retreat. He wrote later that the experience defending the Emmitsburg Road position was even worse than storming the stone wall at Fredericksburg. Second Corps chief Maj. Gen. Winfield Hancock recalled that after the battle, there seemed to be nothing left of Humphreys' division but a mass of defiantly waving regimental flags. Humphreys' brigades spent a restless night on Cemetery Ridge. They were moved to the rear at sunrise the next morning, and spent July 3 in reserve behind the sloping terrain.

Humphreys' heroic performance on July 2 drew almost immediate reward, for just five days later he was promoted to major general and drafted as Meade's new chief of staff, replacing the departed Maj. Gen. Daniel Butterfield. When Hancock's Gettysburg wound finally forced him from the field in 1864, Lt. Gen. Ulysses Grant named Humphreys his successor at the head of the Second Corps. Humphreys held that command until Appomattox four months later.

In 1866, Humphreys was made chief engineer and promoted to brigadier general in the U.S. Army, where he served until his retirement in 1879. He died in 1883 of a heart attack. Charles Anderson Dana, assistant secretary of war, called Humphreys "the great soldier of the Army of the Potomac."

For further reading:

Pfanz, Harry. *Gettysburg: The Second Day.* Chapel Hill, 1987.

Humphreys, Andrew A. *From Gettysburg To The Rapidan. The Army of the Potomac, July 1863 to April 1864.* Dayton, 1987.

Humphreys, Henry H. *Andrew Atkinson Humphreys, a Biography.* Philadelphia, 1924.

Reardon, Carol. "Brig. Gen. Andrew A. Humphreys' Pennsylvania Division at Fredericksburg," in Gary Gallagher, ed. *The Fredericksburg Campaign: Decision on the Rappahannock.* Chapel Hill, 1995.

Round, Harold. "A. A. Humphreys." *Civil War Times Illustrated,* Feb., 1966.

First Brigade

(1,718 men)

Brigadier General Joseph Bradford Carr

Joseph Carr was a bit of a bluenose, for it was remarked that "a profane or objectionable word was never heard from his lips." Despite his rather proper qualities, or perhaps because of them, the men under his command enjoyed razzing their superior. According to a man in the 16th Massachusetts, Carr had taught dancing "in schools of low character," and once news of this got around, he said, the men of the brigade shouted "Right and left!" and "Promenade to the bar!" when he rode by. He looked rather like a dandy, with large

well-groomed side whiskers and a thick mustache.

The thirty-five year old Carr was an upstate New Yorker, born in Albany of Irish parents. He later moved to Troy and was apprenticed to a tobacconist, working his way up through the trade to become a tobacco merchant himself. All the while he had an avid interest in the military, and rose to the rank of colonel in a New York state militia regiment. After Fort Sumter, he recruited the 2nd New York regiment and became its colonel. Stationed at Fort Monroe, Carr's men took part in the first fight (or more properly, skirmish) of the war at Big Bethel.

In June 1862, Carr's regiment joined Brig. Gen. Joseph Hooker's Third Corps division on the Virginia Peninsula, and Carr subsequently found himself in command of his brigade by virtue of his being the senior colonel. The brigade saw sparse action there, and Carr's battlefield leadership was never put to the test. Second Bull Run was an altogether different event. Hooker repeatedly sent Carr's brigade in headlong attacks against the Southern position on the Railroad Cut, and his brigade suffered 393 casualties. Though never able to drive the enemy from his strong position, Carr proved himself a tenacious fighter. Unfortunately, Hooker did not file a report after the battle, so Carr's contributions and abilities remained officially unsung. He was, however, rewarded with a promotion to brigadier general a week after the battle.

By the middle of September 1862, Carr was transferred to the brigade he would lead at Gettysburg after its former leader, Brig. Gen. Cuvier Grover, was transferred to the Department of the Gulf. Carr led the brigade at Fredericksburg, where it was only lightly engaged. At Chancellorsville, Carr's brigade lost over 500 men in heavy fighting, and he took over command of the division temporarily when Maj. Gen. Hiram Berry was killed. Carr was high on Maj. Gen. Daniel Sickles' list of those deserving "especial mention" after the battle.

By the summer of 1863, Carr was a battle-tested brigadier. His health, though, was a question mark, for he suffered from symptoms of malaria during the campaign and needed large doses of medicine just to remain in the saddle.

GETTYSBURG: After undertaking a dangerous, nighttime march on unfamiliar roads near enemy-held territory, Carr's brigade joined the Union army at midnight of July 1-2. The weary soldiers went into bivouac on the southern end of Cemetery Ridge. The entire corps was moved forward in the middle of the following afternoon when General Sickles determined to seize higher ground along the Emmitsburg Road. Carr's brigade manned the right-front of Humphreys' divisional line, facing west on the Emmitsburg Road. The 26th Pennsylvania held the right of Carr's line, about three hundred yards south of the Codori barn. The 11th Massachusetts extended the line south near the Rogers farmstead, while the 16th Massachusetts, 12th New Hampshire, and 11th New Jersey completed Carr's brigade front, which protruded below the Klingle farm buildings.

When the division came under attack about 5:30 p.m., Carr (according to one regimental historian) was far behind the lines and failed to realize his command was under hostile fire (he ordered his own to cease firing). This same author claimed that Carr also blundered by sending the brigade flag to the rear, which would have demoralized the men had they not been such experienced fighters. The initial pressure of the attack fell on Birney's division at Devil's Den and Stony Hill, and orders soon came for Humphreys to refuse his flank and form a new line.

Carr's 11th New Jersey (his left-most regiment) was withdrawn and formed to the left and rear of the Klingle homestead. Before long, the en echelon Southern attack, which at this point consisted of the brigades of Brig. Gen. Cadmus Wilcox and Col. David Lang, engulfed Carr's men, who gamely held on as the enemy foot soldiers threw themselves at their lines.

As the Third Corps salient at the Peach Orchard crumbled on his left, Carr ably shared Humphreys' burden of supervising a fighting withdrawal (as ordered by Birney, who took over command of the corps when Sickles was wounded). The long retreat over a half-mile of ground to Cemetery Ridge was a horrible ordeal for the men experiencing it. Carr's horse was killed under him, and although he was injured in the fall, he continued to direct his brigade. His 790 casualties attest to the nightmarish quality of the fight along the Emmitsburg Road and the retreat eastward. After the Confederate attack had spent itself, Carr's men still had spirit enough to launch a counterattack, which carried to the vicinity of the Emmitsburg Road before retiring once more. Carr's exhausted soldiers spent their second night at Gettysburg on the rear slope of Cemetery Ridge. The brigade was moved to the rear on the morning of July 3 and spent the day in reserve.

Joseph Carr had performed up to expectations on July 2 under extremely difficult circumstances. Humphreys called attention to his "cool courage, determination, and skill ful handling of [his] troops." He was not around to receive any congratulations, however. Sick and hardly able to walk, Carr took leave from the army after the successful termination of the battle. When he returned in September, he was given command of the division (Humphreys had been promoted and transferred) and held it through the remainder of the year. In the March 1864 reorganization, Carr received a division in the newly-reconstituted Second Corps, and there the upward arc of his Civil War career abruptly halted. By May, his brigadier general's commission had still not been taken up and confirmed in the Senate. Although reappointed, the Senate—for reasons not readily apparent—refused to confirm him at the date of his original commission. That left Carr junior to several other officers in his brigade, and he was forced to step down. He was transferred to the Army of the James and led a division of black troops, ending the war as a brevet major general.

Carr returned to Troy, New York, and entered in the manufacturing business. He was secretary of state for New York from 1879 until 1885, when he ran unsuccessfully for lieutenant governor. He died from cancer in 1895.

For further reading:

O'Brien, Kevin E. "'To Unflinchingly Face Danger and Death': Carr's Brigade Defends Emmitsburg Road." *Gettysburg Magazine*, #12, 1995.

Pfanz, Harry W. *Gettysburg: The Second Day.* Chapel Hill, 1987.

SECOND BRIGADE

THE "EXCELSIOR BRIGADE"

(1,837 MEN)

COLONEL
WILLIAM R. BREWSTER

Born in July of 1828 in Goshen, Connecticut, William Brewster worked as a revenue agent before the war. He had no military education, and enjoyed a rather strange and enigmatic army career prior to Gettysburg.

Brewster was living in New York when the Civil War broke out, and he became major of the 28th New York State Militia, a three-month regiment that guarded bridges over the Potomac River while the Battle of Bull Run was fought a few miles away. Named colonel of the 73rd New York Regiment in the Excelsior Brigade when Brig. Gen. Daniel Sickles organized that collection of regiments in October 1861, Brewster led the 73rd in battle at Williamsburg on the Virginia Peninsula in May 1862. For reasons unexplained, he was not with the regiment later that month at the Battle of Fair Oaks, and was still absent while the Seven Days' Battles raged in late June and early July. Brewster was again absent for his regiment's tribulations during the Second Battle of Bull Run—the official report cryptically mentions that he "had been left in Alexandria"—but rejoined it immediately after the fighting. The Connecticut colonel was present for the Fredericksburg Campaign in December 1862, but the regiment did not participate in any fighting. Contrarily, at the Battle of Chancellorsville in May 1863, where the Third Corps was heavily engaged, Brewster was once again absent. A disturbing and unflattering pattern was emerging. When he returned, he discovered (perhaps to his dismay) that he was now the brigade's senior officer. Its previous commander, Brig. Gen. Joseph Revere, had been court-martialed and thrown out of the army for incompetence. Thus Brewster, with no formal military training, little experience under fire, and a questionable service record, was thrust into brigade command on the eve of the Gettysburg Campaign.

GETTYSBURG: After a confusing march on dark, unfamiliar, and twisting country roads that nearly resulted in a an unwanted brush with the enemy near Black Horse Tavern, Brewster's Excelsior Brigade arrived on the battlefield about midnight on July 1-2. The New Yorkers bivouacked with Brig. Gen. Joseph Carr's brigade on the southern end of Cemetery Ridge.

On the afternoon July 2, Brewster advanced his brigade west, in accordance with General Sickles' instructions, to occupy the high ground along the Emmitsburg Road north of the Peach Orchard. The brigade's six regiments did not deploy together, but were instead stuck in the line piecemeal where needed. The 73rd eventually moved left and supported Graham's brigade, while the 72nd took up a position along the Emmitsburg Road, facing west, near the Trostle farm lane. The 71st deployed on the 72nd's right and joined its own right flank with Colonel Carr's 11th New Jersey. Of Brewster's remaining three regiments, the 74th moved north and formed behind the right rear of Carr's brigade, and the 70th and 120th remained in reserve. Thus The Excelsior Brigade regiments stretched from the Peach Orchard north along the road near the Klingle farm.

The New Yorkers watched as Longstreet's large-scale attack opened late that afternoon with Maj. Gen. John Hood's Division sweeping across the Emmitsburg Road and the grounds of the Rose farm into Maj. Gen. David Birney's thinly-spread division. When Brig. Gen. William Barksdale's Mississippians hit the Peach Orchard salient about 5:30 p.m., the force of the assault cracked open the line, causing several of the Excelsior regiments to fall back in a hurry. Brewster's horse went down, but he walked back to his 120th New York and there made a stand, helping to temporarily stem the tide of Barksdale's assault. Under Brig. Gen. Andrew Humphreys' direction, a new line was formed parallel to the Trostle farm lane by swinging back the left. Four of Brewster's regiments participated (70th, 73th, 74th, and 120th), but the new position was soon overwhelmed. The regiments made as orderly a retreat as possible under difficult circumstances back to Cemetery Ridge. During the withdrawal, a private from the 71st New York handed Brewster the blood-soaked bridle he had removed from the colonel's dead horse.

Near dark, as the Confederate attack began to peter out, remnants of the Excelsior Brigade, together with a patchwork of other commands, charged forward south of the Codori barn on Cemetery Ridge and overran Gulian Weir's abandoned Federal artillery pieces. Members of the 71st New York attempted to haul three of them back eastward by hand. Brewster's brigade suffered heavily, and losses tallied 778 men—about every third man. That night the New Yorkers camped once more on Cemetery Ridge. They were withdrawn at sunrise the next morning, and spent July 3 in reserve.

Despite his inexperience, Brewster had done well on July 2 under the close supervision of Humphreys. After the battle, Humphreys commended Brewster for his "courage, determination, and skillful handling of [his] troops." His subsequent record was one of steady service unrewarded by promotion. He continued to command the brigade into the next year, still at the rank of colonel. When the army was reorganized in March 1864, he kept his place at the head of his regiments—still a colonel. Brewster fought steadily through the bloody battles of the Overland and Petersburg campaigns and mustered out in October 1864.

His curious military career drew to a close with a brevet promotion to brigadier general, dated December 2, 1864, for "distinguished services in the present campaign before Richmond." Brewster returned to New York and died in Brooklyn in 1869.

For further reading:

O'Brien, Kevin E. "'To Unflinchingly Face Danger and Death': Carr's Brigade Defends Emmitsburg Road." *Gettysburg Magazine*, #12, 1995.

Pfanz, Harry. *Gettysburg: The Second Day.* Chapel Hill, 1987.

THIRD BRIGADE

(1,365 MEN)

COLONEL
GEORGE CHILDS BURLING

Colonel Burling, together with Col. William Brewster of the Second Brigade of the division, is one of the least recognized Gettysburg commanders. A New Jersey native, he had started the war as a captain in the 6th New Jersey regiment and had worked his way up through the ranks to lieutenant colonel by the time of the Peninsula Campaign. Brig. Gen. Joe Hooker, his division commander, observed Burling's behavior at Seven Pines and singled him out as an "officer of uncommon merit." His brigade commander, Col. Samuel Starr, also mentioned his "coolness under fire" at Seven Pines.

Burling received command of his regiment in August 1862, when its colonel was wounded at the Battle of Second Bull Run. His first experience in regimental command, on the second day of the battle, was not a happy one: the other regiments of his brigade withdrew without notifying him, and Burling had to order his unsupported 6th New Jersey to retreat when attacked by a superior force. After the battle, Burling was among those on a long list of officers cited for "gallant and meritorious conduct" by Colonel Joseph Carr, the brigade's commander. (This "distinction" appears to have been a pro forma exercise extended to all the New Jersey regimental commanders in Carr's post-battle reports.)

Burling's 6th New Jersey was not engaged at Fredericksburg in December 1862, and in May of 1863, Burling was wounded early in the fighting at Chancellorsville. He returned to his regiment the following month. The brigade's commander, Brig. Gen. Gershom Mott, had also been wounded at Chancellorsville, and had not yet returned to duty, so Burling, as senior colonel, took Mott's place at the head of the brigade just before the Gettysburg Campaign opened.

As one of the most important battles of the war loomed, Burling led his new command into Pennsylvania. Although brave, it was unknown whether he was prepared to lead a brigade. His strongest asset was his long association with the organization.

GETTYSBURG: Burling's brigade was one of two Third Corps brigades left behind in Emmitsburg when the rest of the corps moved toward Gettysburg on the afternoon of July 1. The following morning at 1:30 a.m., Burling received orders from Maj. Gen. George Meade to move immediately to join the army at Gettysburg. His men were scattered, and he delayed the departure of both brigades until the morning of July 2, a regrettable decision in view of the urgent circumstances.

The column joined the rest of the division on lower Cemetery Ridge around 10:00 a.m. on July 2. That afternoon, in accordance with Maj. Gen. Daniel Sickles's wishes, Burling moved forward with the rest of Brig. Gen. Andrew Humphreys' division to take up a position along the Emmitsburg Road. Soon, Sickles directed Humphreys to dispatch Burling's men to the left as support for Birney's division. A staff officer guided Burling's six regiments to Trostle's Woods. They did not remain there long. Much like Brewster's brigade, Burling's would be broken up and parceled out where needed.

The Confederate attack against the Union left flank began shortly thereafter, with Maj. Gen. John Hood's Division smashing up against Maj. Gen. David Birney's men on the Rose farm, Stony Hill and Devil's Den. Birney had placed Burling's brigade in a field of rye west of the Trostle Woods, where it could move to either support Graham's brigade at the Peach Orchard or fill the gap that existed between the orchard and Stony Hill. As it developed, Birney parceled out several of Burling's regiments, one by one, to threatened points in the line, effectively leaving the New Jerseyian without a command. His regiments fought well on their own hooks, defending Stony Hill on Colonel de Trobriand's line, assisting Capt. George Winslow's battery, and fighting with ele-

ments of Graham's brigade. Colonel Burling, though, never had the chance to exercise effective control over his own men during the engagement. In his report, General Birney gave him glancing mention for "the valuable aid rendered . . . by the command of Colonel Burling, commanding the Third Brigade of the Second Division."

Gettysburg was Burling's only experience at the head of a brigade, nominal though it was. When Gershom Mott returned to the brigade at the end of August, Burling went back to command the 6th New Jersey. He resigned from the army in March 1864. A year later, he was awarded a brevet promotion to brigadier general for his service at Gettysburg. Burling died in 1885.

For further reading:

Pfanz, Harry. *Gettysburg: The Second Day.* Chapel Hill, 1987.

———

FIFTH CORPS
(11,019 MEN / 26 GUNS)

MAJOR GENERAL GEORGE SYKES

Forty-one-year-old George Sykes was the newest corps commander at Gettysburg. He had risen to the head of the Fifth Corps on June 28, just three days before the battle, taking over the position Maj. Gen. George Meade vacated when he was suddenly called upon to lead the army. Sykes was also the least prepossessing of any of the corps-level leaders. Lt. Frank Haskell, Big. Gen. John Gibbon's aide, described Sykes as "a small, rather thin man, well dressed and gentlemanly, brown hair and beard which he wears full, with a red, pinched, rough looking skin, feeble blue eyes, large nose, with the general air of one who is weary, and a little ill natured." Another described him similarly as "lacking in vigor." Sykes was a career army man, and like many school-trained officers, his time-consuming adherence to regulations had earned him the nickname "Tardy George." Though he earned the moniker at West Point, it stuck with him in the Regular Army where he enhanced his

reputation for having "the slows." It didn't impede his career, however, for the army was an institution which appreciated and valued those who observed established traditions and manners. One fellow officer described Sykes as follows:

It would have been hard to find a better officer in the Army than Sykes. . .he was so thoroughly and simply a soldier, that he knew little of politics and cared less. [He was] one of the coolest men in danger or confusion that we had in the whole Army. He enforced discipline like a machine and had apparently no more sentiment than a gun-stock.

For all his Old Army reserve, Sykes was a likable person. Confederate Maj. Gen. Daniel Harvey Hill, his roommate at West Point, described him as "a man admired by all for his honor, courage, and frankness, and peculiarly endeared to me by his social qualities." (His social qualities must have been considerable indeed to endear Sykes, a New Yorker, to D. H. Hill, a notorious Yankee-hater.) To his subordinates, however, Sykes often came across as stiff and crusty, an unemotional soldier. For him the Army was life and all that it had to offer. Few officers or enlisted men could boast such a single-minded, lifelong commitment to one ideal.

Born in Delaware, he was the grandson of James Sykes, a noted physician and former governor of the state. He was appointed to West Point from Maryland in 1838 after marrying into a prominent family of that state. An unexceptional student, he graduated 39th out of 56 in the Class of 1842 and was immediately dispatched to fight Seminoles in Florida. By 1846 he had been promoted to first lieutenant, and at that rank fought throughout the Mexican War. Afterwards, he served continuously in the lonely outposts of the southwest until the guns boomed at Fort Sumter. Many officers from his adopted state of Maryland were resigning to fight with the South. George Sykes entertained no qualms about his loyalties, and the thought of leaving the U. S. Army never crossed his mind.

Sykes was in his prime in 1861 and recognized as a solid and uncompromising Old Army officer—even if he was a bit overly methodical. Thrust into command of the only Regular infantry on the field in the at First Bull Run, his career soldiers were invaluable in slowing the routed, wild-eyed Union volunteers. His fine showing at Bull Run garnered him a promotion to brigadier general in September 1861. In March 1862, just before the Army of the Potomac embarked for the Virginia Peninsula, Sykes was given charge of a brigade of Regulars, which he led at Yorktown. In mid-May, when the Fifth Corps was organized, Sykes was named to command its Second Division, composed mostly of Regular Army units. Under him, "Sykes' Regulars" (as the soldiers often called themselves) stoutly defended their position at Gaines' Mill on June 27, checking the Confederate attack until the final breakthrough elsewhere on the line. Sykes' name was the first to appear in his corps commander's commendations.

Two months later, at Second Bull Run, Sykes' division again functioned as a rearguard to help save the fleeing army from destruction. Sykes and his men, with the rest of the Fifth Corps, were held in reserve. He received a promotion to major general (the appropriate rank for a division leader) in November 1862. His troops saw light action at Fredericksburg in December, but at Chancellorsville in May 1863, Sykes' Regulars led the Union army's flanking column toward the Lee's rear at the beginning of the campaign. After clashing with a stronger force of the enemy, Sykes was recalled to Chancellorsville by his nervous army chief, Maj. Gen. Joseph Hooker. Following this truncated exchange of gunfire, Sykes and his men went unused for the rest of the campaign.

As the Battle at Gettysburg approached, Sykes had seen little action since the previous summer. He had proven his worth in defense, but never in attack, and he had watched as the rest of the army had caught up in discipline and fighting ability with his

Regulars. It is possible that he would not have advanced beyond his divisional responsibilities if Meade's own advancement had not suddenly thrust him into corps leadership. Still, Sykes had the advantages of a full military education and an army career that included long and reliable service as a division commander. His biggest liabilities stemmed from his newness to command at the corps level—and perhaps, given the situation, his stolid temperament.

GETTYSBURG: On July 1, Sykes marched north from Union Mills, Maryland, to Hanover, Pennsylvania, with his First and Second Divisions. The fighting west of Gettysburg that day prompted General Meade to summon Sykes to Gettysburg at about 7:00 p.m.. The footsore troops had just arrived in Hanover, about 12 miles from the battlefield, but they dutifully reformed their columns and tramped toward their destination. After an exhausting night march, Sykes halted at Bonnaughtown, about five miles east of Gettysburg.

Sykes' two divisions (under Brig. Gens. James Barnes and Romeyn Ayres) took to the road again at daybreak on July 2 and turned south near Brinkerhoff's Ridge, about two miles east of town. There, Sykes' divisions massed briefly in expectation of an offensive against the Confederate left. When Meade abandoned the plan, the Fifth Corps was ordered closer to the army's main body. Sykes turned his men south onto the Baltimore Pike and crossed Rock Creek about 11:00 a.m. The men rested in the shadow of nearby Power's Hill for a few hours. The Third, or Pennsylvania Reserves, Division (under Brig. Gen. Samuel Crawford) had come up from Washington and reached Sykes around noon. In the middle of the day, Meade ordered the Fifth Corps toward the left of the army with orders to support Third Corps commander Maj. Gen. Dan Sickles.

Lieutenant General James Longstreet's corps-level attack against the army's left struck Sickles' front before Sykes and his men arrived. When Meade learned Little Round Top was vacant, he ordered the Fifth Corps to double-quick there and "hold at all hazards." Sykes accordingly sent a messenger to order First Division leader Barnes to dispatch a brigade to the prominent hill. The courier failed to locate Barnes, but he was spotted and hailed by brigade leader Colonel Strong Vincent, who realized the urgency of the situation and agreed to lead his troops onto Little Round Top.

Sykes began to send a stream of reinforcements to Vincent, while also dispatching Col. William Tilton's and Col. Jacob Sweitzer's brigades to plug holes in the Third Corps line. Sykes dispatched Brig. Gen. Romeyn Ayres' division toward the fighting, (though it was soon flanked and put to flight), and then deployed Brig. Gen. Samuel Crawford's Pennsylvania Reserves as they approached. This cobbled and patched line, which fought primarily in the area stretching from Stony Hill to Little Round Top, prevented James Longstreet's Confederates from breaking the Union left completely open and capturing Little Round Top. The fighting rendered Sweitzer's brigade and the two Regular Army brigades under Ayres unfit for further duty; all three had suffered heavy casualties and the survivors were scattered about the vicinity of southern Cemetery Ridge and Little Round Top. Fortunately for Sykes, the bulk of the Sixth Corps arrived late in the afternoon and evening of July 2 to reinforce the area and relieve his shot-up Fifth Corps units. Sykes had done a good and hard day's work on July 2. The Fifth Corps was held in reserve on July 3.

George Sykes never performed again at the level of his Gettysburg showing, although the opportunity to do so never repeated itself. In the fall of 1863, Meade felt Sykes had returned to his "Tardy George" habits, and in the March 1864 army consolidation, Sykes was replaced at the head of the Fifth Corps by Maj. Gen. Gouverneur Warren. The Old Army Regular was transferred west and finished the war in Kansas.

Sykes reverted to his Regular Army rank of lieutenant colonel and was promoted to colonel in 1868. He led a regiment on the frontier and died on active duty, from cancer, in 1880.

For further reading:

Pfanz, Harry. *Gettysburg: The Second Day.* Chapel Hill, 1987.

Powell, William H. *The Fifth Army Corps.* New York, 1896.

Reese, Timothy J. *Sykes' Regular Infantry Division, 1861-1864.* McFarland, 1990.

FIRST DIVISION

(3,418 MEN)

BRIGADIER GENERAL JAMES BARNES

James Barnes was sixty-one in 1863, the oldest of all the generals in the Army of the Potomac with the exception of Brig. Gen. George "Old Pap" Greene of the Twelfth Corps. Barnes would be commanding a division in battle for the first time, and his preparation for that role was questionable. While he had graduated from West Point, his education there was more than three decades past, and he had spent most of the intervening time as a railroad engineer and executive.

Barnes was a Bostonian, had been educated at the Boston Latin School, and engaged in business there for some years before receiving an appointment to West Point. He graduated at the advanced age of twenty-eight, 5th out 46 in the Class of 1829, the same year Robert E. Lee graduated 2nd, and became an instructor of tactics and French at the Academy. He soon tired of this vocation, however, and like many officers bored with the peacetime army, Barnes resigned his commission and went to work in the burgeoning railroad industry. He was successful in this field and became the superintendent of the Western Railroad, working there for the next twenty-two years until shots were fired at Fort Sumter.

With his military connections, Barnes was given the colonelcy of the 18th Massachusetts volunteer regiment in July 1861. He and his regiment went to the Virginia Peninsula with the Army of the Potomac, but during the entire campaign the regiment incurred no casualties to enemy fire. Although the 18th was placed in the hard-fighting Fifth Corps when that organization was created just before the Seven Days' Battles, Barnes' regiment was detached to help the cavalry guard the army's rear. Meanwhile, the rest of brigade suffered terribly in battle after battle. After the campaign, Barnes' commander, Brig. Gen. John Martindale, fell out of favor for proposing surrender rather than withdrawal after Malvern Hill. Martindale was relieved, and Barnes, the senior colonel who had not yet fired a shot in anger, took his place in command of the battered brigade on July 10, 1862.

Barnes was not with his brigade at Second Bull Run. At Antietam, McClellan held the Fifth Corps in reserve, and so Barnes once again found himself a non-combatant, listening to the sounds of heavy fighting from afar. His first taste of combat came as his brigade formed the vanguard of the Union's post-battle pursuit of General Lee's forces. As his men probed the southern bank of the Potomac near Shepherdstown, West Virginia, they were savagely attacked by the Southern rear-guard. Some 200 of his men were shot or drowned in their rush to regain the Maryland bank, and when it was over, the 100 or so who remained on the Virginia side were captives. Despite this debacle and his overall lackluster record, Barnes' enjoyed a promotion to brigadier general two months later, in November 1862—perhaps due to well-placed advocates in Washington.

At Fredericksburg, Barnes and his brigade took part in one of the last attacks on the impregnable Confederate positions on the hills beyond the town. Though he and his men acquitted themselves well, their bravery did nothing more that add 500 names to the Northern casualty rolls. Barnes gained plaudits from his division commander, Brig. Gen. Charles Griffin, who wrote after the battle, "James Barnes. . .is entitled to special notice for his coolness, energy, and marked ability." At Chancellorsville, Barnes' brigade was only lightly engaged; Maj. Gen. Joseph Hooker never fully deployed the Fifth Corps during the battle. The brigade did have the small distinction of being the last Union contingent to retreat across the Rappahannock after the fighting.

When General Griffin went on sick leave immediately after Chancellorsville, Barnes found himself a division commander as his army approached a showdown with its nemesis in Pennsylvania. His age and inexperience as a division commander were two major factors working against him.

GETTYSBURG: While the battle was being fought west of Gettysburg on July 1, Barnes' division was marching north from Union Mills, Maryland, to Hanover, Pennsylvania, with the Fifth Corps' Second Division. That evening, his division moved toward the battlefield, and arrived on Brinkerhoff's Ridge two miles east of Gettysburg during the early morning hours of July 2. His men paused and skirmished briefly with the Southerners in the vicinity while Meade pondered the merits of an offensive against the Confederate left. That plan never came to fruition, and the division tramped southward down the Baltimore Pike, crossed the Rock Creek bridge around 11:00 a.m., then rested for a few hours near Power's Hill.

Some time after 3:00 that afternoon, Maj. Gen. George Sykes ordered Barnes' division toward Little Round Top by way of the Granite Schoolhouse Lane. It had just reached the Taneytown Road with Col. Strong Vincent's brigade in the lead when Barnes and his men were summoned to action against Lt. Gen. James Longstreet's Corps, which was attacking east toward Little Round Top. The chronicler of the 118th Pennsylvania (a man who, it should be said, was inclined to inflate his accounts of his generals), wrote that Barnes exhibited a high standard of personal courage, riding "valiantly amid the. . .fray, encouraging, persuading, directing with that same courageous judgment which had ever been his distinguishing characteristic."

Others, however, paint a different picture of Barnes' behavior during the combat on the afternoon of July 2. According to a soldier in Vincent's brigade, he was not at the head of the column, and "if he gave an order during the battle to any brigade commander I fail to find a record of it in any account I have read." In fact, the heroic and timely defense of Little Round Top by Vincent's infantry—the greatest contribution of Barnes' division to the battle—was primarily attributable to the initiative displayed by Vincent, not Barnes.

Barnes' other two brigades under Cols. Jacob Sweitzer and William Tilton were sent by Sykes through Trostle's Woods and the Wheatfield to assist Maj. Gen. David Birney's embattled men from the Third Corps. It was at this flashpoint of the contest that Barnes' activities engendered subsequent complaint, denial, and recrimination. Soon after Sweitzer and Tilton were situated, Barnes, overly concerned about what he perceived was a gap between the Stony Hill and the Peach Orchard, withdrew them 300 yards from the vicinity of the Wheatfield without permission. A *New York Herald* correspondent on the scene wrote that after Barnes pulled out, he refused to order his brigades back into line, while Colonel Regis de Trobriand asserted that Barnes' men fell back even before being engaged. Birney further claimed that he issued a protest to Barnes regarding the withdrawal, but to no effect. When Brig. Gen. John Caldwell's division arrived, Birney bluntly ordered Barnes' men to lie down, and Brig. Gen. Samuel Zook's brigade passed over their prostrate bodies as they went forward into the firing line. Sweitzer's brigade eventually moved forward and fought gallantly until driven back with heavy losses.

Barnes' most conspicuous appearance with his troops was poorly chosen—he detained Sweitzer's Brigade to deliver a patriotic speech just before they returned to the fight at a time when every minute was critical. Shortly afterward, when a renewed Confederate onslaught once more threatened Sweitzer's brigade, an aide who went to find Barnes could not locate him. Later in the day, when his men had fallen back from their most advanced positions, Barnes and Tilton were sitting their horses behind the blazing line of Federal artillery near the Wheatfield Road when a chunk of shell wounded Barnes in the leg and another killed Tilton's horse. The metal fragment ended Barnes' service at Gettysburg, and he never recovered sufficiently to return to the field.

General Barnes' performance at Gettysburg was mixed at best, although to be fair, his brigades were broken up and dispersed on a confused field, which made it doubly difficult for him to operate. He incurred the criticism of his subordinates and peers, however, which probably would have ended his career with the Army of the Potomac had he not been wounded.

He was given administrative duties in Washington until the close of the Civil War. Brevetted major general in early 1866, Barnes was appointed to a commission to investigate the building of the Union Pacific railroad and telegraph line in 1868, but died of liver congestion the next year.

For further reading:

Pfanz, Harry. *Gettysburg: The Second Day.* Chapel Hill, 1987.

Powell, William H. *The Fifth Army Corps.* New York, 1896.

Reese, Timothy J. *Sykes' Regular Infantry Division, 1861-1864.* McFarland, 1990.

FIRST BRIGADE

(655 MEN)

COLONEL
WILLIAM STOWELL TILTON

Tilton's brief ascent to the command of a brigade occurred on May 5, 1863, when Brig. Gen. James Barnes, the unit's previous brigadier, left to head the division after the Battle of Chancellorsville. Tilton's attainments were not impressive up to that point, but he got the position by virtue of being the senior colonel in the brigade.

A pre-war merchant in his native Boston, Tilton had entered the service as a staff officer in the 22nd Massachusetts in September 1861, and became the regiment's major the next month. The unit was absorbed into the Fifth Corps for the Peninsula Campaign, and participated in the siege of Yorktown. During the Seven Days' Battles, the 22nd Massachusetts fought at Gaines' Mill on June 27. In his report of the battle, Tilton demonstrated a colorful and descriptive style that revealed a more literary soul than possessed by most officers, who usually contented themselves with a bland recounting of events:

The din was incessant on our right, and soon three Yankee cheers told us that there the enemy had been repulsed. Now our extreme left was visited by the vigorous assaults of the

enemy, and they there met a similar fate. . .I now supposed the enemy would abandon the field for the night, but such did not prove to be their design, for, forming in three lines, they made a final and desperate effort to break through our lines, and they were successful, but not until our weary men were trampled upon by the hordes of Jackson's army. The attack, I saw, was desperate, and so was the defense. The noise of the musketry was not rattling, as ordinarily, but one intense metallic din. The sound of the artillery was sublime.

The 22nd's colonel was killed and Tilton wounded through the right shoulder and captured. He was promoted to lieutenant colonel while in captivity and exchanged in August 1862 as the commander of the 22nd Massachusetts. At Second Bull Run, the 22nd had the good fortune of being the one regiment of the brigade to miss the heavy fighting that occurred on August 30. In September, the corps was held in reserve at the Battle of Antietam, but Tilton was with Brig. Gen. James Barnes' brigade days later when it was attacked by the Army of Northern Virginia's rearguard at Shepherdstown, West Virginia, and thrown back to the northern bank of the Potomac River.

A month later, on October 17, Tilton was made colonel and given permanent command of the regiment. Tilton was at the head of his regiment in the disastrous attack at Fredericksburg, though his Bay Staters managed to escape from the fight with a comparatively light loss of 55 men. The regiment did not see any fighting at Chancellorsville.

Thus, Tilton had a rather thin combat record at the head of his regiment when he was elevated to brigade command just weeks before the opening of the Pennsylvania Campaign.

GETTYSBURG: Col. Tilton's command opened the morning of July 1 in Union Mills, Maryland, and marched north toward Gettysburg all that day with the bulk of the Fifth Corps. Its trek toward the battleground continued on July 2, and after 11:00 a.m. Tilton's weary men crossed Rock Creek and fell out for a quick rest near Power's Hill. They reformed and marched about a mile along the Granite Schoolhouse Lane and Taneytown Road toward the Union left flank near Little Round Top about 3:00 that afternoon.

When Lt. Gen. James Longstreet began his attack about 4:30 p.m., Fifth Corps leader Maj. Gen. George Sykes personally directed the brigades of Cols. Tilton and Jacob Sweitzer to bolster Maj. Gen. David Birney's division of the Third Corps in the vicinity of Stony Hill, just west of the Wheatfield. Both brigades moved forward promptly, although neither was very large. Tilton's small brigade was only about the size of an early-war effective regiment, and together with Sweitzer's was only as large as the average single Union brigade at Gettysburg. The latter's went in first, and Tilton's regiments followed at an angle with Sweitzer's brigade in its left front, aligned from left to right as follows: (First line) 22nd Massachusetts, 1st Michigan, 118th Pennsylvania (Corn Exchange Regiment), and (second line)18th Massachusetts. Unfortunately, Tilton's brigade had no infantry support on its right and was largely out of touch with the rest of the Fifth Corps.

There is some confusion as to when Barnes' two brigades formed on the hill, but it was probably just before Brig. Gen. George Anderson's Georgia troops struck the hillock from the front. Soon thereafter Brig. Gen. Joseph Kershaw's South Carolinians advanced and swept over the Emmitsburg Road south of the Peach Orchard and across the Rose farm—straight toward Tilton's right front and his exposed flank. Although Kershaw was ultimately beaten back, both Barnes and Tilton were so concerned about the gap east of their line that a change of front and a withdrawal were ordered. According to the regimental historian of the 118th Pennsylvania, Tilton "personally conducted the delicate maneuver which relieved the brigade of the imminent peril of its first position." Unfortunately, that "delicate maneuver" was in reality a retreat north across the Wheatfield Road and into the western fringe of Trostle's Woods. Tilton's shift exposed Sweitzer's flank, and he too was forced to fall back into Trostle's Woods, leaving a large hole in the Union line. One of Meade's staff officers was worried the brigades would withdraw too far, but the retreat was competently conducted,

if not needed. Tilton's brigade was not seriously engaged at Gettysburg again.

There was no official disparagement of Tilton's performance at Gettysburg. Barnes was very pleased with the performance of both Tilton and Sweitzer, and praised their actions. Barnes' brigades, however, were supposed to *hold* Stony Hill, not fall back; as a result, both he and Colonel Tilton bore the brunt of negative army gossip about their actions on the afternoon of July 2, 1863.

Tilton directed the brigade for the rest of the year. In March 1864, when the army was reorganized, Tilton was forced to step down and return to his regiment. He fought through the Overland Campaign as a colonel and briefly led a brigade at Petersburg. He received a brevet in September 1864 and was mustered out a month later. Tilton died in 1889.

For further reading:

Pfanz, Harry. *Gettysburg: The Second Day.* Chapel Hill, 1987.

Powell, William H. *The Fifth Army Corps.* New York, 1896.

Reese, Timothy J. *Sykes' Regular Infantry Division, 1861-1864.* McFarland, 1990.

SECOND BRIGADE

(1,423 MEN)

COLONEL
JACOB BOWMAN SWEITZER

Sweitzer was a native Pennsylvanian who had no military experience at the beginning of the Civil War. He entered the war as a major with the 33rd Pennsylvania Infantry on Independence Day, 1861, and was promoted to lieutenant colonel of the regiment—which was redesignated the 62nd Pennsylvania—in November of that year. On the Peninsula, Sweitzer participated in the fighting around Yorktown and in June, the 62nd was placed in the newly formed Fifth Corps, which did the lion's share of the

fighting in the subsequent Seven Days' Battles. At Gaines' Mill, the regiment's colonel was killed, leaving Sweitzer in charge. Later in the day, Sweitzer himself led an advance ("gallantly," according to brigade leader Brig. Gen. Charles Griffin), and was badly wounded and left on the field. For this action, he was promoted to colonel during his convalescence.

Sweitzer was back in field command of the 62nd by Antietam in September 1862, although the Fifth Corps was held in reserve during the battle. When Griffin was promoted to division command at the end of October, Sweitzer was given command of the brigade. At Fredericksburg, Sweitzer led his brigade in the division's doomed afternoon assault on Marye's Heights, where it lost 222 men. Sweitzer was replaced in brigade command before Chancellorsville when its senior colonel, James McQuade, returned. When McQuade got too sick to continue in command during the battle, Sweitzer once again took charge, though the brigade was not under fire after this transfer of command.

It is difficult to conclude that Jacob Sweitzer possessed, with such scant credentials, the ability or experience to lead a brigade.

GETTYSBURG: Sweitzer's men started July 1 in Union Mills, Maryland, and marched north toward Gettysburg all day with the bulk of the Fifth Corps. The division arrived and massed briefly on Brinkerhoff's Ridge about two miles east of Gettysburg at mid-morning on July 2, and one of

Sweitzer's regiments skirmished there with the enemy. The corps soon moved on, and Sweitzer and his tired infantrymen crossed Rock Creek bridge on the Baltimore Pike around 11:00 a.m. After a brief respite at the base of Power's Hill, the division was sent down the Granite Schoolhouse Lane and the Taneytown Road to a point near the Union left flank.

When Lt. Gen. James Longstreet's Corps roared across the Emmitsburg Road toward Devil's Den and Stony Hill about 4:30 p.m., Fifth Corps commander Maj. Gen. George Sykes marched Sweitzer's brigade, together with Col. William Tilton's brigade, on Sweitzer's right, to the Stony Hill position. There, his men were to occupy the hillock and bolster Sickles' threatened Third Corps line, in essence the middle of Maj. Gen. David Birney's divisional front, which covered the ground from the Peach Orchard on the right to Devil's Den on the left. Sweitzer was unsure of the exact whereabouts of Col. P. Regis de Trobriand's brigade, one of Birney's units he was to assist, and supposed it was aligned to his left. Sweitzer had but three regiments with him at Gettysburg: the 4th Michigan on the right, the 62nd Pennsylvania in the center, and 32nd Massachusetts on the left, slightly more than 1,000 men and officers. These men held the north end of the woods fronting west toward the Peach Orchard.

When Longstreet's attack reached the Stony Hill sector, Sweitzer shifted his regiments as needed and generally conducted himself well. Division commander James Barnes and Colonel Tilton, however, grew overly concerned about a gap that existed between Tilton's line and the Peach Orchard. Barnes sent word to Sweitzer that when he retreated, he should do so through the woods. Sweitzer notified his regimental commanders, and some confusion ensued as to whether a retreat had actually been ordered. A short while later, while Joseph Kershaw's South Carolinians were pounding Tilton's right front and threatening his flank, Sweitzer watched as his fellow colonel retreated his regiments about 300 yards north beyond the Wheatfield Road and into the Trostle Woods. Barnes soon after ordered Sweitzer to do likewise, since Tilton's withdrawal exposed Sweitzer's right. The long bearded and grim-faced Sweitzer conducted his retreat in good order and aligned his men in the woods along the Wheatfield Road.

After Barnes' troops fell back, assistance from the Second Corps arrived in the form of John Caldwell's division, which formed in the Trostle Woods west of Sweitzer and launched a sweeping attack into the Wheatfield. When Caldwell's division ran into trouble, Sweitzer's brigade advanced to support it. His front, about 300 yards long, moved forward toward the stone wall at the far end of the field. Once past the Stony Hill on his right, fire from that direction prompted him to change front with two regiments to face it. As he faced Kershaw's South Carolinians, elements from two other Confederate brigades pressed in against his center and left, and the small brigade was bent back into a wide V-shaped front, nearly surrounded. Hand-to-hand fighting broke out. It was here that the famous fight for the 4th Michigan's national colors took place, and its colonel, Harrison Jeffords, was bayonetted. Sweitzer's horse was killed under him as he directed the action and a bullet went through his hat. Almost surrounded, his regiments began falling back under the pressure and were forced off the field. Sweitzer had dutifully sent his regiments in twice that afternoon and had made the best of two difficult situations without much direction from above. His efforts cost him more than 400 men, and the brigade would not be fit for further action for the rest of the battle.

Jacob Sweitzer had done well at Gettysburg, especially considering his paucity of experience at that level. General Barnes included Sweitzer in his omnibus praise of his brigadiers after the battle. Sweitzer managed to avoid the mini-controversy that spilled through the army about the Barnes-Tilton performance on Stony Hill. His brigade was considered in good hands after Gettysburg, and Sweitzer continued to lead

his veteran regiments until both he and they were mustered out a year later, in July 1864. Despite his showing at Gettysburg , he never received a promotion to brigadier general. Sweitzer died in 1888.

For further reading:

Pfanz, Harry. *Gettysburg: The Second Day.* Chapel Hill, 1987.

Powell, William H. *The Fifth Army Corps.* New York, 1896.

Reese, Timothy J. *Sykes' Regular Infantry Division, 1861-1864.* McFarland, 1990.

THIRD BRIGADE

(1,336 MEN)

COLONEL STRONG VINCENT

As he watched his brigade march through a small Pennsylvania town toward its destiny at Gettysburg, twenty-six-year-old Strong Vincent declared to an aide, "There could be worse fates than to die fighting here in Pennsylvania." Vincent, true to his first name, was of average height and "well formed" with a forceful personality to match, and had been marked early on as one of the most valuable young officers in the army. Though he had not been trained as a soldier, his assets were many. He was a fine horseman, and struck a very military appearance in the saddle. (His young wife, also a skilled equestrienne, had visited him on the Rappahannock and their long horseback rides, their gaiety, and their striking good looks, had inspired much admiration in the army.) He was personally quiet and gentlemanly, and had a cheerful disposition, but was also a strict disciplinarian. Vincent's regiment, the 83rd Pennsylvania, had been so precise and proficient in drill that on the Peninsula in 1862 army commander Maj. Gen. George McClellan had lauded it as "one of the best regiments in the army."

Born in Waterford, Pennsylvania, to a successful merchant, Vincent toiled for a time in his father's iron foundry in Erie. Convinced that he could further his future in the foundry business with a scientific education, he enrolled in Scientific School in Hartford, Connecticut, transferred to Trinity College in the same city, then finally ended up at Harvard University, where he abandoned his original plans and devoted himself to the study of law. His fine character became evident at this point in his life, for he was a respected figure at Harvard, being elected president of at least one student society and also designated marshal at Class Day ceremonies upon graduation. He was admitted to the Erie County Bar the year before the Civil War began.

After the fall of Fort Sumter, Vincent enlisted in the ninety-day Erie Regiment, and rose from private to regimental adjutant during the regiment's three-month existence. Reenlisting in the 83rd Pennsylvania, he was commissioned lieutenant colonel. The regiment served during the Peninsula Campaign, but Vincent contracted malaria and missed most of the action. The 83rd's colonel was killed at Gaines' Mill, and while Vincent was home recuperating from his disease, the rank and file elected him to be their new commander.

The young colonel returned to the regiment in October 1862, and fought at the Battle of Fredericksburg. At one point during this engagement, his men became pinned down by shellfire, and to help keep up their courage, Vincent calmly strode among his prostrate ranks, oblivious to the deadly projectiles exploding about him. In March 1863, Vincent turned down an opportunity to become the judge advocate general of the Army of the Potomac; a post offered him after his fine performance as a juror in a court-martial. He refused the appointment with a laugh, saying, "I enlisted to fight." Following Chancellorsville, where the brigade was not engaged, Colonel Vincent received command of the brigade on May 20 to "the cheers that broke through the solemn decorum of dress parade."

Thus one of the most celebrated brigadiers of Gettysburg lore was called to battle on his native soil with only five weeks of experience at the head of his unit. Vincent's natural gifts were such that few had any doubts but that he would do well. After a successful performance at one of the early skirmishes in the Campaign, Maj. Gen. George Meade—then still in command of the Fifth Corps—was heard to say, "I wish he were a brigadier general, I'd put him in charge of a division."

GETTYSBURG: After arriving on the battlefield on the morning of July 2, Vincent and his men led Brig. Gen. James Barnes' division to the Union left near Little Round Top in the afternoon, arriving just as Lt. Gen. James Longstreet's attack began driving toward the area about 4:30 p.m. Vincent was in reserve near the Wheatfield with his brigade when he spotted a courier sent by Fifth Corps commander Maj. Gen. George Sykes to deliver orders to Barnes. Hailing the messenger, Vincent learned that Sykes wanted a brigade to occupy "that hill yonder" as soon as possible. Vincent quickly recognized the strategic importance of the rocky eminence, and risked court-martial by ordering his brigade to advance at the double-quick for Little Round Top.

As shells burst in his ranks, Vincent rapidly and expertly deployed his regiments to defend the high ground just minutes ahead of Brig. Gens. Jerome Robertson's Texans and Brig. Gen. Evander Law's Alabamians. The young colonel deployed his four regiments part way down the rocky slope in a crescent front facing generally southwest, toward Devil's Den. His regiments were aligned, from right to left, as follows: 16th Michigan, 44th New York, 83rd Pennsylvania, and 20th Maine (the army's far left).

For the next hour and a half, Vincent's men fought with grit and determination, denying Little Round Top to the Southerners, who doggedly continued to fight their way up its steep slopes a few inches at a time. The attack against his left flank (held by the 20th Maine and Col. Joshua Chamberlain) by Evander Law's Alabamians is well documented.

At the climax of the attack, Vincent rushed forward to cheer on his men and fell mortally wounded by a bullet that passed through his left groin and fractured the thigh bone. He was taken to the rear, and as his condition worsened in the following days, messages were sent to Washington urging Vincent's promotion to brigadier general. For once, the wheels of the military bureaucracy moved quickly, and Vincent received his star shortly before he expired on July 7.

Vincent's bugler wrote:

General Vincent by his soldierly comprehension of the situation, and the promptness of his action, saved to our army the field of Gettysburg that day. . . .Had he hesitated a moment, or waited for orders to reach him through the ordinary channels, when his brigade arrived on [Little] Round Top he would have found it already in possession of the enemy.

For further reading:

Norton, Oliver W. *The Attack and Defense of Little Round Top, Gettysburg, July 2, 1863.* Chicago, 1909.

Pfanz, Harry. *Gettysburg: The Second Day.* Chapel Hill, 1987.

Powell, William H. *The Fifth Army Corps.* New York, 1896.

Wright, James R. "Vincent's Brigade on Little Round Top." *Gettysburg Magazine*, #1, 1989.

SECOND DIVISION
THE "REGULAR DIVISION"
(4,013 MEN)

BRIGADIER GENERAL ROMEYN BECK AYRES

Romeyn Ayres was a career army officer, a competent professional at the head of the only division of professional soldiers in the Army of the Potomac. Six feet tall, he had grown portly and was balding, so as to leave him with a topknot—though he had no shortage of facial hair. Ayres sported a massive, wiry beard and spiked mustache that nearly hid his mouth and ears and made him look older than his thirty-eight years. His high forehead and philosophical gaze imparted the air of an intellectual, while his size helped him assert an authoritative physical presence. He was a very social man in the best sense of the word, considerate of others and capable of having fun without sacrificing his dignity. He had meticulous personal habits and was an immaculate dresser. Despite his cultivated demeanor, Ayres had acquired the reputation of a stubborn fighter who quickly let his men know that they could expect to be driven hard.

Ayres was born along the Mohawk River in upstate New York, the son of a small-town doctor who groomed several sons for professional life. His father singled out

Romeyn for a military career and rigorously tutored him in Latin. Romeyn eventually entered West Point. Despite his father's schooling he was an indifferent scholar, graduating 22nd out of the 38 members of the class of 1847. John Gibbon and Ambrose P. Hill were his classmates. Assigned to the artillery, Ayres entered the humdrum army life of the 1850s, serving in eastern garrisons and on the frontier. He developed the usual Regular Army observance of regulations, but retained a rebellious streak of pragmatism, a paradox that stayed with him throughout his career. A good example of this took place while on duty in Texas, where he pitched his camp near a superior officer. The officer, a stickler for military protocol, had his reveille "at daybreak." After an interview with his superior, Ayres, who liked to sleep in, issued the following order:" Company Orders: Until further orders, daylight in this camp will be at six o'clock."

As a captain in the Battery E, 5th Artillery, Ayres distinguished himself at Bull Run, where his battery's rear-guard action helped save the fleeing Union army. By 1862, he was the chief of artillery for a Sixth Corps division, and served in that capacity on the Peninsula and at Antietam. He was promoted to chief of artillery for the entire Sixth Corps before the Battle of Fredericksburg in December 1862. All of his performances in these battles were followed by numerous commendations by officers who admired his ability.

Since promotion was faster in the infantry, able artillery officers (like Ayres) were often given infantry commissions as a reward for good service. After recovering from a horseback injury, Ayres took over the leadership of the First Brigade of the Second (Regular) Division (which was led at Gettysburg by Hannibal Day) on April 21, 1863. As the historian of Sykes' Regular Division put it, "It was reassuring for the men to learn that this crusty old Regular had been in the field from the start and carried a reputation for quiet dependability." It was also soon apparent that the "crusty old regular" had a low tolerance for cowardliness and behavior unbecoming an officer. When Ayres observed a colonel of his brigade cowering under fire, he dispatched the man the following day into the hottest part of the action. When the colonel was later reported killed, Ayres replied, "Thank God! His children can now be proud of him." Ayres' brigade was only lightly engaged at Chancellorsville in early May 1863.

In the chain reaction of promotions brought about by Maj. Gen. George Meade's ascension to army command, George Sykes took Meade's place at the head of the Fifth Corps, while Ayres replaced Sykes at the head of the Regular Division. These changes occurred only three days before the Battle of Gettysburg. Thus Ayres assumed responsibility for a division on the eve of one of the war's most important battles. But Ayres was a career soldier who had already proven himself as a divisional and corps artillery commander; his character and professional training suited him well for the crisis. In addition, his well-drilled Regulars were perhaps the best prepared to cope with sudden changes in leadership.

GETTYSBURG: On July 1, while the ridges west of Gettysburg rang with the deadly cacophony of battle, Ayres was with the main Fifth Corps column, marching from Union Mills, Maryland, to Hanover, Pennsylvania. He headed toward Gettysburg about 7:00 p.m. His division, together with Brig. Gen. James Barnes', arrived near the battlefield on July 2 at 11:00 a.m. The fatigued men went into camp near Power's Hill, welcoming the opportunity to rest, cook, and boil some coffee.

Ayres' three brigades (under Hannibal Day, Sidney Burbank, and Stephen Weed) were hurried to the Union left with the rest of the Fifth Corps when James Longstreet's First Corps smashed into that flank about 4:00 p.m. Soon after they arrived, the Fifth Corps' commander, Major General Sykes, detached Brig. Gen. Stephen Weed's lead brigade to reinforce Col. Strong Vincent's brigade, which was fighting for its life on Little Round Top. Sykes also directed Ayres to march his two Regular brigades to the support of Brig. Gen. John Caldwell's division, which was counterattacking the Confederates in the area of the Wheatfield.

Ayres resolutely advanced Burbank and Day west from the Plum Run Valley into the Rose Woods on the east side of the Wheatfield. As he discussed the situation with Caldwell, one of his aides noticed that Federal troops near the Emmitsburg Road on their right were breaking and running to the rear. The cause of the Union flight was the Confederate breakthrough in the Peach Orchard, which opened the way for a flood of Southerners, including Brig. Gen. William Wofford's Georgians, to stream past the Wheatfield and against Ayres' right flank, threatening to surround him. While other Confederates pounding his left and center, Ayres' two Regular brigades made quickly for the rear, suffering heavily as they ran a gauntlet of fire. Both rallied north of Little Round Top.

Ayres and his Regulars did not have much of a chance to demonstrate how well they could fight. Ayres rightly escaped any personal blame and was included in Sykes' praise for all three Fifth Corps division leaders.

He continued to lead the Regular Division until the spring of 1864, when he was replaced by Brig. Gen. Charles Griffin in a general reorganization of the army. However, Ayres was too valuable to remain idle for long, and he was placed at the head of another division in June 1864, which he led until the end of the war.

Ayres held a command in the Shenandoah Valley until he mustered out of the Volunteers in 1866, and was on active duty with the 2nd Artillery when he died suddenly in 1888.

For further reading:

Pfanz, Harry. *Gettysburg: The Second Day.* Chapel Hill, 1987.

Powell, William H. *The Fifth Army Corps.* New York, 1896.

Reese, Timothy J. *Sykes' Regular Infantry Division, 1861-1864.* McFarland, 1990.

FIRST BRIGADE
(1,553 MEN)

COLONEL
HANNIBAL DAY

Career soldier Hannibal Day had been associated with the military for most of his fifty-nine years. Yet, fate thrust him into his first field command of the Civil War only three days before Gettysburg.

Day was the son of an army surgeon, and as a boy had been captured twice with his father by the British in the War of 1812. Anything but a military career was out of the question, and he graduated from West Point in 1823 and took an assignment in the infantry. He had served continuously since that time, and his record read like a checklist of America's ante-bellum military deployment. He was first sent to the Great Lakes forts, and subsequently fought in the Blackhawk and Seminole wars before returning to garrison duty on the East Coast. A stretch in California during the Gold Rush followed, after which he served in the Mexican War before once again taking up garrison and recruiting duties. The outbreak of the Civil War found him stationed in the Dakotas, and he was quickly called east to serve in Washington and on recruiting duty in Boston. Military necessity pulled him from his desk job and placed him at the head of the First Brigade of Regulars as it marched north to Gettysburg.

Colonel Day's strikingly snow-white hair and frosty mustache and beard contrasted sharply with his dark, leathery skin. His eyes were deep and piercing, and his Old Army stare of disapproval withered many subordinates. As one would expect of a man with his professional experience, he had a no-nonsense reputation and was a strict disciplinarian. He had no real familiarity with the regiments he was leading into Pennsylvania, however, since he had been with them for only three days. More troubling, perhaps, was the fact that he had never witnessed Civil War combat. Indeed, this would be his first combat command in many years. As for Colonel Day, he had no doubt of his abilities on or off the field, and he looked forward to his combat debut with the brigade.

GETTYSBURG: Colonel Day spent the whole of July 1 marching toward the battlefield from Union Mills, Maryland. On July 2, Day and his men marched over the Rock Creek Bridge on the Baltimore Pike around 11:00 a.m., and camped near Power's Hill, behind the Union center, until about 4:00 that afternoon, when the Fifth Corps was quickly shuffled to the Union left. Day took up a position behind Col. Burbank's brigade as its support, east of the main branch of Plum Run, just northwest of little Round Top. His five United States regiments (the 3rd, 4th, 6th, 12th and 14th) were probably formed in columns rather than line. When John Caldwell's Second Corps division attacked into the Wheatfield, both Burbank and Days were ordered to advance and support Caldwell's left flank. The brigades advanced toward the eastern edge of the Rose Woods, where Burbank's brigade took a heavy fire. Day allowed his men to lie down. As his men were checking their weapons and preparing to enter the fighting near the Wheatfield, Colonel Day leaned over to have his pipe lit by a lieutenant. Just then, a bullet whizzed between the two officers and thudded into the neck of Day's horse, killing the beast. As Day struggled to his feet, he saw Confederates streaming around his brigade's right flank. Day and his men opened fire and waited until Colonel

Burbank's brigade had retreated to their position, and then both brigades made an orderly retreat. Day's Regulars maintained well-aligned ranks as they marched rearward under sheets of crossfire. They regrouped north of Little Round Top, their participation in the battle at an end.

Day's Regulars had been in action less than an hour but lost 382 casualties, most during the withdrawal. Circumstances beyond Day's control did not allow him to demonstrate whether he was a capable brigade commander. The colonel retired from active service less than a month later. The old Army Regular died in 1891.

For further reading:

Pfanz, Harry. *Gettysburg: The Second Day.* Chapel Hill, 1987.

Powell, William H. *The Fifth Army Corps.* New York, 1896.

Reese, Timothy J. *Sykes' Regular Infantry Division, 1861-1864.* McFarland, 1990.

SECOND BRIGADE

(954 MEN)

COLONEL
SIDNEY BURBANK

Colonel Burbank, sixty-one years old at Gettysburg, was in deteriorating health due to the rigors of a long military career. His left

eye had started to "wander," he had contracted hepatitis the year before, and had been forced back into bed with the disease during the winter of 1862-1863. He recovered sufficiently to accept command of a brigade of Regulars in March 1863, but when he arrived in Washington on the way to join his men, he had another relapse and took another twenty days' sick leave. He finally joined up with the army on April 15.

Burbank came from a distinguished Massachusetts military family—his father had been prominent in the Battle of Niagara in the War of 1812. Burbank graduated from West Point in 1829, along with Robert E. Lee and Union division commander Brig. Gen. James Barnes. He had a typical military career, including service on the western frontier and against the Blackhawks and Seminoles, and a stint as an instructor at the Academy. During the early part of the Civil War, Burbank's service, when he wasn't bedridden, included duty in Missouri in 1861 and the command the defenses of Cincinnati during John Hunt Morgan's 1862 Confederate raid. When Col. Dixon Miles was killed following the humiliating surrender of Harpers Ferry in September 1862, Burbank replaced him as head of the 2nd Regular Infantry Regiment. Colonel Burbank, however, did not see action until he joined the Army of the Potomac in April 1863. Chancellorsville, two months before Gettysburg, was his first taste of 1860s combat. His brigade was moderately engaged on the first day of the battle and Burbank was commended, along with both the other brigade leaders, by division leader Maj. Gen. George Sykes.

Aged and in delicate health, with negligible battle experience except again Indians, Colonel Burbank nevertheless had two advantages as he marched with his men toward Gettysburg: a lifetime of Old Army experience, and the knowledge that he was leading well-trained Regular Army soldiers.

GETTYSBURG: After marching toward Gettysburg on July 1, Burbank's brigade neared the town from the east on the morning of July 2. It halted temporarily with the rest of the division near Brinkerhoff's Ridge while Meade considered launching an offensive against the Confederate left from that located. The idea was soon aborted, and Burbank's men crossed the Rock Creek Bridge some time after 11:00 a.m., halting near Power's Hill in the early afternoon. At about 4:00 p.m., the Fifth Corps was hurried to support the Union left near Little Round Top, which was under attack by Lt. Gen. James Longstreet's First Confederate corps.

Burbank's brigade was formed into line east of Plum Run and just northwest of Little Round Top. Day's brigade was posted in his right rear as support. Burbank's regimental alignment is not exactly known other than that the 17th Infantry held the left, and the 2nd Infantry the right. The rest of his line was made up of the 7th, 10th, and 11th regiments. After a short time, he was ordered to advance and support Brig. Gen. John Caldwell's divisional assault into the Wheatfield. The Regulars had just started toward the eastern skirt of the Rose Woods when Confederates from Devil's Den began firing into their left. Burbank's men continued on without firing, tramping out of the marshy low land and up the slope toward the woods. His men double-quicked to a stone wall that bordered the eastern edge of the Wheatfield and stopped as Caldwell's men swept past their front. When Caldwell's men were knocked back out of the field, Burbank's regiments were ordered to advance into the woods and wheeled left about forty-five degrees to do so. As they advanced, Confederates who had recently broken through below the Peach Orchard were discovered moving toward Burbank's right flank and rear. Ayres ordered the brigades to fall back, and the soldiers retreated under heavy enemy fire in the direction of Little Round Top, near which they rallied. Burbank suffered 447 casualties, nearly half his brigade, and the proud Regulars had never been given a chance to show what they could do. After such heavy losses, Burbank's brigade was not fit for further duty in the battle.

The disappointing performance of the Regular Division at Gettysburg was not charged to its commanders, and Colonel Burbank continued in command of his brigade. Before the campaigning in October and November of 1863, both Regular Brigades were consolidated, and Burbank was given the command. In January 1864, he left the Army of the Potomac and field command for good and was sent west to help enforce the draft. Burbank died in 1882.

For further reading:

Pfanz, Harry. *Gettysburg: The Second Day.* Chapel Hill, 1987.

Powell, William H. *The Fifth Army Corps.* New York, 1896.

Reese, Timothy J. *Sykes' Regular Infantry Division, 1861-1864.* McFarland, 1990.

THIRD BRIGADE

(1,491 MEN)

BRIGADIER GENERAL STEPHEN HINSDALE WEED

Stephen Weed was a brigadier general at the age of twenty-eight, and one of the rising stars of the Army of the Potomac. He was a native of New York City and a graduate of West Point (27th out of 54 in the Class of 1854). He served as an artillery lieutenant against the Seminoles and the Mormons before the Civil War, and after the fall of Fort Sumter was assigned to the Fifth Corps artillery. With the Long Arm he saw action in the Seven Days' Battles while attached to

Brig. Gen. George Sykes' Regular Division. At Gaines' Mill, the largest engagement of the Seven Days, he was slightly wounded in the face by a piece of shell, and Sykes warmly commended him for his performance in this battle.

Weed was promoted to chief of artillery of George Sykes' division and fought in that capacity at Second Bull Run and Antietam. In both battles he was little used, but his conduct confirmed the great respect Sykes had for him. In the fall of 1862 he was again promoted, this time to chief of artillery for the entire Fifth Corps, and he served in that capacity at Fredericksburg and Chancellorsville. Since advancement was speedier in the Volunteer army Weed, like many talented artillerymen, transferred to the infantry. With the recommendation of many senior officers, including an enthusiastic endorsement from General Sykes and army artillery chief Brig. Gen. Henry Hunt, Weed's captain's bars were replaced with a brigadier general's star on June 6, 1863, and he was put at the head of the only volunteer brigade in Sykes' Regular Division a couple of weeks before marching toward Gettysburg.

Although he was a gifted young professional, Weed was commanding infantry for the first time and was unfamiliar with the abilities of his volunteer riflemen.

GETTYSBURG: Weed shared the march of the division as it moved toward Gettysburg from Union Mills, Maryland, on July 1, and he arrived on the contested ground just before noon on July 2 by way of the Baltimore Pike. After a halt near Power's Hill in the early afternoon, Sykes' Fifth Corps was called into action about 4:00 p.m., and Weed's brigade led the way for the Regular Division as it hurried to shore up the Union left flank, which was just then being assailed by James Longstreet's two veteran Southern divisions.

Weed's brigade (composed of the 140th and 146th New York and 91st and 155th Pennsylvania regiments) had originally been slated to support Sickles' Third Corps, and Weed rode ahead to ask for directions unaware that this assignment had been canceled. As the head of the brigade crossed the north saddle of Little Round Top, the army's chief engineer, Maj. Gen. Gouverneur Warren, drew off the lead regiment (140th New York under Col. Paddy O'Rorke) to bolster Col. Strong Vincent's embattled brigade already deployed and fighting on the hillside against Maj. Gen. John Hood's Confederates. The New Yorkers rushed up the east slope in columns of four. Their arrival, writes one historian, "must have been a dramatic thing." The regiment, in new Zouave uniforms, ran in some disorder into position on Vincent's right flank—just head of the charging Rebels. The 500 men bolstered Vincent's wavering line and beat back the attackers after a few minutes of heavy fighting. When Weed returned to his command, he led its remaining regiments onto Little Round Top. They extended the line to the right (north) as follows: 91st Pennsylvania, 146th New York and 155th Pennsylvania.

Surveying the fighting in the distance, Weed turned to a fellow officer and remarked, "I would rather die on this spot than see those rascals gain one inch of ground." While standing near a section of Lt. Charles Hazlett's battery on Little Round Top a few minutes later, Weed was hit by a musket ball that paralyzed him from the shoulders down. He asked to see Hazlett, who rode over and kneeled at Weed's side. Another artillery officer close by heard Weed say something to Hazlett about paying some small debts, and then he pulled Hazlett closer. At that moment, Hazlett slumped forward with a bullet in his head.

Weed was carried over the crest of the hill to a medical station. His aide, in an effort to comfort the stricken commander, said "General, I hope that you are not so badly hurt," to which Weed replied, "I'm as dead a man as Julius Caesar." His dire prediction proved true, and he passed away within a few hours.

For further reading:

Norton, Oliver W. *The Attack and Defense of Little Round Top, Gettysburg, July 2, 1863.* Chicago, 1909.

Pfanz, Harry. *Gettysburg: The Second Day.* Chapel Hill, 1987.

Powell, William H. *The Fifth Army Corps.* New York, 1896.

Wright, James R. "Vincent's Brigade on Little Round Top." *Gettysburg Magazine,* #1, 1989.

THIRD DIVISION
THE "PENNSYLVANIA RESERVE DIVISION"
(2,862 MEN)

BRIGADIER GENERAL SAMUEL WYLIE CRAWFORD

Samuel W. Crawford was never shy about taking full credit for his own and others' achievements on the battlefield. He was forty-four, "a tall, chesty, glowering man, with heavy eyes, a big nose and bushy whiskers," as one of his comrades remembered him, who "wore habitually a turn-out-the-guard expression."

This description did not do justice to his spectacular sideburns, which reached all the way to his shoulders. Colonel Joshua Chamberlain used a slightly acid tone when he described Crawford as:

a conscientious gentleman, having the entré at all headquarters, somewhat lofty of manner, not of the iron fiber, nor spring of steel, but punctilious in a way, obeying orders in a certain literal fashion that saved him the censure of superiors—a pet of his State [Pennsylvania], and likewise, we thought, of Meade and Warren, judging from the attention they always gave him—possibly not quite fairly estimated by his colleagues as a military man.

Crawford had an unusual background for a division commander in the Union Army. Born in Franklin County, Pennsylvania, just across South Mountain from Gettysburg, he studied medicine at the University of Pennsylvania and became an army surgeon. He served through the 1850s at Western outposts, and just happened to be garrisoned at Fort Sumter as the post surgeon when the Confederates shelled the fort in 1861. Posted at a loaded cannon, he assumed command of several guns during the historic bombardment. Perhaps this sudden introduction to combat stirred something in him, because a month later he quit the medical corps to accept a commission as major in a Regular Army regiment. After a quiet year in the East, he was promoted to brigadier general of volunteers in April 1862. In May he was assigned to Maj. Gen. Nathaniel Banks' small army in the Shenandoah Valley and given a brigade toward the end of the Shenandoah Valley Campaign. There he marched, countermarched, and sent many messages, but did no fighting.

As Banks' men were moving to join the Army of Virginia under Maj. Gen. John Pope, Crawford led his new brigade at the Battle of Cedar Mountain on August 9. After successfully assaulting the Confederate left flank, his men burst suddenly from a stand of timber upon an unsuspecting portion of the enemy left and put a division to flight—including the legendary "Stonewall Brigade." Crawford's unsupported brigade was smashed by a counter-thrust and driven back with a loss of half of its men, including every field officer in the command. Division commander Brig. Gen. Alpheus Williams reported that Crawford was among the last of his brigade to retreat.

Crawford briefly led the division at Antietam when General Williams moved up to take the place of the mortally wounded Maj. Gen. Joseph Mansfield at the head of the Twelfth Corps. Crawford's stint as division commander was cut short when a bullet hit him in the outside of his right thigh shortly after he took command. He was taken to

Chambersburg, Pennsylvania, to convalesce at his father's house. The wound took eight months to heal.

In May 1863, he was given command of the Pennsylvania Reserve Division in the defenses of Washington. The following month Crawford marched out of the capital with two brigades of the division when they were stripped from the Washington forts and added to the Army of the Potomac for the Gettysburg Campaign. He thus found himself the successor to Maj. Gens. John Reynolds and George Meade, both distinguished former leaders of the Pennsylvania Reserves.

As his men marched toward Gettysburg, Crawford possessed virtually no experience at the division level. His training was as a surgeon, not a soldier. He was also unfamiliar with his command. The march north was hard for everyone and especially taxing on the tenderfooted Reserves, who had just spent six months sitting in the capital's defenses. Just short of the line marking Pennsylvania soil, Crawford halted the division and made a fiery patriotic speech. The Reserves crossed over onto their native sod with bands playing and cheers rending the air.

GETTYSBURG: At about noon on July 2, Sam Crawford and his division brought up the rear as Maj. Gen. George Sykes led his Fifth Corps across Rock Creek behind the Union lines. The Reserves camped near Power's Hill, near the Baltimore Pike, and had their first good meal in three days. That afternoon at about four o'clock, Crawford's division (composed of the brigades of Cols. Joseph Fisher and William McCandless) was again last in line as the Fifth Corps hurried toward the position Sykes had just been assigned on the Union left.

After some confusion on the march, Crawford arrived and parked his division first on the northeast slope of Little Round Top, and then a short distance away north of the Wheatfield Road. Sykes ordered Crawford to move a third time to the northwest slope of the hill, which Romeyn Ayres' division had just vacated. Fisher's brigade formed the first line, while McCandless' deployed behind him. Soon an order arrived from

Sykes to send a brigade to the left to help Col. Strong Vincent on Little Round Top. Crawford dispatched Colonel Fisher, whose men crossed Little Round Top and went into line on Vincent's left where, as it turned out, the fighting was already over for the day.

Crawford stayed with Colonel McCandless' brigade, which had formed for battle just north of Little Round Top looking west into the Plum Run valley. The Pennsylvania Reserves were waiting for the retreating Regular brigades (Burbank and Day) to clear their front and pass through their lines before starting forward. James Longstreet's Confederate assault, which had been sweeping everything before it for the previous two hours, had finally spent itself, and the remnants of three or four different Southern brigades halted at Plum Run in front of McCandless. With a "hurrah" McCandless' brigade rushed down the hill into the valley. The Southerners had already begun pulling back at this time. Crawford, mounted on a "blood bay" horse given to him by Maj. Gen. William S. Rosecrans, grabbed a regimental flag from one of his color bearers and personally led the Reserves down the slope. Charging on the right of the Reserves were the men of Col. David Nevin's Sixth Corps brigade. The attack did not meet much resistance until the Pennsylvanians closed up to the stone wall on the east side of the Wheatfield, where some hand-to-hand combat took place before the Confederates fell back through field and Rose Woods. McCandless' men spent the night near the wall, exhausted but elated over their victory.

Although his casualties had been light—210 for the entire division—Crawford gloried afterward in his association with the defense of Little Round Top and lost few opportunities to describe his exploits there, habitually ignoring the assistance he received from other commands. Brig. Gen. Frank Wheaton of the Sixth Corps commented wryly on Crawford's selfishness: "Crawford's innate modesty never prevented his appropriating his full share of all that was done by his own division and by [Nevin's Sixth Corps brigade] that afternoon at Gettysburg." Although Crawford had attacked but a small contingent of exhausted Confed-

erates, he later claimed he had "completely surprised and routed" most of Maj. Gen. John Hood's Division.

A few months after Gettysburg, Crawford had the nerve to ask Major General Sykes to confirm claims that overstated his division's achievements—to the detriment of Sykes' old Regular Division; a furious Sykes refused Crawford's request. Crawford's attempts to garner undue acclaim reached a pathetic low when, after the conflict, he offered former Confederate Maj. Gen. Lafayette McLaws "a grade in the army" in exchange for a written acknowledgment that the Pennsylvania Reserves had driven back his forces on July 2nd; McLaws declined to do so.

Despite his braggart style, Crawford had some ability and continued to command the Pennsylvania Reserve Division. He fought from the Wilderness through Petersburg, and won brevets through major general in both the Regulars and Volunteers.

Crawford served with his Regular Army regiment at various posts throughout the South until his retirement in 1873, which was forced by complications from his Antietam leg wound. His condition continued to slowly deteriorate until his death from a stroke in 1892.

For further reading:

Norton, Oliver W. *The Attack and Defense of Little Round Top, Gettysburg, July 2, 1863*. Chicago, 1909.

Pfanz, Harry. *Gettysburg: The Second Day*. Chapel Hill, 1987.

Powell, William H. *The Fifth Army Corps*. New York, 1896.

First Brigade
(1,248 MEN)

Colonel
William "Buck" McCandless

"Buck" McCandless started the war at the bottom of the military pecking order with the 2nd Pennsylvania Reserve regiment. He must have shown military talent, however, because when the regiment was reorganized in the first summer of the war, the private was elevated to major. By the time the Pennsylvania Reserves were sent to the Virginia Peninsula to fight the next summer, McCandless was commanding his regiment as lieutenant colonel. He fought well in his first battle at Mechanicsville on June 27, mowing down enemy attackers from a strong position behind Beaver Dam Creek. The 2nd Pennsylvania was among the Union regiments most heavily engaged, and McCandless received "particular thanks" in the official report of division commander Brig. Gen. George McCall. McCandless' regiment was again in the thick of the fighting the next day at Gaines' Mill.

McCandless' service merited a colonelcy in August 1862. The division was assigned to Maj. Gen. John Pope's Army of Virginia that summer, and McCandless was severely wounded at Second Bull Run during James Longstreet's sweeping attack on the battle's second day. He was recuperating during the Battle of Antietam but returned to the head of his regiment before Fredericksburg in December 1862. The Pennsylvania Reserves, under Maj. Gen. George Meade, gave the North its only success in the battle when they temporarily plunged through a gap in the enemy lines. McCandless took over command of the brigade when Brig. Gen. William Sinclair was wounded, and continued to lead it off and on through the winter and spring months of 1863. Stationed at Washington with the rest of the Reserves, McCandless' brigade did not take part at Chancellorsville in May 1863. On June 17, Colonel McCandless forwarded a petition signed by the officers of his brigade asking to join the Army of the Potomac for the defense

of Pennsylvania. On June 25, two brigades, (including McCandless') broke camp and started toward Gettysburg.

William McCandless' battle experience as a brigade commander (at Fredericksburg) had been brief, but he had seen plenty of combat at the regimental level and had distinguished himself consistently at the head of his Reserves.

GETTYSBURG: Colonel McCandless and his brigade crossed Rock Creek about noon on July 2 and camped near Power's Hill, along the Baltimore Pike. At 4:00 p.m., his brigade, together with Col. Joseph Fisher's and the rest of the Fifth Corps, hurried toward the army's threatened left flank.

McCandless first took up a position on northeast slope of Little Round Top, and then a short distance away north of the Wheatfield Road. Crawford ordered him to move yet a third time to the northwest slope of the hill, which Romeyn Ayres' division had just vacated with its advance into Rose Woods. McCandless deployed his regiments in line behind Fisher's brigade, which soon departed for Little Round Top. His Pennsylvania regiments faced west into Plum Run valley deployed in two lines, from left to right as follows: 1st, 11th (Fisher's regiment) and 6th in front, and the 13th and 2nd in the rear. Unfortunately for McCandless, his division commander, Brig. Gen. Crawford, spent the entire day with McCandless' brigade and directed its regiments. Crawford's meddling left the colonel effectively without a command, although he remained and assisted his regiments as much as possible.

McCandless' Reserves watched as the retreating Regular brigades of Cols. Burbank and Day cleared their front before starting forward. Longstreet's sweeping assault had finally spent itself, and remnants of several Southern brigades gathered along Plum Run in front of McCandless. With a "hurrah" McCandless' brigade rushed down the hill into the valley. It was almost dark. The Southerners, who were already in the act of pulling back, retreated before the onslaught. The attack did not meet much resistance until the Pennsylvanians closed up to the stone wall on the east side of the Wheatfield, where some hand-to-hand fighting took place before the Confederates fell back through field and Rose Woods. McCandless' men spent the night near the wall, exhausted but elated over their victory.

The Pennsylvanians remained in place and on July 3, after Pickett's Charge had been beaten back, McCandless was ordered to push his brigade forward to see if the Confederates were retreating. McCandless' men surged across the Wheatfield and into the Rose Woods beyond. McCandless exhibited excellent control of his regiments, which executed difficult maneuvers under fire from one of Brig. Gen. Henry Benning's Southern regiments. The charge captured 200 Confederates and a stand of colors. McCandless was "especially recommended" by Crawford after the battle, and found himself in command of the division—still at the rank of colonel—off and on into the next year, whenever Crawford was absent.

He retained command of his Pennsylvania Reserve brigade in the reorganization of March 1864, but his career came to an end when he lost an arm at Spotsylvania on May 8. Although corps commander Gouverneur Warren worked hard to have McCandless promoted to brigadier general after he was wounded Congress, for reasons unknown, declined to act on his request.

For further reading:

Norton, Oliver W. *The Attack and Defense of Little Round Top, Gettysburg, July 2, 1863.* Chicago, 1909.

Pfanz, Harry. *Gettysburg: The Second Day.* Chapel Hill, 1987.

Powell, William H. *The Fifth Army Corps.* New York, 1896.

THIRD BRIGADE

(1,609 MEN)

COLONEL
JOSEPH W. FISHER

A lawyer from Central Pennsylvania, fifty-year old Joseph Fisher began his Civil War service as lieutenant colonel in the 5th Pennsylvania Reserve regiment in June 1861. Fighting with his regiment in its first combat in the Seven Days' Battles, he distinguished himself at Glendale on June 30, 1862, according to the report of Col. Roy Stone, commanding the nearby Pennsylvania Bucktails. In that battle, the 5th's colonel was killed, and following the campaign, Fisher was promoted to colonel and placed in command of the regiment.

He led the 5th Pennsylvania Reserves into battle at Second Bull Run and at Antietam. In neither battle was the regiment heavily engaged. At Fredericksburg, Fisher's regiment took part in the division's temporary breakthrough in the boggy woods on the Confederate right, the only successful Union attack of the day. Fisher briefly took command of the Pennsylvania Reserves' Third Brigade when Brig. Gen. Feger Jackson was killed. However, brigade command passed to another officer that same day, and records indicate that Fisher was not present with his regiment at the end of the month. He was back at the head of the brigade by the end of January 1863, however, and commanded it in the defenses of Washington during the spring. Stationed there with the rest of the Reserves, Fisher's brigade did not take part in the Chancellorsville Campaign in May.

The First and Third Brigades of Pennsylvania Reserves marched away from Washington to join the Army of the Potomac in the days before Gettysburg, and Fisher was assigned to the head of the Third Brigade by virtue of being its senior colonel. He had only the briefest experience leading a brigade while presiding over the retreat from the Confederate lines at Fredericksburg.

GETTYSBURG: Fisher's Pennsylvania brigade (composed of the 5th, 9th, 10th, 11th and 12th regiments) found itself leading the column during the Pennsylvania Reserve Division's move from its temporary camp near Power's Hill to the Union left about 4:00 on the afternoon of July 2. Fisher first took up a position on northeast slope of Little Round Top, and then a short distance away north of the Wheatfield Road. Crawford ordered his brigade commanders to move yet a third time, and both Cols. Fisher and McCandless marched their men to the northwest slope of the hill, which Romeyn Ayres' division had just vacated with its advance into Rose Woods. Fisher deployed his regiments in line of battle facing west overlooking Plum Run Valley, while McCandless did the same behind him.

Within a few minutes, Crawford received an order from Fifth Corps chief Maj. Gen. George Sykes to send a brigade to support Col. Strong Vincent's brigade on Little Round Top. Even though Fisher's men were more fully deployed and composed his front rank, Crawford selected his brigade for the assignment. Fortunately for the Pennsylvanians, by the time Fisher marched across Little Round Top and took up a position on Vin-

cent's left flank, the fighting was sputtering to a close.

Fisher, in conjunction with Colonel Rice of Vincent's brigade, agreed that Round Top should be taken as soon as possible. Fisher, however, who had the only fresh troops handy, refused to do it except under Crawford's orders, which were soon forthcoming. Fisher posted the 9th and 10th Reserves in line behind a skirmish line composed of the remains of the 20th Maine and began the ascent. The extreme darkness and rocky terrain threw the movement into chaos, and Fisher withdrew his regiments, realigned them, and began anew. They remained unengaged for the remainder of the battle.

Crawford commended Fisher after the battle for occupying Round Top, despite the disorganized effort in the face of no resistance. Fisher continued in command of his Pennsylvania Reserve brigade until June 1864, when he was mustered out of the army. He took command of a new regiment of Pennsylvania militia troops in July, which he commanded in the backwater of Eastern Maryland.

Fisher died in Cheyenne, Wyoming, in 1900.

For further reading:

Norton, Oliver W. *The Attack and Defense of Little Round Top, Gettysburg, July 2, 1863.* Chicago, 1909.

Pfanz, Harry. *Gettysburg: The Second Day.* Chapel Hill, 1987.

Powell, William H. *The Fifth Army Corps.* New York, 1896.

Sixth Corps

(13,599 men / 48 guns)

Major General
John Sedgwick

Following the death of Maj. Gen. John Reynolds on July 1, Maj. Gen. George Meade was left with two highly capable corps commanders. One was the Second Corps' Maj. Gen. Winfield Hancock; the other was Maj. Gen. John Sedgwick, a grandson of a Revolutionary War officer who served under George Washington at Brandywine and Valley Forge. Born on a farm in the Connecticut Berkshires, he had been robust, strong-willed, and a natural leader from boyhood.

Sedgwick's mannerisms belied his prestige and position; he dressed plainly and his mien was placid and unpretentious. He had a pointed Yankee wit that distinguished him from the other, rather humorless senior officers. "He was an old bachelor with oddities," one of his men wrote, "addicted to practical jokes and endless games of solitaire." A weathered-looking man of fifty years, he was described at Gettysburg by Lt. Frank Haskell as "short, thick-set, and mus-

cular, with florid complexion, dark, calm, straight looking eyes, with full, heavy features, which with his eyes, have plenty of animation when he is aroused—he had a magnificent profile—well cut, with the nose and forehead forming almost a straight line, curly short chestnut hair and full beard, cut short, with a little gray in it. He dresses carelessly, but can look magnificently when he is well dressed. Like Meade, he looks, and is, honest." In the field, Sedgwick was frequently found close to the firing line wearing a simple blue coat with no insignia—sometimes he even wore a private's blouse—a red undershirt, muddy boots, and an old black slouch hat.

He may not have been a picture book general, but Sedgwick was a soldier to the core. He had seen more action during his life than most of the officers in either army. Since his graduation from West Point in 1837, he had missed few of his army's major battles. He had seen action at Vera Cruz, Cerro Gordo, Churubusco, and Chapultepec during the Mexican War, winning three promotions for his bravery. He had fought the Seminoles, Cheyennes, Kiowas, and Comanches, and assisted in moving the Cherokees west of the Mississippi on the Trail of Tears. He also served during the Mormon expedition and in "Bleeding Kansas." Through it all, he preferred to be in front showing his men how to be contemptuous of bullets.

Like several other officers in Meade's army, Sedgwick did not owe his high position to great Civil War accomplishments. When the war broke out, he served with the cavalry before being given a general's star in August 1861, and was placed at the head of a volunteer infantry brigade in the Army of the Potomac. Early in 1862, he took over command of the Second Division, Second Corps (led by Brig. Gen. John Gibbon at Gettysburg) after its first commander, Brig. Gen. Charles Stone, was arrested as a scapegoat for the Union fiasco at Ball's Bluff. In the army's first full campaign, on the Virginia

Peninsula in the summer of 1862, he led the division at Yorktown and Seven Pines, although he saw but little action. Ill with camp fever, Sedgwick was unable to sit in his saddle at the beginning of the Seven Days' Battles. On June 29, still sick, he mounted and rode with his men, and at the Battle of Glendale was slightly wounded twice—the first bullet struck his arm and his leg was grazed. While he recovered, he was promoted to major general on July 4, 1862.

Sedgwick returned to the army in time for the Battle of Antietam in September, where Second Corps commander Maj. Gen. Edwin "Bull" Sumner sent Sedgwick's division into the West Woods, where it was struck on three sides and virtually destroyed in less than half an hour. The action in the West Woods was one of the greatest disasters to befall any division in the army's history. Sedgwick himself was severely wounded when a bullet went through his leg and another fractured his wrist. He refused to go to the rear and remained on his horse even though he couldn't control it due to his shattered wrist. A third bullet cut into his shoulder, and he was carried away unconscious. He convalesced and returned to the army three short months later, before his wounds had fully healed. After two more weeks of recuperation in Washington, and said, "If I am ever hit again, I hope it will settle me at once. I want no more wounds." He was restored to his division after the Battle of Fredericksburg, and in February 1863 was placed at the head of the biggest corps in the Union, the 23,000-man Sixth Corps.

There were some who doubted his ability to lead a corps. Brig. Gen. Marsena Patrick, the army's top provost officer, wrote, "Sedgwick, I fear, is not good enough a general for [corps command]. He is a good honest fellow and that is all." Maj. Gen. Joe Hooker's doubts were more specific. He claimed Sedgwick suffered from an "utter deficiency in the topographical faculty, and consequently [has] great distrust in exercising on the field important commands." Despite Hooker's estimation of Sedgwick, at Chancellorsville in May 1863, he placed him in a semi-independent command opposite Fredericksburg with orders relieve the pressure on the main

body of the army by breaking through the enemy lines at Marye's Heights—the same spot where the Union army had come to grief at the Battle of Fredericksburg. Sedgwick captured the Heights against thin opposition, but was stopped at Salem Church by a lone Confederate division and eventually forced to withdraw across the Rappahannock. His failure may be attributed to his inability to perform under discretionary orders; the memory of this flawed performance was still fresh in his mind as he approached Gettysburg less than two months later.

While some may have questioned Sedgwick's competence for high command, few would dispute that he was the most deeply loved of all the high officers in the Army of the Potomac. His men called him "Uncle John," and one staff officer said that Sedgwick was a "pure and great-hearted man. . .a brave and skillful soldier. From the commander to the lowest private he had no enemy in this army." Another officer claimed "his whole manner breathed of gentleness and sweetness, and in his broad breast was a boy's heart."

Sedgwick, a bachelor, had an abiding attachment to his men and made it a point to take good care of them. His solid presence gave the men a feeling of reassurance, and his professionalism never let his paternal feelings for his men erode into slackness or emotionalism. His affection for them was masked by a stern aloofness. "I have heard that a smile occasionally invaded his scrubby beard," one major testified, "but I never saw one there."

Unlike many glory-hungry generals in the Army of the Potomac, Sedgwick never campaigned for promotions, preferring instead to stand on his record as a soldier. Many in the army thought that he could have succeeded Burnside as commander of the army if he had made the effort to cultivate friends in Washington. Secretary of State Salmon Chase was backing Maj. Gen. Joseph Hooker, and Chase's opponents considered Sedgwick as an alternative candidate. Sedgwick was an admirer of Maj. Gen. George McClellan, however, and thought that the army should be returned to him. After

Hooker failed at Chancellorsville, Sedgwick was approached about leading the army, but again deferred, replying, "Why, Meade is the proper one to command this army."

At heart, John Sedgwick was a peaceful man who dreamed in letters home about retiring to the quiet Connecticut River valley. He was not the general to ask for daring decisions. He was a McClellan disciple; constitutionally careful, cautious, and conservative. "Uncle John" was effective only when carrying out direct orders. But he was a hard fighter of imperturbable strength whose men would do anything him.

GETTYSBURG: In the three days before the Battle of Gettysburg, out of a desire to prevent the Army of Northern Virginia from slipping around his army and threatening Washington, Meade advanced the Army of the Potomac cautiously on a wide front. It wasn't until Gen. Robert E. Lee struck on July 1 that Meade realized Gettysburg was where the army needed to concentrate. At that point, Sedgwick's big Sixth Corps was at least a day's march away to the southeast in Manchester, Maryland.

Meade sent a dispatch to Sedgwick to hurry his men to Gettysburg on the afternoon of July 1, while the First and Eleventh Corps were already fighting for control of the high ground around that town. Sedgwick mounted his horse "Cornwall"—named after his home—and got his corps moving at 7:30 p.m. that evening. The Sixth Corps, three divisions made up of eight brigades, trudged on all night through the darkness and all the next day under the merciless July sun. His men marched—sometimes with bands playing to breathe life into the weary columns, sometimes with the men singing in a 10,000-strong chorus, sometimes in silence—for thirty-four miles. It was one of the epic marches of the conflict, and one of the most crucial. The lead elements of the Sixth Corps tramped onto the battlefield by way of the Baltimore Pike at 5:00 on the afternoon of July 2, freeing up the Fifth Corps just in time to allow it to blunt Lt. Gen. James Longstreet's assault on the Union left.

Sedgwick heard the thundering cannon and pattering of musketry as he approached, and when he reached the field with his lead division, he pushed it without rest toward the sound of the heaviest fighting. One brigade, Col. David Nevin's, arrived on the front line near Little Round Top in time to play a minor role in repulsing the last Confederate assault of the day.

On July 3, Meade used the Sixth Corps as the reserve manpower pool for his army, plugging in Sedgwick's units wherever help was needed. Six of Sedgwick's brigades were concentrated north of Little Round Top, but Sedgwick had no control over them, a strange circumstance considering that he was one of the few Union generals with experience at commanding multiple corps. As his brigades were parceled out and put under other officers, a disappointed Sedgwick observed the "he might as well go home." Only 242 men from the Sixth Corps fell as casualties at Gettysburg, fewer men than many regiments left on the field. The corps was never heavily engaged, and most of the casualties resulted from picket activity and long-range shelling.

Sedgwick retained command when the five Union corps were reduced to three in March 1864. On May 9, 1864, while placing his artillery at Spotsylvania, a sharpshooter's bullet hit Sedgwick just under the left eye, killing him instantly. Seconds before he was shot, "Uncle John" had reassured nearby soldiers that the Rebels "couldn't hit an elephant at this distance."

For further reading:

Round, Harold. "'Uncle John' Sedgwick." *Civil War Times Illustrated* 5, Dec. 1966.

Sedgwick, John. *Correspondence of Major-General John Sedgwick.* 2 vols. New York, 1902.

Winslow, Richard E., III. *General John Sedgwick: The Story of a Union Corps Commander.* Novato, 1982.

First Division

(4,215 MEN)

Brigadier General Horatio Gouverneur Wright

Horatio Wright was an engineer by training, a thinking, deliberate soldier in the field, slow moving and competent rather than brilliant. Physically, he was a man of classical attributes—an athletic physique, finely molded head, and luxuriantly curly locks. Though he had some combat experience in other theaters during the first two years of the war, the Gettysburg Campaign would be Wright's debut with the Army of the Potomac.

A Connecticut native, Wright had been in the army for about half of his forty-three years. His career began with an exceptional showing in the classroom, and he graduated 2nd out of 52 students in the West Point Class of 1841. For his outstanding academic performance he was assigned to the engineers, the elite branch of the army. He subsequently taught at the Academy, and for ten years helped construct fortifications and harbor improvements in Florida. He was an assistant to the chief engineer in Washington, D.C. at the opening of the Civil War. When Virginia seceded he took part in the daring expedition to evacuate and destroy the Norfolk Navy Yard on April 20, 1861, and was captured in an unsuccessful attempt to demolish the dry dock.

Released within a month, Wright's career began as chief engineering officer with Col. Samuel Heintzelman's division at First Bull Run in July 1861. The next month he was made chief engineer of the expedition to take Port Royal, South Carolina, the finest natural harbor on the Southern coast. A brigadier's star and a brigade of infantry were his when the expedition sailed south in October. Port Royal fell easily in November, and Wright and his men remained in South Carolina. Given a division in April 1862, he led it in the disastrous Battle of Secessionville on June 16, 1862, where the Union force trying to capture Charleston was badly whipped by half as many Confederates. (Meanwhile, the nation's attention was focused on the climax of the Peninsula Campaign just outside Richmond.)

Despite the unfortunate outcome at Secessionville, Wright was promoted to major general the following month and entrusted with the Department of the Ohio in August 1862. While he served well in that capacity, he was forced to step down in March 1863 when the Senate failed to confirm his nomination for major general. After a brief tenure in command of the District of West Kentucky, in May 1863, Wright was assigned to the Army of the Potomac as the commander of the First Division, Sixth Corps. His predecessor, Brig. Gen. William T. H. Brooks, had been promoted away from the army after coming to grief in the Chancellorsville Campaign at Salem Church. Wright was still trying to adapt to his new surroundings six weeks later as his men hurried northward on the Baltimore Pike toward Gettysburg. With no previous battle experience leading a division, he was a question mark in the Sixth Corps command. It had been a year since he had even seen a battlefield.

GETTYSBURG: Wright arrived on the battlefield with his division by way of the Baltimore Pike some time after 5:00 p.m. on July 2, second in the Sixth Corps column of march. His men rested for an hour or more, then were sent to reinforce the fighting on the army's left. Wright's brigades arrived too late to do any fighting.

Early on the morning of July 3, Wright took Brig. Gen. David Russell's brigade and went to join Col. Lewis Grant's brigade, from the Second Division on the extreme left flank of the army. The two brigades under Wright formed a line facing southwest behind Big Round Top and guarded the approach to the army's left rear, which Lt. Gen. James Longstreet contemplated attacking, unaware Wright's presence. The attack did not take place, however, and Wright's two brigades passed the day uneventfully.

Wright continued to lead his division and was retained in command after the army was restructured in the spring of 1864. In May, after Maj. Gen. John Sedgwick was killed at Spotsylvania, he was promoted to major general and made commander of the Sixth Corps, which he ably led until war's end. Wright served in various army posts after the war and finally advanced to the rank of major general. He was named Chief Engineer of the army in 1879, a position he held until his retirement in 1884. He died of heart disease in Washington, D.C., in 1899.

For further reading:

Pfanz, Harry W. *Gettysburg: The Second Day.* Chapel Hill, 1987.

Sedgwick, John. *Correspondence of Major-General John Sedgwick.* 2 vols. New York, 1902.

Winslow, Richard E., III. *General John Sedgwick: The Story of a Union Corps Commander.* Novato, 1982.

FIRST BRIGADE

THE "NEW JERSEY BRIGADE"

(1,320 MEN)

BRIGADIER GENERAL ALFRED THOMAS ARCHIMEDES TORBERT

Alfred Torbert was a thirty-year-old professional soldier, a West Point graduate from Delaware with enormous mutton-chop sideburns and dark hair which hung over his ears. His pre-war experience included Regular Army service against the Seminoles, in the Mormon Expedition, and on the frontier. Since he was from a border slave state, the Confederate army gave him a commission as a lieutenant of artillery soon after the war broke out, but he chose to honor his vows and remain an officer in the United States Army. Torbert thus could make the rare claim that had held commissions in both the Northern and Southern forces.

In September 1861, Torbert was made colonel of the 1st New Jersey, whose men were veterans of Bull Run. Torbert led the regiment to the Peninsula in the spring of 1862, and fought at Yorktown and during the Seven Days' Battles. At Gaines' Mill, Torbert arose from a sickbed in time to rally his men after the fighting. In late August, Torbert's brigade leader, Brig. Gen. George Taylor, led his New Jersey regiments in a disastrous advance against what turned out to be A. P. Hill's Division at Manassas Junction just two days before Second Bull Run. Taylor was mortally wounded and Torbert assumed command of the stricken brigade, although it was not engaged in the forthcoming battle.

Only a couple of weeks later during the Maryland Campaign, the brigade was back in action at Crampton's Gap on South Mountain, where Torbert was slightly wounded but remained on the field to direct his regiments. Maj. Gen. Henry Slocum, his division commander, praised Torbert and recommended him for promotion for his exploits in this often overlooked engagement. At Fredericksburg in December 1862, his brigade covered the withdrawal of the Sixth Corps across the Rappahannock. As such, Torbert's was the only brigade of the division engaged. The young colonel again received special mention in his new division commander's battle report, and a brigadier general's star was his reward. At the Battle of Chancellorsville, Torbert was forced to leave the field before the fighting began because of a cyst at the base of his spine. He underwent an operation on May 9 and was back with his brigade in time for the Gettysburg Campaign.

Though only thirty, Torbert was already an experienced brigade commander by the time of Gettysburg. He had been at the head of the New Jersey Brigade for ten months. Though he was personally brave, there was a dark side to his fearlessness. He imposed his high personal standards of courage on his staff, whom he insisted accompany him while he paraded along the front line. At times this proclivity was taken to unnecessary levels, and he would go so far as to order additional orderlies, flag-bearers, and a cavalry escort, to accompany him on these ostentatious and needless parades. During one of these exhibitions, his medical director was killed.

GETTYSBURG: Torbert and his New Jerseyians arrived on the battlefield around 5:00 p.m. on July 2, having marched into the town on the Baltimore Pike. After resting for an hour or more they were dispatched to the army's embattled left, which was under assault by Lt. Gen. James Longstreet's Confederate corps, but arrived after the fighting had ceased. Early in the morning of July 3, Torbert and his men were put in the left center of the line just north of Little Round Top, under the overall command of Maj. Gen. John Newton. They were not engaged.

Recognized as a talented professional officer, Torbert had a colorful Civil War career after Gettysburg. He continued to lead his brigade until the army reorganization in March 1864, when he was given command of a cavalry division under Maj. Gen. Philip Sheridan. In August 1864, he was detached to lead the Cavalry Corps of Sheridan's Army of the Shenandoah, and continued to

lead that force after Sheridan was sent to Petersburg in February 1865.

Torbert mustered out as brigadier general in January 1866 and was once again a lowly captain of infantry. He resigned in October after he was not offered a promotion. From 1869 to 1878 he held a succession of minor diplomatic posts in Latin America and France. He drowned in a shipwreck off Cape Canaveral, Florida, in 1880 while en route to Mexico on business.

For further reading:

Slade, A. D. *Alfred T. A. Torbert, Southern Gentleman in Blue.* Dayton, 1992.

Townsend, George A. *Major General Alfred Archimedes Torbert: Delaware's Most Famous Civil War Hero.* Bowie, 1993.

SECOND BRIGADE

(1,325 MEN)

BRIGADIER GENERAL JOSEPH JACKSON BARTLETT

Joseph Bartlett was born in Binghamton, New York, in 1834 and was a practicing attorney when Fort Sumter fell in April 1861. He gave up his civilian livelihood and enlisted in the nearby community of Elmira. Though just twenty-seven at the time, he possessed obvious leadership qualities and dashing good looks, and his company elected him as its captain. When the company was combined with others to form the 27th New York Volunteers, he was elected major of the regiment. The 27th was taken to Washington and fought at First Bull Run within two weeks of mustering in. The 27th's colonel, Henry Slocum, was wounded leading a charge and Major Bartlett took command. According to the official report of brigade commander Col. Andrew Porter, Bartlett rallied the regiment and "by his enthusiasm and valor kept it in action and out of the panic."

Colonel Slocum was promoted, the lieutenant colonel resigned, and Bartlett was ele-

vated to colonel of the 27th New York on September 21, 1861. The regiment was assigned to Slocum's brigade the following month when the Army of the Potomac was organized into divisions. When the Sixth Corps was organized on the Virginia Peninsula in May 1862, Slocum was promoted to division commander and Bartlett took command of the brigade. A man who before the war had never donned a military uniform was commanding a brigade by the end of 1861, a meteoric rise that bespoke his inherent military talent.

The first combat at the head of his brigade came at Gaines' Mill, where Bartlett plunged into the thickest of the fight in support of Brig. Gen. George Sykes' embattled Regulars. Bartlett was commended for his daring by both Sykes and Slocum. Sixth Corps commander Brig. Gen. William Franklin concurred, writing simply "Colonel Bartlett deserves to be made brigadier-general." Slocum again recommended him for promotion after his brigade led the sweep forward over a Confederate-held stone wall at Crampton's Gap in the September Maryland Campaign. Bartlett received his well earned and much-recommended brigadier's star a month later. Bartlett was on sick leave later that year and missed the Battle of Fredericksburg.

The New York general was an avid athlete and often played "base ball" with his troops. One soldier in the Sixth Corps reported that he "frequently plays ball with the boys and is said to be a good player." In the Battle of

Chancellorsville in May 1863, Bartlett's brigade suffered terribly in the division's failed attack at Salem Church, losing more killed that any other brigade in the army during the entire campaign. He later claimed with some remorse that this was the first time an attack by his brigade had been repulsed.

By the Battle of Gettysburg, the twenty-nine year old Bartlett was a highly regarded veteran brigadier. He was a young man of great ability, and there was little he had not seen—except victory in a major battle.

GETTYSBURG: Bartlett's brigade was one of three Sixth Corps brigades that arrived on the battlefield in time to be hurried from the Baltimore Pike to near Little Round Top in the late afternoon of July 2. He was still forming his lines for battle when the final Union counter-attack of the day went forward on his left and ended the action. His men were not engaged. On July 3, Bartlett commanded a Third Division brigade in addition to his own. His commands remained in approximately the same position as the previous day—to the north of Little Round Top—and were not engaged.

Bartlett relieved Brig. Gen. Frank Wheaton in command of the corps' Third Division on the day after the battle and led it through the summer. Thereafter, he alternated between brigade and division command, interrupted occasionally by sick leave for attacks of acute rheumatism, until the end of the conflict. The civilian-turned-soldier received a brevet promotion to major general near the end of the war, and the honor of receiving the stacked arms of the Army of Northern Virginia at Appomattox Court House on April 12, 1865. Bartlett served as diplomat to Sweden and Norway, then as deputy commissioner of pensions under President Cleveland. He died in 1893.

For further reading:

Palfrey, Francis W. *Memoir of William Francis Bartlett*, Boston. 1878.

Wilson, Mrs. H. Neill. *Sketch of the Life of Gen. William F. Bartlett*. Berkshire, MA., 1913.

THIRD BRIGADE
(1,484 MEN)

BRIGADIER GENERAL DAVID ALLEN RUSSELL

David Russell was a man whose talents as a professional soldier continued to improve as he rose in rank. He was born in upstate New York, near Vermont, to a father who became a U. S. Congressman. In the last year of his term, the elder Russell appointed his son to West Point, where his military career started out somewhat inauspiciously: he graduated 38th out of 41 students in the Class of 1845. It was after his posting to the infantry that his extraordinary initiative and talents began to reveal themselves. Russell made a solo trek across Indian Territory to reach Fort Scott, Kansas, his first post. In the Mexican War, which began the following year, he distinguished himself by earning a brevet promotion. After the war he served in garrisons and on frontier duty fighting the Yakima Indians in the Northwest.

When the Civil War began, Russell was stationed in the Washington defenses with his Regular Army unit until he became colonel of the Army of the Potomac's 7th Massachusetts regiment in early 1862. Taking his regiment to the Peninsula, he fought at Yorktown, Williamsburg, and Seven Pines (where he was "conspicuously distinguished" according to Col. Hobart Ward, Russell's brigade commander). At Oak Grove, he led his regiment "in advance of the advance, as usual" according to Brig. Gen. John Peck, who was referring to Russell's habit of reconnoitering with his skirmishers. Despite his constant activity and initiative, Russell's regiment was never seriously engaged in the campaign. His regiment was held in reserve at Antietam and missed the serious fighting done in the Maryland Campaign.

Although he had enjoyed few opportunities to prove himself in combat, Russell was promoted to brigadier general in November of 1862. He was assigned to head a Sixth Corps brigade just prior to the Battle of Fredericksburg, where his command was again only lightly engaged. At Chancellorsville in May 1863, Russell led his brigade as part of a successful dawn amphibious assault in pontoon boats designed to secure a bridgehead below the town of Fredericksburg. Russell's regiments, however, remained in the rear yet again, and were not with the rest of the First Division when it unsuccessfully tried to break through the Confederate defenses at Salem Church on May 3.

By the summer of 1863, Russell had demonstrated sound professional qualities as a soldier and proved he could be counted upon for accurate reconnaissance—which he often conducted himself. Although he had been with his brigade for seven months and had earned the respect of his men, he had not yet been tested in a major battle.

GETTYSBURG: Russell's brigade arrived around 5:00 p.m. on the Baltimore Pike on July 2. After resting for a couple of hours, it was dispatched, with Brig. Gen. Alfred Torbert's brigade, to the threatened Union left flank, which was being rolled back by Lt. Gen. James Longstreet's Southern corps. Russell's brigade arrived too late to take part in the fighting. On the morning of July 3, Russell's regiments were ordered to the extreme left of the Union line, where they formed facing southwest behind Big Round Top. Russell's brigade was teamed up with Col. Lewis Grant's Second Division brigade to guard the approach to the army's left rear. Longstreet considered attacking in this area, but the plan was not adopted. The pattern of coming close to engaging in heavy combat continued to hold true for Russell, and his men spent an uneventful day listening to the thundering cannonade and musketry triggered by Pickett's Charge.

Russell continued in command of his brigade through the fall, praised as a hero after his fine performance in the Battle of Rappahannock Station in November. He took command of the division in May 1864 when Horatio Wright moved up to replace the fallen John Sedgwick. In August 1864, Russell was assigned to a division in Maj. Gen. Philip Sheridan's Army of the Shenandoah, but was killed the next month by a shell fragment that ripped through his heart in the Battle of Third Winchester.

For further reading:

Slade, A. D. *That Sterling Soldier: The Life of David A. Russell.* Dayton, 1995.

SECOND DIVISION

(3,608 MEN)

BRIGADIER GENERAL ALBION PARRIS HOWE

General Howe was a Maine native, a forty-five year old career soldier whose appearance bespoke a serious nature—he wore his hair short, and was clean-shaven except for a long mustache that drooped to his jawline. He had shown outstanding academic ability early in life, and he attracted the attention of the governor of Maine, who saw that he received an appointment to West Point. Howe did not disappoint, graduating 8th out of 52 cadets in the Class of 1841. In view of his high standing, he was posted to the artillery. He served with distinction in the Mexican War, and spent the remainder of his time until the Civil War on duty on the frontier, in "Bleeding Kansas," and teaching at West Point. Howe was among the men led by Robert E. Lee who captured John Brown at Harpers Ferry in 1859.

When the war broke out, Howe remained initially with the artillery and served with Maj. Gen. George McClellan in West Virginia in the summer of 1861. By the conflict's second year, when it became apparent that careers were being made in the volunteer army, he obtained a commission to brigadier general of infantry in June 1862. He was given Brig. Gen. John Peck's brigade in the Fourth Corps two days before the onset of the Seven Days' Battles, after Peck left for division command. In the following week of battles, Howe's brigade was engaged only at Malvern Hill, and there he was placed in a section of the line that was not seriously threatened.

Howe's brigade was attached with the rest of the division to the Sixth Corps for the Maryland Campaign but remained idle, held in reserve along with the rest of the corps, at Antietam. (The division was officially reassigned as Third Division, Sixth Corps a week later.) Howe may have had friends in high places, because despite his slim resume, he was promoted to head the Second Division in November 1862. The next month, at the Battle of Fredericksburg, his division, in the center of the army's line, was not required to heavily engage the enemy. The entire division lost a mere 186 men, mostly to long-range artillery fire.

Howe and the Sixth Corps were more seriously tested at Chancellorsville. There they were called upon to pry the enemy from Marye's Heights above Fredericksburg, the site of the Army of the Potomac's slaughter the previous December. They rolled over the thin Southern lines and seized the heights. As they continued west toward Chancel-

lorsville, however, they suffered terribly from Confederate counterattacks. Howe and his division turned in an excellent performance in repulsing the attacks, but the battle ended with the Sixth Corps furling its banners and retreating across the Rappahannock River. The Maine native was commended in General Sedgwick's report after the battle, but it was generally recognized that the Sixth Corp's performance in the campaign was a disappointment.

Howe, a career soldier who had led his division for more than seven months, was still an unproven quantity by the time the Gettysburg Campaign got underway.

GETTYSBURG: Howe's was the last division of the Sixth Corps to arrive on the battlefield, crossing Rock Creek on the Baltimore Pike at the tail of the column on the evening of July 2. Once on the field, his two brigades were sent to opposite ends of the Union line, and Howe found himself an officer without a command. He led two artillery batteries into position in support of Col. Lewis Grant's brigade on the left end of the line on the morning of July 3. He was a forgotten man after the engagement, and is not mentioned in any battle reports.

By the end of 1863, either army commander Maj. Gen. George Meade or Sixth Corps chief John Sedgwick decided that Howe was not up to leading a division, and he was removed from his command. The demoted officer took over the administration of the artillery depot in Washington, but still received his brevet promotions to major general by war's end.

Howe served in the honor guard at the funeral of Abraham Lincoln, then on the commission which tried the Lincoln conspirators. He retired from the army in 1882, and died of "general giving out of the vital powers," in 1897.

For further reading:

Winslow, Richard E. *General John Sedgwick: The Story of a Union Corps Commander.* Novato, 1982.

SECOND BRIGADE
The "Vermont Brigade"
(1,832 MEN)

COLONEL
LEWIS ADDISON GRANT

Colonel Grant, born in 1828 in Winhall, Vermont, was typical of the scores of officers who entered the volunteer armies of the Civil War with little or no military training, and by hard application to details, books, and operations, transformed themselves into competent generals. The rewards of diligent study were already instilled in Grant, for he had been a school teacher in his native Vermont before preparing for the bar. He was but thirty-one when his wife passed away in 1859, and by then had an established a successful law practice in Bellows Falls.

Grant enlisted in the army as a major in the 5th Vermont regiment in August 1861. He received a promotion to lieutenant colonel the next month, just before his regiment was included in Brig. Gen. William T. H. Brooks' "Vermont Brigade" in October. On the Virginia Peninsula in the spring of 1862, Grant led the regiment at Williamsburg, where the 5th Vermont did but little fighting and lost only one man wounded. In the middle of May he came down with a fever, which prostrated him for about ten days. He returned, still weak and debilitated, in time to lead the regiment in the Seven Days' Battles. On June 29th at Savage's Station, Grant's men routed a Confederate regiment with a bayonet charge ("in gallant style," according to brigadier Brooks), then stood and traded volleys with two enemy regiments and an artillery battery until dark, many men exhausting over 60 rounds of ammunition. The 5th Vermont suffered more than any Northern regiment on that bloody field, losing 209 men (nearly half its force). Grant was among the list of officers thanked by Brooks after the battle.

Two months later, on the day before the Battle of Antietam, Grant was promoted to colonel. His regiment was not used at Antietam because the entire Sixth Corps was held in reserve even though they might have been used to break Gen. Robert E. Lee's thin lines late in the afternoon. At Fredericksburg in December 1862, the 5th Vermont was fortunate enough to be only lightly engaged, but Grant had the bad luck to incur a wound (though he remained on the field). The Vermonter was selected to command a brigade in the Second Division (Albion Howe's), Sixth Corps, and in February 1863 assumed the leadership of the "Vermont Brigade." When fighting commenced again at Chancellorsville in May, Grant led his men as they stormed Marye's Heights, a moment of triumph that resulted in the capture of three enemy battle flags. The achievement earned Grant a Congressional Medal of Honor (awarded in 1893). The next day, however, a Confederate counterattack savaged Grant's regiments and he retreated with the rest of the Sixth Corps after losing 431 men.

The thirty-five year old Colonel Grant was commanding the Vermont Brigade as a colonel when it marched to Pennsylvania in June 1863. Matters other than fighting may have occupied his thoughts, for he was engaged to marry a Vermont woman in September.

GETTYSBURG: After arriving on the battlefield in the early evening of July 2, Grant's brigade was led forward to a position on the extreme left of the army, facing southwest between Big Round Top and the Taneytown Road. His assignment was to guard the approaches to the army's rear and baggage trains. On July 3, aside from some long-range artillery fire, Grant's Vermonters were not engaged.

Lewis Grant obtained a brigadier general's star nine months later in April 1864. He continued in command of his Green Mountain State regiments through the rest of the Civil War, and distinguished himself at Cedar Creek. He occasionally assumed division command in the last year of fighting around Petersburg. Declining a commission in the Regular Army, Grant eventually moved west to Chicago, Des Moines, and finally Minneapolis. His postwar life is rather enigmatic, although he did serve as assistant secretary of war in the early 1890s. He died of heart congestion in Minneapolis in 1918. Only seven of the 583 full-ranking generals were still alive at the time of his death.

For further reading:

Coffin, Howard. *Full Duty: Vermonters in the Civil War.* Dayton, 1995.

Poirier, Robert. *"By the Blood of Our Alumni": Norwich University and the Citizen Soldiers of the Army of the Potomac.* Savas Publishing, 1998.

THIRD BRIGADE
(1,775 MEN)

BRIGADIER GENERAL
THOMAS HEWSON NEILL

Thomas Neill, born in 1826, was a thirty-seven-year-old career soldier, a bachelor whose life revolved around the military. He was a doctor's son from Philadelphia who had attended the University of Pennsylvania until his sophomore year, when he was appointed to West Point. He graduated from the Academy in 1847, 27th out of 38. He missed the action of the Mexican War after being sent to serve on the frontier. In 1853, he returned to his alma mater as an assistant professor of drawing, a position he held until 1857. Neill went west with the Mormon

Early's Confederate division tore into Neill's men, who fought hard and turned back the assault. The Pennsylvanian was injured when his horse was shot and fell upon him; although partially disabled, he remained on the field with his men. The fighting and confusion of the Union retreat that followed cost Neill 850 killed, wounded, and captured—the highest casualty tally of any of Northern brigades that served in the battle.

His superiors commended Neill for his performance at Marye's Heights and Salem Church. The harrowing experience, however, was still fresh in his mind as the armies prepared for the Gettysburg Campaign.

GETTYSBURG: Neill and his brigade arrived at Gettysburg on the evening of July 2. Unlike most of the other Sixth Corps brigades sent to reinforce the left flank, Maj. Gen. George Meade ordered Neill to march in the opposite direction—to Culp's Hill. The Vermonters were eventually positioned on the extreme right of the army, between Power's Hill and Culp's Hill. Neill later reported that his men were constantly in contact with enemy skirmishers. The brigade remained in this location through July 3, but was never directly engaged; Neill lost only 14 casualties during the entire battle.

Neill was still at the head of the Vermont Brigade for the opening of the spring campaign of 1864, and succeeded the wounded Brig. Gen. George Getty in divisional command during the Battle of the Wilderness. He served in that officer's place until Getty returned to the field in July. Thereafter, Neill returned to his original role as a staff officer serving with the Eighteenth Corps and then as inspector general with Phil Sheridan in the Shenandoah valley.

Neill transferred to the cavalry in 1870 and served as commandant of cadets at West Point before being promoted to colonel in 1879. He was stationed in Texas until his retirement in 1883, and died from a stroke in 1885.

Expedition and returned to Philadelphia in 1861.

When Fort Sumter fell, Neill became a staff officer to Maj. Gen. George Cadwalader in the Department of Pennsylvania, where he served until February 1862, when he obtained the colonelcy of the 23rd Pennsylvania Infantry. He led the 23rd to the Peninsula the next summer, where it was assigned to the Fourth Corps. His regiment was only lightly engaged at Williamsburg, but at Seven Pines, Neill led his men in a costly counterattack against the assaulting enemy, losing 129 men. (Despite the fact that his brigade suffered the loss of 629 men, sixty-four-year-old Brig. Gen. John Abercrombie did not see fit to praise anyone after the battle other than his staff.) In the Seven Days' Battles the next month, Neill's regiment was never severely engaged, although it was on the field at Malvern Hill on July 1.

The 23rd Pennsylvania was held in reserve at Antietam, and after that battle the division was redesignated Third Division, Sixth Corps. At the Battle of Fredericksburg in December 1862, Neill assumed command of the brigade when its leader, Brig. Gen. Francis Vinton, was wounded early in the morning. On April 15, 1863, he was appointed brigadier general, to date from November 29, 1862. His first real experience leading the brigade in action came that spring at the Battle of Chancellorsville, where Neill assisted in the triumphant storming of Marye's Heights above Fredericksburg on May 3. The next day, however, Maj. Gen. Jubal

For further reading:

Pfanz, Harry W. *Gettysburg: Culp's Hill and Cemetery Hill*. Chapel Hill. 1993.

Winslow, Richard E. *General John Sedgwick: The Story of a Union Corps Commander*. Novato, 1982.

THIRD DIVISION

(4,740 MEN)

BRIGADIER GENERAL
FRANK WHEATON

When he was just seventeen, Rhode Islander Frank Wheaton, born in 1833, left his upper crust surroundings at Brown University to take the rough job of surveying the border between the United States and Mexico. After five years experience on the frontier, he was appointed directly into the Regular Army—without any formal military training—as a first lieutenant of cavalry in 1855. He fought Indians and went west with the Mormon Expedition, and was a hardened twenty-eight-year-old veteran trooper when the Civil War began.

Wheaton's family was shattered by the secession crisis. His father-in-law was Samuel Cooper, a New Yorker who was adjutant general of the U.S. Army. Cooper's wife was from a distinguished Virginia family, however, and Cooper sided with the South and accepted a brigadier general's appointment in the Confederate Army on March 16, 1861. Cooper's daughter sided with her husband Wheaton, who had just been promoted to captain in the U.S. cavalry on March 3. The guns that roared at Fort Sumter on April 12 signaled the beginning of four painful years for the Wheaton and Cooper families.

Wheaton entered the volunteer service on July 10, 1861, as lieutenant colonel of the 2nd Rhode Island Volunteers. Just eleven days later he was fighting with his regiment at Bull Run. The green Rhode Islanders were in the vortex of the fight, and Col. John Slocum went down mortally wounded, pierced by three bullets. Wheaton took over command of the regiment in the middle of the engagement. Brigade leader Col.

Ambrose Burnside later lauded Wheaton's "admirable conduct." Further combat eluded Wheaton for some time, for his regiment was but lightly engaged during the Peninsula Campaign during the spring and summer of 1862, and was held in reserve during the September fighting at Antietam.

With this meager experience, Wheaton somehow obtained a promotion to brigadier general in November 1862. By the Battle of Fredericksburg in December, however, he still had not formally received his promotion. He remained with his regiment, which was deployed as skirmishers to cover one of the Rappahannock River crossings and thus suffered few casualties. Two days after the fighting ended, Wheaton's promotion was approved and he was transferred to command the Third Brigade, Third Division, Sixth Corps, which he led off the field. At the Battle of Chancellorsville in May 1863, Wheaton's brigade took part in the storming of Marye's Heights on May 3, and was thrown into the line as reinforcements during the Confederate counterattacks the next day. For two days, Wheaton got plenty of experience handling multiple regiments under battle conditions, and his brigade lost 485 men in hard fighting.

By the summer of 1863, thirty-year-old Wheaton was the veteran of one battle as a brigade commander. On the night of July 1-2, a few hours before Wheaton arrived with his regiments on the field, his immediate superior, division commander Maj. Gen. John Newton, was assigned to command the

First Corps after the death of Maj. Gen. John Reynolds on McPherson's Ridge. Newton's elevation meant that Wheaton would command Newton's division, a job for which he had no time to prepare.

GETTYSBURG: Frank Wheaton's division held the van of Maj. Gen. John Sedgwick's Sixth Corps column as it arrived on the battlefield at 5:00 p.m. on July 2 via the Baltimore Pike. Wheaton was immediately sent with his first two brigades to reinforce the embattled Fifth Corps units around Little Round Top. The lead brigade, Col. David Nevin's, arrived in time to participate in the last stages of the day's fighting.

On July 3, Wheaton issued orders that shifted the positions of his three brigades, although none of them were engaged. A few hours after the battle's conclusion, Wheaton was replaced by a new division commander and returned to his brigade. He inherited permanent command of the division in September 1864, and held it until the end of the war. General Wheaton remained in the U.S. Army until his retirement as a major general in 1897. He died from a brain hemorrhage in 1903.

For further reading:

Winslow, Richard E. *General John Sedgwick: The Story of a Union Corps Commander.* Novato, 1982.

First Brigade

(1,770 MEN)

Brigadier General Alexander Shaler

Thirty-six-year-old Alexander Shaler was born in Connecticut and raised in New York City. He was educated in private schools, joined innumerable clubs and societies, and seems to have enjoyed the benefits of a considerable inheritance, judging by the fact that his primary avocations were "non-remunerative positions of public trust." Chief among his hobbies was the militia, and he became major of the famed "Washington

Grays," later the 7th New York State Militia regiment. As a member of that organization, he was one of the first volunteer soldiers to reach Washington in the tense opening days of the conflict.

In the war's first summer, Shaler joined a new volunteer regiment, the 65th New York (also known, somewhat pretentiously, as the "First U.S. Chasseurs"), as lieutenant colonel. He did not see any fighting until the following spring when the 65th was engaged at the Battle of Seven Pines on May 31, 1862. The New Yorkers repulsed an enemy onslaught there, and the colonel of the regiment wrote admiringly in his report that, "Lieutenant-Colonel Shaler evinced during the entire action that presence of mind and military ability for which he is so highly reputed." Shaler was promoted to colonel of the 65th in time for the Seven Days' Battles and led the regiment in heavy fighting at Malvern Hill, where his regiment lost 45 casualties in the final engagement of the campaign.

The next six months were frustrating for Shaler, since he and his men were held in reserve during both the Antietam and Fredericksburg battles. In March 1863, however, brigade leader Brig. Gen. John Cochrane resigned to escape political retribution for trying to oust Maj. Gen. Ambrose Burnside through back channels after the disaster at Fredericksburg. Cochrane's ouster left Shaler, as senior colonel, in charge of the brigade. His first experience leading it in combat was in May during the Chancellorsville Campaign. His regiments were in the second line when the division stormed Marye's Heights, and thus suffered much less than those in front. The next day, during the enemy counter assault, Shaler's men were again spared the brunt of the fighting. His brigade's losses tallied 160 men for the two days of combat—far less than any other such unit in the corps. For no reason readily apparent in the historical record, the Connecticut native was awarded the Medal of Honor in 1893 for his role in the storming of Marye's Heights thirty years earlier.

Shaler was promoted later that month to brigadier general, and in a ceremony on May 26, President Lincoln himself fastened the star on Shaler's shoulder. Touched by Father Abraham or not, it was as a still-untested brigadier that General Shaler marched toward Gettysburg.

GETTYSBURG: Arriving in reserve on the battlefield during the evening of July 2, Shaler's large brigade (the 65th, 67th, and 122nd New York regiments, and the 23rd and 82nd Pennsylvania regiments) was sent to reinforce the army's embattled left flank. By the time Shaler arrived, however, the fighting was winding down and his regiments were not engaged. The next morning on July 3, Shaler was sent to the opposite end of the field at Culp's Hill to reinforce the Twelfth Corps' Brig. Gen. John Geary. He reached that sector about 8:00 a.m. and was held in reserve near the Spangler house for some time. Geary had been instructed not to use Shaler unless absolutely necessary, just in case Shaler had to be moved quickly elsewhere. Despite this admonition, some of Shaler's men were put into Geary's battle line when the third Confederate attack of the morning was launched against Culp's Hill. Shaler selected the 122nd New York for the duty, and the men assisted in repulsing the assault after relieving the 111th Pennsylvania. From their advanced rifle pits, the New Yorkers were able to bag about 75 Rebel prisoners, losing themselves 44 in killed and wounded. Geary utilized each of Shaler's regiments that morning to plug holes in his line and to reinforce threatened points. Shaler's brigade as a whole lost 74 casualties, more than any other brigade in the little-

used Sixth Corps at Gettysburg. That afternoon, Shaler was ordered to shift his brigade to Cemetery Ridge when Pickett's Charge threatened the center. By the time his men arrived, however, the attack had been repulsed.

Shaler led his brigade through the fall, and during the winter of 1863-1864 commanded Johnson's Island, a Confederate prison camp. He returned to the Army of the Potomac in time for the commencement of the spring campaign, but was captured in the Wilderness on May 6, 1864. He was later exchanged, and served out the remainder of the conflict performing occupational duty in New Orleans. After the war, Shaler resumed his active hobnobbing in New York City, where he belonged to numerous clubs and societies. He held various public offices, including the presidency of the city fire and health departments. He died from heart disease in 1911.

For further reading:

Pfanz, Harry W. *Gettysburg: Culp's Hill and Cemetery Hill.* Chapel Hill. 1993.

Winslow, Richard E. *General John Sedgwick: The Story of a Union Corps Commander.* Novato, 1982.

SECOND BRIGADE
(1,595 MEN)

COLONEL
HENRY LAWRENCE EUSTIS

Boston native Henry Eustis was a man of delicate health who, though the son of a U.S. Army general, was more at home in a classroom than on a battlefield. He was already a distinguished scholar and Harvard graduate when he obtained an appointment to West Point. At the Academy he continued to excel, graduating at the top of the famous Class of 1842, and was assigned to the prestigious engineering branch. Military life didn't appeal to Eustis, however, and he resigned from the army seven years later and

went back to Harvard, where he taught engineering.

Eustis was not among the fire-eaters who enlisted in the first few months after the fall of Fort Sumter, preferring instead to remain at his blackboard at Harvard. It wasn't until August 1862—after the Peninsula Campaign had come to a close—that, despite his poor health, he answered the government's call for new troops. In view of his military education, he received a commission as colonel of the 10th Massachusetts regiment, which had lost its commanding officers in the Battle of Malvern Hill two months before.

It would be nine months before he would be tested in battle. At Antietam, his regiment was held in reserve. At Fredericksburg, the only action witnessed by the 10th Massachusetts was an unopposed crossing of the Rappahannock River. At the Battle of Salem Church during the Chancellorsville Campaign, however, Eustis took command of the brigade on May 4 when Col. William Browne fell wounded during the heavy fighting. Eustis spent the rest of that desperate day fighting off one Confederate attack after another, and then retreated toward the river with casualties totaling. 343 men. Sixth Corps chief Maj. Gen. John Sedgwick singled out Eustis in his report and mentioned his "gallant service."

By Gettysburg, the forty-four year old Eustis had seen heavy combat and performed well under fire, although his tenure as commander of his brigade had been brief.

GETTYSBURG: Eustis' command (the 7th, 10th, and 37th Massachusetts regiments, and 2nd Rhode Island) was one the first three brigades to arrive on the battlefield with Sedgwick's Sixth Corps on the afternoon of July 2. His men were immediately led from the Baltimore Pike toward the sound of heavy fighting in the direction of Little Round Top. They arrived after the hill had been secured and were not engaged that afternoon or evening. On the following day, July 3, Eustis' brigade was placed under the supervision of Maj. Gen. John Newton, who put him in line to the left of Brig. Gen. John Caldwell's division on Cemetery Ridge, just north of Little Round Top. The day passed uneventfully for Eustis' command.

Eustis was promoted to brigadier general two months after Gettysburg. However, his poor health drove him to overuse and become dependent on opium, and he left the army in June 1864. Eustis resumed his professorship at Harvard, and continued teaching and writing until his death from lung disease in 1885.

For further reading:

Pfanz, Harry W. *Gettysburg: Culp's Hill and Cemetery Hill.* Chapel Hill. 1993.

Winslow, Richard E. *General John Sedgwick: The Story of a Union Corps Commander.* Novato, 1982.

THIRD BRIGADE

(1,369 MEN)

COLONEL
DAVID J. NEVIN

The most recent addition to the ranks of brigade commanders on July 2 was the 62nd New York's Colonel David Nevin. Nevin had only assumed command when the brigade's former leader, Brig. Gen. Frank Wheaton, was tapped to take Maj. Gen. John Newton's place at the head of the division during the evening of July 1-2. Formerly a coal dealer from New York City, the "impetuous and fiery" Colonel Nevin had

only been in command of the brigade a few hours when it reached the field.

While new to brigade command, Nevin had been at the head of the 62nd New York since the Battle of Seven Pines the previous summer, when the colonel had been killed and Nevin had inherited the regiment's top slot. He was included in a commendation issued by Brig. Gen. John Peck, in whose brigade Nevin served, which praised each of the regimental commanders. He had not been present, however, at the battles of Fredericksburg or Chancellorsville.

Nevin thus had not seen action since his experience under fire the previous summer at Seven Pines, and he had no military education and no experience in brigade command.

GETTYSBURG: Nevin's brigade reached Rock Creek at the head of the arriving Sixth Corps column on the afternoon of July 2, and rested for an hour or two before Maj. Gen. John Sedgwick led it to the vicinity of Little Round Top. Nevin deployed a line just in time to take part in the Union charge across Plum Run by Brig. Gen. Samuel Crawford's Pennsylvania Reserves. His regiments (the 62nd New York, and the 93rd and 139th Pennsylvania), charged west down the slope near the Wheatfield Road, through an abandoned artillery battery (Walcott's), and over Plum Run's marsh. The regiments fell back a short distance to form on more defensible ground. Somehow, the 98th Pennsylvania got lost during the approach march and went into action

behind Crawford on the slopes of Little Round Top. It joined its sister regiments near the J. Weikert farm lane. The final Union push ultimately did little more than adjust the opposing lines, but it did put an end to the fighting for the day. Nevin and his men had the distinction of being the only Sixth Corps brigade engaged on July 2.

Brig. Gen. Joseph Bartlett was assigned to direct Nevin's brigade (in addition to his own regiments) on July 3. The two brigades remained in reserve north of Little Round Top. Wheaton rejoined his brigade the following evening, and Nevin reverted to command of his 62nd New York, having done a good job under extraordinary circumstances.

For further reading:

Adelman, Garry. "The Third Brigade, Third Division, Sixth Corps at Gettysburg." *Gettysburg Magazine,* #11, 1994.

Pfanz, Harry. *Gettysburg: The Second Day.* Chapel Hill, 1987.

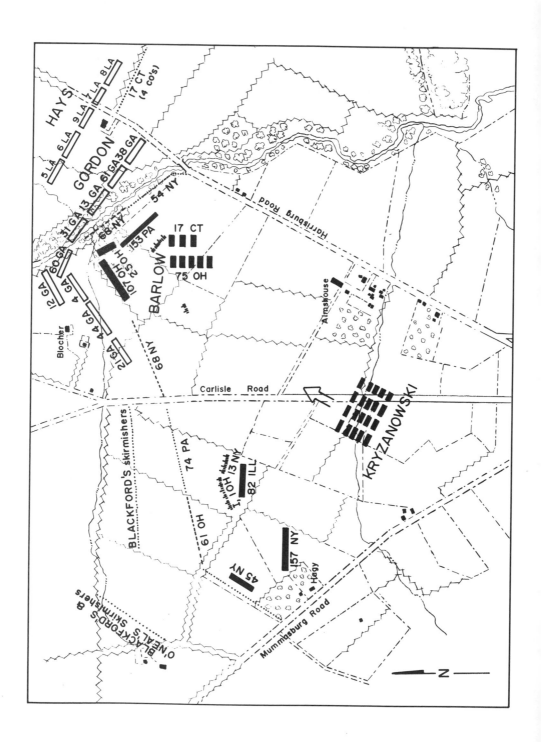

Eleventh Corps

(9,221 men / 26 guns)

Major General
Oliver Otis Howard

In the summer of 1863, the Eleventh Corps, more than any other organization in the Army of the Potomac, was suffering a crisis of confidence. Wracked by self-doubt, rent with petty jealousies and intrigues among the officers, and lacking in discipline, it would have taxed the most experienced officer's ability to mold it into a reliable fighting unit. As it was, approaching Gettysburg the Eleventh was led by the youngest corps commander in the army—and one of the least experienced.

Oliver O. Howard was born in Leeds, Maine, the son of a farmer who died when he was nine. A good student, he graduated from Maine's Bowdoin college and was leaning toward a teaching career, when a congressman uncle offered him an appointment to West Point. Howard accepted and graduated fourth in the Academy's Class of 1854. Undecided about his life's work, he taught mathematics at his alma mater while he studied theology under an Episcopalian priest, with the

idea of going into the ministry. Meanwhile, he married and fathered three children.

A lieutenant when Fort Sumter fell in April 1861, Howard put aside his ministerial plans and devoted himself to the Union cause. He was made colonel of the 3rd Maine Volunteer Regiment in June, and took his men to Washington, D.C. Before long, Howard found himself commanding a brigade, though he retained the rank of colonel. By July, he was leading his neophyte warriors into battle at First Bull Run. Although his brigade was routed along with the rest of the Union army, he was promoted to brigadier general two months later.

In November Howard took command of a brigade that was placed in the Second Corps of the newly-organized Army of the Potomac. During the Peninsula Campaign, at Fair Oaks on June 1, he was hit twice in the right arm while leading a charge; a second bullet shattered the bone near the elbow, and the arm had to be amputed. After a short two-month convalescence, he returned to duty at the head of another Second Corps unit, the Philadelphia Brigade, replacing an officer who had also been wounded on the Peninsula.

Howard's first engagement with his Philadelphians was at Antietam, where his brigade—along with the rest of Maj. Gen. John Sedgwick's Second Division—was ambushed and almost destroyed in a matter of minutes in the West Woods. Howard took control of the tattered division on the field when Sedgwick fell with three wounds. He could do little, however, except to preside over its retreat from the field. That fall, he was promoted to major general on November 29, and continued to lead his division through the Fredericksburg Campaign in December. His was one of the unlucky divisions chosen for the futile, bloody assault against Marye's Heights. Within the span of three months, Howard had the misfortune of being associated with the Second Division during two of the worst disasters to befall the Army of the

Potomac. In February 1863, Maj. Gen. Joe Hooker, the new head of the Army of the Potomac, gave his crony Maj. Gen. Dan Sickles command of the Third Corps. The overlooked Howard, who had seniority over Sickles, protested; after all, Sickles did not even have military training. Another opportunity arose, however, in April when Eleventh Corps commander Franz Sigel resigned because he judged his assignment to a small corps to be incommensurate with his high rank. Hooker gave the corps to the young general from Maine.

Just thirty-two years old in 1863, Maj. Gen. Oliver O. Howard stood five feet nine inches tall, was slight of build, and had a pale complexion. His physical appearance "did not call out from the troops enthusiastic applause," said Maj. Thomas Osborne, his chief of artillery. Osborne wrote that he did not find his commander to be either a profound thinker or an officer with "large natural ability." Another soldier observed Howard's dark, profuse, "flowing moustache and beard, [and] undistinguished" eyes. Despite the general's empty right sleeve, Lt. Frank Haskell somewhat dismissively wrote that, "Howard. . .has nothing marked about him. . .and on the whole appears a very pleasant, affable, well dressed little gentleman."

Many commented on Howard's genteel manner. Osborne described him as "the highest toned gentleman" he had ever known. Col. Charles Wainwright, chief of artillery of the First Corps, commented, "He is the only religious man of high rank that I know of in the army and, in the little intercourse I have had with him, showed himself the most polished gentleman I have ever met." "Howard is brave enough and a most perfect gentleman," continued Wainwright. "He is a Christian as well as a man of ability, but there is some doubt as to his having snap enough to manage the Germans who require to be ruled with a rod of iron."

Wainwright's worry that Howard was overmatched with the command of the Eleventh Corps was echoed by many in the army. It was not a felicitous marriage of a commander and his men. His fidgety gestures and high shrill voice failed to inspire confidence; a serious problem in light of the fact many of his soldiers did not speak English and were more likely to place their faith in a leader with a strong physical presence. Howard's strong Christian beliefs were also well known, and at times he spent Sundays going to hospitals to distribute religious tracts. The Eleventh Corps was largely composed of worldly Germans who had fled religious oppression back home, and who had a deep-seated aversion to being prayed over or preached to. Furthermore, the free-think and free-drinking Europeans often snickered at Howard's prudish behavior. (At West Point, the story was circulated that when he met a girl, the first thing he would do would be to ask her "if she had reflected on the goodness of God during the past night.")

Howard's devoutness was only one of the many unfortunate aspects of the mismatch that existed between him and his corps. He had replaced the Germans' darling, Franz Sigel. "I fights mit Sigel!" had been a proud boast and a recruiting bonanza that brought thousands of immigrant Germans into the Union army eager to show their solidarity with the ideals of their adopted country. Howard addressed his soldiers as "my men," which sounded a bit too patrician to soldiers imbued with a distrust of patronizing members of the gentry. He was also a stern disciplinarian who brought with him the strict Brig. Gen. Francis Barlow to command a division formerly led by a well-liked and easy going commander. General Howard seemed to realize the predicament he was in, and later wrote, "I was not at first getting the earnest and loyal support of the entire command."

Matters worsened after the May 1863 Battle of Chancellorsville. Howard's negligence brought everlasting humiliation to the Eleventh Corps' when he dismissed reports that Confederates were marching past and massing against his unprotected right flank. Howard believed the enemy army was retreating, and thus did not take any steps to verify the reports or strengthen his right—despite having promised Hooker that morning to take measures "to resist an attack from the west." When Jackson's furious onslaught routed the entire Eleventh Corps and the right wing of the army virtually collapsed—despite the courageous attempts of Howard himself, who tucked the American flag under the stump of his missing arm and vainly attempted top rally his terrified men—the rest of the Army of the Potomac never forgot or forgave the "foreign" Eleventh Corps.

When Hooker gave up the battle a few days later, Howard's Eleventh Corps was the obvious choice as scapegoat for the debacle. Major General Carl Schurz, one of Howard's division commanders, wrote his superior a letter so bitter that, said Howard, "I thought I should never survive it, but I have." Hooker encouraged Schurz to use all his influence with Lincoln to have Sigel resume command of the corps, and promised to strengthen his force if Schurz was successful. Secretary of the Treasury Salmon Chase and army bureaucrat Maj. Gen. Henry Halleck also wanted Howard ousted. President Lincoln, however, urged patience, telling critics, "Give him time, and he will bring things straight."

Oliver Howard marched to Gettysburg at the head of an uninterrupted string of battlefield setbacks He was a general desperately in need of a change of luck.

GETTYSBURG: On orders from Maj. Gen. John Reynolds, Howard started his corps from Emmitsburg on a ten mile march north to Gettysburg at about 8:00 a.m. on July 1. At 10:30 he was within sight of the town when an orderly from Reynolds told him the battle had been joined. Howard galloped into Gettysburg and observed the last of the morning's fighting west of town. He learned around 11:30 a.m. that Reynolds was dead and that he was now commanding officer on the field— though at no time did he ride the few hundred yards west to inspect Reynolds' positions or meet with the First Corps generals. Returning instead to Cemetery Hill, Howard selected it as his headquarters and the strong point where he would establish his reserve, Brig. Gen. Adolph von Steinwehr's division.

At 1:00 p.m., Carl Schurz's division came up and passed through Gettysburg to take up a position north of town. Howard accompanied Barlow's division as it followed the path of Schurz's column. A lull had fallen over the battle west of Gettysburg, and Howard took this opportunity to send dispatches to Maj. Gens. Daniel Sickles and Henry Slocum to inform them of the morning fight; he did not

request reinforcements. Half an hour later, he changed his mind and sent the generals new messages asking for help. At 2:00 p.m., Howard informed Maj. Gen. George Meade of the overall situation and mentioned that he had ordered Sickles forward. He finally rode over and approved Maj. Gen. Abner Doubleday's First Corps line on the ridges west of town. When he received a dispatch from cavalryman Brig. Gen. John Buford warning of the approach of Confederates from the north, Howard deployed his two divisions at right angles to the westward facing First Corps line. By 2:00 p.m., Howard's men had taken up positions almost a mile north of town, though the low, flat ground on which they deployed was poorly suited for defense.

Before long, a Confederate division under Maj. Gen. Robert Rodes attacked from the northwest off Oak Hill and crashed up against the salient where the First and Eleventh corps joined. Although his attack was piecemeal and ineptly performed, portions of another Confederate division under Maj. Gen. Jubal Early attacked Howard's vulnerable right rear from the northeast. These unfortunately-timed attacks worked like a giant jaw to crush the Eleventh Corps line, and both of Howard's divisions tumbled back through Gettysburg at a run, losing hundreds of prisoners to the closely pursuing enemy infantry. Yet, despite their second major defeat in as many months, Howard's men were panicked but not shattered. When they saw the 2,000 men of Col. Orland Smith's brigade manning the crest of Cemetery Hill, which was studded with six friendly artillery pieces, they stopped and faced their foe, disorganized but not demoralized. Reynolds' (Doubleday's) First Corps front had collapsed at about the same time, and its refugees were also falling back on Cemetery Hill from the west.

As Howard's men were streaming up the hillside, Second Corps commander Maj. Gen. Winfield Hancock rode up with authorization from General Meade to assume command of all of the troops at Gettysburg. The crestfallen Howard agreed with little fuss and cooperated with the dynamic Hancock. The two divided responsibilities: Howard assumed authority for dispositions of the units to the right of the Baltimore Pike, which included Culp's Hill, while Hancock did the same for the troops to the left of the road. Reinforcements arrived, and a defensive line was assembled. Most of the Eleventh Corps' men assumed positions behind the plethora of stone fences that cross-crossed the hillside's forward slopes. The Confederates did not assail the towering, newly-fortified position southeast of Gettysburg, and the day's fighting ended.

Once Meade arrived that night, Howard's responsibility shrank to that of his Eleventh Corps front, which had been established on the north face of Cemetery Hill. Barlow's division (now under Brig. Gen. Adelbert Ames) was on the right side of the Baltimore Pike on East Cemetery Hill, while Schurz' division was on its left near the cemetery. Von Steinwehr's two brigades were deployed along the Taneytown Road left of Schurz. Howard's position, perhaps the most vulnerable on the whole Union line, would be attacked only once—at dusk on July 2. The primary attack came from two brigades of Early's Division, which advanced from the east side of the town. When the attack sent most of Barlow's division reeling, Howard threw in two of his closest regiments and rushed Col. Charles Coster's brigade (von Steinwehr's division) to the scene as well as a brigade borrowed from the Second Corps under Col. Samuel Carroll. Although Early's men had captured the crest of the hill, they were unable to hold it. Another attack, meant to have been coordinated with Early's, was undertaken by Rodes' Division against Cemetery Hill from the west. Rodes' retreated before the main assault was delivered, however, once he learned Early had been repulsed. Howard's line held, and the Southerners relinquished their gains, falling back to their original positions. At a conference attended by Meade and his corps commanders that evening, Howard confidently asserted that he could defend his position the following day. The army remained in place, and his line was not attacked on July 3.

Oliver Howard's string of bad luck had continued at Gettysburg. His Eleventh Corps lost 3,000 men—half of them captured—and inflicted less than 1,000 casualties. Although it is true that he was the victim of two assaults coordinated by little more than luck (Rodes' and Early's), he knew of the enemy approach in both cases. His deployment north of town on July was awkward and his men had to fight on weak terrain with a vulnerable right flank. Still, though, his soldiers fought as well as possible under these circumstances. According to one historian, the Eleventh Corps was "shredded" by two enemy brigades. "Although they had superior numbers available the 11th Corps had been outnumbered at the point of attack in every instance. It was a classic example of defeat in detail." The corps simply had too much ground to defend, and Howard's decision to remain so far to the rear, commanding from Cemetery Hill, led John Buford to conclude that there was "no directing person on the field."

Howard and the Eleventh Corps were sent west in September 1863, and their luck changed. Major Gen. William Sherman, who appreciated Howard's quiet professionalism, eventually make him commander of the Army of the Tennessee, and he turned in his best service as a Union general away from the Army of the Potomac.

After the war, Howard devoted himself to the welfare of the newly-freed slaves and was made first commissioner of the Freedman's Bureau. His main post-war contribution was his part in establishing Howard University. The one-armed warrior received the Congressional Medal of Honor in 1893, and retired from the U.S. Army in 1894 with the rank of major general. He continued to engage in religious and educational activities until his death from angina pectoris in 1909.

For further reading:

Carpenter, John A. "General O. O. Howard at Gettysburg." *Civil War History*, Sept. 1963.

——. *Sword and Olive Branch: Oliver Otis Howard.* Pittsburgh, 1964.

Greene, A. Wilson. "From Chancellorsville to Cemetery Hill: O. O. Howard and Eleventh Corps Leadership," in Gary Gallagher, ed., *The First Day at Gettysburg.* Kent, 1992.

Hartwig, D. Scott. "The 11th Army Corps on July 1." *Gettysburg Magazine*, #2, 1990.

Howard, Oliver O. *Autobiography of Oliver Otis Howard, Major General United States Army.* 2 vols. New York, 1907.

McFeely, William S. *Yankee Stepfather: General O. O. Howard and the Freedmen.* New York, 1970.

Pfanz, Harry W. *Gettysburg: The Second Day.* Chapel Hill, 1987.

Weland, Gerald. *O.O. Howard, Union General.* Jefferson, Chapel Hill, 1995.

FIRST DIVISION
(2,477 MEN)

BRIGADIER GENERAL
FRANCIS CHANNING BARLOW

At the Battle of Chancellorsville, the First Division of the Eleventh Corps suffered the initial shock of Maj. Gen. Thomas Jackson's devastating flank attack. Corps commander Maj. Gen. Oliver Howard appointed twenty eight year old Francis Barlow, an inspired warrior and strict disciplinarian, to command the division and bring it back to its feet. He found the position a difficult one and soon developed a dislike for his new troops, writing, "These Dutch won't fight. Their officers say so and they say so themselves and they ruin all with whom they come in contact."

Barlow didn't look like much of a fighter himself. He had a boyish face and was slight of build—even frail-looking—with no color in his cheeks. His voice matched his physique, thin and lackluster, and he had a loose-jointed, slouchy manner about him. Period photographs often show him with a black felt hat crumpled in one hand, heavy boots on his feet, and a peaceful expression on his round, clean-shaven face. In stark contrast to Howard, Barlow had little sense of military decorum. He wore a checked flannel lumberjack's shirt, and over that he often wore his uniform coat unbuttoned. He looked, wrote one of George Meade's staff officers, "like a highly independent mounted newsboy." Barlow's choice of swords, however revealed an inner grit that was hidden by his youthful looks and sloppy outward manner. Rather than carrying a regulation officer's sword, he wore a heavy enlisted man's cavalry saber. He used this sturdy weapon to whack the backsides of stragglers—whom he despised—because he wanted to use something that would hurt. The problem of straggling on the march was a personal obsession for Barlow, who developed a unique solution: he detailed a company in skirmish line with fixed bayonets at the rear of the division column with orders drive forward anybody who fell out of the ranks.

Barlow was raised in Massachusetts, a Unitarian minister's son. He graduated first in his class at Harvard and practiced law in Manhattan before the Civil War, occasionally writing editorials for the New York Tribune. A young man with absolutely no military experience, he nevertheless possessed those qualities which could not be taught in an academy—driving energy, determination, and a positive taste for fighting. Five days after Fort Sumter, he left his new bride of one day to go off to war and enlisted as a private. By the time of the Peninsula Campaign of 1862, he was the colonel of the 61st New York.

Barlow saw action at Seven Pines in Oliver Howard's Second Corps brigade. At Glendale, during the Seven Days' Battles, his regiment became separated from the rest of the brigade and Barlow exercised his own initiative by rushing his New Yorkers toward the sounds of fighting. Stumbling upon a Confederate battle line, he led his men in a bayonet charge across a field. The enemy broke and ran, and Barlow picked up a fallen Confederate battle flag and sent it to the rear. He pushed his regiment forward into another enemy line, whose officer challenged, "Throw down your arms or you are all dead men!" Barlow sneered at the request, and "a vigorous fire was kept up on both sides for a long time" until darkness ended the fighting. Two days later, in the final battle of the campaign at Malvern Hill, Barlow's men held their section of the line against repeated Confederate attacks.

At Antietam, Barlow plunged his regiment into the maelstrom of the Sunken Road, where his men captured about 300 of the enemy and where he fell badly wounded with shell fragments in the left groin and face. In his official report of the battle, Brig. Gen. John Caldwell described Barlow's exploits in detail, adding "Whatever praise is due to the most distinguished bravery, the utmost coolness and quickness of perception, the greatest promptitude and skill in handling troops under fire, is justly due to him. It is but simple justice to say that he has proved himself fully equal to every emergency, and I have no doubt that he would discharge the duties of a much higher command with honor to himself and benefit to the country." Caldwell's high praise helped gain Barlow a promotion to brigadier general.

The new general's groin wound healed slowly, and his left leg remained numb through the winter months. An abscess on his back further complicated his convalescence, and he was emaciated and suffering from what doctors called an "influence of malaria." Although he was not fully recovered, he rejoined the army in April 1863 and took command of an Eleventh Corps brigade. At Chancellorsville his brigade was attached to Sickles' Third Corps at the time of Jackson's famous flank attack, and he thus avoided the humiliation visited upon the rest of the Eleventh Corps. At the end of the month, Howard put Barlow in command of the division formerly led by the wounded Brig. Gen. Charles Devens in an effort to stiffen the fighting qualities of its unfortunate brigades. Barlow immediately angered his men by arresting the popular Col. Leopold von Gilsa. "With. . .Barlow banished to the Antipodes, our happiness would have been complete,"

wrote one of von Gilsa's men. "As a taskmaster he had no equal. The prospect of speedy deliverance from the odious yoke of Billy Barlow filled every heart with joy." His men considered him a "petty tyrant."

By the summer of 1863, Barlow was embarking on his first campaign at the head of his division whose men, by and large, disliked him. Yet, Capt. Charles Francis Adams would eventually write, "I am more disposed to regard Barlow as a military genius than any man I have yet seen."

GETTYSBURG: Barlow's division, in the middle of the Eleventh Corps column of march, entered Gettysburg from the south after 1:00 p.m. on July 1, having double-quicked the last several miles from Emmitsburg on orders from corps chief Howard. Barlow drove his two brigades (led by Col. Leopold von Gilsa and Brig. Gen. Adelbert Ames) north of town and deployed them on good ground between the Carlisle and Harrisburg roads, facing generally north. Maj. Gen. Carl Schurz's Third Division, which was deploying to face Maj. Gen. Robert Rodes' Confederate division on Oak Hill, deployed on Barlow's left. Barlow's position was a hillock (since christened "Barlow's Knoll") overlooking Rock Creek, nearly a mile northeast of town. It was the only strong terrain feature he could readily find. Since enemy artillery posted on the knoll would dominate the line already being formed by Schurz to the northwest, Barlow determined to occupy it himself. Although he later described it as an "admirable position," by putting his men so far forward he opened a gap between his left and Brig. Gen. Alexander Schimmelfennig's brigade of Schurz's division. In addition, Barlow's right flank was vulnerable to an enemy force approaching from the northeast. (In fairness to Barlow, he had not been informed of this Rebel advance; nonetheless, his overall troop deployment constituted a significant tactical blunder.) About 2:00 p.m., Maj. Gen. Jubal Early's Confederate division marched into view off Barlow's right front. Within the hour, Brig. Gen. John Gordon's Brigade splashed across Rock Creek and attacked Barlow's Knoll. At the same time, Barlow's men were being pressed on their left by Brig. Gen. George Doles' Brigade (Rodes' Division). The Confederates proved unstoppable and rolled up Barlow's right flank, beginning a chain reaction that soon sent the whole Eleventh Corps fleeing toward Gettysburg.

Barlow was riding in front of his men trying to rally them and form a new line when a bullet struck him in the left side. He dismounted and attempted to walk, and shortly afterward was struck again by a spent bullet in the back. He lay down as the battle roared over him, and another bullet went through his hat, while a fourth round grazed his right hand. The crippled general was carried to the Josiah Benner house by a group of enemy soldiers, and two days later a Confederate surgeon probed the wound in his side. The prognosis, Barlow recalled, was not good, and he was told that the bullet had lodged in the cavity of his pelvis, and "there was little chance for my life."

He was left him behind when the Confederates retreated on July 4. Barlow refused to die, however, and was hospitalized after being rescued by Federal troops. Six months later he still could not mount a horse, and he would not return to the army until April 1864. He commanded a division in Hancock's Second Corps through the Overland Campaign of 1864, with the high point of his military career coming in the "Mule Shoe" at Spotsylvania. He again left the army on sick leave in July 1864, but returned to participate in part of the Appomattox Campaign, and was promoted to major general on May 25, 1865.

Barlow entered politics as a Republican after the war and served as secretary of state of New York (twice), United States marshal, and state attorney general. He was a founder of the American Bar Association, prosecuted the Boss Tweed Ring, and continued practicing law until his death from Bright's disease in 1896.

For further reading:

Greene, A. Wilson. "From Chancellorsville to Cemetery Hill: O. O. Howard and Eleventh Corps Leadership," in Gary Gallagher, ed., *The First Day at Gettysburg.* Kent, 1992.

Hartwig, D. Scott. "The 11th Army Corps on July 1." *Gettysburg Magazine,* #2, 1990.

FIRST BRIGADE

(1,136 MEN)

COLONEL
LEOPOLD VON GILSA

Colonel von Gilsa was a former Prussian officer and major in the Schleswig-Holstein War of 1848-50. After immigrating to New York City, he supported himself by lecturing, singing, and playing piano in music halls along the Bowery. Due to his European service, Von Gilsa was commissioned colonel of the 41st New York volunteer regiment before First Bull Run, where his regiment was in reserve and missed the fighting. His first combat experience on this continent came in the Shenandoah Campaign in the spring of 1862, where he was severely wounded in the fighting at Cross Keys.

While convalescing, he missed the Battle of Second Bull Run in August. His brigade leader, Brig. Gen. Julius Stahel, was promoted to division command, and von Gilsa took over the brigade upon his return in September, which by this time was part of the Army of the Potomac's Eleventh Corps. The corps manned the defenses of Washington during the Maryland Campaign, though von Gilsa led the brigade at Snicker's Gap. After missing the Battle of Fredericksburg, von Gilsa took part in Ambrose Burnside's Mud March at the beginning of 1863.

His first test in combat at brigade level, to his misfortune, was at the May 1863 disaster at Chancellorsville. Von Gilsa's men were on the extreme right flank of the entire Union army when Lt. Gen. Thomas "Stonewall" Jackson's corps came crashing down upon them. In the resulting panic, 265 men of the brigade were lost. The fault was not von Gilsa's, for he had warned corps headquarters about Rebels massing in the woods, though his reports were not taken seriously.

The Prussian von Gilsa was notorious for his genius for profanity in his native German. As one witness joked, "When in difficult straits he was wont to be overcome by a lingual diarrhoea of sonorous expletives in the Bismarckian vernacular." Eleventh Corps chief Maj. Gen. Oliver Howard discovered the extent of von Gilsa's gift for cursing when the two crossed paths on the bitter retreat from Chancellorsville. Howard characteristically reminded the German officer to depend on God, and von Gilsa poured out a stream of oaths in German with such vehemence and profusion that Howard thought he had gone insane. According to Howard, von Gilsa was "a German soldier, who at parades and drills makes a fine soldierly appearance"—which seems to indicate Howard considered him little more than an officer who excelled in parade ground pomp. He also fell rapidly out of favor with his new division commander, Brig. Gen. Francis Barlow, who replaced General Devens after Chancellorsville. The Prussian colonel was not as strict a disciplinarian as Barlow desired him to be; as a result, Barlow placed von Gilsa under arrest on the march north to Gettysburg for allowing more than one man at a time to leave the column to get water.

GETTYSBURG: About 1:00 p.m. on July 1, as Barlow's division was trotting through the streets of Gettysburg to take its place north of town, Barlow realized he needed von Gilsa with his brigade and restored the colonel to command. A Gettysburg resident witnessed the colonel's return:

Past our house came, running at the double quick, Howard's eleventh army corps. They kept the pace without breaking ranks; but they flowed through and out into the battle-field beyond, a human tide, at millrace speed. Far down the road, behind the passing regiments, a roar of cheers began. It rolled forward, faster than the running of the men who made it—like some high surge sweeping across the surface of a flowing sea. Its roar of cheering neared and neared, until we saw a group of officers coming at a brisk trot, with the mighty cheer always at their horses' heels. Among them rode one man in colonel's uniform who held his head high and smiled. He was an officer, a favorite with the soldiers, who had been under arrest until the eve of the battle. Now, released, he was on his way into action, and the whole brigade that knew him was greeting him with the chorus of the lungs.

Colonel von Gilsa's brigade (which consisted of the 54th and 68th New York regiments, and the 153rd Pennsylvania), marched out of town, crossed over the Carlisle Road to the Harrisburg Road, and marched to the Almshouse. There, Barlow ordered him to move north about 400 yards and deploy on Blocher's (later called "Barlow's") Knoll. After some confusion, deployed his New Yorkers and a portion of the 153rd Pennsylvania as skirmishers, with the rest in battalion en masse, and advanced into a heavy skirmish fire. He soon seized the knoll and deployed to defend it. With his Pennsylvanians in the woods on the knoll, he sent a portion of the 68th New York extending westward toward the Carlisle Road on their left, while the balance of the 68th deployed on their right. The 54th New York extended the line to Rock Creek.

It was at once a strong and dangerous position, powerful in front (although it needed more men to adequately defend it) but exposed on both flanks. While Brig. Gen. George Doles' Brigade menaced his front, Brig. Gen. John Gordon's Georgians attacked von Gilsa's right flank. Within minutes the New Yorkers were falling back into the Pennsylvania line, and soon his entire brigade was in full flight, racing backward toward Gettysburg. Von Gilsa had one horse shot from under him, but jumped onto another and desperately tried to stem the retreat. One soldier saw him ride "up and down that line through a regular storm of lead, meantime using the German epithets so common to him." An admiring Confederate soldier remembered, "Their officers were cheering their men on and behaving like heroes and commanders of the 'first water.'" The collapse of the brigade triggered the impending meltdown of the Eleventh Corps line north of Gettysburg on July 1. The skedaddle finally ended at Cemetery Hill.

One the evening of July 2, von Gilsa's regiments were again the target of an attack, this time while situated on the northeast face of Cemetery Hill along Brickyard Lane. Colonel von Gilsa's brigade (which now included the 41st New York, which had brought forward from assignment guarding the trains), was once more sent flying rearward when several regiments of North Carolinians and Louisianians struck its line. Union batteries on the hill, supported by Col. Samuel Carroll's brigade (Second Corps) eventually drove the Confederates back. Von Gilsa had now failed to hold his position three times in two major battles.

In a desire to escape the Eleventh Corps, Brig. Gen. George Gordon, who replaced the wounded Francis Barlow (struck down during the defense of Blocher's Knoll), had his much-maligned division transferred to the coastal islands of South Carolina two weeks after Gettysburg. Colonel von Gilsa reverted to the command of his old regiment. He held several posts in South Carolina and later in the Washington defenses. He was never promoted, and ended the war as a colonel, mustering out in December of 1865.

For further reading:

Greene, A. Wilson. "From Chancellorsville to Cemetery Hill: O. O. Howard and Eleventh Corps Leadership," in Gary Gallagher, ed., *The First Day at Gettysburg*. Kent, 1992.

Hartwig, D. Scott. "The 11th Army Corps on July 1." *Gettysburg Magazine*, #2, 1990.

SECOND BRIGADE
(1,337 MEN)

BRIGADIER GENERAL ADELBERT AMES

General Ames was young for a brigadier general, only twenty-eight at Gettysburg. He was originally a clipper seaman, but he received an appointment to West Point from his native Maine. Ames graduated 5th out of 45 students in the Class of 1861, which completed its studies just after the fall of Fort Sumter. He was assigned to the artillery and fought at Bull Run only two months after graduating. There, he was badly wounded in the right thigh but refused to leave his guns until he was too weak to remain seated on a caisson. (For this heroic performance Ames received a Congressional Medal of Honor in 1893.) Returning to duty, he fought in the Peninsula Campaign the next summer, seeing action at Yorktown, Gaines' Mill and Malvern Hill, where his conduct was referred to as "above praise" by the brilliant and respected Col. Henry Hunt, chief of the Artillery Reserve of the Army of the Potomac.

Ames realized that he could advance in rank more quickly in the volunteer infantry, so he returned to Maine to campaign for a command. State officials were only too happy to indulge the talented young officer, and in August 1862, he became colonel of the 20th

Maine Volunteers, an outfit destined for immortality the next year at Gettysburg. Ames led the 20th in the Maryland Campaign, but it was kept in reserve with the rest of the Fifth Corps at the Battle of Antietam. At Fredericksburg in December, Ames led his regiment in one of the last charges of the day against Marye's Heights. It ended, like all the others, in failure, but mercifully only 36 men in the regiment became casualties. During the Chancellorsville Campaign in May 1863, Colonel Ames—perhaps with an eye toward his own advancement—temporarily relinquished command of his regiment to volunteer as an aide to Fifth Corps commander Maj. Gen. George Meade. On the 20th of May, two weeks after Chancellorsville, Ames received a promotion to brigadier general out of respect for his military talent. (Staff duty with Meade seemed to have this effect on young West Pointers' careers, for staff officer Alexander Webb also became a general at this time). The commander of the Eleventh Corps, Maj. Gen. Oliver Howard, brought Ames and Brig. Gen. Francis Barlow into his First Division to improve the discipline and fighting abilities of his men after their disastrous experience at Chancellorsville. Ames handed over command of the 20th Maine to an obscure colonel named Joshua Chamberlain, and took over the leadership of his brigade.

New York socialite-turned-artilleryman Col. Charles Wainwright found Ames "the best kind of a man to be associated with, cool and clear in his own judgment, gentlemanly and without the smallest desire to interfere." Furthermore, mused Wainwright, ". . .strange thing in this army, I did not hear him utter an oath of any kind [for] three days!"

Ames was new to his brigade and had no experience leading such a unit in action. In fact, the Battle of Fredericksburg was the only occasion upon which he had commanded infantry in combat. Even with such handicaps, however, he was a talented professional officer and was expected to do well in any situation.

GETTYSBURG: General Ames' brigade marched in column behind Col. Leopold von Gilsa's out of Gettysburg, crossed over the Carlisle Road to the Harrisburg Road, and was massed east of the road behind a small ridge upon which sat the county Almshouse. The regiments, aligned in double column of companies, were deployed right to left as follows: 107th and 25th Ohio regiment, 17th Connecticut, and the 75th Ohio in support. The massive enemy build-up opposite von Gilsa's thinly-spread brigade on Blocher's Knoll prompted Barlow to deploy Ames' brigade 400 yards north in support. The 25th Ohio took up a position on the knoll, and the 107th formed on its left, facing northwest. The remaining two regiments were massed in the rear as Barlow's sole divisional reserve.

Soon after 3:00 p.m., von Gilsa was struck from two directions and knocked off the field, exposing Ames' right flank. General Gordon's Georgians smashed into it, collapsing the 25th and 107th Ohio regiments, and Ames ordered up his two reserve regiments. "It was a fearful advance and made at a dreadful cost of life," remembered the 75th Ohio leader, Colonel Andrew Harris. Colonel von Gilsa's retreating men made it difficult for Ames' regiments to stand and fight, and they too were soon driven from Blocher's Knoll. While attempting to rally his division, General Barlow fell with a serious wound, and the youthful Ames inherited command of the division at a time when it was "falling back with little or no regularity, regimental organizations having become destroyed." Ames, together with von Gilsa, somehow succeeded in establishing a new defensive line near the Almshouse, but two more fresh Southern brigades attacked it, forcing a general retreat.

The retreat continued through the streets of Gettysburg and up Cemetery Hill, where Ames' regiments were reorganized on the northeast face, east of the Baltimore Pike. Ames' brigade (led now by Colonel Harris) formed in an L-shaped defensive line, with the shank (17th Connecticut and 25th Ohio) along the Brickyard Lane facing northeast, and the 107th and 25th Ohio regiments forming the bottom of the "L" facing north. This position was struck head-on at dusk on the evening of July 2 by Harry Hays' Louisiana Brigade, which swept it from the crest of the hill. The timely arrival of Col. Samuel Carroll's Second Corps brigade, together with elements from Ames' and von Gilsa's brigades, managed to push the unsupported Confederates off the hill and save the important position. When things quieted down, Carroll requested support for his exposed brigade. Ames replied that his own troops were rattled, and asked Carroll to remain in his front. The fiery Carroll shot back, "Damn a man who [has] no confidence in his troops." The northeast face of Cemetery Hill was not attacked again during the fighting.

Two weeks after the battle, Brig. Gen. George Gordon replaced Ames at the head of the division and took the command to South Carolina, while Ames reverted to command of his brigade. He served the rest of the war in brigade and division commands in various theaters, but never returned the Army of the Potomac.

Ames was assigned to duty in Mississippi after the war and was made military, then provisional governor there. He was elected to as U.S. Senator from that state in 1870, then reelected governor of Mississippi in 1874; his administration was beset by race riots and official misconduct, and he resigned in 1876 to avoid impeachment. He was the last Civil War general to die, in 1933.

For further reading:

Benson, Harry K. "The Public Career of Adelbert Ames, 1861-1876," Thesis, Univ. of VA, 1975.

Greene, A. Wilson. "From Chancellorsville to Cemetery Hill: O. O. Howard and Eleventh Corps Leadership," in Gary Gallagher, ed., *The First Day at Gettysburg*. Kent, 1992.

Hartwig, D. Scott. "The 11th Army Corps on July 1." *Gettysburg Magazine*, #2, 1990.

SECOND DIVISION

(2,894 MEN)

BRIGADIER GENERAL ADOLPH WILHELM A. F. BARON VON STEINWEHR

General von Steinwehr was a Prussian from the Duchy of Brunswick. He looked the part of the stereotypical Teutonic officer, with a bald dome over hawk-like eyes, long straight nose, strong chin, and meticulously groomed martial mustache and side whiskers. Born into a military family—his grandfather had fought in the Prussian army against Napoleon—he was reared to carry on the family tradition and was educated at the duchy's military school. He went on to serve in the army of the Duke of Brunswick, but left for America to fight for the United States during the Mexican War. Although he did not succeed in winning an officer's commission in that conflict, he was retained as an engineer to help survey the new border with Mexico, and later worked on a survey of Mobile Bay, where he met his future wife in 1849. After their marriage, von Steinwehr and his Alabama bride returned to Germany, but by 1854 were back in the U.S., this time to try farming in Connecticut.

When the Civil War broke out, von Steinwehr was given a chance to use his military training in the service of the U.S. He was commissioned colonel of the 29th New York regiment. The German regiment was in reserve during the fight at Bull Run, but it waged a rear guard action that helped protect the routed Union forces. The Prussian was promoted to brigadier general in October 1861, given command of a brigade in December, and sent to fight under General John C. Fremont in the Shenandoah Valley in the spring of 1862. For unrecorded reasons he was absent at the Battle of Cross Keys on June 8. Without proof of his field abilities, Von Steinwehr was given a

division in Maj. Gen. John Pope's Army of Virginia in June 1862. At the Battle of Second Bull Run in late August, however, he had little to do since his division consisted only of the three regiments of his old brigade, commanded by another officer. After Pope's disaster at Second Bull Run, von Steinwehr's division—strengthened to two brigades—became part of the Eleventh Corps, Army of the Potomac. It did not fight again until Chancellorsville, where it was swept up in the rout caused by Lt. Gen. Thomas "Stonewall" Jackson's flank attack.

By the beginning of the Gettysburg Campaign, General von Steinwehr's record boasted participation in multiple defeats. There were some indications, however, that von Steinwehr had real ability. At Chancellorsville his men did some hard fighting before being thrown back, and Maj. Gen. Oliver Howard, the Eleventh Corps' commander, described von Steinwehr's bearing during the battle as "cool, collected and judicious." Brig. Gen. Alpheus Williams, himself a capable and hard-hitting division commander, thought highly of von Steinwehr and described him as a "remarkably intelligent and agreeable person." One subordinate in the 55th Ohio Regiment later recalled the Prussian as "an officer of great merit, trained in the German school and possessing the confidence of his superiors."

GETTYSBURG: In the early afternoon of July 1, Howard deployed the divisions of Maj. Gen. Carl Schurz and Brig. Gen. Francis Barlow north of Gettysburg. General von Steinwehr's division (which consisted of the brigades of Col. Orland Smith and Col. Charles Coster) was held in reserve and given the responsibility of strengthening Cemetery Hill, a strong position southeast of town. Smith's brigade was placed on the crest of the hill to the west of the Baltimore Pike, and Coster's men were aligned east of that thoroughfare, both facing north.

After Maj. Gen. John Reynolds' death, Howard assumed temporary command of the Union forces at Gettysburg, and appointed Schurz to lead the Eleventh Corps in his stead. When Schurz saw the troops of his corps north of the town about to give way, he ordered up Colonel Coster's brigade, leaving von Stein-wehr with only Smith's brigade and a battery on Cemetery Hill. The sight of von Steinwehr's stern defenders lined along the crest of Cemetery Hill, however, helped revive the spirits of the men of the First and Eleventh Corps as they came streaming back through town toward the towering eminence. Coster's brigade was deployed on the northeast edge of town, and after a hard fight was sent retreating to Cemetery Hill.

On July 2, General von Steinwehr was assigned a portion of the line on the northwest side of Cemetery Hill west of the Baltimore Pike along the Taneytown Road. Other than skirmish and artillery fire, his men were not engaged during the day, with the principle fighting taking place far to the south near the Round Tops. At dusk, when the northeast side of the hill was assaulted successfully by the enemy, von Steinwehr threw in two of Coster's regiments to help meet the attack. His own position was to have been assaulted by Robert Rodes' Division, but the attack was canceled and only skirmishing took place on von Steinwehr's front.

The general from Prussia was never tested by a direct attack at Gettysurg, and thus he did not enjoy much of an opportunity in Pennsylvania to prove his abilities as a division commander. The service he did render was competent and purposeful. He continued to lead his division at Chattanooga in the fall, but when the Eleventh and Twelfth Corps were consolidated in April of 1864, von Steinwehr lost his command. He left the army rather than revert to brigade command.

After the war, Von Steinwehr became known as a distinguished geographer and cartographer, teaching at Yale, working as a government engineer, and publishing a number of works before his death in 1877.

For further reading:

Greene, A. Wilson. "From Chancellorsville to Cemetery Hill: O. O. Howard and Eleventh Corps Leadership," in Gary Gallagher, ed., *The First Day at Gettysburg*. Kent, 1992.

Hartwig, D. Scott. "The 11th Army Corps on July 1." *Gettysburg Magazine*, #2, 1990.

First Brigade

(1,217 men)

Colonel
Charles Robert Coster

Charles Coster, a native of New York City, had worked his way up through the ranks. He initially served as a private with the famed 7th New York Militia, one of the first contingents of volunteers to reach Washington, D.C. in the opening weeks of the Civil War. Within a couple of weeks, however, he left the militia to take a commission as first lieutenant with the 12th Regular Infantry regiment—hardened Old Army soldiers. With the Regulars, Lieutenant Coster went to the Peninsula the next summer and was wounded at Gaines' Mill, receiving special commendation for his performance by three different superior officers. After two months of convalescence, he returned to duty in October 1862 and was made colonel of a new volunteer regiment, the 134th New York.

The 134th was assigned to the Eleventh Corps, which was serving in the defenses of Washington during the Battle of Fredericksburg in December 1862. Coster's first combat experience at the head of his regiment came at Chancellorsville in May 1863. Colonel Coster's men were part of Brig. Gen. Francis Barlow's brigade, which was detached to the Dan Sickles' Third Corps at the time of the

Eleventh Corps' infamous rout at the hands of Stonewall Jackson. As a result, neither Coster nor the 134th New York were tested in the battle, and the regiment suffered only eight wounded in the entire campaign.

On June 10th, in a divisional reorganization, Coster's regiment was reassigned to Col. Adolphus Buschbeck's Second Division brigade. Buschbeck, however, was temporarily absent with a wound, and Colonel Coster was placed in command of the brigade. Thus four regiments, two from New York and two from Pennsylvania, headed north in the hands of an inexperienced colonel, whose only real action had come a year earlier on the Peninsula as a lieutenant.

GETTYSBURG: Coster's brigade was hurried forward to cover the retreat of the Eleventh Corps in mid-afternoon of July 1. The colonel marched his regiments past Stratton Street and deployed them, minus the 73rd Pennsylvania, which he left behind as a reserve, near a brickyard. The right end of his line, held by the 134th New York, was posted in a wheatfield behind a strong rail fence, while the regiment in his center, the 154th New York, also enjoyed the slight protection of a fence. Coster's left regiment, the 27th Pennsylvania, was situated with a ridge rising ahead of it, and thus could only fire at a right oblique. The advancing Confederates made it impossible for Coster to alter the 27th's position. The brigade knelt down and waited with orders not to fire until the enemy "were close enough to make our volley effective," remembered on soldier.

They were too little and too late to stem the Confederate tide. Within a few minutes Coster line was heavily assaulted and overrun by a pair of fresh Southern brigades from Maj. Gen. Jubal Early's Division. His infantry mounted a brave but short-lived defense, and before long joined other Eleventh Corps men running through Gettysburg back to Cemetery Hill. Coster's retreat signified the end of the Eleventh Corps' organized resistance on the first day of Gettysburg. Of Coster's battle, von Steinwehr wrote in his report: "Colonel Coster had a severe engagement with the advancing enemy, but was, of course, not strong enough to restore the battle."

The exact role played by Coster's brigade on the evening of July 1 is a small mystery, and Coster's battle report, if he wrote one, was not published. After Coster was defeated in the fight at the brickyard, his regiments were placed in the cemetery on Cemetery Hill. The 73rd Pennsylvania, one of Coster's four regiments, was ordered into town (probably by von Steinwehr) to determine whether the enemy was present it strength. They were, and the regiment fell back to the base of the hill.

The bulk of Coster's brigade was assigned to help cover the north and northwest face of Cemetery Hill. At dusk on July 2, the Confederate attack against East Cemetery Hill overran the northeast face and captured part of the crest. Some of Coster's brigade, primarily the 27th Pennsylvania, assisted in the repulse of this attack, as did Col. Samuel Carroll's brigade of the Second Corps and other elements of the Eleventh Corps. Von Steinwehr recognized Coster's contributions to the final victory in his report of the engagement, writing that he had executed his orders with "zeal," and had exposed himself "freely." Coster, according to his division commander, was "able and gallant."

That fall, soon after the Eleventh Corps was transferred to Chattanooga, Coster resigned from the army on November 12, 1863. He was eventually named as provost marshal of New York's 6th District in May of 1864, and was honorably discharged from this responsibility in April of 1865.

For further reading:

Greene, A. Wilson. "From Chancellorsville to Cemetery Hill: O. O. Howard and Eleventh Corps Leadership," in Gary Gallagher, ed., *The First Day at Gettysburg*. Kent, 1992.

Dunkelman, Mark H., and Michael J. Winey. "The Hardtack Regiment in the Brickyard Fight." *Gettysburg Magazine*, #8, 1993.

Hartwig, D. Scott. "The 11th Army Corps on July 1." *Gettysburg Magazine*, #2, 1990.

SECOND BRIGADE
(1,639 MEN)

COLONEL ORLAND SMITH

Colonel Smith was one of many Union officers who enjoyed profitable railroad careers before the Civil War. He was born and raised in Lewiston, Maine, and worked there as a railroad station agent until 1852. That year, Smith transferred to Chillicothe, Ohio, where he remained as an official of the Marietta and Ohio Railroad until he left to begin his wartime service.

Smith enlisted in November 1861 as the lieutenant colonel of the 73rd Ohio regiment. A month later he was promoted to colonel. The regiment was brigaded with other Ohio regiments, marched into West Virginia and did some skirmishing at the Battle of McDowell on May 8, 1862, but reported no casualties. At the Battle of Cross Keys a month later, Smith's regiment was lightly engaged, suffering seven wounded. Still, Smith was included among the several regimental leaders and artillerymen commended in Brig. Gen. Robert Schenk's report after the battle. Placed in Maj. Gen. John Pope's Army of Virginia later that month, the Ohio brigade, now under Col. Nathaniel McLean, fought at the Battle of Second Bull Run, where Smith finally saw heavy fighting. His regiment lost 148 men during the brigade's critical role in stalling the final Confederate attack. Smith was again commended after the battle by the brigade's commander.

The corps was reorganized in the fall of 1862, and Smith's regiment was now part of the Eleventh Corps of the Army of the Potomac. It was assigned to the Washington defenses and not present at the Battles of Antietam or Fredericksburg. Smith was intermittently in command of the brigade during this stretch, but by Chancellorsville in May 1863, he was in command of his 73rd Ohio. At that contest, the brigade was commanded by Brig. Gen. Francis Barlow, and through the good fortune of being attached to Maj. Gen. Daniel Sickles' Third Corps, was the only brigade from Oliver Howard's Eleventh Corps to miss being stampeded by Stonewall Jackson's flank attack. Smith's regiment only lost two men in the entire campaign.

When Barlow was promoted to head the First Division later in May, Smith assumed command of the brigade, into which new regiments were being shuffled. On the eve of Gettysburg, the thirty-eight-year-old railroad man was commanding unfamiliar regiments, and had no experience leading a brigade in battle.

GETTYSBURG: Smith's brigade, at the rear of the Eleventh Corps column, arrived on Cemetery Hill around 2:00 p.m. on July 1 and was placed in reserve there. His brigade consisted of the 33rd Massachusetts, 136th New York and 55th and 73rd Ohio regiments. From the time he arrived on the hill, Smith was carefully attended to by Brig. Gen. Adolph von Steinwehr and Maj. Gen. Oliver Howard, and was not given much of an opportunity to exercise independent thinking at the brigade level. After Colonel Coster's brigade was advanced into town to try to assist Barlow's men, two of Smith's regiments were sent to East Cemetery Hill to support artillery until Coster's return. The 136th New York sat in the cemetery "amid the tombs of the dead awaiting orders," wrote one soldier, and even the "dullest could see that danger was on every side." Thereafter, Smith's brigade was ordered to move down the west slope and deploy along the Taneytown Road facing west, while the right portion of his line took up a position along the Emmitsburg

Road, facing northwest. The 55th Ohio held the right end of the line, with the 73rd Ohio and 136th New York extending the line to the left. The 33rd Massachusetts was dispatched across Cemetery Hill to reinforce another sector and did not fight under Smith for the remainder of the battle. The brigade was well supported by artillery deployed behind and above it.

By the time Maj. Gen. Winfield Hancock reached the field later that afternoon, troops from the Federal First and Eleventh corps were beginning to fall back through town after their disastrous drubbing beyond Gettysburg. The general was relieved to see Smith's well-formed regiments facing the enemy in their new position and ready to fight. Hancock, who rode along the line and complimented the men on their position, asked to see the brigade's commander. "My corps is on the way, but will not be here in time," he informed the inexperienced colonel. "This position should be held at all hazards. Now colonel, can you hold it?" The young officer from Maine answered, "I think I can," and Hancock shot back, "Will you hold it?" This time Smith's answer was more to Hancock's liking: "I will."

Although Smith's men were never directly assaulted during their three days on Cemetery Hill, their position was targeted for a large-scale attack late on the evening of July 2. Robert Rodes' Division was earmarked to coordinate the thrust with General Early's Division, which successfully captured (albeit temporarily) the crest of East Cemetery Hill. Rodes' attack was late and he canceled it at the last moment; only a heavy skirmishing ensued. Smith's regiments, though, were in a most uncomfortable location and were constantly under fire from enemy skirmishers, long-range artillery, and sharpshooters located in the buildings of the town. By battle's end, Smith's brigade had suffered 345 casualties.

That fall Smith took part in the battles around Chattanooga with the balance of the transferred Eleventh Corps, but was reduced to command of his old regiment a few weeks later. He resigned from the army on February 17, 1864, and was brevetted brigadier general for his services at Gettysburg and elsewhere in March 1865.

After the war, Smith was involved in railroading.

For further reading:

Greene, A. Wilson. "From Chancellorsville to Cemetery Hill: O. O. Howard and Eleventh Corps Leadership," in Gary Gallagher, ed., *The First Day at Gettysburg*. Kent, 1992.

Hartwig, D. Scott. "The 11th Army Corps on July 1." *Gettysburg Magazine*, #2, 1990.

Pfanz, Harry W. *Gettysburg: Culp's Hill and Cemetery Hill*. Chapel Hill. 1993.

THIRD DIVISION

(3,109 MEN)

MAJOR GENERAL CARL SCHURZ

General Schurz was one of the by-products of President Lincoln's policy of naming foreign-born political leaders to positions of military leadership. This tactic helped garner legions of immigrant enlistees for the Union cause, but its also often produced unfortunate results on the battlefield.

Schurz was born near Cologne, Germany, the son of a schoolteacher. He was highly educated, studying at the universities in Cologne and Bonn. Using his gift for oratory, Schurz rose to the leadership of the revolutionary liberal movement in Bonn by the age of nineteen. In 1848 he served as a staff officer when the Liberal revolution broke out in Germany. After the defeat of the revolution, he barely escaped execution by the pursuing Prussians, fleeing through a sewer system and making his way to Switzerland. Then, in an exploit of daring and unselfish heroism that remains the revolution's most legendary single incident, he returned to Germany in disguise, rescued his beloved teacher from Spandau prison, and spirited him out of the country.

Schurz migrated to France, then England, and finally came with his wife to America in 1852. He settled in Wisconsin as a farmer in 1855, but soon began a political and oratorical career as an anti-slavery man, showing the same passion he had given to the revolution in Europe. By 1860 he headed the Wisconsin delegation to the Republican National Convention in Chicago. Lincoln thanked him for his support in the 1860 election, writing Schurz that, "to the extent of our limited acquaintance, no man stands nearer my heart than yourself." Shortly thereafter, the German émigré became the United States' Minister to Spain. By January 1862 Schurz was more interested in the conflict raging back in America, and he returned to push the administration to make emancipation a war aim and to seek a general's commission. Lincoln initially refused the latter, but finally relented and made Schurz a brigadier general of volunteers on April 15, 1862. This was a bald political effort to encourage German-American support for the war, but Lincoln's high opinion of Schurz's abilities undoubtedly played a part. Schurz's first field appointment, in June 1862, placed him in the command of an entire division. (He replaced fellow German refugee Brig. Gen. Louis Blenker, who had been unsuccesful in the 1862 Shenandoah Valley Campaign.) The next year, in March 1863, Schurz advanced to the grade of major general, a move that infuriated many senior, and more competent, experienced officers.

No one denied that Schurz took his military duties very seriously, or that his personal courage was beyond question, but his first experience under fire ended in disaster. At Freeman's Ford on the Rappahannock River during the Second Bull Run Campaign, one of his brigades was roughly handled by the enemy during a poorly conceived attempt to capture elements of Maj. Gen. Thomas "Stonewall" Jackson's supply train. A week later, however, Schurz showed some ability at the head of his division in the Battle of Second Bull Run. In his only other combat experience before Gettysburg, Schurz's division became entangled in the rout of the Eleventh Corps at Chancellorsville in May 1863, though Schurz himself had tried to alert Maj. Gen. Oliver Howard to the peril on his corps' flank. He was horrified by the press' criticism that the German troops—and particularly his own division—had fled in confusion and panic and had not fought well, and he took great pains to point out that it was Brig. Gen. Charles Devens' First Division that was driven back in such a manner, not his own.

With his thick spectacles, broad forehead, tousled brown hair and reddish beard, Carl Schurz at thirty-four looked like a college professor. But he had a charming and animated personality, and was quite capable of using oratorical skills to inspire his men. Unfortunately, he overplayed his part, tending to see himself as the spokesman for every German in the Eleventh Corps. After a while, his superiors began to tire at what they considered to be Schurz's overbearing, self-righteous attitude—and his political intrigues. After Chancellorsville, Howard was rightly suspicious that Schurz was using his influence with Lincoln to have German Maj. Gen. Franz Sigel returned to the head of the Eleventh Corps.

Schurz was still in command of his division in the summer of 1863, and by the Battle of Gettysburg, he outranked every division commander in the army except two: Maj. Gens. John Newton and Abner Doubleday. Despite the fact that he was a novice, more a figurehead than a combat soldier, his political influence continued to be enormous, particularly wherever there were large numbers of German-Americans. He had also acquired a certain level of competence on the battlefield during his year of service.

GETTYSBURG: At 10:30 a.m. on July 1, Schurz rode at the head of his division (composed of two brigades led by Brig. Gen. Alexander Schimmelfennig and Col. Wladimir Krzyzanowski) as it marched northward. He received a dispatch from Howard that the First Corps was fighting west of Gettysburg, and due to the fact that Reynolds had been killed, Howard had assumed overall command of the battlefield; Schurz would temporarily lead the Eleventh Corps and rush it to Gettysburg.

Schurz galloped ahead and reached Howard on Cemetery Hill about 11:30 a.m., where Howard explained that the right flank of the First Corps needed protection, and to that end the Eleventh Corps should occupy the high ground near Oak Hill, northwest of town. When Schurz's division (now led by Brig. Gen. Alexander Schimmelfennig) came double-quicking up around 12:30 p.m., Schurz led the sweat-soaked men through the town and toward the imposing eminence of Oak Hill. It did not take Schurz long to realize that Maj. Gen. Robert Rodes' 8,000-man Confederate Division had gotten there first. In order to occupy Oak Hill, Schurz would have to push the veteran infantry off the prominence.

Schimmelfennig's brigade, under the temporary command of Col. George von Amsberg (45th New York), led the way north along the Mummasburg Road toward Oak Hill. As his men began deploying, Schurz received word from General Howard that a large enemy force was approaching from the northeast. Brigadier General Francis Barlow's division came through town at about this time with instructions from Howard to deploy north of Gettysburg. Without consulting with Schurz (who was busy near Oak Hill), Barlow posted his men far in advance on Schimmelfennig's right on Blocher's (Barlow's) Knoll. Barlow's troops were positioned in such a manner that both of his flanks were unprotected.

Before Schurz could do anything to remedy the situation, Maj. Gen. Jubal Early's Division struck Barlow's front and right rear just as Rodes attacked from Oak Hill. Colonel Krzyzanowski's brigade, just before Rodes' attack, had moved at a right oblique across the Carlisle Road toward Barlow's threatened sector, where it deployed and added some stability for a few minutes. Before long, though, Schurz's line crumbled, Barlow's position was overrun, and both Eleventh Corps divisions tumbled back through Gettysburg, losing almost 50% of their men—half of them captured in the retreat through a badly-congested town. It was another humiliating rout for the Eleventh Corps.

The fault, though, had not been Schurz's. He had shown energy and stayed at the front with his men, losing his horse to enemy gunfire. Certainly he was not responsible for Barlow's flawed disposition. Facing heavy enemy numbers from two directions, Schurz had been forced to deploy four small brigades across too wide a front. But the stain that covered the Eleventh Corps covered him as well.

The German general retained his division when the Eleventh Corps was sent to help relieve Chattanooga that fall, but resigned from the army early the next year. He campaigned actively for Lincoln's reelection, and later served as Henry Slocum's chief of staff in the Carolinas.

Schurz resigned in May 1865, returned to penning political tracts, and was active in various campaigns. He served one term in the Senate and was U. S. Grant's interior secretary. He died in 1906. Gettysburg historian Harry Pfanz concluded that Schurz "learned fast and was a diligent soldier." There are more monuments erected to him than any other foreign-born American.

For further reading:

Greene, A. Wilson. "From Chancellorsville to Cemetery Hill: O. O. Howard and Eleventh Corps Leadership," in Gary Gallagher, ed., *The First Day at Gettysburg*. Kent, 1992.

Hartwig, D. Scott. "The 11th Army Corps on July 1." *Gettysburg Magazine*, #2, 1990.

Pfanz, Harry W. *Gettysburg: Culp's Hill and Cemetery Hill*. Chapel Hill. 1993.

Schurz, Carl. *The Reminiscences of Carl Schurz*. 3 Vols. New York, 1907.

———, *Intimate Letters of. . . [ed.* by Joseph Schafer]. Madison, 1928.

Trefousse, Hans J. *Carl Schurz: A Biography*. Knoxville, 1982.

FIRST BRIGADE

(1,683 MEN)

BRIGADIER GENERAL ALEXANDER SCHIMMELFENNIG

Like his division commander at Gettysburg Carl Schurz, thirty-nine-year-old Alexander Schimmelfennig was a refugee German revolutionary. Unlike Schurz, however, Schimmelfennig was a veteran Prussian military engineering officer. He had served in the Schleswig-Holstein War of 1848-50 against his former army and, like Schurz, was forced to flee to Switzerland, then to England. He finally migrated to Washington, D.C., where he became an engineer and draftsman with the War Department in 1853.

When the Civil War broke out, Schimmelfennig volunteered and in September 1861 was made colonel of a Pittsburgh regiment, the 74th Pennsylvania Volunteers. Passing through Philadelphia en route to Washington with his regiment, his horse fell and severely twisted his ankle. While he remained behind for treatment he contracted smallpox and was absent for several weeks. He rejoined the regiment in camp, and made it, according to one observer, "a model regiment in drill and discipline." Active field duty, however, aggravated his ankle and he had to take sick leave for another seven months. He thus missed the 74th's initial engagement at Cross Keys during the Shenandoah Valley Campaign in June 1862.

Schimmelfennig returned to duty when his regiment was assigned to Maj. Gen. John Pope's Army of Virginia in mid-summer of 1862. He was put in command of a brigade during the subsequent Second Bull Run Campaign, after the brigade's previous commander, Brig. Gen. Henry Bohlen, had been killed at Freeman's Ford on August 22—a Union disaster which Schimmelfennig himself had rashly precipitated by an ill-considered dash across the Rappahannock River against a Confederate wagon train. In the climactic Battle of Second Bull Run, Schimmelfennig's men participated in the massive but unsuccessful effort to pry Maj. Gen. Thomas "Stonewall" Jackson's men out of the Railroad Cut position. The brigade lost 158 men in the campaign, and won little glory.

Schimmelfennig's brigade was absorbed into the Army of the Potomac as part of the Eleventh Corps, and he was promoted to brigadier general in November 1862. However, the corps was not present at either Antietam or Fredericksburg, because it was serving on garrison duty in the Washington defenses. In May 1863, in its first chance to show its mettle with the Army of the Potomac, Schimmelfennig's unfortunate brigade was caught up in the rout of the corps at Chancellorsville. The brigade's list of casualties indicates that it deserves more credit for the resistance it displayed than it has been generally given. The proud career soldier was still stinging from this disgrace as he marched with his brigade toward Pennsylvania in June 1863.

GETTYSBURG: Carl Schurz's division, in which Brig. Gen. Schimmelfennig's regiments marched, was nearing Gettysburg on the morning of July 1 when a fateful dispatch from Oliver Howard was received. The First Corps was fighting west of Gettysburg, it commander John Reynolds had been killed, and Howard was in overall command on the field. Reynolds' death meant that Schurz would temporarily lead the Eleventh Corps, and Schimmelfennig inherited control of Schurz's division. Once the division reached the field, however, Schurz oversaw its deploy-

ment, and Schimmelfennig had little chance to exercise his own command.

Schimmelfennig's men double-quicked forward and at about 12:30 p.m., Schurz led the exhausted soldiers through town and toward a prominent wooded hill, which he had been ordered to occupy. Oak Hill, however, already had occupants dressed in gray and brown, and Schurz was left with no choice except to deploy his men short of his objective. With Schimmelfennig's elevation to division command, his own brigade was under the temporary command of the 45th New York's Col. George von Amsberg. In addition to Amsberg's New Yorkers, the brigade was composed of the 82nd Illinois, 157th New York, 61st Ohio, and 74th Pennsylvania regiments. The brigade made its way north along the Mummasburg Road toward Oak Hill, and deployed between that road and the Carlisle Road to the east. The front was too long to cover with a normal battle line, and thus it was deployed in skirmish order. The 45th New York deployed on the left and facing Oak Hill; the 61st Ohio in the center, facing generally north; and the 74th Pennsylvania on the right, facing northeast toward Blocher's Knoll. The two remaining regiments were held in reserve in line of battle, with the 157th deployed with its left on the Mummasburg Road, and the 82nd behind some Ohio artillery pieces in the center of the line. It would prove a weak position with several deficiencies.

As Schurz and Schimmelfennig deployed their men, word was received from Howard that the enemy was approaching from the northeast. Brig. Gen. Francis Barlow's division had come through town at about this time with instructions from Howard to deploy north of Gettysburg. Without Schurz's knowledge, however, Barlow posted his men well in advance of Schimmelfennig's (von Amsberg's) right flank on Blocher's Knoll, between the Carlisle and Harrisburg roads. Barlow was inviting disaster, and his deployment left both of his flanks unprotected. Before either Schurz or Schimmelfennig could do anything to remedy the situation, Maj. Gen. Jubal Early's Confederate Division struck Barlow's front and right rear just as Rodes attacked Schimmelfennig from Oak

Hill. Schimmelfennig's remaining brigade under Colonel Krzyzanowski had earlier moved across the Carlisle Road and deployed behind Barlow and before long Schimmelfennig's front fell apart, Barlow's position was overrun, and both Eleventh Corps divisions retreated through Gettysburg.

After the Eleventh Corps line collapsed under the weight of the Confederate attack in, Schimmelfennig's troops were swept back through the narrow streets of Gettysburg with enemy infantry following hard on their heels. During this panic-filled scenario, Schimmelfennig was knocked with the butt of a musket—"by the blow of a gun"—as he tried to scale a fence. By the time he regained his senses, the Confederates had overrun the town. Schimmelfennig scrambled into a near-by woodshed (some accounts state the building was in fact a pigsty) and huddled there for the balance of the three day battle, fed secretly by a woman who owned the building while the Confederates held the town. When the battle was over and the Union soldiers reentered Gettysburg, Schimmelfennig came out of hiding and was reunited with his men, who rejoiced to see him alive.

Meanwhile, Schimmelfennig's regiments, still under the command of George von Amsberg, re-grouped on Cemetery Hill and were positioned west of the Baltimore Pike in a small orchard about 100 yards north of the cemetery. The five regiments were deployed in the front line behind a small stone wall (this position today is represented by the northwest wall of the Soldier's National Cemetery). Heavy skirmishing occupied the brigade for the remainder of the battle, but its location prevented a direct assault.

Back in brigade command after the battle, Schimmelfennig was transferred to South Carolina with the division, where he contracted dysentery in the fall. Near the end of the war he retired from the army with terminal tuberculosis, and died seeking treatment in 1865.

For further reading:

Greene, A. Wilson. "From Chancellorsville to Cemetery Hill: O. O. Howard and Eleventh Corps Leadership," in Gary Gallagher, ed., *The First Day at Gettysburg*. Kent, 1992.

Hartwig, D. Scott. "The 11th Army Corps on July 1." *Gettysburg Magazine*, #2, 1990.

Staff of CWTI, "General Schimmelfennig's 'Headquarters.'" *Civil War Times Illustrated*, 10, Feb. 1972.

SECOND BRIGADE
(1,420 MEN)

COLONEL
WLADIMIR KRZYZANOWSKI

Colonel Krzyzanowski was a Polish refugee from the Revolution of 1846 who had fled to New York. From the time he arrived in the United States until the outbreak of the Civil War, he made a living as a civil engineer. When the war began, Krzyzanowski, imbued like many recent European immigrants with a fierce desire to show his patriotism for his adopted country, helped organize the 58th New York Volunteer Infantry, a regiment composed primarily of Germans and Poles. He became its colonel when it was mustered in during October 1861.

Assigned to a brigade led by Brig. Gen. Henry Bohlen, Colonel Krzyzanowski and the 58th New York saw their first fighting under the inept leadership of Maj. Gen. John C. Fremont at the Battle of Cross Keys on June 8, 1862. The regiment lost 29 men in this defeat against Thomas J. "Stonewall"

Jackson's men—the highest casualties of any regiment in Bohlen's brigade. General Bohlen recognized in his report the "gallantry" displayed by Krzyzanowski's regiment, but did not spill a drop of ink in praise any of his regimental commanders. When scattered Union forces were organized into Maj. Gen. John Pope's Army of Virginia later that month, Krzyzanowski received his own brigade of three regiments in Maj. Gen. Franz Sigel's Corps. He led his new brigade in the Battle of Second Bull Run, where his regiments doggedly slugged it out again with Jackson's Confederates in heavy fighting that cost Krzyzanowski 372 casualties.

Pope's army was dissolved after the battle, and Sigel's entire corps was reassigned to the Army of the Potomac and designated the Eleventh Corps. Assigned to the defense of the capital, it missed the battles of Antietam and Fredericksburg. Krzyzanowski was appointed brigadier general in November 1862, but the Senate failed to confirm the appointment. (Fellow refugee Maj. Gen. Carl Schurz joked that it was because no one in Congress could pronounce his name—an attempt at humor that must have fallen flat with the Pole, who was known in the army simply as "Kriz.")

At Chancellorsville in May 1863, Krzyzanowski's regiments had the unfortunate luck of being deployed on the army's far right flank, where they traded numerous volleys with Jackson's onrushing corps before being swept back in the contagion of defeat. Krzyzanowski's extensive casualties, together with eyewitness testimony, proved they had fought as well as anyone could have given the horrendous circumstances they faced. As far as the rest of the army was concerned, however, the foreigners were poor fighters and their rout insured the Union defeat; thus much of the reason for the loss was laid at their doorstep.

Unfair as this might have been, it was under this cloud of shame that Krzyzanowski and his men labored as they marched toward Gettysburg in the summer of 1863.

GETTYSBURG: Krzyzanowski's brigade was second in the Third Division's column (under Carl Schurz) as it neared Gettysburg in the early afternoon of July 1. By this time the First Corps had been engaged in heavy fighting west of Gettysburg, its commander John Reynolds had been killed, and Eleventh Corps commander Oliver Howard was in overall command on the battlefield. This meant Schurz was now temporarily in command of the Eleventh Corps, and Colonel Krzyzanowski's brigade was in a division headed by Brig. Gen. Alexander Schimmelfennig. Matters would soon become even more confused.

Colonel Krzyzanowski's brigade moved forward quickly and at about 1:00 p.m., passed through the town and was ordered by Schimmelfennig to deploy in support of Dilger's artillery battery, which was then engaged with Confederate guns from a position between the Mummasburg and Carlisle roads. The Pole formed his brigade in double column of companies in an orchard northeast of Pennsylvania College. His mixed-state regiments were deployed, from left to right, as follows: 82nd Ohio, 75th Pennsylvania, 119th New York, and 26th Wisconsin (two companies from his 58th New York were also present). The mass of men made a wonderful target, and a several were killed and wounded. As Gettysburg historian D. Scott Hartwig has aptly noted, even though the brigade lost only a few men from the long-range fire, "the effect of artillery is also psychological. Its purpose is to inflict damage but also to break down the will to combat in the enemy."

As Krzyzanowski was deploying his men, Brig. Gen. Francis Barlow's division passed through the town and behind Krzyzanowski's brigade. Without Schurz's knowledge or approval, Barlow marched his brigades well in advance of the Third Division's right flank and onto Blocher's Knoll, a wooded piece of high ground between the Carlisle and Harrisburg roads. When Schurz realized the potential magnitude of the disaster Barlow was inviting—his deployment left both of his flanks unprotected—he send Krzyzanowski's brigade to assist him. The colonel's regiments, aligned in columns for ease of maneuver, were just crossing the Carlisle Road when Maj. Gen. Jubal Early's Confederate Division struck Barlow's front and right rear—just as Rodes was attacking Schimmelfennig's men from Oak Hill. Barlow's front disintegrated within a few minutes. Artillery fire also pounded Krzyzanowski's men. An officer with the 82nd Ohio recalled that "their shells plunged through our solid squares, making terrible havoc." The Polish officer's men continued on, tearing down fences in their attempt to succor Barlow. Forming into a battle line, Krzyzanowski's men gamely began a stand-up musketry fight with George Doles' Confederate brigade. Krzyzanowski's horse was shot under him, and he fell so heavily to the ground that he had trouble breathing. Acting corps commander Carl Schurz urged him to leave the field, but Krzyzanowski refused and stayed with his men. Within a short time his line was overlapped on both ends and, together with most of the Eleventh Corps, was driven back toward Gettysburg with heavy losses. Organized fighting for Krzyzanowski's brigade was over for the rest of July 1.

Krzyzanowski reformed his depleted and bloodied regiments on Cemetery Hill, where Schurz organized his division into two lines. Schimmelfennig's regiments were deployed in the front line behind a small stone wall (this position today is represented by the northwest wall of the Soldier's National Cemetery), and Krzyzanowski's men were positioned behind him in a supporting line. Heavy skirmishing occupied the brigade for the remainder of the battle, but its location near the town prevented a direct assault against them.

At dusk on July 2, General Schurz was near Krzyzanowski and two of his regiments, the 58th and 199th New York, when the Southern brigades of Brig. Gen. Harry Hays and Col. Isaac Avery broke through the Eleventh Corps lines on the northeast face of Cemetery Hill. Schurz dispatched the Polish colonel and his pair of regiments into the fight. Krzyzanowski advanced his men with the 119th in the front line and the 58th behind it, bayonets fixed. The New Yorkers crashed into the Louisiana Tigers with a "vigorous rush" and pushed them down the hill. When they neared the bottom, Krzyzanowski's men went prone to allow the artillery above them to fire canister over their heads at the retreating enemy. Other units also assisting in recovering the hill, including Col. Samuel Carroll's

Second Corps brigade, and the Confederate threat evaporated with heavy loss.

The capable Colonel Krzyzanowski fought with his brigade at Chattanooga in the fall of 1863, but lost his command when the Eleventh and Twelfth corps were consolidated into the Twentieth Corps. He spent the rest of the war in charge of the supply base at Bridgeport, Alabama, and guarding the railroads in that vicinity. Krzyzanowski was brevetted to brigadier general on March 2, 1865. After the war, Krzyzanowski was given a number of minor government appointments, then served as a special Treasury agent at the New York customs house until his death in 1887.

For further reading:

Greene, A. Wilson. "From Chancellorsville to Cemetery Hill: O. O. Howard and Eleventh Corps Leadership," in Gary Gallagher, ed., The First Day at Gettysburg. Kent, 1992.

Hartwig, D. Scott. "The 11th Army Corps on July 1." Gettysburg Magazine, #2, 1990.

Pula, James. For Liberty and Justice: The Life and Times of Wladimir Krzyzanowski. Chicago, 1978

———. The Sigel Regiment: A History of the 26th Wisconsin Volunteer Infantry, 1862-1865. Savas Publishing, 1998.

TWELFTH CORPS
(9,788 MEN / 20 GUNS)

MAJOR GENERAL HENRY WARNER SLOCUM

Henry Slocum was thirty-six, young for a major general. Yet at Gettysburg, he was the ranking general on the field—senior even to army commander Maj. Gen. George Meade. Physically, he was "small and rather spare," wrote Lt. Frank Haskell, "with black straight hair, and beard, which latter is unshaven and thin, large full, quick black eyes, white skin, sharp nose, wide cheek bones, and hollow cheeks and small chin. His movements are quick and angular—and he dresses with a sufficient degree of elegance." Slocum's manner "inspired faith and confidence" said one soldier, while another noted that his sparkling brown eyes gave him a "magnetic power over his troops." He had risen far on these charismatic qualities in the first two years of the war.

Those qualities, however, masked a usually careful and even cautious nature. Self-contained and unemotional, a man who loved discipline and order, Slocum could be agonizingly attentive to detail and protocol. He personified the Old Army way of command, and rarely if ever exceeded his orders. Slocum prided himself on avoiding friction, and sometimes accomplished this by avoiding responsibility. This style of leadership had an up side: the men serving under him never lost a stand of colors or a gun throughout the entire war. Also, once he committed himself to battle, Slocum was one of the army's hardest and toughest fighters.

Ability and activity had marked his whole life. Slocum was born in a small town in upstate New York's Onondaga County, near Syracuse. He went to West Point, were he was a superior student, graduating 7th out of 43 in the Class of 1852 (an achievement made more impressive by the fact that he roomed with Phil Sheridan, who took a full five years to graduate). Commissioned in the artillery, he saw duty against the Seminoles and at Fort Moultrie, South Carolina. Garrison life proved tiresome, so in his off-hours he occupied his restless mind by studying law. In 1857 he left the army and set up a law practice in Syracuse, where he became county treasurer and state legislator while he served as a colonel of artillery in the militia. Shortly after Fort Sumter's fall, he re-entered military service as colonel of the 27th New York Volunteers.

At First Bull Run he was severely wounded in the thigh while leading his regiment. Slocum was promoted to brigadier general during his recuperation, and when the Army of the Potomac was reorganized in October 1861, Slocum was given a brigade. In May 1862, when the Sixth Corps was formed, he was put at the head of its First Division, which he led with distinction in the maelstrom of Gaines' Mill. On July 4, 1862, Slocum was promoted to major general, the second youngest officer in the country to attain that rank.

At South Mountain in September, Slocum drew further notice when he and his officers overrode their indecisive corps commander, Maj. Gen. William B. Franklin, and assault a Rebel line sheltered behind a stone wall at Crampton's Gap. The attack routed the enemy and captured four battle flags. Heroes were few in the Army of the Potomac in 1862, and Slocum's success helped propel him to the head of Twelfth Corps in October. He replaced Maj. Gen. Joseph Mansfield, who had been killed at Antietam while Slocum's division languished in reserve. Thus, in one of the most meteoric rises of any man in the history of the war, Slocum had gone—in the space of about one year—from the head of a regiment to corps command. His ascent must have been inspired in good part by Slocum's intelligence, obvious ability, and vigorous personal qualities, because his only experience in a major battle had been at Gaines' Mill during the Seven Days' Battles.

The Twelfth Corps arrived too late for the carnage of Fredericksburg, so its first battle under Slocum came the following May at Chancellorsville. In fact, in the early stages of that campaign, Slocum was in charge of the three corps that constituted the maneuver element of the army, about 46,000 men. Slocum's force flawlessly executed a flank march and slipped around and behind the Army of Northern Virginia, but commanding Maj. Gen. Joe Hooker halted it at Chancellorsville. The Fifth Corps' Maj. Gen. George Meade advised Slocum to advance into the advantageous open ground beyond the Chancellorsville crossroads. Meade's suggested movement exceeded Hooker's orders, however, and this Slocum would not do. In the battle that ensued, Slocum's Twelfth Corps fought hard and well, losing nearly 3,000 casualties, about 21% of his men.

Slocum was highly critical of Hooker's timidity at Chancellorsville, an opinion that coincided with those in power in Washington. When the decision was made to change the leadership of the Army of the Potomac during the Gettysburg Campaign, it is noteworthy that Slocum, the army's senior

major general, was not seriously considered for the position. Although he had done nothing to cast doubt on his military abilities, by the same turn, little seemed to mark him for higher responsibility. The army command went to Meade, and Slocum graciously consented to serve under him.

Slocum was an able, if not exceptional, corps commander. He had been in command of his corps for eight months—longer than anyone except Maj. Gen. John Sedgwick of the Sixth Corps.

GETTYSBURG: Slocum's occasional habit of avoiding tough assignments resulted in an unfortunate incident on the first day of fighting at Gettysburg. The senior commander on the field, Maj. Gen. Oliver Howard, sent a dispatch to Slocum to come forward with the Twelfth Corps to reinforce the outnumbered Unionists on the field. Slocum spent the entire afternoon vacillating, neither bringing forward his corps nor going ahead himself to take command by virtue of his rank. Evidently he judged that Meade's directives for the occupation of the Pipe Creek line were being subverted by this affair near Gettysburg, which seemed to be going very badly. Heads were likely to roll, and he was taking care that his would not be among them. The messenger who brought Howard's request recorded that he thought Slocum's "conduct on this occasion was anything but honorable, soldierly or patriotic." Officers like Maj. Gens. Winfield Hancock, John Reynolds, or even Daniel Sickles, would have marched to the sound of the guns under those circumstances, but Henry Slocum did not. His dilatory nature eventually earned him the nickname "Slow Come."

Slocum finally put his corps in motion late in the afternoon. He reached the field about 6:00 p.m., when he detached Brig. Gen. John Geary's division to guard the army's left on Little Round Top, and sent Brig. Gen. Alpheus Williams' division to the army's right around Wolf's Hill. Slocum then rode to Cemetery Hill and relieved generals Howard and Hancock, asserting that, in Meade's absence, he was the commander of the army. Meade, in turn, relieved Slocum when he arrived around midnight.

On the morning of July 2, both Twelfth Corps divisions (Geary's and Williams') were summoned and posted on Culp's Hill. Geary's division occupied the main or upper hill (on the left next to Brig. Gen. James Wadsworth's division), while Williams' division took up a line on the right on lower Culp's Hill extending down toward's Rock Creek. Slocum contributed to the army's strategy when he advised against an attack Meade was considering from Culp's Hill (Slocum thought the terrain too rugged for offensive movement.)

But all was not well with the Twelfth Corps. In accordance with a strategy document called the "Pipe Creek Circular," Meade had earlier planned to fight a defensive battle along Pipe Creek in northern Maryland. In accordance with his seniority, Meade had given Slocum command of the "Right Wing" of the army—the Fifth and Twelfth Corps—and he would lead the two to the new line as "developed by circum stances." As historian Harry Pfanz points out, "The command structure of the Twelfth Corps at Gettysburg was an awkward thing, justifiable for a brief time, perhaps, but beyond that a mischief-making incongruity." Its awkwardness stemmed from the fact that Slocum considered himself a "wing commander" for the rest of the battle, and thus he designated Brig. Gen. Alpheus Williams as the temporary commander of the Twelfth Corps, while he continued in his expanded, if irrelevant, role. Williams' "elevation" meant that brigade commander Thomas Ruger led Williams' division, and Col. Silas Colgrove led Ruger's brigade.

Late that afternoon, Lt. Gen. James Longstreet's First Corps struck hard against the opposite end of the Union left near the Round Tops, and Meade summoned assistance from the Twelfth Corps. The evidence is conflicting as to exactly what Slocum's orders were in this regard. It is probable that Meade ordered Slocum to support the crumbling left flank with as much of his corps as possible, and preferably all of it. Alpheus Williams (who was acting as "tem-porary" corps leader in Slocum's stead) advised Slocum that one of the divisions should be left on Culp's Hill. Slocum initially ordered the First Division away to the left; eventually, perhaps at Meade's prompting, the entire Twelfth Corps, less George Greene's brigade, made the march off Culp's Hill—a poor decision, as it turned out. Neither division had any impact on battle for the army's left flank.

Soon after both Twelfth Corps divisions left for the endangered left, Maj. Gen. Edward Johnson's Confederate division charged up Culp's Hill and crashed into Brig. Gen. George Greene's New Yorkers, the lone Union brigade remaining on the hill. Although unable to budge Greene from the crest (General Howard dispatched some seven regiments to assist Greene), Johnson's Southerners were able to capture a large portion of the recently abandoned Union breastworks. Slocum knew nothing of this. He was attending a meeting at Meade's headquarters from shortly before 9:00 p.m. to about midnight (where he contributed his best epigram of the war when he advised characteristically: "Stay and fight it out!"). When he learned of the situation, his response was another laconic gem: "Well, drive them out at daylight." He also made sure the Twelfth Corps divisions dispatched to the left were ordered back to Culp's Hill for the job.

Slocum's divisions moved back to the army's right that evening and after careful planning and arduous preparation during the night, the Twelfth Corps opened the fighting on July 3 with a fifteen minute artillery barrage at daylight. Johnson's Confederates responded with large-scale attacks against Geary's division that were beaten back. For more than seven hours Slocum's troops fought off enemy assaults along the line and delivered localized counterattacks. Shortly before noon the Confederates had enough and withdrew from the hillside. After the danger to Culp's Hill passed, Slocum's job at Gettysburg was done. The action that afternoon passed to the army's center for the final drama—Pickett's Charge.

Meade's report of the battle unintentionally slighted the Twelfth Corps' contribution, and Gettysburg did not enhance Slocum's solid reputation. He was fortunate, however, to have avoided the recriminations that would have befallen him if the First and Eleventh Corps had not held on to Cemetery Hill on July 1 or if General Greene had not held firm on the evening of July 2.

Sent to the west with his corps in September, Slocum continued in positions of high responsibility for the rest of the Civil War, and eventually rose to command of the Army of Georgia under Maj. Gen. William T. Sherman on the March to the Sea and the Carolinas Campaign.

Slocum resigned his commission in September 1865 and returned to the practice of law and politics (running as a Democrat when that affiliation was political suicide). He served three terms in Congress, and died in 1894.

___

For further reading:

Greene, A. Wilson. "Henry W. Slocum and the Twelfth Corps." in Gary Gallagher, ed. *The Second Day at Gettysburg*. Kent. 1992.

Hilton, Thomas E., ed., "To the Memory of Henry Slocum: A Eulogy by Oliver O. Howard." *Civil War imes Illustrated*, vol. 21, March, 1982.

Pfanz, Harry W. *Gettysburg: Culp's Hill and Cemetery Hill*. Chapel Hill. 1993.

Slocum, Charles E. *The Life and Services of Major General Henry Warner Slocum*. Toledo, 1913.

___

FIRST DIVISION

(5,256 MEN)

BRIGADIER GENERAL ALPHEUS STARKEY WILLIAMS

Alpheus Williams had been at his post longer than had any other high-ranking officer in the Army of the Potomac. He had been given command of his division when the Army of the Potomac was first orga-

nized into corps on March 13, 1862. In the fifteen months between that date and Gettysburg, he had commanded his division—and frequently his corps—on several battlefields.

Williams had a curly beard, with a spectacular expanse of hair on his upper lip that flared out on either side of his face. He wore his hair fairly long, curling around his ears. His men called him "Old Pap," not because he was particularly ancient—he was only fifty-three—but because they loved him and the way he would ride about with an unlighted cigar stub gripped in his teeth. Indeed, they probably loved him for some of the same reasons they loved their first army commander, Maj. Gen. George McClellan: Williams good care of his men, and was genuinely anguished when they did not receive the overcoats, shoes, blankets, and tents he had requested. Williams was also overly cautious, consistently reckoning enemy strength at about twice his own, even when the reverse was true; he denounced the public when it asked for bold action, and always thought more time was necessary to prepare. Furthermore, Old Pap often seemed satisfied merely to avoid defeat, and he was averse to bringing the hardships of war to the enemy populace, taking pride in the fact that his softheartedness won him renown among Southern noncombatants as a benevolent Yankee general. Although a hard fighter in battle, he had a soft soul, writing at one point, "Indeed, I feel that all that is needed is kindness and gentleness to make all these people return to Union love."

Williams was born in the village of Deep River, Connecticut. His parents died while he was young and left him with $75,000, a fortune in those days. He graduated from Yale in 1831 with a degree in law, and spent the next few years traveling extensively in the U.S. and Europe before settling in Detroit in 1836, where he married the daughter of one of Detroit's leading citizens. He joined the Brady Guards Militia Company, and from that time forward assumed an increasingly prominent role in the military activities of the city. Over the next decade and a half Williams also served as a judge, bank president, the owner of a newspaper, and as the city's postmaster. When the war with Mexico began, Williams was appointed lieutenant of the Michigan regiment in 1847, but it arrived too late to see action.

His social prominence and military experience prompted the state of Michigan to seek his assistance in training the Badger State's first volunteers for the Civil War. After commanding Michigan's camp of instruction at Fort Wayne, he left state service and became a brigadier general of U.S. volunteers in August 1861. He advanced to lead a division in Maj. Gen. Nathaniel Banks' corps in March 1862, and experienced repeated defeats against Maj. Gen. Thomas J. "Stonewall" Jackson's army in the Shenandoah Valley that spring. Perhaps awed by his opponent's strategic dexterity, Williams' wrote at this time that he believed "a successful retreat [was] often more meritorious than a decided victory."

Incorporated into Maj. Gen. John Pope's Army of Virginia in the summer of 1862, Williams' division fought at Cedar Mountain, where Jackson engaged and defeated Banks' isolated corps. Williams and his men did not reach the scene of Pope's embarrassment at Second Bull Run until the battle had ended. Once Pope's dispirited army was disbanded and incorporated into the Army of the Potomac, Williams became the commander of the newly-minted Twelfth Corps' First Division. At Antietam, the Twelfth Corps saw heavy fighting on the northern portion of the field, and Williams took over command of the corps when Maj. Gen. Joseph Mansfield fell with a mortal wound. In October, Maj. Gen. Henry Slocum received permanent command of the corps, and Williams went back to his division. The Twelfth Corps was en route to join the rest of the army and missed the Battle of Fredericksburg that December. At the Battle of Chancellorsville in May 1863, Williams' division was almost continuously in the thick of the fighting, losing 1,500 casualties while rebuffing numerous enemy attacks near the Chancellor house.

By the late spring of 1863, Williams was beginning to grumble about his lack of advancement. He had watched for months while other less experienced brigadiers gained promotions to major general. Since early in the war he had complained about favoritism enjoyed by West Point graduates (Williams had a hearty contempt for the merits of a military education). "Every such promotion over me," he complained, "as Carl Schurz and twenty others in the last list, is an insult." Part of the problem was Williams' failure to sing his own praises; for example, he refused to solicit the favor of reporters, a common custom in the army.

In a letter written during the early stages of the Gettysburg Campaign to his daughter, Williams was clearly demoralized by Chancellorsville and the army's disheartening string of defeats of the past year. While his letters show that he was openly pessimistic on the eve of the critical battle, General Williams' determination to do his best was never impaired. He had more battle experience than did any other division commander of the army, and he had led his division for about 15 months—the longest tenure of command at the head of the same unit than any other general in the Army of the Potomac. Yet, he seemed trapped in his role as the army's forgotten general.

GETTYSBURG: Riding at the head of his division of two brigades, Alpheus Williams neared the battlefield on the Baltimore Pike, after a hot and difficult march, about

5:00 p.m. on July 1. He received an order from General Slocum to occupy Benner's Hill east of Gettysburg, and so turned his division north off the pike and marched to that point. He was also notified that he was the temporary Twelfth Corps commander since Slocum believed he was now the commander of the army's "right wing." When Williams reached Benner's Hill, one of Slocum's staffers met him there and informed him of the defeat of the First and Eleventh corps. Since it seemed likely the advancing enemy would cut off his division, he was to return to the Baltimore Pike. Retracing their steps, Williams and his men withdrew and slept east of Wolf's Hill that night. Williams was uneasy that night since, as the corps' acting commander, he knew nothing of the whereabouts of John Geary's division. When told it was posted at the opposite end of the field near the Round Tops, Williams "slept most splendidly until daylight."

Williams rose early on July 2 and received orders from Slocum to dispatch his First Division (now under Thomas Ruger) to the Hanover Road area east of Gettysburg. The First division (composed of the three brigades led by Archibald McDougall, Henry Lockwood, and Silas Colgrove—the latter having assumed Ruger's command), deployed facing north and lightly engaged the Stonewall Brigade, after which George Sykes' Fifth Corps arrived from the east and deployed on Ruger's right flank. When it was decided by Meade that the army would not launch an offensive from that flank, Slocum ordered Williams to withdraw the division and deploy it on Culp's Hill on the right of John Geary's division— the army's extreme right flank. Williams aligned McDougall's brigade on the south slope of the lower hill behind and above Geary's right flank; Colgrove's brigade on McDougall's right, stretching east to near Rock Creek; and Lockwood's small brigade behind Colgrove, bent back south toward the Baltimore Pike. Brig. Gen. Henry Lockwood's brigade had marched from the Baltimore defenses and had only just been attached to the First Division, Twelfth Corps. All was quiet on Williams' front.

Late that afternoon, James Longstreet's First Corps launched a large assault and hammered the Union left near the Round Tops, rolling it back for some distance. Although the evidence is conflicting, it is probable that Meade ordered Slocum to support the crumbling left flank with as much of his corps as possible, and preferably all of it. Williams (who was still acting as "temporary" corps leader within Slocum's awkward and dangerous command structure) counseled caution and advised Slocum that a full division should be left on Culp's Hill. Thus Slocum initially ordered the First Division away to the left; eventually, perhaps at Meade's prompting, the entire Twelfth Corps, less "Old Pop" Greene's brigade, made the march off Culp's Hill. Williams, who oversaw the march, believed Geary had been left on Culp's Hill. By the time the First Division arrived on southern Cemetery Ridge, the fighting had almost ended. Williams deployed his brigades near the west end of Trostle's (or perhaps Weikert's) Woods, but only Lockwood's engaged the retreating enemy before the fighting concluded. Meanwhile, the other Twelfth Corps division under John Geary blundered off the battlefield and did not contribute anything to the defense of the Union left.

With his division on its way back to the army's right flank, Williams (by virtue of his "corps" level status) attended the famous generals' meeting held at Meade's headquarters from 9:00 p.m. to past midnight. After it was decided the army would remain and fight at Gettysburg, Williams rode to Culp's Hill, where he discovered to his dismay that the Confederates had attacked just after the Twelfth Corps had withdrawn and now occupied large segments of the abandoned Federal line.

Williams labored all night to orchestrate an artillery barrage and morning assault to dislodge the Confederates clinging to Culp's Hill. With Geary's division back on Culp's Hill, he deployed the First Division on the right, with Lockwood's men in reserve behind Greene's brigade. Although it took the entire morning of July 3, from daybreak to about 11:00 a.m., during which Williams' front was under heavy pressure from Johnson's attacking Confederates, Williams finally managed to drive the enemy from their foothold on the hill and regain his original line.

Williams had performed extremely well at Gettysburg. His defense and counterattack on the battle's final morning was his most notable achievement. "In my judgment," wrote one of his staff officers later, "General Williams was one of the finest military commanders in the eastern army, and had he been fairly treated would have found his proper place at the head of it. He had all the attributes of manhood, was brave as a lion, was thoroughly versed in all the arts of war, and had a genius that inspired him where other men failed in a pressing emergency."

Williams spent the balance of the war in the Western Theater, where he rendered valuable service, eventually at the head of a corps. After the war, Williams' wonderfully insightful letters home to his daughter were published in book form and made widely available; it is often found described as one of the 100 best books on the Civil War. He never made major general.

For further reading:

Foster, Greg. "Alpheus Williams—'Old Pap.'" *Civil War*, 10, July/August, 1992.

Greene, A. Wilson. "Henry W. Slocum and the Twelfth Corps." in Gary Gallagher, ed. *The Second Day at Gettysburg*. Kent. 1992.

Pfanz, Harry W. *Gettysburg: Culp's Hill and Cemetery Hill.* Chapel Hill. 1993.

Quaife, Milo M. *From the Cannon's Mouth: The Civil War Letters of General Alpheus S. Williams.* Detroit, 1959.

FIRST BRIGADE

(1,835 MEN)

COLONEL
ARCHIBALD L. MCDOUGALL

Archibald McDougall was a distinguished, handsome figure with a bald dome, silver sideburns, and neatly trimmed beard. He was forty-six at Gettysburg, old for a colonel. Not a career soldier, he had entered the Civil War in mid-summer 1862, when he organized and became colonel of the 123rd New York regiment, upstaters from a county bordering Vermont. The regiment joined the First Division, Twelfth Corps of the Army of the Potomac on September 30, 1862, as the army was licking its wounds after the Battle of Antietam.

It wasn't until May 1863, at Chancellorsville, that McDougall and his regiment saw the enemy in combat. When Thomas "Stonewall" Jackson's Corps bore down on the Twelfth Corps after routing the Eleventh, enemy shell fragments and minie balls began to zip through McDougall's regiment for the first time. The colonel jumped onto a log and waved his sword and yelled, "For God's sake, boys, stand your ground! Don't let it be said the boys of Washington County ran!" That day and the next, the regiment stayed in the middle of the heavy fighting, suffering 148 casualties.

The terms of enlistment of many of the veteran regiments in Brig. Gen. Alpheus Williams' division expired after Chancellorsville. The first two brigades of the division were consolidated, and McDougall's 123rd New York became part of the First Brigade. When Lee's Army of Northern Virginia headed north, McDougall's brigade commander, Brig. Gen. Joseph Knipe, was assigned to take charge of a Pennsylvania militia brigade, in order to bolster the confidence of the Keystone State's nervous residents. That move made McDougall, who was the brigade's senior colonel, the new leader of the newly-consolidated brigade.

As he approached the battlefield, Colonel McDougall certainly reflected on his curious situation. He had no pre-war military education or experience, was the veteran of only one battle, and was new to the intricacies of leadership at the brigade level.

GETTYSBURG: McDougall's brigade (composed of the 5th and 20th Connecticut, 3rd Maryland, 123rd and 145th New York, and 46th Pennsylvania regiments), participated in all the peregrinations of Williams' division on July 1 and 2 without directly engaging the enemy. His troops wore out their shoe leather tramping twice from the Baltimore Pike north to the Hanover Road and back; then into position on Culp's Hill (in two lines on the right of John Geary's division); then to the Union left near Weikert's Woods when Lt. Gen. James Longstreet's attack threatened that flank; then back to Culp's Hill, which in their absence had been occupied by General Edward Johnson's Rebels.

Late on the night of July 2, Williams' First Division, including McDougall's brigade, moved back toward Culp's Hill with an eye toward regaining its lost field works. McDougall crossed the Baltimore Pike and moved toward the woods on the south slope of the lower hill, forming his men in a double line of battle in the open fields to the south. Two companies went forward a skirmishers. It was quickly discovered that the woods were held in force

by Confederates, and a brisk skirmish fire ensued. McDougall's men spent the night in line of battle on the high ground between McAllister's Woods and the Lightner buildings near the pike. Colonel Colgrove's (Ruger's) brigade formed northeast of McDougall above Rock Creek in McAllister's Woods.

The battle for Culp's Hill began at daybreak and continued for seven hours until just before noon, when the Confederates were finally pushed from its slopes. McDougall's brigade was not heavily engaged, although the 20th Connecticut played a key role by moving forward early in the morning west of Spangler's Spring, where it engaged the 10th Virginia and prevented the enemy from turning Geary's right flank. During the entire engagement, McDougall's brigade suffered only 80 casualties.

The novice officer performed competently in his new responsibilities at Gettysburg, but General Knipe returned to lead the brigade in late July, and McDougall went back to his regiment. He never commanded a brigade again. In May of 1864, he was wounded in the leg during the Atlanta Campaign at the Battle of New Hope Church and died shortly thereafter.

For further reading:

Greene, A. Wilson. "Henry W. Slocum and the Twelfth Corps." in Gary Gallagher, ed. *The Second Day at Gettysburg*. Kent. 1992.

Pfanz, Harry W. *Gettysburg: Culp's Hill and Cemetery Hill*. Chapel Hill. 1993.

Quaife, Milo M. *From the Cannon's Mouth: The Civil War Letters of General Alpheus S. Williams*. Detroit, 1959.

SECOND
(INDEPENDENT) BRIGADE
(1,818 MEN)

BRIGADIER GENERAL
HENRY HAYES LOCKWOOD

Delaware native Henry Lockwood was a West Point graduate, ranking 22 out of 49 in the Class of 1836. A year after his graduation, after campaigning against the Seminoles as an artillery lieutenant, he resigned and went into farming. The Naval Academy at Annapolis soon hired him as a mathematics professor, and when war was declared on Mexico in 1846, he shipped out on the *USS United States* and served in the navy off the California coast. He returned to his classroom after the Mexican War, where he taught until the outbreak of the Civil War.

Only weeks after the fall of Fort Sumter Lockwood was commissioned colonel of the 1st Delaware Volunteers, and at the end of the war's first summer was promoted to brigadier general. His entire career until late June 1863 was spent overseeing and commanding the peaceful military district that encompassed the Eastern Shore of Maryland and occupied Virginia. Lockwood did not see any action during this period.

The Army of Northern Virginia's advance into Pennsylvania in late June 1863 interrupted Lockwood's idyllic assignment. He was ordered to report with his men to the Twelfth Corps, and Lockwood stripped two regiments from the defenses of Baltimore and southern Maryland and marched them into Pennsylvania. A third regiment would arrive to bolster his brigade at Gettysburg in the early morning hours of July 3.

Lockwood's regiments were easy to pick out—their uniforms were near new, their knapsacks were over-packed, and their rosters were huge, having never been depleted by enemy bullets or active campaigning. Although Lockwood and his men had never experienced fighting, they were well disciplined and excited about the prospects of a battle. Lockwood was a capable career military man, but his obvious liability was his lack of combat experience.

GETTYSBURG: When Col. Lockwood marched his brigade (composed of the 1st Maryland Potomac Home Brigade and the 150th New York—the 1st Maryland, Eastern Shore, arrived July 3) onto Culp's Hill to take his place in Brig. Gen. Alpheus Williams' division on the morning of July 2. By virtue of his early-war promotion to brigadier general, Lockwood found himself the army's senior brigadier—a fact that caused no little consternation within the Twelfth Corps. With Williams as an acting corps commander, Lockwood—by virtue of his rank would displace Brig. Gen. Thomas Ruger, the extremely able and seasoned veteran who was acting as commander of the First Division. Williams, who wrote that Lockwood appeared to be a "pleasant gentleman," contrived to solve the problem by telling Lockwood to regard his command as an "unattached brigade pending the existing operations." By this expediency Williams observed military protocol, gave no offense to Lockwood, and kept Ruger as the division's ranking brigadier.

Late that afternoon Williams' division, with Lockwood's fresh brigade in the lead, marched off Culp's Hill to reinforce the

Union left, where a Confederate attack launched by James Longstreet's First Corps threatened to roll up the Union line. The brigade marched by way of Granite Schoolhouse Lane. His large regiments—the 1st Maryland Potomac counted 674 bayonets and the New Yorkers had about 609—marched four abreast and were soon throwing away their bedrolls and packs to lighten their loads. The division as a whole arrived too late to do any serious fighting, but Lockwood's men were the first on the scene on the south end of Cemetery Ridge. Williams ordered Lockwood to advance and "occupy the woods" in his front.

Without taking the time to deploy his first regiment, the 1st Maryland Potomac Home Brigade, into line, Lockwood sent it into the west end of Trostle's Woods, followed at a distance by the 150th New York. George Willard's Federals were attacking the enemy on Lockwood's right. The Rebels had mostly retired from the area, but for Lockwood and his rookie men it was warfare at once horrible and exciting. They surged ahead through woods and to the Trostle Farm and beyond in the fading light, "amid the most terrific firing of shells and musketry," according to Lockwood, who can be forgiven the exaggeration due to his dearth of battle experience. They recovered three of Bigelow's field pieces previously overrun by the enemy. The New Yorkers, following behind, did not fire a shot during the advance. After they had rushed nearly as far as the Peach Orchard, Lockwood was recalled and the entire First Division was ordered to return to Culp's Hill, where its men were chagrined to find the enemy occupying the breastworks they had left earlier in the day. Williams made preparations to drive the Confederates off the hill, and Lockwood's units were initially deployed along the Baltimore Pike northwest of the Lightner buildings.

Williams opened the battle near dawn with an artillery barrage, and then proceeded to beat back a number of Confederate assaults against Culp's Hill. Lockwood's largest regiment, the 1st Maryland Potomac Home Brigade, was ordered to advance early that morning into the woods

and meadow in its front to near Spangler's Spring and lost about 80 men before falling back, unsupported in its effort. Thereafter, Lockwood's regiments (all three were now on the field), were moved north to upper Culp's Hill and placed at General John Geary's disposal. The regiments replaced some of Geary's regiments in the front-line breastworks and skirmished, sometimes heavily, with the enemy there. Lockwood's total losses were 174 men.

While it appears Lockwood turned in an able performance, his superiors gave his regiments only grudging praise and labeled his service as "efficient." Thereafter, Lockwood served in the backwater of the war pretty much as he had before his experience with the Army of the Potomac. He commanded a department in Maryland for a time, and some provisional troops called out to oppose Jubal Early's Valley Raid in 1864. He again returned to his classroom after the war and in 1870 was assigned to the Naval Observatory in Washington. He retired in 1876, and died in 1899.

For further reading:

Greene, A. Wilson. "Henry W. Slocum and the Twelfth Corps." in Gary Gallagher, ed. *The Second Day at Gettysburg*. Kent. 1992.

Pfanz, Harry W. *Gettysburg: Culp's Hill and Cemetery Hill*. Chapel Hill. 1993.

Quaife, Milo M. *From the Cannon's Mouth: The Civil War Letters of General Alpheus S. Williams*. Detroit, 1959.

THIRD BRIGADE

(1,598 MEN)

BRIGADIER GENERAL
THOMAS HOWARD RUGER

(COLONEL SILAS COLGROVE)

Thomas Ruger was a young career soldier, extremely able and intelligent. The son of an Episcopal minister, he was born in New York and moved to Wisconsin at the age of thirteen. He graduated 3rd out of 46 cadets in the West Point Class of 1854, just

ahead of Oliver Howard, the future leader of the Eleventh Corps. Ruger served for less than a year with the engineers before he resigned and returned to Wisconsin to study and practice law.

When Fort Sumter was bombarded, Ruger returned to the army and by September was colonel of the 3rd Wisconsin Volunteers. The following spring, he and his regiment saw their first action under political general Maj. Gen. Nathaniel Banks at Winchester in the Shenandoah Valley Campaign. After that battle, Ruger was singled out by his brigade commander, Col. George Gordon, for the "steadiness and perfect discipline" with which he handled his men. Ruger and the 3rd Wisconsin fought again at Cedar Mountain on August 9, where Gordon noted the Wisconsin troops exhibited "commendable coolness." Ruger had his troops had seen heavy combat in both battles, and the regiment lost about a hundred men in each engagement. Ruger's men, with the bulk of Banks' corps, did not see action at Second Bull Run.

In September, Banks' corps reorganized as the Twelfth Corps of the Army of the Potomac and saw action at the Battle of Antietam. There, Ruger took command of his brigade when Gordon had to temporarily lead the division, and he suffered a slight wound in the head. When he recovered, he briefly took charge of the First Brigade of the division in October, and in November

was promoted to brigadier general. The following February in 1863, Gordon was transferred away from the army and Ruger permanently took his place at the head of the Third Brigade. At Chancellorsville, Ruger and his brigade heroically engaged in a gory slugfest on May 3. At one point, surrounded on three sides by the enemy, Ruger and his brigade helped drive back three Confederate charges before pulling out; suffering a horrendous 614 casualties in the process.

By the summer of 1863, after gritty fighting in the Shenandoah and at Cedar Mountain, Antietam, and especially Chancellorsville, Ruger and his brigade were some of the finest, most battle-tested veterans in the army. The Wisconsin general was a favorite of his division commander, Brig. Gen. Alpheus Williams, who described Ruger as "modest as a girl but of most thorough and sterling character." This modesty prevented Ruger from getting the attention he deserved in an army of full of less capable but more self-seeking officers.

GETTYSBURG: After following the orders of Twelfth Corps commander Maj. Gen. Henry Slocum and twice countermarching his brigade on the east side of Rock Creek during the evening of July 1 and morning of July 2, Ruger finally crossed the watercourse and took up a position on Culp's Hill shortly before noon. Before long, Williams appointed Ruger to lead the First Division while he acted in Slocum's stead at the head of the Twelfth Corps. This command shuffle took place because Slocum was under the (mistaken) impression he was commanding the "right wing" of the army (fifth and Twelfth corps). Ruger essentially remained as the acting division commander throughout the battle.

The afternoon of July 2 passed quietly while Ruger's division (composed of the brigades of McDougall, the "unattached" Lockwood, and his own brigade under Colgrove) completed defensive earthworks to strengthen its lines on Culp's Hill. When Lt. Gen. James Longstreet's assault hit the Union left near the Round Tops, Williams led Ruger's men off Culp's Hill toward the action on the opposite end of the line. They marched along the Granite Schoolhouse Lane and then south on the Taneytown Road until they reached the southern end of Cemetery Ridge. Although the action was winding down, Lockwood's brigade entered the action by charging into the Trostle Woods and beyond; the balance of Ruger's division was not engaged there. Soon, Slocum ordered the return of the division to Culp's Hill, and Ruger marched his men back again in the moonlight. As they approached their earlier position, Ruger had the foresight to order a skirmish line forward to probe the darkness; the action discovered Rebels had captured the earthworks in their absence.

Williams and Ruger spent all night arranging their men to defend the hills and drive off the enemy, and placed fieldpieces on nearby hills to "shell hell out of them" in the morning. Ruger's (Colgrove's) brigade formed on the division's right flank in McAllister's Woods near Rock Creek in a tight U-shaped line, with the 2nd Massachusetts on the left, the 13th New Jersey in the center, the 27th Indiana on the right, and the 3rd Wisconsin in reserve. Colonel McDougall's regiments took up a position between Colgrove and the Baltimore Pike, while Lockwood's large rookie brigade aligned itself along the pike northwest of McDougall's position. On the morning of July 3, the artillery barrage began at daylight, with the most vigorous action taking place against Geary's division just to the north on upper Culp's Hill. The most unfortunate incident of the fight occurred in Ruger's division, however, when his old brigade under Col. Silas Colgrove's leadership misunderstood Ruger's order for a reconnaissance-in-force. Colgrove was to cross the Spangler meadow in his front and if the enemy was "not in too great a force," he was to "advance two regiments, and dislodge him from the breastworks."

Colonel Colgrove was forty-seven on July 3, 1863, a native of New York domiciled in Indiana. Like many officers, he was a lawyer and had been active in local politics. He had worked himself up through the ranks and was a "feisty" officer and a solid

veteran. Although he had his doubts about the order, he moved forward the 2nd Massachusetts (whose commander thought the directive little short of "murder") and 27th Indiana. The regiments advanced separately and were defeated that way, one by one. The Bay Staters moved out first on the left, several minutes in advance of the 27th Indiana and to northwest. The regiment passed just east of Spangler's Spring, where it was beaten back by General William Smith's Virginians, who occupied a strong position on the other side of the meadow. As the Massachusetts men withdrew to their left, the Indianians advanced in line and made it about half-way across the field before they, too, were thrown back with heavy loss.

After seven hours of fighting, the Confederates were thrown off Culp's Hill for good. With the recapture of Culp's Hill, Ruger's service at the Battle of Gettysburg—and Colgrove's as well—was largely over. Ruger had performed with seamless competence in his increased responsibilities.

Transferred to the Western Theater with the rest of the corps in September, Ruger retained command of his brigade when the Eleventh and Twelfth Corps were consolidated the next year. He was promoted to the command of a division in November 1864, and ended the war in North Carolina (the officer who led his brigade at Gettysburg, Silas Colgrove, was brevetted brigadier general in August 1864 for his distinguished war record and died in 1907.)

Maj. Gen. Oliver Howard described Ruger as "deliberative, cautious, and yet fearless; persistent, and if unfairly pressed, obstinate to the last degree."

For further reading:

Greene, A. Wilson. "Henry W. Slocum and the Twelfth Corps." in Gary Gallagher, ed. *The Second Day at Gettysburg*. Kent. 1992.

Pfanz, Harry W. *Gettysburg: Culp's Hill and Cemetery Hill*. Chapel Hill. 1993.

Quaife, Milo M. *From the Cannon's Mouth: The Civil War Letters of General Alpheus S. Williams*. Detroit, 1959.

SECOND DIVISION

(3,964 MEN)

BRIGADIER GENERAL JOHN WHITE GEARY

John Geary had experienced a lifetime of leadership before he ever set foot on a Civil War battlefield. Forty-four years old, he certainly had the perfect physique for a leader. He was a huge man, six feet six inches tall, well over two hundred pounds and solidly built (his large size helped make him an easy target: by Gettysburg he had already been wounded nine times). One of his men described him as "a man of large stature, fine black eyes, very robust physique, and when mounted upon his horse was a figure of commanding presence. He was a strict disciplinarian, withal a warm-hearted, emotional man, and although some of the men feared him, they all respected him." Geary had a violent temper which, together with his size, made a terrific impression on many in the army who learned to give him a wide berth.

Geary was born in the Allegheny Mountains near Pittsburgh, Pennsylvania. He was attending Jefferson College when his father died, leaving him the head of the family and responsible for his father's debts. He left school and worked odd jobs, then went to Kentucky as a surveyor. He speculated in land there and made enough money to return to college in Pennsylvania to study civil engineering. He worked as an engineer constructing the Allegheny Portage Railroad. Geary had been active in the militia from the age of sixteen, and led a Pennsylvania regiment during the Mexican War in the assault on the fortress at Chapultapec, where he was wounded five times. After this exploit, he was named the regiment's colonel and returned home a war hero.

Following the Mexican War, Geary traveled west and was appointed postmaster of San Francisco, an appointment he lost when the presidential administration changed in 1849. He remained in that quickly-growing California town and became its first mayor in 1850. His wife's ailing health, however, required him to vacate the officer after about one year and go back to Pennsylvania. After her death, President Franklin Pierce offered Geary the governorship of the Utah Territory, but he refused the appointment. In 1856 Geary, an anti-slavery man, accepted the governorship of the Kansas Territory. The new governor was unable to stop the bloodshed in "Bleeding Kansas," and remained in this strife-torn post less than a year before returning to Pennsylvania.

A wealthy man by the time of the Civil War, Geary left his farm to raise the 28th Pennsylvania Volunteer Infantry Regiment and "Knap's Artillery Battery" in June 1861. Patrolling the Potomac near Harpers Ferry in March 1862 with his regiment, he was wounded below the knee by a piece of shell and captured. Geary was exchanged and promoted to brigadier general on April 25 and given command of a brigade in Maj. Gen. Nathaniel P. Banks' corps. He served with Banks in the Shenandoah Valley Campaign of 1862 against Maj. Gen. Thomas "Stonewall" Jackson. His brigade was incorporated into Maj. Gen. John Pope's Army of Virginia in late June. While fighting with his men at Cedar Mountain on August 9, Geary was again seriously wounded. "A ball struck me in the ankle, and almost at the same instant a ball passed through my left arm," he wrote. Returning to duty in October with his arm in a bandage, he rose to command his division, replacing Maj. Gen. Christopher Auger, who had also been wounded at Cedar Mountain. Banks' old corps had been absorbed into the Army of the Potomac as the Twelfth Corps, and was now under the leadership of Maj. Gen. Henry Slocum.

Although the Twelfth Corps missed the army's next engagement at Fredericksburg in December 1862, Geary's division— known as the "White Star" division—was heavily engaged at Chancellorsville the following May in 1863. When General Winfield Hancock was ordered to form with his division around Chancellor House, an angry Geary called to Hancock's troops to cover his retreat, yelling "Charge, you cowards, charge!" Two of Hancock's men were so insulted they lowered their bayonets in Geary's direction until an adjutant stepped in. He came within a hair's breadth of suffering a fatal wound in the battle when a cannonball just missed his head, knocking him unconscious. When he came to, Geary could speak no louder than a whisper for several weeks.

The general, as attested by his numerous wounds and veteran status, was a fearless man. According to Maj. Gen. Oliver Howard, Geary "reconnoitered without regard to personal safety," and he demanded similar bravery from those around him. By the summer of 1863, Geary had been in command of his division for the better part of a year, long enough to know it inside and out.

GETTYSBURG: The entire corps marched north from Frederick, Maryland, on June 29 and reached Littlestown, Pennsylvania, about 2:00 p.m. the following day. By 9:00 a.m. on July 1, Geary's division, bringing up the rear of the corps, was on the march via the Baltimore Pike to Gettysburg, ten miles distant. It arrived there a little after 5:00 p.m., just after the end of the day's fighting. Second Corps commander Maj. Gen. Winfield Hancock placed Brig. Gen. Thomas Kane's brigade behind Cemetery Hill as a reserve and escorted the other two brigades (those of Charles Candy and George Greene) to the army's left,

where Geary's men slept on and around Little Round Top. His aggressive skirmishers pushed as far west as the Emmitsburg Road.

At daylight the next morning, July 2, Geary's men were awakened and countermarched to the Baltimore Pike, then to Culp's Hill—the army's far right—where they went into line on the crest of the hill facing northeast. Brig. Gen. "Old Pop" Greene's brigade of New Yorkers was aligned on the most important part of the eminence, on the south slope from near the peak to the saddle between the upper and lower hill. Brig. Gen. Thomas Kane's brigade (under the command of Col. George Cobham) was deployed on Greene's right, while Col. Charles Candy's men were held in reserve behind Greene. James Wadsworth's battered First Corps division was dug in on Greene's left flank. Geary acceded to Greene's suggestion to construct defensive earthworks to strengthen the line, even though Geary thought that fighting behind barricades dissipated the men's fighting spirit.

Geary men could hear the rumble of heavy fighting from the army's left late that afternoon. About three hours later, at 7:00 p.m., a staff officer rode up to Geary and ordered him leave Greene's brigade on Culp's Hill and follow Brig. Gen. Alpheus Williams' First Division, which was just pulling out. Unfortunately, the instructions didn't say where Williams was going and that division was soon out of sight. Geary's men, with Candy in the lead, turned south on the Baltimore Pike. Geary had last seen William's men moving in that direction, so he headed down the pike past Maj. Gen. Henry Slocum's "Right Wing" headquarters on Power's Hill and didn't stop, even when he reached Rock Creek, wandering with his two brigades completely off the battlefield.

His march in the darkness carried him beyond the small road Williams' division had used to reach the Union left. As one modern historian has written, "As far as the Battle of Gettysburg is concerned, Geary's two brigades had stepped off the map." It was, wrote one of his men, "a singular blunder." In his defense, Geary later wrote that he "received no specific instructions as to the object of the move, the direction to be taken, or the point to be reached, beyond the order to move by the right flank and to follow the First Division."

By a mistaken order he deployed his men there, in the dark, miles from where he was wanted. He remained completely out of touch until 9:00 p.m. that night. His reputation was saved by the fact that he ultimately was not needed at his intended destination on the Union left. Why he failed to dispatch a courier to Slocum, or seek out more specific instructions when it became obvious he had lost touch with Williams' column, is a mystery. The Union right flank, though, was weakened and vulnerable to attack.

Slocum eventually located Geary and ordered him back to Culp's Hill. His men marched back up the pike and were within a couple hundred yards of their old lines when an enemy volley met them. By midnight it was obvious the Confederates had made a strong lodgement on Culp's Hill and were holding some of their old lines. General Williams, the acting corps commander in place of General Slocum, intended to seal off the breach and drive them off the hill the following morning; much of the night was spent preparing to accomplish the task. It took until past 1:00 a.m. for Geary's two brigades to file into carefully improvised lines, with Kane's (Cobham's) brigade taking up a position on Greene's right flank, and Candy's regiments extending the line back toward the Baltimore Pike.

An artillery barrage opened the battle before dawn on July 3 and Edward Johnson's Confederate Division opened the infantry action with a series of heavy attacks up the hill. Geary's infantry bore the brunt of the Twelfth Corps' successful effort to beat back the Confederates and regain control of Culp's Hill, which was accomplished after seven hours of fighting, by about 11:00 a.m.

Geary's career suffered no obvious ill effects from his single-handedly subtracting a division from the army's strength during its moment of peril on July 2. Perhaps this was so because the snafu was caused by bad staff work and Slocum's awkward "Right Wing" chain of command structure. Geary continued to command his division for the rest of the war, largely in the Western Theater, where he did well.

A lifelong Democrat, Geary retired from the army and was elected governor of Pennsylvania on the Republican ticket. In 1873, eighteen days after the end of his second term, he died suddenly.

For further reading:

Beers, Paul. "General John W. Geary: A Profile." *Civil War Times Illustrated*, 9, June 1970.

Geary, John W. *A Politician Goes to War: The Civil War Letters of . . .* University Park, 1995.

Greene, A. Wilson. "Henry W. Slocum and the Twelfth Corps." in Gary Gallagher, ed. *The Second Day at Gettysburg*. Kent. 1992.

Hilton, Thomas F., ed., "To the Memory of Henry Slocum: A Eulogy by Oliver O. Howard." *Civil War Times Illustrated*, 21, March, 1982.

Pfanz, Harry W. *Gettysburg: Culp's Hill and Cemetery Hill*. Chapel Hill. 1993.

Tinkom, Harry Marlin. *John White Geary, Soldier-Statesman*. Philadelphia, 1940.

FIRST BRIGADE

(1,798 MEN)

COLONEL
CHARLES CANDY

Kentuckian Charles Candy was an Old Army private. He had enlisted in the 1st Dragoons when he was nineteen and served a five-year hitch in this mounted branch of the service, then served another five years with the 1st Infantry until January 1861. He had been out of the military service for merely three months when Fort Sumter fell.

Due to his experience, Candy entered the volunteer army in September 1861 at the rank of captain and was placed in staff positions in western Virginia. He served during the Union defeat at Ball's Bluff in

October and by December, was commissioned colonel and given command of the newly organized 66th Ohio regiment.

Candy and the 66th Ohio were put in an Ohio brigade in Brig. Gen. James Shields' division and "saw the elephant" in a losing effort during the Shenandoah Valley Campaign's engagement at Port Republic. The Buckeyes were in the thick of the fight and lost 205 men. After that battle, Candy was mentioned in the list of regimental commanders commended by brigade leader Brig. Gen. Erastus Tyler. At Cedar Mountain on August 9, Candy ascended to the command of the brigade when its new leader, Brig. Gen. John Geary, went down with two wounds.

The brigade was not engaged at Second Bull Run, Candy was absent during the Battle of Antietam, and the corps was not present for the Battle of Fredericksburg in December. As a result, Candy's first chance to lead his brigade into action came at Chancellorsville in May 1863. There, he got more than he bargained for—Confederate infantrymen were positioned on his flanks and across the front of his brigade on May 3, and they directed an intense hail of lead at Candy's men. Forced to abandon their position, Candy's Ohioans suffered a terrific 523 casualties.

Although Candy had been leading the same brigade for almost eleven months—a long time in the Army of the Potomac—he had not received a brigadier general's commission by the summer of 1863. This may have due in part to his having served as a private in the Regular Army, a position that allowed him to cultivate few friends in high places.

GETTYSBURG: Candy's mixed brigade of Ohioans and Pennsylvanians arrived by the Baltimore Pike after 5:00 p.m. on July 1 with the rest of Geary's division, and was shuffled to the opposite end of the Union line that evening, going into bivouac near Little Round Top.

It was moved early on the morning of July 2 to Culp's Hill and took up a position behind George Greene's brigade, which was deployed on the south slope of upper Culp's Hill. The sound of the battle raging on the army's left, where James Longstreet's attack was pounding its way onto Little Round Top and southern Cemetery Ridge, was plainly heard by all of Geary's division. About 7:00 p.m., Candy's men were pulled off the hill with Kane's brigade and directed to march after Alpheus Williams' First Division, which was headed to reinforce the embattled flank. Greene was left in place. Geary mistakenly led Candy and Kane too far south on the Baltimore Pike and over Rock Creek, where Candy deployed his brigade in line of battle in the darkness. Both units were unavailable to the army until after 9:00 p.m., when one of Henry Slocum's staff officers located Geary and ordered the men back to Culp's Hill.

When they approached their old positions on Culp's Hill, Candy found that Maj. Gen. Edward Johnson's Division had made a lodgement on the hillside and had captured some of their recently-abandoned works. Williams, as temporary commander of the Twelfth Corps, together with General Geary, planned to attack the next morning, seal the breakthrough, and drive the Confederates back off the hillside. It took considerable time to position the men for the endeavor. Kane's brigade filed into position on the right of George Greene's brigade, while Candy aligned his men in two segments: four regiments—the 28th Pennsylvania, and 7th, 29th and 66th Ohio—were held behind Greene's right rear, and two others—the 147th Pennsylvania and 5th Ohio, were deployed facing east and angled back toward the Baltimore Pike, fronting what would soon be called Pardee Field.

The 66th Ohio was the first of his regiments called to succor Greene's men, and it marched over the hill and took up a position on his far left flank in a way to enfilade attacking Confederates. In the battle for Culp's Hill that ensued just before daybreak on July 3 and lasted some seven hours, Candy's men were used mostly to relieve regiments in Greene's hard-pressed brigade line. They fought well and the Confederates were pushed off the hill by 11:00 that morning in fighting which killed and wounded 130 men in Candy's brigade.

Candy performed ably in a limited role at Gettysburg. He must have had the confidence of Geary, because he kept his position when the Eleventh and Twelfth Corps were consolidated the next year, and commanded his brigade through the rest of the war. Despite his erstwhile service, however, Candy never obtained the appropriate rank of brigadier general.

For further reading:

Greene, A. Wilson. "Henry W. Slocum and the Twelfth Corps." in Gary Gallagher, ed. *The Second Day at Gettysburg.* Kent. 1992.

Pfanz, Harry W. *Gettysburg: Culp's Hill and Cemetery Hill.* Chapel Hill. 1993.

O'Brien, Kevin E. "'A Perfect Roar of Musketry': Candy's Brigade in the Fight for Culp's Hill." *Gettysburg Magazine,* #9, July 1993.

SECOND BRIGADE

(700 MEN)

BRIGADIER GENERAL
THOMAS LEIPER KANE

(COL. GEORGE A. COBHAM, JR.)

Thomas Kane was described by First Division commander Brig. Gen. Alpheus Williams as being small, precise, and full of "pluck and will." Kane's forty-one years

had been filled with one improbable episode after another. Born into a wealthy Philadelphia family, he was educated in the United States and Paris. Although he studied law under his father, who was a Federal judge, he was averse to actual practice, preferring instead to shuttle between a variety of appointed offices. Kane's trans-Atlantic education had made him a dedicated abolitionist. When the Fugitive Slave Act was passed in 1850, he resigned his post as a U.S. commissioner rather than help reinforce this edict that demanded Federal officials help return escaped slaves to their owners. His father considered Kane's position on this issue an insult to the law and threw him into jail for contempt of court. Kane the younger was freed by an order of the United States Supreme Court, whereupon he assisted in helping slaves escape on the legendary Underground Railroad.

Though not a Mormon himself, Kane was a friend of Brigham Young and associated himself with the Mormons during the 1850s. During the Mormon Expedition of 1858, Kane helped prevent a shooting war between the Mormon settlers and the U. S. Army. Returning east, he founded the town of Kane in the wooded hills of northwestern Pennsylvania shortly before the Civil War.

In the weeks following Fort Sumter, Kane recruited soldiers in the towns and hamlets of backwoods Pennsylvania, putting up placards announcing that he was authorized to accept for service "any man who will bring in with him to my headquarters a Rifle which he knows how to use." He recruited mainly the woodsmen and lumberman of the area, men who were used to hunting for subsistence, who could survive in a forest, and who had the strength of mind and body that came from a life of rugged work. After successfully filling his ranks with these coarse denizens of the forest, Kane drilled them while carrying a delicate umbrella for a sunshade.

During the regiment's formative period, one of Kane's recruits ornamented his hat with the tail from a deer's carcass that was hanging in a butcher shop. The other men liked this sartorial appendage, and thus was born the regiment's distinctive headgear and famous nickname: the "Pennsylvania Bucktails." The Bucktails built four large log rafts and floated down the Susquehanna River to Harrisburg, where they were mustered in. Once the regiment was assembled, Kane stepped down to second in command in order to let an officer with military experience command the regiment.

Kane was a visionary. He taught the Bucktails what would become known as "skirmisher tactics"—to scatter under fire, to make use of whatever cover the ground offered, to press continually forward along advantageous ground, and fire only when they could see their target. In complete contradiction of the military thinking of the day, Kane stressed individual responsibility in his soldiers. He held target practice, which was also an innovative idea at the time. He stressed long-range firing, and developed his men into fine sharpshooters.

The Bucktails were assigned to the "Pennsylvania Reserve" Division, Fifth Corps and carved out a very successful early-war career. When the regiment's first colonel resigned to enter Congress, Kane took over and developed quickly into an excellent officer. In his first action at Dranesville, Virginia, on December 20, 1861, an enemy round wounded Kane in the right side of his face, knocking out some teeth and producing long-term difficulty with his vision.

He rejoined the Bucktails in time for the frustration of the Shenandoah Valley Campaign in the spring of 1862, where he was wounded a second time in June near Harrisonburg, Virginia, by a bullet that split the bone below his right knee. Faint from shock and loss of blood, he was left on the field. When he tried to rise after the fighting was over, an enemy soldier broke Kane's breastbone with a savage blow from the butt of his rifle. The unconscious officer was captured.

Exchanged in August 1862, Kane returned to the Bucktails for the Second Bull Run Campaign, although he was so weak that another officer had to lead the regiment. He was promoted to brigadier general in September and put at the head of a Twelfth Corps brigade in the First Division in October, though at first he had to be helped onto his horse and could not walk without crutches. (His Harrisonburg wound continued to reopen for two years.) The brigade was mustered out in March 1863 and never saw action under Kane's command.

Kane was reassigned to a new brigade in March 1863, and led it in the Battle of Chancellorsville in May. His command was spared the terrible losses of the other two brigades of the division, but still suffered 139 casualties in the fighting on May 3. While crossing the Rapidan River in the early stages of the Chancellorsville Campaign, Kane's horse stumbled and toppled him into the water. Still weak from his prior wounds, Kane developed pleurisy. A few days after the battle his condition worsened into pneumonia and he was forced to leave the army.

When he heard about the impending showdown in Pennsylvania at the end of June, however, he rose from his sickbed in Philadelphia and, after a hard journey by railroad and buggy—and avoiding capture by Maj. Gen. "Jeb" Stuart's cavalry by disguising himself in citizen's dress—he arrived on the battlefield at 6:00 a.m. on the morning of July 2.

GETTYSBURG: Kane found his brigade, under the command of its senior colonel, George A. Cobham, Jr., in reserve behind

Cemetery Hill. Although he attempted to resume command of his regiments, he again turned the brigade over to Cobham "being too much prostrated to continue it." For the rest of that day and the next, active command went back and forth between Kane and Cobham, depending on how well Kane was feeling. Cobham—a native of England who had seen limited combat duty at Chancellorsville with the 111th Pennsylvania—seems to have actively led the brigade during most of the strenuous fighting on Culp's Hill. Kane was among the best of the civilian brigadiers, but his abilities were negated by his pneumonia at Gettysburg.

Later on July 2, Kane's brigade was assigned to Culp's Hill, and spent the afternoon building breastworks on the right flank of George Greene's New York brigade. The sound of the battle raging on the army's left between Dan Sickles' Federal Third Corps and James Longstreet's First Corps was plainly heard by Kane's Bucktails. About 7:00 p.m., his men were pulled off the hill with Charles Candy's brigade in the lead and marched after Alpheus Williams' First Division, which was headed to reinforce the embattled flank. Greene was left in place. General Geary mistakenly led Kane and Candy too far south on the Baltimore Pike and over Rock Creek, where Candy deployed his brigade in line of battle in the darkness. Both units were unavailable to the army until after 9:00 p.m., when one of Maj. Gen. Henry Slocum's staff officers located Geary and ordered the men back to Culp's Hill.

When they approached their old positions on Culp's Hill, Kane's men found that Maj. Gen. Edward Johnson's Division had made a lodgement on the hillside and had captured some of their recently-abandoned works. Williams, as temporary commander of the Twelfth Corps, together with General Geary, planned to attack the next morning, seal off the breach, and push back the Confederates. It took considerable time to position the men for the endeavor. Kane's brigade—which consisted of the 29th, 109th, and 11th Pennsylvania infantry—filed carefully into a position (facing south-

east) on the right flank of Brig. Gen. George Greene's brigade, which had maintained its line on the crest of the hill. The battle for Culp's Hill began with an artillery barrage just before daybreak on July 3 and lasted seven hours. Although Greene's line was hard-pressed, there was less stress placed against Kane's narrower and deeper front. The Pennsylvanians met the attack with "an unswerving line of deadly fire," wrote a member of the 109th, "a smothering fire of bullets" exclaimed another Bucktail. At one point Colonel Cobham, forgetting his was a brigade-level officer, borrowed a rifle from a soldier and shot a Confederate hiding in a rock pile through the head. Kane's–Cobham's Pennsylvanians fought well, and the Confederates were pushed off the hill by 11:00 that morning in fighting that killed and wounded 98 men of the brigade.

General Kane, however, was a broken man and he never recovered his health. His festering facial wound, lingering chest problems, and impaired vision forced him to return to Philadelphia soon after Gettysburg. He resigned from the army four months later in November 1863. Kane returned to Pennsylvania and was the first president of the State Board of Charities, a railroad president, and author. He died in Philadelphia in 1883.

For further reading:

Greene, A. Wilson. "Henry W. Slocum and the Twelfth Corps." in Gary Gallagher, ed. *The Second Day at Gettysburg*. Kent. 1992.

Imhof, John D. "Two Roads to Gettysburg: Thomas Leiper Kane and the 13th Pennsylvania Reserves." *Gettysburg Magazine*, #9, July, 1993.

Pfanz, Harry W. *Gettysburg: Culp's Hill and Cemetery Hill*. Chapel Hill. 1993.

Thomson, O. R. Howard, & William Rauch. *History of the Bucktails*. Dayton, 1988.

THIRD BRIGADE

(1,424 MEN)

BRIGADIER GENERAL
GEORGE SEARS GREENE

"Old Man Greene," his soldiers called him, or sometimes, "Old Pop"—at sixty-two, George Green was the oldest general in the army, though he was far from doddering or ineffectual. He was a hardy war-horse, a man who spent most of his time in the saddle, an officer who insisted on hard drilling and discipline in camp and hard fighting on the battlefield. Harsh in his manner, Greene was not a man who won immediate affection; but those under his command soon learned to appreciate his ability. He was a colorful figure, with a full head of silver hair, a huge mustache, a large grizzled spade-like beard, and an easy-going style of dress that made him look more like a farmer than the Old Army regular he was.

To the New Yorkers of his brigade, most of who were under twenty-one, the old man seemed an ancient out of the Revolution or the War of 1812. In fact (though he was a relative of Revolutionary War hero Nathaniel Greene), he was a native of Warwick, Rhode Island, the son of a shipowner who was financially ruined by the War of

1812. It had been intended that young George would enter Brown University, Rhode Island's famous institution of higher learning, but his father's sudden plunge into poverty made this impossible. Instead Greene went to work in New York City. He received an appointment to West Point, and graduated 2nd in his class of 35 cadets in 1823, six years before Robert E. Lee. He was posted to the artillery and for thirteen year interspersed teaching engineering at the Academy with dull garrison duty in New England. Restless, he left the army to enter civil engineering, and for the next quarter century built railroads and designed municipal sewage and water systems for Washington, Detroit, and several other cities. The Central Park reservoir in New York City was his handiwork, along with the enlarged High Bridge over the Harlem River.

Greene didn't re-enter the army immediately following Fort Sumter, as did most West Pointers. He waited until January 1862, quitting work on the Croton Reservoir in Central Park to take command of the 60th New York Volunteers, men from New York State's "North Country" along the St. Lawrence River. In April 1862 he was promoted to brigadier general and in May was given command of his brigade. His first duty was in the Shenandoah Valley Campaign, but Greene and his men did not fight there. His first action was at Cedar Mountain in August 1862, where he succeeded to the command of the division after Brig. Gen. Christopher Augur was wounded and Augur's first replacement, Brig. Gen. Henry Prince, was captured. Both Auger and Army of Virginia leader Maj. Gen. John Pope praised him after the battle.

Greene led the division through the August battle at Second Bull Run, where it was only lightly engaged. At Antietam in September, he pushed his brigades forward in what would be the strongest penetration of the enemy left flank to occur on that bloody autumn day. He was not properly supported in his exposed position, however, and was forced to retreat after hard fighting and heavy casualties. In October, command of the division was transferred to

Brig. Gen. John Geary, who had returned to the army after being wounded at Cedar Mountain. Geary outranked Greene, (Geary's appointment to brigadier general pre-dated Greene's by three days), and "Old Man Greene" went back to leading his brigade, which was reorganized in April 1863 so as to be composed entirely of New York regiments. At Chancellorsville, Greene again assumed division command in the middle of heavy fighting after Geary was knocked unconscious by a near hit from a cannonball. Greene's brigade of New Yorkers, meanwhile, fought well, but assaulted from two directions, lost a terrific 528 men before falling back.

By the summer of 1863, "Old Pop" Greene was a seasoned veteran with enough battle experience at or above brigade level to allow his superiors to feel comfortable in his abilities. He had been in command of his brigade for more than a year, since the Shenandoah Campaign.

GETTYSBURG: Greene and his New Yorkers arrived with the rest of Geary's division by the Baltimore Pike shortly after 5:00 in the afternoon of July 1. He was directed to the army's left, and his men bivouacked that evening on or near Little Round Top. His brigade was moved to Culp's Hill the next morning, where Greene's substantial engineering skills proved invaluable to the army when he convinced Geary to permit the men to construct defensive field works to strengthen their positions along the crest. As a result, his men dug in near the crest on upper Culp's Hill to the right of a battered First Corps division led by James Wadsworth. Greene's line faced almost due east. His New York regiments were aligned, from left to right, as follows: 78th, 60th, 102nd, 149th, and 137th. With Thomas Kane's Bucktail's on his own right and Charles Candy's regiments in reserve, Greene felt reasonably confident about the strength of his position.

The sound of the battle began about 4:00 p.m., when the Confederates struck the left flank of the Union army, and was plainly heard by Greene's men on Culp's Hill. About 7:00 p.m., Greene's men watched with something approaching dismay as the other two brigades of the Second Division were pulled off the hill and marched after Brig. Gen. Alpheus Williams' First Division, which was headed to reinforce the embattled flank. Worried about his exposed flanks, Greene extended his right flank by placing the 137th New York on the top of the lower portion of Culp's Hill, almost perpendicular to his main front. It was an incredible blunder by higher-ups: Greene's brigade was left alone to defend Culp's Hill.

His preparations proved crucial when he was attacked in the growing darkness by Maj. Gen. Edward Johnson's Division across his entire front. Confederates from Maryland Steuart's Brigade took over a line of recently abandoned trenches on the lower hill and turned and enfiladed the 137th New York, which was driven back some distance up the hill. Greene's men, sheltered behind their breastworks, were able to hang on to most of their embattled line against a hillside full of surging Confederates. His tenacious defense saved Culp's Hill—the key to the army's right—and turned back a serious threat to the entire Union position at Gettysburg. Twelfth Corps commander Maj. Gen. Henry Slocum attributed "the failure of the enemy to gain possession of our works . . . entirely to the skill of General Greene and the heroic valor of his troops."

When the rest of Geary's division returned after dark that night, they found the enemy in possession of much of their lines, and thus filed into new positions adjacent to the right of Greene's weary defenders, extending the line to near the Baltimore Pike. At daybreak, around 4:00 a.m. on July 3, the fighting for the hill resumed, with Greene's men still on the crest where the bullets flew the thickest. Johnson's Confederates launched another series of attacks and again Greene's New Yorkers, with assistance from Candy's Ohioans and Pennsylvanians, grimly held on to the wooded and rocky crest. By 11:00 that morning, Johnson's battered Confederates brigades had been pushed out of the lines they had captured the night before and off the hill, and the Union army's right flank was safe. George Greene's men had done the lion's share of the fighting by the Twelfth Corps on July 2 and 3. Consequently, they suffered 303 casualties—more than any other brigade in the corps.

After his distinguished performance in a crisis at Gettysburg, Greene continued in command of his brigade until he was severely wounded in the face at the Battle of Wauhatchie near Chattanooga on October 29, 1863.

Greene resumed his career as a civil engineer after the war, and was the president of the American Society of Civil Engineers. He died in 1899 at the age of 98.

For further reading:

Pfanz, Harry W. *Gettysburg: Culp's Hill and Cemetery Hill.* Chapel Hill. 1993.

Greene, George Sears. "The Breastworks at Culp's Hill." in Johnson and Buel, eds. *Battles and Leaders of the Civil War,* 4 vols. (vol. 3). New York, 1884-7.

Motts, Wayne E. "To Gain a Second Star: The Forgotten George S. Greene." *Gettysburg Magazine,* #3, July, 1990.

Pfanz, Harry W. *Gettysburg: Culp's Hill and Cemetery Hill.* Chapel Hill. 1993.

CAVALRY CORPS

(11,856 MEN / 52 GUNS)

MAJOR GENERAL
ALFRED PLEASONTON

According to Lt. Frank Haskell, an aide–de–camp in the Second Corps, Alfred Pleasonton, the leader of the Army of the Potomac's cavalry force, was a man of the world, "a nice little dandy. . .with an unsteady eye, that looks slyly at you, and then dodges." Short and slight of build, he had a finely trimmed, waxed moustache, and wore a perky little straw hat with a broad black band cocked rakishly on his head. He habitually carried a cowhide riding–whip, wore white kid gloves, and fitted himself out in dapper uniforms with stylish accouterments. Mounted atop his light–colored charger, he presented a striking picture. Pleasonton also exhibited a certain high style in his dining tastes. He eschewed the drudgery of army rations and instead dined on champagne, oysters, and other delicacies he took pains to stock in his headquarters mess even during active campaigning. His manner was polished and personable, and his conversation was witty and charming, especially when the ladies were present (though he never married).

In short, Pleasonton had all the stereotypical attributes of a dandified cavalry officer in an age where the romantic ideal of the beau sabreur still had its place in the public imagination. But Pleasonton had another trait as easily distinguishable as his taste in clothes and food—a thirst and for military fame, combined with a complete lack of scruples about how to achieve it. When the war broke out, he was in Utah, keeping an eye on the Mormons with the 2nd Dragoons, about as far from the main arena as he could possibly be. But Pleasonton showed early on that he possessed an unerring eye for the centers of power. He personally marched his cavalry regiment overland from Utah back to Washington D.C., and by the time of the Army of the Potomac's first campaign on the Peninsula in the summer of 1862, Pleasonton was commanding a regiment at army headquarters, right under the eye of army commander Maj. Gen. George B. McClellan. McClellan, also a man fond of military ceremony and pomp, took notice of Pleasonton, and in the week following the Seven Days' Battles he was jumped from major to brigadier general and given a brigade in the army's new Cavalry Division.

Thirty-nine years old at Gettysburg, Pleasonton's record suggested professional competence. He had graduated 7th in the Class of 1844 at West Point, and had served in Mexico, against the Seminoles, and in Bloody Kansas. During the early days of the Civil War, the Union cavalry had an inferiority complex and was often out-performed by the Rebel horsemen. Pleasonton's swagger inspired confidence amongst his troopers, and he worked diligently prove to them he wasn't afraid of anybody, and that he was someone they could follow with confidence. At the same time he was courting the favor of his soldiers, Pleasonton was careful to woo the press, and form journalistic and political connections.

In August 1862, Maj. Gen. John Pope proceeded to demonstrate, in the Second Bull

Run Campaign, the disastrous consequences of misusing a cavalry force. To introduce reform, McClellan placed Pleasonton at the head of his Cavalry Division. At Antietam, Pleasonton's cavalry charged through Confederate cavalry fire to secure a bridge. Though this was a relatively small operation, and Pleasonton was far to the rear at the time, his official battle report turned the action into an epic event and he took credit for the heroism of his men. The story was soon picked up and exaggerated further in Northern newspapers, and Pleasonton's reputation benefitted as a result. When Maj. Gen. Jeb Stuart embarrassed the Union cavalry by riding around McClellan's army for a second time, Pleasonton's poor performance in the affair was conveniently overlooked.

The main business of the cavalry arm was reconnaissance and intelligence gathering, and at this Pleasonton was a spectacular failure. His dispatches to headquarters were unreliable due to his inability to break the Confederate cavalry screen, his gullibility in believing wholeheartedly information obtained from enemy prisoners, and his penchant for fanciful speculation. Some snickering reporters not under the spell of his magnetic personality dubbed Pleasonton the "Knight of Romance." When Gen. Robert E. Lee crossed the Potomac with 40,000 men at the start of the Maryland Campaign, for example, Pleasonton dashed off breathless dispatches to McClellan putting the Rebel strength at 100,000, then 110,000. Later, when Lee marched north again prior to Gettysburg, Pleasonton wrote, "My opinion is, that . . . they will turn westward toward Pittsburgh," an option that stretched the limits of feasibility, given the difficulty of supplying any army attempting to march across the intervening mountains.

In February 1863, new commanding Maj. Gen. Joe Hooker passed up Pleasonton for the command of the newly organized Cavalry Corps in favor of his rival, Brig. Gen. George Stoneman. Pleasonton's reputation, however, received a boost in typical style at the Battle of Chancellorsville in May. Stoneman left Pleasonton behind with one brigade to accompany the main body of the army as he dashed off to grab glory in a major cavalry raid. The scheme backfired. While Stoneman thrashed around ineffectually in the Confederate rear, Pleasonton found himself in the thick of the action when Maj. Gen. Thomas "Stonewall" Jackson's corps crushed the Federal right wing. One of Pleasonton's regiments, the 8th Pennsylvania, found itself cut off from the main body of the army and had to fight its way to the Union lines through a band of advancing Rebels. Pleasonton again embellished his role in this charge in his official report, claiming he had "ordered the 8th Pennsylvania Cavalry to proceed at a gallop, attack the Rebels, and check the attack at any cost till we could get ready for them." Later he added the claim that "Jackson was mortally wounded by our troops in his attack upon our right at this time." Thus, according to Pleasonton, he was not only responsible for only saving the Pennsylvanians, but for also killing the legendary Jackson.

The 'Knight of Romance' also inaccurately bragged in this report that he had personally helped collect and supervise the placement of twenty-two pieces of artillery that faced down and slowed the oncoming enemy. Pleasonton maintained he ordered a devastating fire of "canister for about twenty minutes, and the affair was over." Others remembered the episode differently; the senior artillery officer at the scene reported that eighteen of the cannon were readied under his orders while Pleasonton was fully occupied in placing one battery of horse artillery. Nevertheless, Pleasonton's version of events was accepted at face value by many. A few days after the battle, when Abraham Lincoln visited the humiliated army, Joe Hooker, desperate to find a positive note in the campaign, produced the cavalryman and exclaimed, "Mr. President, this is General Pleasonton, who saved the Army of the Potomac the other night!"

A few days after the Battle of Chancellorsville, Hooker replaced the discredited Stoneman. In view of Pleasonton's recent 'exploits,' and the fact that his commission pre-dated by eleven days that of the able cavalryman Brig. Gen. John Buford; Hooker crowned Pleasanton's career on May 22 by naming him head of the Cavalry Corps with the rank of major general.

There was considerable grumbling from below. The new Maj. Gen. Pleasonton had by now become notorious for lack of bravery among the men "who have served under him and seen him under fire." One cavalry surgeon wrote, "Poor little pusillanimous Pleasonton wants to. . .have Stoneman's place—& he is about as fit for it as any 2nd Lieutenant in the command." As a captain in the 1st Massachusetts saw it, Pleasonton was "pure and simple a newspaper humbug . . . He does nothing save with a view to a newspaper paragraph." As another officer observed, "it is the universal opinion that Pleasonton's own reputation, and Pleasonton's late promotions are bolstered up by systematic lying." Pleasonton soon used his new power to purge the cavalry's non–American born brigade commanders, believing them insufficiently patriotic because of their foreign origins. His troopers were also antagonized by his growing reputation as a cold blooded martinet, and soon yearned for Stoneman's return. One cavalry officer pointed to Pleasonton's "tyrannical & illegal exercise of military authority," and considered him a exceedingly brutal disciplinarian. Earlier in the War, one critic had warned army headquarters, "I sincerely believe that somebody will be wanted before long to prefer charges against him."

No one had followed this course, however, and the man that had been in charge of three regiments and a battery at Chancellorsville was, two months later, at the head of nearly 13,000 mounted men. For all his ineptitude in the field, it must be said that Pleasonton was a gifted administrator and organizer. In the few weeks that he was in command of the Cavalry Corps before Gettysburg, the thirty–nine year old general used his political connections to replace the considerable losses from Stoneman's wasteful raid in the Chancellorsville campaign and make far–reaching personnel changes in the command structure of the corps. In typical fashion, he pulled political strings to strip Hungarian Maj. Gen. Julius Stahel from his 3,600–man cavalry division stationed in the defenses of Washington and redesignating it the Third Division of his own Cavalry Corps only three days before Gettysburg.

Pleasonton led strictly from the rear, and his reports were always better than his fighting. Heading into Pennsylvania, he had no experience leading the corps in a major battle, and had only been at its head for little more than a month.

GETTYSBURG: Pleasonton upheld his reputation as a desk general in the three days of Gettysburg. On July 1, as Buford was scouting the enemy, protecting advantageous terrain and holding off Southern infantrymen until reinforcements could arrive, Pleasonton was far to the rear in Frederick, Maryland.

On July 2, his main influence on the battlefield was the bungling removal of Buford's division—only lightly damaged the day before—from the army's left flank, when they were the only cavalry on the field. Pleasonton then proceeded to forget to replace them. The Army of the Potomac operated without cavalry to guard its left on the day when Lee targeted that flank for a furious assault.

When Brig. Gen. David Gregg achieved his success east of Gettysburg on July 3, Pleasonton was again nowhere near the scene of the fighting. Pleasonton's main involvement in this scenario consisted of trying to recall Brig. Gen. George Custer's brigade from the field at the moment when it was most needed.

Pleasonton failed to provide the Army of the Potomac with accurate intelligence throughout the entire engagement. Not only did he continue to demonstrate his lack of ability in able reconnaissance, he at times demonstrated a complete disregard for it, ignoring Buford's valuable dispatches.

Pleasonton continued to serve as cavalry chief for another year, until Lt. Gen. Ulysses Grant replaced him with Maj. Gen. Phil Sheridan in July 1864 and sent Pleasonton to Missouri.

After the war, Pleasonton reverted to a Regular Army major. Disgusted by his plummeting prospects, he resigned in 1868. He held minor government appointments until he retired in 1888, and he died in1897.

For further reading:

Longacre, Edward G. *The Cavalry at Gettysburg.* Lincoln, 1986.

Starr, Stephen. *The Union Cavalry in the Civil War: Gettysburg to Appomattox.* vol. 2. (Baton Rouge, 1995.)

———

FIRST DIVISION

(4,073 men)

BRIGADIER GENERAL JOHN BUFORD

Artilleryman Col. Charles Wainwright spoke for many of his peers when he described John Buford as "straight–forward, honest, conscientious, full of good common sense, and always to be relied on in any emergency," and "decidedly the best cavalry general" in the Army of the Potomac. In fact, Buford was one of the finest cavalrymen in American history. He was a man who liked to lead from the front, and frequently he could be found observing combat from the skirmish line while accompanied by and aide carrying his divisional flag. A former Indian fighter, he was all business, driving himself as relentlessly as he drove his men, with the result that six months after Gettysburg he would be dead of what the doctors called "exposure and exhaustion." Buford's hard–bitten attitude was reflected in his facial expression. One observer claimed he had "a good–natured disposition, but [was] not to be trifled with," a

"singular–looking party. . .with a tawny mustache and a little, triangular gray eye, whose expression is determined, not to say sinister."

Buford was quiet and sober, quite in contrast to the flamboyant types that so often gravitated toward the cavalry. "He is kind, and always on hand when there is fighting to be done . . . He don't put on so much style as most officers," wrote one grateful subordinate in the 8th Illinois. The man might have been speaking of Buford's plain, unpolished manner, or his wardrobe. In the field he usually wore an old officer's sack coat "ornamented with holes," ancient blue corduroy breeches tucked into a pair of ordinary cowhide boots, and always had a big pipe and tobacco pouch sticking out of his shirt pockets. It was obvious this trooper was made of sterner stuff than was his "nice little dandy" superior, Maj. Gen. Alfred Pleasonton, with whom he had campaigned on the Plains. Buford was not shy about advertising his hard attitude. He once hanged a guerrilla, in an area seething with Secessionist sympathies, and left the corpse dangling from a tree limb under the sign "This man to hang three days; he who cuts him down before shall hang the remaining time."

Coming from a family whose tradition of turning out soldiers dated back to England's Wars of the Roses, Buford was born in Kentucky and raised in Rock Island, Illinois. He attended West Point and graduated in the upper half of the Class of 1848. Assigned to the dragoons, he saw his first combat in the Sioux campaign of 1855, then went west with the Mormon expedition and stayed in Utah until the commencement of the Civil War, when his regiment marched 1,100 miles overland to return to Washington, D.C.

Buford's War career was slow getting started, however. In the summer of 1862, when Maj. Gen. John Pope came to Washington to take command of the Army of Virginia, he was surprised to find that Buford had held an unimportant staff job in the capital since the previous November. Pope at once saw to it that Buford was promoted to brigadier general, and gave him command of the Reserve Cavalry Brigade of his Army of Virginia. Buford was one of the few officers to emerge from Pope's disastrous Second Bull Run Campaign with an enhanced reputation. He showed talent at reconnaissance operations and consistently provided Pope's headquarters with timely intelligence about the approach of Maj. Gen. James Longstreet's Right Wing to the battlefield (which was fatally ignored). During the actual Battle of Second Bull Run, Buford ordered a charge against Rebel horsemen, marking one of the first times in the War that Union cavalrymen initiated a stand–up cavalry fight. In the clash, Buford was wounded so badly in the knee that he was left on the field for dead.

The wound incapacitated Buford until the next year. In the meantime, during the Antietam and Fredericksburg Campaigns, he acted as cavalry advisor to Maj. Gens. George McClellan and Ambrose Burnside. When Hooker consolidated the cavalry into an army corps in February 1863, Buford returned to the command of the elite Reserve Brigade, where he exercised his talents in training recruits. He particularly advocated the advantages of fighting on foot rather than in the saddle, techniques from his old dragoon days that would become Union cavalry doctrine as the War wore on.

Although Buford performed well in the Chancellorsville Campaign, cavalry chief Brig. Gen. George Stoneman's abortive raid took him away from most of the important action. When Stoneman was replaced, Buford was considered as a replacement. But Buford was modest, and cultivating connections with newspapermen and garnering the favor of influential politicians was beneath him. As a result, commanding Maj. Gen. Joe Hooker gave command of the cavalry to the flashier, publicity–savvy Alfred Pleasonton. (In his latter years, Hooker admitted Buford would have been the better choice.) Buford was given a division.

At Brandy Station on June 9, Buford did not distinguish himself; he fought a passive defensive battle all afternoon. As the Gettysburg Campaign developed throughout the following couple of weeks, however, he was again energetic and invaluable in reconnaissance, passing on crucial information about the enemy that went unappreciated by Pleasonton. Though still physically weakened by his knee wound, Buford was a seasoned,

supremely talented officer in his prime in the summer of 1863.

On the evening of June 30, as his troopers already trading pot shots with Confederate infantrymen to the west of Gettysburg, Buford told brigade leader Col. Tom Devin, "The enemy must know the importance of this position and will strain every nerve to secure it, and if we are able to hold it we will do well." Buford's signal officer noticed "He seemed anxious, more so than I ever saw him."

GETTYSBURG: Buford was the first to make contact with Gen. Robert E. Lee's army, and became the first hero of the battle for realizing that he needed to protect the good terrain about Gettysburg until the rest of the Union army could arrive in the area. His men used dragoon tactics—three–quarters of his troopers fighting in a heavy skirmish line while the remaining quarter held their horses—and held the advance of Lt. Gen. A. P. Hill's Rebel infantrymen to a crawl until Maj. Gen. John Reynolds arrived with the advance units of his First Corps. When the infantry deployed, Buford's men dropped off to the flanks to provide protection, while at the same time continuing to provide timely intelligence on the arrival of new Confederate units. It was an example of a consummate professional showing an eye for good ground, tactical sense, and tenacity at a moment of crisis. When the Federal infantry retreated to Cemetery Hill in the late afternoon, Buford helped deter a Confederate advance by taking a menacing position on the Union left, near the Emmitsburg Road.

The next morning, July 2, Buford's men patrolled a broad area around the Peach Orchard, performing the valuable duty of guarding the army's left flank and reporting enemy movement. Pleasonton, however, withdrew Buford's entire force to Westminster in order for it to rest and be refitted in the army's rear. Buford's 2,600 troopers rode off the field in the late morning of July 2 with nobody to replace them—a fact that would have dire consequences for the Union left later that day. They would never reenter the battle.

In the fall of 1863, exhausted and weak from non–stop service, Buford contracted typhoid. The Union lost an irreplaceable cavalry soldier when he died from the disease in December.

For further reading:

Longacre, Edward G. *The Cavalry at Gettysburg*. Lincoln, 1986.

——. *General John Buford*. Conshohocken, 1995.

Peterson, John. *"The Devil's to Pay": General John Buford, USA*. Gettysburg, 1995.

Starr, Stephen. *The Union Cavalry in the Civil War: Gettysburg to Appomattox*. vol. 2. (Baton Rouge, 1995.

Wittenberg, Eric. "John Buford and the Gettysburg Campaign." *Gettysburg Magazine*, #11, July, 1994.

FIRST BRIGADE

(1,600 men)

COLONEL
WILLIAM GAMBLE

A forty–five year old native of Ireland William Gamble still spoke with the brogue of his County Tyrone birthplace. A faint smile can be detected on many of Gamble's wartime photographs, and they project and affable, friendly image of the man. Though corps commander Pleasonton was doing his best to weed all foreign–born officers out of brigade commands, Gamble didn't arouse his resentment, perhaps because the Irishman with the fluffy muttonchops and broad, florid face had spent most of his life in the United States.

Gamble had already served a stint as a dragoon in the British Army before immigrating to America in 1838 at the age of twenty, where he immediately enlisted in the 1st Dragoons, U.S. Army. He fought the Seminoles, then left the army after four years. He went to Chicago to return to the civil engineering career he had begun in Ireland. For the next eighteen years he worked for the Board of Public Works in Chicago, involved with the canal and river system.

When the Civil War began, Gamble's Old Army dragoon service, though it had ended almost twenty years before, was enough qualification for Congressman John Farnsworth to get Gamble commissioned lieutenant colonel of Farnsworth's 8th Illinois volunteer cavalry regiment in September 1861. As the highest ranking officer with any experience in the regiment, Gamble was largely responsible its for training. One of Gamble's sergeants mentioned him in a letter home during this period:

I particularly admire our Lt. Colonel. He is a perfect soldier. Rough to be sure, but frank and open–hearted. A man who says what he means and means what he says. We Orderly Sergeants get some pretty severe reprimands from him occasionally, but we like him all the better for that. He was Orderly Sergeant himself for some years in the regular service and knows perfectly well what our duties are and the difficulties we have to encounter.

The following summer the 8th Illinois was attached to the Pennsylvania Reserve Division, and saw active duty in the Peninsula Campaign. On August 5, 1862, more than a month after the end of the campaign but before the Army of the Potomac departed the Peninsula, Gamble led a cavalry charge during a skirmish with Rebel pickets near the scene of the recent battle on Malvern Hill. He was severely wounded by a bullet that entered his chest, skipped off a rib and lodged in his back, and he spent the next three months convalescing.

When he returned to the army in the fall, Gamble took command of the 8th Illinois from Brigadier General Farnsworth, who had been bumped up to command the newly formed cavalry brigade. Gamble was promoted to colonel on December 5, 1862, just before the Battle of Fredericksburg, though the 8th Illinois did no fighting there.

Farnsworth had already been elected to Congress, and when he resigned in January 1863 to begin his term in office, Gamble took command of the brigade. Winter was hard on his health, however. He got a medical furlough in March, suffering from "rheumatism and neuralgia" and continuing problems with his Peninsula wound, and missed the Chancellorsville Campaign in early May and the Battle of Brandy Station on June 9. Col. Benjamin 'Grimes' Davis, a 'proud tyrannical devil' who loved to fight, commanded the brigade in both engagments. Davis was killed at Brandy Station, and when Gamble returned from leave on four days after the battle, his lack of aggressiveness in the early phases of the Gettysburg Campaign contrasted sharply with the recently departed Davis' fiery leadership.

Gamble's own military philosophy was summed up in an order to the 8th Illinois: "The first duty of a soldier is a prompt and cheerful obedience to all lawful orders, and no one is fit to command, in any capacity, that is not himself willing to obey." Gamble was learning brigade command on the job during the Gettysburg Campaign. He had yet to express talent for an independent command, and though not particularly aggressive, he seemed capable of adequate service when supervised and prodded by a superior officer.

GETTYSBURG: At the Battle of Gettysburg Gamble was suffering from a bad cold or allergies, constantly sniffing, sneezing, wheezing, and wiping his nose and watery eyes on his coat. Gamble's was the first brigade to block the path of Lt. Gen. Ambrose P. Hill's men as they advanced toward Gettysburg on the Cashtown Pike on the morning of July 1, and they fought with grit, slowing the enemy to a crawl for three hours while Maj. Gen. John Reynolds summoned his First Corps. They performed so well fighting dismounted that the enemy soldiers thought they were combating Union infantry.

When Reynolds' men arrived around 11:00 a.m., Gamble led his men off to the infantry's left flank where they proceeded to guard against enemy movements as well as delivering an enfilading fire against the advancing Southerners. When the First Corps line collapsed and the Union defenders fled to Cemetery Hill, Gamble's men withdrew to the vicinity of the Peach Orchard.

On July 2, Gamble's participation in the fight ended when Pleasonton withdrew Buford's entire division to the army's rear. Gamble, however, had only lost 99 men on July 1, and still could have rendered valuable service.

Gamble continued to command his brigade in the army's fall maneuvers. When the Overland Campaign began the next spring, though, Gamble was transferred to the command of the cavalry in the defenses of Washington. He remained with the army after the war, but contracted cholera accompanying his regiment to California via Central America, and died in 1866.

For further reading:

Longacre, Edward G. Cavalry at Gettysburg. Lincoln, 1986.

———. General John Buford. Conshohocken, 1995.

Starr, Stephen. The Union Cavalry in the Civil War: Gettysburg to Appomattox. vol. 2. (Baton Rouge, 1995.

SECOND BRIGADE

(1,148 men)

COLONEL
THOMAS CASIMER DEVIN

Tom Devin's cheery, boyish face and youthful vitality belied his forty–one years of age, though in fact he was older than the average cavalry leader. He was a courageous and aggressive fighter, but he balanced this pugnacity with the careful habit of taking all precautions necessary to secure success.

Devin was born in New York City of Irish immigrant parents. After a limited education in the public schools, he became a house painter, and by the fall of Fort Sumter was a partner in a New York City paint, oil, and varnish company—an unlikely spawning ground for a tough cavalry leader. However, he had been a lieutenant colonel in the New York Militia's cavalry for years, and when the Civil War began, he enlisted in the volunteer cavalry. With his militia service to recommend him, he was made colonel of the 6th New York Volunteer cavalry in November 1861. When the War Department sent an old Regular to test Devin on his understanding of the mounted arm, the veteran came away amazed, writing, "I can't teach Col. Devin anything about cavalry; he knows more about the tactics than I do!" By early 1862, Devin's unit was "the best drilled Regiment in the service," according to one observer.

Devin led his regiment at South Mountain and Antietam, then rose to command of the brigade at the Battle of Fredericksburg when the former leader, Brig. Gen. David Gregg, was transferred to the head of another brigade.

At Chancellorsville, Devin's brigade was the only cavalry unit present with the main body of the army after the rest of the cavalry was sent away on Brig. Gen. George Stoneman's ineffectual raid deep in the enemy rear. Initially, Devin and his troopers led the way for three full army corps during the successful

Union flank movement that preceded the battle. Finding themselves in the thick of the fighting on May 2 and 3, Devin and his brigade repeatedly distinguished themselves. At one point they desperately counterattacked Maj. Gen. 'Stonewall' Jackson's victorious Confederates after the rout of the Union Eleventh Corps. (Brig. Gen. Alfred Pleasonton would later take the full credit for this audacious move.) The brigade lost almost 200 men in the battle, unprecedented casualties for a cavalry brigade. With this recent adventure under their belts, Devin's troopers were considered as the hardest fighting brigade in the Cavalry Corps by the Gettysburg Campaign. Devin, a favorite of Brig. Gen. John Buford, his tough division commander, had won the sobriquets "Old War Horse" and "Buford's Hard Hitter" for his rugged leadership style.

GETTYSBURG: At the opening of the battle on the morning of July 1, while Gamble's brigade was fighting Maj. Gen. A.P. Hill's infantrymen advancing along the Cashtown Pike, Buford posted Devin and his men as far north as the Mummasburg road, and ordered them to keep a watch for any enemy troops approaching from the west or the north. Once the infantrymen of the Federal First Corps came up, Devin slid his brigade clockwise to the low ground north of the town, since his pickets had informed him of Rebels coming from that direction.

Around noon, Devin rode up the Heidlersburg Road to the northeast and concentrated on delaying the approach of Maj. Gen. Jubal Early's Division, successfully buying time until Brig. Gen. Francis Barlow's Eleventh Corps division could deploy to defend against this new threat. When Barlow arrived, Devin and his men slid clockwise again to the York Pike to guard Barlow's right. At that point, friendly batteries on Cemetery Hill mistakenly shelled Devin's men, causing them to withdraw into Gettysburg just as Early's men were preparing to assault the right and rear of the Eleventh Corps. Without protection on their flank, the Union line quickly dissolved in the face of Early's charge. Devin then pulled his men back to the fields south of Gettysburg. Parts of his brigade skirmished with Confederates advancing through the town streets during the flight of the Eleventh and First Corps to Cemetery Hill. After the crisis had passed, Buford withdrew Devin's and Gamble's brigades to the vicinity of the Peach Orchard, where they spent the night.

Pleasonton withdrew Buford's entire division from the battle the next day, July 2, in order to refit and resupply. Devin's brigade did not really need the relief—they had lost only 28 men in the fighting of July 1.

Devin continued as one of the army's indispensable cavalry brigadiers, fighting in all its campaigns until the end of the Civil War. He was promoted to brigadier general for his performance at Cedar Creek, in the 1864 Shenandoah Campaign.

Devin remained in the army after the war and died in New York in 1878 on sick leave, at the rank of colonel.

For further reading:

Longacre, Edward G. Cavalry at Gettysburg. Lincoln, 1986.

——. General John Buford. Conshohocken, 1995.

Starr, Stephen. The Union Cavalry in the Civil War: Gettysburg to Appomattox. vol. 2. (Baton Rouge, 1995.

RESERVE BRIGADE
(1,321 MEN)

BRIGADIER GENERAL WESLEY MERRITT

Wesley Merritt had a boyish, beardless face that belied his Regular Army philosophy—he was a tough disciplinarian, stringent and demanding enough so that some volunteers regarded him as a martinet (one called his temperament "miserable"). Those who knew him better wrote of his "genial, though rather . . . reticent manner." Capt. James H. Kidd, an officer who served with him, wrote admiringly, "Modesty that fitted him like a garment, charming manners, the demeanor of a gentleman, cool bearing in action, were his distinguishing characteristics." At Gettysburg, Merritt, who had just turned twenty–nine two weeks before, had yet to achieve fame.

He was one of a trio of talented young cavalry captains (with Brig. Gens. Elon Farnsworth and George Custer) whom the new cavalry chief, Maj. Gen. Alfred Pleasonton, had promoted from staff positions to brigadier generals and placed at the head of brigades—three days before the battle.

Merritt was the fourth of eleven children born to a New York City lawyer who was financially ruined by the Panic of 1837 when Wesley was three. Four years later, Merritt's father abandoned his profession and moved the family from New York to Illinois. Wesley attended the Christian Brothers school, then studied law in Salem before accepting an appointment to West Point. There he did not excel in academics, but shone in military tactics and leadership, graduating 22nd out of 41 cadets in the Class of 1860.

After graduation, Merritt was posted to Capt. John Buford's 2nd Dragoons, serving in Utah. Although he only served a few months with Buford, that officer made a life–long impression on Merritt, who absorbed Buford's dismounted cavalry tactics as well as his attitude toward discipline and proper military behavior. When the Civil War began, the 2nd Dragoons made a cross–country trek to return to Washington, where Merritt waited for an assignment. In February 1862, Merritt was made aide–de–camp on the staff of Brig. Gen. Philip St. George Cooke, commander of the Union cavalry during the subsequent Peninsula Campaign. After Brig. Gen. "Jeb" Stuart made a mockery of Cooke's command,

Brig. Gen. George Stoneman took over the cavalry in July 1862, but kept Merritt on his staff. By the time of the Chancellorsville Campaign in May 1863, Stoneman had enough confidence in Merritt to send his young staff officer with a 50–man detachment on a successful bridge–destroying mission. (Stoneman's entire raid, however, was poorly conceived and didn't have the desired effect of making Gen. Robert E. Lee pull his army back from its defensive position on the Rappahannock River).

Brig. Gen. Alfred Pleasonton was made cavalry chief after Stoneman's Chancellorsville fiasco, and he also saw Merritt's ability and retained him on his staff. At Brandy Station on June 9, Merritt temporarily relinquished his staff duties and rode into battle with his old unit, the 2nd U.S. Cavalry. Late in the day, he found himself in a saber fight with a large Rebel officer, who got the better of him, slashing his scalp and leg. Fortunately, Merritt was protected from the full impact of the blow to the scalp by his thick hat and the handkerchief he used as a sweatband. The officer rode off, and a gang of Rebel horsemen soon surrounded Merritt. Characteristi-cally, Merritt demanded their surrender. Startled, the gray-clad troopers peered through the battle smoke for other Union horsemen, and Merritt seized the moment and bolted to safety.

Merritt had never led a group larger than 50 men, but on June 22, during a period of ongoing cavalry skirmishes that characterized the Gettysburg Campaign, Pleasonton sent the following message to army headquarters:

I desire to inform the general commanding that the losses my command has sustained in officers require me to ask for the promotion of good commanders. It is necessary to have a good commander for the regular [Reserve] brigade of cavalry, and I earnestly recommend Capt. Wesley Merritt to be made a brigadier–general for that purpose. He has all the qualifications for it, and has distinguished himself by his gallantry and daring. Give me good commanders and I will give you good results.

Five days later, on June 28, Merritt was put in charge of the elite, almost 2,000–man Reserve Brigade of Buford's First Division, the only Regular cavalry regiments in the Army of the Potomac. On June 29, Merritt was made brigadier general. On June 30, Merritt called on the Regular Army officers over whose heads he had been promoted to secure their support and inspect their camps. On July 1, the Battle of Gettysburg began.

GETTYSBURG: During the first day's fighting, Merritt's brigade carried on reconnaissance work and did picket duty in the left rear of the army around Mechanicsburg, Maryland, 18 miles to the southwest of Gettysburg. On the morning of July 2, Merritt and his troopers advanced to Emmitsburg, ten miles south of the battlefield.

At noon on July 3, Merritt's brigade moved toward Gettysburg, called on by Brig. Gen. Judson Kilpatrick to move into the enemy's left rear in the general vicinity of the Round Tops. Merritt first detached 400 men to raid what were reported to be the enemy's wagon trains. (Brig. Gen. William 'Grumble' Jones' cavalry brigade, it turned out, accompanied the trains, and Merritt's detachment was nearly annihilated, losing 242 men.) Merritt's main body reached the Confederate right flank, occupied by Maj. Gen. John Hood's Division, about 3:00 p.m. Kilpatrick ordered Merritt to attack at about 4:30 p.m., and Merritt made the mistake of dismounting his men in clear terrain ideal for mounted tactics. The Confederate left flank was covered easily by Brig. Gen. George Anderson's Georgians, and Merritt's men were stopped, flanked, rolled up, and sent flying.

Despite his disappointing debut as a brigadier at Gettysburg, Merritt's Civil War career continued to soar after the engagement. He commanded the division during Buford's absence later that summer, then took over permanently when Buford contracted typhoid and had to relinquish command on November 21, 1863. Merritt eventually standardized the dragoon tactics that were Buford's legacy to the Army of the Potomac. By the war's end, he commanded the Cavalry Corps and had risen to the rank of major general.

Thereafter, Merritt fought indians as a lieutenant colonel and served as superintendent of West Point. By 1895, he had risen through the grades to major general. In the Spanish-

American War, Merritt, along with Admiral Dewey, received the surrender of Manila. He died in 1910.

For further reading:

Alberts, Don E. *General Wesley Merritt, Nineteenth Century Cavalryman.* Novato, 1980.

Longacre, Edward G. *The Cavalry at Gettysburg.* Lincoln, 1986.

Wittenberg, Eric J. "Merritt's Regulars on South Cavalry Field: Oh, What Could Have Been." *Gettysburg Magazine,* #16, 1997.

SECOND DIVISION:

(2,614 MEN)

BRIGADIER GENERAL DAVID McMURTRIE GREGG

Unlike many officers that flocked to the mounted service, David Gregg was quiet and modest, and for that reason was easily overshadowed by flashy horsemen like Maj. Gen. Alfred Pleasonton and Brig. Gens. Judson Kilpatrick and George Custer, who watched for their names in the newspapers as closely as they did for the approach of an enemy column. Gregg, in fact, had a positive dislike for journalists and barred them from approaching him, telling them, 'I do not propose to have a picture reputation." One newspapermen who got close enough to get a good look at him, however, described a man with an urbane appearance. "His heavy blue eye and regular features bear English characteristics . . . Put him in peg–tops and a round hat, and he would typify the class of well–drawn thoroughbreds seen frequently in the London Punch."

Gregg was indeed well bred, born in Huntingdon County in central Pennsylvania and reared in prosperous circumstances, he was already attending a university when he received his appointment to West Point. He was a good student, graduating 6th out of 34 cadets in the Class of 1855. After years of service fighting Indians, he was sent to duty at Fort Tejon in California, and was there when the Sumter crisis erupted in April 1861.

Gregg was brought east and made a colonel of a regiment of volunteer cavalrymen from his native state, the 8th Pennsylvania, in January 1862. He led it on the Peninsula that summer and received "favorable notice" from Brig. Gen. Alfred Pleasonton after the campaign. Gregg took part in the Maryland Campaign in September, then obtained leave to marry on October 6, 1862. In November he won a promotion to brigadier general, and was given a brigade in Pleasonton's cavalry division of Maj. Gen. Ambrose Burnside's army. In the middle of the Battle of Fredericksburg, on December 13, Gregg was transferred to command Brig. Gen. George Bayard's brigade when that brilliant, unlucky officer was struck and killed by shrapnel while standing near headquarters—his brigade's only casualty in the battle.

When Maj. Gen. Joseph Hooker ascended to lead the Army of the Potomac, he reorganized the force in February 1863, and created the Cavalry Corps. Gregg received his reward for the notice he had won the previous year when he was given command of the Cavalry Corps' Third Division. During the Chancellorsville Campaign in early May 1863, Gregg participated in Brig. Gen. George Stoneman's ill-conceived raid into the Confederate rear. In the cavalry battle at Brandy Station on June 9, Gregg showed combativeness, but sent in his units piecemeal, ensuring their eventual repulse.

Still, Gregg remained universally liked and respected as a highly capable leader by his peers and subordinates. His unassailable calm was an amazement to all that served with him. Once, when he became the target of an enemy battery and cannonballs began to tear by him and his staff, he trotted to safety, all the while puffing imperturbably on his meerschaum pipe. When he saw his aides galloping to the rear wild–eyed with terror, he called out, "Be calm, gentlemen—no occasion for haste!" He assumed the same composed, deliberate manner in every bit of business he attended to. His subordinates appreciated this combination of ability and self–control; one officer wrote, "I was more or less in awe of him . . .one could not have been under a more considerate and finer commander."

David Gregg, a career cavalryman, had shown ability at every level of command. He had led his division since February, though, since Pleasonton had reorganized it after Brandy Station, Gregg might not have been entirely familiar with its new configuration. Gregg was bothered by an intestinal ailment on the march toward Pennsylvania. Even so, the thirty–year old could be expected to perform well under any circumstances.

GETTYSBURG: Advancing on the right of the Army of the Potomac as it neared Gen. Robert E. Lee's army, Gregg, with Col. McIntosh's and Col. J. Irvin Gregg's brigades, spent July 1 marching and countermarching in the area of Hanover Junction—25 miles to the east of Gettysburg— trying to follow a confusing series of orders from Pleasonton.

On the morning of July 2, Gregg's column rode west along the Hanover Road and arrived at the junction of the Low Dutch Road, nearly three miles east of Gettysburg, just before noon. There he halted and let his men rest, awaiting further orders. After 6:00 that evening, increased skirmishing near Gettysburg on Brinkerhoff's Ridge prompted Gregg to send over a portion of his artillery and several dismounted regiments, which engaged the Stonewall Brigade guarding the rear of Maj. Gen. Edward Johnson's Division as it assaulted Culp's Hill that evening. Gregg's presence was crucial to the eventual repulse of the Culp's Hill assault, since it kept the Stonewall Brigade busy in the rear, effectively removing it from the front line.

On July 3, Gregg was assigned the task of guarding the army's right on the east side of Rock Creek. He formed a long skirmish line across Wolf's Hill to the Hanover Road with his two brigades, then placed Brig. Gen. George Custer's brigade (borrowed from Brig. Gen. Judson Kilpatrick's division) a mile to the east, at the intersection of the Low Dutch Road and the Hanover Road. Ordered by Pleasonton to return Custer's men to Kilpatrick, but spotting large menacing columns of Confederate cavalry coming into view to the north, Gregg jeopardized his career by ordering Custer to stay. Gregg then confronted the Rebel horse soldiers with McIntosh's and Custer's brigades while keeping J. Irvin Gregg's brigade in its skirmish line on Wolf's Hill.

The cavalry battle began shortly after 3:00 p.m. north of the Hanover Road. The open fields rang with the tumult of thundering charges and slashing countercharges, cannon firing canister, saber duels and dismounted volleys. Both sides finally pulled back and the affair ended in a draw.

The cavalry battle was not much noticed afterward—the publicity–hungry Pleasonton had not been anywhere near the action, and Gregg, who had guided the Union troopers, was too modest to seek attention for his accomplishment. Gregg's ability, however, insured that he would stay as division commander throughout the rest of the War, until he abruptly resigned in February 1865.

Gregg was a farmer after the war until President Grant made him a diplomat to Pargue in 1874. He served only briefly, then settled in Reading, Pennsylvania, and lived there until his death in 1916.

For further reading:

Longacre, Edward G. *The Cavalry at Gettysburg.* Lincoln, 1986.

Patterson, Gerard A. "Friends More Than Enemies." *Civil War Times Illustrated*, 36, June, 1997.

Weigley, Russell F. "David McMurtrie Gregg." *Civil War Times Illustrated*, 1, Nov. 1962.

FIRST BRIGADE

(1,311 MEN)

COLONEL
JOHN BAILLIE MCINTOSH

Son and great–nephew of military heroes, thirty–four year old Floridian John McIntosh had military experience as a youth serving during the Mexican War in an unlikely venue for a future cavalry leader—as a midshipman on the USS Saratoga. Resigning from the Navy soon after the conflict, he took up residence with an uncle in Brunswick, New Jersey and married in 1850. For the next decade, until the opening of the Civil War, he engaged in business with his father–in–law. He was shamed into volunteering for the Union army after his brother James disgraced the family honor (to John's mind, at least) by joining the Confederacy. (James eventually rose to brigadier general before being killed at the Battle of Pea Ridge in March 1862).

In consideration of his heritage and military experience, John was commissioned directly into the regular army cavalry in June 1861. He distinguished himself as a lieutenant with the 5th U.S. regular cavalry in the Peninsula Campaign in the summer of 1862, at one point having his horse shot under him as he led what Col. William Averell praised as an "impetuous dash" pell–mell across a bridge into the enemy's camp. After service with the 5th U.S. in the Maryland Campaign in September, he was given his own regiment of volunteer cavalrymen, the 3rd Pennsylvania, in November. For some reason he was not present with his regiment at the Battle of Fredericksburg.

When the Cavalry Corps was organized in February 1863, McIntosh received a brigade in the division of his old friend, now Brigadier General Averell. The division fought well at the Battle of Kelly's Ford in March, where Union cavalrymen first showed themselves equal to their Confederate foes. Averell's official report of the battle states that McIntosh "showed during the day that he possessed the highest qualities of a brigade commander."

McIntosh and his brigade, along with Averell's entire division, were held out of the fighting in the Chancellorsville Campaign, and in May, commanding Maj. Gen. Joseph Hooker sacked Averell. McIntosh's continuing friendship with the discredited Averell, along with his Southern roots and his conservative Democratic politics, may have worked to deny him a brigadier's star—after Chancellorsville, the cavalry was reorganized and McIntosh was returned to his regiment. Brigade leader Col. Percy Wyndham was wounded at Brandy Station on June 9, however, and McIntosh was put in command of Wyndham's brigade in time for the Gettysburg Campaign.

McIntosh was experienced and aggressive. Averell had described him as a brigade commander second to none (although that was a bit of an exaggeration). McIntosh's weakness was his unfamiliarity with his brigade—he had been in command of the recently organized unit for only three weeks. He had a more immediate problem, however. As his troopers approached the battlefield, McIntosh became too sick to continue in command, as an intestinal ailment contracted weeks before had become re–aggravated by the grueling march northward. After the attention of a regimental doctor he returned to the head of the column as it reached the field, though he was still shaky and unsteady.

GETTYSBURG: Around noon on July 2, McIntosh and his troopers arrived east of Gettysburg on the Hanover Road with Col. J.

Irvin Gregg's brigade. They halted and rested during the afternoon near the intersection of the Low Dutch Road. That evening, McIntosh's men were rushed westward toward nearby Brinkerhoff's Ridge, where they had a sharp fight with a regiment from the Stonewall Brigade. The action had the important effect of keeping that entire brigade of veteran Virginian infantrymen guarding the rear and out of the spearhead of the Stonewall Division's assault on Culp's Hill.

On July 3, after being initially posted as skirmishers around Wolf's Hill's to bar access to the Union army's right rear, McIntosh's men were hurried to the northeast in mid–afternoon to take part in the cavalry battle with Maj. Gen.'Jeb' Stuart's troopers north of the Hanover Road. Aiding Brig. Gen. George Custer's brigade, McIntosh's men were able to fight the vaunted Rebel horsemen to a draw. All this activity took only a small toll on McIntosh's force, however; he reported a loss of only 35 men in the entire battle.

Gettysburg solidified McIntosh's position as brigade leader. He continued in that role until he was injured by the fall of his horse in October. After being given temporary control of all the cavalry in the Washington defenses in early 1864, he was back in command of a brigade for Ulysses Grant's Overland Campaign that summer. He served well until he lost a leg at the Battle of Third Winchester in September 1864.

After the war, McIntosh stayed in the Regular Army, retiring in 1870 with the rank of brigadier general. He died eighteen months later of heart complications arising from his leg wound.

For further reading:

Longacre, Edward G. *The Cavalry at Gettysburg.* Lincoln, 1986.

Starr, Stephen. *The Union Cavalry in the Civil War: Gettysburg to Appomattox.* vol. 2. (Baton Rouge, 1995.

THIRD BRIGADE

(1,255 MEN)

COLONEL
JOHN IRVIN GREGG

Tall, lanky, and with a great, pirate–like beard, J. Irvin Gregg was nicknamed "Long John," by his troops. Gregg was an iron merchant from Centre County, Pennsylvania, who had shown a talent for military leadership during his service in the Mexican War, where he had enlisted as a private at the age of nineteen and risen to the rank of captain before the two–year conflict was over. He took advantage of his knack for soldiering, joining the Regular Army after the War, and spent ten years in the military before entering the iron business.

The War Department commissioned Gregg again a month after the fall of Fort Sumter, and he was given command of a company in the 6th U.S. Cavalry. In the Peninsula Campaign in the summer of 1862, he was among a handful of cavalry officers "recommended to favorable notice" by brigade commander Brig. Gen. Alfred Pleasonton. In November of that year, he was made colonel of the 16th Pennsylvania Volunteer Cavalry Regiment. The 16th was placed in McIntosh's brigade of Brig. Gen. William Averell's division in January 1863, and at Kelly's Ford in March, Gregg led his regiment in battle for the first time, winning success with a loss of only 1 man slightly wounded. 'Long John's' career suffered a reverse in the Chancellorsville Campaign in May as he and his troopers were out of the fighting, sitting useless at an outpost with the rest of Averell's division.

In the cavalry reorganization after Chancellorsville, Gregg was given a brigade for the first time, and led it in the cavalry fighting at Brandy Station, Middleburg, and Upperville in the early stages of the Gettysburg Campaign. By the middle of June, his brigade had been assigned to the division of his cousin, David Gregg. Through it all, Col. J. Irvin Gregg had shown a low-key, unflappable, reliable temperament, a man who did his job with little fanfare. A member of the 16th Pennsylvania regiment recalled Gregg as having been a "very tall, quiet, soldierly captain."

GETTYSBURG: Arriving around noon on July 2 from the east by the Hanover Road, J. Irvin Gregg and his men were halted at the intersection of the Low Dutch Road three miles east of Gettysburg and spent the rest of the afternoon resting in a nearby field. In the late afternoon one of Gregg's regiments skirmished with Rebels on Brinkerhoff's Ridge to the west. The clash escalated that evening, but Gregg's men were kept in the rear as a reserve.

The next morning, July 3, Gregg's men fanned out in a skirmish line to guard the approaches to the Union rear around Wolf's Hill. When the cavalry battle commenced that afternoon northeast, Gregg's men were again kept in reserve around Wolf's Hill. Spared any major fighting, they lost only 21 casualties in the entire battle.

Even though his participation in the fighting at Gettysburg was slight, Gregg remained a fixture in the cavalry of the Army of the Potomac, in command of his brigade for the rest of the war. Gregg remained in the Regular Army after the war, retiring with the rank of colonel in 1879. He died in 1892.

For further reading:

Longacre, Edward G. *The Cavalry at Gettysburg*. Lincoln, 1986.

Starr, Stephen. *The Union Cavalry in the Civil War: Gettysburg to Appomattox.* vol. 2. (Baton Rouge, 1995.

THIRD DIVISION
(3,902 MEN)

BRIGADIER GENERAL [HUGH] JUDSON KILPATRICK

Maj. Gen. William Sherman had a gift for the brutally apt pronouncement. Summing up Judson Kilpatrick in 1864, he said, "I know that Kilpatrick is a hell of a damned fool, but I want just that sort of man to command my cavalry on this expedition." On June 28, three days before the Battle of Gettysburg, Cavalry Corps commander Maj. Gen. Alfred Pleasonton might have been thinking the same thing when he chose Kilpatrick to lead his newly acquired Third Division.

Physically, Kilpatrick was a candidate for least heroic looking of any general in the army. Only twenty-seven years old, a fellow officer described him as "A wiry, restless, undersized man with black eyes [and] a lantern jaw." He sported huge, stringy sand-colored sideburns, had bandy legs that gave him a rolling gait, and spoke in a shrill voice. He constantly attempted to advance himself by aggressiveness and bluster. The combined effect was comical—a member of Maj. Gen. George Meade's staff wrote in his diary that it was hard to look at Kilpatrick without laughing. Yet, at the same time, Kilpatrick was not easy to overlook. He was relentlessly ambitious, and had predicted a major generalcy for himself. He also believed that if he survived the War he would become the governor of his native New Jersey, and then President of the United States.

The Civil War began while Kilpatrick was still a student at West Point. There, he had already been noticed as fighting cock. Ardently pro–Union and anti–slavery, he engaged in a slew of fistfights with Southern cadets. Graduating 17th out of a class of 45 cadets in May 1861, he realized that the quickest road to promotion was with the volunteers, and rushed into service as captain of the flashy 5th New York volunteer regiment, also called "Duryea's Zouaves." It took just one month for him to land in the headlines. In the first infantry fight of the Civil War, at Big Bethel in June, he was hit in the buttock by a grapeshot and assisted off the field, to be lauded in gung–ho Northern newspapers as the first Union officer wounded in the War. While recuperating he traded on his new fame and landed himself a commission in the mounted service, joining the 2nd New York cavalry as lieutenant colonel in September 1861. For the next several months, while the War was largely inactive in the East, he served as a staff officer and took part in cavalry skirmishing in Northern Virginia. When the Second Bull Run Campaign began in August 1862, Kilpatrick seized on his opportunities for self–promotion, making a successful raid on a Confederate railroad line early in the campaign. During the Battle of Second Bull Run, he ordered a cavalry charge in the twilight at the end of the first day's fighting which succeeded only in annihilating a squadron under his command. The fireworks produced by the nighttime charge were sensationally picturesque, however, and Kilpatrick drew the adulation he wanted as a hell–for–leather fighter. He was promoted to colonel of the 2nd New York in December 1862.

Kilpatrick's tireless effort to gain attention helped win for him the leadership of a brigade when Maj. Gen. Joseph Hooker created the Cavalry Corps in February 1863. In the following Chancellorsville campaign, Kilpatrick led the most successful of the raiding parties that cavalry chief Brig. Gen. George Stone-man sent into the Confederate rear. Although the expedition as a whole failed in its goal of throwing the Army of Northern Virginia into a retreat toward Richmond, Kilpatrick engaged in a flashy series of wagon captures and bridge burnings, riding completely around the Rebel army and penetrating to within two miles of Richmond. This was heady stuff for a Union cavalry force that had been earlier embarrassed by the similar exploits of their foes.

At Brandy Station on June 9, Kilpatrick made a typically vigorous if not highly successful showing. Later that month, he performed erratically but aggressively at Aldie and Upperville. On June 28, new cavalry commander Maj. Gen. Alfred Pleasonton was looking for a fighter to lead his Third Division, and he chose Kilpatrick. This promotion came despite the fact there were a spate of misgivings about Kilpartick's ability. First was his insensitivity to his men and mounts. He had shown a tendency to take off on wild goose chases without a thought to the waste of horseflesh such adventures involved, and to order reckless charges which slaughtered his troopers—as at Second Bull Run. These traits would earn Kilpatrick the nickname "Kill Cavalry" among his men. His tactical repertoire had lately hardened into an unswerving determination to attack on horseback regardless of the circumstances. His discipline and attention to detail was also uneven, for although his command fought well and paraded well, their clothing and equipment were frequently neglected, carbines were dirty, and the horses showed poor grooming.

There were also questions about Kilpatrick's honesty and personal character. He had lain in jail for weeks in 1862 under suspicion that he had sold confiscated Confederate livestock and provisions for personal gain. He had been jailed again for defaming government officials while on a drunken spree in Washington. He had even been implicated in a graft scheme whereby certain horse brokers had paid him off in order to get contracts selling horses to his brigade. As if all this were not enough, he was a known devotee of prostitutes, though he was married and his wife was with child. He drank hard liquor while at the same time professing temperance. His official reports of battle were notoriously fictionalized, with exaggerated accounts of heroic behavior and enemy casualties. One officer remarked disgustedly that Kilpatrick's campaign reports were "great in 'the most glorious charges ever made,' 'sabering right and left,' and such stuff." Another observer called him a "frothy braggart, without brains," while a third saw him as an "injudicious boy, much given to blowing and who will surely come to grief."

Many others had made similar predictions since 1861. And yet against all this, Kilpatrick showed a fearlessness and a positive love of fighting that the Army of the Potomac badly needed in its officers. He showed "a great impatience and eagerness for orders," a trait which endeared him to superiors. It was because he was such a fighter that at Gettysburg his star was still ascending.

GETTYSBURG: On June 30, Kilpatrick's two brigades fought a sharp skirmish with Maj. Gen. "Jeb" Stuart's cavalry at Hanover, 15 miles east of Gettysburg, after which Kilpatrick failed to maintain contact with the enemy horsemen. Mistakenly supposing that he would find Stuart further north at East Berlin, Kilpatrick wasted July 1 wandering fruitlessly between the two towns, disobeying commanding Maj. Gen. George Meade's directions to make accurate information –gathering the "most important and sacred" duty of the mounted arm. (On the other hand, Pleasonton—who never appreciated cavalry's intelligence–gathering role, was thrilled with Kilpatrick's empty exploit at Hanover.)

On the morning of July 2, Kilpatrick received orders to move toward the battlefield, and directed his brigades to Hunterstown, five miles northeast of Gettysburg. Arriving in mid–afternoon, he clashed with Brig. Gen. Wade Hampton's Brigade, where both sides made reckless charges and then pulled back. At 11:00 that night, Kilpatrick withdrew from Hunterstown and moved south, reaching Two Taverns, five miles southeast of Gettysburg, between 3:00 and 4:00 in the morning.

At 8:00 a.m., July 3, Kilpatrick was ordered to move west toward the Emmitsburg Road and come into position on the Army of the Potomac's left, south of the Round Tops—the flank from which Brig. Gen. John Buford had been ordered the day before. As Kilpatrick was leaving Two Taverns, Second Division commander Brig. Gen. David Gregg rode up to the rear of the column and commandeered Brig. Gen. George Custer's rear brigade, leading it back up the Baltimore Pike to join his regiments guarding the army's right rear. Unaware of this subtraction, Kilpatrick headed west with only one of his two brigades.

Late in the morning, Kilpatrick approached the left of the Union army line at Big Round Top, itching to attack. Before reaching the Emmitsburg Road, he turned Brig. Gen. Elon Farnsworth's brigade to the north. The terrain was too rocky and rugged for a cavalry attack, but, about 5:30 p.m., Kilpatrick gave the order for a foredoomed, senseless charge by Farnsworth against well–posted Confederate infantry. Farnsworth was killed and dozens of his men were shot or captured during the suicidal assault. (Pleasonton declared himself "highly delighted" with Kilpatrick's operation.)

Despite earning his nickname "Kill–Cavalry" at Gettysburg, Kilpatrick showed no signs of learning from Farnsworth's disaster. Remaining in place as Third Division commander, he devised and led a miscarried raid on Richmond the next spring. Sherman then transferred him to fight in the West, where he finished out the war.

Kirkpatrick resigned from the army in 1865 to become President Johnson's minister to Chile. After returning to America in 1868, he ran unsuccessfuly for Congress in 1880, and the next year was reappointed to Chile, where he died in 1881.

For further reading:

King, George W. "The Civil War Career of Hugh Judson Kilpatrick." Thesis, Univ. of SC, 1969.

Longacre, Edward G. "Judson Kilpatrick." *Civil War Times Illustrated*, 10, Apr., 1971.

Pierce, John E. "General Hugh Judson Kilpatrick in the American Civil War: A New Appraisal." Thesis, PA State Univ, 1983.

FIRST BRIGADE

(1,925 MEN)

BRIGADIER GENERAL
ELON JOHN FARNSWORTH

For the first two years of the war, Elon Farnsworth served as adjutant in his uncle's cavalry regiment, the 8th Illinois Volunteer Cavalry. John Farnsworth, an abolitionist and U.S. Representative from Chicago, had formed the 8th in September 1861 and had become its colonel, appointing Elon, his twenty–four year old nephew, to his staff as first lieutenant.

There was a skeleton in the closet of the dark–complexioned and mustachioed Farnsworth—he had been expelled from the University of Michigan in 1858 following a drunken prank during which another student was killed. Farnsworth had headed west following this tragedy, finding work as a civilian forager for the U. S. Army's Mormon Expedition until the advent of the Civil War. Although his appointment to lieutenant was obviously due to his uncle's connections, he was soon highly regarded by the men of the regiment, among whom his "shrewdness and wit were proverbial."

By the end of 1861 he had been promoted to captain. Early the next year, on occupation duty in Alexandria, Virginia, Farnsworth gained renown when he hauled an Episcopalian minister out of his pulpit at Saint Paul's Church and had him arrested for refusing to read the required prayer for the U.S. President. (The preacher was subsequently released.) Over the next year and a half, Farnsworth accompanied the 8th Illinois in forty–one battles and skirmishes. During the Chancellorsville Campaign, he was with the regiment on Brig. Gen. George Stoneman's Raid in the enemy rear, at one point saving the horse artillery's ammunition chests by floating them over a river. At Brandy Station, he ably commanded the 8th Illinois during the early part of the battle.

New Cavalry Corps commander Maj. Gen. Alfred Pleasonton appointed Farnsworth to his staff in the early stages of the Gettysburg Campaign. This may have been a political move by the savvy Pleasonton. Pleasonton coveted for his own force the cavalry division in the Washington defenses commanded by Maj. Gen. Julius Stahel, and in a June 23 letter to his old cavalry buddy John Farnsworth, now back in Washington strolling the halls of the Capitol Building, Pleasonton disparaged Stahel's fitness for command. Pleasonton enclosed a short note from Elon in this communiqué, in which the youthful cavalryman informed his representative uncle that "Genl. [Pleasonton] speaks of recommending me for Brig[adier General]. I do not know that I ought to mention it for fear that you will call me an aspiring youth. I am satisfied to serve through this war in the line. . . . But if I can do any good anywhere else of course 'small favors &c.' Now try and talk this into the President and you can do an immense good."

Only five days later, the War Department relieved General Stahel of command of his division and added its nearly 4,000 troopers to Pleasonton's command. That same day, Pleasonton jumped young Farnsworth in rank from captain all the way to brigadier general and gave him one of Stahel's two cavalry brigades, now part of the Army of the Potomac. Pleasonton gave his reason as wanting to place in high command "officers with the proper dash to command cavalry." At the age of twenty–six, never having led anything bigger than a company for more than a few hours, Farnsworth found himself at the head of a brigade for the first time, three days before one of the largest battles of the Civil War. He was so fresh in his position that he had to borrow brigadier's coat from Pleasonton.

In spite of his inexperience, early indications of Farnsworth's ability were encouraging—at Hanover, on the eve of the big battle, Farnsworth rode at the head of his new brigade into the teeth of Maj. Gen. "Jeb" Stuart's troopers and drove them from the town.

GETTYSBURG: On June 1, the day after Hanover, Farnsworth participated in division commander Brig. Gen. Judson Kilpatrick's futile search for Stuart's elusive cavalry column.

Moved to Hunterstown, five miles northeast of Gettysburg, on July 2, Farnsworth aided Brig. Gen. George Custer in a back–and–forth fight with Brig. Gen. Wade Hampton's Southern cavalry brigade. That evening and the next day, Kilpatrick moved the division across the rear of the Union army to the opposite flank. Farnsworth's brigade was brought up to face north against the right flank of Maj. Gen. John Hood's Division south of Big Round Top.

Ordered by Kilpatrick to make a mounted charge across broken ground into a well–posted line of infantry, Farnsworth protested that it was suicide but agreed to lead the charge. "My God, Kil is going to have a cavalry charge. It is too awful to think of," Farnsworth moaned in disbelief to one of his subordinates. Farnsworth was right in his apprehension—the attack was a bloody fiasco during which Farnsworth toppled dead from his horse with five bullets in his body.

For further reading:

Longacre, Edward G. *The Cavalry at Gettysburg*. Lincoln, 1986.

Starr, Stephen. *The Union Cavalry in the Civil War: Gettysburg to Appomattox*. vol. 2. (Baton Rouge, 1995.)

SECOND BRIGADE
(1,934 MEN)

BRIGADIER GENERAL GEORGE ARMSTRONG CUSTER

George Custer had more pictures taken of himself during the Civil War than did any other officer in the Union army. A broad–shouldered six–footer with a slim waist and muscular legs, he was a man fond of extravagant dress; "one of the funniest–looking beings you ever saw . . . like a circus rider gone mad" was how one witness described his appearance. As he rode to meet his new cavalry brigade on the eve of Gettysburg, Custer had improvised a uniform which included shiny jackboots, tight olive corduroy trousers, a wide–brimmed slouch hat, tight hussar jacket of black velveteen with silver piping on the sleeves, a sailor's shirt with silver stars on its collar, and a red cravat. He wore his hair in long, glistening ringlets liberally sprinkled with cinnamon–scented hair oil.

Custer, the son of a farmer and blacksmith from Ohio, had always aspired to a soldier's life. Appointed to West Point, he was a mischievous student prone to pulling pranks. He accumulated so many demerits that he came close to expulsion in each of his four years at the academy, and graduated dead last in the

Class of 1861, just as the Civil War was starting. Assigned to the 2nd Cavalry, he reached the Federal army on the eve of the Battle of Bull Run, detailed to carry dispatches for commanding Brig. Gen. Irvin McDowell. The next year, he served at the rank of captain on the staff of Maj. Gen. George McClellan during the Peninsula Campaign. Custer was not one to let an opportunity to gain notice go to waste, and one occasion when McClellan and his well–heeled staff were reconnoitering the Chickahominy River, they came upon a potential crossing point, but could not determine the exact depth of the river at this point. Captain Custer overhead "Little Mac" mutter "I wish I knew how deep it is," turned to a companion and said, "I'll damn soon show him," and rode his horse, splashing and stumbling, out to the middle of the river. Custer then turned to the astonished officers and said triumphantly, "That's how deep it is, General!"

He continued to serve on the staffs of General McClellan and Brig. Gen. Alfred Pleasonton through the Antietam and Chancellorsville Campaigns. He became Pleasonton's protégé, and boasted that no "father could love his son more than Genl. Pleasonton loves me." He imitated Pleasonton's sartorial affectations, and began strutting about in flashy clothes. He also acquired his mentor's knack for political maneuver and for placing himself where it would do him the most good. Pleasonton ascended to the command of the Cavalry Corps after the Battle of Chancellorsville, and when he received a new division of troopers from the defenses of Washington just three days before the Battle of Gettysburg, he placed Custer—a staffer who had never commanded anything—at the head of one of its brigades. At the same time, Pleasonton promoted Custer from captain to brigadier general, a fantastic jump in rank that made Custer the youngest general in the Union forces.

Known as "Armstrong," "Autie" (his own childhood pronunciation of the former), "Fanny" (a nickname from his freshman year at West Point), or "Curly," with a reputation as one of the finest horsemen in the army, Custer had undeniable military talent. He was bold, alert, brave . . . and lucky. His tactical repertoire consisted primarily of leading whatever friendly troopers were at hand on hell–for–leather charges into the teeth of the nearest enemy force. He would have eleven horses shot from under him before the War was over. A West Point comrade observing him about the time of Gettysburg described Custer as "careless, reckless," but also as "a gallant soldier, a whole–souled generous friend, and a mighty good fellow." His bravery had a dark side—he was viciously contemptuous of those who were less strong–willed than he, testing the members of his staff by leading them where the bullets flew thick and fast, watching for any betrayal of weakness.

At Hanover on June 30, fighting against Stuart's troopers, Custer's brigade of Michigan troopers saw him for the first time. There, the massed fire of Custer's men collapsed Maj. Gen. "Jeb" Stuart's left flank.

GETTYSBURG: Custer moved as part of Brig. Gen. Judson Kilpatrick's column on a unsuccessful search for Stuart's men between Hanover and East Berlin on June 1. On June 2, after Kilpatrick moved the division to Hunterstown five miles northeast of Gettysburg, Custer took part in an ill–considered charge ordered by Kilpatrick and had his horse shot out from under him. He was saved by one of his troopers who galloped up, shot the Rebel nearest him, pulled Custer onto his horse and dashed to safety. That night, Kilpatrick's division moved south to Two Taverns, five miles southeast of Gettysburg.

As Kilpatrick's column pulled out the next morning bound for the Union left flank, Second Division commander Brig. Gen. David Gregg pulled Custer's brigade out of the rear of the column and posted it near his two brigades, at the intersection of the Hanover and Low Dutch Roads three miles east of Gettysburg. Pleasonton subsequently ordered Custer to resume his place with Kilpatrick's division, but in mid–afternoon, at the moment he prepared to pull out, Stuart's cavalry hove into view in the fields to the north and Gregg ordered Custer to stay and fight with him. Toward the end of the ensuing cavalry battle, Custer led a mounted charge by one of his regiments against two enemy brigades, crying "Come on, you Wolverines!"

The enemy forces met head–on with such force that horses flipped end over end, crushing their riders.

Both sides eventually retired, content to let the fray end in a draw. Custer's brigade had lost 257 men at Gettysburg, more by far than any other cavalry brigade. Custer survived, and continued to make aggressive attacks a staple of his command style throughout the conflict. His Michigan brigade became one of the most celebrated cavalry units of the War, and Custer would eventually command a division as a major general.

After the war, Custer was appointed lieutenant colonel of the newly authorized 7th Cavalry. He fought Indians with his regiment until his death in the massacre at Little Big Horn in 1876.

For further reading:

Longacre, Edward. *Custer and his Woverines: The Michigan Cavalry Brigade.* Conshohocken, 1997.

Monaghan, Jay. *Custer: The Life of General George Armstrong Custer.* Lincoln, 1971.

Riggs, David F. *East of Gettysburg: Custer vs. Stuart.* Bellevue, 1970.

Starr, Stephen. *The Union Cavalry in the Civil War. Gettysburg to Appomattox.* vol. 2. (Baton Rouge, 1995.

Urwin, Gregory. *Custer Victorious: The Civil War Battles of George Armstrong Custer.*

Wittaker, Frederick. *A Complete Life of General George A. Custer. Sheldon,* 1876

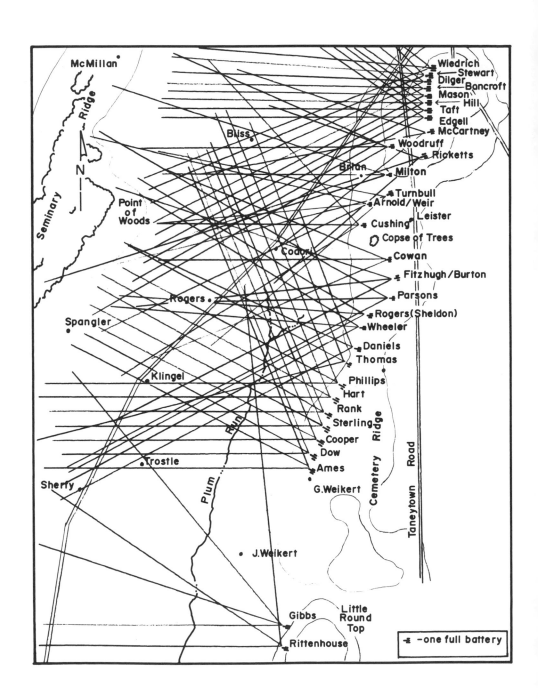

McMillan

Seminary Ridge

N

Bliss

Brian

Point of Woods

Codori

Rogers

Spangler

Klingel

Trostle

Sherfy

Plum Run

J.Weikert

Gibbs

Rittenhouse

Little Round Top

Wiedrich
Stewart
Dilger
Bancroft
Mason
Hill
Taft
Edgell
McCartney

Woodruff
Ricketts
Milton
Turnbull
Arnold/Weir
Leister
Cushing
Copse of Trees
Cowan
Fitzhugh/Burton
Parsons
Rogers (Sheldon)
Wheeler
Daniels
Thomas
Phillips
Hart
Rank
Sterling
Cooper
Dow
Ames
G.Weikert

Cemetery Ridge

Taneytown Road

⫞ —one full battery

ARTILLERY

BRIGADIER GENERAL HENRY JACKSON HUNT

Henry Hunt was too stuffy and conservative, too stiff and "Old Army" to ever be popular with his men, but his prompt decisive direction of the artillery arm of the Army of the Potomac had already been crucial to several battles in the two years before Gettysburg.

Hunt was the great artillery general of the Civil War. He had a genius for organization, and his keen knowledge of the science of gunnery drew admiration from his Confederate foes—even though they were the victims of Hunt's belief in densely supplied salvos of gunfire from massed batteries. He particularly liked to focus every available gun on one Confederate battery at a time, pulverizing the target with a hail of iron before moving on to the next enemy gun position. Hunt did not advocate indiscriminate cannon fire, and he sternly preached that each gun crew should take the time to carefully sight and aim its piece before every shot. Even in the hottest action, he consid-

ered a gun firing at a rate quicker than one round every two minutes to be firing wildly and wasting ammunition. (One story has Hunt castigating one of his artillery officers when he appealed for more ammunition in the midst of a battle. "Young man," Hunt scolded, "are you aware that every round you fire costs $2.67?") He even associated the quick expenditure of ordnance with cowardice, for he thought that any crew which rapidly discharged its ammunition did so because it was anxious to hitch up the guns and head rearward. To combat this, he forbade any battery to retire just because the chests were empty; batteries were required to send the caissons back for resupply and then sit under fire—every man at his post—while they waited for it to return.

Hunt was born into a military family stationed at the frontier outpost of Detroit in 1819. As an eight-year-old boy, he accompanied his infantry officer father on the expedition that established Fort Leavenworth. Orphaned at age ten, he graduated from West Point at twenty and chose the artillery arm of the service. He earned fame for his bravery a few years later in the Mexican War, when he ran his fieldpiece right up to an enemy cannon and destroyed it in a muzzle-to-muzzle duel. By 1856, he was already one of the most distinguished authorities on the gunner's art in the Regular Army, chosen as a member of a three-man board to review light artillery tactics. The report of the board was adopted in 1860 and composed into a manual that served as the "bible" for artillerymen on both sides in the Civil War.

After the Civil War began, Hunt made himself conspicuous in his first battle, heroically covering the retreat of the Union army from an exposed position with his four-gun battery at Bull Run. By the time of the Peninsula Campaign the next spring, he was already the Army of the Potomac's top gunner, in command of its Artillery

Reserve. At Malvern Hill, the last action of the Seven Days' Battles, he directed his massed and well-sited guns so well that one admirer was reminded of "an organist pulling the stops." Hunt's fieldpieces caused such slaughter amongst the Rebel attackers that the battle was won with only the moderate participation of the Federal infantry.

Hunt was promoted to brigadier general in September 1862, and made Chief of Artillery by Maj. Gen. George McClellan in the middle of the Maryland Campaign. An immediate indication of Hunt's value to the Union army was the nickname the Confederate veterans gave to the September 17 Battle of Antietam: "Artillery Hell."

At Fredericksburg in December, Hunt spent a week or more posting 140 guns in a line on Stafford Heights, a ridge on the Union side of the Rappahannock River. It was Hunt's intimidating array which deterred General Robert E. Lee from counterattacking the decimated and otherwise vulnerable Federal infantry formations as they staggered away from their disastrous assault against Marye's Heights.

The army's next commander, Maj. Gen. Joe Hooker, had an unfortunate antipathy toward Hunt and stripped him of his command, leaving him with only administrative duties. This cost the Federal army dearly at the Battle of Chancellorsville in May 1863, where the traditional advantages in the quality and volume of fire of the Union batteries were squandered through mismanagement. Hooker (and many other Union officers) recognized this problem, and he belatedly restored Hunt to his active battlefield role on the third day of the battle, though the move came too late to change the outcome.

As the Army of the Potomac headed toward Pennsylvania in the early summer of 1863, Hunt's value to the army was freshly vindicated and universally acknowledged. When Maj. Gen. George Meade took command three days before Gettysburg, the army had a new chief who, like Hunt, was thoroughly professional and rather stiff. Although the two generals were not close personal associates, they enjoyed

mutual respect for one another, and Hunt considered Meade a "gentleman." Meade, in turn, often sought Hunt's opinion and implicitly trusted his judgment, frequently using him as his surrogate on the battlefield.

GETTYSBURG: On July 1, after spending the entire first day of the battle in the rear at army headquarters in Taneytown, Hunt received an order from Meade sometime after 7:00 p.m. to move the Artillery Reserve to Gettysburg—an act which effectively committed the Army of the Potomac to do battle there. Hunt rode to Gettysburg with Meade's small party of seven that night, leaving around 10:00 a.m. and arriving on Cemetery Hill at 11:30 a.m.

At about 2:00 in the early morning of July 2, Hunt and Meade rode south along the army's line in the moonlight from Cemetery Ridge to near Little Round Top, then to the army's right, where the Baltimore Pike crossed Rock Creek. Having scouted the excellent defensive ground upon which his army was deployed, Meade instructed Hunt to continue to study the terrain and supervise the placement of the army's artillery. By 10:30 that morning, the efficient Hunt had 108 cannon from the Artillery Reserve on hand, as well as a surplus stock of ammunition from which all the army's batteries would gratefully borrow in the days ahead.

It was a little after 10:00 a.m. when Hunt returned to army headquarters from Culp's Hill and became involved in the dispute between Meade and Third Corps' leader Maj. Gen. Daniel Sickles. Sickles was worried about his corps' position on the army's left, an issue that became one of the great controversies of the battle. Meade declined to go over the ground with Sickles personally, and he sent Hunt instead. Sickles pointed out to Hunt the advanced position he wanted to take, on the high ground along the Emmitsburg Road about three-quarters of a mile in front of his assigned position. When Sickles asked if he should advance to the new line, Hunt shook his head: "Not on my authority." At that point, a cannonade opened on Cemetery Hill, and Hunt rode off to give his attention to the gunfire, making a point to go by headquarters and tell Meade of the line Sickles proposed. Later, after Sickles had advanced his line without permission, Hunt rode back to the Third Corps and helped ready its artillery for the impending Southern assailment. When the Confederate attack commenced, Hunt galloped to Devil's Den, the endpoint of Sickle's line, to observe the posting of one of his batteries. Hunt dismounted to confer with the artillery officer there, and as he made his way back to his horse, was nearly trampled in a bizarre stampede of terror-stricken cattle. He remained to direct his guns in the desperate fighting on Sickles' sector for the rest of the afternoon.

That night, Hunt worked with Brig. Gen. Robert Tyler of the Artillery Reserve to ensure that damaged equipment was repaired, ammunition chests were refilled, decimated batteries were reorganized, and that the available serviceable guns were readied for service by the next morning. At dawn on July 3, when the Twelfth Corps batteries opened the battle on Culp's Hill, Hunt was there to help direct their fire. When the fighting eased at that point in late morning, he went to inspect the field pieces on Cemetery Hill, and observed the Confederate artillery buildup on the ridge to the west. Hunt allowed the enemy to continue their emplacements during an informal "artillery truce."

At 1:00 p.m., when Hunt was on Little Round Top resting from his morning's inspection, the 150-gun Confederate cannonade commenced. The guns were aimed at the Union defenders on Cemetery Ridge, the focal point for "Pickett's Charge" scheduled to begin later in the afternoon. Hunt rode back to the Artillery Reserve to see about fresh batteries and ammunition, then trotted to Cemetery Ridge. While the shells hissed and exploded amongst his batteries, Hunt moved up and down the line, checking the condition of his guns and crews and making sure they fired slowly and deliberately. After an hour or so, in spite of his efforts at conservation, ammunition began to run low. It occurred to Hunt that if the Union batteries ceased firing, the Rebels might be fooled into thinking their bombardment had effectively reduced the capability of the Federal cannoneers, so he rode along the ridge ordering his guns to go silent. About 3:00 p.m., the Confederate batteries stopped firing and the mile-long line of Pickett's Charge appeared. Hunt's batteries still had long-range ammunition in their chests, and they began to mercilessly punish their attackers' flanks. (In the middle of the Union line, the gunners were out of shot and shell where Maj. Gen. Winfield Hancock had ordered the guns at this location to keep blasting away during the cannonade to inspire the infantry.) At the climax of the attack, as the Southerners clambered over the wall and closed in on one of his batteries, Hunt appeared among the guns on horseback, firing his revolver into the Rebels until his horse was shot, and he fell pinned beneath his dead mount. Pulled free, he mounted his sergeant's horse and spurred off to another portion of the line. His guns played a large role in turning back the last attack of Gettysburg.

Henry Hunt continued as the indispensable chief of artillery for the rest of the war, but the last two years of the conflict offered few opportunities for the spectacular employment of his guns. Hunt got along well with Lt. Gen. Ulysses S. Grant, who put Hunt in charge of batteries involved in the Petersburg siege operations, which began in June 1864.

Hunt remained in the army and was stationed in the South during Reconstruction (where he gained a reputation for fairness). He retired in 1883 and became governor of the Soldiers' Home in Washington, D. C., where he died of pneumonia in 1889.

For further reading:

Longacre, Edward G. *Henry Hunt: The Man Behind the Guns.* South Brunswick, 1977.

———, "The Soul of Our Artillery," *Civil War Times Illustrated,* 12, June, 1973.

ARTILLERY RESERVE
(2,988 MEN / 114 GUNS)

BRIGADIER GENERAL
ROBERT OGDEN TYLER

Robert O. Tyler was a competent professional, a thirty-one-year-old artillery officer who had spent most of the war around the heavy siege guns of the Washington defenses.

Born in the Catskill Mountains of New York and raised in Hartford, Connecticut, he graduated from West Point in 1853 in the upper half of his class and went into the artillery. His wide-ranging Regular Army service in the eight years before the Civil War took him from Florida to the Pacific Northwest, from Arizona to Minnesota.

Tyler witnessed the beginning of the war firsthand when he watched the shelling of Fort Sumter from the deck of the relief ship that tried in vain to supply the stronghold. Returning North, served at the quartermaster depot in Alexandria, Virginia, and was then made colonel of the 4th Connecticut Volunteers in late August 1861. These men were converted into the gunners of the 1st Connecticut Heavy Artillery in January 1862, and manned the heavy guns that safeguarded the nation's capital.

That spring, Tyler was put in charge of Maj. Gen. George McClellan's siege train in the Peninsula Campaign, directing the heavy artillery that was intended to reduce the Richmond defenses to rubble. Tyler's resourcefulness, however, was put to the test while protecting his weaponry during McClellan's retreat, and he managed to save all but one of his guns. After the Army of the Potomac left the Peninsula, Tyler went back to manning the Washington defenses.

In November 1862, he was promoted to brigadier general, making him only the second general in the artillery, after Brig. Gen. Henry Hunt. He was transferred back to the field for the Fredericksburg Campaign and commanded artillery on the Stafford Heights during the December battle, then returned again to the Washington forts in January 1863.

When the artillery arm of the Army of the Potomac was reorganized after Chancellorsville in May 1863, the Artillery Reserve was doubled to five brigades consisting of 118 guns, and Tyler was brought back to command it under the direction of Chief of Artillery Hunt. This arrangement centralized control of a large part of the army's artillery and made it more responsive to the army's needs. Working together, Hunt and Tyler could rush guns to critical points to give the army overwhelming firepower where it was needed.

GETTYSBURG: Tyler and the Artillery Reserve spent the greater part of July 1 at army headquarters in Taneytown. About sundown, receiving orders to move to Gettysburg and report to General Hancock, Tyler moved north with two brigades—nine batteries. Apparently not understanding that Hancock had been recently assigned to go forward and oversee the battlefield, Tyler stopped his batteries when he reached the bivouac of Hancock's Second Corps on the Taneytown road, about 10:30 p.m.

When the Second Corps moved out the next morning, July 2, Tyler followed, parking his batteries in the southeast corner of the junction of the Granite Schoolhouse Lane and Taneytown Road when he arrived at the battlefield that morning. At about 10:30 a.m., ten more batteries arrived from the south, making a total of 108 guns, along with their ammunition train, available to the Army of the Potomac. From 3:30 that afternoon on, Tyler sent a steady stream of batteries to the Third Corps' front, the scene of desperate fighting, only a few hundred yards to the west of his artillery park. As the fighting proceeded northward along the Union line as the afternoon progressed, Tyler dispatched batteries to Cemetery Ridge, then Cemetery Hill.

After dark, Tyler worked with General Hunt to resupply, refit, and reorganize all the army's batteries—those attached to the individual corps as well as the Reserve. Seventy wagonloads of ammunition were distributed to the guns that had been employed that day, with more than 10,000 rounds going to batteries outside the Reserve.

On July 3, when the 150-gun Confederate cannonade opened about 1:00 p.m., Tyler was riding behind the lines overseeing the artillery and double-checking the location of ammunition wagons. A hissing shell, one of hundreds that sailed over Cemetery Ridge and exploded in the rear among the parked guns, killed his horse. Tyler spent the next hour or so supervising the movement of the Reserve's guns further to the rear, out of danger. Working in the extreme heat and humidity of July weather, Tyler became prostrated by sunstroke. He was forced to leave his command, though he recovered and returned to duty by dusk.

Artillery chief Hunt expressed his "indebtedness" to Tyler after the battle, and Tyler continued in command of the Reserve until December. In January 1864 he was given command of a division of infantry in the Washington defenses, and in late May, during Lt. Gen. Ulysses Grant's Overland Campaign, Tyler brought a oversized "division" of green Heavy Artillery regiments to Spotsylvania. On June 3, while leading a brigade of these new infantrymen at Cold Harbor, several bones in Tyler's foot were fractured by a gunshot. The lameness which resulted forced him from the army.

Tyler was made duputy quartermaster for the army after the war, and remained in that position until his death from heart disease in 1874.

For further reading:

Allardice, Bruce. "Out of the Shadows." Civil War Times Illustrated, 33, Jan./Feb., 1995.

Longacre, Edward G. Henry Hunt: The Man Behind the Guns. South Brunswick, 1977.

Warner, Ezra. "Who Was General Tyler?" Civil War Times Illustrated, 9, Oct., 1970.

ARMY OF NORTHERN VIRGINIA:
(70,247 MEN / 283 GUNS)

GENERAL
ROBERT E. LEE

Napoleon said that "the personality of the general is indispensable, he is the head, he is the all of the army." This was never truer than with Robert E. Lee and the Army of Northern Virginia. The character of Lee suffused the army from the time he took its command in June 1862, providing inspiration and élan for the Rebel soldiers who made up its storied ranks.

Lee had hardened and strengthened his famous character through a lifetime of almost Biblical self-denial. He had lived his life strictly by devotion to the self-sacrificing virtues of duty and religion. There is thus a certain impenetrability to Lee's personality; he presents a profound enigma to anyone raised after the advent of Freud, accustomed as we are to looking for dark corners in the hopes of finding the keys to a man's character. Even in his own time, Confederate diarist Mary Chesnut mused in her journal, "Can anyone say that they know Robert E. Lee?"

His own father's misspent life provided Lee with a disturbing cautionary tale about the consequences of the lack of self-control. Robert E. Lee was the son of "Light Horse Harry" Lee, a Revolutionary War hero whose reputation had become blackened by vain financial schemes. By 1807, when Robert was born, the family mansion was already a cheerless, barren place with chains placed across the doors to keep out creditors. Before Robert was two, his father had served two stretches in debtor's prison. In 1813, Light-Horse Harry, who had been badly injured in a Baltimore political riot, boarded a boat for a retreat in Barbados, and his family never saw him again.

By the age of twelve Robert, the youngest of five children, was the only one still at home when his mother's health worsened, and the youngster shouldered the burdens

of managing the household and ministering to his ill parent. As he approached late adolescence, Lee found his options limited by his family's poverty. Although he loved the soil and would have found fulfillment in a planter's life, there was no earth for him to till—his father had lost all of the family land. There were signs that he was interested in a career in medicine, but the family could not afford the cost of the necessary education. Since Robert had long been interested in the military, he accepted an appointment to Military Academy at West Point, to prepare for the only profession for which his family could afford to train him.

Lee performed brilliantly as a student, graduating with high honors, 2nd among the 46 cadets in the class of 1829, with a sterling record of conduct. West Point regulated cadets' behavior with a demerit system. Demerits, called "crimes," were given for tardiness or absence at roll calls, meals, chapel, drill, and inspections. They were issued for dirty quarters or equipment, visiting after taps, disturbances during study hours, any of a number of lapses in personal grooming, smoking in the barracks, improper behavior toward cadet officers and academy officers, and altercations or fights. The system was so comprehensive and administered so rigidly that only one cadet in the history of the Academy ever passed the four-year course of instruction without committing a "crime." That cadet was Robert E. Lee.

The top graduates were given their choice of assignments, and Lee chose to go into the engineers, the elite branch of the army. He was a stunning, handsome young officer, vibrant and gregarious, a man who enjoyed flirting with young, pretty ladies. This carefree post-graduate period was no more than a brief interlude, however, ended by Lee's ready adherence to a tradition of five generations of Lee men—that of bettering their status by marrying well.

In 1831, just two years out of West Point, he married his childhood playmate and distant cousin Mary Custis, the only daughter of George Washington's adopted son, George Washington Parke Custis. Robert and Mary were wed in the Custis family mansion at Arlington overlooking the Potomac River. The house had become a shrine to the memory of George Washington, full of articles used by the venerated Father of the Country. In addition to bettering Lee's status, he realized the marriage had made him an heir to the Washington tradition. Washington had always been Lee's hero. Now, as he ate on Washington's china and took up Washington's knife and fork, Lee also took up Washington's view of duty, and acted as he thought Washington would. His self-conscious effort to emulate Washingtonian tact and grave self-discipline caused Virginia governor Henry Wise to remark, "General Lee, you certainly play Washington to perfection."

Lee's wife's health started to deteriorate in 1831, beginning thirty years of nearly constant illness that would in the end reduce her to a total invalid. During the decades before the Civil War, Lee moved from military assignment to assignment, separated from his wife and children (who would eventually number four daughters and three sons). Here again the Washingtonian virtues prevailed, for Lee tried to accept the demanding personal burdens of his duty without complaint. The long separations from his family were hard on the young officer, however, and by the 1850s had produced in him a state of melancholy. Lee's letters in this period were often tinged with discouragement at his condition and the painfully slow promotion rate among the engineers in the Regular Army. By 1855, he had risen only to lieutenant colonel in the 2nd Cavalry. A theme of personal suffering as God's retribution for his sins became present in his letters. When he left home for Jefferson Barracks near St. Louis in 1855, he viewed the separation as "a just punishment for my sins," and prayed that "I may truly repent of the many errors of my life, that my sins may be forgiven." By 1857, he was considering leaving the army, as he indicated in this letter to future Confederate general Albert Sidney Johnston:

I can see that I have at least to decide the question, which I have staved off for 20 years, whether I am to continue in the Army all my life, or to leave it now. My preferences which have clung to me from boyhood impel me to adopt the former course, but yet I feel that a man's family has its claims too.

When the Civil War came in 1861, the private wilderness of self-doubt that had plagued Lee for a decade disappeared. Lee had always been held in high esteem by his fellow military men, both for his abilities and character. He had no greater admirer than the highest-ranking officer in the United States, Mexican War hero General Winfield Scott. He had won Scott's undying respect for his brilliant service as a staff officer during the Mexican War campaign from Vera Cruz to Mexico City. Lee had been praised in Scott's battle reports more than any other officer, and in the banquet after the final victory, the victorious Scott had risen, rapped on the table, and proposed a toast to "the health of Captain Robert E. Lee, without whose aid we should not now be here."

When Sumter fell, President Abraham Lincoln and Scott tried to make Lee the principal Union field commander. When

Virginia seceded, however, Lee's visceral allegiance to the soil of his native state would not allow him to take up arms against it, and he declined the offer when it was tendered on April 18, 1861. On April 23, he accepted the command of Virginia's army and navy, and worked tirelessly for the next three months organizing the Old Dominion's fledgling military forces.

In late July 1861 he was given his first field command, in western Virginia. His first campaign in September-October 1861 was a disaster, and Lee's popularity plunged. His seemingly tentative behavior in this rugged mountainous region earned him the disparaging nickname "Granny Lee." When Jefferson Davis reassigned Lee to the department of the Carolinas and Georgia in November 1861, the locals protested the appointment. Davis wrote later of "the clamor which then arose followed him when he went to South Carolina, so that it became necessary on his departure to write a letter to Governor of that State, telling him what manner of man he was."

Lee became President Davis' military advisor in March 1862, though his appointment to this post went virtually unnoticed in Southern newspapers. His tenure in Richmond did garner him another contemptuous moniker, the "King of Spades," for his insistence on having earthworks constructed around the Southern capital. When Lee took command of the Confederate army on June 1, after its previous commander Gen. Joseph E. Johnston had been wounded at Seven Pines, the *Richmond Examiner* announced: "Evacuating Lee, who has never yet risked a single battle with the invader, is commanding general."

This moment, however, marked the emergence of one of history's most successful commanders. Lee named his divisions the "Army of Northern Virginia" and proceeded to attack Maj. Gen. George McClellan's larger and better-equipped force in the Seven Days' Battles. His offensives, while bloody and clumsy—Lee's plans were complex and far too difficult for inexperienced officers to perform—drove McClellan back from the shadows of Richmond to the cover of his gunboats on the James River.

Satisfied McClellan had been turned aside, Lee moved to deal with Maj. Gen. John Pope's Army of Virginia, which was coalescing outside Washington. During the Second Manassas Campaign, Lee audaciously divided his army in the face of the enemy, sending Maj. Gen. Thomas J. "Stonewall" Jackson on a long flank march into the enemy rear. Pope was bewildered by his opponent's move to the point that the Confederates were able to unite forces in the middle of a battle and rout Pope's army at Second Manassas. Winfield Scott's former staff officer had taken over command of an outnumbered army with its back to Richmond, and then defeated two larger Union armies in two months. With the enemy thrown back to Washington, D.C., the epithet "Granny Lee" disappeared from the headlines.

Lee was loath to withdraw after such an exhilarating triumph as Second Manassas. In Thomas Jackson and James Longstreet Lee had found two able corps (or wing) commanders, his men were tired but victorious veterans, and the spirit of the army was high. Lee wanted to maintain an offensive to take the war onto the Union-occupied soil of Maryland, where he hoped to catalyze the enlistment of Marylanders into the Confederate ranks. With his opponent disorganized, perhaps a victory there would bring assistance from overseas. And so Lee crossed the Potomac in September 1862.

The move was a desperate one and his army, though victorious, was ill-shod and poorly-equipped, and thus not fit for the enterprise. Under the guidance of General McClellan, the Union army recovered from Pope's debacle sooner than expected and marched to meet Lee. Fighting a battle that would have been better avoided at Sharpsburg, Lee was fortunate to be able to retreat across the Potomac at the end of the Maryland Campaign, although his casualties had heavily bled the army. At the year's end, he recovered his earlier good fortune and dealt the Union war effort another blow at the Battle of Fredericksburg, where the Army of the Potomac's new commander, Maj. Gen. Ambrose Burnside, obliged

Lee by hurling division after division against his impregnable defensive positions.

The opening of the 1863 campaign season opened with Lee's most perfectly-orchestrated victory at the Battle of Chancellorsville in early May. Outnumbered two-to-one and initially outmaneuvered by the Army of the Potomac's latest chief, Maj. Gen. Joseph Hooker, Lee took bigger risks than ever before, dividing his army in the face of a superior enemy, and then dividing it again. A flanking force under Stonewall Jackson crushed the Union right flank, setting in motion a series of Union reverses that took the fight out of Hooker and sent the sullen enemy host back across the Rappahannock River. To capitalize on his momentum, Lee once again decided to march north, this time aiming at Pennsylvania. This invasion (or, more properly, "raid," since the incursion was never intended to permanently hold enemy territory), promised to bring about a climactic engagement. On June 3, his men quietly slipped out of their works at Fredericksburg and began marching toward the Shenandoah Valley, triggering the beginning of the Gettysburg Campaign.

What made Lee such a great commander? Some have argued that Lee's abilities were rooted in the "cavalier tradition" of Virginia. This tradition was an aristocratic holdover from England that held that the "best men" of society were born to lead, victory being guaranteed by the wholehearted backing of those born to follow. While historians have begun to question the impact such a arcane holdover had in developing differences between the North and the South, it does seem that Lee took very seriously that he, as a gentleman, was entitled to possess and judiciously apply authority. He was able to maintain a subtle balance between his ability to dominate and inspire by his mere presence, while not becoming intoxicated by such power.

The second component—Lee's essential humility—was evident in the manner in which he waged his battles. He rarely made himself conspicuous, preferring to lead by his moral strength while trusting the execution of his orders to other professional sol-diers with a formal military education (for him, warfare was too important to entrust to amateurs). His command style derived from his twin guiding principles of duty and religion. He confided to a Prussian visitor the essential features of his leadership: "I plan and work with all my might to bring the troops to the right place at the right time," he said. "With that I have done my duty. As soon as I order the troops forward into battle, I lay the fate of my army in the hands of God." There were obvious practical defects in this philosophy, and sometimes his subordinates were paralyzed by the discretion Lee afforded them. Yet, Lee's command technique repeatedly succeeded in his first year with the Army of Northern Virginia because he had surrounded himself with lieutenants who were not afraid to act on their own initiative and who understood his desires.

Another facet of Lee's cavalier credo went a long way toward explaining the success of his army—his ability to work well with a wide assortment of high-strung prima donnas in subordinate positions. Lee believed that a gentleman "does not needlessly and unnecessarily remind an offender of a wrong," and not only forgives "but can forget." Lee was constitutionally non-confrontational; he avoided humiliating his subordinates, even when he believed they had failed him. Instead he would reassign or relieve ineffectual commanders, such as he had with Maj. Gens. John B. Magruder, Benjamin Huger, and Theophilus Holmes after the Seven Days' Battles.

Perhaps the biggest conundrum of Lee's personality was how his legendary calm could exist side-by-side with the audacity that became the most striking feature of his generalship. President Davis' aide, Col. Joseph Ives, made a fascinating prediction in a conversation with Col. E. Porter Alexander just after Lee took over the Virginia army. At a time when the newspapers were calling the general "Granny Lee," Ives informed Alexander: "[Lee] will take more desperate chances and take them quicker than any other general in this country, North or South. . .His name might be Audacity." Maj. Gen. Henry Heth later seconded this opinion, writing of Lee at Gettysburg, "This determination to strike his enemy was not from the position he found himself [in], but from a leading characteristic of the man. General Lee, not excepting Jackson, was the most aggressive man in his army." Lee had been unfailingly aggressive ever since the Seven Days. While this behavior cowed his early adversaries and made his army legendary, it also bled the Confederacy of its manpower. Lee's thrilling assaults were winning astounding victories in the short run, but over the course of the war they would eventually rob him of his offensive power and condemn him to a defensive conflict he could not win.

But what Southerner would not have sacrificed himself for a commander such as Lee? The general was at the height of his power during the Gettysburg Campaign, and many of those who encountered him during this period remarked on the magnificence of his appearance. British observer Arthur J. L. Fremantle judged him "the handsomest man of his age I ever saw . . . tall, broad shouldered, very well made, well set up, a thorough soldier in appearance." Lt. Col. G. Moxley Sorrel, Longstreet's staff officer, commented on "the perfect poise of head and shoulders," and wrote "his white teeth and winning smile were irresistible" (features that are not visible in any photograph). Age had given additional gravity to what had always been a dignified bearing. In his fifty-seventh year, his hair had turned gray, and he sported a full gray beard. Five feet ten inches tall and 165 pounds, he was short in the legs, so when he rode a horse he seemed much taller. In this campaign he wore a worn long gray jacket and a black felt hat. His blue trousers were tucked into high leather boots that came up to cover his knees. His only insignia of rank were three stars on his collar. As always, he did not carry any weapons. Notwithstanding his weathered coat, Fremantle called his appearance "smart and clean."

There were issues, however, that were cause for concern. Lee was campaigning without Jackson for the first time, for the

corps commander had been mortally wounded at Chancellorsville. Jackson's loss resulted in an army-wide reorganization from two corps to three. The reconstituted army now possessed two new lieutenant generals and Lee was operating for the first time with three primary subordinates. He was not in good health, being weakened by pleurisy and an infection he had contracted in April; he may also have been suffering from a heart condition.

As he crossed the Mason-Dixon Line, the ramifications of the campaign began to weigh on Lee, creating an unusual tension in him. A number of observers noted that Lee was uneasy, anxious, uncharacteristically excitable. He fretted about the disappearance of Maj. Gen. "Jeb" Stuart, whose absence meant that Lee was receiving little in the way of accurate intelligence, even as he moved deep into enemy territory. It augured poorly that for the first time anyone could remember, Lee's many concerns, in Lt. Gen. James Longstreet's words, "threatened his superb equipoise."

GETTYSBURG: Lee woke on the morning of July 1 at his headquarters on the outskirts of Chambersburg, about 25 miles west of Gettysburg. He expected that a battle was imminent somewhere along the Chambersburg-Gettysburg Pike, and he conferred with Lt. Gen. A. P. Hill, the new commander of the Third Corps. Hill's men were headed eastward that morning, and Lee stressed his desire that he not trigger a general engagement before the army could concentrate. Lee had given orders for the army to group at Cashtown on the Chambersburg Pike eight miles west of Gettysburg, but it would take most of the day for Lt. Gen. Richard Ewell's Second Corps to arrive from the north and for the rest of the army to snake along the single road over South Mountain from Chambersburg. He determined to move his headquarters forward to Cashtown that morning.

As he rode toward Cashtown with First Corps commander James Longstreet, he heard the rumble of cannon from the east. Arriving in Cashtown about 11:00 a.m. he knew from the rolling thunder that a substantial fight was underway. Lee had only recently learned that the Army of the Potomac had marched north after him, and that Maj. Gen. George Gordon Meade had replaced Joe Hooker. Knowing that Meade outnumbered him, he became acutely anxious that Stuart's cavalry, his "eyes and ears," return soon from a wide-ranging raid into the enemy rear. After listening intently to the sound of the guns, Lee felt he had no choice but to ride ahead to see for himself what was happening.

Sometime after 1:00 p.m. he reached a ridge one mile east of Herr Ridge just west of Gettysburg. What he learned must have disturbed him. Hill's leading division under Maj. Gen. Henry Heth had been mauled badly on the outskirts of town by elements of the Army of the Potomac. Although Heth had withdrawn, far off to the left he could see Confederates (Maj. Gen. Robert Rodes' Division, Richard Ewell's Second Corps) on Oak Hill attacking the Federals in front of Heth from the north. Heth rode up begging for orders to attack in concert with Rodes, but Lee at first would not permit it, still reluctant to commit his army to battle with so little information about the enemy in front of him. About 2:30 p.m., however, Lee realized a magnificent opportunity was at hand to crush the Union First Corps, and gave Heth the order to attack. Maj. Gen. Dorsey Pender's Division, Hill's Corps, was behind Heth in support.

The overwhelming combination swept the First Corps off the ridges west of town. Another stroke of good luck for Lee was the appearance of Maj. Gen. Jubal Early's Division of Ewell's Corps, which arrived from the northeast during the heavy afternoon fighting. Taking position on Rodes' left, Early's brigades outflanked and routed the enemy Eleventh Corps. In the late afternoon, masses of enemy soldiers from both corps were running back through Gettysburg to rally on Cemetery Hill, a prominent eminence just south of town. Lee's men were pursuing and rounding up thousands of prisoners as the commanding general rode forward to Seminary Ridge to observe the spectacle. He had just witnessed a substantial Confederate victory, but the Federal forces had not been thoroughly crushed

and there were still several hours of daylight remaining. Lee was unsure of what to do next.

Longstreet's corps was not up, and Lee was uncertain as to the enemy's strength. He halted Maj. Gen. Richard H. Anderson's arriving division (Third Corps) two miles west of town as a reserve. Yet, Cemetery Hill was clearly the key to the battlefield, and had to be taken if possible. According to Lee's report of the battle, he sent Second Corps chief General Ewell instructions "to carry the hill occupied by the enemy, if he found it practicable, but to avoid a general engagement until the arrival of the other divisions of the army, which were ordered to hasten forward." What, exactly, did this confusing order mean? Ewell was unsure. Although he had several fresh brigades coming up, the enemy had deployed a number of guns on the eminence and were rapidly fortifying it. Ewell, who had previously operated exclusively within Stonewall Jackson's rigid command system, was now faced with a discretionary order. He felt constrained by Lee's directive not to bring on a full-fledged battle, was lacking fresh troops in large numbers, and night was rapidly approaching. After some consideration, Ewell decided an attack that evening was not justified. Lee's overly discretionary and complicated order to Ewell was partially to blame for the malaise that struck down the Confederate drive.

That evening, Longstreet joined Lee and urged him to move the army to the right, around the Union left, taking up a strong position between the Federal army and Washington. This, claimed Longstreet with some justification, would force the Federals to attack them. By that time, however, Lee considered a battle at Gettysburg unavoidable. "No," he said, "the enemy is there, and I am going to attack him there." His army, though, was awkwardly positioned on exterior lines and communications between both ends were difficult and time-consuming. The Federal position, by contrast, was rather compact and anchored on both flanks by hills and wooded terrain. Sometime before sunset, Lee rode from Seminary Ridge over to Ewell's headquarters near Gettysburg to make plans for the next day. Ewell and his subordinates were reluctant either to attack from their present location or to withdraw and come to the right to shorten the army's lines. Their solution was that Longstreet should come up and attack on the right. As Lee headed back to his tent for the night, he had still not finalized his plans for the next day.

The general spent the morning of July 2 near his headquarters tent, which was pitched on the west slope of Seminary Ridge just south of the Chambersburg Pike. There, a meeting was underway with a variety of officers, including Longstreet, Hill, and Maj. Gens. Lafayette McLaws and John, Hood. Jeb Stuart and his cavalry had not yet reported, so Lee still knew little more about the strength or position of the Army of the Potomac than what he could see from the Seminary, but he felt he had to maintain the initiative by attacking. Shortly after sunrise, Lee sent a scouting party to Little Round Top to examine the enemy left. They returned three hours later and reported that they had seen no sign of the enemy there in force. (Given that thousands of Federals were active in the area that morning, the report is one of the most puzzling mysteries of the battle).

After receiving this news, Lee decided to attack from his right with Longstreet's two available First Corps divisions (McLaws and Hood; George Pickett was still marching to join the army). Within a short time, Lee gave McLaws orders to move south without being seen and place his brigades across the Emmitsburg Road. He was to attack en echelon toward Gettysburg, driving in the Federal left flank with Hood's Division in support—a move similar to Jackson's flanking attack at Chancellorsville. Longstreet was visibly upset by Lee's plan to attack the enemy and disputed Lee's tactical arrangements with McLaws' Division, to no avail.

About 9:00 a.m. Lee rode again to Ewell's headquarters. The Second Corps commander persuaded Lee to let his men stay in place so they could attack and create a diversion whenever they heard the sound of Longstreet's guns. This diversion, Ewell further argued, could be converted to an all-out attack on the enemy on Culp's Hill and Cemetery Hill if a good opportunity presented itself. Lee acquiesced and rode back to Seminary Ridge, where Longstreet was finalizing his arrangements to move his divisions toward their jump-off positions near the Peach Orchard. Richard Anderson's Division of Hill's Corps was filing south on Seminary Ridge. Anderson's men, who would be on Longstreet's immediate left flank, would continue the attack when "Old Pete" swept the enemy in front of their position. By about 11:00 a.m., Lee had marked out the responsibilities for the day's attack, with every division on hand (except Pender's and Heth's, which had been badly cut up on the first day of battle) slated to participate in some capacity. Much like the Seven Days' Battles, however, Lee's directive required close coordination between two widely-separated flanks.

For a variety of reasons, Longstreet did not get into position until about 4:00 p.m., when his two divisions reached the area fronting the Peach Orchard opposite the Union left flank. Longstreet and his commanders were shocked to find Federals posted there in strength and strongly supported by artillery. Lee had ridden south to be with Longstreet in mid-afternoon, and the plan to attack up the Emmitsburg Road was quickly changed: Hood would now form on McLaws' right flank and begin the attack north up the Emmitsburg Road. McLaws would attack next, and Anderson's men would follow.

Once his corps were in position Lee typically did not interfere with his subordinates. Instead, he went back to the Lutheran Seminary to watch the progress of the engagement. One man said his face betrayed no anxiety, while another reported that he received and sent only one message (which if true demonstrates a remarkably detached command style). Longstreet's men dutifully opened the attack and crushed the Federal Third Corps, driving it and reinforcements from other Federal corps back some distance onto southern Cemetery Ridge. Despite some of the hardest fighting of the war, the Union line remained intact. Meanwhile, Ewell's men on the opposite end of the line attacked hours after Longstreet's engagement began and, because of a Federal blunder that left Culp's Hill all but unoccupied, made a lodgment on that wooded and rocky eminence. Lee's army had suffered horrendous casualties and was stretched thinner than ever, yet he was still optimistic that another offensive the following morning would bear fruit. Strengthened by the arrival of Maj. Gen. George Pickett's Division, he intended to reinforce Longstreet and renew the assault on the Union left at dawn; Ewell would support the assault as he had on the previous day.

Three things immediately went wrong with this plan. First, when dawn arrived Pickett's brigades were still far to the rear—possibly because Lee was so exhausted he forgot to give proper orders to Pickett. (Another possibility exists that Lee gave the orders to Longstreet, who then failed to transmit them.) Next, Ewell was himself attacked on Culp's Hill by the entire Union Twelfth Corps at daybreak. Last, when Lee rode to Longstreet's headquarters that morning, he found Longstreet preoccupied with his own plans for an attack around the enemy left, a fixation that had preoccupied "Old Pete" since the beginning of the battle.

With an early and coordinated attack no longer possible, Lee rode back toward his headquarters and called a conference of his generals to discuss a new plan. Still determined to assault the enemy, Lee shifted his attention north to a section of Cemetery Ridge on the right center of the Union line opposite Hill's front. The area had been penetrated by a single Confederate brigade at dusk on July 2, and perhaps the brief lodgment had influenced Lee's thinking. It was a desperate plan, for the approach was open for almost one mile, dozens of pieces of enemy artillery could be brought to bear on his men, and that section of Meade's line was readily reinforceable. Pickett's Division would spearhead the attack on the right, joined on its left by Henry Heth's Division (now led by Brig. Gen. Johnston Pettigrew), and half of Pender's Division (soon to be

led by Maj. Gen. Isaac Trimble). Two brigades of Anderson's Division would provide support on Pickett's right. Lee's selection of troops composing the left half of his force is astonishing. Heth's and Pender's brigades had been devastated on July 1 and were hardly suitable to make such an attack. It is unlikely Lee realized the full extent of their disorder and losses, although it was his responsibility to know such things. The attacking divisions would converge on an umbrella-shaped clump of trees on the crest of Cemetery Ridge. The assault would be opened by a cannonade from 150 massed guns, the heaviest so far in the war. The barrage was intended to pulverize and silence the Federal artillery and drive away or demoralize the Union defenders.

Longstreet did not like the plan and said so. Lee insisted it be made and commanded by Longstreet himself—even though the majority of the attacking column were men from A. P. Hill's Third Corps, and the attack would be delivered on Hill's front. During the lengthy preparations of that morning, Lee rode up and down the lines, consulting with Longstreet and others and inspecting positions and troops. It was not until this time that he realized how badly shot up were Hill's divisions; scores of men stood in line with blood-soaked bandages from wounds suffered on July 1. "Many of these poor boys should go to the rear; they are not able for duty," Lee said to Isaac Trimble, whom he had only minutes earlier selected to head Pender's pair of brigades in the attack. Lee could have stopped the attack entirely or substituted others in their place, but chose not to do so. Many observers mentioned a nervousness in his manner that morning, but there were no indications that he ever faltered in his decision to strike Cemetery Ridge.

Once the men and guns were in position, Lee committed the battle to Longstreet and sat quietly nearby. The guns, under the overall direction of E. P. Alexander, opened fire about 1:00 p.m. At one point during the cannonade, Lee rode out in front of Pickett's men, who shouted and pleaded with him to leave for a place of safety; he waved his hat and rode on. The infantry moved forward about 3:00 p.m. and, as Longstreet had predicted beforehand, were torn to pieces. Only small clumps of men managed to actually enter the Union lines; thousands more were left crumpled on the wide open fields between the ridges. As mangled brigades drifted back to Seminary Ridge, Lee again rode forward trying to assuage his bloodied soldiers by telling them, "The fault is mine. . .It will be all right in the end," and "Go back and rest yourself." Fremantle called his conduct at this terrible moment "perfectly sublime." Although Lee, Longstreet, and others prepared Seminary Ridge for a counterattack by the victorious Union defenders, the counterstroke was never delivered. The battle of Gettysburg was over. As Lee later explained to Longstreet, "It is all my fault. I thought my men were invincible."

Next to Malvern Hill, the second and third days at Gettysburg represented the nadir of Lee's generalship. By the summer of 1863, however, Lee more than any other embodied the Southern cause, and blame for the defeat was deflected from his shoulders. Although he offered to resign, President Davis asked him—Who else was capable of taking his place? The casualties he had sustained at Gettysburg so crippled his army, however, that he could not again mount a sustained offensive campaign into enemy territory.

Although his days of wide-ranging strategic offensives were over, some of Lee's best generalship was still ahead. His battles against Meade and U. S. Grant from the Wilderness through Cold Harbor in the spring of 1864 are exhibitions of defensive genius, and his nine-month defense of Petersburg and Richmond while the rest of the Confederacy crumbled around him was magnificent. When his lines were finally broken on April 2, 1865, Lee evacuated the Southern capital and fled west, where he was trapped and surrendered at Appomattox Court House in April.

As president of Washington College in Lexington, Lee spent the five remaining years of his life educating Virginia's young men. He died in October 1870, and was buried there.

For further reading:

Alexander, Edward Porter, *Fighting for the Confederacy: The Personal Recollections of*, Gary Gallagher, ed. Chapel Hill, 1989.

Connelly, Thomas L. *The Marble Man: Robert E. Lee and His Image in American Society.* New York, 1977.

Dowdey, Clifford. *Lee.* Boston, 1965.

Freeman, Douglas S. *Lee's Lieutenants: A Study in Command.* vol. 3. New York, 1944.

——. *R. E. Lee: A Biography.* 4 vols. New York, 1934-5.

Gallagher, Gary, ed. *Lee the Soldier.* Chapel Hill, 1997.

Nolan, Alan. *Lee Considered: General Robert E. Lee and Civil War History.* Chapel Hill, 1991.

Pfanz, Harry W. *Gettysburg: Culp's Hill and Cemetery Hill.* Chapel Hill. 1993.

——. *Gettysburg: The Second Day.* Chapel Hill, 1987.

Thomas, Emory. *Robert E. Lee: A Biography.* New York, 1995.

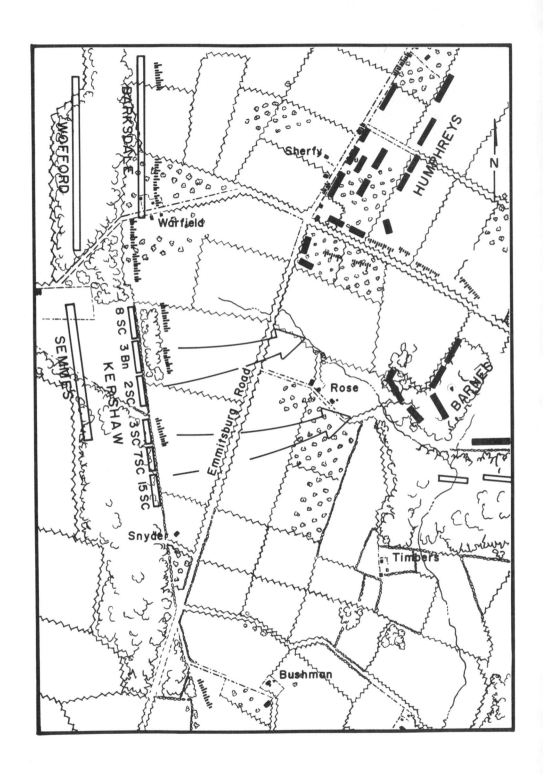

FIRST ARMY CORPS

(20,935 MEN / 87 GUNS)

LIEUTENANT GENERAL JAMES LONGSTREET

James Longstreet was the dean of the Southern corps commanders at Gettysburg. The forty-two year old had been in corps command twice as long as anybody else on either side, and it was he who would command the Army of Northern Virginia if Gen. Robert E. Lee became incapacitated. Longstreet was a devoted poker player, and as such was the oppositeof a gambler. He was a man who studied the averages and calculated the odds very carefully. Never one to force his chances, he preferred to wait for Fredericksburg-type situations—where he could prepare his defenses on advantageous terrain and then await his enemy's attack. If the odds were not in his favor, he would wait for the moment when he held the high card. Longstreet, also in the nature of a good poker player, approached his business dispassionately. To him, victory was the result of thoughtful planning, not heroism or a careless roll of the dice. While he supported Lee's bold strategic offensives, it was always with an eye to fighting a defensive battle at the climax of each campaign. He felt that conserving the lives of his soldiers was the best way to gain equality with the numerically superior Union army, and he rued the high casualty counts brought on by costly assaults. Longstreet thus dealt in human life with a conservatism lacking in many military men—especially in the South—and showed constant concern for their well-being. At Fredericksburg, for instance, when his engineers protested to him that artillerymen were digging their emplacements too deep, Longstreet refused to stop the spade-wielding gunners: "If we only save the finger of a man, that's good enough," he said.

Longstreet's appearance was like that of his personality: oversized, blunt and rugged. Six feet two inches tall and burly, he gave the impression of solidity and dependability rather than dash or brilliance. His aide, Lt. Col. G. Moxley Sorrel, described him at First Manassas:

A most striking figure. . .a soldier every inch, and very handsome, tall and well proportioned, strong and active, a superb horseman and with an unsurpassed soldierly bearing, his features and expression fairly matched; eyes, glint steel blue, deep and piercing; a full brown beard, head well shaped and poised. The worst feature was the mouth, rather coarse; it was partly hidden, however, by his ample beard.

Completely unfettered by nervous habits, Longstreet's calm presence on the battlefield imparted a feeling of well-being to those around him. Longstreet maintained a magnificent fearlessness. At Sharpsburg, one witness recalled that, under fire, he was "as cool and composed as if on dress parade. I could discover no trace of unusual excitement except that he seemed to cut through his tobacco at each chew." Longstreet later revealed his philosophy to a colonel on the battlefield of Chickamauga. When an artillery shell shrieked by, the colonel flinched. "I see you salute them," chided Longstreet. "Yes, every time," the colonel answered. "If there is a shell or bullet over there destined for us," Longstreet mused, "it will find us." His imperturbability, which seems to have been his preeminent trait, may have had something to do with the fact that he was slightly deaf. At any rate, few ever saw him get excited about anything, good or bad.

Of Dutch descent, Longstreet was born in 1821 in South Carolina but grew up mostly in Georgia. He was accepted at West Point, but was a poor student who preferred the physical side of military life; he graduated only 54th out of 62 in the Class of 1842. After graduation, he served a tour of duty at Jefferson Barracks outside St. Louis, Missouri, where he fell in love with the regimental commander's daughter, Louise Garland. She was only 17, and her parents insisted the couple wait until she was older to marry. The smitten Longstreet departed to serve in the Mexican War with Louise's daguerreotype in his pocket. He was wounded in the thigh while carrying the flag forward in the storming of Chapultapec, and when the veteran officer returned in 1848, the couple wed. They eventually had ten children together (oddly, Longstreet neglected to mention her in his memoirs). Life settled down into a dreary succession of dusty outposts, and he became content with the safe but dull duties of a post paymaster.

When the Civil War began in 1861 Longstreet joined the Confederate army with the intent of continuing as a paymaster. Instead, he was made a brigadier general, and within a fortnight was commanding a brigade in the First Manassas Campaign. In those two weeks, he imposed discipline, drilled the brigade three times a day, and saw to the care of his men. His brigade saw light action at a skirmish near Blackburn's Ford, but was not heavily involved at First Manassas. Longstreet's strong presence, though, did gain notice from his peers. Cavalryman Fitzhugh Lee recalled seeing him and thinking, "there is a man that cannot be stampeded." By the fall of 1861, Longstreet and Brig. Gen. Thomas J. "Stonewall" Jackson were already marked as the two outstanding brigadiers in the Confederate army. On October 7, both were promoted to major general, and Longstreet was given command of the Third Division of the army.

His aide, Thomas Goree, wrote during this time that Longstreet's "forte as an officer consists in the seeming ease with which he can handle and arrange large numbers of troops, as also with the confidence and enthusiasm with which he seems to inspire them. . . .If he is ever excited, he has a way of concealing it, and always appears as if he had the utmost confidence in his own ability to command and that of his troops to execute." He could be difficult, however, and at times sulked and pouted. Goree noticed that when someone displeased him, "he does not say much, but merely looks grim. We all know now how to take him, and do not talk much to him without we find if he is in a talkative mood. He has a good deal of the roughness of the old soldier about him."

When the war heated up in the spring of 1862 with Maj. Gen. George McClellan's arrival on the Peninsula, Longstreet displayed ability in the early fighting at Williamsburg. At Seven Pines, however, he not only performed miserably but tried to place the blame on a fellow officer. However, in the Seven Days' Battles, where Jackson faltered, Longstreet performed admirably. Following the action on the swampy Peninsula, Lee divided his army into two wings, giving one each to Jackson and Longstreet.

At Second Manassas in late August Longstreet displayed both of his prominent tendencies: his methodical preparations while getting into position to deliver a blow, and his ability to manage large numbers of men in a sweeping attack which, when finally delivered, swept John Pope's army from the field. A few weeks later, at Sharpsburg, wearing carpet slippers and riding sidesaddle on account of a boot-chafed heel, Longstreet rode up and down the lines, holding his men in place along the center and right of Lee's broken army through the critical hours of the late afternoon. When the fight was over and Longstreet reported back to headquarters, Lee exclaimed, "Here comes my war horse from the field he has done so much to save!" When Lee promoted both men to lieutenant general in the fall and organized the army into two corps, he submitted Longstreet's name ahead of Jackson's, which gave him a slight edge in seniority. He was a "War Horse" to Lee, "Pete" or "Old Pete" to his men, "Dutch" to his West Point cronies, sometimes "Bull" or "Bulldog" to others. Few colorful stories attached themselves to him, however, because of his phlegmatic personality. It was not always so.

During the first year of the war, Longstreet was outgoing and gregarious; indeed, his headquarters had been a center of socialization where visitors could expect a good time, a fine meal, plenty of whiskey—and a convivial game of poker. "He was rather gay in disposition with his chums," wrote Sorrel. Then in January 1862, three of his children died in a single week during a scarlet fever epidemic in Richmond. When the bereaved general returned to the army from the heartbreaking funeral, he was, said Sorrel, "a changed man." The poker parties stopped, he rarely drank thereafter, and he became a devout Episcopalian. While he had always on the taciturn side by nature, after the death of his children he became more withdrawn, often saying little beyond a gruff "yes" or "no."

During operations between Sharpsburg and Fredericksburg, General Lee followed the custom of pitching his tent close to Longstreet's. Although the two often differed fundamentally in their philosophy of how the conflict should be waged, Lee valued Longstreet's opinions and liked "Old Peter"—even if he was at times presumptuous when he advanced his recommendations to Lee. Perhaps this is the trait that most endeared Lee to Longstreet and Jackson, for in an army where most generals were disposed to await instructions, these two advanced their own ideas in their own forceful ways.

Longstreet considered Fredericksburg to be the most instructive battle of the war. His veterans, well positioned on Marye's Heights and supported by artillery, repulsed wave after wave of Federal attackers. Appreciating the power of the defensive as few generals did, Longstreet sought to repeat this scenario. Perhaps Fredericksburg spoiled him by giving him the notion that if he got in position and stayed there, impatient Union generals would crash headlong into his prepared defenses like Union commander Maj. Gen. Ambrose Burnside did on that December day.

In February 1863, Longstreet was detached with two of his divisions and sent below Petersburg with a set of contradictory orders that eventually resulted in a large foraging expedition to Suffolk, Virginia. Thus he was not present for the army's spectacular victory at Chancellorsville in May. While some have argued he was deliberately slow in returning—and could have been present for some of the fighting at Chancellorsville—a careful reading of the evidence does not support such a conclusion. The campaign resulted in the death of Jackson and the reorganization of the army from two corps into three, which in turn required a pair of new corps commanders.

After Lee reunited the army and appointed Richard Ewell and A. P. Hill to lead the new Second and Third Corps, respectively, Longstreet discussed the strategy of the upcoming operation with Lee. He came away with the impression that Lee intended to fight a defensive battle.

As the army marched north into Maryland and Pennsylvania, James Longstreet was the rock upon which Lee relied. He was at the height of his military career as the armies moved toward battle on July 1, 1863.

GETTYSBURG: Longstreet's two lead divisions under Maj. Gens. John Bell Hood and Lafayette McLaws, started July 1 in Greenwood, a town about 17 miles west of Gettysburg located on the western face of South Mountain. Lee ordered Longstreet to move to Gettysburg, but "Old Pete's" men were forced to wait for the slow 14-mile-long wagon train of the Second Corps to pass by on the Chambersburg Pike, the only road over the mountain. Longstreet's men finally got moving from Greenwood around 4:00 p.m. and marched 13 miles by midnight, halting near Marsh Creek, about 3 1/2 miles west of Gettysburg.

Longstreet had ridden ahead on July 1 and had found General Lee about 5:00 p.m. standing on Seminary Ridge observing the Union position on Cemetery Hill. Longstreet took out his field glasses and surveyed the enemy position for a few minutes, then turned to Lee and said he did not like the look of things, and urged a move to the right, which would take the Confederate army past the Union left beyond the Round Tops. There, Longstreet advocated, the army could place itself between the Army of the Potomac and Washington, and the Federals would be forced to attack to restore their communications with the capital. Lee disagreed. The Union army was in front of him, he said, and he would strike it there. If the enemy army is there tomorrow, Longstreet retorted, it is because he wants you to strike him. The discussion was dropped for the time being.

About 3:00 a.m. the next morning, July 2, Longstreet's column resumed its march and advanced a mile or so to near Seminary Ridge, where the men stopped and rested while Longstreet and Hood went to Lee's headquarters; McLaws was the last to arrive. Lee was mulling over plans for the day's battle, and a little after 9:00 a.m., he gave Longstreet orders to march McLaws and Hood's divisions unseen opposite the Union left—which he apparently considered to be somewhere north

and west of Little Round Top—and attack it, rolling it up Cemetery Ridge (George Pickett's Division was still not up). Lee wanted McLaws to attack perpendicular to the Emmitsburg Road so as to envelop the enemy flank. Longstreet corrected Lee, explaining the his division should be formed parallel to the road, but Lee repeated his previous order. Hood would move forward after McLaws.

Longstreet requested and received Lee's approval to await the arrival of Evander Law's Brigade, of Hood's Division, before moving out, and Lee agreed. To Longstreet's way of thinking, it made sense to have all of your men in hand before striking (the delay absorbed some forty minutes and Law arrived about noon). Longstreet finally started McLaws and Hood, in that order, south along the west side of Herr Ridge toward their destination opposite the Union left. Longstreet was under orders to move without being seen by the enemy—Lee had provided a guide for that purpose. The Confederates belatedly discovered that when the route over the southern end of Herr Ridge was visible to Union scouts on Little Round Top. Longstreet halted his men short of this stretch and gave the order to countermarch—they would begin again and try another approach.

After the column had retraced its steps, the two divisions marched three miles along a hidden route to Pitzer's Woods. The frustrating countermarch took hours to complete, but it was in compliance with Lee's directive that it be conducted without being seen. According to Colonel Moxley Sorrel, Longstreet failed to conceal some anger at Lee's orders to attack in spite of his several objections, although evidence that this anger delayed or adversely affected the march of his divisions is open to debate.

What is not open to debate is that the Union left was not where Lee supposed it to be. When McLaws' men reached their destination opposite the Peach Orchard, it was bristling with enemy troops and several batteries. Another delay ensued while Hood's Division was deployed to the right (south) of McLaws. This improvisation required Hood's soldiers to begin the onslaught, and it was designed as an en echelon assault (Hood, then McLaws, then Anderson's Third Corps division).

Longstreet's men were finally in place about 4:00 p.m. Hood sought a further modification of the attack plan by seeking permission to move his division around Big Round Top and attack the enemy in flank and rear. Longstreet refused his request three times. "Already our line was dangerously extended," wrote the astute observer E. Porter Alexander, "and to have pushed one or two divisions past the 3d corps would have invited their destruction." It also would have further delayed the attack and required new orders be issued up and down the line. Whether Longstreet refused Hood out of tactical considerations or had temper is hard to tell.

Sometime around 4:00 p.m. Alexander's artillery opened on the enemy lines. Hood's Division jumped off about one-half hour later and drove across the Emmitsburg Road and lashed out against the Rose Farm and woods, Stony Hill and Devil's Den sectors of Dan Sickles' advanced Third Corps line. Once Hood's men were well engaged, timing McLaws' jump-off was Longstreet's next task. When Union reinforcements caused Hood's attack to falter, Longstreet sent in McLaws' Division about 5:00 p.m. His attack was well-timed, for the surge of his four fresh brigades smashed the Peach Orchard salient, overran the Federal line along the Wheatfield and Emmitsburg roads, bore down into the Wheatfield, and threatened the collapse of the entire Union left flank.

Enemy reinforcements from the Federal center and elsewhere bolstered the imperiled left flank. Longstreet's attack was designed to be continued on his left with the advance of Maj. Gen. Richard H. Anderson's Division of Hill's Third Corps. As portions of McLaws' Division swept up southern Cemetery Ridge, Anderson launched his brigades east against troops aligned generally along the Emmitsburg Road and on the ridge itself in an effort to exploit the weakened Union center. The assault, however, lacked the proper coordination and failed to push the Unionists off Cemetery Ridge.

Hood's men fought just below the crest of Little Round Top and in Devil's Den, and the critical area around the Wheatfield changed hands several times. Exhausted and badly bloodied, however, the Confederates began to lose their cohesion and energy. By the onset of darkness, Longstreet's massive July 2 attack on the Union left petered out with the Federal line withdrawn and severely punished—but still intact. Longstreet called the assault "the best three hours of fighting ever done by any troops on any battlefield." His eight brigades had knocked out thirteen Union brigades from the Union Second, Third, and Fifth Corps, but had fallen short of their intended goal.

Longstreet's third division under George Pickett arrived near the field on the afternoon of July 2; it was the only division in the army that had not yet been engaged. After the day's fighting ended, the exhausted Longstreet declined to ride to headquarters to meet with Lee, who therefore sent an order to his "War Horse" calling for the use of Pickett's fresh division in a renewed attack at daylight the next morning in conjunction with Ewell's attack against the opposite end of the line. The next morning, however, at the hour when the attack was supposed to have started, Lee rode to Longstreet's headquarters to find his subordinate still trying to figure out how to work his way around the Union left. Pickett was not yet even in position (neither Lee nor Longstreet had informed Pickett of the morning plan to attack), and Lee was forced to scrap the idea. Lee and Longstreet then rode up Seminary Ridge and examined the Union line on the parallel ridge to the east. Lee pointed to the right center of the ridge and designated it as the target of the day's assault. It would be softened with a massive artillery barrage to open the way for the infantry. Longstreet objected—how many men were to be in the attacking force? Lee gave the figure at 15,000, to which Longstreet replied as follows: "General, I have been a soldier all my life. I have been with soldiers engaged in fights by couples, by squads, companies, regiments, divisions, and armies, and should know, as well as any one, what soldiers can do. It is my opinion that no fifteen thousand men ever arranged for battle can take that position."

While Lee would not change his general plan, he did relent and agree to leave Hood and McLaws in place on the army's right flank. Longstreet would instead attack the Union center with Pickett's Division, Maj. Gen. Henry Heth's Division (now under Brig. Gen. Johnston Pettigrew), which had been bled severely during July 1, and half of Maj. Gen. W. Dorsey Pender's Division (now under Maj. Gen. Isaac Trimble). Half of Anderson's Division would be aligned to support the expected breakthrough. Longstreet balked again at the idea of such a frontal attack, though he finally resigned himself to Lee's plan and personally directed Pickett's men into their positions behind Seminary Ridge. He supervised the placement of Hill's attacking divisions less carefully. Then Longstreet wrote to Alexander: "Colonel, let the batteries open."

During this bombardment, which drew a furious response from the Union guns on the opposite ridge, Longstreet showed himself at his most fearless. With the shells screaming and exploding all around him, he was observed by Brig. Gen. James Kemper of Pickett's Division:

Longstreet rode slowly and alone immediately in front of our entire line. He sat his large charger with a magnificent grace and composure I never before beheld. His bearing was to me the grandest moral spectacle of the war. I expected to see him fall every instant. Still he moved on, slowly and majestically, with an inspiring confidence, composure, self-possession and repressed power in every movement and look, that fascinated me.

Nearly two hours later, when the bombardment slackened, Longstreet still could not bring himself to give the order to attack. Pickett had to ask his chief, "General, shall I advance?" and Longstreet merely nodded in reply. The assault was torn apart, and only a small fraction of the attacking infantry managed to reach the Union lines, where most either fell or surrendered. Longstreet watched helplessly from Seminary Ridge as the columns receded back toward his position in defeat. He reacted quickly after the disaster by getting artillery ready to repulse an expected Union counterattack, pulling McLaws' and Hood's Divisions back to a position west of the Emmitsburg Road, and helping to rally Pickett's men. The counterattack was not forthcoming; the battle of Gettysburg was over.

There was never any question that Longstreet would stay in his place at the head of the First Corps after Gettysburg. However, his conduct during the battle remained a subject of heated controversy—especially after Lee died. According to Moxley Sorrel, "There was apparent apathy in his movements. They lacked the fire and point of his usual bearing on the battlefield." According to Lafayette McLaws, "during the engagement he was very excited giving contradictory orders to everyone, and was exceedingly overbearing," although he wrote his assessment after his own feud over another issue broke out between the two men. It is worthy of note that Lee never blamed Longstreet for losing the battle at Gettysburg—as others would do following Lee's demise in 1870—and in fact assumed the responsibility himself.

After stellar offensive performance in North Georgia that fall at the Battle of Chickamauga, Longstreet performed less ably around Knoxville, Tennessee, and returned to the Army of Northern Virginia in the early spring of 1864. He was arrived just in time to save Lee's collapsing right flank in the Wilderness in May, and was critically wounded in a manner eerily reminiscent of Stonewall Jackson's mortal wounding at the height of a counterattack that was rolling up the Federal left flank. Although he returned to duty in October a weakened and crippled soldier, Lee's "Old

War Horse" was with his chief at the surrender at Appomattox Court House in April 1865.

Longstreet depended after the war on political appoints for a living and became a Republican—which resulted in his being ostracized by much of the South. He is perhaps best known during those years for his running feud with General Jubal Early over his role at Gettysburg. Longstreet died in 1904.

For further reading:

Alexander, Edward Porter, *Fighting for the Confederacy: The Personal Recollections of*, Gary Gallagher, ed. Chapel Hill, 1989.

Krick, Robert K. "'If Longstreet. . .Says so, it is Most Likely Not True': James Longstreet and the Second Day at Gettysburg," in Gary Gallagher, ed., *The Second Day at Gettysburg*, Kent, 1993.

Greezicki, Roger J. "Humbugging the Historian: A Reappraisal of Longstreet at Gettysburg." *Gettysburg Magazine*, #6, 1992.

Longstreet, James. *From Manassas to Appomattox: Memoirs of the Civil War in America*. Bloomington, 1960.

Piston, William G. *Lee's Tarnished Lieutenant: James Longstreet and His Place in Southern History*. Athens, 1987.

Rollins, Richard. "'The Ruling Ideas of the Pennsylvania Campaign': James Longstreet's 1873 Letter to Lafayette McLaws." *Gettysburg Magazine*, #17, 1997.

Sorrel, Moxley. *Recollections of a Confederate Staff Officer*. Dayton, 1978.

Wert, Jeffrey. *General James Longstreet: The Confederacy's Most Controversial Soldier: A Biography*. New York, 1993.

MCLAWS' DIVISION:

(7,153 MEN / 16 GUNS)

MAJOR GENERAL
LAFAYETTE MCLAWS

"Square" and "solid" were adjectives that applied equally to Lafayette McLaws' character and appearance. His complexion was swarthy and his hair curly and very black; his beard was enormous and bushy and half-covered his broad face; and his eyes—"coal black" according to observant Rebel artilleryman Robert Stiles—peered out in a rather owlish way. He was short, compact, and burly, with big square shoulders, deep chest, and large, muscular arms. For his type, wrote Stiles, "he is a handsome man."

McLaws personified stolidity and reminded Stiles of the Roman centurion who stood at his post in Herculaneum "until the lava ran over him." He was a capable soldier without flair, whose steady performance never produced a high moment. His reliability and dogged tenacity rubbed off on his men, however, and made them as hard to dislodge as any in the army. He exuded unflinching fortitude, with the downside being that he lacked military imagination; McLaws was at his best when told exactly what to do and closely supervised by superiors. Although he developed a mastery of profanity, and could appear blunt and coarse, McLaws' martial demeanor hid a sensitive soul. He was a literate man who frequently poured out his experiences in candid, often sentimental letters to his wife. During the Fredericksburg Campaign,

McLaws and Brig. Gen. William Barksdale would wander along the bank of the Rappahannock River at night and listen quietly to the Yankee bands playing the army favorites about lives and loves lost.

A native Georgian born in 1821, McLaws was a student at the University of Virginia when he received his appointment to West Point, where he graduated 48th out of 62 students in the Class of 1842. Soon after, he married President Zachary Taylor's niece. During the antebellum years, he made the army his life, serving in the infantry in Mexico, on the frontier, and in the Mormon Expedition. In 1845, he was wounded in the left hand during a shooting accident that maimed the appendage for life, and he often hid the mangled hand when sitting for a photograph. McLaws had been a captain of infantry for almost ten years when the Fort Sumter crisis erupted in April 1861.

McLaws resigned from the United States army, received a colonel's commission in the Confederate army, and was assigned to the 10th Georgia regiment in June 1861. He was sent to the Peninsula and was helping to construct defenses there during the Manassas Campaign. McLaws impressed his superior, Brig. Gen. John Magruder, who promoted him to brigadier general in September and gave him a division in the Yorktown defenses in November. The fighting below Richmond began in earnest with the arrival of Maj. Gen. George McClellan's Army of the Potomac the next spring. After an impressive performance in the operations around Yorktown, for which he was highly commended by both Magruder and army commander Gen. Joseph Johnston, McLaws was made major general on May 23. The rapidly-rising McLaws had established himself as a general to watch even before the climax of the Peninsula Campaign during the Seven Days' Battles.

McLaws' Division saw fighting in the Seven Days' Battles at Savage's Station and Malvern Hill, but it was Magruder who directed most of its operations. In July, after that week of combat had dimmed Magruder's star and added luster

to Maj. Gen. James "Pete" Longstreet's, McLaws's Division was added to Longstreet's command, an association which would last for the two following years of almost constant campaigning. McLaws missed the Second Manassas Campaign in August 1862 when he and his men, together with D. H. Hill's Division, were left behind to protect Richmond.

McLaws' and Hill's divisions were summoned by Lee for the Maryland Campaign in September. There, McLaws made a poor showing which impaired his standing with Lee. After assisting in the capture of Harpers Ferry, it took his division forty-one hours to march from there to Sharpsburg at a time when Lee was desperate to concentrate his forces; he barely arrived in time for the battle. (In contrast, A. P. Hill's Division covered the same route in nine hours later that day under more strenuous conditions.) In his report after Sharpsburg, Lee came as close to censure as he ever did in written comments on his officers' performances when he penned that McLaws' "progress was slow, and he did not reach the battlefield at Sharpsburg until sometime after the engagement of the 17th began."

Three months later at Fredericksburg, McLaws put himself back in Lee's good graces. The defensive preparations above the town were the type of work for which McLaws was best suited. Under Longstreet's supervision and with the help of corps engineers, he dug pits for his batteries and strengthened parts of his line with obstructions. He also carved a long ditch that traversed his divisional front along a stone wall and then banked the dislodged dirt against it. With stacks of loaded muskets by their sides, his men carpeted the ground in front of the roadway with Union dead during the ensuing battle. Fredericksburg was the one of the most lopsided Confederate victories of the war, and the reports of both Longstreet and Lee praised McLaws.

His star, though, dimmed again in the Chancellorsville Campaign. On May 3, McLaws was directed to move east toward Fredericksburg and assist Maj. Gen. Jubal Early in driving back and overwhelming the isolated Union Sixth Corps, which was moving against Lee's rear. Even though McLaws was the highest ranking major general in the Confederate army, the deferential officer allowed Early to direct the operation. McLaws was always happier obeying a direct order instead of using his own discretion. At Salem Church however, some initiative was needed to solve the puzzle of how to move against the enemy—and McLaws was nearly paralyzed with indecision. When his attack finally got under way, it was hesitantly executed, and the enemy host escaped.

The loss of "Stonewall" Jackson at Chancellorsville was the catalyst for a reorganization of the army that Lee had been contemplating for months. Jackson's and Longstreet's two corps would become three, necessitating a pair of new corps commanders. Longstreet recommended McLaws, who thought himself deserving of corps command by virtue of his seniority and his reliable service. When Lee chose Maj. Gens. Richard Ewell and Ambrose P. Hill for the new posts, McLaws was shattered. Both of the men chosen were from Virginia, and McLaws felt that favoritism for natives of the Old Dominion had deprived him of his rightful standing in the army. Disgruntled, he requested a transfer. But there was more to McLaws' failure to advance than the fact that he was a Georgian. He had been ill the previous winter, and his listless performance at Chancellorsville had disappointed Lee and recalled his similar failure before Sharpsburg the previous fall. Lee simply did not think McLaws' performance over the last year indicated that he was deserving of further advancement.

Despite this disappointment, McLaws' strengths as a division commander were appreciated by his troops. He attended closely to the needs of his men and had earned their respect. "He was an officer of much experience and most careful," noted Longstreet's aide Lt. Col. G. Moxley Sorrel. "Fond of detail, his command was in excellent condition, and his ground and

position well examined and reconnoitered; not brilliant in the field or quick in movement there or elsewhere, he could always be counted on and had secured the entire confidence of his officers and men." His tendency to be cautious—he sometimes sent out pickets as far as eight miles—and his fussiness and rigidity in enforcing regulations (his men nicknamed him "Make Laws") made his division a reliable one. He had led his division longer than anybody in Lee's army and knew it inside and out.

GETTYSBURG: On July 1, McLaws' Division was in Greenwood, Pennsylvania with orders from Lee to march east over South Mountain to Gettysburg, about 17 miles distant. The men, however, were prevented from using the only road over the mountain by Lt. Gen. Richard Ewell's wagon train, which clogged the road for ten hours, until 4:00 p.m. Finally falling in behind the trains, McLaws' men marched until midnight and halted at Marsh Creek, about 3 1/2 miles west of Gettysburg.

On the morning of July 2, McLaws rode up to Lee's headquarters, where he joined Longstreet. After some discussion, McLaws was instructed to make a hidden march with Maj. Gen. John Hood's Division opposite the enemy's left flank, where he would launch an attack north along Cemetery Ridge. He also received personal instructions from Lee on how to place his division for the day's attack, which was perpendicular to the Emmitsburg Road at the Peach Orchard. The major general rejoined his command and marched it back to Herr Ridge, where he waited for Longstreet to give the signal for the trek to their destination.

Longstreet waited for Evander Laws' Brigade to arrive from the west, and the march was delayed until about noon. When the two-division-long column finally got moving to the south, it soon came to a stretch of road visible to enemy scouts on Little Round Top. To achieve surprise, the column would have to start over and find a hidden approach. McLaws still wanted to lead the march (as he was instructed by Lee to open the assault), so rather than simply turning the column around and allowing Hood's Division to carry the van, McLaws' men marched back to the Chambersburg Pike, wasting valuable time. The troubled march was finally finished around 3:30 p.m. when it reached the woods along Seminary Ridge opposite the Peach Orchard. To McLaws' dismay, enemy infantry and artillery of Dan Sickles' Third Federal Corps were already firmly in control of the area. He was also shocked to find that the Federal line extended past his front to the right, angling off toward the direction of Devil's Den and Little Round Top. If he positioned his troops as Lee had indicated, his right flank would be exposed and destroyed.

McLaws deployed his own division with a two-brigade front, with Brig. Gen. Joseph Kershaw on the right and Brig. Gen. William Barksdale on the left. Brigadier General Paul Semmes was put in a second line behind Kershaw, and Brig. Gen. William Wofford was aligned behind Barksdale. His attack column was narrow, deep and powerful. As his men were forming, Hood's Division passed behind to take up a position on his right. McLaws reported the situation confronting him and thereafter received a courier from Longstreet inquiring why he had not attacked? McLaws explained the situation, but the courier returned again and repeated the order for him to move forward. McLaws agreed to do so, but another order soon arrived instructing him to await the deployment of Hood's brigades. Longstreet then rode up at a time when tempers were growing short and the day was winding down too quickly for the Confederates. Tense words were exchanged between the veteran officers about the placement of a battery, and the growing emotional chasm between them widened.

About 4:00 p.m., Longstreet's artillery opened up and shortly thereafter Hood's brigades plunged forward across the Rose Farm, into the Rose Woods and toward Little Round Top and Devil's Den. Longstreet remained with McLaws near Kershaw's South Carolinians, and together the officers monitored Hood's progress. With "Old Peter" next to him, there was not much for McLaws to do except steady his men and tell them to be patient. This arrangement, which McLaws bitterly resented, may have been the result of Longstreet's earlier promise to Lee that he would give personal attention to McLaws and his division. "I thus became responsible for anything that was not entirely satisfactory in your command from that day," he subsequently informed McLaws, "and was repeatedly told of that fact [by Lee]." McLaws "knew nothing about this arrangement between Lee and Longstreet," writes historian Jeff Wert, "and as a consequence, the command relationship portended trouble within the First Corps."

Finally, around 5:00 p.m. or shortly thereafter, Longstreet gave the signal and Kershaw's Brigade moved out, followed by Semmes' behind him. Barksdale's and Wofford's Brigades got tangled up in the batteries dotting the Confederate line and were delayed (Kershaw's left flank suffered heavily because of this mix-up), but soon they too were away, and in a matter of minutes stormed through the Union lines in the Peach Orchard. As they poured forward, they outflanked the Northern brigades in the Wheatfield fighting Kershaw and Semmes and sent them back in a rout. McLaws' actions after the battle commenced are in many respects a mystery. For some time he remained behind with Longstreet while his four brigades stormed eastward, and he does not seem to have exercised a tight rein of command over his units, which fought largely on their own hook. Each was in capable hands, however, and each performed admirably against a tough and defiant enemy. Although they managed to smash the Peach Orchard salient and push the Federal line back across southern Cemetery Ridge (Anderson's division on the left attacked after McLaws' brigades went forward and assisted in the effort), McLaws' brigades ran out of steam and the attack petered out in the dying light of July 2.

Longstreet—still keeping a firm hand on McLaws' command—ordered them back before they were annihilated by the fresh Federal reserves flooding into the area. That night McLaws' brigades occupied the western fringe of the Rose Woods and Stony Hill.

The combined divisions of Hood and McLaws had fought with deadly ferocity and had inflicted about 9,000 casualties among the Third, Second, and Fifth Federal Corps. McLaws' casualties for the day were about 2,200, or 30% of his force (Hood's were similar). The disparity in the respective losses is extraordinary, especially considering that the Confederates were on the tactical offensive. On July 3, McLaws' Division remained in and around the Rose Woods-Stony Hill sector, but was pulled back to the west side of the Emmitsburg Road after the failure of Pickett's Charge.

McLaws apparently did not write a report after the Battle of Gettysburg. He later said that the attack of July 2 was "unnecessary and the whole plan of battle a bad one." Longstreet did not commend McLaws in his report of the battle—and thus the rift between the two Georgians grew wider than ever.

McLaws never again served with the Army of Northern Virginia. He went west with Longstreet's Corps in the autumn and his relationship with his corps leader continued to slide; there, Longstreet charged him with lack of cooperation and negligence during the disappointing Knoxville Campaign. Although a court found McLaws guilty of some of the charges, the next May Jefferson Davis ordered that he be allowed back in the army. Lee declined to accept him, however, and assigned McLaws to the Carolinas, where he spent the rest of the war.

McLaws held mundane jobs after the war, including insurance agent, tax collector, and postman. He died in 1897.

For further reading:

Greezicki, Roger J. "Humbugging the Historian: A Reappraisal of Longstreet at Gettysburg." *Gettysburg Magazine*, #6, 1992.

Longstreet, James. *From Manassas to Appomattox: Memoirs of the Civil War in America.* Bloomington, 1960.

McLaws, Lafayette. "Gettysburg." *Southern Historical Society Papers,* vol. 7, 1879.

Pfanz, Harry. *Gettysburg: The Second Day.* Chapel Hill, 1987.

Piston, William G. *Lee's Tarnished Lieutenant: James Longstreet and His Place in Southern History.* Athens, 1987.

Rollins, Richard. "'The Ruling Ideas of the Pennsylvania Campaign': James Longstreet's 1873 Letter to Lafayette McLaws." *Gettysburg Magazine*, #17, 1997.

Sorrel, Moxley. *Recollections of a Confederate Staff Officer.* Dayton, 1978.

Wert, Jeffrey. *General James Longstreet: The Confederacy's Most Controversial Soldier: A Biography.* New York, 1993.

KERSHAW'S BRIGADE

(2,183 MEN)

BRIGADIER GENERAL JOSEPH BREVARD KERSHAW

Joseph Kershaw was the embodiment of the Confederate gentleman-turned-soldier ideal, and a lawyer from the "Cradle of the Rebellion," South Carolina. He was intelligent, literate, and dignified, a reli-

giously devout man of high character who had been an orphan at age seven. Blond, with light blue eyes, refined features and a resolute expression, he was clean-shaven except for a drooping blond mustache. He had the bearing of command and a clear voice that seemed to inspire courage when it was raised in battle. Maj. Gen. Lafayette McLaws described him as "Gallant and pious. . .cool and judicious."

Kershaw was admitted to the bar in 1843. Meanwhile, he picked up some military experience as a lieutenant in South Carolina's Mexican War "Palmetto Regiment." While a member of the South Carolina legislature and of his state's secession convention, he raised a militia regiment that mustered into Confederate service as the 2nd South Carolina Regiment when the Civil War began. When he went off to war, his beautiful wife Lucretia made herself a necklace and bracelets woven from locks of his hair.

The 2nd South Carolina was present at Fort Sumter and First Manassas where, after the latter action, Kershaw irritated commanding general Brig. Gen. P. G. T. Beauregard by writing a self-promoting article for a South Carolina newspaper. Beauregard later referred to him as "that militia idiot." After Beauregard was transferred away from the Virginia army, Kershaw took command of a brigade in January 1862 when its previous commander, Brig. Gen. Milledge Bonham, resigned in a huff over a seniority dispute. Two weeks later Kershaw was promoted to brigadier general.

Joseph Kershaw led his brigade in action on the Virginia Peninsula at Williamsburg and again at Savage's Station during the Seven Days' Battles. His division commander, Maj. Gen. Lafayette McLaws, made special mention of the South Carolinian in his official report: "I beg leave to call attention to the gallantry, cool, yet daring, courage and skill in the management of his gallant command exhibited by Brigadier-General Kershaw." Much was expected of the man as the army headed north into Maryland in September of 1862. Kershaw's soldiers forced Union soldiers off

Maryland Heights before the capture of Harpers Ferry (during which some of them had to load and fire while using one arm to keep from rolling down the mountainside). McLaws praised Kershaw once more for his solid performance on the field of Sharpsburg.

One of Kershaw's finest hours came at Fredericksburg, where his South Carolinians reinforced Brig. Gen. Thomas Cobb's Brigade behind a stone wall on Marye's Heights; Kershaw took command of that embattled sector when Cobb was mortally wounded. Leading his brigade on horseback, the gallant Kershaw was a conspicuous and defiant target, seen and admired by thousands on both sides. It was said later that when he reined in his horse, the Yankees withheld their fire as if out of respect, and that Kershaw took off his cap in acknowledgment before he disappeared behind the stone wall. Kershaw's troops were but lightly engaged at Salem Church during the Chancellorsville Campaign.

By the summer of 1863, the forty-one year old Kershaw had been a brigadier for a year and a half, and had distinguished himself in almost every battle. He displayed an ability for quick and rational decisions, and he never endangered his men rashly. McLaws had complete faith in him and his brigade, and he was much admired by his fellow South Carolinians. The official reports Kershaw wrote were graceful, tempered, literate, and restrained. He was a man who passed among the whistling bullets and shrieking shells with a calm center, never losing his dignity.

GETTYSBURG: Kershaw was in the van of Lt. Gen. James Longstreet's two divisions as they marched east from Greenwood, Pennsylvania over South Mountain on the night of July 1-2. His brigade was again in the lead at noon on July 2 when the two divisions of McLaws and Hood started their march from Herr Ridge to the jump-off point for their attack against the Union left flank. After a frustrating series of countermarches, Kershaw's men reached the front about 3:30 p.m., trudging into Biesecker's Woods and into view of the Federals occupying the Peach Orchard. Kershaw began deploying for battle on extreme right of McLaws' Division behind a rock wall that ran along the edge of the woods on the southern end of the crest of Seminary Ridge. His South Carolina regiments were deployed, from left to right as follows: 8th, 3rd Battalion, 2nd, 3rd, 7th, and 15th.

When he peered through the trees he was astounded to see Union infantry and artillery in strength in his front. Complicating matters was the fact that he was receiving "sundry messages" from McLaws and Longstreet, and was in personal communication with both officers. He had expected his own brigade to be in the front line of Longstreet's attack, but the unexpected presence and strength of the enemy required a new plan. Maj. Gen. John Hood's Division, now deploying on Kershaw's right, would attack first and drive in the Union left. Kershaw would await a signal and advance thereafter. The careful officer made an important decision while viewing the terrain in his front, resolving to guide the center of his long line of battle against the Stony Hill, while his left regiments swept into the rear of the Peach Orchard and his right engulfed the Rose farm buildings.

Hood's men moved forward after the artillery opened at about 4:00 p.m., and Longstreet gave the signal for McLaws' Division to move forward about one hour later. There was trouble almost immediately. Brig. Gen. William Barksdale's Brigade, which was to have moved out and supported Kershaw's left flank, was delayed in its advance. As a result, Kershaw's men—especially those on the left—suffered cruelly from artillery and musketry flanking fire coming from the Peach Orchard. Even so, his men moved forward "with the precision of a brigade drill." The three left regiments turned near the Rose buildings and swept north toward the Federal batteries aligned along the Wheatfield Road, while the other half of the brigade pushed forward to Stony Hill, now held by elements of the Third and Fifth Federal Corps. Kershaw later

recalled "the clatter of grape" smacking the Rose buildings as he passed.

During an effort to un-bunch his regiments, an order was misconstrued by his left wing regiments, which were closing in on the flaming batteries in their front. The well-drilled units turned right and exposed their flank to the guns, which ripped them to shreds. "Hundreds of the bravest and best of Carolina fell," Kershaw later grieved, "victims of this fatal blunder." While the shattered regiments reformed to advance again in conjunction with the belated Barksdale, Kershaw's left units, with "Tige" Anderson's Brigade on his right, pounded the Federals on the wooded Stony Hill. Hood's men were barely hanging on around the Wheatfield on the other side of the Stony Hill, and Kershaw's appearance materially aided their efforts.

Kershaw eventually forced several Northern regiments off the Stony Hill and then occupied it. Federal reinforcements in the form of Brig. Gen. John Caldwell's division advanced into the fight from the Trostle Woods to recover the position. The brigades of Brig. Gen. Samuel Zook and Col. Patrick Kelly fell heavily on Kershaw's right and forced it rearward. Wofford's Brigade, however, stormed into the action on Kershaw's left, outflanking Caldwell's brigades and forcing them to retreat. Kershaw's men went forward again, and with the help of Wofford's soldiers (and perhaps others), drove back a volunteer and two Regular brigades (all from the Fifth Corps). By the time the Fifth Corps' Pennsylvania Reserve Division appeared on the scene, Kershaw's force was spent. Longstreet gave the order to retire, and Kershaw's men withdrew to the Peach Orchard. Kershaw was withdrawn to the wall in Biesecker's Woods the following day, where they had formed for the attack only 24 hours before.

Joseph Kershaw deservedly appeared on Longstreet's post-battle list of those "most distinguished for the exhibition of great gallantry and skill." His star was still on the rise. After the Knoxville Campaign in the fall, he succeeded to command of the division when McLaws was relieved and arrested by Longstreet. Kershaw was made major general in May 1864, and remained in command of the division for the rest of the war—a proud exception (with Maj. Gens. Wade Hampton and John B. Gordon) to Gen. Robert E. Lee's rule that a division commander must be a professionally-trained soldier.

After the war, Kershaw resumed his law practice and reentered politics. He was elected to the state senate in 1865 and circuit court judge in 1877, holding the latter office until failing health forced him to resign in 1893, a year before his death.

For further reading:

Dickert, D. Augustus. *History of Kershaw's Brigade.* Dayton, 1976.

Freeman, Douglas Southall. *Lee's Lieutenants: A Study in Command*, vol. 3. New York, 1944.

McDowell, John E. and William C. Davis, "General Joseph B. Kershaw." *Civil War Times Illustrated*, 8, Feb., 1970.

McLaws, Lafayette. "Gettysburg." *Southern Historical Society Papers*, 7, 1879.

Pfanz, Harry. *Gettysburg: The Second Day.* Chapel Hill, 1987.

Wyckoff, Mac. *A History of the 2nd South Carolina Infantry.* Fredericksburg, 1994.

———. "Kershaw's Brigade at Gettysburg." *Gettysburg Magazine*, #5, 1991.

SEMMES' BRIGADE:

(1,334 MEN)

BRIGADIER GENERAL PAUL JONES SEMMES

Forty-eight year old Paul Semmes had been a banker and plantation owner in Columbus, Georgia before the Civil War. He had also been an officer in the militia, and he was made colonel of the 2nd Georgia Volunteer Regiment and sent to Virginia with his men when the Southern states seceded. His brother, naval commander Raphael Semmes, would become the Confederacy's most famous sea raider as captain of the *CSS Alabama*.

Tall and ruddy, with his lordly mustache and beard, Semmes was distinguished looking in the romantic tradition of the times. He dressed elaborately for battle with a red turban, polished boots, and an elegant uniform with a red sash around the shoulders and waist. Semmes' regiment was initially sent to the Peninsula, and by the spring of 1862 he was already a brigadier general at the head of Maj. Gen. Lafayette McLaws' old brigade. He ably led his regiments at Williamsburg, and at Savage's Station and Malvern Hill in the Seven Days' Battles, where Semmes received a commendation from McLaws for "cool courage and knowledge of his duties." He had so expended himself during the engagement at Malvern Hill that two of his men had to assist him back to camp.

In the Maryland Campaign in September, Semmes led his brigade in late fighting at Crampton's Gap and again at Sharpsburg a few days later. McLaws included him in an omnibus commendation of his brigadiers. At Fredericksburg, he was present but was held in reserve and was not engaged in the division's famous defense of Marye's Heights. During the Chancellorsville Campaign the following spring, Semmes' Brigade was at the head of the column which stopped the advance of Maj. Gen. George Sykes' Regular Division on May 1. This action caused Union commandi*ng general Joe Hooker to withdraw to Chancellorsville crossroads and cede the initiative to General Lee. On May 4, Semmes' men suffered heavily in the terrific fighting against the Union Sixth Corps relief column at Salem Church. The Georgian was not bashful about claiming his brigade's share of credit in the fight, boldly (and falsely) exclaiming that half of the Federal 5,000 losses were inflicted by his infantry.

Paul Semmes had proven himself a worthy and capable brigadier by the time of Gettysburg, frequently employed in supporting roles in several of the army's battles. In Pennsylvania, he and his brigade were expected to render the same able service they had provided over the past fifteen months.

GETTYSBURG: Semmes' Brigade marched with McLaws' Division from Greenwood, Pennsylvania east over South Mountain on the night of July 1-2 to a bivouac near Marsh Creek, about 3 1/2 miles west of Gettysburg. The next day Semmes' men marched south from Herr Ridge about noon with the rest of McLaws' Division, followed by Hood's brigades. After a frustrating and time-consuming series of marches, Semmes' men reached their destination in Biesecker's Woods, the jump-off point for the attack against the Union left flank, about 3:30 in the afternoon. Semmes filed his men into line behind Brig. Gen. Joseph Kershaw's Brigade and aligned his four Georgia regiments behind the left flank of Kershaw's line, from left to right as follows: 10th, 50th, 51st, and 53rd. About 150 yards separated the brigades, and McLaws instructed his brigadiers to retain this separation during their advance.

Although it was initially intended that McLaws' men would open the attack, the strength and location of the Union left necessitated a change of plans. As Semmes marked time, Hood's Division was shuttled behind the lines and deployed to the south, from which point it would begin the assault.

Hood's Division moved forward after the First Corps artillery opened at about 4:00 p.m. About one hour later, Longstreet gave the signal for McLaws' Division to advance into action. Semmes' regiments were again in a supporting role, this time adding depth and weight to Kershaw's spearheading attack. As Kershaw's regiments pushed to the Stony Hill and swung north to confront the artillery along the Wheatfield Road, Semmes advanced behind his right and rear, across the Rose Farm and into the woods. By the time the Federals of Brig. Gen. John Caldwell's division pushed back Kershaw's men, Semmes had his regiments in line and advanced. The brigade came on "handsomely" Kershaw later wrote, and together with Anderson and his South Carolina regiments, blunted and then threw back Col. John Brooke's brigade's push into Rose's Woods.

At about this time, Semmes fell with a wound in his thigh in an unidentified location. Although one officer's account has Semmes hit by a shell fragment in Biesecker's Woods *before* the attack began, Kershaw's battle report indicates clearly that he had a discussion with the general on the Rose Farm *during* the assault. The South Carolinian believed Semmes was struck in an open field near a fence—probably on the Rose Farm. Colonel Goode Bryan, the brigade's senior colonel, probably took over as Semmes' successor and led the regiments for the balance of the action. Unfortunately, neither Bryan nor any of the brigades regimental commanders filed reports following the close of the campaign. Semmes was struck down so quickly so it is impossible to assess his performance at Gettysburg.

While the battle raged, someone applied a tourniquet to stem the blood loss and Semmes was taken off the field. He was transported back to Martinsburg, West Virginia, where he died on July 10. His last words were reported as: "I consider it a privilege to die for my country."

For further reading:

Derry, Joseph T. *Georgia, Confederate Military History*, vol. 6, ed. by Clement A. Evans. Atlanta, 1899.

Pfanz, Harry. *Gettysburg: The Second Day*. Chapel Hill, 1987.

BARKSDALE'S BRIGADE:
(1,620 MEN)

BRIGADIER GENERAL
WILLIAM BARKSDALE

Even in an army full of fire-eaters, William Barksdale stood out. Division commander Maj. Gen. Lafayette McLaws referred to him as "The fiery impetuous Mississippian." Large and heavy, he did not present a classic figure on a horse, and when he rode into action he leaned forward as if trying to push his horse faster out of sheer eagerness to get at the Yankees. "He had a thirst for battle glory," said one of his men. Many noticed that Barksdale achieved a kind of incandescence when he was about to go into a fight. This effect was partially due to his light complexion and thin, wispy white hair, which shone during a charge "like the white plume of Navarre," wrote one captain.

A Tennessee native and a graduate of the University of Nashville, Barksdale moved to Mississippi to practice as a lawyer, but left his practice to edit the pro-slavery newspaper *Columbus Democrat*. He took part in the Mexican War as a quartermaster, but frequently appeared at the front during heavy fighting, often coatless and carrying a large sword. After that war he

entered Congress, where in the 1850s he attained national prominence as a hot-headed States' Rights Democrat. He was alleged to have stood by the side of his friend and fellow representative, Preston S. Brooks, when Brooks nearly killed Massachusetts abolitionist Senator Charles Sumner in the Senate Chamber by beating him repeatedly over the head with a gutta-percha cane. In another shoving match in the House, Barksdale lost his wig.

When the South seceded in the spring of 1861, Congressman Barksdale resigned his seat in the House to become quarter-master general of Mississippi's forces. In May, however, he was made colonel of the 13th Mississippi. He was with his regiment at First Manassas that summer, where it participated in a critical attack on the Federal flank. That fall, however, Colonel Barksdale got so drunk that his superior, Brig. Gen. Nathan "Shanks" Evans (himself a notorious tippler), brought him up on charges. Barksdale escaped punishment by giving "a solemn pledge" not to touch a drop for the duration of the conflict.

He devoted the following months to training his regiment and learning the ropes of command. On the Peninsula the following spring, Barksdale's brigade leader, Brig. Gen. Richard Griffith, was killed by a stray shell at Savage's Station on June 29. Barksdale took over command of the brigade and led it two days later at Malvern Hill. Robert E. Lee wrote that Barksdale, by "seizing the colors himself and advancing under a terrific fire of artillery and infantry," displayed "the highest qualities of the soldier." He was made brigadier general in August 1862.

In the Maryland Campaign, Barksdale served for the first time under the divisional leadership of Lafayette McLaws. His Mississippians, along with Brig. Gen. Joseph Kershaw's soldiers, pried a Federal regiment off rugged Maryland Heights and helped seal the doom of the Union garrison trapped below at Harpers Ferry. A few days later at Sharpsburg, McLaws' Division rushed onto the field and crushed

Maj. Gen. John Sedgwick's division in the West Woods. At Fredericksburg in December 1862, Barksdale and his men won lasting renown with their solitary, gritty defense of the waterfront, where they obstinately resisted Federal attempts to bridge the Rappahannock River by firing from cellars and rifle pits along the river's edge. The Mississippians clung to their position even after a concentrated Federal artillery bombardment pounded the buildings into rubble.

Barksdale's unique leadership style was illustrated by the prayer service and pep rally he held for his men one evening during the Chancellorsville Campaign in May 1863. While the ex-Mississippi governor Albert Gallatin Brown and other politicians delivered speeches, Barksdale gave "a very interesting 'family talk,'" explained one of his soldiers. "He is very much attached to the boys, as the boys are to him." Barksdale's difficult assignment in that campaign was to hold the heights above Fredericksburg with his lone brigade. When John Sedgwick's 23,000-strong Sixth Corps overran his position, Barksdale showed pluck and resilience: "Our center has been pierced, that's all," he glibly reported; "we will be all right in a little while." He managed to evacuate his survivors, rally his brigade, and with reinforcements, take back the lost ground the next day.

Forty-two years old, Barksdale was one of the Confederacy's most inspirational brigadiers, and his brigade of rangy, straight-shooting Mississippians was second to none. While the political general had never demonstrated any real tactical sophistication, he was a charismatic leader who had performed well both offensively and defensively. Marching into position at Gettysburg, the general is said to have worn trousers trimmed with gold braid, a short round jacket trimmed with gold braid on its sleeves, and Mississippi's star-emblazoned buttons; three gold stars were sewn on either side of his collar. Barksdale's fine linen shirt was fastened with studs bearing the Masonic emblem.

GETTYSBURG: Barksdale's Brigade marched with McLaws' Division from Greenwood, Pennsylvania, east over South Mountain on the night of July 1-2 and camped at Marsh Creek about 3 1/2 miles west of Gettysburg. At about noon on July 2, his infantrymen marched with McLaws' other brigades on a long and frustrating, back-and-forth route from Herr Ridge to a line facing east from Pitzer's Woods. From this woodlot, they were to launch their onslaught on the Union left flank—a flank thought to be somewhere north of the Wheatfield Road. The brigade arrived in place at about 3:30 p.m.

Barksdale's Mississippians were aligned in the woods just west and north of the J. Snyder farm, from left to right as follows: 18th, 13th, 17th, and 21st. He could see through the trees that the Peach Orchard immediately opposite his line along the Emmitsburg Road, though supposedly empty, was instead full of enemy infantry and artillery. The Union presence forced a change of strategy, and McLaws' brigades waited for Maj. Gen. John Hood's Division to deploy to the south and begin the sweeping attack. Barksdale's Brigade was aligned on Joseph Kershaw's left, with William Wofford's Brigade deployed about 150 yards behind him. His advance would strike the Peach Orchard directly and cover Kershaw's left flank. Hood's men moved to the attack about 4:00 p.m., and immediately thereafter Barksdale chafed to get into the battle, especially since artillery shells were raining on his position and inflicting casualties. His pleas to McLaws did no good, so the general sought out Longstreet when the corps commander rode along his line. "I wish you would let me go in, general," he pleaded. "I will take that battery in five minutes." To this, Longstreet patiently replied, "Wait a little; we are all going in presently." While they waited, Barksdale instructed his officers that only he and likely his staff would enter the battle mounted; all others would advance on foot. Pointing his finger in the direction of the enemy, he said, "The line before you must be broken—to do so let every officer and man animate his comrades by his personal presence in the front line."

About 5:00 p.m. or later, Longstreet gave the order for McLaws' Division to advance. Kershaw's Brigade, on Barksdale's immediate right, stepped over a stone wall and moved forward, but Barksdale's brigade did not. For some unexplained reason his men were late in advancing. One report has his regiments entangled with artillery. Whatever the reason, the delay was paid for with the blood of Kershaw's men, who suffered heavily without support on their exposed flank.

Barksdale made a short speech, then shouted, "Attention, Mississippians! Battalions, Forward!" and the brigade exploded from the woods opposite the Sherfy orchard. It was, by all accounts, an irresistible tide, one of the most breathtaking spectacles in the war. One Confederate called it "the most magnificent charge I witnessed during the war." A Northern colonel was quoted as saying, "It was the grandest charge that was ever made by mortal man." Barksdale's tightly-packed line surged forward and did not stop even when Union musketry and artillery fire began to tear holes in it. The Mississippians swept up and over the Federal front and smashed Brig. Gen. Charles Graham's brigade manning the Peach Orchard—and still the charge hurtled ahead.

While the bulk of Barksdale's regiments turned north and continued advancing, the 21st Mississippi continued heading east against a line of infantry and artillery. The Federal line along the Emmitsburg Road north of the Trostle land was manned by Andrew Humphreys' division, which was struck by Barksdale's men on the left and two other Southern brigades (Wilcox and Perry) in front. The Federals crumpled and fell back a full half-mile to Cemetery Ridge. Barksdale kept urging the men on, yelling, "Brave Mississippians, one more charge and the day is ours."

The Mississippians turned back east and swept on toward Cemetery Ridge, into the skirt of trees lining Plum Run. A fresh Federal brigade could be seen deploying to confront the advance; heavy casualties, disordered lines, and fatigue slowed the attack. Barksdale's men had advanced about one mile when Col. George Willard's "Harpers Ferry" brigade counterattacked, driving them back. Unfortunately, Barksdale was no longer leading his men. According to a private in the 13th Mississippi, he found the general lying on the ground, badly wounded and alone. He claimed he gave Barksdale a drink from his canteen until he saw water leak from a wound in the general's chest.

The mortally wounded officer was later picked up and carried on a litter to a Union field hospital along the Taneytown Road. Credible accounts claim he was placed in the yard on a bed of blankets— no one knew who he was at this point— and given water with a spoon. When it was discovered the wounded officer was General Barksdale, a surgeon examined his injuries, which included a left chest wound "too large to have been made by a minie ball," and a fracture and two wounds in his leg. He was given morphine and asked the doctor several times whether his wounds were mortal. He supposedly told the surgeon "Beware! You will have Longstreet thundering in your rear in the morning!" The general eventually lost consciousness and expired sometime during the night. A Federal who had known him from his days in the House of Representatives saw him the next day "with open unblinking eyes. . .uncovered in the sunshine. There he lay alone, without a comrade to brush the flies from his corpse." The general was buried in a temporary grave near the Hummelbaugh house, and his remains were later returned to Mississippi.

For further reading:

Hawley, Steve C. "Barksdale's Mississippi Brigade at Fredericksburg." *Civil War History*, 40, March, 1994.

McKee, James W. "William Barksdale: The Intrepid Mississippian." Ph.D. diss., Mississippi St. U., 1966

McNiely, J. S. *Barksdale's Mississippi Brigade at Gettysburg: "Most Magnificent Charge of the War."* Gaithersburg, 1987.

Pfanz, Harry. *Gettysburg: The Second Day.* Chapel Hill, 1987.

Rand, Clayton. *Men of Spine in Mississippi.* Gulfport, 1940.

Winschel, Terrence J. "Their Supreme Moment: Barksdale's Brigade at Gettysburg." *Gettysburg Magazine*, #1, 1989.

WOFFORD'S BRIGADE:
(1,627 MEN)

BRIGADIER GENERAL
WILLIAM TATUM WOFFORD

William Wofford was born and raised in the mountainous region of Habersham County, Georgia. His father died shortly after he was born, and his mother raised the boy. The driven young man went on to study law after an inauspicious education at the Gwinnett County Manual Labor School, and by his thirties was a prosperous plantation owner and lawyer in Cassville, Georgia. He was also elected to the state legislature and edited a weekly newspaper. A Unionist Democrat, he opposed secession and voted against it at the Georgia secession convention, although he volunteered for Confederate service when the Civil War began.

Wofford had no formal military education, but he had been captain of a company in the Mexican War in his early twenties. Those credentials were enough to get such a prominent citizen his own regiment, and in April 1861 Wofford was made colonel of the 1st Georgia State Troops, which was redesignated the 18th Georgia Volunteers. Initially posted in North Carolina, by the spring of 1862 Wofford and his regiment were part of Brig. Gen. John B. Hood's "Texas Brigade" (the Georgians were "adopted" by the Lone Star soldiers). They served with this unit on the Peninsula in the battles of Yorktown, Eltham's Landing, West Point, and the Seven Days' Battles, where the brigade won fame with its heroic breakthrough attack at Gaines' Mill. Wofford again led the 18th Georgia when the Texas Brigade spearheaded Maj. Gen. James Longstreet's crushing assault at Second Manassas in August 1862. Official recognition of Wofford appeared for the first time in Hood's report after this battle, albeit only in an all-encompassing commendation of his regimental commanders.

In the Maryland Campaign, Hood was given command of a division and Wofford led the Texas Brigade at Sharpsburg, where it incurred a horrendous 513 casualties in the Cornfield during some of the war's bloodiest fighting. He received some notice after the battle from both Longstreet (who included Wofford in a rather long list of "most prominently distinguished" officers) and Hood (who merely called both his brigadiers "conspicuous.").

In November Wofford and his 18th Georgia were transferred to the Georgia brigade of Brig. Gen. Thomas Cobb. At the Battle of Fredericksburg, Cobb's Brigade played a central role behind the famous stone wall on Marye's Heights, where Cobb was mortally wounded. On January 17, 1863, Wofford was made brigadier general and two days later was officially given command of Cobb's old brigade. At Chancellorsville in May 1863,

Wofford led his new brigade ably, battling both wings of the Union army along with the rest of Maj. Gen. Lafayette McLaws' Division. McLaws had to fight off accusations that he had not been aggressive enough at Salem Church, and he singled out no one for after-battle praise.

In trying to win a reputation, William Wofford was perhaps aggressive to the point of being rash. One colonel remarked that "we all know that he was but too prone to go forward. . .even into disaster." McLaws' described the Georgian as "very ambitious of military fame and one of the most daring of men." By mid-1863 Wofford, one year shy of forty, had seen plenty of action and had led his brigade for six months.

GETTYSBURG: Wofford and the rest of McLaws' Division spent July 1 on the west side of South Mountain waiting for Lt. Gen. Richard Ewell's supply trains to pass. At 4:00 p.m. the division started east on a 13-mile march over the mountain and reached Marsh Creek, 3 1/2 miles west of Gettysburg, at midnight.

Up at daylight, Wofford's Brigade edged near Seminary Ridge, then moved back to Herr Ridge, where it waited all morning. At noon, Longstreet's First Corps (minus Pickett's Division, not yet up) started south to get into position for a flank attack against the Federal left. Though this destination was only three miles away, it took Wofford's troops nearly four hours of exhaustive marching to reach its jump-off point in Pitzer's Woods and deploy. The delay was compounded when it was discovered that the enemy was strongly posted in their front. What had been intended as a flank attack would now be a head-on charge—a grim prospect to the men in the ranks.

Wofford's Georgia Brigade was deployed behind Brig. Gen. William Barksdale's Mississippians on the left half of McLaws' divisional front. His brigade was composed of the 16th, 18th and 24th regiments, Cobb's Georgia Legion, and Phillips' Georgia Legion. Its exact deployment is somewhat obscure—Wofford's report is missing—although at least half of the brigade was aligned south of the Wheatfield Road.

After Maj. Gen. John Hood's Division passed behind McLaws' men and formed on the right, the First Corps artillery opened and Hood jumped off to the attack at about 4:30 p.m.. Wofford waited with the rest of McLaws' brigades for approximately an hour and Longstreet gave the signal to advance. The right side of McLaws' divisional line (Kershaw and Semmes) plunged ahead. Wofford's men, though, had to wait for Barksdale's regiments to begin their assault, and by the time Wofford finally started forward, he got tangled up with some friendly batteries and more minutes were lost. During this episode, one battery officer saw Wofford and was awed by his military magnificence. "Oh, he was a grand sight," wrote the artilleryman, "and my heart is full now while I write of it. . . .Long may Gen. Wofford live to lead his men to victory!"

The delay, while costly to Kershaw, proved advantageous to Wofford, for by the time he gained the Peach Orchard, Barksdale's Brigade had already swept its defenders aside. Most of the Mississippi regiments turned north and continued their attack, but Wofford's Georgians headed east, their front bisected by the Wheatfield Road. The 21st Mississippi continued east as well, protecting Wofford's left flank.

His advance could not have been better timed nor more advantageously positioned, and his brigade gave new hope to the Southerners struggling around the Stony Hill and intimidated the Federals before them. As he went forward, Wofford, in conjunction with others (primarily Kershaw) pushed Barnes' division (the brigades of Sweitzer and Tilton) out of Trostle's Woods, which in turn exposed the flank of what remained of Brig. Gen. John Caldwell's division of four small brigades battling in the Wheatfield.

The domino effect continued when Caldwell's collapse exposed the flank of a Regular brigade led by Col. Sidney Burbank, which also fell back hastily from the Wheatfield. Wofford's men, in turn, poured a deadly fire into each of these Federal organizations.

By the time Wofford's Georgians reached Plum Run, they had lost momentum and had outrun their supports. They took up an advanced position behind a stone wall and remained there for some time until General Longstreet wisely called them back before arriving Federal reinforcements surrounded them. At least one of Wofford's regimental commanders complained directly to Longstreet, to no avail. McLaws, who was west of Trostle's Woods, watched as Wofford's Brigade withdrew, its angry general behind it with pistol in hand. McLaws did not know that Longstreet had ordered the brigade back (another example of Longstreet acting in McLaws' stead and watching over the division, as he promised Lee he would), and inquired as to the move's necessity. Wofford was "apprehensive that his coming back might be misconstrued," McLaws explained later. The division commander posted Wofford's battered brigade "under the woods" and later agreed that his withdrawal was wise. Wofford's men were not engaged on July 3, and withdrew after Pickett's defeat later that afternoon.

Despite its string of tactical successes on the afternoon of July 2, Wofford's Brigade lost only 334 men—less than any other Confederate brigade engaged against the Union left. Curiously, Longstreet did not include Wofford's name in his post-battle list of those deserving commendation; McLaws did not write a report. Though he turned in a solid performance, Gettysburg did not enhance the Georgian's reputation, and he was never viewed as a luminary brigadier slated for higher command. William Wofford continued to lead his brigade through the many of the rest of the army's difficult battles until he transferred away from the Army of Northern Virginia in the last few months of the war.

Wofford turned once again to politics and was elected immediately after the war to the House of Representatives from Georgia. He was active for the rest of his life in railroading, politics, and education. He died in 1884.

For further reading:

Conyos, Lucy J. *The History of Bartow County, Georgia*. Jefferson, 1933.

Derry, Joseph T. Georgia, Vol. 6 of *Confederate Military History*. ed. by Clement A. Evans, Atlanta, 1899. [Vol. 7 of the extended edition. Wilmington, 1987.]

Pfanz, Harry W. *Gettysburg: The Second Day*. Chapel Hill, 1987.

Smith, Gerald J. *"One of the Most Daring of Men:" The Life of Confederate General William Tatum Wofford*. Murfreesboro, 1997.

HOOD'S DIVISION:
(7,375 MEN / 19 GUNS)

MAJOR GENERAL
JOHN BELL HOOD

Outside of Gen. Robert E. Lee, Maj. Gen. John Bell Hood enjoyed arguably the greatest popularity among the Southern people in the summer of 1863. Called "Sam" by his intimates, the magnificent and grave-faced Kentuckian was still a bachelor at age thirty-two. Over six feet tall and lanky, with a booming and a full head of blond hair, Hood's looks—combined with his unparalleled record in battle—had an electric effect on people, particularly women. When he appeared in Richmond, he transfixed Civil War diarist Mary Chesnut. "When he came with his sad face—the face of an old crusader who believed in his cause, his cross, and his crown—we were not prepared for that type as a beau ideal of wild Texans," she wrote.

Against the wishes of his father, a doctor who wanted his son to follow in his footsteps, Hood entered West Point and graduated an undistinguished 44th out of 53 students in the Class of 1853. He served in frontier Texas with the cavalry unit commanded by Robert E. Lee. The future army leader became a mentor for the young Hood, and the relationship would be reestablished years later when the two fought together in the Army of Northern Virginia. In Texas, Hood established his reputation as a brave soldier. In an Indian fight in 1857, when an arrow pinned his left hand to his bridle, he broke off the arrowhead, pulled out the shaft and continued fighting. He was partially incapacitated by the wound for the next two years.

Hood was serving near the Rio Grande when the Civil War broke out, and when his native Kentucky did not secede he linked himself with Texas troops. Sent to the Peninsula defenses, he began as a lowly cavalry lieutenant but was rapidly promoted. By March 1862, when the Army of the Potomac arrived to threaten Richmond, he was a brigadier general at the head of the only brigade of Texans in the Eastern army, regiments that he had personally drilled and instructed to high efficiency. He achieved his first notice for "conspicuous gallantry" during the skirmish at Eltham's Landing on May 7, and at Gaines' Mill on June 27, he led a charge by the Texans that broke the Federal defensive line. This achievement gave him renown as the leader of some of the fiercest combat troops in Robert E. Lee's Army of Northern Virginia.

After his notable performance on the Peninsula, Hood was given command of a division that consisted of his Texans and another brigade. His men added to their reputation as superior shock troops in August 1862 at Second Manassas, when Hood spearheaded the crushing attack of Maj. Gen. James Longstreet's wing that nearly destroyed Maj. Gen. John Pope's Federal army.

An incident following the battle illustrates the man. Hood became embroiled in a dispute over captured Yankee ambulances with Brig. Gen. Nathan "Shanks" Evans. General Longstreet sided with Evans and Hood was arrested and ordered to Culpeper Court House. Lee wisely intervened and Hood was allowed to ride at the rear of his division when the army marched into Maryland. During the Battle of South Mountain, his men, resenting the fact they were being committed to combat while deprived of their leader, began to yell, "Give us Hood!" Lee heard the ruckus and raised his hat to the angry warriors, telling them, "You shall have him, gentlemen!" He brought Hood up from the rear of the column and offered him back his command if he would offer a simple statement of regret over the ambulance incident. Hood flatly refused. Lee, undaunted, announced that the arrest was suspended while there was fighting to be done, and put the charismatic general back at the head of the division. A few days after that episode, at the height of the bloody fighting in the Cornfield at Sharpsburg, Hood's men were thrown in to stop the Confederate left from being crushed. "It was here that I witnessed the most terrible clash of arms, by far, that has occurred during the war," Hood wrote after the fight.

With a combat record unequaled by any in the army at his level, Maj. Gen. "Stonewall" Jackson recommended Hood for promotion to major general in October 1862. Lt. Col. G. Moxley Sorrel, Longstreet's aide, entered his opinion that the tall, gangly Hood was the "ideal" soldier. At Fredericksburg in December, Hood's Division, now expanded to four brigades, occupied a relatively quiet section of front and lost less than 400 men during the campaign. In the spring of 1863, Hood's Division, together with that of Maj. Gen. George Pickett, was detached to participate in the Suffolk Campaign in southeastern Virginia, where they foraged successfully while Lee and Jackson won a dramatic victory at Chancellorsville against Maj. Gen. Joseph Hooker's army.

While he was a fine combat leader, Hood was not a talented administrator. When his division was in bivouac he relaxed and was inclined to be careless. An inspection of the Texas Brigade in November 1862 revealed a dirty camp, with arms in bad order and only a third of its men decently clad.

Maj. Charles Venable, of Lee's staff, once said he had often heard of the "light of battle shining in a man's eyes." He had only seen it once, however, when he approached Hood with an order from Lee in the middle of heavy fighting. The man was transfigured, said Venable. "The fierce light in Hood's eyes I can never forget." At the time of Gettysburg, it seemed to be a universal opinion in the Confederacy that, of any division commander in the army, Hood the was the most likely to have a brilliant future.

GETTYSBURG: On July 1, while the men of Lt. Gens. A. P. Hill's and Richard Ewell's corps were fighting on the battle's first day, Hood was with his division (minus Brig. Gen. Evander Law's detached brigade) in Greenwood, about 17 miles west of Gettysburg. After waiting all day for Ewell's wagons to pass on the road into Gettysburg, Hood's men finally got moving around 4:00 p.m.. They trod 13 miles over the mountain, halting at midnight at Marsh Creek, about 3 1/2 miles west of Gettysburg.

Early the next morning, July 2, Hood's men followed Maj. Gen. Lafayette McLaws' Division on the approach to Gettysburg. They fell out in the fields west of Seminary Ridge near the Chambersburg Pike while Hood went a short distance forward to Lee's headquarters to confer with his commander. Lee's plan was for Hood to follow behind McLaws and

attack up the Emmitsburg Road toward Gettysburg, driving in the Union left after a two-mile march to the south to get astride the Union flank. Hood's men spent the rest of the morning filing back toward Herr Ridge, and waiting for the march south to begin.

Longstreet's two divisions began their trek to their jump-off positions around noon, moving south along the west side of Herr Ridge with Hood riding at the rear of the column with Lee and Longstreet. Shortly after the march started, the column stopped near Black Horse Tavern, where the road was visible from Little Round Top. McLaws suggested starting over and using a new route, and insisted on keeping his place at the head of the procession; Hood and his men waited while McLaws' Division filed back along the column. The march resumed south down Willoughby Run. As he neared the end of the movement, Hood sent some of his Texan scouts ahead to locate the enemy flank. It soon became clear that the Union left was not where Lee had said it would be—the Federal line extended much further south than expected. To adjust to the new situation, Longstreet sent Hood and his men further south, into Biesecker's Woods, and changed the attack plan. Hood's Division would now attack first up the Emmitsburg Road, drive in the Yankee left, and assist McLaws' men when they attacked later. Richard Anderson's Third Corps Division, beyond McLaws' left flank, would advance after McLaws' men were well engaged.

Hood deployed his division in Biesecker's Woods in two lines of two brigades each, one line behind the other. His front line consisted of Brig. Gen. Evander Law's Brigade on the right, and Brig. Gen. Jerome Robertson's Texas Brigade on the left. Behind them were the brigades of Brig. Gens. Henry Benning on the right and George "Tige" Anderson on the left. Hood's scouts returned with news that the enemy line ended just north of Little Round Top. Hood requested a change in the attack order and asked Longstreet if he could skirt the enemy left around Big

Round Top and come in behind the Union defenders. Longstreet refused. The attack was already behind schedule, and the move would take a substantial amount of time. Hood thought the Union position so strong that he asked a second time to be allowed to improvise a move around the enemy left, and again Longstreet refused. A third time Hood asked, and Longstreet's reply was a peremptory demand to attack immediately as ordered. Although many consider Hood's proposed flank attack one of the great "what ifs" of the Battle of Gettysburg, the Federals fed significant reinforcements into the area which would likely have isolated the lone division.

Hood rode to his accustomed place in front of the Texas Brigade and gave a short speech, then stood in his stirrups and boomed, "Fix bayonets, my brave Texans; forward and take those heights!" Law's and Robertson's Brigades thundered out of the woods. Instead of moving north along the Emmitsburg Road, as Lee apparently intended, they advanced east toward the Round Tops on their own initiative. Hood rode forward with Robertson for a short distance and stopped in a peach orchard to watch the progress of his brigades.

Twenty minutes into the attack a shell from the Union batteries about 1,300 yards to the north exploded above his head, and metal fragments shredded his entire left arm. Hood reeled in the saddle from the shock and was lowered to the ground by his aides. As he was taken to an ambulance in the rear, where his arm was wrapped in bandages, Hood later wrote that he experienced "deep distress of mind and heart at the thought of the inevitable fate of my brave fellow-soldiers, who formed one of the grandest divisions of that world-renown army." While he may have convinced himself after the war that he suffered "deep distress" while leaving the field, contemporary evidence confirms he was so insensible from shock that he paid almost no attention when another shell struck the roof of an ambulance near his head. Regardless, the blond giant was out of the battle. Lee would later dramat-

ically refer to Hood's wounding as the moment the battle was lost.

Evander Law succeeded Hood in command of the division, and the four brigades continued fighting until sundown, capturing the Stony Hill, Rose Woods, Devil's Den and Big Round Top. Hood's men came within yards of seizing Little Round Top, but were driven from its slopes as the sun was setting on the day's battle. Losses for the division were about 2,000, perhaps more. The Gettysburg wound added to Hood's favorable reputation at large, although he was injured so early in the fight it is impossible to assess his performance.

Hood's months of glory were forever behind him. With his arm in a sling, Hood rejoined his division as it passed through Richmond on its way west to reinforce the Army of Tennessee, where he lost his right leg to a bullet in the thigh at Chickamauga. With his mangled body grotesquely hewn by combat, Hood was given a corps in the Army of Tennessee. He led it during the Atlanta Campaign and eventually succeeded Joe Johnston as commander of the army in front of Atlanta in July 1864. Like many others, Hood finished the war a victim of what would later be described as "The Peter Principle": he was promoted too high for his capabilities. After losing Atlanta and leading his army to disaster at Franklin and Nashville, he resigned his commission.

Hood's tragic bad luck continued after the war. He settled in New Orleans and became a prosperous merchant until an 1878 financial crisis wiped him out. The following year in a yellow fever epidemic he, along with his wife and one child, died. They left behind a number of orphans.

For further reading:

Dyer, John. *The Gallant Hood.* Indianapolis, 1950.

Freeman, Douglas Southall. *Lee's Lieutenants: A Study in Command.*, vol. 3. New York, 1944.

McMurry, Richard M. *John Bell Hood and the War for Southern Independence.* Lexington, 1982

O'Connor, Richard. *Hood: Cavalier General.* New York, 1949.

Pfanz, Harry. *Gettysburg: The Second Day.* Chapel Hill, 1987.

Polley, Joseph B. *Hood's Texas Brigade: Its Marches, Its Battles, Its Achievements.* New York, 1910.

Simpson, Harold B. *Hood's Texas Brigade: Lee's Grenadier Guard.* Waco, 1970.

LAW'S BRIGADE:
(1,933 MEN)

BRIGADIER GENERAL
EVANDER McIVOR LAW

South Carolinian Evander Law had a heritage of gritty backwoods fighting. His grandfather and two great-grandfathers had been soldiers under the personable and flamboyant "Swamp Fox," Francis Marion, during the Revolution. The 26-year-old Law was himself charismatic figure in uniform, "one of the handsomest of men, as straight as an arrow, with jet black beard and dashing appearance," wrote a contemporary. " The grace of his manner was flawless."

Law was a professor before the war and a graduate of the South Carolina Military Academy (now The Citadel). He taught history and belles-lettres at King's Mountain Military Institute before establishing his own Military High School at Tuskegee, Alabama, where he was serving as principal when the South seceded. He recruited a company largely from his own school when the conflict began, and was soon promoted to lieutenant colonel of the 4th Alabama, also called the "Alabama Zouaves." The regiment fought at First Manassas in July 1861, where its colonel was killed and Law was severely wounded in the arm. The wound left his elbow stiff and his entire left arm practically useless. He returned to the regiment in late October 1861 and was promoted to colonel. On the Peninsula the following spring, the former company commander was given command of an entire brigade when its leader, Brig. Gen. William Whiting, was promoted to head the division. After being lightly engaged at Seven Pines on May 31, Law led his Alabama Brigade in fierce combat at Gaines' Mill the next month where, in tandem with Brig. Gen. John Hood's Texas Brigade, he spearheaded the triumphant assault that cracked the Federal lines. Law and Hood attacked again, this time with tragic results, four days later at Malvern Hill. At Second Manassas in August 1862, Maj. Gen. James Longstreet used both Law and Hood to land another sledgehammer blow in the assault that collapsed the Federal left and almost destroyed Maj. Gen. John Pope's Army of Virginia. Law's veterans saw hard action once again at Sharpsburg in September, where his men were thrown into the teeth of a Union attack across the Cornfield at the cost of 454 killed and wounded.

Law had led his brigade well in three successive campaigns at the rank of colonel, and he was finally given his overdue brigadier's wreath on October 3, two weeks after Sharpsburg. His men were but lightly engaged at Fredericksburg in December, and he was not present at the Battle of Chancellorsville in May 1863, as his brigade was with the rest of the Maj. Gen. John Hood's Division operating around Suffolk. The lone complaint against Law was extended by Col. William C. Oates of the 15th Alabama. Though Law was a "brave man and a good fighter," grumbled Oates, he was negligent in writing official reports after battles, and thereby failed to get the brigade due credit for its accomplishments on the battlefield.

By the middle of the summer of 1863, Law was the senior brigadier in what was generally acknowledged to be Lee's most outstanding combat division. The Palmetto State general had military training, dash, youth, experience, ability, and familiarity with his men—a formidable package in combat.

GETTYSBURG: Law's Brigade was detached from Hood's Division at Greenwood on July 1, spending the day instead at New Guilford, about 3 miles to the southeast, where it guarded the approaches from the south. Law did not move toward the battlefield with the rest of the division that evening, but started his march over South Mountain toward Gettysburg about 3:00 a.m. on July 2, arriving shortly before noon at Herr Ridge. His men were not allowed to rest after the 24-mile march, but instead joined Hood's column as it headed toward the jump-off point opposite the Union left flank for the day's attack in that sector. A frustrating, back-and-forth, stop-and-start march of several miles ensued before his men were able to move to take up a position in Biesecker's Woods. By the time they were deployed for the attack just before 4:00 p.m., Law's Alabamians were extremely fatigued from their 13-hour effort to reach the battlefield.

Evander Law's Brigade was aligned facing east on the extreme Confederate right behind a stone wall east of the Emmitsburg Road and directly opposite Bushman's Woods and Big Round Top. Law's five Alabama regiments were deployed, from left to right, as follows: 4th, 47th, 15th, 44th, and 48th. Skirmishers covered the brigade's front. Like his division commander, Law knew little about the enemy in front of him, and thus he dispatched six of his men to determine how far the Union line extended in the area of the Round Tops. Meanwhile, Law learned from some prisoners that a lightly guarded wagon train was parked behind Round Top. His returning scouts confirmed that Round Top itself was unoccupied. Law sought out Hood and set forth (he later claimed) four reasons why the planned frontal attack should be abandoned and a flanking effort undertaken instead. He was overruled.

The Alabamians were in their accustomed place in the first line of Hood's attack, and were ordered to swing to the left and head north on the right side of the road. Whether because of the terrain or because he disregarded orders, Law took the liberty of attacking straight east toward Devil's Den and the Round Tops. His men advanced after 4:00 p.m. The ground over which Law advanced was covered with fences, rocks, trees, and bushes, which served further to exhaust his men. The line passed to the right of the Bushman farm buildings, with Robertson's Brigade trying to keep in contact with Law's fast-moving left. As the left three regiments (4th, 47th and 15th) continued straight ahead and up the wooded slope of Round Top, Law sent his two right regiments (44th and 48th) veering sharply north behind the line toward Devil's Den to silence a deadly battery firing from its rocky confines.

At some point thereafter Law was notified that General Hood had been severely wounded and taken to the rear—leaving the South Carolinian in command of the division. When and exactly how he exercised his new command is unclear, but his leadership for the rest of the day appears to have been ineffectual. He forgot to appoint a new commander for his own brigade until the fighting was over for the day, and his regiments fought that afternoon with no one to coordinate their efforts. Neither Brig. Gens. Robertson, Anderson, or Benning mentioned receiving any orders from Law during the whole afternoon, which strongly suggests, as one historian has written, that Law's "control of the division as a whole that afternoon was not very active or strong." Although the regiments populating Hood's Division fought well as individual units, they crashed against Union strong points from Little Round Top to the Wheatfield without any sense of unified purpose or a firm guiding hand. The division knocked many Union brigades out of action, but failed to completely shatter the Union line and wrest control of Little Round Top from the Federals. If Law had done a more forceful job at the head of the division, it is doubtful whether Lee would have made the statement that the loss of Hood was the biggest reason for the Confederate army's defeat. Most of Law's regiments, meanwhile, marched over Round Top and attacked up the slopes of Little Round Top, where they were beaten back with heavy loss. It was here, on the far right of the Confederate army, that the 15th Alabama under Colonel Oates engaged in his immortal combat with Joshua Chamberlain and the 20th Maine on the wooded and rock-strewn slopes of Little Round Top. Darkness ended the action.

The next day, July 3, Law pulled three of "Tige" Anderson's regiments out of line and faced them south between Big Round Top and the Emmitsburg Road, where they easily repulsed Brig. Gen. Judson Kilpatrick's bungled cavalry attack that afternoon.

Law's ineffectual performance on July 2 did not immediately provoke comment—in fact, Longstreet even listed Law in his post-battle report as one of the officers "most distinguished for the exhibition of great gallantry and skill." In September, however, as the division entrained to head west to reinforce the Army of Tennessee, Longstreet reattached the brigade of Brig. Gen. Micah Jenkins to Hood's Division. Jenkins outranked Law and would have effectively replaced him at the head of the division, but Hood's return temporarily ended the issue. When Hood rose to corps command at Chickamauga and Jenkins failed to reach the field before the battle, Law led the division. While Longstreet purportedly expressed his "admiration and satisfaction" with his performance, Jenkins led the division at Chattanooga

and Knoxville. Relations between Longstreet and Law soured to the point that Law tendered his resignation and Longstreet brought him up on charges. After Longstreet was wounded in the Wilderness in May 1864, Law again led a brigade in the Army of Northern Virginia and was badly wounded at Cold Harbor.

Evander Law moved to Florida after the war, where he was active in education, journalism, and veterans' affairs. He never regained the use of his left arm, but lived a long life—until 1920.

For further reading:

Law, Evander McIvor. "The Struggle for 'Round Top," *Battles and Leaders of the Civil War*, ed. by Johnson and Buel, vol. 3. New York, 1888.

Oates, William C. *The War Between the Union and the Confederacy. . History of the 15th Alabama Regiment*. Dayton, 1974.

Pfanz, Harry. *Gettysburg: The Second Day.* Chapel Hill, 1987.

ANDERSON'S BRIGADE:
(1,874 MEN)

BRIG. GEN. GEORGE THOMAS "TIGE" ANDERSON

Never called anything but "Tige" (short for "Tiger"), George Anderson was born in Georgia in 1824 and attended Emory

College. While he never took any courses related to warfare, he did acquire some military training in the Mexican War as a lieutenant of Georgia cavalry. Later, in 1855, he received a captain's commission in the Regular cavalry, but resigned after three years. When the South seceded in 1861, Anderson—who owned considerable property in his native Covington, Georgia—was made colonel of the 11th Georgia Regiment in view of his local prominence and Old Army experience. He had a striking, well-defined face with dark wavy hair and a full but neatly-trimmed beard.

Anderson's regiment was mustered in too late to fight at First Manassas, but was brigaded with regiments that had fought there under Col. Francis Bartow, who was killed in the battle. Anderson was given command of the Georgia Brigade in the first part of 1862, surrendered it to Brig. Gen. David R. Jones, and regained it again in May when Jones became division commander. He led it during the Peninsula Campaign at Yorktown and in the Seven Days' Battles. When the new colonel of the 11th Georgia disappeared at Malvern Hill, Anderson, wrote one of his men, "left his horse and took it afoot rite with us. . . .Some of the companies runn clean off." Anderson, he said, "spoke out plain and publicly." If he couldn't get his old regiment to follow him, at least his old company would. "Boys, stick to your colors," Anderson yelled, and headed up the hill toward the blazing Federal line. The men who followed him suffered 72 casualties in the next few minutes. Despite such courage, Jones did not mention him in his list of commendations after the battle.

In the Second Manassas Campaign, Anderson and his men were in the lead of Maj. Gen. James Longstreet's column when it fought its way through Thoroughfare Gap. Two days later, Anderson's Brigade attacked with the rest of Longstreet's corps and drove in the enemy left, tearing asunder Maj. Gen. John Pope's Union force. The next month Anderson's Brigade fought at South Mountain, then at Sharpsburg, where it served mostly in reserve and suffered relatively little. In Longstreet's report of the campaign, however, he included Anderson in his long list of those who had distinguished themselves. The brigade was transferred to Maj. Gen. John B. Hood's hard-fighting division at the end of October 1862. "Tige" himself was finally made brigadier general on November 1; his men had been petitioning the War Department for months, and the promotion was long overdue, for he had been leading his brigade as a colonel for six months. At the Battle of Fredericksburg in December, Anderson's men were spared again, losing only ten casualties. The brigade was with the rest of Hood's Division at Suffolk in May, and was not present for the Battle of Chancellorsville.

Unlike many of Lee's brigadiers, "Tige" Anderson had enjoyed little chance to distinguish himself. Gettysburg would be his first heavy fighting since Second Manassas the previous summer, and his first real combat as a brigadier general. While his superiors were not overly impressed with him, his men loved him. Anderson "stands up to us like a father," wrote one of his privates. "He is always at his post," wrote another.

GETTYSBURG: On July 1, Anderson, with most of General Hood's Division, made the long evening march over South Mountain from Greenwood to Marsh Creek. On the morning and afternoon of July 2, Anderson's Brigade likewise shared the tedium and frustration of waiting for orders that eventually started it on the long and fitful march south to where the Emmitsburg Road passed through Biesecker's Woods, where the brigade formed into a line of battle in preparation for an attack against the Union left flank. The brigadier did not describe his position with any great detail other than that it held the left of Hood's Division and was in the rear of Robertson's Texas Brigade. His Georgia regiments were arranged, from left to right, as follows: 9th, 8th, 11th and 59th. His fifth regiment, the 7th Georgia, was detached to the south to "watch the movements of the enemy's cavalry." Thus, when it advanced Anderson's Brigade numbered only about 1,400 men.

When Longstreet launched his attack around 4:30 p.m., Anderson's men were withheld until he received a request for help from Brig. Gen. Jerome Robertson, who was locked in head-on combat in Rose's Woods near Devil's Den. At about this time Anderson saw the wounded Hood being carried to the rear. He responded to Robertson on his own initiative, moving his men out of the woods, across the Emmitsburg Road, and into the Rose Woods. His line advanced at an oblique into the timber with its left regiments near the Stony Hill. The Georgians, in conjunction with elements from Henry Benning's and Jerome Robertson's brigades, struck Brig. Gen. Hobart Ward's brigade in the eastern end of Rose Woods and the front of Col. Regis de Trobriand's brigade, which was holding the southern end of the Wheatfield and part of the Stony Hill. Stalled in his advance, Anderson pulled his men rearward and regrouped. While walking alone behind his regiments near a large rock, a bullet struck him in the flesh of his right thigh, knocking him from the fight. Brigade command fell to Lt. Col. William Luffman of the 11th Georgia.

While Tige was being assisted from the field, Luffman did a credible job with the brigade. Together with Joseph Kershaw's newly-arrived brigade on his left, he pushed the line forward a second time and Ward's men fell back before the onslaught. The brigade was re-formed facing generally north and with Kershaw again on the right, the Georgia regiments charged forward yet again, this time striking the brigades of Jacob Sweitzer, Regis de Trobriand, and perhaps a portion of William Tilton's as well. As de Trobriand's regiments retired, John Caldwell's division of the Second Federal Corps attacked across the Wheatfield and threw back Anderson's (Luffman's) regiments, which regrouped yet again in time to help sweep Caldwell's men from the area. The brigade was not engaged on the following day, July 3.

Anderson was among those commended as "most distinguished for the exhibition of great gallantry and skill" by General Longstreet after the fight. The Georgian was back with his brigade two months later for the Knoxville Campaign, and he served in workmanlike fashion through the rest of the war, leading his brigade until the surrender at Appomattox. After the war, Anderson was a railroad freight agent and the chief of police in Atlanta, Georgia, and Aniston, Alabama, where he died in 1901.

For further reading:

Derry, Joseph T. "Georgia," vol. 6, *Confederate Military History*, ed. by Clement A. Evans. Atlanta, 1899 [vol. 7 of the extended edition, Wilmington, 1987.]

Jorgensen, Jay. "Anderson Attacks the Wheatfield." *Gettysburg Magazine*, #14, 1996.

Pfanz, Harry. *Gettysburg: The Second Day*. Chapel Hill, 1987.

THE TEXAS BRIGADE:
(1,734 MEN)

BRIGADIER GENERAL JEROME BONAPARTE ROBERTSON

Jerome Robertson's grateful infantrymen called their forty-eight year old commander "Aunt Polly" because of his devotion to their well being. He was described as a man of strong sense, kindly, with warm impulses and genial manners, but "not much cultivated or polished." He had lived a full life before his Civil War career began.

Born in Kentucky in 1815, his father died when he was twelve, and in order to earn a living he apprenticed with a hatter. When his first master died, he was transferred to another in St. Louis, where at the age of eighteen he bought his release from the last three years of his contract. Though relatively uneducated, a St. Louis physician took Robertson under his wing, employing the teenager as a office assistant and also tutoring him. The doctor's

schooling enabled Jerome to enter Transylvania University as a medical student. His course of study at the University was only three months, truncated by the advent of Texas' war for independence from Mexico. The 20-year-old Robertson quit college to raise a company of Kentuckians to go south and join Sam Houston's Texan army. When he arrived in Texas in 1836, the Battle of San Jacinto had already been fought and independence was assured, but Robertson and his company remained in the Lone Star Republic until 1837, when they were formally mustered out. Robertson settled in Washington on the Brazos, Texas, where he married and began to practice medicine. He took time out each year between 1838 and 1844 to participate in at least one campaign against the Indians, and became a renowned Indian fighter. His fighting fame and social standing resulted in his being elected to both houses of the Texas state legislature, and in 1861 he was a pro-secessionist delegate to the state secession convention.

Robertson was middle-aged when the South left the Union, and as he had done a quarter-century earlier, he left his physician's practice and raised a company of volunteers, leading them to the capital of a new revolution. Arriving in Richmond, his company became integrated in the 5th Texas Infantry and Robertson again became a captain in a rebel army. The 5th was brigaded with other Texas regiments and would soon win fame in Virginia as "Hood's Texas Brigade." In early June 1862, James J. Archer, the first colonel of the 5th Texas, was given his own brigade, and Robertson was promoted to take his place at the head of the regiment in time for the Seven Days' Battles. The Texans won glory in their triumphant assault at Gaines' Mill, their first large fight. Robertson was slightly wounded in the shoulder, but was back in command of the 5th Texas two months later at Second Manassas, where the Texas Brigade added to its luster by spearheading another powerful Confederate attack. At one point in the action, Robertson discovered that the right of his regiment had raced ahead of the rest of his command. Instead of recalling these companies, the fiery Robertson pushed the remainder of his men to catch up with their enthusiastic brethren. The entire regiment hurtled on in the advance of the Confederate onslaught, and Robertson was shot in the groin as he urged him men forward.

Although he tried to stay with the army during the subsequent Maryland Campaign, Robertston had to be taken off the field at South Mountain after collapsing from exhaustion and the effects of his recent wound; he was too weak to fight at the Battle of Sharpsburg three days later. Nevertheless, he was promoted to brigadier general on November 1, 1862, and given command of the vaunted Texas Brigade, taking the place of that other Kentuckian-turned-Texan, John B. Hood.

Robertson would not have a chance to prove what he could do with a full brigade until the next summer at Gettysburg. At Fredericksburg, the division was not seriously threatened, and the Texas Brigade lost only six men. Robertson's men were with the rest of Hood's Division at Suffolk, out of harm's way during the battle fought at Chancellorsville in early May.

GETTYSBURG: On July 1, Robertson and his brigade marched eastward with the rest of Hood's Division on the Chambersburg Pike from Greenwood to Marsh

Creek. On July 2, the Texans shared their division's frustrating stops, starts, marches and countermarches, from Marsh Creek to the starting point for the attack against the Union left. They finally reached their intended destination of Biesecker's Woods before 4:00 p.m., and formed into line of battle in the edge of the woods.

Robertson's Texas Brigade was deployed for Hood's attack, as usual, in the first line and to the left of Brig. Gen. Evander Law's Brigade, thus forming a two-brigade front. His line overlapped those of Brig. Gens. Henry Benning and Tige Anderson, which had formed behind him. Robertson's four regiments were deployed astride the Emmitsburg Road, from left to right, as follows: the 3rd Arkansas and 1st Texas on the left, north of the road; and the 4th and 5th Texas regiments below or south of it. The entire brigade faced generally east.

Evander Law's Brigade opened the infantry attack and moved forward about 4:30 p.m., and Robertson and his men marched from the woods just moments later. Robertson had been ordered to keep his right closed on Law 's left flank and to keep his own left flank on the Emmitsburg Road, in conformity with Gen. Robert E. Lee's wishes that the assailment move northward. Law, however, had sent his brigade almost directly east against the Round Tops, and Robertson soon found that he had to either abandon the road or disconnect himself from Law. Reasoning that Maj. Gen. Lafayette McLaws would soon strike on his left, he decided to break with the road rather than with Law, and he directed his own brigade eastward, directly at the Devil's Den. During the advance over hundreds of yards of broken terrain, "exposed to a destructive fire of canister, grape, and shell," the distance between the wings of his brigade lengthened; Robertson lost contact with his two right regiments (4th and 5th Texas). He was informed that they had drifted into and were entangled with the middle of Law's Brigade, so he requested Law to look after them, and concentrated on his two remaining regiments (1st Texas and 3rd Arkansas), which were heavily

engaged just north of Devil's Den and in Rose Woods against Hobart Ward's Federal brigade and Smith's Federal battery.

As the fighting dragged on, Anderson became aware that McLaws' brigades were not appearing on his left as soon as he expected, and he sent back for reinforcements—a request complicated by the fact that Hood was being carried off the field with a shredded left arm. Robertson's request reached corps commander Lt. Gen. James Longstreet and Brig. Gens. "Tige" Anderson and Henry Benning, and the latter two brigades advanced up on either side of Robertson's two regiments. In conjunction with Benning and Anderson, Robertson's men moved forward and after severe close quarter fighting dislodged Ward's Federals, securing Devil's Den and the Rose Woods for the Confederates. As Robertson fought with his pair of regiments just above Devil's Den, his errant 4th and 5th Texas regiments attacked off the northwest face of Big Round Top and up the southwest face of Little Round Top, where they were beaten back with heavy losses. He saw nothing of their actions.

By this time darkness was beginning to fall and Robertson's small demi-brigade was disorganized and exhausted. An enemy round wounded Robertson above the right knee, and he was unable to walk. He left the brigade with his senior colonel and retired 200 yards to tend the wound. Nothing further was required of the Texans, and Robertson's men slept in their positions around Devil's Den during the evening of July 2. His brigade was ordered withdrawn late in the afternoon after the failure of Pickett's Charge.

Robertson had not performed well at Gettysburg and was not among those commended by Longstreet after the battle (Evander Law, the acting division commander, never wrote a report). Robertson's post-Gettysburg career was a checkered one, for he was twice removed from the head of the Texas Brigade for various reasons, once by Braxton Bragg in North Georgia and a second time by Longstreet in East Tennessee. The latter episode resulted in a courts martial trial, which found Robertson not guilty of "ulterior motives," but guilty of "bad conduct," and he was relieved of his command. A staff officer with Longstreet's command believed that Robertson had been "unjustly dealt with," but admitted that he was not "considered a good officer." The men of his brigade, however, were entirely on the side of their dear "Aunt Polly," and would have revolted en masse but for Robertson's intervention. Robertson never held another active field command.

After the war, Robertson returned to Texas and resumed his medical practice, became state superintendent of immigration (in 1874), and involved himself in railroad building. He died from cancer in 1891.

For further reading:

Laney, Daniel M. "Wasted Gallantry: Hood's Texas Brigade at Gettysburg," *Gettysburg Magazine*, #16, 1997.

McMurry, Richard M. *John Bell Hood and the War for Southern Independence.* Lexington, 1982.

Pfanz, Harry. *Gettysburg: The Second Day.* Chapel Hill, 1987.

Piston, William G. *Lee's Tarnished Lieutenant: James Longstreet and His Place in Southern History*, Athens, 1987.

Simpson, Harold B. *Hood's Texas Brigade: Lee's Grenadier Guard*, Waco, 1970.

Wright, Marcus J., comp., and Harold B. Simpson, ed., *Texas in the War, 1861-1865*, Hillsboro, 1965.

BENNING'S BRIGADE:
(1,420 MEN)

BRIGADIER GENERAL
HENRY LEWIS BENNING

Henry Benning was an inspiring sight: six feet tall, solidly built, with a full head of curly iron-gray hair and a trimmed gray bear. His formidable appearance, along with his solid combat record, earned him the nickname "Old Rock." The forty-nine year old also possessed a deep and guttural voice with which he distinctly enunciated each syllable of his speech. His bearing and presence befitted the Georgia Supreme Court justice he was. A native of Columbus, Georgia, he graduated first in the 1834 class of Franklin College (later the University of Georgia) and the next year was admitted to the bar at the age of twenty-one. Married in 1839 to the daughter of his law partner, he fathered six children while achieving success as a lawyer, legislator, and judge on the Georgia Supreme Court. Benning was known to all as a man of the highest integrity, and he was compared in character to that earlier champion of the South, John Calhoun. He was one of the most industrious and capable men in the Confederacy.

Politically, Benning had diligently sought secession for the South. He believed in the formation of a "consolidated" Southern Republic of the states of the deep South with strong centralized powers, so that slavery could be put "under the control of those most interested in it." When secession finally came in 1861, he was a prime candidate for a cabinet post in Jefferson Davis' new administration, but he had already decided to be a soldier and was at work organizing the 17th Georgia Volunteer Regiment. In August 1861, the regiment was mustered in with Benning as its colonel.

As part of a brigade led by volatile Georgia politician Brig. Gen. Robert Toombs, Benning's 17th Georgia was not heavily engaged in its first campaign on the Peninsula. Benning fought a battle of another sort in July 1862, when, ever the jurist, he disputed the constitutionality of the conscription act and refused to obey orders based on it. Through the interference of another Georgian politician-soldier, Col. Thomas R. R. Cobb, he escaped arrest and court martial. In the ensuing Second Manassas Campaign in August, Toombs was off on political business and Benning found himself commanding the brigade at the Battle of Second Manassas. There, perhaps unaccustomed to his new responsibilities, Benning suffered a rare loss of his composure after a sudden Federal strike. He jumped on an artillery horse, galloped back to Maj. Gen. James Longstreet, and cried, "General, I am ruined; my brigade was suddenly attacked and every man was killed; not one is to be found. Please give orders where I can do some fighting." The imperturbable Longstreet drawled, "Nonsense, Colonel. You are not so badly hurt. Look about you. I know you will find at least one man, and with him on his feet, report your brigade to me, and you two shall have a place in the fighting line." This ridicule sobered Benning, and he turned around, rallied his men, and went back to the fighting.

At Sharpsburg in September, Benning was again asked to lead Toombs' Brigade, this time in the crucial defense of "Burnside's Bridge." In an exploit that became part of the lore of the Army of Northern Virginia, Benning and his regiments harassed and prevented Union Maj. Gen. Ambrose Burnside from crossing his Ninth Corps over the bridge for much of the day. Toombs, who returned to the brigade late in the day and suffered a hand wound, was effusive in his praise of Benning after the battle. Benning led the brigade in light action at Fredericksburg in December during Toombs' absence, and was promoted to take his place at the head of the unit in April 1863, when Toombs resigned in a huff after being passed over

for promotion. Participation in the Suffolk Campaign caused him to miss the Chancellorsville Campaign in May 1863.

As Hood's men headed north to join in the Pennsylvania invasion, "Old Rock" was at the head of his brigade, a proven commander. His noble bearing provided strong leadership and bolstered the confidence of the men under him.

GETTYSBURG: Henry Benning and his brigade marched with the rest of Hood's Division, moving east on the Chambersburg Pike from Greenwood to Marsh Creek on July 1. On July 2, the Georgians endured the perambulations of Hood's Division as it wandered about the countryside behind Lafayette McLaws' Division trying to reach the starting point for the attack on the Union left flank. Benning's soldiers finally arrived at Biesecker's Woods a bit before 4:00 p.m. and were deployed on the far right in the second line of Hood's divisional attack formation.

His Georgia regiments were aligned, from left to right, as follows: 15th, 20th, 17th and 2nd. Brig. Gen. "Tige" Anderson's Brigade was deployed on Benning's left, and the brigades of Brig. Gens. Jerome Robertson and Evander Law were deployed probably 100 or more yards in front of him. Evidently, Benning was not privy to any information about the strength or exact location of the Federal position in Hood's front; he saw it for the first time when he advanced with his men.

Benning's rather vague orders were to follow and support Brig. Gen. Evander Law's Brigade. Hood's Division moved forward to the attack around 4:30 p.m., with Law's men leading the way. Benning waited for a while, for Hood's orders were for him to follow at a 400-yard interval. When he ordered his own regiments forward, long-flying artillery shells landed in his ranks before he even reached the Emmitsburg Road. His line angled to the left and crossed Slyder's lane, heading toward Plum Run between Devil's Den and the Rose Woods. He stopped his line twice to preserve the proper distance between his brigade and the line he could just make out ahead through the smoke and confusion. Without any direction from Hood or anyone else, he continued on.

Benning learned eventually that he was following the left flank elements of Robertson's Brigade, which was advancing on Law's left and getting into trouble around Devil's Den. Law's men had disappeared in the trees and smoke. The Georgian's advance, though, came at a critical moment and in the right place. With Robertson and "Tige" Anderson (who had come in on Robertson's left), Benning's men decimated the Brig. Gen. Hobart Ward's Third Corps brigade in their front. His right regiments swarmed up and over Devil's Den, while his left regiments carved their way through Rose's Woods, but suffered heavy casualties and could go no further. Consolidating his position around the great pile of rocks, Benning could do little else that evening as the sun set; ahead was reinforced Little Round Top, whose slopes were already carpeted with Confederate dead. The Georgians held their position until the afternoon of July 3, then withdrew after Pickett's Charge ended in failure.

Although Henry Benning was not among those singled out for commendation in Longstreet's report after the battle (a curious circumstance and one that has not been fully explained), he had certainly performed honorably at Gettysburg. The brigadier remained at that rank for the rest of the war and continued to serve honorably and well at the head of his brigade until the surrender at Appomattox. Benning resumed his law practice in Columbus, Georgia, until he suffered a stroke and died in 1875.

For further reading:

Adelman, Garry E. "Benning's Georgia Brigade at Gettysburg." *Gettysburg Magazine*, #18, 1998.

Cobb, James C. "The Making of a Secessionist: Henry L. Benning and the Coming of the Civil War." *The Georgia Historical Quarterly*, 60, no. 4, Winter, 1976.

Derry, Joseph T. "Georgia," vol. 6, *Confederate Military History*, ed. by Clement A. Evans. Atlanta, 1899 [vol. 7 of the extended edition, Wilmington, 1987.]

Pfanz, Harry. *Gettysburg: The Second Day.* Chapel Hill, 1987.

PICKETT'S DIVISION:
(5,473 MEN / 18 GUNS)

MAJOR GENERAL
GEORGE EDWARD PICKETT

Affable George Pickett was one of the most popular officers in the Army of Northern Virginia. He combined conviviality with a swashbuckling image. "Dapper," and "dashing," were the two words most frequently on the lips of witnesses; one man spoke of his "marvelous pulchritude." G. Moxley Sorrel, Lt. Gen. James Longstreet's aide, called him "a singular figure indeed!"

He was medium-sized, slender and well built, and carried himself gracefully and erect. He rode a sleek black charger and wore a small blue kepi, with buff gloves over the sleeves of his immaculately tailored uniform. An elegant riding crop was in one of his hands at all times, and his boots were always polished and his gold spurs were shiny—as were the double row of gold buttons on his coat front. Pickett wore a mustache that drooped gracefully beyond the corners of his mouth and then turned upward at the ends. His hair was a conversation topic in itself—"long ringlets flowed loosely over his shoulders, trimmed and highly perfumed, his beard likewise was curling and giving out the scent of Araby." Pickett's locks were the subject of a light moment on the march north to Gettysburg, when a female admirer asked Gen. Robert E. Lee for a lock of his hair. He replied that he had none to spare. . .but suggested she ask Pickett. The joke produced plenty of laughter from the staff, but Pickett, who was present, was not amused.

The dandy Southern general came from an Old Virginia family and was known, if not related, to everybody of importance east of Richmond. As a young man he had gone to Springfield, Illinois to study law and became acquainted with a lawyer named Abraham Lincoln, who gave him helpful bits of advice. Pickett received an appointment to West Point, where his strengths and weaknesses were brought clearly into focus. At the Academy he was the class clown and among the most well-liked cadets, but he also showed evidence of a meager intellect and an aversion to hard work: he graduated dead last in the Class of 1846.

Sent to serve in the Mexican War within months of graduation, Pickett was the first to climb the parapet during the storming of the fortress at Chapultepec. After having taken a flag from the wounded James Longstreet, Pickett unfurled it over the castle while bullets flew all around him, an exploit that made newspapers all over the country. Twelve years later, stationed in Puget Sound, he made news again and won his government's approval by providing the climactic moment of a territorial dispute called the "Pig War," when he faced down a British force of three warships and one thousand men while commanding an American garrison of just sixty-eight. "We'll make a Bunker Hill of it," were his defiant words, reprinted nationwide for an admiring public. While there, he also worked well with the region's native Indians. He learned their language, translated the Lord's Prayer and several hymns, and became a teacher to them; they called him "Great Chief."

It was not a surprise to anyone when Pickett went with Virginia after Fort Sumter. He had to return cross-country from Oregon, and thus missed First Manassas. Made colonel and assigned to the defense of the lower Rappahannock in September 1861, the energetic officer attracted the attention of his superior, Maj. Gen. T. H. Holmes. Probably through the efforts of Holmes, he was commissioned brigadier general in February 1862, and later that same month took over a leaderless brigade after Brig. Gen. Philip Cocke, its fifty-two year old general, put a pistol ball through his temple the day after Christmas 1861.

Pickett led his new regiments to the Peninsula in the spring of 1862, where they earned the collective nickname "Game Cock Brigade" in fighting at Williamsburg, Seven Pines, and Gaines' Mill. (This is the same brigade Richard Garnett would lead at Gettysburg.) At Gaines' Mill, Pickett was knocked off his horse by a bullet in the shoulder, just before the charge that carried the day. Though the wound would add to his military mystique, the episode was actually less than heroic. Pickett was found by a staff officer in a hollow "bewailing himself," crying out for litter bearers because he was mortally wounded. The officer examined the wound, saw it was not critical, and rode away since Pickett was "perfectly able to take care of himself."

Though the wound was a minor one, Pickett was slow to mend and took three months to return to the army. (The arm would still be stiff the next summer at Gettysburg.) When he reported for duty in late September 1862, he received a windfall promotion to major general—due almost entirely to the influence of Maj. Gen. James Longstreet, his corps commander and Mexican War colleague. Their friendship had been cemented by Pickett's kindness upon the death of Longstreet's children the previous winter. Though Pickett now had a division of two brigades, he would have little chance to show what he could do with it until Gettysburg. At Fredericksburg, the division was only lightly engaged, and not one man was killed. At Chancellorsville, Pickett's Division had been detached, along with two others under Longstreet, to the relatively uneventful Suffolk Campaign in southeastern Virginia.

By the mid-summer of 1863, Pickett must have been itching for a chance to prove himself as a division commander; he was still receiving solicitous attention from Longstreet. Moxley Sorrel told how "taking Longstreet's orders in emergencies, I could always see how he looked after Pickett, and made us give him things very fully; indeed, sometimes stay with him to make sure he did not get astray." Sorrel himself didn't have a very high regard for Pickett, characterizing him sarcastically as a "good brigadier" long after he had graduated to major general. Sorrel also had little patience with Pickett's love life, for the thirty-eight year old widower was head-over-heels in love with LaSalle "Sally" Corbell, a teenaged Virginia girl. During the Suffolk Campaign, Pickett had "commuted" back and forth between his fiancé and the front, which provoked Sorrel to conclude, "I don't think his division benefited by such carpet-knight doings in the field."

Though he was a career soldier and had been a division commander for ten months, Pickett was still untested at that level. However personally well liked, it was largely the opinion of the other officers that he owed his high rank to the patronage of Longstreet—and not native ability.

GETTYSBURG: On July 1, Pickett's Division was at Chambersburg, detached to guard the army's rear while the other two divisions of Longstreet's First Corps were at Greenwood, about seven miles to the east. All three were waiting to march over South Mountain toward the battle raging at Gettysburg about 20 miles away. Pickett's Division was ordered to remain in Chambersburg until relieved by Brig. Gen. John Imboden's tardy cavalry brigade, and it wasn't until that night that Pickett received orders to move toward Gettysburg.

His men got a late start, and made much of their march during the hot daylight hours of July 2, arriving exhausted about three or four miles east of Gettysburg late in the afternoon. Although Pickett reported to Lee that the men would be ready to pitch into the fighting that evening if given a couple of hours rest, Lee sent back word to go into camp—they would not be needed that day. The Virginians (the brigades of Brig. Gens. Richard Garnett, James Kemper and Lewis Armistead) rested in their bivouac on the Chambersburg Pike until the morning of July 3. Although Lee intended an attack early that morning, someone—probably Longstreet—failed to issue marching orders to Pickett until 3:30 a.m., making the dawn assault impossible.

A new offensive thrust was constructed around Pickett's three fresh Virginia brigades. The attack would also include all four of Maj. Gen. Henry Heth's previously bloodied brigades under Johnston Pettigrew's command, and two of Maj. Gen. W. Dorsey Pender's brigades under the leadership of Isaac Trimble. Two additional brigades from Maj. Gen. R. H. Anderson's, Division were also selected to support the column. This force, about 12,000 men, would assault the right center of the Union line on Cemetery Ridge. The Confederates would focus their efforts on a large umbrella-shaped copse of trees on the crest of the ridge—about one mile distant—close to where one of Lee's brigades under Brig. Gen. Ambrose "Rans" Wright had nearly made a breakthrough about sunset on the previous day's fighting. A massive 150-gun cannonade would precede the infantry.

After daylight, Pickett led his division forward to a spot "into a field near a branch," probably Pitzer's Run, a few hundred yards behind the main Confederate line on Seminary Ridge. The men fell out and relaxed in the morning air for about twenty minutes, formed battle lines, and advanced east a few hundred yards before they were ordered to lie down. They advanced again through Spangler's Woods and again hugged the ground behind another crest on which Confederate artillery pieces were unlimbered. Here Pickett aligned his men for the attack, placing the brigades of Brig. Gens. James Kemper and Richard Garnett in the first line, right to left, with Brig. Gen. Lewis Armistead behind in support. During these preparations Pickett was "cheerful and sanguine," according to artilleryman Col. E. Porter Alexander, and in fact "thought himself in luck to have the chance." Another colonel remembered Pickett "in excellent spirits," expressing great confidence in his ability to "drive" the Yankees after the artillery had demoralized them.

About 1:00 p.m. on July 3, Confederate artillery began a large-scale bombardment of the Union lines. About 150 guns opened up at once the biggest artillery barrage in the history of the North American continent—and thundered with bone-jarring ferocity for nearly two hours. The Virginians, lying under a hot sun, suffered casualties when Federal shells overshot their targets and burst in their ranks. Pickett made a dangerous ride along the lines while answering Union shells burst around him, seemingly oblivious to the danger. Just before 3:00 p.m. (the timing of the bombardment and advance are open to some speculation) while he was writing a letter to his fiancée, a note came to Pickett from Alexander: "For God's sake, come quick, or we cannot support you. Ammunition nearly out." Pickett read the note and took it to Longstreet. "General, shall I advance?" he asked. Longstreet, who held little hope for the attack's success, could not speak and merely nodded his assent. Pickett saluted and said, "I shall lead my division forward, sir," and galloped over to his waiting brigades. Pickett's men rose to their feet and the general made "a brief, ani-

mated address," that ended with the ringing phrase, "Charge the enemy, and remember old Virginia!"

Pickett began his advance from the bottom of a swale, but within five minutes his infantry came to the top of a low rise, where the whole line came into enemy view. The other two divisions on his left also marched forward at this time. According to everyone present on both sides, the infantry maintained perfect order and the steady advance gave a sense of overwhelming power. "Beautiful, gloriously beautiful," wrote one Federal observer. Pickett remained alert and active, dispatching aides with messages in all directions. His men, however, were suffering a substantial number of casualties from the well-arrayed Federal artillery firing from Little Round Top to Cemetery Ridge. When Pickett reached a crest upon which advanced Confederate guns were posted, the order "Left Oblique!" was given, and the brigades shifted toward the copse of trees on the crest. About half way across, a protective swale allowed Pickett to redress his ranks and prepare to close the final distance. One Rebel soldier remembered him personally ordering the division to double-quick at the end of the advance.

It is unclear from where Pickett watched the assault after it crossed the Emmitsburg Road, but he probably halted at the Codori farm, a couple of hundred yards from Cemetery Ridge. Although some have criticized Pickett for not advancing further, the Codori farmstead was a proper distance and location for a division commander to observe and assist the attack. By this time the Federal infantry had opened on the packed Confederate lines, which were bunching together into masses of men, and canister was tearing great gaps from the ranks. Armistead's men closed with the men of Garnett's and Kemper's brigades, and together they pressed on toward the low stone walls and crouching Federal infantry. Federal regiments advanced and turned, pouring a killing enfilade fire into the right elements of Pickett's Division.

It probably took at least twenty minutes for the Confederate host to cross the shallow valley and hit the stone fence behind which the Federals crouched. The other two divisions on Pickett's left were having an even harder time, and some of the units were already falling back. In the end only handfuls of men managed to breach the Federal line at the "Angle," just north of the copse of trees, where they fought hand-to-hand with the Federal defenders. By this time the attack was melting away toward Seminary Ridge, and those within the Angle were either killed, wounded, or taken prisoner; only a few managed to escape. The magnificent attack, known to history as "Pickett's Charge"—although he Pickett commanded only his division— ended in less than one hour in a tragic loss of life and the near annihilation of Pickett's Division as a organized force.

When the attack ended, wrote Longstreet, "Pickett's division was gone." Lee and Longstreet rode out to greet the survivors and form a defensive front to contend with the counterattack both believed would be launched. When Lee asked Pickett to reform his division to repulse it, he replied, "I have no division now." Although Lee admitted that the fault was his own, Pickett was in tears and bitter about the destruction of his division: about one-half of his warriors lay crumpled on the field or in enemy hands.

Although neither Lee nor Longstreet ever disparaged Pickett's efforts on July 3, his hour of glory had passed. He kept his command until near the end of the war, and it was his defeat at Five Forks on April 1, 1865 (while he was in the rear eating shad), that forced Lee's evacuation of Richmond. A postwar meeting between Pickett and Lee was "icy," according to one witness. Afterward, Pickett turned to the comrade and said that Lee "massacred my division." Pickett became an insurance agent in Norfolk, Virginia, and died of a liver abscess in 1875.

For further reading:

Freeman, Douglas Southall. *Lee's Lieutenants: A Study in Command*, vol. 3. New York, 1944.

Georg, K. R., and Busey, J. W. *Nothing But Glory: Pickett's Division at Gettysburg.* Hightstown, 1987.

Longacre, Edward G. Pickett, *Leader of the Charge: A Biography of General George E. Pickett, C.S.A.* Shippensburg, 1996.

Pickett, George E. *The Heart of a Soldier: As Revealed in the Intimate Letters of General George E. Pickett, C.S.A..* New York, 1913.

Pickett, LaSalle C. *Pickett and his Men.* Philadelphia, 1913.

Rollins, Richard. *Pickett's Charge: Eyewitness Accounts.* Long Beach, 1995.

Stewart, George. *Pickett's Charge: A Micro History of the Final Attack at Gettysburg, July 3, 1863.* Boston, 1959.

KEMPER'S BRIGADE:
(1,634 MEN)

BRIGADIER GENERAL
JAMES LAWSON KEMPER

The youngest of Pickett's brigadiers and the only non-professional among them, James Kemper was a forty-year old politician from the Virginia Piedmont. Fellow soldiers could easily discern Kemper's political background, for he still had the habit of delivering high-flown orations to anyone within the sound of his voice. "Judging by manner and conversation alone," an observer wrote, "he would have been classed as a Bombastes Furioso." Kemper also had the looks to go along with the voice, including a long and full black beard and piercing eyes. He shared a special camaraderie with his men, who were proud to be known as "Kemper's Men" long after the war ended.

Kemper had a military pedigree, for his grandfather had served on George Washington's staff in what Southerners liked to call the "earlier Revolution." His own military training consisted only of some instruction in military drill during his college days. He had graduated with a B.A. from Washington College, studied law, and had started a legal practice when war

with Mexico was declared in 1846. He enlisted and was commissioned a quartermaster captain, but reached the army too late for active service.

Back in Virginia, he went into politics and in 1853 he was elected to the first of three terms in the Virginia legislature, where he rose to become Speaker of the House of Delegates. Perhaps most importantly, he became chairman of the Military Affairs Committee in the years before the Civil War, and insisted on a high level of military preparedness. His efforts would pay off when the fighting began at First Manassas, where 43 of the 47 Confederate cannon on the field were provided by the Old Dominion State.

Kemper's high station made it easy for him to get a commission as a colonel commanding the 7th Virginia Volunteers. He fought with his regiment at First Manassas (where the brigade was commanded by Brig. Gen. James Longstreet), then again the next year during the early stages of the Peninsula Campaign at the battles of Yorktown and Williamsburg (where the brigade was commanded by Kemper's childhood friend from Culpeper, Brig. Gen. A. P. Hill). On May 27, 1862, Hill was promoted to head what would be called the "Light Division," and a few days later, after a valorous performance at the Battle of Seven Pines on May 30, Kemper was made brigade commander and commissioned brigadier general. In the Seven Days' Battles at the end of June,

Kemper's Brigade rushed ahead of their support at the Battle of Glendale and lost 414 men. That engagement, however, was Kemper's only action during the week-long series of battles; his regiments suffered less in the campaign than any others in their division.

In the Second Manassas Campaign in August, Kemper was temporarily put in command of a division of three brigades. (The division would become Maj. Gen. George Pickett's in the fall, after he returned from a shoulder wound suffered at Gaines' Mill). This division took part in Maj. Gen., James Longstreet's sweeping attack against the left flank of John Pope's army at the Battle of Second Manassas. Kemper was back at the head of his brigade at Sharpsburg that September. There, he was posted south of the town and was called on to blunt the Union Ninth Corps' afternoon attack. His brigade did not perform particularly well, and folded in the face of the advancing enemy; its withdrawal exposed the right flank of Lee's army to destruction. Fortunately for all concerned, A. P. Hill's Light Division marched up from Harpers Ferry and reached the field just in time to stem the Federal advance.

Although no one could know it then, Sharpsburg was the last action Kemper's Virginians would experience until Gettysburg. They were held in reserve at Fredericksburg, and missed the Chancellorsville Campaign while participating in the foraging expedition around Suffolk. Since he had not seen combat for nearly ten months, the able politician-turned-general was likely looking forward to a chance to get into a fight as he led his high-spirited brigade into Pennsylvania.

GETTYSBURG: With the rest of Pickett's Division, Kemper and his men spent July 1 in Chambersburg, detached to guard the army's rear while the other two divisions of Longstreet's First Corps were at Greenwood, about seven miles to the east. All three of Pickett's brigades were waiting to march over South Mountain toward the battle raging at Gettysburg about 20 miles distant. That night, Kemper received orders to prepare to march toward Gettysburg. His brigade spent most of July 2 tramping east and arrived near the town late in the afternoon. Kemper's Virginians, together with the Virginians from Richard Garnett's and Lewis Armistead's brigades, rested in their bivouac on the Chambersburg Pike until the morning of July 3.

After daylight on the third day of the battle, Kemper led his brigade into a field near Pitzer's Run, a few hundred yards behind the main Confederate line on Seminary Ridge. The men fell out and relaxed in the morning air for about twenty minutes, formed a battle line, and advanced east a few hundred yards before they were ordered to lie down. They advanced again a short time later through Spangler's Woods and again hugged the ground behind another crest on which Confederate artillery pieces were unlimbered. It was in this location that Kemper's placement in the forthcoming attack was formalized. The division was organized with two brigades in the front and one behind in support. The front line would consist of Kemper's men on the right—the extreme right of the spearhead, as it turned out—and Brig. Gen. Richard Garnett's on the left; Brig. Gen. Lewis Armistead's men comprised the second line.

The pending assault was designed around George Pickett's three fresh Virginia brigades, and would also include brigades from three other divisions. Eleven brigades (50 regiments) would directly participate, a total of about 12,000 men. They were to assault the right center of the Union line on Cemetery Ridge. The focus of their efforts was a large umbrella-shaped copse of trees on the crest of the ridge, which lay about one mile distant over open ground. One Southern brigadier claimed to have made it all the way to the ridge and back the previous evening; now more than ten times as many would attempt it. A massive 150-gun cannonade would precede the infantry.

During the artillery battle which raged between 1:00 and 3:00 p.m., Kemper's men lay in a swale south of Spangler's Woods, immediately behind a ridge on which Confederate pieces were dueling with the enemy. Though they were not directly exposed to shell fire, Kemper complained to James Longstreet, the First Corps commander, that his men suffered terribly from Union shells that overshot their targets. After the artillery subsided, Kemper's Virginia regiments rose with the others of Pickett's Division and started forward in perfectly dressed lines at route step—110 strides per minute. They were aligned, from left to right, as follows: 3rd, 7th, 11th and 24th. Kemper, astride his sorrel horse, moved his troops forward through the bursting shells, which knocked men out of the ranks immediately. All three of Pickett's brigades obliqued left while still west of the Emmitsburg Road and headed for the clump of trees. A short distance later, about half way across the field, Kemper dressed his ranks in a swale near the Emmitsburg Road that protected his men from the shot and shell that was raining over them. The worst was still ahead.

When the advance began anew, the Union line on the ridge erupted with sheets of gunfire that tore through his ranks. Canister and shell fire continued to extract a large toll as well. A line of Federals swung out from the crest of the hill beyond Kemper's right and sent a volley into his exposed flank that brought down scores of men, crowding his survivors to the left and into Brig. Gen. Richard Garnett's Brigade. Kemper exacerbated the problem when he rose in his stirrups, pointed left with his sword, and cried; "There are the guns, boys, go for them!" By this time much of the brigade's organization was gone and Pickett's Division as a whole was little more than a charging mass of gray and brown humanity.

At that moment, a minié ball ripped into the inside of Kemper's left thigh near the femoral artery. The bullet glanced up the thighbone, caromed through his body cavity, and lodged near the base of his spine. The crippling shot knocked Kemper off his horse and out of the battle.

Federal soldiers captured Kemper after the attack was beaten back, and he ended up in Gettysburg's Lutheran Seminary. He was exchanged in late September. Although the wound healed relatively well, the bullet was never removed. In pain and with his left leg practically useless, Kemper was unable to return to the field. He was given instead command of Virginia's reserve forces for the rest of the war.

After the war, Kemper returned to politics and won election to governor of Virginia in 1874. He suffered with pain from his groin wound, and movement was increasingly difficult. He died in 1895.

For further reading:

Freeman, Douglas Southall. *Lee's Lieutenants: A Study in Command*, vol. 3. New York, 1944.

Georg, K. R., and Busey, J. W. *Nothing But Glory: Pickett's Division at Gettysburg*. Hightstown, 1987.

Greenburg, Henry J. "Pickett's Charge: The Reason Why." *Gettysburg Magazine*, #5, 1991.

Riggs, David F. *Seventh Virginia Infantry*. Lynchburg, 1982.

Rollins, Richard. *"The Damned Red Flags of the Rebellion": The Confederate Battle Flag at Gettysburg*. Redondo Beach, 1997.

———. *Pickett's Charge! Eyewitness Accounts*. Redondo Beach, 1995.

Stewart, George. *Pickett's Charge: A Micro History of the Final Attack at Gettysburg, July 3, 1863*. Boston, 1959.

Woodward, Harold R., Jr. *Major General James Lawson Kemper, C.S.A.: The Confederacy's Forgotten Son*. Natural Bridge Station, 1993.

ARMISTEAD'S BRIGADE: (1,946 MEN)

BRIGADIER GENERAL LEWIS ADDISON ARMISTEAD

At forty-six, Lewis Armistead was Pickett's eldest brigadier. His friends nicknamed him "Lo," short for "Lothario," which was meant to be a joke, because, unlike the Shakespearean lover, Armistead

was a widower with a shy and silent mien. He receding hair was gray, as was his close-cropped beard.

Armistead came from a military family; his father and four uncles had fought in the War of 1812, and it was one of those uncles who had commanded Fort McHenry during the attack witnessed by Francis Scott Key. Young Lewis was sent to West Point to continue the family tradition, but was expelled for breaking a plate over the head of fellow cadet Jubal Early. (The incident only hastened his inevitable dismissal for his failing grades.) Despite this setback, he refused to be denied a career as a soldier and was commissioned directly into the infantry in 1839 at the age of twenty-two. He distinguished himself in the Mexican war, where he was wounded at Chapultepec and earned two commendations for bravery. Otherwise, he spent his pre-war years in the Old Army's frontier posts. When the South seceded, Armistead had been in the army for twenty-two years, but had risen only to captain of infantry due to the glacial promotion rate of the peacetime army.

Armistead was assigned to the little village of Los Angeles when the war began. On June 15, 1861, as tradition has it, Capt. Winfield S. Hancock's wife threw a party for the several officers who had resigned their commissions and were about to leave to join the Confederate army. Despite the awkward situation, everyone parted good friends. As the party was breaking up, Col. Albert Sidney Johnston's wife sat down at the piano and sang "Kathleen Malvourneen." (A song of loss, with mournful lyrics that went in part, "It may be for years, and it may be forever.") According to Mrs. Hancock, Captain Armistead walked across to his host, and put his hands on his friend's shoulders as the tears streamed down his face: "Hancock, good-by; you can never know what this has cost me."

In mid-September 1861, back in Richmond after a grueling cross-country trek, Armistead was made colonel of the 57th Virginia Volunteer Regiment. The next April, before he had seen any fighting, he was promoted to brigadier general and given command of a brigade serving near Norfolk in the southeastern part of the state. He fought with his brigade at the Battle of Seven Pines. During a Federal counterattack on the second day of the fight, his regiments retreated, leaving Armistead to face an entire enemy brigade with only about thirty stalwart men. This courageous episode was noted admiringly by Maj. Gen. D. H. Hill in his report after the battle. A month later at Malvern Hill, Armistead was chosen to spearhead the attack after the Confederate artillery had softened up the Federal position, indicating that General Lee had faith in Armistead's ability and judgment. As it happened, Armistead's unfortunate brigade lost 388 men in one of the worst conceived and executed assaults of the war.

At Second Manassas in August 1862, Armistead was situated on the extreme right of Maj. Gen. Longstreet's assaulting corps. As darkness was falling and the battle winding down, cavalryman Maj. Gen. "Jeb" Stuart rode upon the scene and called upon Armistead to deliver an attack. Armistead refused, believing that a night attack would be futile and the danger of collision with friendly infantry too great. A reluctant Stuart acquiesced. The episode serves as an indication of Armistead's backbone and belief in his own judgment.

Twenty-two years of Old Army service had made Armistead crusty and blunt,

qualities that didn't endear him to the numerous civilians in the officer corps of the volunteer Confederate army. One of his colonels quit, stating that "on every occasion Brig. Gen. Armistead's manner and tone are so offensive and insulting that I can but believe he. . .wishes to force me to resign." Armistead replied, "I have felt obliged to speak to him as one military man would to another and as I have passed nearly all my life in camps my manner may not be understood or appreciated by one who has been all his life a civilian." A good indication that Armistead was widely known as a hard-bitten, no-nonsense soldier was the fact that Lee made Armistead the army's provost marshal, its "chief of police," during the Maryland Campaign. It was a frustrating assignment. Desertions were at a high point in the Army of Northern Virginia because of exhaustion, lack of shoes, bad diet, and a widely-held belief that invasion of the North was wrong. General Lee felt he needed a tough man to keep straggling to a minimum. Armistead was back at the head of his brigade at the Battle of Fredericksburg, but the entire division was held in reserve. His participation in the expedition to Suffolk in southeastern Virginia caused him to miss the army's next large-scale operation around Chancellorsville.

By the early summer of 1863, Armistead was known for his toughness, sound judgment and great personal courage. However, his brigade had had the least contact with the enemy of any in the Army of Northern Virginia over the previous year. Armistead and his men, with their unfortunate experiences at Seven Pines and Malvern Hill a full year past, were in fine fettle and eager for another chance to engage the enemy.

GETTYSBURG: Armistead was with the rest of Pickett's Division at Chambersburg on July 1, detached to guard the army's rear while the other two divisions of Longstreet's First Corps were at Greenwood, about seven miles to the east. All three of Pickett's brigades were waiting to march over South Mountain toward the battle raging at Gettysburg about 20 miles distant. That night, Armistead received orders to prepare to march toward Gettysburg.

His brigade spent much of July 2 marching east, and arrived near the town late in the afternoon. His Virginians, together with those from Richard Garnett's and James Kemper's brigades, rested in their bivouac on the Chambersburg Pike until the morning of July 3. Thus far they had been spared the hard fighting the rest of the army had experienced. It was beginning to look as though circumstances would once again leave Armistead out of the action.

On the morning of July 3, Armistead's men, along with those of from the brigades of Brig. Gens. Garnett and Kemper, were brought forward to take up a position in a swale in front of Spangler's Woods, behind a low ridge occupied by Southern artillery. They were to assault the right center of the Union line on Cemetery Ridge. The focus of their efforts was a large umbrella-shaped copse of trees on the crest of the ridge, about one mile distant over open ground. One Southern brigadier, Ambrose "Rans" Wright, claimed to have made it all the way to the ridge and back the previous evening. Getting there, he said, was not that difficult; remaining there was the problem. Eleven brigades (50 regiments) from four divisions totaling some 12,000 men would make the attempt, which would be preceded by a massive 150-gun cannonade.

Armistead aligned his men for the forthcoming attack. The division was organized with two brigades in the front and one behind in support. The front line would consist of Kemper's men on the right and Garnett's on the left. Armistead's men formed a second line, although there is some confusion as to whether he advanced behind Garnett or Kemper.

His men lay exposed to the hot summer sun during a nearly two-hour long artillery duel from 1:00 to 3:00 p.m. Armistead spent the time dangerously exposing himself to the hissing Union metal. One of his men rose to protest, fearing the general would be killed, but Armistead ordered him back down, saying, "Never mind me; we want men with guns in their hands." After the artillery duel had subsided—during which Armistead's Brigade suffered numerous casualties—the infantrymen stood and prepared for the assault which would become known to history as "Pickett's Charge." Armistead addressed his men briefly, telling them, "Men, remember your wives, your mothers, you sisters and your sweethearts." His Virginia regiments were aligned, from left to right, as follows: 38th, 57th, 53rd, 9th and 14th.

As his brigade started forward in precise synchronization with the rest of the division, Armistead, going forward on foot, took his old black slouch hat and placed it on the point of his sword, holding it high for the men to see and follow. Unfortunately, the point of the sword pierced the fabric, and the hat descended slowly along the blade, finally resting on the hilt. It sat on his fist as Armistead approached the Union lines, until he put it again at the tip. All three of Pickett's brigades continued forward and about one third of the way across obliqued left while still west of the Emmitsburg Road and headed for the clump of trees. A short distance later, about half way across the field, the Virginians entered the safety of a swale, where Armistead dressed his ranks.

Leaving the shallow valley, Armistead guided his men across the Emmitsburg Road, and with a rush they sprinted for the enemy. By this time his men were intermingled with Garnett's regiments in front, and the large mass surged forward toward the clump of trees, just below the "Angle," which was formed by the intersection of two stone walls. Armistead by this time was the only brigadier left on his feet, for both Garnett and Kemper had been shot down. As he breasted the stone wall, sensing that his men were hesitating, Armistead called out, "Come on boys, give them the cold steel! Who will follow me?" He stepped over the wall toward a battery of Union guns; somewhere between 100 and 300 men followed him across the barrier. A solid line of blue regiments with flashing rifles greeted them. Just before reaching one of the Union pieces, three bullets hammered into Armistead's chest and arm. He staggered forward, put his hand on a cannon to steady himself, and fell mortally wounded.

Armistead was carried behind the Union lines to a surgeon, who later described him as "seriously wounded, completely exhausted, and seemingly broken-spirited." The doctor told Armistead that he was dying. According to the doctor's disputed account, Armistead replied, "Say to General Hancock for me, that I have done him, and you all, a grievous injury, which I shall always regret." The meaning of these words, and whether they were even uttered, are still heatedly debated today. "Lo" Armistead died two days later in a Union hospital.

For further reading:

Georg, K. R., and Busey, J. W. *Nothing But Glory: Pickett's Division at Gettysburg.* Hightstown, 1987.

Krick, Robert K. "Armistead and Garnett: The Parallel Lives of Two Virginia Soldiers," in Gary Gallagher, ed., *The Third Day at Gettysburg and Beyond.* Chapel Hill, 1994.

Motts, Wayne *"Trust in God and Fear Nothing": Gen. Lewis A. Armistead. CSA.* Gettysburg, 1994.

Poindexter, James E. "Address on the Life and Services of Gen. Lewis A. Armistead." *Southern Historical Society Papers*, vol. 37, 1909.

Rollins, Richard. *Pickett's Charge! Eyewitness Accounts.* Redondo Beach, 1995.

Stewart, George. *Pickett's Charge: A Micro History of the Final Attack at Gettysburg, July 3, 1863.* Boston, 1959.

GARNETT'S BRIGADE:
(1,455 MEN)

BRIGADIER GENERAL
RICHARD BROOKE GARNETT

Dick Garnett should have been in the hospital instead of leading his brigade up the slope of Cemetery Ridge. He was ill with a fever, suffering severe pain from a recent kick in the ankle by his horse. However, there was a deeper pain that Garnett could only assuage by taking his usual place with his men, riding toward the enemy lines at the head of his brigade on his big black charger.

Garnett, forty-five, had been born into the Virginia Tidewater aristocracy, growing up on the family estate in Essex County. He applied numerous times over three years to get into West Point. His tutor referred to his scholastic abilities rather evasively as "rigidly moral," with an "ardent desire" to do well in his studies. Garnett was finally accepted and graduated an unremarkable 29th out of 52 cadets in the Class of 1841. After graduation, he showed that his forte was fighting rather than studying, and he became one of the most noted Indian fighters in the U.S. Army. He gained experience in the Seminole Wars, on the Mormon Expedition, and in frontier garrisons from Florida to California, and from Texas to the Dakotas. Due to the snail's pace of promotion in the army, however, he was only a captain when the Civil War began.

Garnett was a strong Unionist. When war loomed he made one strong public plea to preserve the Union—then followed his state when it seceded early in 1861. He on duty in Los Angeles at the time, where he attended the legendary dinner party given by Capt. Winfield Hancock's wife for the officers about to go over to the Confederacy; Col. Albert Sidney Johnston was present, as was Capt. Lewis Armistead.

During the first months of the war Garnett served as a major of artillery. In November 1861, he was made brigadier general and given command of the most famous brigade in the Confederacy, the Stonewall Brigade, on December 7, when its namesake commander, Maj. Gen. Thomas J. "Stonewall" Jackson, was elevated to command the troops in the Shenandoah Valley. In the weeks that followed, Garnett, a handsome man who made friends easily, gained the confidence of the officers and men. Even Jackson, still with a proprietary interest in his old command, agreed that Garnett was able and energetic. However, word circled through the ranks that Garnett was pampering the brigade, always trying to grant the men's requests, acting as their guardian as much as their superior officer. Jackson strenuously objected to such "soft" behavior.

In the Romney Campaign early in 1862, Garnett ran afoul of Jackson for the first time when he halted to rest his tired, hungry, and freezing men. Jackson sharply reprimanded Garnett and told him to push the men ahead. At the Battle of Kernstown in the early days of what would evolve into a brilliant campaign in the Valley, Garnett did the unthinkable: he ordered his men to fall back after they had run out of ammunition and were in danger of being flanked by a superior enemy. His subordinates supported his wise decision, but Jackson, who couldn't stand the idea of the Stonewall Brigade retreating under any circumstances, arrested Garnett and brought charges against him. Jackson even went so far as to try to keep Garnett from being reassigned anywhere else in Confederate service. A seething Garnett tried to convene a court martial so he could clear his name, but the constant fighting of 1862 kept Jackson too busy to participate. By August a court was convened and a few of the charges were heard, but the proceeding was cut short by the Second Manassas Campaign. Most officers in the army were familiar with Jackson's unbending

manner, and most sympathized with Dick Garnett, whose reputation was spotless.

General Lee, knowing better than to waste a talented brigadier like Garnett, put him in charge of Brig. Gen. George Pickett's Brigade for the Maryland Campaign while Pickett was recuperating from a shoulder wound. Garnett served well at Sharpsburg and was given permanent command of the brigade when Pickett was elevated to lead a division in October 1862. "While he was not a man of much mental force," wrote a colonel of the 8th Virginia regiment, "he was one of the noblest and bravest men I ever knew." Garnett was in reserve with the rest of Pickett's Division at Fredericksburg, then languished around Suffolk during the Chancellorsville Campaign in May 1863. All the while he bore the stain of Jackson's court martial, waiting to restore his military honor. When Jackson died of his Chancellorsville wound, Garnett showed the generosity of his nature and grieved for him while marching in the line of officers who bore the coffin to the grave.

During the first hours of July Garnett rode painfully toward Gettysburg in a new gray uniform, a tragic figure attempting to live down the undeserved shame of Kernstown. While we know his physical condition, we may not know what Dick Garnett looked like—a curious circumstance for so famous a general. Family members claim that the image of the swarthy and dapper officer popularly identified as Richard Brooke Garnett is actually Robert Garnett, his brother. Descendants, who claim there is no picture in existence of Richard, noted in 1908 that he "was a man of just the opposite type, having light hair and blue eyes, and wore no full beard." It seems Garnett, even in death, could not escape litigation, for a court case in 1986 was convened to investigate the issue.

GETTYSBURG: Garnett guarded the army's rear at Chambersburg with the rest of the division on July 1. All three of Pickett's brigades were waiting to march over South Mountain toward the battle raging at Gettysburg 20 miles distant. That night, Garnett received orders to prepare to march. His brigade spent much of July 2 heading east and arrived near the town late that afternoon. His Virginians, together with those from Brig. Gens. Lewis Armistead's and James Kemper's brigades, rested near the Chambersburg Pike until the morning of July 3.

Garnett and his men advanced during the morning and eventually formed in a swale in front of Spangler's Woods. The lines were dressed out of sight behind a sloping ridge, where the Confederate artillery was unlimbering in preparation to bombard the enemy line. The men were ordered to lie down and wait. Pickett's Division was going to assault the right center of the Union line on Cemetery Ridge. The focus of its efforts was a large umbrella-shaped copse of trees on the crest of the ridge, about one mile distant over open ground. A Third Corps brigadier, Ambrose "Rans" Wright, claimed to have made it all the way to the ridge and back the previous evening. Getting there, he said, was not that difficult; remaining on the crest under fire was the problem. In addition to Pickett's men, eight other brigades from three other divisions (a total, including Pickett, of 50 regiments) would make the attempt. The 12,000-man assault would be preceded by a massive 150-gun cannonade. "This is a desperate thing to attempt," Garnett exclaimed when he saw the strength of the Union position for the first time.

Garnett's Brigade was placed on the left in the first line of Pickett's Division, with Kemper's men deployed on their right. Armistead's regiments formed behind him as a second supporting line. Two other divisions (Maj. Gens. Henry Heth's and Dorsey Pender's) were also forming some distance to the left. During the lull before the artillery bombardment, Garnett conferred with Pickett and Col. Birkett Fry, who belonged to Heth's Division (led this day by Brig. Gen. Johnston Pettigrew) to arrange for coordination during the assault. Pettigrew's brigades were ordered to converge on Garnett during the attack in order to arrive on Garnett's immediate left when they hit the enemy line. It would

be a difficult tactical feat to perform while under fire. Garnett took lunch with Brig. Gen. Cadmus Wilcox—cold mutton washed down with whiskey and water.

The artillery opened about 1:00 p.m. and continued firing for about two hours. Pickett had ordered his officers to advance on foot to save lives, but Garnett was allowed to ride because of his injury. (By the time the advance was underway, numerous officers were riding into the action.) The order was given and the men started forward. When Garnett's infantry reached the crest of the ridge they were cheered by their gunners as the passed between the guns. Beyond, they performed a skillful left oblique movement amid bursting artillery shells in order to connect with Pettigrew's Division. Artilleryman Col. E. Porter Alexander, an old friend of Garnett's, rode forward with the general for a little way before they parted.

About half way across the field, the Virginians entered the safety of a swale, where Garnett dressed his ranks. Within a few minutes they left the shallow valley and Garnett directed his men across the Emmitsburg Road and up the steepening slope to the clump of trees. Garnett rode his black horse up and down behind his lines. "Steady, men! Close up!" he shouted. "A little faster; not too fast! Save your strength!" The brigade was well formed and despite numerous casualties from artillery fire, tightly aligned and under control. The ill brigadier impressed Maj. Charles S. Peyton of the 19th Virginia, who described him there as "totally devoid of excitement or rashness [as he] rode immediately in the rear of his advancing lines, endeavoring by his personal efforts, and by the aid of his staff, to keep the line well closed up and dressed."

The final two hundred yards were murder at every step. By this time Garnett's men were being shot down by the score and crowded on the right from Kemper's men. One volley of Federal musketry unhorsed every member of Garnett's staff and courier, save one. Garnett's men leveled their own weapons about seventy-five yards away and returned the fire before charging forward. The Union line began to crumble and Garnett called up Armistead to hurry his men forward; he had too few left to carry and hold the position. Somehow Garnett was still unhurt, despite the storms of canister and musketry that greeted the Confederates. The mass of commingled soldiers surged forward toward the "Angle," which was formed by the intersection of two stone walls.

Federal reinforcements arrived in the form of the 72nd Pennsylvania, whose men stood, took aim, and fired. Some say Garnett was struck in the head by a bullet, while others contend canister tore his body asunder. Whatever the projectile, Garnett fell dead from his mount. Many who knew him learned of his death when they saw his horse, Red Eye, galloping toward the rear without a rider. His death took place, claimed one of his aides, "within fifteen or twenty paces of the rock wall, a little to the right of the point of the angle known as the 'bloody angle' as we faced the enemy."

The charge was beaten back shortly after Garnett's fall, and the retreat prevented the Confederates from securing the corpse. Garnett's uniform was evidently stripped of its insignia in the orgy of post-battle souvenir gathering, and his body was never identified. He was probably buried in a mass grave with his men, and later reinterred in Hollywood Cemetery in Richmond, Virginia, where a memorial was erected for Garnett in 1991.

For further reading:

Davis, Steve. "The Death and Burials of General Richard Brooke Garnett." *Gettysburg Magazine*, #5, 1991.

Georg, K. R., and Busey, J. W. *Nothing But Glory: Pickett's Division at Gettysburg*. Hightstown, 1987.

Krick, Robert K. "Armistead and Garnett: The Parallel Lives of Two Virginia Soldiers," in Gary Gallagher, ed., *The Third Day at Gettysburg and Beyond*. Chapel Hill, 1994.

Longacre, Edward G. Pickett, *Leader of the Charge: A Biography of General George E. Pickett, C.S.A.* Shippensburg, 1996.

Rollins, Richard. *Pickett's Charge! Eyewitness Accounts*. Redondo Beach, 1995.

Stewart, George. *Pickett's Charge: A Micro History of the Final Attack at Gettysburg, July 3, 1863*. Boston, 1959.

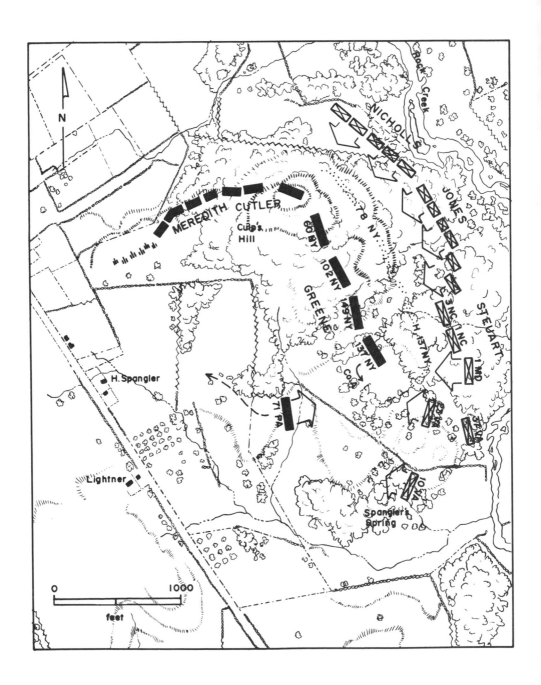

Second Army Corps:

(20,224 MEN / 78 GUNS)

LIEUTENANT GENERAL RICHARD STODDERT EWELL

On May 10, 1863, Lt. Gen. Thomas "Stonewall" Jackson, the most celebrated military figure in the Confederacy and one of Gen. Robert E. Lee's two corps commanders, died. Who would take his place? On May 23, an announcement came from headquarters: Richard S. Ewell had been promoted from major to lieutenant general and appointed to command the Second Corps.

Dick Ewell inspired men in spite of, not because of, his appearance. Rather short at 5 feet 8 inches, he had just a fringe of brown hair on an otherwise bald and bomb-shaped head. Bright bulging eyes protruded above a prominent nose, creating an effect which many likened to a bird—an eagle, some said, or a woodcock—especially when he let his head droop toward one shoulder, as he often did, and uttered strange speeches in his shrill, twittering lisp. He had a habit of muttering

odd remarks in the middle of normal conversation, such as "Now why do you suppose President Davis made me a major general anyway?" He could be spectacularly profane. He was so nervous and fidgety he could not sleep in a normal position, and often spent nights curled around a campstool. He had convinced himself that he had some mysterious internal "disease," and so subsisted whenever possible almost on frumenty, a dish of hulled wheat boiled in milk and sweetened with sugar. A "compound of anomalies" was how one friend summed him up. He was the reigning eccentric of the Army of Northern Virginia, and his men, who knew at first hand his bravery and generosity of spirit, loved him all the more for it.

Like Lee, Ewell was a Virginian from a well-connected family in straitened circumstances. He grew up on a farm called "Stony Lonesome" near Manassas, and despite his family's poverty, received an appointment to West Point, where he graduated 13th out of 42 students in the academy's Class of 1840. He fought Indians on the Southwest frontier as a dragoon, served in the Mexican War, then returned to more Indian warfare. By 1861 he had developed a reputation as a stout fighter and expert horseman.

Although he was personally against secession, Ewell entered Confederate service when the Civil War began. Due to his lifetime of service (and despite his claim that in twenty years in the cavalry he had learned all about commanding fifty dragoons and had forgotten everything else), he rose rapidly in rank. He made lieutenant colonel in April 1861, colonel in May, brigadier general in June (in time to command an infantry brigade at First Manassas), and major general in January 1862. He was given a division under Maj. Gen. Thomas "Stonewall" Jackson, and became his most trusted subordinate during the celebrated 1862 Shenandoah Valley Campaign, where he defeated Maj. Gen. Nathaniel Banks at Winchester and Maj. Gen. John Fremont at Cross Keys. During the Seven Days' Battles, Ewell's marches were well-ordered and prompt, and at Gaines' Mill and Malvern Hill, he seemed to be always at hand with his brigades. No officer was mentioned more often or more appreciatively in the reports of others.

Everything changed for Ewell with the Second Manassas Campaign. He was renowned as a man who often led his division from the front, the same way he had led his dragoon company. In the bloody duel with the Union Iron Brigade at Brawner's Farm, he once again yielded to his love of being in the middle of a fight. Leading one of his regiments forward in person, he was hit by a bullet that split his left kneecap, shattered the head of the tibia, then traveled down the marrow of the bone for six inches, fragmenting it into splinters. Surgeons amputated the leg the next day, and Ewell was out of the war for nine months, missing the battles of Sharpsburg, Fredericksburg, and Chancellorsville.

His recuperation took longer than necessary when Ewell slipped on ice while walking with his crutches on Christmas Day 1862. Another inch of bone snapped off during the accident and caused the leg to hemorrhage badly. Already frustrated with the slow pace of his recovery, he was again flat on his back for weeks. Prostrated and weakened as he was, he displayed the essential generosity of his nature. A genuinely modest and decent man, he never looked for public recognition for himself, but fought hard for the reputations of his subordinates and superiors alike. He was convinced that the officer who had taken over his division in his absence, Brig. Gen. Jubal Early, had earned recognition as its permanent commander. From his bed, he wrote Early:

When I am fit for duty, they may do what they please with me, but I think your claims to the Division, whether length of time or hard service be considered, are fully equal, if not superior, to mine. I don't presume they will interfere with you. What is very certain is that I won't ask for any particular duty or station, but let them do as they see proper with me.

A campaign of an intimate nature occupied him while he healed. Ewell was a romantic and a man of fine sentiments, and admired women of quality. There were few such women on the frontier, and as a result Ewell was one of the army's most notorious bachelors. In his time off, he wooed Lizinka Brown, a cousin and the wealthy widow of a Mississippi plantation owner. When she said yes to his proposal of marriage Ewell, who had always been of modest means, could hardly believe his luck, and he was heard to introduce his new bride as, "My wife, Mrs. Brown."

When he returned to the army at the end of May 1863 to head Jackson's Corps, many unanswered questions swirled about "Old Bald Head," as his men affectionately called him. Had the loss of his leg affected his ability? Had the acquisition of a wife tempered his fighting qualities (as it had moderated his profanity)? Would he be able to handle a corps as well as he had handled a division? Would he perform well under Lee—whose command style allowed his subordinates considerable discretion—as well as he had performed under Jackson, who always spelled out exactly what he expected?

The immediate indications were that Jackson's successor would continue in the victorious Stonewall tradition. It was Ewell's Second Corps which led the incursion into Maryland and Pennsylvania. In the two weeks prior to the Battle of Gettysburg Ewell performed flawlessly. On the march north he won a sweeping victory at Second Winchester, where he captured 28 guns, some 4,000 prisoners, and mountains of supplies at the cost of only 300 Confederate casualties. Ewell's had exercised decisiveness on the field of battle and his directions were clear and forceful. The officers and staff were all convinced of his corps-level abilities. Sandie Pendleton, Jackson's adjutant, wrote,

The more I see of him the more I am pleased to be with him. In some traits of character he

is very much like General Jackson, especially in his total disregard of his own comfort and safety, and his inflexibility of purpose. He is so thoroughly honest, too, and has only one desire, to conquer the Yankees. I look for great things from him, and am glad to say that our troops have for him a good deal of the same feeling they had towards General Jackson.

Ewell traveled at the rear of the column in a buggy, with his favorite horse "Rifle," a "flea bitten gray," near at hand. His wooden leg prevented him from mounting, so he had to be lifted into the saddle and strapped on to avoid falling off. A born fighter, Ewell had shown early promise as a corps commander, but he yet to lead his divisions in a pitched battle with the stubborn Army of the Potomac.

GETTYSBURG: On the morning of July 1, Ewell marched Maj. Gens. Robert Rodes' and Jubal Early's divisions south from Carlisle (25 miles north of Gettysburg) to rejoin the rest of the army, under orders from Lee to "proceed to Cashtown or Gettysburg, as circumstances might dictate." Ewell was traveling at the rear of Rodes' column, which had not quite reached Middletown, when he got a message from First Corps commander Lt. Gen. A. P. Hill around 9:00 a.m. that he was moving from Cashtown toward Gettysburg. Ewell reasoned he was more likely to find a fight in Gettysburg than Cashtown, so he ordered Rodes' Division to turn toward Gettysburg once he reached Middletown. He also ordered Early's Division to march to Gettysburg from Heidlersburg.

By the time Ewell's men approached Gettysburg from the north, the first day's battle had been raging for some time. Rodes' brigades marched onto Oak Hill, a prominent piece of wooded terrain on the vulnerable right flank of the Maj. Gen. John Reynolds' embattled Union First Corps, drawn up west of town to oppose Hill's advance. Although Ewell was under orders from Lee not to bring on a general engagement until the rest of the army was up, he felt such favorable circumstances warranted ignoring those instructions. "I determined to push the attack vigorously," he

later explained. He ordered Rodes to attack the First Corps' right flank, and also ordered Jubal Early to move his division forward on the left of Rodes and attack at once. Unfortunately, Rodes' division was poorly handled and badly mauled in the process, and the Federal Eleventh Corps, led by Maj. Gen. Oliver Howard, began fanning out north of town to help protect the First Corps' vulnerable flank. Ewell enjoyed position and superior numbers, however. When Early's Division appeared to the northwest, it outflanked the Eleventh Corps on its right and drove it back at a run. With Rodes' Division prying the stubborn First Corps defenders off Seminary Ridge and A. P. Hill pressing the attack from the west, the Federal line collapsed and streamed through the narrow streets of Gettysburg, where Ewell's men captured large numbers of the enemy. By 5:00 p.m., the disorganized remnants of the Union First and Eleventh corps were attempting to regroup on Cemetery and Culp's Hills, immediately southeast of the town.

It was a stunning victory, but the day was not yet over. Lee, who was now on the field with Hill's men, had no way of knowing what condition Ewell's Corps was in or the strength of the enemy before him. He therefore suggested that Ewell should take Cemetery Hill if he thought it "practicable," and without bringing on a general engagement. Ewell's assault had lost its momentum after Union resistance was crushed north of town. The town itself had become an obstacle to swift movement, especially since Federal sharpshooters and skirmishers were still harassing the advance of the Confederates. Many Confederate units had been disorganized as a result of the afternoon's fighting, and the men were fatigued. There were also thousands of prisoners to round up and guard.

As Ewell's subordinates looked to these concerns, the general examined Cemetery Hill. The Union position looked formidable from the town. The enemy was regrouping on the hill and digging in behind stone walls. In addition, they had placed several batteries in key positions, and there were few good positions for Rebel artillery to effectively bombard the heights. As Ewell pondered his options Brig. Gen. William "Extra Billy" Smith warned that the enemy was approaching from the east along the York Pike. Early sent two brigades, Brig. Gen. John Gordon's and Smith's, to guard against these potential dangers; if an assault was to be launched, they would be unavailable.

For all these reasons, Ewell decided to wait for Maj. Gen. Edward Johnson's Division, which was just arriving from the west along the Chambersburg Pike. Before Johnson could file through town and get into position east of Gettysburg, however, darkness had fallen and Ewell abandoned the struggle for the day. Though his subordinates, primarily General Early, had pleaded with him to attack, he had exercised his discretion and decided against it. His decision not to mount an assault in the fading hours of July 1 created one of the most nagging controversies in a battle replete with them.

That evening, Lee rode over to confer with Ewell about an offensive the next morning against the Federal right, which was now firmly entrenched on powerful defensive terrain. Four generals conversed, including Lee, Ewell, Early and Rodes. Ewell sat silently while his subordinate, General Early, gave a number of reasons why the Second Corps should not make an attack. Rodes concurred. Since the Second Corps could do little in its current position and the army was thinly extended, Lee proposed withdrawing it to shorten his lines. Early strenuously objected. Ewell concurred with Early, as did Rodes. Perhaps Ewell had lost his ability to make decisions, or perhaps he was just using the more articulate Early as a spokesman, but the fact remained that Lee could not get Ewell to move the Second Corps forward or back. When Lee left, the understanding was that an assault would be launched from his other flank as early as possible, and Ewell would demonstrate before the enemy and turn it into a full-scale attack if deemed appropriate.

Later, Ewell received a report that Culp's Hill was undefended, and determined to march Johnson's Division to occupy it.

Thereafter, a message arrived that agitated Ewell: Lee had determined the Second Corps should be withdrawn and marched to the right flank of the army. Ewell went personally to Lee to get permission to remain where he was and seize the wooded heights. Pleased with Ewell's new-found aggressive attitude, Lee assented. Culp's Hill, however, was by this time heavily defended and remained out of Southern hands. The decision to leave the corp east of Gettysburg was a poor one, for it was isolated and communication with it was difficult and time-consuming. As a result, the army's efforts were crippled by a lack of coordination on the last two days of the fight.

By the morning of July 2, Johnson's Division was on Ewell's left across Rock Creek, facing southward toward Culp's Hill. Early's Division stretched from the middle of town east to the Hanover Road, while Rodes' Division occupied a line from Gettysburg west along the Fairfield Road to Seminary Ridge. Lee instructed Ewell that when Lt. Gen. James Longstreet started his offensive against the enemy left, he was to "make a simultaneous demonstration upon the enemy's right, to be converted into a real attack should opportunity offer." However, Ewell was beset with problems. He could find no good artillery positions beside Benner's Hill, which was exposed to counter battery fire and too small to accommodate many fieldpieces. The town itself interfered with the deployment of his corps, and the hills in front were steep and rocky, unsuitable to attack. When Longstreet launched his corps against the Round Tops and the Peach Orchard about 4:00 that afternoon, Ewell was only able to get thirty-two artillery pieces into action and none of his infantry. His artillerists were outgunned by the Federal batteries on Cemetery Hill and driven off Benner's Hill by 6:30 p.m.

At about 7:30 that evening, as Longstreet's attack was beginning to wind down, Ewell decided the time was right to send in the Second Corps. According to Ewell's plan, Johnson's brigades would confront the enemy on Culp's Hill, while Early assailed Cemetery Hill from the northeast and Rodes join the onslaught from the northwest. The attack on Cemetery Hill, while initially promising, proved a fiasco. Although Early managed to get a portion of his division up the hill and capture its crest, Rodes was unable to deploy his division quickly enough to assist before Early was thrown back off.

While Johnson's attack on Culp's Hill did not go as smoothly as planned, the Confederate brigades were in luck. Nearly the entire Twelfth Corps, under Maj. Gen. Henry Slocum, had been removed from the area to reinforce the threatened Union left flank. Only a single brigade remained to defend the critical piece of terrain. Even so, Johnson's men were unable to seize the crest and had to settle for a portion of the Union line, much of which had been abandoned earlier that night. Brig. Gen. George Greene's New York brigade, still manning the defenses on the crest of the hill, proved to be impossible to drive out. The responsibility for the failure of these attacks on the evening of July 2 belongs to Ewell—especially in regard to Rodes' tardiness. With so much at stake, Ewell should have been more aggressive in seeing to it that Rodes' large division was in position on time.

Ewell and Lee saw opportunity in the advantage that Johnson had gained on Culp's Hill, and worked during the night to exploit it the next morning. Two brigades from Rodes' Division and one from Early's were added to Johnson's force on the hill. Lee's plan was for Ewell to attack at dawn, in concert with an attack by Longstreet on the other end of the line. Unfortunately for the Southerners, the enemy had reinforced the nearly empty hill and was planning to retake the old line of works. Although Ewell did his part by hurling Johnson's augmented division forward at about 4:30 a.m. on July 3, word was received a short time later that Longstreet was not ready to attack. By that time, however, Johnson was committed on the rocky and wooded slopes of Culp's Hill. Slocum's Twelfth Corps, aided by well-placed artillery which Ewell could not match, defeated Johnson and Ewell's men were leveraged out of their foothold with heavy casualties by 11:00

a.m. In an odd anti-climax to his role at Gettysburg, Ewell was shot in his wooden leg by Union sharpshooter as he rode with General Gordon down an exposed street around noon. Ewell chirped to Gordon, "Suppose that ball had struck you: we would have had the trouble of carrying you off the field, sir. You see how much better fixed for a fight I am than you are? It don't hurt a bit to be shot in a wooden leg."

After the tragic waste of life suffered by Johnson's men, the focus of the battle shifted south opposite the Federal center, which was attacked later in the day in an assault known as "Pickett's Charge." Ewell's Second Corps no longer figured prominently in the battle. Ewell was later criticized for his failure to act aggressively under discretionary orders from Lee. With characteristic modesty, Ewell freely admitted that "it took a dozen blunders to lose Gettysburg and I committed a good many of them."

In 1864, Ewell was in and out of command due to poor health and injuries, and at Spotsylvania was relieved of his corps duties and transferred to command the defenses of Richmond. Ewell was with the Army of Northern Virginia in the Appomattox Campaign until he was captured at Sayler's Creek, two days before Lee's final surrender. After the war, Ewell retired to a farm in Tennessee until his death in 1872.

For further reading:

Ewell, Richard S. *The Making of a Soldier: Letters of.* Ed. by Percy Hamlin, Richmond, 1935.

Haines, Douglas C. "R. S. Ewell's Command, June 29-July 1, 1863." *Gettysburg Magazine*, #9, 1993.

Hamlin, Percy G. *"Old Bald Head" (General R. S. Ewell), The Portrait of a Soldier and the Making of a Soldier: Letters of R.S. Ewell.* Gaithersburg, 1988.

Martin, Samuel J. *The Road to Glory: Confederate General Richard S. Ewell.* Indianapolis, 1991.

Pfanz, Donald. *Richard S. Ewell: A Soldier's Life.* Chapel Hill, 1998.

Pfanz, Harry W. *Gettysburg: Culp's Hill and Cemetery Hill.* Chapel Hill. 1993.

EARLY'S DIVISION:
(5,424 MEN)

MAJOR GENERAL
JUBAL ANDERSON EARLY

Everybody respected Jubal Early for his combat accomplishments in the two years of fighting before Gettysburg; almost nobody liked him. In Pennsylvania, Irish stragglers under his command were quoted as saying that there were many Confederates who would shoot him "just as quick as they would a damned Yankee." Early was derisive of subordinates, overbearing with his peers, and abrasive with all. A non-stop talker, he spoke in a snarling rasp, and was opinionated and dogmatic on every subject. Though he was an accomplished scholar, his conversation was rough, full of poor grammar, and profane. Nor was he physically attractive. Balding, with black hair and flashing black eyes, he seldom bothered to trim his graying beard. He chewed tobacco, and had a habit of shifting his quid from one cheek to the other during moments of excitement. Though slender and about six feet tall, he had rheumatism, which twisted him and forced him to stoop over when he walked. One soldier said Early, when mounted, looked as "solemn as a country coroner going to his first

inquest." As a result, he appeared much older than his forty-six years.

Early's disciplinary tactics were so strict as to often verge on vindictiveness. Once, when a regiment failed to protect a wagon train to his satisfaction, he rode up and roared that he would put the regiment on the front line "where he hoped every one of them would get killed and burn through all eternity." He did what he promised, and the unit suffered heavy losses; one survivor of this affair mixed a grudging admiration for the general in with his resentment, writing that Early was "a queer fish. . .but no humbug." Even the precious few who discerned a warm human being under the harsh exterior admitted the general almost never betrayed tender emotion. One such man, John Daniel, recalled such a moment during the Battle of the Wilderness when Early got news of the death of a young cousin who had recently served him as an aide. "Poor Robert," he heard Early remark, and saw a lone tear glisten on his cheek.

While it is true that "Old Jubilee" was notorious among the men for his unsavory personality, his record in battle prior to Gettysburg was unsurpassed. After leading a brigade at First Manassas, he was promoted to brigadier general (ranking from July 21). He demonstrated aggressive tendencies, but directed an ill-considered assault at Williamsburg in May 1862, where he was severely wounded by a bullet that went through his back from shoulder to shoulder. When battle loomed outside Richmond in late June, Early returned to duty and was given the command of a new brigade at the Battle of Malvern Hill on July 1, though he was still so feeble from his wound that he needed assistance mounting his horse.

His new brigade, one of the largest in the army with seven regiments, belonged to Maj. Gen. Richard Ewell's Division. He led the brigade well during the Second Manassas Campaign in the fighting that flared across Northern Virginia. He was perhaps the most conspicuous figure on the field at the Battle of Cedar Mountain, and was gritty and steadfast when his brigade was later stranded by high water on the enemy's side of the Rappahannock. It was Early who went to Maj. Gen. A. P. Hill's rescue at a critical moment on Jackson's embattled left during the Battle of Second Manassas. Ewell, who was put out of action with the loss of a leg at Brawner's Farm on the eve of the latter battle, joined Jackson in lauding Early's performance.

During the September bloodshed at Sharpsburg, Federal troops faced Early from three sides, but he made his dispositions shrewdly and not only held his ground but, according to Jackson, "attacked with great vigor and gallantry." When acting division commander Brig. Gen. Alexander Lawton was wounded during the battle, Early took his place. His actions were commended by Lee, who recognized his capabilities and rewarded him by permanently keeping him in this post. At Fredericksburg in December, Early again came to A. P. Hill's rescue, this time when Maj. Gen. George Meade's Pennsylvanians hit a hole in Hill's front and threatened to collapse the army's right flank. Told that Hill's line had been pierced, Early's men came on the run, shouting, "Here comes old Jubal! Let old Jubal straighten out that fence!" Meade's men tumbled back, and the line was restored.

Early received an overdue promotion to major general in April 1863. His division, which at Fredericksburg was still being called "Ewell's Division," was permanently handed over to "Old Jube" with Ewell's blessing. His new prestige made him no less bad-tempered. Early, a life-long bachelor, rekindled the resentments of his men when he petitioned Jackson to order all the visiting wives, mothers, and sisters to stay away, citing them as an interruption in the army's work. Jackson read Early's letter and roared to those standing anxiously nearby, "I will do no such thing. I wish my wife could come to see me!"

During the Chancellorsville Campaign in May, Early was put in the precarious position of holding the Fredericksburg lines with his lone division (augmented by Brig. Gen. William Barksdale's Brigade). The assignment was an indication that Lee considered Early the division commander he most trusted with an semi-independent command. Hampered by confusing orders, Early was overrun by the Union Sixth Corps, but kept his head while he withdrew. In the last stage of the battle, he reoccupied the lost ground and organized a counterattack that ended the Union threat. Boxed in, the offending Sixth Corps withdrew across the river and ended the battle.

The man who had thus achieved so much in so short a time was from the Blue Ridge hills of southwest Virginia. Early graduated from West Point in the top third of the Class of 1837, but left the army shortly thereafter and hurried back to Virginia to study law. He interrupted his practice in 1841 to serve in the state legislature as a Whig, then in 1846 to participate in the Mexican War as a major of volunteers (where he saw no fighting). Being a Whig, Early strongly opposed secession and voted against it at the 1861 secession convention, but once it was an accomplished fact, he offered his services to the Confederacy. He was sent to Lynchburg to raise three regiments, one of which, the 24th Virginia, was assigned to him. Though still a colonel, he was given a brigade in June 1861, with which he started his Civil War career at First Manassas a month later.

Early had weaknesses as a commander. He had a poor sense of direction, which he exhibited early on when he had trouble finding the battlefield at First Manassas (and in delivering his attack at Williamsburg). At Malvern Hill he had floundered through forest and swamp, and frequently thereafter his command arrived late at its destination due to Early's inability to grasp the guiding features of the ground over which he operated. His unpopularity with those he had scorched with his arrogance and irascibility, which included just about everybody, hampered somewhat his ability to handle men effectively. One notable exception was Lee himself, for even though Early was the only officer ever heard to swear in Lee's presence, the army leader had a certain affection for him, calling him "my bad old man."

As the army approached Gettysburg, Jubal Early was once again serving under the familiar direction of Richard Ewell, the new commander of the Second Corps. In the combination of their personalities was potential for trouble. Ewell, the superior, was by nature generous and agreeable; Early, the subordinate, was by nature arrogant, overbearing, and independent-minded. It was foreseeable that their roles might become confused at a critical time. Capt. Robert Stiles, an observant Southern artilleryman, vividly remembered that the fire of combat was upon "Old Jube," as he went into battle on Gettysburg's first day. Even his "glossy black ostrich feather, in beautiful condition, seem[ed] to glisten and tremble upon the wide brim of his gray-brown felt hat, like a thing of life."

GETTYSBURG: In mid-morning of July 1, Early, moving his division west from York to rejoin the army, received a message from Ewell to march south to Gettysburg when he reached Heidlersburg. As he approached Gettysburg ahead of his division's column, he heard the thud of distant artillery fire. About a mile north of Gettysburg he passed over a rise and surveyed the Union Eleventh Corps, which was deploying to contest Maj. Gen. Robert Rodes' Division, which was attacking from Oak Hill to the west. Seeing his chance, Early skillfully deployed three of his four brigades (Brig. Gens. Harry Hays and John Gordon, and Col. Isaac Avery; Brig. Gen. William Smith's was operating east along the York Pike) and threw his men forward. They hit the Eleventh Corps' right flank north of town on Blocher's Knoll and routed that unlucky Union force, which lost thousands of casualties and prisoners in a pell-mell dash through the town to the safety of the hills beyond. It was a masterful performance by Early, and his rugged attackers inflicted three times as many casualties as they incurred.

Before a pursuit beyond the town could be organized, Early received word from "Extra Billy" Smith that the enemy was approaching from the east along the York Pike. Early took the precaution of sending Gordon's Brigade to join Smith's, two miles east of town, to guard against the threat. Old Jubal rode into Gettysburg in the late afternoon, where he again received word of enemy presence to the east from Smith. Although Early didn't believe the threat was real, he couldn't disregard it. Together with Ewell and Rodes, Early rode east of town to scout the York Pike, though no enemy was seen. Prudently, Early left his two brigades to protect the approach until the next day. Although he strongly advocated a joint attack by Ewell and A. P. Hill against the Cemetery Hill position, Ewell refused and darkness put an end to the discussion.

That evening, Lee rode over to confer with the Second Corp leaders, asking specifically if the Second Corps could storm Cemetery Hill at daylight. While Ewell remained silent, Early, never at a loss for words, presumed to speak for the Second Corps, answering that Cemetery Hill was too steep to assail from its northern side, and that tomorrow's attack should be made on Lt. Gen. James Longstreet's front instead. In that case, Lee asked, shouldn't the Second Corps be withdrawn to shorten the lines? Early answered (when his superior Ewell would have been expected to do so) that it would hurt morale to give up the ground the men had gained, and the terrain in the Second Corps front was good for defense. It was a vintage Early performance—presumptuous and argumentative. Lee bought it.

By mid-day of July 2, Gordon's Brigade was recalled from the York Pike and put into position behind Brig. Gen. Harry Hays' and Col. Isaac Avery's Brigades, which were placed on low ground just southeast of town. From this point, it was expected they could charge Cemetery Hill if a favorable opportunity presented itself. Smith's Brigade was left to guard the York Pike approach. A little before dusk, Maj. Gen. Edward Johnson's Division struck across Rock Creek against Culp's Hill, which was the signal for Early to attack Cemetery Hill in conjunction with Rodes' Division on his right. Old Jube ordered Avery's and Hays' brigades forward (from left to right) in the dying light. For some reason, Gordon's remained near town and did not advance up the hill. The Louisianians and North Carolinians overran the Eleventh Corps regiments and batteries deployed to defend the northeast slope of the hill, but were thrown back after reaching the crest when reinforcements failed to arrive. Rodes, who had experienced a disappointing day on July 1, took too long to form his division and thus no cooperation was accomplished. For several minutes Early's men were just a few hundred yards away from the Baltimore Pike, a major logistical artery for the Army of the Potomac. The nighttime assault on East Cemetery Hill was perhaps the true high point of the Confederate effort at Gettysburg, an honor usually bestowed upon Pickett's Charge.

During the night, Early detached Smith's Brigade to Johnson for an all-out attempt to capture Culp's Hill on the morning of July 3. His other brigades remained near the town and were not further engaged in the battle. His division suffered 1,188 casualties at Gettysburg, a smaller amount than the average of 2,000 men lost by most of the other divisions in Lee's army.

Lee's high opinion of Early's qualifications for independent leadership was enhanced by his performance at Gettysburg. During the next year Early led the corps several times in Ewell's absence. At the end of May 1864, Early was made lieutenant general and given the Second Corps after Ewell suffered a breakdown at Spotsylvania and was transferred to command the Richmond defenses. Old Jube took the depleted corps into the Shenandoah Valley to threaten Washington. He succeeded in this task, but was subsequently soundly defeated by Maj. Gen. Philip Sheridan in the Valley. Lee was forced by public opinion to remove Early from command in the last days of the Confederacy.

After the war, Early settled in Lynchburg, where he resumed his law practice. He refought the war with his vitriolic pen for the rest of his life, and died in 1894.

For further reading:

Early, Jubal A. *Autobiographical Sketch and Narrative of the War Between the States*. Philadelphia, 1912.

Gallagher, Gary W. "East of Chancellorsville: Jubal A. Early at Second Fredericksburg and Salem Church." in *Chancellorsville: The Battle and Its Aftermath*. Chapel Hill, 1996.

Gannon, James P. *Irish Rebels Confederate Tigers: The 6th Louisiana Volunteers, 1861-1865*. Campbell, 1998.

Osborne, Charles C. *The Life and Times of General Jubal A. Early, CSA, Defender of the Lost Cause*. Chapel Hill, 1992.

Pfanz, Harry W. *Gettysburg: Culp's Hill and Cemetery Hill*. Chapel Hill. 1993.

HAY'S BRIGADE:
(1,292 MEN)

BRIGADIER GENERAL HARRY THOMPSON HAYS

Forty-three years old, with a full head of wavy brown hair and a large brown beard streaked with gray, Harry Hays was a New Orleans lawyer at the head of a brigade of tough Louisiana soldiers. His men were a cosmopolitan mix of nationalities from Irishmen to French Creoles; many were lawbreakers recruited from alleys, docks, and jails. Born near Nashville, Tennessee, Hays was orphaned at an early age and reared by an uncle in Wilkinson County in the southwestern corner of Mississippi. He was educated at Saint Mary's Catholic School in Baltimore, and he studied law after graduation with one of the city's leading lawyers. He moved to New Orleans to practice, but interrupted his career to serve as lieutenant and quartermaster of the 5th Louisiana Infantry Regiment in the Mexican War. Back in New Orleans, Hays formed a successful legal firm and became active in Whig politics.

When the South seceded, Hays was made colonel of the 7th Louisiana, a New Orleans outfit nicknamed the "Pelican Regiment." Hays led the regiment at First Manassas "with satisfactory coolness and skill," according to the official report of army commander Gen. P. G. T. Beauregard. The next year, his regiment was brigaded

the enemy, he slammed his hat down and shouted, "Those Louisiana fellows can steal as much as they please now!" The attack cost Hays 370 men, but the threatened Sixth Corps withdrew back across the river, ending the battle.

By mid-summer 1863, Hays and his tough, colorful Tigers had established a reputation as fearless fighters. Although Hays was not a professional soldier, he was hard-bitten enough to get good results out of his New Orleans toughs. He had been in command for ten months at the head of his brigade, and had seen enough hard fighting to know how to handle his men in action.

GETTYSBURG: The Louisiana Brigade entered the battle from the north along the Harrisburg Road on the afternoon of July 1 after a march of about 12 miles. Hays was in the second line of Early's divisional attack, and he deployed his regiments, from left to right, as follows: 8th, 7th, 9th, 6th and 5th, with the roadbed cutting through the center of the 9th Louisiana.

With the brigades of Brig. Gens. John Gordon and George Doles fighting for control of Blocher's (Barlow's) knoll in advance, Hays pushed his men forward, with Col. Isaac Avery's Brigade ahead on his left. The combined weight of Early's attack (coupled with Maj. Gen. Robert Rodes' assault on the right), caved in the right flank of the Union Eleventh Corps north of Gettysburg. Hays' Louisianians crossed Rock Creek around 3:30 p.m. and drove through successive lines of resistance, finally entering the town (perhaps the first Confederate brigade to do so) and "clearing it of the enemy and taking prisoners at every turn." Despite his hard fighting and rapid advance, Hays put his casualties at only 63 men on July 1, though he estimated enemy casualties at six times that number. The combative brigadier urged Early to let him try and take Culp's Hill, but Early did not have orders to do so, and Hays was halted on one of the "upper southern streets." At midnight, Hays received instructions from Ewell to reconnoiter between his position in the outskirts of town and that of the enemy. As a result of his reconnaissance, Hays moved his brigade

with other Louisiana organizations under Brig. Gen. Richard "Dick" Taylor. The brigade distinguished itself in Maj. Gen. Thomas "Stonewall" Jackson's brilliant Valley Campaign of 1862, where Hays was wounded by a bullet in the shoulder in the Battle of Port Republic on June 9. Hays was promoted to brigadier general while he was recovering, and Taylor was promoted to the command of a district in the Trans-Mississippi theater. Hays, in turn, was given Taylor's Brigade, now nicknamed the "Louisiana Tigers" after a particularly notorious battalion of that name was disbanded and its members spread throughout the brigade's regiments. (The Louisianians had terrorized friendly civilians and comrades with their disciplined rioting and pillage, and the city of Richmond rejoiced when the Tigers departed for the front.) Hays returned to duty on the day of the Battle of Sharpsburg, where more than half the brigade fell as casualties in the Cornfield.

The Louisiana Brigade was only lightly engaged at Fredericksburg. In May 1863 during the Chancellorsville Campaign, Hays' men were stationed in the Fredericksburg sector opposite the Union Sixth Corps. Heavy skirmishing and advance picket duties cut up some of Hays' regiments, and eventually his men, with the rest of Early's Division, were forced back by the Federals. When General Early saw Hays' Brigade break through the Union lines at Salem Church in an effort to throw back forward to a ravine southeast of the town around 2:00 a.m. on July 2.

Hays expected to attack Cemetery Hill from this position after dawn that morning, in concert with an assault by Lt. Gen. James Longstreet's First Corps at the other end of the line. Longstreet's attack, however, was delayed until after 4:00 p.m., so Hays and his men spent the entire miserable day in the shallow ravine within range of Union sharpshooters on Cemetery Hill. It was almost certain death for a man to stand upright, and the hot July sun pounded down upon them. The attack would go forward with the entire line, Early explained that afternoon, and Hays was to hold his men in readiness to advance at a given signal.

With Avery's North Carolina Brigade deployed on his left, Hays was finally ordered forward after 8:00 p.m. (Hays had been given temporary command of both brigades). His own was deployed with its right flank near the Brickyard Lane, and his men guided on that for some distance before wheeling to the southwest, marching up the slope and crashing into Ohio and Connecticut troops from the Federal Eleventh Corps posted along the lane itself. Avery's men had a greater distance to traverse, and struck the line a short while later. "They moved forward as steadily, amid [a] hail of shot and minnie ball, as though they were on parade far removed from danger," wrote an admiring Federal colonel. The Federal canister and musket fire was largely ineffective, wrote Hays, because the darkness hid his men and caused the enemy to overshoot. As the first line of Federals fell back, Hays' Tigers continued driving forward, smashing the center of a line held largely by Colonel Leopold von Gilsa's Germans.

The Louisianians advanced through three separate defensive lines of works and reached the summit where, "by a simultaneous rush from my whole line, I captured several pieces of artillery, four stands of colors, and a number of prisoners," wrote Hays. The fighting there was vicious and often hand-to-hand.

Several minutes passed. Heavy masses of infantry could be heard approaching his position, but Hays did not know their identity. The line stopped about 100 yards away and "a simultaneous fire was delivered." Hays reserved his own fire until confident he was facing the enemy, but superior numbers forced him off the hill and back to his original position. The promised supports (Rodes' Division on the right and Gordon's Brigade in his rear) never arrived. Hays lost about 200 men in the effort to capture East Cemetery Hill, and the survivors were infuriated by the lack of support. They were veteran enough to know someone had bungled things. At daylight on July, 3, Hays withdrew his exhausted men into the town and remained there throughout the day. Their part in the battle was over.

Harry Hays performed well at Gettysburg and was commended by General Early after the battle. He continued to lead his brigade and on occasion commanded the division in Early's absence. While directing both of the army's Louisiana brigades in operations around Spotsylvania, Hays was badly wounded on May 9, 1864. He was assigned to recruiting duty in Louisiana in August 1864, and never again led troops in action. He was promoted by General Kirby Smith to major general, and was paroled at this rank.

After the Civil War, Hays returned to his New Orleans law practice and briefly served as sheriff there (before being removed from office by General Philip Sheridan). He died of Bright's disease in 1876.

For further reading:

Gannon, James P. *Irish Rebels Confederate Tigers: The 6th Louisiana Volunteers, 1861-1865.* Campbell, 1998.

Jones, Terry L. *Lee's Tigers: The Louisiana Infantry in the Army of Northern Virginia.* Baton Rouge, 1987.

Pfanz, Harry W. *Gettysburg: Culp's Hill and Cemetery Hill.* Chapel Hill. 1993.

Seymour, W. J. *The Civil War Memoirs of Captain William J. Seymour.* Baton Rouge, 1991.

GORDON'S BRIGADE:
(1,807 MEN)

BRIGADIER GENERAL
JOHN BROWN GORDON

The longest arc of any Confederate career was that of John Brown Gordon. A civilian from the hardscrabble northwest corner of his native Georgia, a region dependent upon coal mining, Gordon raised a company of mountaineers called the "Raccoon Roughs" in the opening weeks of the war. When Gordon's raw recruits, all wearing coonskin caps, reached Atlanta, they were told they were not needed, so Gordon fired off telegrams offering their services to all the Southern governors. Alabama finally found room for them, and they boarded a train for Montgomery.

Married and with two children, Gordon arranged to leave his children in his mother's care so he could devote himself to campaigning. His wife came with him to the front, following so devotedly that it became a tradition in the army that when Mrs. Gordon was seen on her way to the rear, it was a signal that action was about to open. With no military experience whatsoever, but with the natural instincts of a born leader, the persuasive power of an orator, and incredible luck at escaping death, Gordon rose from the head of his company to corps command during the last months of the war.

Gordon was "the most prettiest thing you ever did see on a field of fight," testified one of his soldiers. "It 'ud put fight into a whipped chicken just to look at him."

After leading the Raccoon Roughs at First Manassas in July 1861, Gordon was elected colonel of the 6th Alabama regiment the following April, just before the serious campaigning began on the Peninsula. At Seven Pines, where he was thrust suddenly into brigade command when Brig. Gen. Robert Rodes was wounded, he distinguished himself by leading his men in a charge through murderous fire. Every one of his field officers was killed; he alone survived—though his horse was shot beneath him and bullet holes were discovered in his coat. Still suffering from his wound, Rodes turned command of the brigade back over to Gordon after Gaines' Mill, and the Georgian led it in a costly charge at Malvern Hill. Gordon was temporarily blinded when dirt from an exploding shell hit him in the eyes, while four hundred members of his brigade became casualties.

Left in southeastern Virginia with the rest of Maj. Gen. D. H. Hill's Division during the Second Manassas Campaign, Gordon's 6th Alabama regiment rejoined Lee's army for the Maryland Campaign in September. Stationed on the Confederate left at South Mountain, Rodes' Brigade plunged boldly into action. Although the other regiments were soon shattered, the 6th Alabama stayed intact under the flawless bearing and inspirational leadership of Colonel Gordon. According to Rodes, Gordon handled the 6th Alabama "in a manner I have never heard or seen equaled during this war." At the climax of the campaign three days later at the Battle of Sharpsburg, Rodes' Brigade defended the Bloody Lane in the Confederate center. While repulsing multiple Northern assaults, Gordon suffered (and somehow survived) five wounds, one of which hit him in the face and pitched him forward unconscious with his face in his kepi. He would have drowned in his own blood but for the hole in his kepi, courtesy of another Federal bullet. After the battle, division commander Hill styled Gordon the "Christian hero" and asserted that Gordon "had excelled his former deeds" at Seven Pines and Malvern Hill. "Our language," Hill concluded, "is not capable of expressing a higher compliment."

Promoted to brigadier general in November 1862 while he mended, Gordon returned to the army in April 1863 after seven months of convalescence and was assigned temporarily to the command of Brig. Gen. Alexander Lawton's Brigade of Georgians (Lawton had resigned after despairing of receiving the promotion he thought he deserved). During the Chancellorsville Campaign in May, Gordon was selected to lead an attack to retake Marye's Heights, just behind Fredericksburg, from the Union Sixth Corps. He called on every man willing to follow him up the Heights to raise his hat. According to Henry Walker of the 13th Georgia, every man did so. "I don't want you to holler," Gordon told them. "Wait until you get up close to the heights. Let every man raise a yell and take those heights. . .Will you do it? I ask you to go no farther than I am willing to lead!" Gordon had once again found the right note of inspiration—"We all stepped off at quick time," Walker wrote. Although they found Marye's Heights undefended, fighting later in the day claimed 161 of his men. By the next morning the Federals had retreated across the Rappahannock River.

So completely had Gordon won the hearts of his fellow Georgians at Fredericksburg that before the Gettysburg Campaign, the officers of the brigade unanimously petitioned that Gordon remain their chief. The sole stipulation of one of the men was that Gordon should not again address them before they went into battle. When asked why, the soldier replied, "Because he makes me feel like I could storm hell."

GETTYSBURG: On July 1, Gordon's Brigade was marching at the head of Maj. Gen. Jubal Early's Division as it approached the battlefield from the north on the Harrisburg Road. About 3:00 p.m., Early deployed the Georgian in a field west of the road, facing generally south, as support for Robert Rodes' Division's embattled left flank, which was engaged with advance elements of the Federal Eleventh and First corps near Oak

Hill a few hundred yards to the west. Gordon's advantageous position placed him on the front and flank of Brig. Gen. Francis Barlow's Union division around Blocher's (Barlow's) Knoll, a piece of high ground a mile or so north of Gettysburg. Gordon aligned his Georgia regiments from left to right as follows: 38th, 61st, 13th, 31st, and 60th; the 26th had been left behind to support a line of artillery.

Gordon approached the enemy slowly since his men were badly fatigued. With parts of Doles' Brigade beginning to fall back on his right front, he moved to within 300 yards of the enemy and rushed forward "as rapid as the nature of the ground. . . would permit." Captain Robert Stiles, a Confederate artilleryman, described the general as the Georgians moved to the attack:

Gordon was the most glorious and inspiring thing I ever looked on. He was riding a beautiful coal-black stallion, captured at Winchester, that had belonged to one of the Federal generals in [Maj. Gen. Robert] Milroy's army—a majestic animal whose 'neck was clothed with thunder. . . .[The horse] followed in a trot, close upon the heels of the battle line, his head right in among the slanting barrels and bayonets, the reins loose upon his neck, [with General Gordon] standing in his stirrups, bareheaded, hat in hand, arms extended, and, in a voice like a trumpet, exhorting his men. It was superb, absolutely thrilling.

Splashing over Rock Creek and up the knoll, Gordon's well-executed assault fell on Col. Leopold von Gilsa's small brigade of Germans, who fought well for a few minutes before breaking and running to the rear. In conjunction with some of Doles' men, Gordon drove his regiments several hundred yards to the Almshouse, where the Federals were desperately attempting to form a second line. The sheer weight and order of Gordon's advance collapsed the remnants quickly. General Early, however, spotted a fresh line of Federals forming in the distance beyond Gordon's left (Col. Charles Coster's brigade) and ordered him to halt. The division commander called up his second line, composed of the brigades of Brig. Gen. Harry Hays and Col. Isaac

Avery, to finish the rout of the Union Eleventh Corps.

After the Federals had been sent reeling through town, Early received an alarm from Brig. Gen. "Extra Billy" Smith, who sent two dispatches that "a large force" of the enemy was approaching from the east on the York Pike. Early ordered Gordon and his men to reinforce Smith's men east of town and guard the approach from that direction. Gordon, who believed that a complete victory was at hand if only if he were allowed to make one more thrust against the beaten enemy, protested bitterly but was overruled. The force Smith thought he saw never materialized, and Gordon spent the rest of July 1 isolated behind the army's left-rear with Smith's men out on the York Pike.

Gordon never reentered the battle. His official report contains this curious statement: "The movements during the succeeding days of the battle [July 2 and 3], I do not consider of sufficient importance to mention." In reality, at least one matter of "sufficient importance" transpired in which Gordon played a small role. At dusk on July 2, he was brought back to Gettysburg and put in reserve for Early's dusk attack on East Cemetery Hill. Although two of Early's brigades managed to drive the Federals from the hillside and hold the crest for several minutes, Robert Rodes' Division failed to cooperate on the northwest slope, and Early's troops were driven back down. Gordon's men sat and watched southeast of town and never advanced. Early later wrote that Gordon's participation would have been a "useless sacrifice of life," although Harry Hays probably would have concluded otherwise—especially if Gordon had arrived in conjunction with his Louisiana troops.

Early commended Gordon in his Gettysburg report. After another impressive demonstration of initiative the next May at the Wilderness, Gordon delivered a powerful countercharge that helped seal the breach inside the Mule Shoe at Spotsylvania. Lee rewarded the Georgian with a promotion to major general and placed him in command of a division. He was one of only three non-professionals to be so honored by Lee (the others were Joseph B. Kershaw and Wade Hampton). His strong service continued in the Shenandoah Valley Campaign of 1864, and in the Petersburg defenses. By war's end, Gordon was leading a corps, which he surrendered at Appomattox Court House.

John Gordon was the war idol of the people of Georgia for four decades. He was elected governor in 1886 and served three terms as a U. S. Senator. He was commander-in-chief of the United Confederate Veterans from 1890 until his death in 1904.

For further reading:

Eckert, Ralph L. *John Brown Gordon: Soldier, Southerner, American.* Baton Rouge, 1989.

Gordon, John B. *Reminiscences of the Civil War*, New York, 1903.

Pfanz, Harry W. *Gettysburg: Culp's Hill and Cemetery Hill.* Chapel Hill. 1993.

Tinkersley, Allen P. *John B. Gordon: A Study in Gallantry.* Atlanta, 1955.

SMITH'S BRIGADE:
(802 MEN)

BRIGADIER GENERAL
WILLIAM "EXTRA BILLY" SMITH

At sixty-six years of age, William Smith was old enough to be the father of many Civil War generals, and a grandfather to most of the enlisted men. Born in the previous century, the Virginian was a career politician, one of the most magnetic leaders in the South. A practicing lawyer since 1818, he had been Governor of Virginia during the Mexican War, and when the Civil War began was serving out his fourth term in Congress. His nickname, "Extra Billy," by which he was known to everyone North and South, was a result of questionable perks he had gotten as a mail contractor in President Andrew Jackson's administration in the 1830s. He had owned the contract for a daily postal route between

Washington, D.C. and Milledgeville, the capital of Georgia at the time. Smith had extended it to numerous spur routes, for which he received extra payments. When Postmaster General William T. Barry came under political attack for increasing payments to contractors, Smith's "extras" were uncovered, and his sobriquet was born.

When the Old Dominion State seceded, Smith turned down a brigadier general's commission, saying he was "wholly ignorant of drill and tactics." When the war was only weeks old, however, he happened to be at Fairfax Court House when a detachment of Union cavalry charged through the town, killing the Confederate commander on the scene. Smith directed the defense in the ensuing skirmish, and found the smell of gunpowder to his liking. Despite his complete lack of military experience, he asked for and received a commission as colonel of the 49th Virginia regiment, organized just three days before First Manassas in July 1861. During the battle, Smith brought his companies and remnants of others to the Henry Hill sector and introduced himself to General Beauregard: "I am Col. Smith, otherwise Gov. Smith, otherwise Extra Billy Smith." When asked what his men could do, Smith responded, "Put us in position and I'll show you." Smith led the regiment into the hottest part of the battle and fought remarkably well.

In November, Smith was elected to the Confederate Congress, but returned to the 49th Virginia when Maj. Gen. George McClellan's Army of the Potomac started up the Peninsula in the spring of 1862. Smith fought with the regiment at Williamsburg and received a severe contusion on the thigh by a spent bullet at the Battle of Seven Pines on May 31, where half of his regiment went down as casualties. Smith appears to have done a credible job and was reported by his superior as "conspicuous. . .for coolness and courage. His exposure of his person was perhaps almost a fault." Smith and his men were only lightly engaged during the Seven Days' Battles, but his brigadier mentioned Smith's "characteristic coolness" and "fearlessness" a second time.

By the time of the Second Manassas Campaign in August, Extra Billy had become well known for his contempt of "West P'inters." A military education, he proclaimed, was next to worthless in battle, where only good common sense was needed. One yarn described a incident when his men were held up by obstructions in a fight. They were suffering heavily from Federal sharpshooters while instructed to hold their fire. "Colonel," one of them cried, "we can't stand this! These Yankees will kill us before we get in a shot!" Smith exploded, "Of course you can't stand it boys; it's all this infernal tactics and West P'int tomfoolery! Damn it, fire, and flush the game!"

"Extra Billy" also displayed contempt for military dress. At Chantilly in early September he carried a blue cotton umbrella and topped his uniform with a tall beaver hat. When a thunderstorm broke, Smith calmly raised his umbrella and moved nonchalantly through the brigade. "Come out of that umbrella," his men would cry. "I see your legs; come out of that hat, I want it to boil the beans in!"

At Sharpsburg on September 17, Smith took command of the brigade while Brig. Gen. Jubal Early led the division. During the course of the action he suffered three wounds but remained in control of his men. Maj. Gen. "Jeb" Stuart observed the old colonel fighting valiantly with blood streaming from his left shoulder, leg, and arm, and reported that Smith was "conspicuously brave and self-possessed." By the time the action was over, Smith was prostrate; unable to move, he had to be carried off the field. President Jefferson Davis recognized the need for more brigadiers (and the need for Smith's political support) and promoted the old colonel in April 1863, to date from January 31, 1863. Smith resigned his congressional seat and returned to the army, where he was put back in charge of Early's Brigade in time for the Chancellorsville Campaign, where his deployments were awkward and his brigade's performance far from efficient.

The general could always be counted on to enliven the drudgery of his brigade's marches with his colorful personality and gift for speechifying. On the march toward Gettysburg, when Early's Division entered York, Pennsylvania, Smith's Brigade was at the head of the column. He rode into town with his hat off, bowing right and left to the amused crowds, saluting the girls "with that manly, hearty smile which no man or woman ever doubted or resisted."

When the head of the column reached the town square, the men stopped to deliver a hearty cheer for the old Governor. The townspeople crowded forward and the Confederate column, thus surrounded, could go no further. Smith, who never met an audience he didn't like, couldn't resist an opportunity for some silver-tongued oratory. He cleared enough room for his men to stack arms and launched into "a rattling, humorous speech" from his saddle, applauded wildly by Pennsylvanians and Confederates alike. The legendarily irritable Jubal Early soon arrived from the rear, however, and barged impatiently toward the center of the crowd. Smith, sailing ever higher on the gusts of his own eloquence, was unaware that his nasty-tempered superior had joined the party until Early caught his blouse, jerked him around and screamed, "General Smith, what in the devil are you about, stopping the head of this column in this cursed town!" "Having a little fun, General," Smith replied good-naturedly, "which is good for all of us." At that, General Early cooled off; this was,

after all, the former governor of the state of Virginia.

There was the prospect that Smith might soon resign to once again become Governor of Virginia, an office for which he was an active and favored candidate. One soldier expressed the opinion that "Extra Billy" received a heavy vote in the Army because the Virginia soldiers wished to get rid of him as a commander; while no one questioned his courage, by the time of the Gettysburg Campaign, it had become apparent that Smith's generalship was deficient. Early judged it advisable to keep Smith's men in close proximity to Brig. Gen. John Gordon's so that Gordon could exercise what amounted to a joint command. Early's concern had a personal edge, because Smith's Brigade had once been his own, and he didn't want to see its splendid record ruined by the incompetence of its commander. Smith was the oldest general on the field, and he was showing the wear and tear of the army's campaigns.

GETTYSBURG: On July 1, Smith's Brigade was at the rear of Early's column as it approached the field from the northeast by the Harrisburg Pike. In mid-afternoon, when Early deployed his division for its attack on the flank of the Union Eleventh Corps north of town, Early held Smith's men a half-mile in the rear as a reserve and to watch the division's left flank.

After the rest of the division had put the Federals to rout, Early twice ordered Smith to join in the pursuit, but Smith refused, claiming instead that a large body of the enemy was approaching from the east. Smith headed his brigade instead out on the York Pike nearly two miles east of town. As it turned out, there were no Federals approaching on the roadway. (One lieutenant later swore that what Smith saw was in fact a fence with a growth of small trees.)

Smith's alarm, however, caused Early to defer his attack on Cemetery Hill and resulted in the siphoning off of Gordon's Brigade—in addition to Smith's—to guard against a non-existent threat. All this came at a time when Lt. Gen. Richard Ewell was making the important decision of whether or not to attack the Federals then attempting to rally on Cemetery Hill. With two of Early's brigades unavailable and darkness falling, the attack was never made.

Smith's Brigade remained east of town on the York Pike throughout July 2, remote from the desperate battles on Cemetery and Culp's hills. Just after daybreak on July 3, Ewell sent Smith and his regiments to reinforce Edward Johnson's Division, which had gained a foothold on Culp's Hill on the evening of the 2nd. Smith was guided into place on the left of Brig. Gen. "Maryland" Steuart's Brigade, along a wall near Rock Creek. There, Smith's Brigade replaced the 2nd Virginia and faced generally south, his left flank next to the stream.

What happened next is open to some speculation. One Confederate staff officer later wrote that Smith led his brigade, "taking the highest pos[ition] he could find, reckless of shot and shell, with bare head & sword in hand, pointing to the enemy." "Hurrah for Governor Smith!" rose along the lines "like an electric current, mingling with the sullen roar of the enemy cannon." A member of Smith's 52nd Virginia saw things differently. Smith, he claimed, led them too far forward without orders and left the men there doing nothing while the brigade was badly cut up. Ultimately, Johnson's Division was driven off the hill by the Federal Twelfth Corps and the serious fighting in that sector ended before noon.

Governor Smith was the only brigadier in the division not commended by Early after the battle. He at least had the good sense to know when to depart, and within a week resigned his command. Smith received a cosmetic promotion to major general in August and returned to Virginia to help with recruiting. He was inaugurated as Governor of Virginia on New Year's Day of 1864, a post he held for the rest of the war.

Smith spent his years after the war farming on his estate, although he returned to public office as a member of the Virginia house of delegates at the age of eighty, from 1877 to 1879. He died in 1887.

For further reading:

Bell, John W. *Memoirs of Governor William Smith of Virginia: His Political, Military and Personal History.* New York, 1891.

Fahrner, Alvin A. "The Public Career of William 'Extra Billy' Smith." Ph.D. diss., University of North Carolina, 1953.

——, "William 'Extra Billy' Smith, Governor of Virginia, 1864-1865: A Pillar of the Confederacy." *Virginia Magazine of History and Biography,* 74, 1966.

Pfanz, Harry W. *Gettysburg: Culp's Hill and Cemetery Hill.* Chapel Hill. 1993.

HOKE'S BRIGADE:
(1,242 men)

COLONEL
ISAAC ERWIN AVERY

Thirty-five year old Colonel Avery was the youngest of four brothers who enlisted in the Confederate service from Morganton, North Carolina. He was a large and powerful man, weighing over 200 pounds. He came from a distinguished family, and his grandfather, Waightstill Avery, had been the state's first attorney general. Isaac attended the University of North Carolina but left school after one year to manage one of the family farms. In the late 1850s, after ten years as a farmer, he went into business with others for the purpose of building the Western North Carolina Railroad, an enterprise interrupted by the fall of Fort Sumter. One of his partners, Charles Fisher, was authorized to organize a regiment of volunteer infantrymen, and Avery and a third partner, Samuel Tate, both raised companies. When the regiment was mustered in as the 6th North Carolina, Fisher was its colonel and Tate and Avery were captains.

The 6th North Carolina fought at First Manassas in July 1861, where Avery was wounded and Fisher was killed. Dorsey Pender took Fisher's place as colonel of the regiment, and the next spring on the Peninsula Avery fought with the regiment at Seven Pines at the end of May 1862. When Pender was promoted to command his own brigade after the battle, Avery was promoted to colonel and put in charge of the 6th. Capt. John A. McPherson described Avery as always being with his regiment and always cheerful and in good spirits. He also wrote "there was no fall back in Avery." Avery led his regiment into the thick of the fighting at Gaines' Mill, where he was severely wounded.

The wound kept him out of action for months, and in January 1863, the 6th North Carolina was transferred to Col. Robert Hoke's Brigade. Avery returned to duty in the spring of 1863, and during the Chancellorsville Campaign, after brigade commander Hoke had his arm shattered leading an assault on Salem Heights, Avery took command of the brigade in the middle of the attack. He remained in command of Hoke's Brigade after the battle, and it was considered to be in good hands. Avery was known for insisting on a high level of discipline and drill, and Gens. Pender, Hood and Early all recommended him for promotion. Others mentioned his "high moral worth," "genial nature," and "chivalrous bearing."

Though his peers had confidence in him, in Pennsylvania Avery would be going into battle for the first time at the head of a brigade of men who did not know him well.

GETTYSBURG: Entering the battle from the north by the Harrisburg Road in the early afternoon of July 1, Colonel Avery and his men descended on the right flank of Eleventh Corps position north of Gettys-

burg. As the brigades of Brig. Gens. George Doles (Rodes' Division) and John B. Gordon moved forward to assault the Federals atop Blocher's (Barlow's) Knoll, Avery's North Carolinians were deployed in line of battle north of Rock Creek and east of the Harrisburg Road, from left to right as follows: 57th, 21st, and 6th. Together with Harry Hay's Louisianians on their right, Avery's men formed Early's second line of battle.

When Gordon's men broke the Union position and sent it streaming toward the rear, General Early spotted a new Federal threat forming in front of Gordon in the distance on the northeast side of town. The division commander ordered Hays and Avery to advance while Gordon remained near the Almshouse. Avery crossed Rock Creek about 3:30 p.m. and moved directly against the Federal line, which turned out to be Col. Charles Coster's brigade. Overlapping the Federal right, a sharp stand-up engagement ensued, memorialized as the "Brickyard Fight." Coster's men broke and fled for the rear and Avery's regiments captured hundreds of Federals in and around Gettysburg, driving the rest back through the streets in a rout. Avery pursued the enemy through Gettysburg and halted just southeast of town, where his men came under Union artillery fire from Cemetery Hill. The men were ordered to lie down, and there they spent the night.

Although Avery was instructed to be ready to attack the next morning when he heard the sound of Lt. Gen. James Longstreet's assault on the other end of the line, that effort was delayed until late afternoon. It was a miserable day for Avery's men, who cringed in low, open ground while the deadly bullets of Federal sharpshooters hissed constantly around them. Finally, some time after 8:00 p.m., Avery got the word to attack East Cemetery Hill in the dying light of July 2. With his men aligned in the same order as the previous day's fight, he rode forward with them through an orchard and over open fields, angling his men to the west to strike the Union line along the Brickyard Lane. Avery's North Carolinians marched in tandem with Hays' Louisianians on their right, although his regiments had almost double the distance to traverse before reaching the enemy. Protected somewhat by darkness and smoke so thick that they "could not see ten yards ahead," they were slowed by the uneven ground and a series of rock walls. As he climbed the slope with his men, a bullet hit Avery on the base of the right side of his neck and knocked him from his horse. From that time until the end of the night's battle, the North Carolinians were leaderless. Although the regiments assisted Hays in breaking through to the crest of East Cemetery Hill, no supports were forthcoming and the men were forced to withdraw soon after.

As he lay dying alone in the darkness, Isaac Avery took out a pencil and a piece of paper and scribbled a note to his friend, Major Samuel Tate: "Major: Tell my father I died with my face to the enemy. I. E. Avery."

For further reading:

Dunkelman, Mark H., and Michael J. Winey. "The Hardtack Regiment in the Brickyard Fight." *Gettysburg Magazine*, #8, 1993.

Iobst, Richard W. *The Bloody Sixth: The Sixth North Carolina Regiment*. Raleigh, 1965.

Pfanz, Harry W. Gettysburg: *Culp's Hill and Cemetery Hill*. Chapel Hill, 1993.

JOHNSON'S DIVISION
"THE "STONEWALL DIVISION"
(6,343 MEN / 16 GUNS)

MAJOR GENERAL
EDWARD JOHNSON

Among the ten division commanders of the newly-reorganized Army of Northern Virginia in June 1863, only Edward "Allegheny" Johnson was a complete newcomer to the army. Lt. Gen. Thomas "Stonewall" Jackson had asked for Johnson earlier in the spring, claiming that Johnson "was with me at McDowall and so distinguished himself as to make me very

desirous of having him as one of my Division commanders."

The question was whether Johnson would be able to walk and ride well enough to return to the field. After beginning the war leading a regiment in Gen. Robert E. Lee's ill-starred Cheat Mountain Campaign in western Virginia, he spent the winter of 1861-2 at the head of a brigade-sized contingent with the grand title of the "Army of the Northwest," holding the crest of the Allegheny Mountains—where he was given his nickname "Allegheny." His little army came under Jackson's command, and in May 1862 fought at the Battle of McDowell. There, Johnson went down with a bad wound to the ankle, but not before he made a strong impression on Jackson. It would take Johnson a full year to heal, the ankle-bones did not knit well, the leg stiffened, and Johnson mended slowly.

Johnson made the most of his long convalescence by retiring to Richmond, where he owned property and had relatives and friends. He particularly enjoyed the social scene, where he was the source of considerable amusement and fascination. Johnson was a heavy set, rough looking character, still a bachelor at age forty-seven with uncouth manners, a booming voice, and an eye for the ladies. Before long there was much talk and shaking of heads about his ham-handed amorous exploits. One story circulated that he had been heard propos-

ing marriage to one belle, and, not a week later he admitted to "paying attention" to one of his cousins. As a result of a wound received in Mexico, he had an affliction in one eye that caused it to wink uncontrollably, which contributed to the impression among many women that he was being overly familiar and downright impertinent. He caught the attention of the Confederate diarist Mary Chesnut, who wrote that his head "is strangely shaped, like a cone or an old-fashioned beehive. . .there are three tiers of it; it is like a pope's tiara." While photographs show Ed Johnson was not a handsome man, Mrs. Chesnut's description seems a bit embellished.

While Johnson was on sick leave, Brig. Gen. Raleigh Colston led his division for the first time. Colston performed poorly at the Battle of Chancellorsville in May 1863, and Lee sent him to Georgia and summoned Johnson to the army. On May 8, exactly one year after he received his wound at McDowell, Johnson left the diversions of Richmond to join the Army of Northern Virginia.

Johnson's pre-war resume followed the ordinary pattern for a professional U.S. Army soldier. Born in Virginia and raised in Kentucky, he graduated from West Point 32nd out of 45 students in the Class of 1845. After service in Florida against the Seminoles he served in the Mexican War, winning brevets for bravery in three different battles. Between these wars, Johnson had toured the usual frontier posts and participated in the expedition against the Mormons.

Catapulted into the command of Stonewall's former division, Johnson was an outsider with no real experience above the brigade level. Jackson's former soldiers—who called him "Old Clubby," because he had to walk with the help of a heavy hickory staff that looked like a fence rail—did not take kindly to him from the start. Even after his success in their first battle together at Second Winchester, in the opening days of the Gettysburg Campaign, they developed no affection for him. He swore at them and hit skulkers with his huge staff, attributes that did little for his popularity. One of his men called him a

"brute;" another described him as being one of the "wickedest men I ever heard of," and later wrote, "The whole division suffered through the folly of our hard fighting Johnson. He has none of the qualities of a general, [but] expects to do everything by [head-on] fighting."

While Johnson was a talented and professionally-schooled soldier, he had little battlefield experience. He was also unfamiliar with the qualities and limitations of his four new brigadiers, all of who would likewise be leading their brigades into combat for the first time. As Johnson's Confederates headed toward the crossroads hamlet of Gettysburg, Maj. Henry Kyd Douglas, a staff officer in the division, remembered that "Allegheny" "seemed to be spoiling for a fight with his new division."

GETTYSBURG: Johnson's Division was separated from the rest of Lt. Gen. Richard Ewell's Second Corps, and approached the battle on July 1 from the west, along the Chambersburg Pike. After trudging 15 miles over South Mountain, his soldiers could hear the sounds of the first day's battle, and the last five miles was traversed with a renewed sense of urgency. Ewell, whose other two divisions had mauled the Union Eleventh Corp north of Gettysburg that afternoon, was waiting for Johnson's Division to arrive before attempting to carry the Union rallying point on Cemetery Hill.

By the time Johnson's men began to stream over Seminary Ridge and into town, however, sundown was near and Ewell was no longer thinking of Cemetery Hill. His scouts led him to believe Culp's Hill was vacant of enemy troops, and Ewell told Johnson to move his division there and, if indeed it was unoccupied, to take it. Johnson's soldiers moved east in the twilight, crossed to the east side of Rock Creek and then moved south, not quite reaching the Hanover Road. There, Johnson deployed his four brigades in one line, from right to left as follows: Brig. Gens. Nicholls (under Col. J. M. Williams), Jones, Steuart, and Walker. The division faced south, and Culp's Hill was about one mile away. After pickets were thrown forward, Johnson dispatched a reconnoitering party to examine the dark and foreboding eminence. Unfortunately, several members of the scouting team were captured. Federals were indeed on Culp's Hill, but unknown to Johnson, only in regimental strength (the 7th Indiana). Darkness fell and Johnson allowed his 6,000-man division to sleep on its arms one mile distant from the key eminence.

Dick Ewell, though, knew none of this. He believed Johnson had already taken possession of the hill in accordance with his orders of the previous evening. After telling General Lee as much in a late night meeting, he sent a messenger to Johnson on the early morning of July 2 with a direct order to occupy Culp's Hill if he hadn't already done so. The courier found Johnson preparing his brigades for a morning assault—well north of Culp's Hill. Johnson explained the situation as he understood it—the hill was solidly in Federal hands—and that he would refrain from attacking and await further orders. Ewell's messenger returned with even more disturbing news: Johnson's scouts had captured a Federal courier carrying a dispatch that confirmed that the Federal Twelfth Corps was on the field, and the Fifth Corps would arrive within a short time. Johnson had squandered his chance for an easy conquest of one of the field's key pieces of terrain.

According to Lee's new plan for July 2, the divisions of Johnson and Maj. Gen. Jubal Early would attack Culp's and Cemetery Hills, respectively, when they heard Lt. Gen. James Longstreet's assault commence on the other end of the line. The assault was scheduled for some time that morning. Due to a series of delays on Longstreet's end—during which Johnson's men waited in frustration while they listened to the Federals on Culp's Hill "plying axe and pick and shovel" to improve their defenses—his attack against the Peach Orchard-Round Tops line was not begun until about 4:00 p.m.

Johnson's own belated attack was troubled from the outset. When Major Joseph Latimer's artillery battalion opened from Benner's Hill, his fieldpieces were quickly overmatched, smothered with counter battery fire, and forced to withdraw. Brig. Gen. James Walker's Stonewall Brigade, meanwhile, was engaged with Union cavalry astride the Hanover Road on Brinkerhoff's Ridge. The threat to Johnson's left-rear had to be taken seriously, and thus Walker's Brigade was subtracted from the attacking column in order to stay and deal with it. The balance of the division was deployed with John M. Jones' Brigade on the right, Nicholls' in the center, and "Maryland" Steuart's on the left. It was about 7:00 p.m.

The division advanced over Rock Creek and began climbing the rocky northeast face of Culp's Hill in the twilight. Johnson would finally enjoy a bit of good fortune that evening. The Union Twelfth Corps, which had been manning the defenses of Culp's Hill, had pulled out to help repulse Longstreet's attack on the opposite end of the line, leaving behind nothing but Brig. Gen. George Greene's brigade on the crest. Although the New Yorkers were sheltered behind heavy breastworks, under ordinary circumstances they should not have presented a significant problem to an aggressive division. The growing darkness and heavy terrain, however, prevented the Confederates from realizing one of the golden opportunities of the battle. Johnson's attack fell directly against Greene's men, with Jones pounding his left, Nicholls his center and Steuart his right. Steuart's line managed to flank around a portion of Greene's right and occupied the abandoned Union trenches on lower Culp's Hill, where his men stopped for the night. Unable to make much headway, Johnson's attack ended.

During the night Lee and Ewell agreed that Johnson should consolidate his gains by continuing the attack in the morning. (As on the previous day, the plan was for Longstreet to attack at the same time.) Johnson would have to attempt his breakthrough without artillery support, since there were no good positions for cannon on the steep and wooded slopes. He did, however, manage to obtain heavy reinforcements. Walker's Stonewall Brigade finally arrived from Brinkerhoff's Ridge, and Brig.

Gen. Junius Daniel's and Col. Edward O'Neal's Brigades marched over from Maj. Gen. Robert Rodes' Division. In addition, Early sent Brig. Gen. William "Extra Billy" Smith's Brigade from his division. The brigades were aligned with Johnson's Division in the front line with Walker behind Maryland's Steuart's men, and O'Neal and Daniel extending the second line to the right. (Smith's Brigade arrived later in the morning.) There was no finesse in their instructions: each would plunge directly forward and pound the Union lines, trying to locate a weak point.

The plan went awry, however, because the Federals, with the Twelfth Corps back in position, struck first at about 4:30 a.m. on July 3. A furious short-range pounding by twenty-six well-sited Union guns opened the contest and kept up their thundering for the next six hours. During that time, the Federals remained largely behind their protective earthworks and smashed each of Johnson's attempts to claim the hilltop. At the southern end of the action, a determined Union assault recaptured the trenches held by Steuart's soldiers. Limited thrusts and counterthrusts occupied the area around Spangler's Spring and Pardee Field. (Similar to the previous day, Longstreet's expected simultaneous assault was postponed until the afternoon, when Pickett's Charge was launched.) By 11:00 a.m. it was over; the works on Culp's Hill were back in Union hands, and Johnson had been forced to withdraw to the marshy low ground just west of Rock Creek.

The Culp's Hill fighting had been a disaster for Confederate arms. The division had suffered around 2,000 casualties with absolutely nothing to show for its losses, and Johnson's part in the battle had sputtered to a disappointing end. The entire Second Corps withdrew to the hills west of Gettysburg that night.

Though Ewell was saddened by Johnson's failure to take Culp's Hill on the first night of the engagement, he still commended Johnson and his two other division commanders in his after-battle report. Lee's opinion of Johnson as a solid professional appears not to have been damaged by the dismal experience of Gettysburg—after all, how many of his division and corps level commanders had turned in strong performances?

During the next year, Johnson led his division at the Wilderness, and on May 12 at Spotsylvania Court House, a massive Union attack overran the Mule Shoe salient. The sector was defended by "Old Clubby's" troops, and Johnson, along with tens of hundreds of his soldiers, was captured and his division was nearly annihilated. Johnson returned to his Virginia farm after the war and died in 1873.

For further reading:

Hotchkiss, Jed. "Virginia," vol. 3 of **Confederate Military History**, Ed. by Clement A. Evans. Atlanta, 1899. [vol. 4 of the extended edition, Wilmington, 1987.]

Patterson, Gerard. "'Allegheny' Johnson." *Civil War Times Illustrated*, 5, Jan. 1967.

Pfanz, Harry W. *Gettysburg: Culp's Hill and Cemetery Hill*. Chapel Hill. 1993.

STEUART'S BRIGADE:
(2,116 MEN)

BRIGADIER GENERAL
GEORGE HUME STEUART

The sobriquet "Maryland" was applied to George Steuart in order to distinguish him from the famous Rebel cavalryman whose last name was pronounced the same but spelled differently. It was an obvious choice for a soldier who dropped to his knees and kissed the cherished soil of his native state after his brigade crossed the Potomac in the early days of the Gettysburg Campaign. "We loved Maryland," explained his aide. "We felt that she was in bondage against her will, and we burned with desire to have a part in liberating her."

The thirty-five year old Steuart was a professional soldier who had graduated from West Point in 1848 and spent the next thirteen years as a cavalryman fighting Indians

in the West. When he resigned after the fall of Fort Sumter and offered his services to the Confederacy, he was eagerly welcomed and introduced into the army as "one of Maryland's gifted sons" in the hope that more men of that state would follow his example and rally to the Confederate flag. Steuart led the 1st Maryland regiment at First Manassas, where it participated in the charge that helped put the green Union army to rout. He was promoted to colonel that same day.

Initially the men of the 1st Maryland disliked Steuart because of his unbending discipline. He had spent years in the U.S. Regulars and ran his command according to exacting Old Army regulations. It was said that he once had his men sweep the bare earth of their bivouacs. In another of Steuart's more eccentric episodes, the old frontier fighter tested his regiment's sentinels by attempting to infiltrate past them and shouting "Indians!" With time, however, the men of the regiment appreciated his efforts, and credited him with the unit's "fine state of discipline."

Promoted to brigadier general in March 1862, Steuart led a brigade composed of his own 1st Maryland and three Virginia regiments at the beginning of Stonewall Jackson's Shenandoah Campaign. On May 24, Jackson transferred Steuart to command two cavalry regiments (the 2nd and 6th Virginia regiments). At the Battle of Winchester on May 25, Jackson wanted Steuart to use his cavalry to exploit this Southern victory, but "Maryland" and his horsemen could not be located. When a staff officer finally found him, Steuart refused to accept the order because it did not come through Maj. Gen. Richard Ewell, his immediate commander. Although this incident and a generally lackluster performance as a cavalryman did not result in a court-martial, the angry Jackson reassigned Steuart to his infantry brigade. He led his men at Cross Keys on June 8, where a canister ball stuck him in the back of the shoulder and broke his collarbone. Steuart was carried off the field in an ambulance and did not begin to improve until the projectile was finally cut out in August.

The collarbone did not knit properly, and Steuart was unable to return to duty until May 28, 1863, as Lee's army was preparing for its summertime incursion into Pennsylvania. Steuart, who had never served with the Army of Northern Virginia and had missed its best days on the field, was put in command of a troublesome brigade whose former leader, Brig. Gen. Raleigh Colston, had just been relieved of duty by Lee after a disappointing performance at the head of a division at Chancellorsville. In addition to the 2nd Maryland, the brigade consisted of the 1st and 3rd North Carolina, and the 10th, 23rd and 37th Virginia. Unpleasant state rivalries had risen amongst the various regiments and a resolution was needed. It was decided that "Maryland" Steuart, as an old Regular Army man, would be able to handle such efficiency draining and morale-sapping problems.

As Steuart's Brigade marched toward Gettysburg, its leader had been in the field for only a month following a year of recuperation. Although he was a stranger to Lee's army, Steuart's superiors counted on him to improve the performance of his bickering unit—which was still unfamiliar to him. His only experience at brigade-level command had been at Cross Keys, but the upcoming fight promised to be a much larger contest than that Shenandoah Valley engagement.

GETTYSBURG: Steuart shared the 20-mile approach march of Maj. Gen. Edward

Johnson's Division on July 1 from the west, arriving in Gettysburg on the Chambersburg Pike about sunset. Third in the column, Steuart's Brigade pushed through town with the rest of the division, marched along the railroad tracks east of town, and forded Rock Creek. The exhausted troops finally halted north of the Hanover Road and faced southwest toward Culp's Hill, which was about a mile away. Johnson deployed his four brigades in one line, from right to left as follows: Nicholls (under Col. J. M. Williams), Jones, Steuart, and Walker.

Steuart woke his men early the next morning on July 2 and prepared to assault Culp's Hill, but was told to stand down after a couple of hours and wait for the sound of Lt. Gen. James Longstreet's assault on the other end of the Confederate line. Hours passed and nothing of substance transpired. Finally, about 4:00 p.m., the thunder of Longstreet's guns was heard by the troops along the Hanover Road. Their own artillery support went into action a while later, but the pieces were pounded into submission and forced to withdraw. It wasn't until about 7:00 p.m. before Steuart was finally ordered to move forward. Dusk was drawing near as Steuart's mixed-state brigade advanced toward Culp's Hill with skirmishers from the 23rd Virginia in advance. Steuart's brigade now held the far left flank of Johnson's line because Walker's Stonewall Brigade had been engaged with Federal cavalry on Brinkerhoff's Ridge and was held there to keep an eye on that sector. It was not a pleasant march for Steuart. The men tramped over rough and wooded terrain, and were forced to cross Rock Creek at a point where it was chest deep with steep banks. Such obstacles shattered alignments and slowed the pace to a crawl. By the time Johnson's line began the tiring ascent of the steep and rocky northeast face of Culp's Hill, darkness was rapidly approaching.

As it turned out, Steuart was about to enjoy a small stroke of good fortune. The Union Twelfth Corps, which had been manning the defenses of Culp's Hill, had pulled out to help repulse Longstreet's attack on the opposite end of the line. Left behind on the crest was a single brigade led by Brig. Gen. George Greene. Although Greene's New Yorkers were sheltered behind breastworks and rock fences, their right flank was vulnerable and undefended. The gloomy dusk—accented by the timber—prevented Johnson and his generals from realizing the extent of their good fortune.

It was Steuart's men who were opposite Greene's right front and flank. The Confederate brigadier's regiments were aligned, from left to right, as follows: 10th, 23rd and 37th Virginia, 1st Maryland, and 3rd North Carolina; the 1st North Carolina was behind Steuart's Virginia regiments in reserve, facing almost south to keep an eye on his own exposed left flank. As they advanced, his right two regiment drifted away to keep in touch with Nicholls' Brigade, and Steuart's brigade temporarily separated into two separate wings. The 1st Maryland and 3rd North Carolina ran into a heavy fire and were quickly bogged down on the wooded slope while Steuart's left three regiments continued advancing. On the other side of the division, Johnson's attack fell directly against Greene's men, with Jones pounding his left, Nicholls his center. With the smoke and darkness, no one could even see the opposing lines, and thus Johnson did not realize that he was facing only one brigade.

The only location on the field for any tactical option other than a frontal attack was on Steuart's front, and he took advantage of it when his 23rd Virginia tumbled into the dark and empty trenches prepared and abandoned by the enemy. On the flank of Greene's right regiment, the 137th New York, the Virginians unleashed a devastating volley. As the 137th fell back, the 10th and 37th also advanced and captured a line of works. Steuart's men occupied the terrain between lower Culp's Hill and the wall of stone near Spangler's Spring. His 10th Virginia used the wall as a guide and slid along it to further flank the enemy. Unfortunately for Steuart, Federal reinforcements were arriving on Culp's Hill in the form of Cutler's brigade, and his advance stopped. When Steuart heard more Federals coming up from beyond his flank, he solidified his position and halted, moving the 1st North Carolina over to extend his left flank. The costly night battle sputtered to a close. Both sides prepared to resume the fighting the next morning.

That night, Steuart heard what he optimistically thought was the sound of enemy wagons retreating from his front; in reality, he was listening to Union artillery being wheeled into line to blast his men in the morning. The Twelfth Corps also returned and aligned itself to throw back the Confederates. General Johnson intended an assault by the entire division in the early morning of July 3, hoping to press the advantage Steuart had won the previous evening. Walker's Stonewall Brigade arrived and took up a position behind Steuart, while two other brigades from Rodes' Division also joined Johnson.

Just before daybreak, however, around 4:30 a.m., the Union guns that had assembled during the night pounded Steuart's exposed front and much of Johnson's line. Daylight brought on the musketry, which continued unabated with the artillery fire for the next six or seven hours. None of Johnson's brigades were in a position to make any headway except Steuart, who was surprised when he received orders from Johnson to resume the offensive; he objected to no avail.

Shifting some of his men into the woods overlooking Pardee's Field while his right stretched beyond the stone wall, he led them forward about 10:30 a.m. The charge against the fortified position was bloody, quick, and forlorn. Johnson finally ordered his brigades to withdraw out of harm's way to the creek bottom about 11:00 a.m., and the disastrous fight for Culp's Hill was over. The division lost about 2,000 men, while Steuart's Brigade accounted for almost 700 of them—far more than any other brigade in the division.

Rather uncharitably, Edward Johnson did not cite any of his officers in his report, even though Steuart had given a gritty performance under extremely difficult circumstances. The Marylander remained in command of his brigade until he was captured at Spotsylvania Court House on May 12,

1864, along with Johnson and the bulk of the division. Exchanged that same summer, he returned to Lee's army and commanded a brigade in Maj. Gen. George Pickett's Division until the end of the war.

After the war, Steuart settled on a farm in Maryland and stayed active in veterans' affairs. He died from an ulcer in 1903.

For further reading:

Elmore, Thomas L. "Courage Against the Trenches: The Attack and Repulse of Steuart's Brigade on Culp's Hill." *Gettysburg Magazine*, #7, 1992.

Goldsborough, William W. *The Maryland Line in the Confederate States Army.* Baltimore, 1869.

Howard, McHenry. *Recollections of a Maryland Confederate Soldier and Staff Officer under Johnston, Jackson and Lee.* Baltimore, 1914. Reprint, Dayton, 1975.

McKim, Randolph. *A Soldier's Recollections.* New York, 1910.

Ptanz, Harry W. *Gettysburg: Culp's Hill and Cemetery Hill.* Chapel Hill. 1993.

JONES' BRIGADE:
(1,460 MEN)

BRIGADIER GENERAL JOHN MARSHALL JONES

During the Battle of Chancellorsville on May 3, 1863, Brig. Gen. John R. Jones, whose bravery had already been questioned at Sharpsburg and Fredericksburg, excused himself from the leadership of his brigade in the middle of heavy fighting and left the field because of an "ulcerated leg." His regiments subsequently refused to charge the enemy, and Brig. Gen. Stephen Ramseur's brigade was forced to step over Jones' men to make its advance. Apparently the sore on Jones' leg also kept him from writing an official report after the battle, for he neglected to explain the whole episode. Whether on orders from above or out of chivalry, none of his staff discussed his strange behavior, either. What is known is

that John R. Jones left Confederate service under a cloud of shame, and never again fought with a Confederate army.

The officer who replaced him after the battle was John M. Jones. The "new" John Jones was a mature forty-three year old staff officer, a West Point man who had graduated in the bottom quarter of the Class of 1841. His poor academic standing may have had something to do with his social habits, for his heavy drinking earned him the nickname "Rum" Jones among his classmates. After graduation, he had remained at the Academy for seven years as an assistant instructor of infantry tactics, and so missed combat service in the Mexican War. Assigned to the infantry, he endured the tedious service of the antebellum army of the 1850s and rose to captain of the 7th Infantry.

His Civil War career got off to an inauspicious beginning. After "going South" in May 1861 to serve his native Virginia, Jones was promoted to lieutenant colonel in the Confederate army in September, but still was not assigned to a regiment. In January 1862, he was removed from duty due to ill health and went home to Charlottesville to recuperate. When he returned in the spring, he was made adjutant general and inspector general on the divisional staff of Maj. Gen. Richard Ewell, who was then campaigning with Maj. Gen. Thomas "Stonewall" Jackson in the Shenandoah Valley. After Ewell was wounded just before Second Manassas in August 1862, Jones continued on the staff of Ewell's successor, Brig. Gen. Jubal Early, through the spring of 1863.

Jones had been unfailingly described as "very gallant and efficient" in his staff work on most of the army's battlefields. Ewell regularly praised him, and a Louisiana staffer called Jones "one of the best officers. . .in the army." Why then, did an officer with his military background spend half the war without a field command? Others with his rank (or below) from the old army were now brigadiers or major generals. The answer is simple: Jones was an inebriate. His nickname said as much, and he had readily produced a flask of whiskey at Cross Keys; a few days later Jones was found drunk in a hotel "in a perfectly limp state." Given his personal habits and continued problems with the bottle, the army was unwilling to place him at the head of a brigade. By early 1863, however, he appears to have gotten himself sufficiently under control to warrant the opportunity to lead men in battle, and he was entrusted with John R. Jones' regiments after that officer's poor showing at Chancellorsville. Lee may have been alluding to Jones' condition when he penned a highly unusual proviso to his new assignment in a letter to Jefferson Davis: "Should [Jones] fail in his duty," wrote Lee, "he will instantly resign." The newly-minted brigadier inherited six troublesome Virginia regiments that sorely needed the discipline and attention he was capable of providing.

(It is also worthy of note that the transfer of a brigade to a staff officer who had never commanded men in battle may also be a sign that, by the summer of 1863, the Army of Northern Virginia was running out of available men with the proper experience to command a brigade.)

John Jones was under close scrutiny as he marched his brigade north with the rest of Allegheny Johnson's Division in late June 1863. He was new not only to the responsibilities of brigade leadership, but to his brigade and his division. One can only imagine the stress Jones experienced during the campaign into Pennsylvania.

GETTYSBURG: Jones' Brigade was second in line as Maj. Gen. Edward Johnson's Division's marched 20 miles east over South Mountain to Gettysburg on July 1. Hurried through the town and over to the east side of Rock Creek in the gathering darkness, Jones' men halted with the rest of the division just north of the Hanover Road, facing southwest toward Culp's Hill a mile distant. Johnson deployed his four brigades, from right to left as follows: Nicholls (under Col. J. M. Williams), Jones, Steuart, and Walker.

Jones woke his men early on July 2 for a planned early-morning attack on Culp's Hill with the rest of the division. They were instructed to stand down after a couple of hours of tedious waiting, for Lt. Gen. James Longstreet's attack on the opposite end of the line would not commence until later in the day, and Johnson's brigades were to coordinate their effort with it. Longstreet's attack was delayed until shortly after 4:00 p.m.

When "Old Pete's" artillery was heard thundering away to the south, Johnson ordered his artillery battalion under Major Latimer to shell Union positions from Benner's Hill, and he instructed Jones' men shortly afterward to advance and form a line just south of the hill to support the artillery. Nicholls' Brigade (led by Col. Jesse Williams) and Brig. Gen. George Steuart's Brigade followed and formed on Jones' left. When the three commands united, they would advance upon Culp's Hill, with Jones' Virginians holding the division's far right flank.(Walker's Stonewall Brigade had been engaged with Federal cavalry on Brinkerhoff's Ridge that afternoon and was held there to keep an eye on that sector.)

Rough terrain hampered the advance, and though Jones' men forded a relatively shallow section of Rock Creek, Union skirmishers on Culp's Hill slowed them down once they crossed the stream. The exact order of alignment of Jones' regiments is difficult to determine with certainty, although once over the creek his front probably was a single line of six regiments. The darkness made it difficult to see, and

by the time the men clambered up the steep slope, sheets of "heavy" musketry from Brig. Gen. George Greene's New York brigade sprayed through the foliage and found plenty of targets. Culp's Hill, remembered Jones, was "steep, heavily timbered, rocky, and difficult of ascent."

Unbelievably, Greene's men were the only Northern regiments on Culp's Hill. The Union Twelfth Corps, which had been manning its defenses earlier in the day, had pulled out to help repulse Longstreet's attack on the opposite end of the line. George Greene's brigade was the only one left behind. Although his New Yorkers were sheltered behind breastworks, trees, and rocks, their right flank was vulnerable and undefended. Greene's left flank, against which Jones was attacking, connected with another Federal corps, which meant Jones' men did not have a prayer of success. The descending darkness and thick smoke prevented any of the Confederates from realizing as much.

Johnson's three brigades pressed the Federals; only Steuart, on the left side of the line, experienced some success which ultimately proved fleeting and expensive. The Confederates gained nothing of lasting value and suffered heavily in casualties. One of these was General Jones. "When near the first line of intrenchments, moving with my troops," he wrote in his report almost three months later, "I received a flesh wound through the thigh." The injury bled excessively, and Jones had to be carried off the field and out of the battle. Command of the brigade fell to Colonel John C. Higginbotham of the 25th Virginia, who in turn fell wounded himself a short time later. The next morning, with the Twelfth Corps back in position, the Federals opened the fighting about 4:30 a.m. and forced Johnson's reinforced division off Culp's Hill for good.

Unfortunately, John Jones never had an opportunity to prove his worth as a brigade commander. He convalesced in Virginia and returned to the army for the fall campaigning. Although he led his brigade in the brisk fight on November 27 at Payne's Farm in the Mine Run Campaign—conspicuously riding a horse up an down his lines—he fell early in the action with a wound to the head that kept him off the field for a few days.

On May 5, 1864, his brigade opened the Battle of the Wilderness. For the third straight time, perhaps trying to disprove any lingering doubts that may still have been hovering over his command, Jones placed himself conspicuously in harm's way when his brigade came under fire. After his Virginians were driven back in confusion in the early fighting, Jones refused to retreat and sat "gazing at the approaching enemy." He died amidst a hail of Northern gunfire.

For further reading:

Howard, McHenry. *Recollections of a Confederate Soldier and Staff Officer under Johnston, Jackson, and Lee.* Baltimore, 1914. Reprint, Dayton, 1975.

Pfanz, Harry W. *Gettysburg: Culp's Hill and Cemetery Hill.* Chapel Hill. 1993.

THE STONEWALL BRIGADE:
(1,319 MEN)

BRIGADIER GENERAL
JAMES ALEXANDER WALKER

After Lt. Gen. Thomas "Stonewall" Jackson's death in the Battle of Chancellorsville, the First Brigade of his old division became formally recognized by the Confederate War Department as the "Stonewall Brigade"—the only command of its size with an official name on the Confederate roster. At the same moment that this most famous brigade in the Confederacy was achieving its apotheosis, however, its command structure was disintegrating.

The brigade's leader, Brig. Gen. Elisha Paxton, had been killed at Chancellorsville. Such a famous command deserved an equally capable brigadier, and General Lee combed through the dwindling number of available competent officers to find one. He finally determined that thirty-one year old Col. James A. Walker of the 13th Virginia

was the man for the job—even if he was from Maj. Gen. Jubal Early's Division. There was an immediate outcry from the officers of the Stonewall Brigade, and all of the regimental commanders promptly resigned. Instead, they named three officers they said they would accept as their brigadier; General Lee quietly averted a crisis by tactfully declining the resignations of the offended officers.

For his part, Walker seemed almost oblivious to this cold reception. He was an extrovert who loved to fight, a two-fisted drinker and practical joker who enjoyed life too much to engage in petty bickering with his new subordinates. His attitude soon won over the entire brigade. By the end of his first month, the Virginians affectionately called the tall and muscular fighter "Stonewall Jim."

Walker had previously been associated with Stonewall Jackson under less than auspicious circumstances. In 1852, when he was a senior at the Virginia Military Institute, Walker was involved in a classroom disturbance and was ordered from the room by none other than Professor Thomas J. Jackson. After a sharp exchange of words, the brash young Walker challenged Jackson to a duel. Jackson debated the question, but eventually Walker was court-martialed and expelled. For the next eighteen months he worked for the Chesapeake and Ohio Railway as a terrain engineer, then studied law at the University of Virginia. He graduated and married in 1854, and moved to Pulaski County in the hills of southwest Virginia to set up his practice. After John Brown shocked Southerners with his raid on Harpers Ferry in 1859, Walker organized a local militia company called the "Pulaski Guard."

When the Civil War broke out two years later, Walker took his company into Confederate service. He was assigned to the 4th Virginia Infantry in a brigade led by his old nemesis, the former professor and now brigadier general, Thomas Jackson. A larger and common enemy occupied their attention, and no animosity seemed to remain between the two. (In fact, during the war, VMI's school board sent Walker his diploma, supposedly at Jackson's request.) Walker performed so well in the first weeks of campaigning that he was quickly promoted to lieutenant colonel and transferred in June 1861 to Col. A. P. Hill's 13th Virginia Infantry. In February 1862, when Hill was promoted to brigadier general; Walker was elevated to colonel and given command of the regiment.

Walker fought with his regiment in the Shenandoah Campaign until June 8, when he took over command of Brig. Gen. Arnold Elzey's Brigade after Elzey was wounded in the Battle of Cross Keys. Walker's debut performance in brigade command the next day at the Battle of Port Republic was a comical embarrassment. He and three of his regiments got "lost in the mountains," according to the blunt report of division commander Maj. Gen. Richard Ewell, and failed to find their way back to the battle until the fighting was over. When Jackson's army was transferred to the Peninsula later that month for the Seven Days' Battles, Walker's fortunes improved slightly. Back with his regiment after Elzey's return, he and his men fought well and hard at Gaines' Mill, but did not achieve a Confederate breakthrough. The unlucky Elzey was again wounded, and Walker assumed brigade command—only to discover that he could not find three of the brigade's regiments. He continued in command of the brigade through the remaining days of fighting on the Peninsula, and at

Malvern Hill a shell buried itself beneath Walker, "elevating him a few feet." The next time Walker saw action, his career began to soar. Back in command of his 13th Virginia at the Cedar Mountain on August 9, Walker performed so well that he won ringing recommendations for promotion to brigadier general from both Ewell and Brig. Gen. Jubal Early (who had permanently replaced Elzey). Early called Walker "a most efficient and gallant officer, who is always ready to perform a duty." His men, continued Early, "are capital fighting men, there being none better in the army." This was high praise from a general who had little good to say about anyone.

Walker fought again at Second Manassas at the end of August, where his regiment lost 46 men in defensive fighting along the Railroad Cut, and at Sharpsburg on September 17, where he led Trimble's Brigade. During the latter fight, Union fire injured Walker, killed his horse, and caused 228 casualties (including three of the four regimental colonels) in a brigade that numbered less than 700 men. Early called attention to Walker's "most conspicuous gallantry and good conduct" in the battle and added that he should be promoted for his bravery. On October 27, Lee recommended Walker for promotion to brigadier general, though it turned out Walker would have to wait until after Chancellorsville to get his brigadier's wreath.

Walker again led a brigade with impressive ability at Fredericksburg, this time pitching Early's Brigade forward to stop a Union threat when George Meade's Pennsylvanians poured through a gap in the front of Stonewall Jackson's line. In April 1863, after being admitted to the hospital with a urethral stricture, he went on sick leave until after the Battle of Chancellorsville. A proven and appreciated quantity, Lee selected Walker (Early's Brigade was by now in the hands of another) to lead the Stonewall Brigade after Chancellorsville. Thus Walker was promoted to brigadier general in May and assigned to Jackson's already-legendary regiments.

By the end of June, as they marched toward Gettysburg, the men of the

Stonewall Brigade had warmed to Walker's style and would fight hard for him. The brigade was so decimated by losses that it would never again equal its earlier formidability, but Walker was a brawler, proud of his new command and eager to find a fight.

GETTYSBURG: Walker's Stonewall Brigade was in the rear of Maj. Gen. Edward Johnson's Division as it hiked 20 miles to reach Gettysburg on July 1. Arriving in Gettysburg around 7:00 p.m., Walker's men followed the column as it streamed through town, kept marching east along railroad tracks, forded Rock Creek, and went south almost to the Hanover Road, where it faced southwest toward Culp's Hill about a mile away. Walker's Virginians were on the far left of the division's line. There they slept on their arms.

Thus situated, Walker's men represented the far left of the Army of Northern Virginia, and they were charged with watching the army's flank. They spent much of the day on July 2 skirmishing with various enemy units, fulfilling in many respects the role of the army's largely-absent cavalry. The shooting began at dawn, when the Stonewall men began exchanging shots with elements from the Union Twelfth Corps which had come onto the north slope of nearby Wolf's Hill early that morning. The Twelfth Corps' infantry retired, and a regiment from the arriving Fifth Corps took their place. Later in the afternoon, the Fifth Corps regiment likewise marched away to rejoin its brigade, and the fight was taken up by Brig. Gen. David Gregg's exhausted cavalrymen, who had been on hand for most of the day. As the fighting with the cavalry progressed through the evening, it became serious enough to cause Walker to make the questionable decision to stay at the scene (Brinkerhoff's Ridge) while the other three brigades of Johnson's Division made a desperate and short-lived attack against Culp's Hill. After dark, Walker left some pickets in place to face the cavalry and marched to join Johnson on Culp's Hill, but he was too late to help in the nighttime assault.

The Stonewall Brigade crossed Rock Creek about 2:00 a.m. and was placed on the left, behind Brig. Gen. George Steuart's Brigade, to press the advantage Steuart had won the evening before when he occupied a section of abandoned Union entrenchments. Steuart's success was the result of a spectacular Federal blunder the previous day, when the entire Twelfth Corps, less one brigade, evacuated Culp's Hill and scurried south to oppose James Longstreet's assault against the Round Tops. The Federals returned on the night of July 2, however, and prepared throughout the early morning hours of July 3 to throw the Confederates off the hill.

The battle commenced anew on July 3. "At daylight. . .Steuart's Brigade, which was immediately in my front, became hotly engaged," reported Walker, "and, on receiving a request from General Steuart, I moved up to his support." Walker's left regiment, the 2nd Virginia, had a lively time of it and assisted in repulsing a regimental-size thrust by the 1st Maryland, Potomac Home Brigade. His entire line was hotly engaged, with no gains to show after "five hours of incessant firing." Unable to crack the line, the Stonewall Brigade was withdrawn during the middle of the morning to replenish ammunition and clean its rifles. General Johnson personally directed Walker to shift his brigade and renew the assault. Since the 2nd Virginia was still on the other side of Rock Creek and engaged, Walker's force consisted of just four depleted regiments: the 4th, 5th, 27th, and 33rd, about 1,000 men.

Walker took up a position on the right flank of Brig. Gen. Junius Daniel's Brigade, where the brigades of Nicholls and O'Neal had already tried and failed that morning. Neither Walker nor any of his regimental commanders specified the alignment of the brigade, although almost certainly the left regiment, whichever it was, began the attack in the depression leading up to the saddle between the hills. The Virginians dutifully charged up Culp's Hill directly into the teeth of George Greene's heavily entrenched New York brigade at the crest. "I was ordered. . .to renew the attack, which was done with equally bad success as our former efforts," lamented Walker. "The fire became so destructive I suffered the brigade to fall back to a more secure position, as it was a useless sacrifice of life to keep them longer under so galling a fire." Many Confederates all along Johnson's line, trapped close to the enemy and unwilling to make a run back down the lead-swept hill, surrendered. Before falling back to Rock Creek with the rest of the division, Walker advanced yet again to hold the enemy in check and prevent a counterattack while Johnson disengaged his brigades. By 11:00 a.m., the fighting for Culp's Hill was over. Divisional casualties totaled some 2,000 men, and about 350 of those were from the Stonewall Brigade. It was no consolation to Walker and his men that his brigade suffered the fewest casualties in the division.

The action passed from Culp's Hill to the Union right center that afternoon, where Pickett's Charge advanced and receded, ending the Battle of Gettysburg. Johnson pulled back over Rock Creek and withdrew west of Gettysburg that night. Though Johnson did not commend any of his brigadiers in his report, the Stonewall Brigade's commander had done as well as anyone could have under the circumstances and was worthy of his command.

"Stonewall Jim" led his brigade until he lost an arm in the division's annihilation the next May at Spotsylvania. He returned briefly at the end of the war to lead a division. After the conflict, Walker resumed his law practice and entered politics. He was elected to the Virginia house of delegates in 1871 and lieutenant governor in 1876. Later, as a Republican, he was twice elected to Congress, from 1895 to 1899, and was severely wounded in a shootout with a legal opponent. He died in 1901.

For further reading:

Caldwell, Willie W. *Stonewall Jim: A Biography of General James A. Walker. C.S.A.*, Elliston, 1990.

Pfanz, Harry W. *Gettysburg: Culp's Hill and Cemetery Hill.* Chapel Hill. 1993.

Riggs, David F. *Thirteenth Virginia Infantry.* Lynchburg, 1988.

Robertson, James I., Jr., *The Stonewall Brigade.* Baton Rouge, 1963.

NICHOLL'S BRIGADE:
(1,101 MEN)

COLONEL JESSE MILTON WILLIAMS

No photograph of Colonel Williams has been located.

After the Battle of Chancellorsville, each of the brigades in Stonewall Jackson's former division (led by Raleigh Colston at Chancellorsville) required a new commander. The army was scoured and brigadiers were found for three of the four brigades. A suitable replacement for Brig. Gen. Francis Nicholls' Louisiana Brigade, whose commander had lost a foot during Jackson's flank attack on May 2, could not be found. Thus its regiments remained under the 2nd Louisiana's colonel, Jesse M. Williams, who led the brigade at Chancellorsville after Nicholls was carried from the field. The fact that an officer of proper rank could not be located was an ominous sign that the well from which capable brigade leaders were drawn was running dry.

Unfortunately, the brigade did not perform well under Williams in the Chancellorsville fighting. On May 3, while Jackson's corps was fighting desperately to overrun the Federal defenses around Chancellorsville and reunite with the rest of the Confederate army, the brigade became disordered and Williams was unable to get his veterans to attack. Even more disgraceful, the men of the brigade were so completely without leadership that they were almost thrown out of their own defenses, unable to even to keep up a strong fire against the approaching Federal infantry. Nicholls' men, obviously demoralized, were saved only by a counterattack mounted by other Southern regiments.

Thirty-two years old, Col. Williams was a resident of the northwest Louisiana town of Mansfield. He was a company commander in the 2nd Louisiana regiment when the Civil War began, and fought on the Peninsula at the Battles of Yorktown and Malvern Hill, where the regiment's colonel was mortally wounded. The field officers of the regiment were so decimated at Malvern Hill that Williams, a lowly captain, was promoted to colonel and given command of the regiment. He led the 2nd Louisiana well at Cedar Mountain and again at Second Manassas, where after exhausting their ammunition in the latter battle, the Louisianians picked up rocks and threw them at charging Federal soldiers. At Sharpsburg in September, "Williams was severely wounded by a Minie-ball, which passed through his chest, while gallantly leading his regiment in the first charge," Edmund Pendleton, the acting brigade commander, wrote in his report. This was the first time in the war that Williams had been formally recognized in a superior's battle report. He was taken prisoner in Maryland and was eventually exchanged. Williams convalesced for months and returned to the army in time to participate in the Chancellorsville Campaign, where command of the brigade fell on his shoulders when an artillery shell severed Francis Nicholls' foot.

The fact that Lee unsuccessfully sought a replacement for Nicholls (and it wasn't Williams) meant that the commanding general did not entertain great expectations from the Louisiana colonel, even though he left him at the head of the brigade as the army marched north into Pennsylvania.

GETTYSBURG: Williams and his men led the 20-mile march of Maj. Gen. Edward "Allegheny" Johnson's Division on July 1, from Scotland east along the Chambersburg Pike to Gettysburg. After marching through the town some time around 6:00 in the evening, Williams led the division along the railroad tracks east of town, forded Rock Creek, then turned south and went into line 500 yards north of the Hanover Road facing Culp's Hill, about a mile away to the southwest. The rest of the division extended the line in the growing darkness on Williams' left and settled down for the night.

Williams had his men up early on July 2 for Johnson's planned early-morning attack on Culp's Hill in coordination with James Longstreet's planned assault against the other flank of the Union army. The attack was delayed when it was learned that Longstreet's attack would not commence until later in the day. When his guns were heard thundering away to the south at about 4:00 p.m., Johnson ordered his own artillery battalion under Major Joseph Latimer to shell Union positions from Benner's Hill. Jones' Brigade moved out first and the brigades of Williams and Brig. Gen. George Steuart followed and formed on Jones' left. When the three commands united, Johnson informed them, they would advance over Rock Creek and up Culp's Hill. Williams' Louisianians held the center of the division line. (Walker's Stonewall Brigade had been engaged with various infantry and cavalry units on Brinkerhoff's Ridge throughout the day and remained there to keep an eye on that sector.)

The attack moved forward about 7:00 p.m., as dusk was about to descend. After crossing Rock Creek, "[We] engaged the enemy near the base of these heights," recalled Williams after the battle, "and, having quickly driven his front line into the intrenchments on their crest, continued forward. . ." The skirmishers he was driving in belonged to the 78th New York of Brig. Gen. George Greene's brigade. Greene was the only part of the Federal Twelfth Corps left on Culp's Hill. The corps, which had been manning the hill's defenses that day, had only recently been yanked from its works and sent south to help repulse Longstreet's attack on the opposite end of the line. Now only Greene's five New York regiments remained. Although he had all the advantages of terrain, breastworks, trees, and rocks, Greene's right flank was vulnerable and undefended, while his left connected with the Eleventh Corps. Williams' men were moving directly against the 102nd, the right of the 60th, and the left of the 149th—the very center of Greene's powerful line. They did not stand a chance of success.

The growing darkness and spreading clouds of smoke prevented any of the Confederates from realizing that they faced but a single brigade. Williams' Louisiana troops began the ascent of the steep and rocky northeast face of Culp's Hill and "reached a line about 100 yards from the enemy's works." They could go no further. We engaged him with an almost incessant fire for four hours," wrote Williams, who sent his men forward on several forlorn charges that day to try to pierce Greene's line. "Several attempts to carry the works by assault [were made, but] being entirely unsupported on the right (Jones' brigade having failed to hold its line on the right)" wrote a frustrated Williams, "were attended with more loss than success." In fact, Williams had no success at all that evening. Only Steuart's Brigade on the left managed to gain a solid foothold higher up the hill, and his lodgement was a brief one.

Williams men remained in place that night so close to the enemy lines they had to speak in whispers to keep their position secret. The balance of the Federal Twelfth Corps returned late that night and early the following morning, intent on driving Johnson's men off Culp's Hill. Johnson, meanwhile, was reinforced with several additional brigades and determined to sweep the Federals from the crest. The Federals opened the fight just before daylight on July 3, and it continued with unrelenting fury for some seven hours. Williams attacked the same place in the line (with Col. Ed O'Neal's Brigade formed on his left and Brig. Gen. James Walker's in his left-

rear). His infantrymen were met by Union fire that was "the most terrific and deafening that we ever experienced," recalled one officer. The gun smoke at times became smoke so thick that only muzzle flashes indicated the position of the opposing lines.

If his men enjoyed any good fortune, it was the fact that they were so close to the Union lines, for much of the enemy fire went over the heads of the Louisianians; their charge, however, went nowhere. Williams withdrew his men to Rock Creek late that morning while the Stonewall Brigade made a futile advance over the same ground. By 11:00 a.m., Johnson withdrew the entire division, and the battle for Culp's Hill ended, as did Williams' part in the Battle of Gettysburg.

Williams had been dealt a tough hand in the battle, and it is difficult to imagine anyone accomplishing more with the low cards he was dealt. His superiors judged from his performance that he was not the man to permanently command Nicholls' Brigade. Thus Williams returned to the 2nd Louisiana, and another colonel, Leroy Stafford from Hays' Louisiana Brigade, was elevated to brigadier and put in command in time for the fall campaigns.

Colonel Jesse Williams was shot through the head with a Federal minie ball at Spotsylvania Court House on May 12, 1864.

For further reading:

Jones, Terry L. *Lee's Tigers: The Louisiana Infantry in the Army of Northern Virginia*. Baton Rouge, 1987.

Pfanz, Harry W. *Gettysburg: Culp's Hill and Cemetery Hill*. Chapel Hill. 1993.

RODES' DIVISION:
(7,831 MEN / 16 GUNS)

MAJOR GENERAL
ROBERT EMMET RODES

Unlike Lt. Gen. Richard Ewell and Maj. Gens. Jubal Early and Edward Johnson— the other three high-ranking commanders

of the Second Corps—Robert Rodes looked every inch the heroic leader of men. He cut a majestic yet slender six-foot figure astride his black charger, with a mop of blond hair, a sandy mustache that drooped below the corners of his mouth, and a strong dimpled chin and flashing blue eyes. Historian Douglas Southall Freeman especially enjoyed describing Rodes. The Virginian "stepped from the pages of Beowulf," he wrote with a flair, "a Norse God in Confederate gray," and a "Wotan still young." Freeman also paid Rodes one of his highest compliments by terming him "the personification of the new type of Confederate leader."

In the summer of 1863, Rodes was one of the Army of Northern Virginia's brightest stars. Certainly part of his mystique was due to his dashing looks, but he had won his major generalcy mainly because of his effective, up-front style of combat leadership. He was the only division commander in Lee's army who hadn't graduated from West Point. A native of Lynchburg, Virginia, he had gone to the Virginia Military Institute instead, graduating with distinction in the Class of 1848. Appointed assistant professor that year, he applied for a professorship in 1850, but Thomas (later "Stonewall") Jackson was chosen instead. Rodes, like many officers of that time, went to work for the railroad. Moving to Alabama, he worked for various rail lines both as a civil engineer and executive. After he married in Tuscaloosa in 1857, Rodes

moved back to Virginia and accepted the professorship of Applied Mathematics at his alma mater—the job previously held by Jackson. He held the position only briefly before the war broke out.

Rodes volunteered at the first clash of arms and organized a company of Alabamians called the "Warrior Guards" in May 1861. Within days he was made colonel of the 5th Alabama regiment. Commended by General P. G. T. Beauregard as an "excellent officer," Rodes was promoted to brigadier general and given a brigade in October 1861. He led his men in battle for the first time on the Virginia Peninsula in the summer of 1862. Rodes displayed martial prowess in a series of attacks at Seven Pines, continuing to fight even after he was wounded in the arm by a bullet. He relinquished command at the end of the day's action but was back on duty within the month and fought again at Gaines' Mill. Still suffering from his arm wound, however, he relinquished field duty just before Malvern Hill. Rodes emerged from the Peninsula with a reputation as a hard-hitting brigadier, and high-ranking officers like James Longstreet commented on the VMI graduate's "coolness, ability, and determination" in battle. South Mountain found his isolated brigade gallantly holding back an entire Union division for much of the afternoon. At Sharpsburg, he was again wounded, this time only slightly, when a shell fragment struck him in the thigh during the contest waged at the Sunken Road.

Although his brigade was not directly engaged at Fredericksburg, Rodes had demonstrated on several fields that he was capable of additional responsibilities. His chance for higher command came in January 1863, when Maj. Gen. Daniel H. Hill was sent to North Carolina. Brig. Gen. Edward Johnson, whom Jackson wanted to take command of the division, was still convalescing from an ankle wound, and Rodes was put in charge by virtue of being the division's senior brigadier.

In May at the Battle of Chancellorsville, Rodes's Division played a prominent role in Jackson's crushing attack on the Union right flank. One Confederate wrote that

Rodes' "eyes were everywhere, and every now and then he would stop to attend to some detail of the arrangement of his line or his troops, and then ride on again, humming to himself and catching the ends of his long, tawny moustache between his lips." His fiery battle cry, delivered in a clarion voice heard above the din, was "Forward, men, over friend or foe!" After the battle, the mortally wounded Jackson urged for a "battlefield promotion" for Rodes, whose leadership he described as "magnificent." Such promotions, Jackson thought, were "the greatest incentives to gallantry in others." Lee, who wished both to reward Rodes and please Jackson, made the young officer a major general for the coming campaign in Pennsylvania.

Rodes had not only consistently distinguished himself as a brigadier, but was a splendid success in his first performance as a division commander. Though not as experienced at this level of command as some in the army, he was a rising star and much was expected from him. His only liability was an overconfidence that had the potential to lead to recklessness.

GETTYSBURG: On July 1, Rodes planned to continue the previous day's march south from Carlisle in response to Lee's orders to concentrate the army around Cashtown. He had his division on the road at sunrise. Some time before 9.00 a.m., new Second Corps commander Lt. Gen. Richard Ewell learned that Lt. Gen. A. P. Hill's Third Corps was fighting west of Gettysburg. In response, he ordered Rodes to turn south toward that town upon reaching Middletown. By 11:30 a.m. Rodes had approached close enough to hear gunfire, and turned his lead brigade onto the northern spur of Oak Hill in order to come in on the flank of the Federals drawn up and opposing Hill. In hindsight this was probably a mistake, for if he had kept to the road, he would have sped into the unguarded rear of the First Corps before most of its men were deployed.

After advancing for a mile through the dense woods on Oak Hill, Rodes was able to observe the flank of the enemy line to the south. He deployed his division with Brig.

Gen. George Doles', Col. Edward O'Neal's, and Brig. Gen. Alfred Iverson's brigades in his first line (from east to west or left to right), while Brig. Gens. Stephen Ramseur and Junius Daniel took a position anchoring his rear line. With some of his artillery up, Rodes' began shelling the enemy—another bad idea, since it announced his presence on the Federal's flank and gave them time to redeploy to meet his challenge.

Rodes' brigades were fully deployed by 1:30 p.m., with his first line occupying a mile of ground between the Carlisle Road and the Mummasburg Road. With advance elements from the Federal Eleventh Corps pushed north of town to oppose his left, Rodes led off his attack piecemeal and with Colonel O'Neal, his least experienced brigade commander. O'Neal bungled his attack by moving forward only three of his five brigades while he remained behind with the 5th Alabama. As Rodes angrily reported, O'Neal "was repulsed quickly, and with loss."

Next to go forward was Iverson, who failed to deploy skirmishers and was ambushed by Henry Baxter's Federals, hidden behind a low stone wall. The brave North Carolinians were practically annihilated. This second costly disaster within a time span further eroded Rodes' initial advantage of position on the enemy flank. Iverson's collapse also jeopardized the next of Rodes' brigade assaults by Daniel on Rodes' far right. As Iverson's men were being mowed down and their commander inflicted with a wave of hysteria, Daniel's Brigade advanced at an oblique and was caught in a deadly crossfire from positions on his right flank and front.

Just when matters were beginning to look rather grim for Freeman's "Norse God in Confederate Gray," Ramseur's Brigade (probably the best in the division) advanced on Daniel's left. Elements from Hill's Third Corps moved up to support Daniels's right, and the weight of the attack, coupled with portions of O'Neal's Brigade, Doles' Brigade, and Maj. Gen. Jubal Early's rolling divisional assault on Rodes' left against the Eleventh Corps, forced the exhausted brigades of the enemy to give way and scramble back toward the town.

In conjunction with Jubal Early's Division on his left, Rodes pushed his brigades as quickly as possible to and through Gettysburg, stopping them on the opposite side of the town before they could storm Cemetery Hill (which angered O'Neal's and Ramseur's men, whose blood was up and who believed they could have continued the pursuit successfully). Rodes met with Early and Ewell in the town square. According to later reports, the pair of division chiefs urged Ewell to press the attack against the retreating Federals, to no avail. It had been an exhausting and not particularly good day for Rodes—and it was not yet over.

Fatigued and in a more passive state of mind, Rodes advised against sending Maj. Gen. Edward Johnson's newly-arrived division to attack Culp's Hill. When Lee rode up that evening to confer with Rodes, Early, and Ewell about the proper use of the Second Corps, Rodes spoke little but agreed that any attack the next day should not be delivered by the Second Corps. Rodes' Division ended the day with Doles', Iverson's, and Ramseur's brigades in the town, O'Neal's Brigade in their right rear along the railroad bed near the Chambersburg Pike, and Daniel further to the west on Seminary Ridge.

When plans were finalized late that night, it was determined that Rodes would attack with Ewell's other two divisions on July 2 in concert with Lt. Gen. James Longstreet's First Corps' assault against the opposite end of the Federal line; Johnson would go in first against Culp's Hill, and then Early and Rodes, in that order, would assail Cemetery Hill from the northeast and northwest, respectively. As it happened, Longstreet's attack did not get underway until about 4:00 p.m., and it was almost dark by the time Johnson moved against Culp's Hill and Early moved out two of his brigades against East Cemetery Hill.

Rodes, however, who was well aware of how his men were positioned and the difficulties of the approach to Cemetery Hill from the town, did not begin his attack preparations in time to be of assistance to anyone. The movement of his brigades from the town's narrow streets and the fields west into a position to assault the northwest face of Cemetery Hill took much longer than Rodes had anticipated.

By the time his infantrymen were in position, Early's successful assault was ending. Hays and Avery captured the crest but were thrown back when reinforcements did not arrive. Rodes, in a most curious move, turned over command of the advancing division to one of his brigadiers, Dodson Ramseur, who called off the attack after advancing halfway to the enemy lines in the dark. Rodes recalled his brigades and ordered his men to stand down in the Long Lane leading southwest out of Gettysburg, where they faced southeast toward Cemetery Hill. Early was enraged by Rodes' lack of support, and he complained bitterly about his July 2 command lapse for the rest of his life, calling it "the solitary instance of remissness on the part of any portion of the corps in the battle." Officially, Ewell was more forgiving, reporting only that "Major-General Rodes did not advance, for reasons given in his report." However, at least one member of Ewell's staff held the opinion that Ewell agreed with Early regarding Rodes' tentative July 2 behavior. Detailed information on Lee's division commanders is remarkably thin for Gettysburg, and so it is with Robert Rodes. One source, though, claims the general was sick with a fever during the battle, which could well explain his several costly mistakes.

During the night, Rodes sent the brigades of Daniel and O'Neal to reinforce Johnson's Division, which had made a lodgment on Culp's Hill that evening. Rodes now only had three brigades, including Iverson's decimated command, remaining under his direct control. His division maintained its position in Long Lane and was not called upon for offensive action on July 3.

The Rodes of pre-Gettysburg days reappeared after the army abandoned Pennsylvania, and he continued to perform well at the head of his division until he was killed in Jubal Early's 1864 Shenandoah Valley Campaign at Third Winchester in September 1864. Although he was not the only

Confederate general to experience an "off day" at Gettysburg, his performance there may have had an adverse effect on his career. Rodes, who was considered by almost everyone to be a rising talent after Chancellorsville, was never seriously considered for corps command.

For further reading:

Freeman, Douglas S. *Lee's Lieutenants: A Study in Command.* vol. 3. New York, 1944.

Griffin, D. Massy. "Rodes on Oak Hill: A Study of Rodes' Division on the First Day of Gettysburg." *Gettysburg Magazine*, #4, 1991.

Peyton, Green. "Robert E. Rodes," in Memorial, V.M.I. Ed. by Charles D. Walker. Philadelphia, 1875.

Wert, Jeffry E. "Robert E. Rodes." *Civil War Times Illustrated*, 16, Dec. 1977.

DOLES' BRIGADE:
(1,319 MEN)

BRIGADIER GENERAL
GEORGE PIERCE DOLES

George Doles was called "one of the bravest, best loved and most accomplished soldiers Georgia furnished to the Confederate army." Thirty-three years old, Doles was a handsome man with penetrating eyes under a high forehead, wearing a beard but no sideburns. Though he was a vigorous commander, he was by habit a quiet man, self-assured and intelligent.

He had an early hankering for the military life. A teenager when the Mexican war was declared, he ran away to join the army, but was caught waiting for the stagecoach and returned home. He settled for an active career in the militia while he prospered as a businessman in Milledgeville, the Georgia state capital. Doles rose to captain a company called the "Baldwin Blues," one of the oldest and best-trained military units in the state.

When Fort Sumter fell, Doles led his militia company into Confederate service, where it became part of the 4th Georgia regiment. His military abilities were well known to his fellow Georgians, and the men of the 4th elected him their colonel. After serving in the Norfolk area of Virginia, Doles and his regiment were moved to Richmond and attached to Maj. Gen. Benjamin Huger's Division for the Peninsula Campaign. At Seven Pines in May 1862, Doles' regiment mistakenly marched away from the fighting due to confused orders from the divisional commander. At the outset of the Seven Days' Battles a month later, the regiment manned Richmond's thin defensive line at Oak Grove while the bulk of Lee's army attacked McClellan's force across the Chickahominy. Doles' Georgians saw action at Malvern Hill, where they lost 101 men. On that bloody slope Doles was wounded by a shell, but remained with the army while he recovered. After the campaign, both Brig. Gen. Ambrose "Rans" Wright and division commander Huger commended Doles' "attention to his duties as well as his gallantry in action." A newspaperman reported that "the Fourth Georgia fought like devils."

The 4th Georgia was placed into Brig. Gen. Roswell Ripley's Brigade for the Maryland Campaign. After the fighting at South Mountain, there was complaining within the regiment that the inactive Ripley "did not draw trigger." In addition, during the withdrawal from South Mountain, Ripley completely forgot the 4th Georgia and the regiment was saved from certain capture by an alert colonel who notified Doles that the rest of the brigade had pulled out. When Ripley was wounded three days later at Sharpsburg, Doles took over the brigade. He was given permanent command of the unit six weeks later in late October, and promoted to brigadier general on November 1. Doles' Brigade was in reserve at Fredericksburg but made up for lost time at Chancellorsville, where he and his men were conspicuous in the front line of Jackson's punishing flank attack that crushed the Federal right. His brigade suffered more than 400 casualties, and Doles was commended by division commander Robert Rodes "for great gallantry and efficiency in this action."

On the eve of Lee's Pennsylvania Campaign, George Doles had earned a reputation for being among the Southern army's most daring, hard-fighting brigadiers.

GETTYSBURG: By 11:30 a.m., Doles' soldiers had marched close enough to Gettysburg on the Carlisle Road to hear the battle raging between Lt. Gen. A P. Hill's Confederates and the Federal First Corps. Rodes, the division commander, turned his lead brigade onto the northern spur of Oak Hill in order to come in on the flank of the Federals opposing Hill west of town. Doles' Georgians were placed on the left of the division's front line, on the clear east slope of Oak Hill. It was soon shifted even farther to the left, across the valley north of Gettysburg, to link with Maj. Gen. Jubal Early's Division, which was approaching the town on the Harrisburg Road.

With portions of the Union Eleventh Corps advancing in strength from Gettysburg to reinforce the threatened right flank of the First Corps, Doles held his ground and waited anxiously for Early to appear. In the distance on his right front was the Federal brigade of Alexander Schimmelfennig, deployed north and west of the Mummasburg Road; Union artillery was unlimbered and firing in his front, and additional Federal infantry was marching north in his direction. With skirmishers well forward, Doles aligned his four Georgia regiments, from left to right, as follows: 12th, 4th, 44th, and 21st. His three right-most regiments were aligned west of the Carlisle Road, while the 12th Georgia was on the east side, not too far distant from the Blocher house. Tense moments ensued when the two brigades (Iverson's and O'Neal's) supporting Doles' right collapsed, isolating Doles and placing him at a distinct numerical disadvantage until Early's brigades arrived and pitched into the Eleventh Corps' right flank.

By this time Francis Barlow's Federal division had assumed control of Blocher's (later Barlow's) Knoll to the left front of Doles, and Early's men were pitching into it. Without waiting for orders from Rodes, Doles seized the initiative and attacked the Federals in his front. With his left flank near Rock Creek, Doles drove his men forward on the right flank of Brig. Gen. John Gordon's brigade and cracked Federal Brig. Gen. Barlow's divisional line into pieces. During this attack, Doles' powerful sorrel horse seized the bit in his teeth and ran full tilt toward the Union lines. About fifty yards shy of the enemy, Doles was thrown off into a wheat field. Fortunately for the general, the Federals had other concerns and were preparing to retreat, and thus ignored him.

Leading his men temporarily on foot, Doles watched as another Federal brigade under Col. Wladimir Kryzanowski advanced over the Carlisle Road and sent his 21st Georgia men, on his far right, tumbling to the rear. He turned his brigade to meet the threat, and the combined force of Doles and Gordon sent the Federals into a quick withdrawal. With his brigade aligned on the west side of the Carlisle Road, Doles headed south to try to intercept the retreating Federals of the First Corps, but was not in time to do so. His exhausted brigade moved through the west side of Gettysburg pursuing the beaten Federals, but was halted by Rodes before it could advance further toward Cemetery Hill. Doles' men spent the night in town camped on the left of Rodes' Division on West Middle Street. Although he could not have known it, Doles had already done his last fighting of the battle.

On July 2, Rodes' Division was called upon to attack in concert with the rest of Ewell's Corps in conjunction with Lt. Gen. James Longstreet's First Corps assault against the opposite end of the Federal line; Johnson's Division would go in first against Culp's Hill, Jubal Early's Division would strike next at East Cemetery Hill, and Rodes men would assail the same hill from the northwest. Longstreet's attack did not begin until about 4:00 p.m., and it was almost dark by the time Johnson moved against Culp's Hill, and Early moved out two of his brigades against East Cemetery Hill.

When the order to move arrived, Doles dutifully guided his brigade through town to Long Lane southwest of Gettysburg in preparation for the attack. The overall division's movement from Gettysburg's narrow streets and the fields west of the town into a position to assault the northwest face of Cemetery Hill took much longer than Rodes had anticipated. By the time Doles infantrymen were in position on the left flank of the first line of attack, Early's assault—which had captured the crest of the hill but was thrown back when reinforcements did not arrive—was over. When the three brigades of Doles, Iverson and Ramseur crept forward in the darkness, however, Ramseur—under whose authority Rodes had placed the attack—stopped the line. He found Doles and Iverson and the three officers conferred. The generals decided that the enemy defenses were too strong and halted their troops. Rodes soon recalled them, and the attack was not made. The men retraced their steps to Long Lane, where they spent that night and all of July 3, and were never seriously engaged again.

Doles was one of the three brigade leaders commended by Rodes after the battle (Daniel and Ramseur were the other two). Although his brigade lost only 179 men in the entire campaign, Doles' performance on July 1, in a perilous situation against superior numbers, contributed significantly to the Confederate victory that day, reinforcing his status as one of Lee's ablest brigadiers.

The well-liked and respected Georgian continued in command of his regiments until he was killed by a sharpshooter on June 2, 1864, near Cold Harbor.

For further reading:

Derry, Joseph T. "Georgia," vol. 6 of *Confederate Military History*, ed. by Clement A. Evans. Atlanta, 1899 [vol. 7 of the extended edition, Wilmington, 1987.]

Freeman, Douglas S. *Lee's Lieutenants: A Study in Command*. vol. 3. New York, 1944.

Thomas, Henry W. *History of the Doles-Cook Brigade*. Dayton, 1981.

RAMSEUR'S BRIGADE:
(1,023 MEN)

BRIGADIER GENERAL
STEPHEN DODSON RAMSEUR

Reared in the rolling hills of North Carolina Piedmont region, young Ramseur—known as "Dodson" to his friends and "Dod" to his intimates—impressed his friends with a unique combination of personal gentleness ("womanly tenderness of feeling," one called it) and reckless daring. Raised in a devout Presbyterian home, Ramseur attended Presbyterian Davidson College, where he befriended the mathematics professor, Daniel Harvey Hill. With former West Pointer Hill's recommendation, Dodson Ramseur won appointment to the academy and graduated 14th out of 41 cadets in the Class of 1861, the last class to graduate before the Civil War began. He chose the artillery so that he could stay in the East, where he had the best chance of meeting girls.

When the first Deep South states seceded, Ramseur did not wait for his native state to follow, rushing instead to Montgomery, Alabama, to join the Confederacy's forming army. However, he was soon elected to captain of the Ellis Light Artillery of Raleigh, North Carolina, and he hurried back to join his new unit in time to fire the opening salute—one hundred cannon blasts—on the lawn of the state capitol when the Tarheel State voted to leave the Union. In the spring of 1862, the 49th North Carolina Infantry regiment was mustered in near Ramseur's home. Ramseur, always ambitious, successfully pursued an appointment as its colonel, and he left his artillery battery to take command of the new regiment. After two months of drill—but before the worried Colonel Ramseur thought his men were ready—the regiment was summoned to Richmond to help drive McClellan's Union army away from the Confederate capital. The 49th saw its first heavy combat at Malvern Hill, the last of the Seven Days' Battles. Ramseur led his regiment forward in a futile charge into an artillery "fire the intensity of which is beyond description," he wrote, and was hit in the right arm above the elbow. Ramseur at first refused to leave his men, but was finally removed to a hospital.

His limb was so badly mangled and paralyzed he had to return home to heal. When Brig. Gen. George Anderson was mortally wounded at Sharpsburg in September General Lee sought out Ramseur to take his place on the basis of his performance at Malvern Hill and his superlative training of his artillery and infantry units. He was promoted to brigadier general on November 1. Rather suddenly, Ramseur found himself, at twenty-five, the youngest general in the Confederate army. While convalescing back in North Carolina, he met his future wife

Nellie, a small attractive brunette of similarly strong Presbyterian faith.

By January 1863, Ramseur felt well enough to return to Virginia and join his new brigade of four veteran North Carolina regiments. His right arm still hung in a sling and was giving him trouble. As one of his colonels later remembered, Ramseur "at once disarmed criticism by his high professional attainment and great amiability of character, inspiring his men, by his own enthusiastic nature, with those lofty martial qualities which distinguish the true Southern soldier." Indeed, the young general cut an inspiring figure, carrying his slim, slight frame with a martial bearing. He further attempted to disguise the boyishness of his face by growing a great, bristling black beard while shaving his hair to the scalp. He was a magnificent, graceful horseman, and the Richmond press called him the "Chevalier Bayard of the War." Though intensely ambitious, he hid his vanity from public view (only a single wartime photograph has been found). "He abhorred newspaper puffs, gotten up to make a false reputation for those not worthy of it," reported a friend. He was not indifferent to newspapers, though, and in letters home asked friends to clip all his notices. Ramseur remained profoundly devout to his faith during combat. Once, at a moment of battlefield crisis, Ramseur turned to his courier and in a sudden outburst shouted, "Damn it, tell them to send me a battery! I have sent for one a half a dozen times." He then stopped short, threw up both arms, looked upward and within earshot of his entire brigade said, "God Almighty, forgive me that oath."

At the Battle of Chancellorsville, Ramseur's Brigade participated in Stonewall Jackson's flank attack that crushed the Federal Eleventh Corps. Leading his brigade forward the next day against the advice of fearful fellow officers, Ramseur strode over the prostrate bodies of fellow Confederates who had lost the heart for attack. His command plunged into sheets of fire, running over Federal breastworks with a shout. However, the brigade soon ran short of ammunition and found itself exposed and alone in an advanced position. Ramseur's predicament finally galvanized the Stonewall Brigade to come to his support and consolidate the gains made by his men. One of Ramseur's colonels thought the general handled troops under fire with more ease than any officer he knew. Maj. Gen. J. E. B. Stuart, temporarily in command of Jackson's Corps, ordered cheers for Ramseur's North Carolinians when they emerged from the fighting, and declared that Ramseur deserved a major general's commission. Ramseur's Brigade lost more than half its men in the Chancellorsville fighting, the heaviest casualties of any Confederate brigade in the battle. The young general was painfully hobbled by a shell fragment that hit him in the shin on the evening of May 3. In return for this bravery and sacrifice, Ramseur won plaudits from numerous officers, including Lee, Jackson, Stuart, and A. P. Hill.

Together with Robert Rodes and a few others, Dodson Ramseur was one of the brightest lights in Lee's army as it approached the field at Gettysburg. Though still able to use only one arm, he was fully aware of the great expectations surrounding him, and was confident he could meet them. Maj. Gen. D. H. Hill stated that Ramseur "reveled in the fierce joys of strife," and that "his whole being seemed to kindle and glow amid the excitements of danger." His only distraction from his military duties was his constant struggle against the urge to return home to Nellie. "I must overcome these longings," he wrote. Duty, "stern and high, must reign supreme."

GETTYSBURG: Because his was the last brigade in the line of march, Ramseur was held in reserve when Rodes' Division moved onto Oak Hill about 1:00 p.m. on July 1. From there the Confederates could see and hear the battle raging between Lt. Gen. A P. Hill's Third Corps and the Federal First Corps, just west of town on McPherson's Ridge. The Oak Hill position was on the right flank of the Federals opposing Hill.

The division did not get off to a good start. The first two brigades to attack ahead

of Ramseur were Col. Edward O'Neal's and Brig. Gen. Alfred Iverson's. They went in separately against troops from Brig. Gen. John Robinson's division at the northern end of the Union line on Seminary Ridge; both were thrown back with heavy loss (especially Iverson's). Ramseur's turn was next.

By the time the conspicuous officer—he was the only officer mounted on that part of the field—pushed his North Carolinians forward about 3:00 p.m., Brig. Gen. Henry Baxter's disorganized Union brigade had left the field and had been replaced by Brig. Gen. Gabriel Paul's brigade, which was formed in a wide U-shaped defensive line with refused flanks. Ramseur's North Carolina regiments were aligned from right to left as follows: 14th, 30th, 2nd, 4th. The Mummasburg Road cut through the left-center of his brigade line as it advanced against the strong timber-covered position. With a shout Ramseur's right pair of regiments fell heavily against the front of Paul's line, while the left pair struck his right front and flank. The resistance was fierce for some time. Ramseur, whose horse was killed just a few yards from the enemy line, called for reinforcements, and at one point took effective control of both O'Neal's and Iverson's brigades (although so little was left of either that it made almost no difference).

Paul's brigade, which was in effect covering the retreat of the First Corps, was running low on ammunition. When the 2nd and 4th North Carolina regiments appeared in their right flank and rear, Paul's men had had enough and broke rearward. Ramseur reported that in the face of his onslaught, the Federals "ran off the field in confusion, leaving [their] killed and wounded and between 800 and 900 prisoners in our hands."

Ramseur pursued the routed enemy through the west side of town, but to the dismay of his men, Rodes ordered Ramseur to halt before he could assault the enemy rallying point on Cemetery Hill. The first day's fighting had come to a close, and Ramseur's men camped in the town along debris-strewn West Middle Street. Ramseur would fight no more at Gettysburg.

On July 2, Rodes' Division was selected to attack in conjunction with the rest of Ewell's Corps in concert with Lt. Gen. James Longstreet's First Corps assault against the opposite end of the Federal line. Maj. Gen. Edward Johnson's Division would attack first against Culp's Hill, followed by Maj. Gen. Jubal Early's Division, which would strike East Cemetery Hill, and Rodes' men, who would assail the same hill from the northwest. Longstreet's attack did not begin until about 4:00 p.m., and it was almost dark by the time Johnson moved against Culp's Hill, and Early moved out two of his brigades against East Cemetery Hill.

When Ramseur got the order to move his men out of town, he guided his brigade out to Long Lane, which ran southwest of Gettysburg. His brigade formed the far right of the first line of attack, which also included the brigades of Iverson and Doles. Daniel's men took up a line behind Ramseur, and O'Neal's men aligned themselves on Daniel's left. It was here they learned they were to attack Cemetery Hill, and would do so at the point of the bayonet. Since great confusion was anticipated, they were to use the phrase "North Carolina to the rescue!" to distinguish friend from foe. The maneuver had been so time-consuming, however, that it was dark before all the brigades were in position.

By then, Early's temporarily successful assault was over. When the three brigades of Doles, Iverson and Ramseur crept forward in the darkness and ran into enemy skirmishers, Ramseur—under whose authority Rodes had placed the attack—stopped and discussed the situation with Doles and Iverson. The generals decided that the enemy defenses were too strong, the circumstances inauspicious, and halted their troops. Ramseur explained the situation to Rodes, who recalled them, and the attack was not made. The men retraced their steps to Long Lane, where they spent that night and all of July 3, and were never seriously engaged again.

After the battle, Ramseur was remembered for the glory of the first day's triumph. One of three brigadiers commended by Rodes in his report (the other pair were Doles and Daniel), Ramseur's career was still on the rise. He left the army to be married in the fall, but the next June, after the Battles of the Wilderness and Spotsylvania, Ramseur was promoted to major general and put in command of Maj. Gen. Jubal Early's former division. It was while serving in this capacity that he was shot through both lungs and mortally wounded at the Battle of Cedar Creek in October 1864.

For further reading:

Allen, T. Harrell. *Bryan Grimes of North Carolina: A Fighting General to the Last.* Campbell, 1998.

Cox, William R. "Major General Stephen D. Ramseur: His Life and Character." *Southern Historical Society Papers*, vol. 18, 1990.

Gallagher, Gary "One of the Best of Lee's Young Generals: Stephen Dodson Ramseur at Chancellorsville." *Civil War Quarterly*, 6, 1986.

——. *Stephen Dodson Ramseur: Lee's Gallant General.* Chapel Hill, 1985.

Griffin, D. Massy. "Rodes on Oak Hill: A Study of Rodes' Division on the First Day of Gettysburg." *Gettysburg Magazine*, #4, 1991.

Taylor, Michael W. "Ramseur's Brigade in the Gettysburg Campaign: A Newly Discovered Account." *Gettysburg Magazine*, #17, 1997.

DANIELS'S BRIGADE:
(2,048 MEN)

BRIGADIER GENERAL
JUNIUS DANIEL

Daniel was from the tidewater city of Halifax, North Carolina, the son of a prominent state congressman and attorney general. He was a professional soldier, trained at West Point, Class of 1851, after which he spent seven years as a Regular Army infantry officer. In 1858 he left the army to manage one of his father's plantations in Shreveport, Louisiana. When the

South seceded, Daniel entered the Confederate army as the colonel of the 14th North Carolina, but soon transferred to command of the 45th North Carolina after a reorganization in the middle of April 1862. His rise was a quick one, and by the time of the Seven Days' Battles, Daniel was leading a brigade. His only combat experience there, however, was enduring a long-distance shelling at Malvern Hill, where his brigade lost 24 men. After the Peninsula battles he was detached from the Army of Northern Virginia for less exciting duty guarding Drewry's Bluff on the James River below Richmond. During the winter of 1862-3, he and his brigade served uneventfully in North Carolina.

General Lee brought up three brigades from the North Carolina theater for the movement north into Pennsylvania, and one of them was Daniel's. As the brigade marched into Carlisle, Pennsylvania, one of Daniel's regiments, the 32nd North Carolina had the honor of unfurling for the first time the official battle flag of the Confederate States, the red flag with its cross of blue spangled with white stars, which would become the most familiar Confederate banner. A group of Richmond ladies had sewn one of the new banners shortly after the Confederate Congress adopted this design, and the banner was sent to General Lee for his approval and for presentation to the regiment he judged most worthy to carry it. Lee, in honor of the deceased Jackson,

deferred this privilege to Lt. Gen. Richard Ewell, who commanding Jackson's old corps. Ewell, according to Brig. Gen. Isaac Trimble, passed it on to "his favorite division commander," Robert Rodes, who in turn sent the emblem to General Daniel, whom Rodes considered as "his most favored brigadier." This decision may have been a political gesture of good will, for Daniel was the newest brigadier in Rodes' Division.

General Daniel had a remarkably deep, stentorian voice that one listener said was "audible a quarter of a mile or more away." He combined this unique gift with an imposing presence, being about five feet ten inches tall and weighing 200 pounds. At the age of thirty-five, Daniel, according to an observer, had "the essential qualities of a true soldier and successful officer, brave, vigilant, and honest. . .gifted as an organizer and disciplinarian, skilled in handling troops." This opinion was shared by many, and it was this excellent reputation that Daniel brought to the Army of Northern Virginia as it headed northward for Pennsylvania in the summer of 1863. Never before, however, had he led a brigade in a large battle like the one that awaited him at Gettysburg.

GETTYSBURG: About 1:00 p.m. on July 1, Junius Daniel formed his regiments about 200 yards behind Brig. Gen. Alfred Iverson's Brigade on Oak Hill. Rodes' Division was advantageously situated on high wooded ground northwest of town, and Oak Hill commanded the right flank of the Federal First Corps, then battling with A. P. Hill's Confederates west of Gettysburg on McPherson's Ridge. Daniel's orders were to support Iverson's men as they advanced. He moved his men moved forward, keeping to the right and rear of Iverson, who unexpectedly veered his men to the left toward a low stone wall—where they were slaughtered by the hundreds. When Iverson asked for assistance, Daniel dispatched three-fifths of his brigade (the 32nd, 43rd, and 53rd regiments) to the left, while his two remaining regiments, the 2nd Battalion and 45th, continued southeast toward the unfinished railroad cut where other Confederates from the Third Corps had come to grief earlier that morning (the remnants of that earlier attack, from Brig. Gen. Joseph Davis' Brigade, refused to assist Daniel despite his request).

Daniel's pair of Tarheel regiments, in what was the first of three distinct efforts, struck the middle of the First Corps line on Seminary Ridge at an oblique, with the 45th North Carolina striking as far south as the Railroad Cut. The Southerners encountered what one officer called "the most destructive fire ever witnessed," before they were turned away with serious losses by determined regiments from Col. Roy Stone's Federal brigade. Other Federal regiments in a wood in front of Daniel contributed their lead to the attack as well.

Daniel's powerful presence and booming voice enabled him to rally his brigade almost single-handedly. He ordered his disordered line to halt and reform on him, and they did so almost to a man. His men attacked once more, this time with the assistance of the other three regiments, but the 2nd Battalion and 45th regiment bore the brunt of the enemy's wrath a second time. The attack ground to a halt and the Confederates traded volleys with the enemy less than 100 feet away. Another advance and a desperate fight around the Railroad Cut ensued before Daniel's men were forced back a second time.

By this time Maj. Gen. Jubal Early's Division had arrived on the left of Rodes' Division and was beginning to drive the Eleventh Corps rearward. Brig. Gen. Stephen Ramseur's Brigade was launched forward on Daniel's left against Brig. Gen. Gabriel Paul's Federals, and Maj. Gen. Dorsey Pender's Division, Hill's Third Corps, had come up and was ready to attack on Daniel's right. When Daniel advanced a third time, throwing the 32nd North Carolina across the Railroad Cut to link with Pender's men, the whole line swept forward and Federal resistance buckled, then broke. Daniel's men surged forward in pursuit of the Federals streaming back through Gettysburg, capturing prisoners and participating in one of the most spectacular days of the war for the South.

As he went into camp that evening near the Lutheran Seminary, Daniel could count 750 casualties—more than a third of the brigade was lying on the bloody field.

On July 2, Daniel was ordered to take part in Rodes' attack on the northwest face of Cemetery Hill. This movement had been designed to coincide with Longstreet's assailment of the Union left flank near the Round Tops, and Maj. Gen. Edward Johnson's attack on Culp's Hill. It was also to be timed with Early's thrust up East Cemetery Hill. It was nearly dark, however, when Daniel's North Carolinians, again posted on the right of their division's second battle line, moved from the Lutheran Seminary forward to the division's jump-off position in the Long Lane southwest of the town. The lines moved forward some distance but were halted while Brig. Gen. Dodson Ramseur, under whose authority the attacking column had been effectively placed, debated the merits of continuing. By this time Early's assault had been beaten back and it was too late to assist him. Daniel and his men fell back to Long Lane.

That night, Daniel received orders to march his men through town to Culp's Hill, where Johnson's Southern division had made a lodgement. After a long and difficult march, Daniel's exhausted infantry was moved into position about 4:00 a.m. in support of the right of Johnson's line, which had been stopped cold by Brig. Gen. George Greene's dug-in New Yorkers. When Daniel saw the formidable Northern defenses, he became very pessimistic about their chances. The position "could not have been carried by any force," he later wrote. The dutiful brigadier took part in the assault launched on the morning of July 3. Later in the morning, Daniel was shifted to the left to take possession of the enemy works that Brig. Gen. George Steuart's Confederates had found abandoned the night before. Confused fighting followed for the next few hours. Daniel's men made several brave rushes toward the Union lines, but the unfavorable results Daniel had predicted prevailed, and the Confederates tumbled back to the bottom of the hill. The battle for Culp's Hill was over before noon, and Daniel's weary troops saw no more combat at Gettysburg. The Second Corps was withdrawn to the ridges west of town that night.

Daniel won glowing praise from Rodes after the battle: "The conduct of General Daniel and his brigade in this most desperate engagement elicited the admiration and praise of all who witnessed it," he wrote. Daniel had certainly proved his mettle with the Army of Northern Virginia.

Though he left the army with hepatitis later that month, Daniel was back by September, and he led his brigade through the fall campaigns. He was shot through the abdomen while trying to recapture the trench lines inside the Bloody Angle (the "Mule-Shoe") at Spotsylvania on May 12, 1864, and died the next day.

For further reading:

Freeman, Douglas S. *Lee's Lieutenants: A Study in Command.* vol. 3. New York, 1944.

Pfanz, Harry W. *Gettysburg: Culp's Hill and Cemetery Hill.* Chapel Hill. 1993.

IVERSON'S BRIGADE:
(1,380 MEN)

BRIGADIER GENERAL
ALFRED IVERSON, JR.

Alfred Iverson, Sr., had paved the path for his son. The elder Iverson was a former Senator from Georgia, one of the earliest and most fiery advocates of secession—and a close friend of former Senator Jefferson Davis. Senator Iverson decided on a military career for his son, and began by sending young Alfred to school at the military institute at Muskegee, Alabama. When Alfred was seventeen, the Mexican War began. The Senator raised and equipped a Georgia volunteer regiment, took his son out of school, and commissioned the teenager to serve in the conflict as a 2nd lieutenant.

With his pedigree and Mexican War experience, young Iverson was commissioned

directly into the U.S. Army as a 1st lieutenant of cavalry in 1855 and served in "Bloody Kansas" in the late 1850s. When the South seceded in 1861, Alfred, now thirty-two years old, resigned from the U. S. Army and received a commission from his father's old friend, President Davis, as colonel of the 20th North Carolina. Iverson's 20th was stationed in North Carolina until it was called to the Peninsula in June 1862. During the Battle of Gaines' Mill, his first fight, Iverson demonstrated promise as an officer. Division commander Maj. Gen. D. H. Hill sent five regiments to storm a troublesome enemy battery, but only Iverson reached the guns. His capture of the annoying pieces allowed the rest of the Hill's Division to move forward, although Iverson himself was seriously wounded early in the charge, and his regiment suffered 272 casualties.

The promising young Georgian recovered in time to lead his regiment at South Mountain in September, where the entire brigade skedaddled after its commander, Brig. Gen. Samuel Garland, went down with a mortal wound. Three days later at the Battle of Sharpsburg, the shaky brigade broke and ran again, though Iverson rallied his regiment later in the day. None of this was to Iverson's credit, though it did not slow his rise through the ranks.

The brigade's poor performance while under the reins of a temporary commander

at Sharpsburg prompted General Lee to look about for a more suitable leader. It may have been as a result of pressure from patrons in high places that Alfred Iverson was promoted to brigadier general, and placed in command of the brigade in the army reorganization of November 1862. Iverson was in command of the brigade for the first time at the Battle of Fredericksburg, but there the brigade was held in reserve and the new brigadier was not put to the test.

Iverson's relationship with the 20th North Carolina had always been rocky. The field officers of the regiment had never liked Iverson much, and Iverson reciprocated the feeling. When he was promoted to brigade command, Iverson tried to import a friend from outside the regiment to take his place as colonel of the 20th. Outraged, twenty-six field officers of the regiment signed a petition protesting the move. When Iverson refused to forward the petition, the aggrieved officers disregarded the proper channels and sent it over his head to army headquarters. On December 27 Iverson retaliated by placing the officers under arrest, though they eventually remained in their positions. Iverson's friend was not placed as the new colonel, but Iverson continued to fuel the feud all winter by rejecting all subsequent appointees to the post. There was a certain vindictive streak running through the Senator's son.

Iverson's problems were not limited to his relationship with subordinates. In February 1863, he insisted that Lt. Gen. Thomas "Stonewall" Jackson grant his request for furlough under threat of resignation. Jackson promptly replied that while it would be unfortunate for Iverson to resign, he would rather Iverson leave the army than approve a furlough when a battle might be fought at any time. Iverson's bluff had been called, and he stayed put.

At Chancellorsville, Iverson's Brigade was posted on the far left of the first line of Jackson's monumental flank attack against the Federal Eleventh Corps. Driving the fleeing Federals before him, Iverson led his brigade with some competence and lost 470 men fighting in the baffling woodland of the Wilderness. Yet, it was fellow brigadiers George Doles and Stephen Ramseur who won favorable notice. Iverson worsened the ill feelings between him and his men when he went to the rear to get support for his left flank during the fighting and his officers concluded he was shirking.

Iverson's mediocre performance with the Army of Northern Virginia up through the spring of 1863 had been full of turmoil. Whispered rumors that his advancement had been the result of family influence remained unabated among the troops in his command as Lee's army marched into Pennsylvania. His men hated him, and the rancor seething within Iverson's regiments was a recipe for disaster.

GETTYSBURG: On July 1 at Gettysburg, the Senator's son showed clearly that he was unequal to the job of leading a brigade. Iverson's men led the march of Maj. Gen. Robert Rodes' Division onto the crest of Oak Hill about 1:00 p.m. Seeing the opportunity offered by having arrived squarely on the flank of the Union First Corps on Seminary Ridge, which was engaged with the Confederate Third Corps, Rodes quickly assembled his first three brigades into a battle line. Iverson's troops were deployed on the right with his own right near the Mummasburg Road, while Col. Edward O'Neal's Brigade extended the line to the left, and George Doles' Brigade continued it in that direction; the brigades of Junius Daniel and Dodson Ramseur were formed behind in reserve. Unsure about exactly when to advance, Iverson did not coordinate his movement with the more impetuous Colonel O'Neal, and Rodes exercised little guidance in the matter. O'Neal attacked first and quickly suffered a bloody repulse.

Iverson's North Carolina regiments were aligned, from left to right, as follows: 5th, 20th, 23rd, and 12th. His orders were to strike the left flank of Brig. Gen. Henry Baxter's Federal brigade, which had been facing generally north and had just repulsed O'Neal. His flank, it was believed, was ripe for an attack, as it did not connect with Cutler's brigade on Baxter's left. By the time Iverson started forward around

2:30 p.m., things went awry at once. His first sin was that he did not accompany his brigade during its advance—an unpardonable act for a brigadier in Lee's or any other army. Telling his infantry to "Give them hell," Iverson ordered his men to advance while he stayed in the rear. Worse, Iverson ordered his men forward without having previously reconnoitered the ground ahead or putting out skirmishers. "Unwarned, unled as a brigade, went forward Iverson's deserted band to its doom," wrote one North Carolina scribe. As Iverson advanced, Junius Daniel's large brigade followed in his right rear.

Without warning to Daniel or anyone else, Iverson's advance veered left toward what appeared to be an unmanned stone wall running very roughly perpendicular to the Mummasburg Road. The Federals had seen the threat in time for Baxter to change front to left. When Iverson's regiments, in perfect lines advanced at an oblique to within less than 100 yards of the wall, Baxter's men rose up as one and ambushed the surprised Confederates, pouring a deadly fire at point blank range into scores of young men from North Carolina. Many of the dead of Iverson's Brigade fell in a straight line, as if on dress parade; Baxter's tactic resulted in perhaps the most intense and one-sided ten second slaughter of the war. Those still alive stood on perfectly open terrain. Realizing their horrible predicament, they fell into a shallow dip in the ground for whatever meager protection it offered. Although the men attempted to return fire, the position was such that it was nearly impossible to do so effectively; retreat was virtually impossible. When someone raised a small white cloth in an attempt to stop the firing, Iverson, according to one historian, "went to pieces and became unfit for further command." He even went so far as to tell Rodes that some of his men were cowards and had surrendered. In fact, they were brave veterans and a large percentage of them were dead because of Iverson's incompetence. A sharp counterattack by some of Baxter's men netted several flags and more than 300 prisoners. Within minutes, Iverson's Brigade lost

458 killed and wounded (in addition to the captured).

One of Iverson's captains rallied some of the men and led them until the Federals had been chased through Gettysburg. "Arriving in the town and having but very few troops left," Iverson later wrote, "I informed General Ramseur that I would attach them to his brigade, and act in concert with him." For the rest of the battle, Iverson led his fragments under Ramseur, more as a colonel than a brigadier. The men formed for the night on West Middle Street in Gettysburg.

On July 2, it was decided that Rodes' Division would attack in conjunction with the rest of Ewell's Corps, in concert with Lt. Gen. James Longstreet's First Corps assault against the opposite end of the Federal line. While Maj. Gen. Edward Johnson's Division attacked Culp's Hill, Maj. Gen. Jubal Early's Division would pummel East Cemetery Hill, and Rodes' men would assail the same hill from the northwest. Longstreet's attack began about 4:00 p.m., but it was almost dark by the time Johnson moved against Culp's Hill and Early moved out a pair of his brigades against East Cemetery Hill. Iverson was aware the something was happening, but no one chose to inform him. "I had received no instructions," he explained, "and perceiving that General Ramseur was acquainted with intentions of the major-general [Rodes]," cooperated with him.

Iverson moved in conjunction with Ramseur's men out of town and deployed along Long Lane, which ran southwest out of town. His men—they could not have numbered more than a good-sized regiment—were placed between Ramseur and Doles in the front line of attack (an odd alignment, given what they had just experienced). Rodes had moved his division too late to help Early's men, however, and by the time they advanced, it was dark and the fighting on East Cemetery Hill was all but over. Enemy skirmishers began firing on them and Ramseur halted the line to discuss the situation with Doles and Iverson. "I perceived as I believe everyone did," explained Iverson, "that we were advancing to certain destruction." The attack was called off and Iverson's handful of survivors spend the rest of July 2 and all of July 3 in Long Lane.

It was an especially long retreat for the North Carolinians of Iverson's Brigade. Regaining his composure, Iverson performed well during the withdrawal. In a delicious twist of irony, he found the enemy fighting Southern cavalry at Hagerstown, Maryland, where he then proceeded to "fixed an ambuscade, and I believe killed, wounded, and captured as many of the enemy as I had men."

Some of the officers and men refused to serve with Iverson after Gettysburg. One colonel, dying from a mortal wound, told some his men he would make sure that "the imbecile Iverson" would never lead them into battle again. General Lee agreed. When the army retreated across the Potomac, Iverson was given the post of temporary provost marshal—a polite way of removing him from field command. In late July, he was transferred for a short time to another brigade, but in October Lee removed him from the army and ordered him back to Georgia to organize cavalry.

Iverson marginally redeemed himself by leading a cavalry brigade during the Atlanta Campaign, during which he captured General Stoneman and about 500 Federal troopers at Sunshine Church. He surrendered his own command when he learned of Lee's capitulation. After the war he engaged in business in Florida, where he grew oranges. He died in Atlanta in 1911.

For further reading:

Derry, Joseph T. "Georgia," vol. 6 of *Confederate Military History*. ed. by Clement A. Evans. Atlanta, 1899. [vol. 7 of the extended edition, Wilmington, 1987.]

Freeman, Douglas S. *Lee's Lieutenants: A Study in Command*. vol. 3. New York, 1944.

Krick, Robert K. "Failures of Brigade Leadership." in Gary Gallagher, ed., *The First Day at Gettysburg*. Kent, 1992.

Pfanz, Harry W. *Gettysburg: Culp's Hill and Cemetery Hill*. Chapel Hill. 1993.

O'NEAL'S BRIGADE:
(1,685 MEN)

COLONEL
EDWARD ASBURY O'NEAL

Edward O'Neal had absolutely no military experience before the war, and as such was a rarity among the officers in Robert E. Lee's army. Raised by his widowed mother, he had lived his whole life in Northern Alabama. Trained as a lawyer, he was defeated for Congress in 1848, but became one of the state's leading secessionist politicians. When the South seceded, he entered the Confederate army as captain of an Alabama company called the "Calhoun Guards." Before he saw his first combat a year later on the Peninsula, he had been promoted to colonel of the 26th Alabama.

O'Neal battled Maj. Gen. George McClellan's Federals on the Peninsula with a fearlessness and disregard for his own safety. He was wounded by a shell fragment during Brig. Gen. Robert Rodes' Brigade's costly charge at Seven Pines, but returned to action for the Seven Days' Battles. Rodes cited his bravery after Gaines' Mill, and acting brigade commander Col. John B. Gordon recognized his "gallant conduct" at Malvern Hill. At South Mountain in September 1862, O'Neal was again wounded at the head of his regiment, this time in the thigh. Furloughed home to Alabama to recover, he reported back that winter. In January 1863, when division leader Maj. Gen. D. H. Hill transferred to North Carolina and Rodes took his place, O'Neal, as senior colonel, took Rodes' position at the head of the brigade. Rodes was not in favor of O'Neal's elevation, but O'Neal was nevertheless still in command at the Battle of Chancellorsville, where his brigade was clumsily handled. After hours of preparation, he miscued when Lt. Gen. Thomas "Stonewall" Jackson gave the go-ahead to commence his corps' famous flank attack, and he forgot to start the skirmishers forward ahead of his brigade. The main line overtook them within the first couple of minutes, and the whole attack came to an abrupt halt while O'Neal stopped to allowed the skirmishers to move ahead. The next day O'Neal was wounded a third time, struck by what he called "the fuse of a shell," which disabled him for a day.

O'Neal's ability to command was called into question at Chancellorsville, but by this time Lee was running out of able brigadiers, and he was forced to leave O'Neal at the head of Rodes' old brigade despite Rodes' vocal disapproval of the arrangement. Lee, in fact, recommended O'Neal for promotion to brigadier general and permanent command of the brigade, and the commission was issued and forwarded to Army of Northern Virginia headquarters bearing the date June 6, 1863. Lee, however, kept the commission in his pocket for the time being, evidently unsure of O'Neal's ability. Thus O'Neal fought as a colonel during the Gettysburg Campaign.

GETTYSBURG: The test of O'Neal's competence came on July 1, the first day of fighting at Gettysburg. When Rodes hurriedly deployed his division on Oak Hill to strike the northern flank of the Union First Corps shortly after noon, O'Neal's Brigade was in the middle of the front line, with Brig. Gen. George Doles on his left and Brig. Gen. Alfred Iverson on his right. About 2:00 p.m., when Rodes was ready to order the advance against the Union line, O'Neal was forced to admit that neither he

nor his staff officers had any horses at hand nor any mounted couriers with them to take orders to the regiments. After the brigade was finally ordered forward, O'Neal failed to start two of his five regiments, leaving only three to press the attack. These three were deployed to advance with the 6th on the left, 26th in the center, and 12th on the right. The 5th Alabama had been held behind O'Neal's left to keep a connection between O'Neal and the right flank of Brig. Gen. George Doles' Brigade, while the 3rd Alabama ended up with Brig. Gen. Junius Daniel's Brigade. "Why my brigade was thus deprived of two regiments, I have never been informed," O'Neal pathetically stated in his report.

Other problems crept up and bit Rodes' acting brigadier. With only a segment of his brigade in hand, he misunderstood the objective of his attack and started his brigade in the wrong direction. Poor coordination with Iverson's Brigade meant O'Neal's infantry lurched ahead alone. Worst of all, O'Neal did not go forward with his advancing regiments—an unforgivable error for a brigadier. When he finally entered the action, he did so on foot, which made it extremely difficult for him to communicate with his regimental officers. As the advance drew within 200 yards of the enemy, volleys began to crackle from Brig. Gen. Henry Baxter's regiments, and the 45th New York of Alexander Schimmelfennig's brigade (Eleventh Corps) wheeled left and smacked O'Neal's exposed flank, which was also struck with artillery fire. Robert Rodes' first attack of the afternoon unraveled within minutes. "The whole Brigade. . .was repulsed quickly, and with loss," a disgusted Rodes reported afterward.

Later that afternoon, when Brig. Gen. Stephen Ramseur started his brigade forward, O'Neal joined in the advance and assisted in finally driving the right flank of the First Corps off the ridge and pell-mell through the town. After moving through Gettysburg, O'Neal, perhaps seeking to redeem himself in the eyes of his division commander, argued for an immediate attack on Cemetery Hill. O'Neal purportedly became enraged when Rodes called a halt to the onslaught and tried to get Brig. Gen. George Doles to take charge of the division and lead it up the hill. Fortunately for both of them, Doles ignored O'Neal's mutinous suggestion. O'Neal's Alabamians slept that night in the railroad bed just west of town.

July 2 was a relatively quiet day for the entire division. O'Neal took part in Rodes' twilight deployment southwest of town in preparation for an attack on the northwest slope of Cemetery Hill in conjunction with Maj. Gen. Jubal Early's thrust up East Cemetery Hill. After dark, the division advanced about halfway to the hill, at which time it was discovered that Rodes' deployment was too late and Early's attack had already come to grief. An anxious conference of brigadiers ensued, and General Ramseur (under whose authority the attack had been placed) decided to abort the effort, and the division returned to its starting place.

O'Neal's men were destined to get little rest that night. About 2:00 a.m. on July 3, they were detached with Daniel's Brigade and marched to Culp's Hill to add weight to Maj. Gen. Edward Johnson's planned morning assault, where Johnson's veterans had effected a lodgment in the Union lines the previous evening. O'Neal arrived about 4:00 a.m. and deployed in the center of Johnson's front in reserve behind Nicholls' Louisiana Brigade. The battle started raging just thirty minutes after O'Neal arrived, and when the Louisianians were spent, O'Neal's men were ordered forward about 8:00 a.m. "The attack was made with great spirit," he wrote later, "under a terrific fire of grape and small arms." After a short advance to what O'Neal claimed was a "hill near the enemy's works," which he described as a "log fort," the Alabamians "held it for three hours, exposed to a murderous fire." The defenders belonged to Brig. Gen. George Greene's New York brigade, and O'Neal gained nothing but losses. The attack was called off before noon and the hill was conceded to the Federals. The brigade was pulled back that night to the ridges west of town along with the rest of the corps, and O'Neal's trying experiences at Gettysburg drew to a close.

Edward O'Neal's name was conspicuously absent from the list of brigadiers commended in Rodes' report of the battle. Influenced by O'Neal's spectacular show of incompetence on July 1, Lee discarded O'Neal's brigadier general's commission. Later that month he replaced him at the head of the Alabama Brigade with a junior colonel, Cullen Battle, and O'Neal returned to the 26th Alabama for the fall campaign. His regiment was detached from the army to the Western Theater in early 1864, and he finished the war chasing deserters in Northern Alabama.

O'Neal resumed his law practice and reentered politics, winning two terms as governor of Alabama in 1882 and 1884. He died in 1890.

For further reading:

Wheeler, Joseph. "Alabama," vol. 7 of *Confederate Military History*. Ed. by Clement A. Evans. Atlanta, 1899. [vol. 8 of the extended edition, Wilmington, 1987.]

Freeman, Douglas S. *Lee's Lieutenants: A Study in Command*. vol. 3. New York, 1944.

Griffin, D. Massy. "Rodes on Oak Hill: A Study of Rodes' Division on the First Day of Gettysburg." *Gettysburg Magazine*, #4, 1991.

Krick, Robert K. "Failures of Brigade Leadership." in Gary Gallagher, ed., *The First Day at Gettysburg*. Kent, 1992.

THIRD ARMY CORPS:

21,882 MEN / 84 GUNS

LIEUTENANT GENERAL
AMBROSE POWELL HILL

A. P. Hill was inconsistent and enigmatic throughout his career with the Army of Northern Virginia. At times he could perform what Lt. Gen. James Longstreet called "prodigies," but at other moments Hill's combat behavior was disappointing and lackluster. At thirty-seven, he was the youngest of the corps chiefs, thin-faced and pale, with a chiseled nose, deep-set eyes, and high cheekbones jutting above a full auburn beard; a look perfectly in tune with the romantic times.

To these natural gifts he added grace and an instinctive sense of style. He wore his flowing hair parted on the left side and brushed straight back over his ears, long in the back. (Longstreet joked that there was "a good deal of 'curled darling'" about Hill.) He dress was picturesque, particularly when he donned his red wool hunting shirt when fighting was in the offing. Wearing such a garment within sight of the enemy implied swagger and a combative attitude; Hill called it his "battle shirt," and when the word was passed down "Little Powell's got on his battle shirt!," they would begin to check their weapons.

Hill was narrow-chested and frail, and his fragile health was the result of complications from the advanced stages of gonorrhea, which he had contracted as a cadet at West Point. Always emotional, he was so high-strung before battle that he had an increasing tendency to become unwell when the fighting was about to commence. With the rank and file he could be extraordinarily affectionate and was always concerned with their welfare. He maintained, however, a strict formality with his subordinate officers, regarding it as an important part of discipline. Though backslapping or embracing a comrade was against his nature, his warm manner and his thoughtfulness made him popular among his junior officers and staff. One officer even called him "the most lovable of all Lee's generals." His expression was described as "grave but gentle," and "his manner so courteous as almost to lack decision."

Hill, however, rarely seemed to want for decision. Indeed, he was often heedless and impetuous. His policy could was often to pitch headlong into whatever lay in his path, with little regard for its strength or position. So far in the war, though, his impulsiveness and fast marching had benefited the Confederacy, and Hill had provided the winning punch in battle after battle since the Peninsula.

His career began inauspiciously at Mechanicsville, where his impatient attack opened Lee's Seven Days offensive but incurred heavy losses. At Cedar Mountain, his quick march and rapid deployment on the field saved Stonewall Jackson from suffering a sharp defeat, and at Sharpsburg, his late-afternoon attack after a grueling 17-mile march from Harpers Ferry saved the entire army from a ruinous and potentially fatal setback. Lee's reference to him in his official Sharpsburg report, "And then A. P. Hill came up," had become a byword in the army. Hill and his "Light Division" had become the embodiment of the Confederate army's offensive spirit. It is reported that both Jackson and Lee called for Hill in their dying delirium. Hill's association with these tales, whether true or not, indicates the mythic stature he achieved during his tenure with the Confederacy.

The Federals were awed as well. By the Gettysburg Campaign, they had the impression that whenever they were being pushed especially hard, they were probably fighting A. P. Hill—and a legend based on fact was developed to account for his fury. Before the conflict, Hill had asked for the hand of the beautiful Ellen Marcy. She was willing, but, her father, a Regular Army officer, disapproved, as Hill was a mere lieutenant of modest means, a Southerner on top of that, and Marcy had higher aims for his daughter. Ellen obeyed her papa, and his judgment was soon rewarded when a wealthy, up-and-coming railroad president asked her to marry. This time, Ellen accepted. The new husband was George McClellan, and within a year he was a major general commanding the Army of the Potomac, with Ellen's father along as his chief of staff. The Federal soldiers, therefore, believed Hill's ruthless charges were a means of carrying out his grudge against Marcy and his Yankee son-in-law. Hence, it was reported that one morning, when musket fire crackled out of the stillness and Hill's Light Division came swarming into view with a fiendish Rebel yell, a harried Federal veteran wailed, "God's sake, Nelly—why didn't you marry him?" (Unfortunately for the legend, Hill had married the beautiful sister of Kentucky raider John Hunt Morgan, a woman so devoted to her husband it sometimes took a direct order from Lee to remove her from the lines before a battle.)

While Hill was gentle with those under his command; his attitude with superiors was notoriously prickly. It began after the Peninsula Campaign, when a columnist in the Richmond Examiner glorified Hill's performance at the expense of other commanders. Many of the ignored officers became angry and jealous; particularly Longstreet, Hill's immediate superior. A quarrel ensued between the two, and Longstreet placed Hill under arrest, and the two men were soon on the verge of a duel. Lee solved the crisis by detaching Hill's Division to join Stonewall Jackson's corps, which was then facing Maj. Gen. John Pope's Union army. However, Hill got along no better with Jackson, who soon had him under arrest for disregarding marching procedures. Although circumstances quickly forced Jackson to restore Hill to duty, Hill took umbrage at the incident and sought vindication through a courts-martial until Jackson's death. Neither Jackson nor Longstreet could bring themselves to make more than a cursory mention of the rebellious Hill in their battle reports, no matter what feats his hard-fighting Light Division performed.

Perhaps the fact that he was the son of a Culpeper, Virginia, merchant and not from the landed aristocracy of the South made Hill so pugnacious about his rights and his honor. He graduated from West Point in 1847, 15th in a class of 38. His fourteen years of pre-war service were of the standard Regular Army pattern. He served with the 1st Artillery in Mexico and against the Seminoles, and after 1855, in the Washington, D.C. office of the U.S. Coast Survey. When he entered Confederate service in March 1861, he was made colonel of the Shenandoah Valley's 13th Virginia regiment, with which he won notice in western Virginia in June. Already marked for advancement, Hill was in reserve at First Manassas in July. Promoted to brigadier general in February 1862, his ability attracted further attention during the early Peninsula actions at Yorktown and Williamsburg. Longstreet applauded his brigade's behavior in the latter action as "perfect throughout the battle, and it was marched off the field in as good order as it entered it." He fought so well that he was promoted to major general on May 26 and given a division in time for the Seven Days. Though he was the lone unproven division commander when Lee took charge of the army in June, Hill quickly demonstrated ability at his new level. One of Lee's staff reported: "[Hill's] defenses are as well advanced as those of any part of the line. His troops are in fine condition. . .Hill is every inch a soldier and is destined to make his mark." He named his division, which he led with such impetuosity, the "The Light Division," presumably for its speed in executing maneuvers. With it, he was the first into action at Mechanicsville and Gaines' Mill on two successive days.

After his distinction in the Seven Days and his transfer to join Stonewall Jackson in Northern Virginia, Hill and the Light Division fought well at Cedar Mountain, where they were held in reserve but plunged into the battle on Hill's own initiative. But at Second Manassas, Hill stumbled. Although his men fought well in defense along the Railroad Cut, Hill's front crumbled when he failed to close a gap between two of his brigades, and Maj. Gen. Jubal Early's Division had to come to his rescue. Hill redeemed himself in the Maryland Campaign, where much of the burden of maneuver in capturing Harpers Ferry was given to his Light Division. After the Union surrender there, Hill's men were left behind to inventory the booty and parole prisoners. When the battle was joined at Sharpsburg on September 17, he marched from Harpers Ferry to Sharpsburg in just nine hours (it had taken Maj. Gen. Lafayette McLaws' men forty-one to make the same trek) and attacked immediately upon arriving, saving the day and the army. With that exploit, the Light Division and its leader passed into Confederate legend. In his letter to President Davis on October 2, after recommending Jackson and Longstreet for promotion, Lee wrote, "Next to these two officers, I consider A. P. Hill the best commander with me. He fights his troops well and takes good care of them."

At Fredericksburg in December there was a reprise of the situation that had developed along the Railroad Cut at Second Manassas. Hill again left a gap between two of his brigades in what he thought was an impenetrable marshy patch of woods. An attacking Union division found the gap, pried it open, and threatened to break the Confederate line. Early's Division again came to the rescue, counterattacking, driving the Federals back, and restoring line. Hill's poor deployment resulted in the only tense moment Lee's army experienced all day, and Hill's responsibility for the gap was noted in Jackson's battle report. Hill's rising and ebbing fortunes rose once again at Chancellorsville. His division marched with Jackson on his famed maneuver around the Union right flank and his men fought well during the ensuing assault. After the Union wing had been crushed and Jackson wounded in the gathering darkness, Hill briefly took command of the corps but was himself wounded minutes later by a bit of metal which lacerated his calves. Unable to walk or ride a horse, he was forced to relinquish command for three days.

After unequal fortune in the previous ten months (potent to the point of rashness in attack but careless in defense), Hill was among the half-dozen candidates for command of Jackson's corps after Jackson succumbed in May. "I think upon the whole," Lee wrote in a letter to Jefferson Davis, that Hill "is the best soldier of his grade with me." Though Lee finally decided to place Maj. Gen. Richard Ewell at the head of Jackson's old corps, the day after he named Ewell to command the Second Corps he announced the formation of another corps-sized organization, the Third Corps, under the direction of Hill. The prickly merchant's son, so full of petty rebellions when placed under anyone less than Lee himself, was finally a lieutenant general at the head of his own corps.

Hill's appointment to corps command sparked considerable negative reaction. Many, Longstreet in particular, thought that Hill had been chosen primarily because he was a Virginian. The rejected candidates—Maj. Gens. John Hood, D. H. Hill, Lafayette McLaws, and R. H. Anderson—were all from states other than the Old Dominion. Thus, Hill had plenty to prove as he approached Gettysburg in an unaccustomed role and unfamiliar with many of his subordinates. It did not bode well that as rifles crackled on the army's approach to the crossroads town, Hill started to suffer from an unidentifiable illness.

GETTYSBURG: Hill precipitated the Battle of Gettysburg on June 30 when he discounted Brig. Gen. Johnston Pettigrew's concerns about meeting Federal infantry from the Army of the Potomac in Gettysburg that day. Pettigrew had taken his brigade into the small town to search for supplies (primarily shoes), but when he ran into enemy soldiers he prudently withdrew and rode to Cashtown to inform his superiors. Maj. Gen. Henry Heth, Pettigrew's division commander, was listening to the report when Hill joined them. Hill dismissed the idea outright. "If there is no objection, then," asked Heth, " I will take my division tomorrow and go to Gettysburg and get those shoes." Hill replied with a nonchalance that typified the Army of Northern Virginia in the early summer of 1863: "None in the world."

By July 1, however, Hill was ailing and out of sorts. When Heth's Division approached Gettysburg from the east on the Chambersburg Pike that morning, it unwittingly ran into advance elements of the Army of the Potomac's cavalry. Two brigades from Heth's Division, Brig. Gens. Joe Davis' and James Archer's, deployed and were sent forward. Unbeknownst to them, the head of Maj. Gen. John Reynolds' First Corps was approaching the field. Neither brigade was handled well, both were shattered, and Archer was captured. A distressed Heth, who was new to division command (and showing it), brought up his remaining two brigades (Pettigrew's and Col. John Brockenbrough's) and reorganized his front. When General Lee questioned Hill in Cashtown as to the sounds of battling rolling in from the east, the obviously ill corps commander claimed ignorance and mounted his horse to investigate.

When Hill reached the front with Lee, Heth filled in the generals on the status of his division. Despite not knowing exactly what he was up against—and with a sizeable segment of his corps already out of action with nothing to show for it—Hill decided to renew the battle on a larger scale. Maj. Gen. William Dorsey Pender's Division was called up—in direct contradiction of Lee's explicit orders to avoid a general engagement until the entire army was concentrated. While Heth's Division regrouped and Pender's Division deployed in the early afternoon, Lee reiterated his orders not to bring on a general engagement until the army was well in hand. Hill relented and the opposing sides contented themselves with dueling long-range with artillery.

As the hours passed, the sound of a fresh battle rolled down from the northeast about 2:30 p.m. Richard Ewell's Second Corps was arriving—directly on the flank of the Federal First Corps. The first troops to make their presence visible from Hill's position were those belonging to Maj. Gen. Robert Rodes' Division, who attacked the enemy right flank from Oak Hill. When Heth asked to renew his attack and aid Rodes, who was having a much harder time of it than he expected, Hill referred Heth directly to Lee, who refused because Longstreet's First Corps was not up. Before long, however, Rodes' attack was rolling up the right flank of the First Corps and it became obvious to Lee that a general engagement was already taking place—and the Union line was crumbling. Lee ordered Hill to drive forward and assist Rodes' Division.

Heth struck with his two fresh brigades and ran into a firestorm from the staunch Union First Corps brigades opposing him. After Heth was struck in the head with a spent minie ball and knocked nearly unconscious, Hill sent Pender's Division surging forward to clear the final bit of resistance from McPherson's Ridge. The Federals fell back, pounded on the front by Hill and on the right by Rodes. A new stand was made on Seminary Ridge, which Pender's men swept clean a short time later after a bitter struggle. Federal resistance collapsed west and north of Gettysburg, and the exhausted and beaten Federals retired on the double-quick through the town and out to Cemetery Hill. Hill's pursuit of the defeated enemy netted more than 2,000 prisoners.

Lee and Hill now faced the decision whether or not to attack Cemetery Hill, the Union rallying point. The usually combative Hill, still feeling unwell and looking "very delicate" according to British observer Arthur Fremantle, complained that his troops had been exhausted and disorganized by six hours of fighting. Even though Hill had some fresh brigades, Lee did not press him on the issue and did not consider a fresh attack by the Third Corps for the remainder of the evening. (In the recriminations that followed the battle, Hill escaped all blame for the failure to attack Cemetery Hill in the fading daylight of July 1 because Lee was with him. The fault was instead heaped on Lt. Gen. Richard Ewell and his Second Corps.)

Hill positioned most of his corps for July 2 along Seminary Ridge stretching south from the Fairfield Road. Pender's Division took up a position on the left with its flank near the road, while Maj. Gen. Richard Anderson's Division extended the line down the spine of the ridge. Heth's battered brigades (now under their senior brigadier, Johnston Pettigrew) were in reserve behind Pender. Hill's movements on July 2 are largely a mystery—as biographies of the man aptly demonstrate. He apparently displayed little vigor in his leadership, and he was still suffering from an undisclosed illness. Perhaps it was because he was overshadowed by Lee, who apparently spent large segments of the day with Hill near the Lutheran Seminary. Hill probably learned of James Longstreet's planned assault against the far left of the Federal army almost as soon as Longstreet himself. One of his divisions, Richard Anderson's, would cooperate in the assault. Hill's communications with Anderson were so poor or unclear, however, that Anderson did not know until after he was fully deployed that Longstreet would be forming on his right and that he was to assist in the attack. Hill advised Anderson that the attack would take place at right angles to his line (up the Emmitsburg Road) and that he should join in, en echelon, when the fighting reached his right flank.

Lee rode down his line to Anderson's right flank and personally reiterated the order—as opposed to Hill doing so—to Brig. Gen. Cadmus Wilcox, whose brigade would be the first of Anderson's Division to enter the approaching action. Hill seemed to consider the entire assault the affair of his old nemesis Longstreet, and he did not supervise Anderson's attack at all. As a result, Anderson did not receive any support when he had some chance of carrying Cemetery Ridge in the fading daylight. Ultimately, Longstreet's epic attack did not achieve its objective of rolling up and destroying the Federal army, and nightfall ended the action.

Hill was present at the meeting held soon after sunrise on July 3 where Lee and Longstreet discussed the plans for the third day's assault. Heth's and Pender's Divisions from Hill's Corps, despite their weakened condition, were transferred under Longstreet's authority for the purpose of attacking the right center of the Union line. With two of the three divisions in the assault from his own corps, it would have been natural for Hill to lead the onslaught, but Lee obviously believed Hill was not up to the task or he would have given it to him. Hill's duties that day were to "hold the center at all hazards" according to Lee's written orders. In reality, however, Hill spent the last day of the Battle of Gettysburg virtually without an independent command. Before Pickett's Charge was launched, Hill approached Lee with a request to lead his entire corps in the attack. Lee refused.

As Gettysburg and subsequent battles would prove, Little Powell had finally been promoted into a position where he did not excel, and his health deteriorated. He continued in command of the Third Corps and led its advance elements into a disastrous ambush at Bristoe Station that fall. He turned in a mixed performance the following May at the Battle of the Wilderness, where his lines were again haphazardly formed and broken, and he was forced to relinquish command thereafter—again because of illness. He was probably dying of gonorrhea-related renal failure (kidney disease), although no one knew it at the time. Some of Hill's finest fighting took place during the Siege of Petersburg, where on the morning of April 2, 1865, Union troops shot him dead during a Federal breakthrough that captured the city.

For further reading:

Craig, Douglas. "A. P. Hill's Advance to Gettysburg." *Gettysburg Magazine*, # 5, 1991.

Hassler, William W. *A. P. Hill: Lee's Forgotten General*. Richmond, 1957.

Martin, David. *Gettysburg. July 1, 1863*. Conshohocken, 1996.

Pfanz, Harry W. *Gettysburg: The Second Day*. Chapel Hill, 1987.

Robertson, James I., Jr. *General A. P. Hill: The Story of a Confederate Warrior*. New York, 1987.

Schenck, Martin. *Up Came Hill: The Story of the Light Division and of Its Leaders*. Harrisburg, PA, 1958.

ANDERSON'S DIVISION:
7,100 MEN / 17 GUNS

MAJOR GENERAL RICHARD HERON ANDERSON

In an army full of contentious generals, "Dick" Anderson was notable for his modesty, amiability, and unselfishness. Tall, strong, and from a distinguished South Carolina family, he did not fit the stereotype of the aristocratic firebrand from the "Cradle of the Rebellion." He never indulged in any of the boastfulness that came naturally to many of his fellow officers, nor did he become insubordinate toward his superiors; and he had no inclination to advertise or advance himself by courting newspapermen and politicians. His easy-going ways, combined with his competence and professionalism, made him one of the most well liked officers in the Army of Northern Virginia. His deficiencies could be seen as the flip side of the same coin, as Anderson lacked the strong,

magnetic personality with which the best officers often inspired their men. Also, his lack of self-promotion caused some disgruntlement among his officers when he failed to call attention to their gallantry and achievements in his combat reports.

Forty-two years old at Gettysburg, he was a career soldier in his twenty-first year of military service after graduating from West Point in 1842 (along with Lt. Gen. James Longstreet and Maj. Gen. Lafayette McLaws). He was distinguished in the Mexican War and received a sword from the state of South Carolina for his "gallant conduct" in that conflict. Anderson served on the frontier as a captain of dragoons for the next thirteen years before resigning in March 1861 to enter Confederate service. He had already been made colonel of Charleston's 1st South Carolina before the bombardment of Fort Sumter in April. After Brig. Gen. P. G. T. Beauregard left for Virginia, Anderson took command of Confederate forces in Charleston harbor, and was promoted to brigadier general in July. After a transfer to Pensacola, where a musket ball broke his left arm on October 9 in an attack at Santa Rosa Island, Anderson joined the Virginia army in February 1862 and was put in command of a South Carolina brigade that had fought at First Manassas the summer before.

Anderson did well on the Peninsula in the spring of 1862. At Williamsburg and again at Seven Pines, he directed his own brigade and parts of others as well, executing difficult assignments with professional surety. Both Maj. Gen. D. H. Hill and James Longstreet praised him for his success, and army commander Gen. Joseph Johnston suggested his promotion. During the Seven Days' Battles he took charge of Longstreet's entire division at Frayser's Farm while that officer directed the overall engagement. In Longstreet's report on Gaines' Mill and Frayser's Farm, "Dick" Anderson's name was the first on his list of officers deserving praise. (Anderson, surely to his officers' dismay, did not file a report of the campaign.) Two weeks later he was promoted to major general and given command of Maj. Gen. Benjamin Huger's former division, which was now attached to Longstreet's wing of the army.

At Second Manassas that August, Anderson and his brigades joined the army on the evening of the first day of battle and almost blundered into Union lines. Anderson made up for his carelessness the next day by hitting hard in the furious attack that sent the Union army reeling back to Washington. At Sharpsburg in September, Anderson was in command at the Bloody Lane when he was hit in the thigh and knocked from his horse. Without his leadership, his division lost its drive and took heavy casualties before abandoning the position in a headlong retreat that threatened the Confederate center. This episode demonstrated how much his efficient division depended on Anderson's personal influence. Anderson was back with his brigades in time for the Battle of Fredericksburg, where his command was not heavily engaged.

It was at Chancellorsville in May 1863 that Anderson demonstrated talents evidencing his capacity for higher command. Acting without the presence of General Longstreet, "Fighting Dick" demonstrated considerable tactical sophistication in battling the Federal army to a standstill in the opening hours of the clash on May 1. On May 2, his soldiers held the Confederate right while Maj. Gen. Thomas "Stonewall" Jackson struck on the left, with Anderson's men attacking heavily on May 3. The following day, Anderson marched in the opposite direction and brought the weight

of his division to bear in the attack on the Union Sixth Corps, which ended the battle. Lee rewarded Anderson by calling him his "noble old soldier." Though he was too reserved to ask for it, Anderson was one of the five or six generals considered for the post of corps commander in the post-Chancellorsville reorganization of the army. The promotion to head the Third Corps went instead to A. P. Hill, under whom Anderson's Division was now slated to serve. Anderson had never worked with Hill, and a period of adjustment was to be expected. Longstreet had been blunt and firm, while Hill was less forceful and more erratic.

Of Anderson's service with the army, Longstreet's observant chief of staff, Lt. Col. G. Moxley Sorrel, wrote: "His courage was of the highest order, but he was indolent. His capacity and intelligence were excellent, but it was hard to get him to use them. Withal, of a nature so true and lovable that it goes against me to criticize him." Sorrel added that Longstreet could get "a good deal out of him, more than any one else." Given Anderson's pre-Gettysburg record, Sorrel's charge of indolence seems incorrect.

GETTYSBURG: On the morning of July 1, Anderson's Division was still far to the west in Fayetteville, the most distant of Hill's three divisions (18 miles) from Gettysburg. Soon after daylight, Hill ordered Anderson east over South Mountain to join Maj. Gens. W. Dorsey Pender and Henry Heth. After a fitful march, Anderson's men filed into Cashtown between 10:00 and 11:00 a.m. They waited there for an hour or two, listening to the murmuring guns to the east. After a short meeting with Lee, Anderson was ordered forward toward the fighting. The congestion of troops and wagons on the Chambersburg Pike made for a difficult march, and when he arrived he arrayed his men in a line of battle on Herr Ridge about 4:00 to 5:00 p.m. Ordered to go into bivouac, a surprised Anderson rode forward to meet with Lee, who told him that the army was not all up, and that he wanted to keep Anderson's men back for a time as a reserve. It was an odd situation, for the army had already fought a large-scale battle on July 1; Anderson's Division was available for immediate employment at a time when every available Confederate should have been moving to assault Cemetery Hill.

Confederate preparations on A. P. Hill's front on the morning of July 2 are difficult to pin down. During the morning Hill ordered Anderson forward from Herr Ridge to a position facing on Seminary Ridge, on Pender's right flank occupying McMillan's, Spangler's, and Pitzer's Woods. By the time Anderson deployed his brigades it was at least noon. From left to right, Anderson placed into line the brigades of Brig. Gens. William Mahone, Carnot Posey, Ambrose Wright, Col. David Lang, and Brig. Gen. Cadmus Wilcox. Anderson rode with Wilcox and placed his brigade, bending it back to protect his (and at this point, the army's) right flank. The enemy line was in plain view 1,200 yards away on Cemetery Ridge.

Shortly after Wilcox's men formed into line they had a short but fierce fight with Col. Hiram Berdan's elite Sharpshooters, who had been sent forward by Maj. Gen. Dan Sickles to scout the Union Third Corps front. It was the first serious fighting of the day (Anderson called it a "sharp skirmish") and would have a significant impact on Sickles' tactical arrangements; it was all but ignored by the Confederate high command.

Not long after Berdan's men pulled back, Anderson learned of Lee's plan for that afternoon which called for James Longstreet to deploy his First Corps on Anderson's right flank and attack up the Emmitsburg Road. Longstreet, apparently, would align his divisions at nearly a right angle to Anderson and drive the enemy across his front. After Longstreet went in, Anderson was to continue the attack by brigade, one after another, all of which was intended to drive in and crush the Union left flank. In mid-afternoon Longstreet's men filed south behind Anderson's Division, deployed in the woods there, and started their echelon attack from the far right about 4:30 p.m. About 5:30 p.m., Maj. Gen. Lafayette McLaws' Division, on Anderson's immediate right, sprang ahead with a shout and crushed the Federal line in the Peach Orchard. It was now Anderson's turn.

Cadmus Wilcox's Alabama Brigade swept forward about 6:20 p.m., striking the front of Brig. Gen. Andrew Humphrey's Federal division, aligned along the Emmitsburg Road, in conjunction with Brig. Gen. William Barksdale's Mississippi Brigade, which was attacking from the south through the Peach Orchard. Humphrey's men buckled under the weight and eventually streamed rearward. David Lang's Floridians jumped off next, striking the line north of the Rogers' farm, where they hit Brig. Gen. Joseph Carr's New Englanders. Ambrose "Rans" Wright's Brigade was next, and the Georgians started forward toward the now vulnerable center of Cemetery Ridge near the Codori farmstead. This sector of the enemy line had been denuded of Union troops in a desperate attempt to stem the Confederate tide rolling up from the south. Wright's men penetrated farther than any Confederate brigade that day (at least according to Wright), and for a few minutes, his riflemen stood on Cemetery Ridge. Carnot Posey's regiments, however, had advanced only piecemeal and a short distance on Wright's left flank, and on Posey's left, William Mahone's Brigade remained idle on Seminary Ridge.

Wilcox, Lang, and Wright were all savagely counterattacked. It was now sunset, and with his assault out of steam and troops on his right falling back, Wilcox's ordered his infantry to withdraw, which prompted Lang's men to do likewise. Wright's soldiers encountered similar opposition and fell back over the same fields that Pickett's men would attack across the following afternoon. Anderson's attacking brigades, which suffered almost a 40% casualty rate, were betrayed on the cusp of victory by a breakdown in the division's communications. Posey's regiments, for example, had not gone forward much beyond the Bliss farm because Mahone (on Posey's left) did not advance—even after Posey sent a plea for assistance that he do so; Mahone, though, claimed he had orders from Anderson to stay where he was, even when one of Anderson's aides went to Mahone with orders to advance.

Unfortunately for the Confederates, Anderson seems to have chosen the early evening of July 2 to confirm Moxley Sorrel's charge of "indolence." He made his headquarters in a blind ravine in the rear of Seminary Ridge, where he had no view of his brigades. When a messenger from Wilcox's staff sought out Anderson for assistance, he found Anderson's horse tied to a tree and his aides lounging about as though no attack was under way. Further, Anderson's plan of attack was flawed by a lack of depth (although his deployment may have been ordered by either Hill or Lee, and it was Hill who had ordered the attack "by brigades"). His division had been deployed in one thin line, and each brigade advanced alone with its flanks exposed—and each was defeated in detail. It is thus hard to imagine how any of his brigades could have held any portion of the enemy line for long (Longstreet's divisions, for example, were in double lines). When some of his brigadiers were subjected to criticism after the battle, Anderson accepted the blame as his own, manfully admitting that his brigades advanced, or failed to advance, according to his orders. A modern historian summed up the entire affair when he cogently penned, "Something was wrong in Anderson's division that evening."

On July 3, Lee determined to advance a strong assault column against the Union right center on Cemetery Ridge. The attack, popularly known as "Pickett's Charge," was comprised of elements from four divisions—including Anderson's, which remained on Seminary Ridge until the assault was underway. Two of his brigades, Wilcox's and Perry's (Lang's) had been selected to support the column on the right (whether that actually meant they were to advance with the column is open to some debate), while his other three (Wright, Posey, and Mahone) were held in readiness "to move up in support." Practically speaking, since Longstreet was effectively controlling the assaulting column, Anderson was more or less a spectator.

When the assaulting brigades moved forward against the Union position on Cemetery Ridge, the brigades of Wilcox and Lang remained idle for about 20 minutes. Wilcox, who was also in control of Lang's men, advanced when he received orders to do so, and Lang followed orders to conform to Wilcox's movements. Both brigades, however, marched straight over the Emmitsburg Road instead of angling north toward Pickett's right flank, and both were soon driven back to Seminary Ridge with some loss. Other than cavalry action, both Anderson's role at Gettysburg and the battle itself had ended.

A. P. Hill's thin report on the Pennsylvania Campaign does not contain any words of appreciation for Richard Anderson's services; indeed, there is an implication of censure in his words. The battle was a curious break in a string of well-fought engagements by Anderson. His performance was not held against him—perhaps because so many other able Confederate generals were similarly afflicted.

Richard Anderson opened the 1864 campaigns at the head of his division, and was given command of the First Corps when Longstreet was severely wounded at the Battle of the Wilderness. His march to Spotsylvania saved the army serious embarrassment and possible defeat, although his performance at the corps level overall is perhaps best described as "adequate." Anderson was promoted to lieutenant general, and when Longstreet returned in October, Anderson was given command of General Beauregard's old corps, which was little more than a single division. He directed this force until it was virtually destroyed in the Appomattox Campaign.

Anderson was unable to avoid poverty after the war, and was serving as South Carolina state phosphate agent when he died suddenly in 1879.

For further reading:

Elliott, Joseph C. *Lieutenant General Richard Heron Anderson: Lee's Noble Soldier.* Dayton, 1985.

Freeman, Douglas S. *Lee's Lieutenants: A Study in Command.* vol. 3. New York, 1944.

Hassler, William W. "'Fighting Dick' Anderson." *Civil War Times*. Vol. 12, Feb., 1974.

Pfanz, Harry W. *Gettysburg: The Second Day*. Chapel Hill, 1987.

Walker, C. Irvine. *The Life of Lieutenant General Richard Heron Anderson*. Charleston, 1917.

WILCOX'S BRIGADE:
(1,721 MEN)

BRIGADIER GENERAL CADMUS MARCELLUS WILCOX

Cadmus Wilcox was perhaps the most disgruntled brigadier in Gen. Robert E. Lee's army during the march to Gettysburg, disgusted at being overlooked for a promotion to major general. He was too much of a gentleman, however, too genial and good-natured—and too adverse to controversy—to agitate for the rank he believed he deserved. At the age of thirty-nine, he was older than most of the other professional soldiers who commanded brigades. At West Point, he had been in the Class of 1846 with George McClellan, Stonewall Jackson, and George Pickett; the class that followed had contained A. P. Hill, and John Hood had left the Academy in 1853. Yet, Wilcox was junior to them all of them in grade. Wilcox had saved the entire army with his delaying action at Salem Church during the

Battle of Chancellorsville, and still promotion eluded him; he was pondering leaving the army.

In an army of bearded men, Wilcox's strong jaw was clean-shaven. He stood six feet tall with high cheekbones, a well-tended mustache, and not a hint of gray in his short dark hair. His careful barbering reflected his "no nonsense" approach to soldiering. But beside this habit of being "precise and insistent on precision" with a military exactness in his speech and manner while on duty, he was amiable in camp, generous, friendly, and informal, with the ability to laugh at himself. He was known for his non-regulation attire—a short jacket and a battered straw hat. His men liked him and called him "Old Billy Fixin."

Cadmus Wilcox had been born to a Connecticut Federal father in the mountains of North Carolina and raised in Tennessee, where he attended the University of Nashville before receiving his appointment to West Point. After graduating near the bottom of his class at the young age of eighteen, he served as an aide in the Mexican War, seeing enough action to bring home tales of harrowing exploits at Chapultepec and Mexico City. In the thirteen years between wars, while most career soldiers were fighting dust, flies, boredom, and occasionally Indians in dreary frontier outposts, Wilcox taught tactics for five of them at West Point, then studied for two more in Europe. He wrote a manual, *Rifle and Infantry Tactics*, and translated an Austrian manual on infantry tactics.

When the Civil War came, Wilcox quit the U.S. Army and entered Confederate service as colonel of the 9th Alabama. At the early date of October 1861, he was promoted to brigadier general, and was already commanding a brigade when the fighting started in earnest on the Peninsula the next spring. Wilcox led his brigade with reliability and professionalism at Williamsburg, Seven Pines, and in the Seven Days' Battles. In the latter week of fighting he lost more than a thousand men—the highest number of casualties suffered by any brigade in the Confederate army. Wilcox himself escaped being wounded, though six bullets pierced his clothing in ferocious fighting at Frayser's Farm.

Maj. Gen. James Longstreet had enough confidence in Wilcox to put him in command of a three-brigade division at Second Manassas in August, where his performance was a bit uneven. He failed to get his brigades moving during a crucial counterattack, and brought only one brigade forward when Longstreet desired that all three become involved in the action. Later that fall, Longstreet promoted George Pickett over Wilcox to lead a new division. Longstreet may have based his decision on Wilcox's Second Manassas performance, or it may have stemmed from "Old Pete's" personal affection for Pickett. Regardless, Wilcox was not pleased when he was passed over for advancement in favor of a junior officer. In November he informed General Lee that he wished to leave the Army of Northern Virginia for another command. Lee, however, could not afford to lose such an experienced brigadier, and refused to transfer the unhappy Alabamian.

Between Second Manassas and Chancellorsville in May 1863, Wilcox did not play a conspicuous part in the army's success. He was absent sick during the Maryland Campaign, and his men were not engaged at Fredericksburg. At Chancellorsville, however, Wilcox enjoyed perhaps his best day on a battlefield. Stationed to guard a ford near Fredericksburg while the rest of the army fought near the Chancellor House (a circumstance he did not relish), Wilcox noticed that there were fewer Federal pickets on the opposite bank than usual. Peering through his binoculars, he observed that the remaining videttes were wearing their haversacks; were they preparing to march? Wilcox, astutely deducing that the enemy did not intend to force a crossing at his ford, took the bulk of his brigade to join the battle. His action was indeed fortuitous, for Maj. Gen. John Sedgwick and his 23,000-strong Union Sixth Corps had broken through a token Confederate force left at Fredericksburg and was descending on Lee's rear. Wilcox placed his men in the path of the advancing Federal column near Salem Church and carried out a classic

delaying action. His lone brigade forced Sedgwick to repeatedly deploy, which in turn bought time for Confederate reinforcements to arrive from Chancellorsville and save Lee's army from being caught between two powerful pincers.

By mid-summer 1863, a few weeks after Chancellorsville, Wilcox had been in the military service for twenty-one years. He was a bachelor, married only to the army, and had been immersed in army routine since he was a teenager. His independent-minded service had just helped rescue the Army of Northern Virginia, and he was still waiting for advancement.

GETTYSBURG: Wilcox's Brigade led Anderson's Division's stop-and-start march from Fayetteville on July 1. When the division went into bivouac on Herr Ridge late that afternoon, Wilcox's men were posted on the right, about one mile south of Chambersburg Pike near Black Horse Tavern. That night, Brig. Gen. Andrew Humphreys' Union division took a wrong road as it approached the battlefield and almost bumped into Wilcox's men in their camps. At 7:00 a.m. the next morning, July 2, Wilcox filed back onto the Pike and advanced to Seminary Ridge and then south along the ridge to Pitzer's Woods, where Anderson personally placed Wilcox's Brigade in line with its flank refused. Wilcox's Alabama regiments (the 8th, 9th, 10th, 11th, and 14th) took up their new position about noon. The 10th held the far right, with the 11th on its left flank; the exact alignment of the other regiments at this time is unclear. Wilcox held thus the right flank of the division, and at that time comprised the extreme right flank of the Army of Northern Virginia.

Just as Wilcox was completing the deployment of his brigade (he was still in the process of sending the 10th Alabama to the right), an enemy force in heavy skirmish order advanced into Pitzer's Woods and directly into the 10th regiment from the south. The Federals, about 100 men from Berdan's Sharpshooters and another 200 from 3rd Maine Infantry, had been dispatched to reconnoiter the woods to determine if the Confederates were opposite

Maj. Gen. Dan Sickles' Federal Third Corps in strength. A short but sharp exchange followed in which the 10th lost 10 killed and 28 wounded, and the enemy 67 killed and wounded. It was the first serious fighting on July 2. Although none of the Confederates deemed the engagement important, Berdan himself exaggerated the number of men he engaged and his report convinced Sickles he was about to be attacked. Sickles, in turn, advanced his corps to occupy the high ground along the Emmitsburg Road—directly in the path of Longstreet's forthcoming assault.

After the brush with Berdan, Wilcox's men watched as Longstreet's two divisions filed south past their rear on the way to their marshaling positions for the late-afternoon attack on the Union left. Wilcox belatedly learned that he would take part in the day's assault and would advance toward Cemetery Ridge when Longstreet's men, attacking at right angles to his own, moved forward on his right. Lee personally discussed with Wilcox his assignment that day. The brigadier pointed out for Lee where he believed the Union left was (about 600-800 yards in his front), and confirmed that he could carry out his assignment. With some of his regiments facing south, though, it was impossible to directly attack the enemy. For reasons that remains unknown, his brigade was not shifted into a better position to carry out his attack.

Longstreet opened his attack with Hood's Division about 4:30 p.m., and McLaws' moved out about one hour later. By 6:00 p.m., Longstreet's assault reached Wilcox's front. Before him was Brig. Gen. Andrew Humphreys' Federal division, aligned along the Emmitsburg Road. The Federals were already feeling heavy pressure from Brig. Gen. William Barksdale's Mississippians, who had just advanced on Wilcox's immediate right. Because of his unusual alignment, Wilcox had to file his men several hundred yards to the left into the low ground between Spangler's Woods and the Spangler house, where he took a position on the right flank of Edward Perry's (Col. David Lang's) small Florida Brigade. When finally deployed, the 8th Alabama was positioned on the right on the Staub farm, with the 10th, 11th, 14th, and 9th regiments extending the line north past the Spangler farm. A large gap of some 200 yards apparently existed between the 8th and 10th regiments, although no one seems to have noticed at the time. The almost solid mass of the enemy to his front caused an officer in the 9th to pray for strength.

Wilcox's advance through the gathering dusk was immediately greeted with heavy artillery fire, which cut the general's bridle and killed and wounded many. Colonel Lang, who had orders to "advance with General Wilcox," moved his Floridians forward on Wilcox's left flank. The Alabamians crashed into Humphreys' line, mostly between the Klingle and Rogers farms. Although the Federals put up a terrific fight, the combined weight of his attack, with Barksdale's Brigade on one side and Lang on the other, drove Humphrey's brigades to the rear. Wilcox's regiments eventually fought their way several hundred yards beyond the road to near Plum Run, where they finally stopped to reorganize. Wilcox, who had captured a number guns, sent three separate requests for reinforcements to General Anderson to support the final assault on Cemetery Ridge; none came. Although Wilcox was bitter about the way Anderson handled his division that afternoon and evening, it is hard to imagine where reinforcements for Wilcox would have come from.

The 262 men of Col. William Colvill, Jr.'s 1st Minnesota watched in stunned disbelief as the Confederate assault swept all before it. For some distance on either side of them there was nothing but empty terrain and a single battery of guns. Maj. Gen. Winfield Hancock rode upon the regiment and, pointing to the flag of the 11th Alabama, ordered Colvill to advance and take it. A well-ordered bayonet charge ensued and the Minnesotans advanced to the creek, where they blasted a volley into Wilcox's already disorganized line. A protracted shoot-out took place which shredded Colvill's regiment. The valiant assault, however, plugged a critical gap on the ridge and convinced Wilcox it was time to withdraw. He had pierced deep into the Union line, but was unable to advance safely without support on his flanks. Unwilling to risk the utter destruction of his brigade in the growing darkness, the Alabamian ordered his men back in the gloaming. Three of the brigade's four regimental commanders and 577 men were left lying on the field—fully one-third of its strength. Afterward, Wilcox was offended when Lee wrote in his report that the Alabamian had been "compelled" to retire.

On July 3, when Lee decided to launch a massive strike against the Union right center on Cemetery Ridge, Wilcox's Brigade, together with Perry's three regiments (which were under his charge), were selected to support the right flank of the attacking column. They moved up to within 200 yards of the Emmitsburg Road to support the Confederate guns that battered the enemy in preparation for Pickett's Charge. After the attacking column advanced about 3:00 p.m., however, Wilcox did not, Whether he was to have advanced together with Pickett is open to question. Some evidence suggests Wilcox received no less than three orders to advance, while others claim he was not ordered forward until twenty minutes after Pickett moved out. Col. E. Porter Alexander later wrote that Wilcox's Brigade advanced past his line of guns "some ten minutes after the crisis was over . . .As they passed us I could not help feeling a great pity for the useless loss of life they were incurring, for their was nothing left for them to support." Wilcox realized as much, writing later with disgust, "Not a man of the Division that I was ordered to support could I see." Although he did not engage enemy infantry, his brigade retired after suffering 204 casualties from heavy artillery fire. Wilcox was in tears after this futile bloodletting that signaled the end of the battle.

While neither Anderson nor A. P. Hill offered any commendations for the work performed by their subordinates at Gettysburg, Wilcox's star remained bright. On August 1, two weeks after Maj. Gen. W. Dorsey Pender died from his Gettysburg wound, Lee recommended Wilcox as the best man available to fill the vacancy at the head of Pender's Division. President Jefferson Davis accepted the recommendation, and two days later Wilcox was at last a major general. The choice was a popular one—especially with those who knew Wilcox. He served steadily during the rest of the war as a division chief.

Settling in Washington, D.C. after the war, Wilcox enjoyed nation-wide esteem and held a number of government appointments, serving as chief of the railroad division of the Land Office from 1886 until his death from a brain hemorrhage in 1890.

For further reading:

Evans, Clement A., ed., *Confederate Military History.* Vol. 8, New York, 1962.

Freeman, Douglas S. *Lee's Lieutenants: A Study in Command.* Vol. 3. New York, 1944.

Pfanz, Harry W. *Gettysburg: The Second Day.* Chapel Hill, 1987.

Stewart, George. *Pickett's Charge.* Boston, 1959.

Wilcox, Cadmus M. "'Four Years With General Lee'—A Review by C. M. Wilcox." *Southern Historical Society Papers,* 6, Richmond, 1878.

———. "General C. M. Wilcox on the Battle of Gettysburg." *Southern Historical Society Papers,* 6, 1878.

MAHONE'S BRIGADE:
(1,538 MEN)

BRIGADIER GENERAL WILLIAM MAHONE

"He was every inch a soldier, though there were not many inches of him," said one Confederate soldier of William Mahone. There was some disagreement about just how tiny "Little Billy" was, but nobody guessed his height at more than five feet six inches (some said he barely cleared five feet). His weight was estimated at 125 pounds at most, and some swore he weighed less than 100. He was so thin that after the Battle of Second Manassas, when his wife was told that he had received a

flesh wound, she said, "Now I know it is serious, for William has no flesh whatever." One young Confederate officer wrote that Mahone was "the sauciest little manikin imaginable" and "the oddest and daintiest little specimen" he ever saw.

In his wardrobe Mahone put comfort above convention. A comrade remembered, "On a certain hot summer's day that I recall he was seen . . . wonderfully accoutered! A plaited brown linen jacket, buttoned to trousers of the same material, like a boy's; topped off by a large Panama hat of the finest and most beautiful texture, met our eyes, and I must say he looked decidedly comfortable." On some occasions, Mahone wore a linen duster, which was so long it almost covered the tip of his sword. Pacing nervously in front of his tent as he often did, he presented a comic figure: "He looked like the image of a bantam rooster or gamecock," said one veteran. Mahone wore his hair long, and his eyes were blue beneath bushy brows. He had a straight, dainty nose, and a drooping brown mustache and long beard that touched his chest covered the lower half of his face. His voice was high and piping, like that of a falsetto tenor.

Mahone suffered from dyspepsia and could eat little more than tea, crackers, eggs, and fresh milk on a consistent basis. He was so dependent on milk he tethered his own cow to his headquarters wagon. Possibly due to his poor digestion, Mahone was extremely irritable—some even said

tyrannical—and was not a popular general; his subordinates gave him a wide berth out of respect for his quick temper and famous cussing fits. On one occasion, he formed his brigade to witness the punishment of two men convicted of stealing property they had been sent to guard. The prisoners were stripped to the waist and their hands tied to crossbars above their heads. When Mahone determined that the two soldiers selected to inflict the thirty-nine lashes were not applying themselves forcefully enough, he arrested them and ordered another set to carry out the punishment. His men retaliated against this cruelty when they got the chance, and on one occasion stole the turkeys Mahone was planning to eat for a Christmas dinner. The phrase "Who stole Mahone's turkeys?" evoked laughter among the soldiers of his brigade for the rest of the war.

Mahone had grown up in Virginia, the son of a tavern owner. A gambler, drinker and a mischief-maker, he was the sort other boys' mothers told their sons to avoid. He had grit, however, and made friends easily. Early on, he was marked as someone with that "something special" that others were attracted to. Aided financially by friends, he was enrolled at the Virginia Military Institute, though he admitted later that he didn't have the academic preparation for it. When he graduated, he taught school while continuing his education in engineering. Full of restless, driving energy, his rise was swift— at the age of thirty-three he was named the president, chief engineer, and superintendent of the new Norfolk and Petersburg Railroad, which he succeeded in constructing across the bottomless Dismal Swamp. Settling in Norfolk, by 1861 he was dreaming of railway consolidations by which he could link the Virginia coast with the Mississippi and ultimately with the Pacific.

When Virginia seceded, Mahone, an ardent pro-secessionist, interrupted his railroad career and accepted the colonelcy of the 6th Virginia. When Union forces evacuated Norfolk, Mahone and his men occupied the city. He was promoted to brigadier general in November 1861, and marched to join the Confederate forces defending Richmond when the Army of the Potomac began its Peninsula Campaign. Due to his experience in construction, Mahone was called upon to help to help build the defenses of Drewry's Bluff. During his initial taste of combat at Seven Pines, Mahone retreated without orders when the Confederate line began to crumble. This action led to a shouting match between Mahone and his superior, Maj. Gen. D. H. Hill, both excitable officers. Mahone considered proposing a duel, but was talked out of it. He redeemed himself with a brave but futile effort at Malvern Hill a month later where his brigade lost 329 men in the assault—26% of its total strength.

At Second Manassas, Mahone led his brigade in Maj. Gen. James Longstreet's crushing corps-level assault. At the moment of truth, however, when his brigade was poised to make the final attack on the crumbling Federal line, Mahone hesitated. Later wounded by a bullet in the chest, he was taken from the field and remained absent from the army throughout September and October. "Little Billy" returned in time for the Battle of Fredericksburg in December, and although his brigade wasn't heavily engaged, he was commended for suggesting some advanced artillery positions that proved valuable in repulsing the waves of Federal attackers. During the winter of 1862-3, Mahone, a savvy political operator, embarked upon a campaign for promotion to major general. He was able to muster the support of thirty-five Virginia state legislators, the governor of Virginia, and many respected army officers. According to General Richard Anderson, Mahone was "a thorough disciplinarian and unites to military education great skill and untiring activity in the field." Robert E. Lee concurred with the idea of Mahone's promotion—but pointed out that there was no command available for a new major general. Mahone fought competently but without distinction in the Battle of Chancellorsville and a month later, still at the head of his brigade, marched with the army into Pennsylvania.

Mahone had established himself as a competent and experienced brigade leader, but also as one who was perhaps too ill-tempered to inspire great deeds from his men.

GETTYSBURG: Sharing the march of the division from Fayetteville on July 1, Mahone turned south off the Chambersburg Pike onto Herr Ridge with the rest of Anderson's brigades around 4:00 or 5:00 p.m. His men camped there for the night.

On the morning of July 2, Mahone marched forward along the Pike and filed south along Seminary Ridge before noon, where his Virginians took up a position on the far left of the Anderson's Division, facing east from McMillan's Woods. James Longstreet's First Corps would assault the Union left flank that afternoon, attacking up the Emmitsburg Road with two divisions. The attack was to be taken up by Anderson's Division, en echelon by brigades. The first of Anderson's brigades, Cadmus Wilcox's, jumped off about 6:00 p.m., and the rest followed suit, advancing toward Cemetery Ridge about one mile distant. When it came his turn to strike, Mahone remained stationary. Requests for reinforcements poured in from the advancing brigades, and still Mahone sat idle.

Mahone's failure is one of the most impenetrable mysteries in a day full of Confederate mistakes. Mahone's report of the battle is little more than a paltry 100 words in length, and reveals nothing about his orders or his actions (which in itself makes it a curious document). After Brig. Gen. Carnot Posey had moved tentatively toward the Union lines on Mahone's right, he asked Mahone for support, and wrote in his report that "Little Billy" refused because he had been "ordered to the right," (although such an order is mentioned nowhere else). Anderson dispatched an aide to Mahone with orders to advance, but Mahone refused. He justified his incredible combination of inertia at a time of extreme urgency and insubordination in the face of a direct order by responding that he had been ordered to stay put by Anderson himself. It is likely that Mahone was initially withheld as the division's reserve brigade, but his refusal to come forward when called up to do so (if in fact he was), is inexplicable.

Just as inexplicable is his idleness on July 3. At a time when Lee was scouring his army for fresh units to place in the attacking column he was planning to send against Cemetery Ridge, Mahone's Brigade—which had yet to trade a shot with enemy infantry—was not called upon to participate in Pickett's Charge. Instead, it was assigned to protect artillery positions during the climactic onslaught. Perhaps Lee believed a large and fresh brigade was needed if Pickett's attack failed and a counterattack was delivered. Neither Lee, A. P. Hill, Richard Anderson, nor Billy Mahone ever discussed the matter further.

Despite this curious set of circumstances, Mahone's career with the army did not suffer because of his inactions at Gettysburg—perhaps because he was one of only five brigadiers who had held that rank for a full year. In May 1864, after some of his men accidentally wounded Longstreet in the Wilderness, Mahone was raised to command Anderson's Division after Anderson was elevated to fill Longstreet's post at the head of the First Corps. Little Billy was made a major general on July 30, 1864. Strangely enough, he performed much better at the head of his division than in his role as a brigade commander. By the end of the war Mahone was one of Lee's most conspicuous—and trusted—subordinates.

Mahone returned to his railroad after the war and finished creating his Norfolk and Western system. He also built a strong political machine around himself, winning the Senate election of 1880 on the unpopular Republican ticket. He died in Washington in 1895.

For further reading:

Blake, Nelson M. *William Mahone of Virginia: Soldier and Political Insurgent.* Richmond, 1935.

DePeyster, John W. "A Military Memoir of William Mahone, Major-General in the Confederate Army." *History Magazine,* 7, 1870.

Dufour, Charles L. *Nine Men In Gray.* Lincoln, 1993.

Gottfried, Bradley M. "Mahone's Brigade: Insubordination or Miscommunication?" *Gettysburg Magazine,* #18, 1998.

Pfanz, Harry W. *Gettysburg: The Second Day.* Chapel Hill, 1987.

WRIGHT'S BRIGADE:
(1,409 MEN)

BRIGADIER GENERAL
AMBROSE RANSOM "RANS" WRIGHT

Colorful anecdotes did not attach themselves to "Rans" Wright, even though he led a brigade in the Army of Northern Virginia through most of the Civil War. The heavily-bearded Georgian with the long, dark curly hair had been a lawyer in civilian life, and seemed to be a no-nonsense individual. Wright had grown up red-dirt poor in Georgia. He elevated his status by working a small patch of land while he studied at night by the light of a pine knot. By dint of such hard work he managed to become a successful lawyer in Augusta, prominent in Georgia public affairs. He tried politics but was generally unsuccessful as a candidate, probably because he did not advocate secession. Despite his Unionist sentiments, when Fort Sumter fell in the spring of 1861, Wright enlisted in the Confederate army and was named colonel of the 3rd Georgia.

The 3rd was stationed first at the important Virginia port of Norfolk. After its abandonment, the regiment was united with the Virginia army in time for the Battle of Seven Pines. It was assigned to Maj. Gen. Benjamin Huger's ill-starred division—the one that never found its way into the fighting. When the brigade's commander, Brig. Gen. A. G. Blanchard, resigned two days later, Wright was given command and promoted to brigadier general. His first test of his brigade leadership came on June 25 at Oak Grove, the first day of the Seven Days' Battles. When Huger's Division was attacked by strong Federal forces, Wright helped stymie them with slashing counterthrusts. At Malvern Hill, which closed out the battles, Wright led his men forward only to find his brigade completely alone on the slope in a hail of lead and iron. "It is astonishing that every man did not fall," wrote one of his soldiers. Wright lost nearly 400 men in the disastrous attack.

At Second Manassas in August, Wright joined Longstreet's crushing assault on the battle's second day. Wright, however, failed to sense his advantage on the Union flank and did not press his effort. As his brigade advanced into action at Sharpsburg, a cannonball horribly mangled Wright's horse, and as he continued forward on foot, a bullet hit him in the chest. He recovered in time for the Battle of Fredericksburg in December, but his brigade was not engaged. At Chancellorsville in May 1863, Wright's Brigade was employed in several phases of the week's fighting but lost only 260 men, light casualties compared to some of the other Confederate brigades in that battle. Wright himself was hit in the knee by a piece of shrapnel, but did not leave the field.

Wright's battle reports were florid, longwinded affairs, full of statements like "deadly volleys," "dashing charges," "masters of the field," and "driving the enemy before me like chaff." Some would say they were highly imaginative as well. All in all, however, the thirty-seven year old Wright was considered a well-tested capable combat veteran by the time of Gettysburg— even if his reports did tend to exaggerate his exploits.

GETTYSBURG: On July 1, Wright's Brigade was in the middle of Anderson's column as it approached Gettysburg along the Chambersburg Pike. In the early afternoon, Wright got sick and had to leave his command as it marched toward the sound of the fighting. He returned to his brigade at 7:00 a.m. on July 2, which was camped on Herr Ridge, two miles short of the battlefield. With the rest of Anderson's Division, Wright's regiments tramped forward to Seminary Ridge and then filed south along its spine. Wright occupied the middle of the divisional front as it deployed facing east, and was posted in a thin strip of trees between McMillan's Woods and Spangler's Woods. After getting into position about noon, Wright learned that he would participate in an attack later that day when the Florida Brigade moved forward on his right. Brig. Gen. Carnot Posey, stationed on Wright's left, would then go forward as well. The en echelon attack would begin with James Longstreet's First Corps far to the south, which at that time was marching into position to assail and crush the Union left flank. Longstreet would attack up the Emmitsburg Road with his two divisions, and Anderson's Division would join in by brigades.

The first of Anderson's brigades under Cadmus Wilcox moved forward at 6:00 p.m., followed by the Florida Brigade, led by Col. David Lang. Wright's Georgians emerged from the woods with the 22nd deployed on the right, the 3rd in the center and the 48th on the left. His 2nd Battalion was stretched across the front as skirmishers. Without specific orders as to where to strike, Wright moved his men forward on the Floridians' left, intent on attacking whatever appeared before him. The Georgians were almost immediately exposed to a "sheet of fire" from Federal batteries. Wright double-quicked his men, reformed them in a small swale, and then advanced again, moving forward south of the Bliss farm buildings. Men of the 48th Georgia, on Wright's left flank, were dismayed to find that Posey's Mississippians remained behind on the Bliss farm. Who would support their flank? "Get up and fight!" they shouted. "Come forward Mississippians!" A number of them did, advancing into battle with the Georgians, but the bulk of Posey's Brigade advanced no further.

Much to Wright's chagrin, the 2nd Battalion skirmishers, who were supposed to form on the brigade's left, melted instead into the main line or intermingled with some of Posey's men. As a result Wright was effectively denied the use of a cohesive organization. The smoke and darkening sky made it difficult for Wright to see where he was going, and visibility was only about 100 yards. Federal small arms fire from a pair of regiments from General Harrow's brigade, stationed along the Emmitsburg Road, began striking Wright's men. As he pressed forward near the Emmitsburg Road and the two Union regiments fell back, Wright realized for the first time that Posey's Brigade was not advancing on his left. He sent a dispatch back to Anderson asking that this force be hurried forward. The courier returned later and informed Wright that Posey had already been ordered to advance, and that Wright should continue pressing ahead regardless. Wright obeyed, but as he approached the Union defenders on Cemetery Ridge, he noticed that the Floridians had retreated on his right, and now both his flanks were unprotected and alone.

The Georgians pressed on "in splendid order," wrote one Federal officer. Wright's front flowed around the Codori buildings and up the slope of the ridge to near the rock walls just south of the soon-to-be-famous Copse of Trees. Artillery splintered the ranks and a number of regiments from Brig. Gen. John Gibbon's Second Corps blasted the Georgians with musketry. Wright later breathlessly wrote that his men scaled "the side of a mountain . . . so precipitous...that my men could scarcely climb it." While his report was a wild stretch of the imagination, Wright's men had lodged themselves on top of Cemetery Ridge. "We were now complete masters of the field," Wright later wrote, "having gained the key, as it were, of the enemy's whole line."

Wright's moment of triumph was fleeting, however, as Federal counterattacks closed upon his force and reinforcements never arrived to exploit his small tactical victory. With darkness upon them, Wright's Georgians had to cut their way out, falling back across the fields over which they had advanced. The brigade lost 688 men, almost half its strength, and three of his four regimental commanders.

In view of their crippling losses, Wright's Georgians were not called upon to advance in support of Pickett's Charge on the afternoon of on July 3. "The trouble is not in going there [to Cemetery Ridge]," Wright explained to artillerist Porter Alexander on the morning of the attack. "The trouble is to stay there after you get there." His troops remained on Seminary Ridge while the battle played out over the same few yards of rock fencing on Cemetery Ridge where they had been repulsed in the dying light the previous day. Afterward, Longstreet instructed Wright to move forward and help form the stragglers and survivors of the attack.

Wright performed admirably at Gettysburg, and he held his place at the head of his brigade until the next summer, when he went away on sick leave. In the fall of 1864, Wright left the Army of Northern Virginia. He was made major general, and given a division command in Georgia at the request of the governor of that state.

After the war ended, Wright bought two Augusta, Georgia, newspapers. He was elected to the House of Representatives in 1872, but died before he could take his seat.

For further reading:

Derry, Joseph T. "Georgia," vol. 6 of *Confederate Military History*. Ed. by Clement A. Evans. Atlanta, 1899 [vol. 7 of the extended edition. Wilmington, 1987.]

Freeman, Douglas S. *Lee's Lieutenants: A Study in Command*, vol. 3. New York, 1944.

Gottfried, Bradley. "Wright's Charge on July 2, 1863: Piercing the Union Line or Inflated Glory?" *Gettysburg Magazine*, #17, 1997.

Pfanz, Harry W. *Gettysburg: The Second Day*. Chapel Hill, 1987.

POSEY'S BRIGADE:
(1,318 MEN)

BRIGADIER GENERAL
CARNOT POSEY

"The dashing Mississippian" Carnot Posey exemplified the flower of the plantation South. At forty-four, he was a striking figure in uniform; tall, slender, handsome, with coal-black hair, a neatly trimmed spade beard, and dark piercing eyes. One of Posey's Mississippians described him as "singularly mild in character, he was energetic in action, wise in counsel, brave, temperate, good."

Born in Wilkinson County in the southwest corner of Mississippi, he went to college across the state line in Louisiana, then studied law at the University of Virginia. He returned to Mississippi to live the life of the gentleman planter at Sligo Plantation for several years. In 1844, he became a partner in a lucrative law practice, establishing a reputation as a meticulous lawyer, aggressive but fair—and impeccably honest. His practice was interrupted by the Mexican War, and he volunteered to serve. He fought as a lieutenant under Col. Jefferson Davis, and suffered a slight wound at the Battle of Buena Vista. His conduct earned him frequent honorable mentions from Davis, and endeared him to the future president of the Confederacy. Posey returned home after the war and was

appointed as a United States district attorney by President Buchanan, a prestigious position which he held until Mississippi's secession in 1861. Posey was a deeply religious man; devoted to his family, he was an affectionate father who inculcated in his children the same noble qualities he tried so hard to embody. Family, faith, and law were the watchwords of his life.

Posey was an ardent States' Rights Democrat, and when the Civil War began he organized a company of Mississippi volunteers called the "Wilkinson Rifles." When the company was placed in the newly organized 16th Mississippi in June 1861, Posey was elected colonel of the regiment. The Mississippians saw their first action in October 1861 at Ball's Bluff, where they performed well and helped rout a small Federal force. In the spring of 1862, Posey and his men took part in Maj. Gen. Thomas "Stonewall" Jackson's Shenandoah Valley Campaign. At Cross Keys in June, Maj. Gen. Richard Ewell noted that Posey's regiment was "the closest engaged." Posey was wounded in the fight and carried by litter bearers to the rear, winning commendation by Ewell for "valuable service." Incapacitated for two months, he returned to duty before his wound fully healed. A surgeon later said that he had expected Posey to die from this wound because he was so despondent, nervous, and easily depressed.

Back on duty in time for the Second Manassas Campaign in August, Posey led two Mississippi regiments at Kelly's Ford on the Rappahannock and repulsed a sortie by Federal troopers. He also fought well at Second Manassas, and was placed in charge of the entire brigade for a few hours at the end of the battle. At Sharpsburg, Brig. Gen. Winfield Featherston, the brigade's commander, was absent sick, and Posey led the brigade. Unfortunately, the brigade did not do well there: it fell into confusion in the Sunken Road, its battle line collapsed, and Posey and his men were chased away by the advancing Federals with a loss of 319 men. Even so, Posey was commended as "most prominently distinguished" by Maj. Gen. James Longstreet after the battle.

Despite his disastrous experience at Sharpsburg, Robert E. Lee recommended Posey be elevated to brigadier general—a move he knew would surely be applauded by Posey's old friend, Jefferson Davis—and recommended that he permanently take Featherston's place, a politician who was not highly regarded as a soldier. Featherston, however, upset Lee's plan by returning suddenly from sick leave and taking control of his brigade. The brigade was not engaged at Fredericksburg (where Posey led his regiment), and Featherston requested a transfer to the Mississippi Theater after the battle. With Featherston out of the way, Posey had his brigade.

Chancellorsville was Posey's first chance to show what he could do with his own brigade, and his strong performance entirely justified his promotion. The Mississippian distinguished himself on several occasions during the campaign, and Maj. Gen. Richard Anderson made it a point to mention his good service in his campaign report.

Anderson's sterling recommendation must have pleased Lee, for Posey's fine performance came at a time when the South's supply of able brigadiers was drying up. For the first time after a major campaign, Lee was forced to leave colonels in charge of brigades for lack of better officers to take their places. Although his experience at the brigade level was rather limited, Posey was a vast improvement over Featherston, and anyone in the army who was paying attention realized it.

GETTYSBURG: On July 1, Posey and his Mississippians shared the division's fitful march from Fayetteville, about 18 miles east of Gettysburg, along the Chambersburg Pike to Herr Ridge, about two miles short of town. There, Posey's men went into bivouac in the late afternoon and remained there until early the next morning.

On the morning of July 2, Posey's Brigade continued its march toward Gettysburg, turned off the pike at Seminary Ridge and filed south along the crest for some distance before being ordered to stop. Anderson's Division was deployed in the trees along the spine of the ridge, facing the visible Union line on the open slope of Cemetery Ridge about 1,200 yards to the east. From north to south, Posey's Brigade was posted second among the division's five brigades (William Mahone was on his left, and Ambrose Wright was on his right), in a thin strip of trees just south of McMillan's Woods. The deployment was complete about noon.

Posey learned a short time later that his brigade would be participating in an attack that afternoon. The en echelon assault would begin with James Longstreet's First Corps well to the south, which at that time was marching behind Posey to take up a position to assail and crush the Union left flank. Longstreet would attack up the Emmitsburg Road with his two divisions, and Anderson's Division would join in by brigades. Posey was instructed to advance when he saw the Wright's Brigade moving forward. Posey's Mississippi brigade consisted of the 12th, 16th, 19th, and 48th regiments.

Before the main attack commenced, however, Posey received orders from Anderson to advance two of his regiments as skirmishers. He already had parts of the 16th and 19th deployed in that capacity near a fence about half way to the Bliss farm directly in front of his position. He complied with the order by sending out the rest of the 19th as well as the entire 48th regiment. Their advance stirred up a sharp and protracted engagement around the Bliss buildings that continued well after Longstreet's (and then Anderson's) assault got underway. As the fight escalated, Posey threw in the balance of the 16th Mississippi as well, leaving just the 12th regiment and a few companies of the 16th back on Seminary Ridge. The fighting "skirmish" line west of the Bliss land was organized by the senior colonel there, Nat Harris of the 19th regiment. Harris held his men in place behind the fence and waited for the Georgians on his right to advance. Posey remained on Seminary Ridge, a poor decision he would later come to regret.

Cadmus Wilcox, whose brigade held the far right of Anderson's line, stepped off to continue Longstreet's attack about 6:00

p.m. As his Alabama regiments moved forward, Col. David Lang, who commanded Edward Perry's small Florida Brigade on Wilcox's left, also advanced. After a stressful thirty minutes, Colonel Harris watched from near the Bliss farm as Wright's men tramped forward from the timber on Seminary Ridge about 6:30 p.m. When the advancing lines reached Harris' position, he ordered his own line forward. The Mississippians jumped the fence and quickly cleared the last Federal resistance from the Bliss orchard and buildings. Posey's regiments were now aligned, from right to left as follows: 48th, 19th, and 16th.

Posey's officers halted the line on and around the Bliss farm and reorganized it there. As the Georgians marched past, many yelled jibes at the stationary Mississippians. "Get up and Fight!" screamed one, while another stated, "Come forward Mississippians." Against the wishes of their officers, a sizeable number of them did just that. The advance was spontaneous and without much order or alignment. The bulk of the brigade, though, remained behind near the Bliss farm, and General Wright commented on this in his report. Despite Wright's claim that Posey's Brigade did not advance, he is only partially correct. Hundreds eventually advanced several hundred yards, supporting Wright's left flank during this critical phase of the attack. Colonel Harris' 19th Mississippi drove the gunners from a Federal battery (Brown's) away from their pieces on three separate occasions.

Unaware of the situation at and beyond the Bliss farm (the smoke and growing darkness made it difficult to see much of anything), Posey advanced the remaining companies of the 16th Mississippi toward the farm. When he learned they were meeting strong opposition, he advanced himself with the 12th Mississippi. The general was shocked to learn that his line had advanced to near the Emmitsburg Road, and "had driven the enemy's pickets into their works and the artillerists from their guns in their front." Without orders to proceed farther, and with no sign of Mahone's men on his left, Posey sent a courier to General Anderson seeking direction. Posey remained on the Bliss Farm watching with the 12th Mississippi, peering through the smoke at the culmination of the battle for Cemetery Ridge while his brigade was hopelessly strung out between those two points. Posey had lost control of his brigade.

Meanwhile, the fragments of his brigade near the Emmitsburg Road were thrown back in disarray, unable to remain where their legs had carried them. As the Mississippians fell back to the Bliss farm, Posey and his officers quickly organized them for further action. Unfortunately, the day's fighting was over, and Anderson eventually recalled the men to Seminary Ridge. While history would record that the attack of Anderson's Division weakly petered out on Posey's front, those of his men who went forward fought well. Posey's Brigade lost a mere 83 men in the day's fighting (including the lengthy but brisk engagement at the Bliss farm) and was as fresh as any in the army on July 3. Much as in Billy Mahone's case, when Lee was trying to find fresh brigades to include in the attacking column popularly known as Pickett's Charge, Posey's men were overlooked and not even assigned a supporting role. The Mississippians spent the day in their lines on Seminary Ridge, harassed by artillery but unengaged.

Posey marched out of Pennsylvania with the dubious distinction of leading the brigade that suffered the least number of casualties of any such unit in the Army of Northern Virginia. There was no recorded concern over Posey's competence, however, and he continued to lead the brigade until he was mortally wounded by a shell fragment in the left thigh at the debacle of Bristoe Station on October 14, 1863.

For further reading:

Freeman, Douglas S. Lee's Lieutenants: A Study in Command, vol. 3. New York, 1944.

Hooker, Charles E. "Mississippi," vol. 7 of Confederate Military History. Ed. by Clement A. Evans. Atlanta, 1899 [vol. 9 of the extended edition. Wilmington, 1987.]

Pfanz, Harry W. Gettysburg: The Second Day. Chapel Hill, 1987.

Winschel, Terrence J. "Posey's Brigade at Gettysburg." *Gettysburg Magazine*, #4 & 5, 1991.

PERRY'S BRIGADE
"THE FLORIDA BRIGADE":
(739 MEN)

COLONEL
DAVID LANG

Colonel David Lang was just twenty-five years old when Brig. Gen. Edward Perry, his brigade commander, came down with typhoid after the Battle of Chancellorsville. As senior colonel, Lang inherited command of the Florida Brigade for the summer campaign into Pennsylvania.

Lang had come a long way in the chain of command since the outbreak of the Civil War, as he had begun the conflict as a private. Born in Camden County, Georgia (which bordered Florida near Jacksonville) and graduated from the Georgia Military Institute in 1857, he had ignored a military career and instead had gone to work surveying in Florida. When the war began a short time later, he enlisted as a private in the 1st Florida regiment and rose to sergeant by the time his year-long enlistment expired. He raised his own company of Floridians and journeyed with them to

Virginia, where they became part of the 8th Florida Infantry Regiment, in Brig. Gen. Roger Pryor's Brigade. Lang's first action was at Second Manassas in August 1862, where because of poor handling by Pryor, the brigade belatedly entered the fight and spent its time futilely chasing the retreating Federal army. A few weeks later at Sharpsburg, Pryor's Brigade arrived to reinforce the Sunken Road sector, but became disordered and fled while the losing 382 men—many of whom were shot in the back.

General Robert E. Lee had seen enough of Pryor and transferred him away from his army. His brigade was divided up and Lang's regiment was put in another Florida brigade under the command of Brig. Gen. Edward Perry. The new "Florida Brigade" fought first at Fredericksburg. There, Lang, who after Sharpsburg had been bumped up two grades and was now colonel of the 8th Florida, was sent into the town with his regiment to help repulse the Union crossing of the Rappahannock River. His Floridians fought alongside Brig. Gen. William Barksdale's Mississippians from rifle pits dug along Fredericksburg's riverfront, and picked off Federal engineers as they attempted to span the river with a pontoon bridge. Union artillery eventually bombarded the position for hours, mercilessly pounding Lang's men. The regiment lost 31 killed and wounded before Lang received a serious wound to the head and was carried off the field.

This head wound kept Lang out of the Battle of Chancellorsville. Perry was ill when he returned, and Lang ascended to temporary command of the brigade just before the Gettysburg Campaign. While Lang had been in three battles, he had fought in two of the engagements as a captain and he had never led a brigade in combat. It was clear he was serving in an emergency situation, and would have to be carefully watched.

GETTYSBURG: Lang's Floridians were escorting the corps wagons at the rear of Maj. Gen. Richard Anderson's divisional column during the approach to Gettysburg along the Chambersburg Pike on the morning of July 1. Lee held the division out of the fighting that day, and Lang's Brigade encamped on Herr Ridge with the rest of the division that evening, about two miles east of town.

On the morning of July 2, the division marched toward Gettysburg and filed south along Seminary Ridge. Lang's three small regiments were posted facing east from Spangler's Woods, just to the left of Brig. Gen. Cadmus Wilcox's Brigade, who was then on the army's extreme right. Lang threw out skirmishers and aligned his regiments, left to right, as follows: 2nd, 8th, and 5th. The plan for the day was for Lt. Gen. James Longstreet's two divisions to go into position on Wilcox's right for an attack up the Emmitsburg Road against the enemy's left flank. When the attack reached Anderson's Division, its brigades were to advance in "unison," although the way the orders were presented, the result was more en echelon. The inexperienced Lang was given careful instructions to let his movements be guided by those of Wilcox, a professional soldier and veteran brigadier. Opposite Wilcox and Lang was Brig. Gen. Andrew Humphrey's Federal division, aligned along the Emmitsburg Road and well supported by artillery. Directly opposite Lang was the Rogers farm and Brig. Gen. Joseph Carr's brigade.

When the moment for the attack arrived (Lang said it was about 6:00 p.m.), Wilcox's men stepped off and Lang's regiments hurried to follow suit. His men walked directly into a "murderous fire of grape, canister, and musketry." In order to close on Wilcox's rapidly-advancing flank—which must have been disappearing into the smoke—and pass as quickly as possible over the artillery-swept field, Lang double-quicked his men. Although the Floridians were plastered with shell, Lang had the good fortune of overlapping the right end of Humphreys' divisional line along the Emmitsburg Road, which was being pressed at the same time in front by Wilcox and to the south by Brig. Gen. William Barksdale's Mississippians (McLaws' Division). This pressure, with the added weight of Brig. Ambrose Wright's Georgians beyond Lang's left flank, col-lapsed the Federals and forced them back hundreds of yards in what was essentially a fighting withdrawal.

Crossing the Emmitsburg Road between the Rogers and Codori farms, Lang's men moved forward perhaps another quarter mile or so under increasingly heavy artillery and musketry fire from Humphreys' stubborn defenders. According to Lang, his men "gallantly met and handsomely replied" to the fire poured into them. When Wilcox and Lang reached Plum Run, they stopped to reorder their ranks, and both men sent to Anderson for reinforcements. None appeared, and Wilcox finally withdrew his men while under pressure from repeated Federal counterstrokes. A messenger reached Lang from the right to tell him that Wilcox had fallen back. Riding that way through the smoke and gathering darkness, he discovered to his mortification that "the enemy was then some distance in rear of my right flank." Facing a chance that he would be surrounded and cut off, Lang withdrew his brigade to the road, where he was unable to rally it safely, and then back toward Seminary Hill. The small Florida Brigade suffered terribly in the attack, losing 300 men, or more than 40% of its strength.

Early the next morning, July 3, Lang was ordered by divisional headquarters to conform all of his movements to Wilcox's Brigade, and that he would receive no further orders from General Anderson; this directive effectively gave Wilcox control of his Floridians, although exactly why this was done is unclear. On July 3, Lang and his remaining men, along with Wilcox's, were called to advance and support a line of Confederate guns near the Emmitsburg Road in preparation for their supporting role in Pickett's Charge. It is difficult to determine whether Lang ever learned of his role in the assault before it actually commenced. Wilcox (and thus Lang) was ordered to support the right flank of Pickett's Division in its advance; Lang clearly writes that Wilcox did not move forward until "General Pickett's troops retired behind our position." Stannard's Vermonters, who had poured such a devastating flanking fire into Pickett's right flank just minutes before, now turned and delivered a similarly destructive fire into Lang's exposed left and front as well. Before several minutes had passed, Lang was forced to retreat, and the Vermonters managed to capture much of the 2nd Florida regiment and its colors. More than 150 men did not return to Seminary Ridge.

Lang exercised only semi-independent control of his brigade on July 2-3, and seems to have performed with some competence on both days under difficult conditions (especially on July 3). When General Perry returned from his illness in September, Lang returned to his 8th Florida regiment. He led it through the bloody battles of the next year, and was again called upon to command a brigade (Finnegan's) in front of Petersburg in the final months of the war. He was never promoted to brigadier general, although he deserved the rank. After the war, Lang served in a variety of civil and military appointments and died when America was about to enter another war, in 1917.

For further reading:

Elmore, Thomas L. "The Florida Brigade at Gettysburg." *Gettysburg Magazine*, #15, 1996.

Freeman, Douglas S. *Lee's Lieutenants: A Study in Command*, vol. 3. New York, 1944.

Pfanz, Harry W. *Gettysburg: The Second Day*. Chapel Hill, 1987.

Stewart, George. *Pickett's Charge*. Boston, 1959.

PENDER'S DIVISION:
(6,645 MEN / 16 GUNS)

MAJOR GENERAL
WILLIAM DORSEY PENDER

At twenty-nine years of age, W. Dorsey Pender was the youngest and one of the fastest-rising major generals in the Army of Northern Virginia by the time of the Gettysburg Campaign. He had just been placed at the head of Lt. Gen. A. P. "Little Powell"

Hill's old "Light Division," one of the best in the army. Gen. Robert E. Lee and his fellow officers predicted a great future for the capable North Carolinian.

Pender was thin and handsome, with dark hair, and an olive complexion; he wore his beard neatly trimmed, short and pointed. With soft brown eyes and a kindly expression, he combined a sweet and gentle disposition with a strict sense of discipline—and men who did their duty found him good-natured. "Firm, very courteous," was how one officer described his manner. He was modest and said little in his languid Carolina drawl. He was sensitive about his receding hairline, referring to himself half-jokingly in a letter to his wife as "quite bald," especially after a superficial head wound at Second Manassas.

Pender was rather short, another sensitive point, but was "well formed and graceful," according to his brother. One exploit suggests he was powerfully built. Serving as a dragoon in the Northwest against the Indians, he was riding alone when he found himself in face-to-face combat with an Indian chief at the Battle of Spokane Plains. With no time to draw his sword, Pender grabbed his attacker's arm as it was raised to strike him, then grabbed the man's neck. He held the Indian powerless with his two hands and spurred his horse into a gallop toward his dragoons. When he reached his men he threw the Indian down among them.

Pender's feelings about the Civil War were complicated, for he wrote often that he was "sick of soldiering and especially the fighting part." His wife accused him of having a "cold, unfeeling nature," and he admitted to being a man who did not much express emotion. Instead, Pender expressed himself through heroic deeds in battle. A doctor called Pender "a very superior little man though a strict disciplinarian . . . brave as a lion," who "seemed to love danger." One officer summed him up: "He was one of the coolest, most self-possessed and one of the most absolutely fearless men under fire I ever knew."

The son of North Carolina farmers, Pender received his early education in the county schools, and worked as a clerk in his brother's store before his appointment to West Point at the age of sixteen. There, he graduated 19th out of 46 in the Class of 1854. Afterward, he served until the Civil War on the West Coast, in the artillery and dragoons, participating in numerous Indian fights. Pender married Fanny Sheppard, the daughter of a Congressman, in 1859. Two sons, Turner and Dorsey, followed in the next two years. In 1861 he offered his services to the Confederacy even before most of the states, including his own, had seceded. Given the job of training recruits, he missed the First Manassas. Thereafter, he joined the Virginia army as colonel of the 3rd North Carolina Volunteers in August 1861.

When Maj. Gen. George McClellan moved to the Virginia Peninsula in the spring of 1862 with his army, Pender's regiment did not see action until the Battle of Fair Oaks (Seven Pines) on June 1. President Davis had ridden out from Richmond to observe the battle and happened to stop where he could see Pender's regiment. Ordered forward, Pender found his command alone, without promised support. About to be surrounded by three Federal regiments, Pender displayed an incredible presence of mind and shouted "the only possible combination of commands that could have saved us from capture," in the words of a lieutenant. Redeploying his men at right angles to their original line, Pender

charged, stunning the enemy long enough for his beleaguered North Carolinians to withdraw to safety. President Davis rode over and addressed him: "General Pender, I salute you." The young colonel thus enjoyed the heady experience of being promoted to brigadier general on the field of battle by the president of the Confederacy.

Pender was assigned a North Carolina brigade in a new division under Maj. Gen. A. P. Hill, one that would win immortality as the "Light Division." His was soon the most efficient brigade in that excellent organization. Pender and Hill shared a hard-hitting intensity in combat, and their friendship grew with every battle. The division fought first in the Seven Days' Battles, where Pender received a flesh wound in the arm at Malvern Hill.

Transferred to Stonewall Jackson's command and facing Maj. Gen. John Pope, the division fought at Cedar Mountain on August 9, and at Second Manassas at the end of that month, where Pender was knocked down by the explosion of a shell but refused to leave the field. He was fortunate; his heavy felt hat had provided some protection, and his wound was nothing more than a relatively minor cut. Pender was with his brigade and the Light Division in Maryland that September, where it played a key role in capturing Harpers Ferry. On September 17, A. P. Hill led the division's epic march to Sharpsburg and launched an army-saving attack as he reached the field. At Fredericksburg, where the division held the Confederate right, a bullet passed through Pender's left arm, but no bones were broken. He continued to ride along the line with the injured limb hanging down and blood dripping from his fingers.

The North Carolinian was again in the thick of the high drama at Chancellorsville, where he tramped with Jackson on his famous flank march on May 2, and led his brigade in the sweeping surprise attack that crushed the Union Eleventh Corps. When Hill was wounded that evening, Pender took command of the Light Division. On May 3, attacking headlong into the Federal lines, Pender grabbed a regimental flag and carried it on horseback at the head of his men straight into the Federal trenches. The next day a spent bullet struck Pender while he stood behind an entrenchment. The ball, which had killed an officer in front of him, produced only a slight bruise to his right arm near the shoulder. However, in a few days the arm was stiff. He became ill, but returned to his brigade on May 13.

When Hill was promoted to command the new Third Corps after Chancellorsville, his first priority was to find a successor to lead the beloved Light Division. He was anxious to see that it preserved its "pride in its name . . . its 'shoulder to shoulder feeling' and good feelings between the brigades." With this in mind, he recommended his most intimate subordinate for the position, writing, "Gen. Pender has fought with the Division in every battle, has been four times wounded and never left the field, has risen by death and wounds from fifth brigadier to be its senior, has the best drilled and disciplined Brigade in the Division, and more than all, possesses the unbounded confidence of the Division." Lee himself noted: "Pender is an excellent officer, attentive, industrious and brave; has been conspicuous in every battle." The promotion to major general and head of Hill's Division came on May 27, 1863, just before the Gettysburg Campaign. Privately, Lee was quoted as saying that Pender was the most promising of the younger officers of the Army.

The new major general continued to write extremely tender, emotional letters to his wife, right up to the moment he rode onto the battlefield at Gettysburg. There, for some reason, he wore a colonel's uniform, with three braid loops, three un-wreathed stars, and the light blue trousers of an infantry officer. Although he was inexperienced as a major general, he had commanded the division before and done well; he was expected to do well again. His wife, though, was steadfastly against the raid into Pennsylvania because she did not think the Lord would bless Southern arms if the Confederacy assumed an offensive strategy.

GETTYSBURG: Dorsey Pender's Division, camped on the northern side of the Chambersburg Pike in the Cashtown Gap, got onto the road at 8:00 a.m. on July 1 and marched toward Gettysburg in the rear of Maj. Gen. Henry Heth's Division. Col. Abner Perrin's Brigade was in the lead, followed by the brigades of Brig. Gens. Alfred Scales, James Lane and Edward Thomas. At 9:30, as Perrin reached Marsh Creek, Pender heard the boom and crackle of Heth's fight just ahead, and stopped to form a line of battle about two miles east of McPherson's Ridge where the battle was being fought. The subsequent slow advance through the fields on that hot morning fatigued the men and kept Pender's brigades from joining the desperate fight between Heth and the Union First Corps. (It is unknown whether Pender would have been thrown into the battle even if his brigades had been available, given Lee's order not to bring on a general engagement). Pender's brigades finally reached Herr Ridge a little before noon, just as Heth's men were being repulsed in their front. There he was held in place while Lee and Hill discussed the morning events with Heth and settled on a course of action.

Pender deployed his men in line of battle on Herr Ridge and there his brigades rested until around 2:30 that afternoon. By this time, another division from Lt. Gen. Richard Ewell's Second Corps, under Maj. Gen. Robert Rodes, was attacking the right flank of the Federal First Corps, and when it became obvious to Lee that a general engagement had developed, Heth's Division, with two fresh brigades, renewed its attack against McPherson's Ridge in Pender's front. Pender's brigades were held behind Heth as support. The advancing Confederates got more than they bargained for from the tough First Corps defenders on McPherson's Ridge, and at the height of the attack Heth was struck in the head by a minie ball, badly dazed but not mortally wounded.

With Heth's four brigades pounded into disorder, A. P. Hill, who was closely monitoring the situation, sent Pender forward. (Evidence on exactly when Pender was ordered to advance is in some dispute). By this time the Federals had slowly fallen back and taken a position on Seminary Ridge—the last line of defense short of the town itself.

It was not until about 4:00 p.m. when Pender got the order from Hill to launch his attack. His line stretched for about one mile in length, from the Chambersburg Pike south to the Fairfield Road. Scales' men held the left flank near the pike, Perrin's the center, and Lane's the right. Thomas' brigade was held in reserve to exploit any advantage uncovered by his other three brigades. Pender's men marched through Heth's exhausted warriors with the steady step of veterans. By the time they reached the low ground some 200 yards in front of Union line, Scales' North Carolinians had been nearly obliterated by a storm of musketry and canister and shell fire. With Lane's men held up on the right by dismounted Federal troopers fighting from behind stone walls and fences with Sharps carbines, Perrin's Brigade continued the charge alone. After about a half-hour of bloody fighting, Perrin broke through the Federal line, which was being rolled up on the right by Ewell's Corps at about the same time. The shattered Federals retreated through the town and took up a position on the heights beyond. Disorganized after the bloody victory, Pender pursued the retreating men, then halted in and west of town. That evening, with Thomas's Brigade brought up, the division was posted on Seminary Ridge facing east. Pender's debut as a division commander had been outstanding.

On July 2, Pender's Division held the left of Hill's Corps, with his own left around the Lutheran Seminary extending down Seminary Ridge to Maj. Gen. Richard Anderson's Division. Pender's men held the quietest sector of Lee's long and overextended line, with Lane on the left, Scales to his right, Perrin behind Lane, and Thomas in front of Scales. That afternoon, James Longstreet's First Corps launched an attack against the Union left flank, which was followed by Anderson's Division as the assault rolled northward. As the attack was working its way up the front, Pender was sitting on a large granite rock near the left of his line. When the sound of battle got closer, he mentioned the attack to a fellow officer and they mounted to ride down the line toward the firing. Just before sunset, he was struck in the thigh by a two-inch-square piece of shell. He had a penchant for attracting enemy metal, and Pender did not think the wound mortal; he regretted turning over his command to Lane. He was carried to the rear and taken by ambulance on the long and painful ride back to Virginia.

Pender safely reached Staunton, Virginia, and there suffered a ruptured artery. In an attempt to save his life, surgeons amputated his limb on July 18, but he died a few hours later. Before his passing, Pender had quietly told the surgeon: "Tell my wife that I do not fear to die. I can confidently resign my soul to God, trusting in the atonement of Jesus Christ. My only regret is to leave her and our two children. I have always tried to do my duty in every sphere in which Providence has placed me." Fanny's intuition of disaster north of the Potomac had been right on two counts: the army was defeated, and the gallant Pender was no more.

For further reading:

Freeman, Douglas S. *Lee's Lieutenants: A Study in Command*, vol. 3. New York, 1944.

Hassler, William W. "Dorsey Pender, C.S.A.: A Profile." *Civil War Times Illustrated*, 1, Oct. 1962.

Pender, William D. *The General to His Lady: The Civil War Letters of William Dorsey Pender to Fanny Pender*. Ed. by William W. Hassler, Gaithersburg, 1988.

Pfanz, Harry W. *Gettysburg: The Second Day*. Chapel Hill, 1987.

Schenck, Martin. *Up Came Hill: The Story of the Light Division and of Its Leaders*. Harrisburg, PA, 1958.

MAJOR GENERAL
ISAAC RIDGEWAY TRIMBLE

At sixty-one Isaac Trimble was one of the oldest generals on either side at Gettysburg, yet the huge, scowling, martial mustache that blazed across his face advertised the fact that behind it was one of the most pugnacious commanders on the field. On battlefield after battlefield in 1862 he had driven himself and his brigade past the limits of their comrades, making him a favorite with his legendarily relentless commander, Maj. Gen. Thomas "Stonewall" Jackson. Stoking his inner fire was naked ambition. "Before this war is over," he had told a delighted Jackson, "I intend to be a major general or a corpse."

Trimble was a restless soul, a Culpeper, Virginia, native who had gone west and had been appointed to West Point out of Kentucky; he later identified himself with the state of Maryland. Graduating from West Point at the age of twenty, he served in the artillery branch of the Old Army for ten years, then in 1832 doffed his uniform and entered the fast-growing railroad industry, where there was unlimited opportunity for such a fiery competitor. In the nearly thirty years before the Civil War, he engineered a number of railroad lines in the Mid-Atlantic region and became a distinguished superintendent.

In the early weeks of the war, Trimble used his acumen to try bring victory to the South in one quick stroke by burning the railroad bridges north of his adopted Baltimore, thereby obstructing the passage of Northern troops bound for Washington and rendering the capital defenseless. When that failed and it became clear that Maryland would not secede, he went home to Virginia. In May he enlisted in the Engineers and went to work constructing battery emplacements. Although Gen. Joe Johnston initially had a low regard for his military abilities, Trimble managed to get himself commissioned brigadier general by August and placed with a brigade by November 1861.

Trimble's first chance to show what he could do came the next spring in Stonewall's Shenandoah Campaign at Cross Keys on June 8, 1862. While placed in the front line of Maj. Gen. Richard Ewell's command, he drew an attack by Maj. Gen. John C. Fremont's Federals. Trimble ordered his men to hold their fire, then the entire brigade blasted a volley into the faces of the Federals, who staggered and ran. Trimble advanced after the enemy until they were a mile ahead of other Confederate brigades. Not yet content, he heatedly insisted on another attack. Ewell refused his request but remembered his ardor: "Trimble won the fight," he would confide later, "and I believe now if I had followed his views we would have destroyed Fremont's army."

To the men Trimble appeared old and cranky, with an eccentricity of dress which made him right at home in the command of the eccentric Jackson and "Old Baldy" Ewell. Once, when someone mentioned the subject of "fancy soldiers," Jackson pointed to Trimble, "sitting on the fence, with black army hat, cord and feathers, [and said] 'There is the only fancy soldier in my command.'" Another distinguishing feature was his bull voice. One of his men remembered, "Trimble gave the loudest command I ever heard, to 'Forward, guide center, march!' I could hear the echo . . . for miles."

Trimble displayed his aggressive tendencies again at Gaines' Mill, and at Malvern Hill he vainly begged Jackson to let him make a night assault, unwilling to give up without one more effort even though 5,000 Confederates casualties already covered the ground. In the early stages of the Second Manassas Campaign, Trimble routed one Federal brigade at Freeman's Ford on the banks of the Rappahannock. Later, after Jackson had mercilessly driven his flanking column around Pope's army and into its rear, Trimble volunteered his exhausted brigade for one more march to the Federal supply depot at Manassas Junction. Jackson gratefully accepted. Trimble's men, numbed with lack of sleep, aching and foot-weary, legged out the additional distance and rushed forward and captured two Federal batteries. In September, after Trimble was wounded in the Battle of Second Manassas (hit above the left ankle by an explosive bullet), Jackson recommended him for promotion to major general, extolling his virtues as an aggressive and capable leader. Confederate regulations, however, required that Trimble be well enough to serve with the troops before such a promotion could be effected.

Trimble's injury healed slowly, and he developed numerous infections and complications. True to form, Trimble went on the offensive from his sickbed, writing enraged letters to the Adjutant General and Secretary of War, demanding his promotion at once. The letters bore fruit, and on January 19, 1863, Trimble was promoted to major general and given command of one of Jackson's divisions—though he had still not recovered. When he fell sick again in April, Maj. Gen. Edward "Allegheny" Johnson took over command of the division after the Battle of Chancellorsville in May. Meanwhile, Trimble was given command of the quiet Shenandoah Valley District.

When the army marched north across the Potomac River, Isaac Trimble could not remain in his quiet backwater when battle was promised in Maryland or Pennsylvania, a region he knew like the back of his hand from his railroading days. Trimble joined Lee in the third week of June, and after he wore out his welcome at army headquarters, rode north and joined his old chief, Lt. Gen. Richard Ewell, in Carlisle on June 28. With but a single brigade Trimble volunteered to take the capital of Pennsylvania (about whose defenses or garrison he knew absolutely nothing), an offer Ewell was wise enough to brush aside. On June 30, however, orders came from Lee for the army to concentrate, and Ewell moved south with the garrulous Trimble always at his ear.

GETTYSBURG: Trimble accompanied Ewell during the whole of July 1, giving unsolicited advice with the receipt of every dispatch from Lee and at every turn in the road. Trimble's close association with Ewell ended at a stormy meeting in the late afternoon, after the retreat of the Union Eleventh Corps and after Ewell had received Lee's order to take Cemetery Hill "if practicable," but avoid a general engagement. Trimble buzzed excitedly, "General, don't you intend to pursue our sweep and push the enemy vigorously?" According to Trimble's later recollections in 1883, Ewell only paced about, cited Lee's order not to bring on a general engagement, and looked confused. Trimble urgently advised taking Culp's Hill—"you should send a brigade with artillery to take possession of that hill," he cautioned the corps commander—which he saw as the key to the whole Union position. "Give me a division," he said, according to one witness, "and I will engage to take that hill." When this was declined, he said, "Give me a brigade and I will do it." When this was declined, Trimble said, "Give me a good regiment and I will engage to take that hill." Ewell snapped back, "When I need advice from a junior officer I generally ask for it." Trimble warned Ewell that he would regret not following his suggestions for as long as he lived, threw down his sword, and stormed off, saying he would no longer serve under such an officer.

On July 2, Trimble stood by in his status as major-general-at-large, for he had no command to lead anywhere. On July 3, though, two of Hill's divisions earmarked for the climactic charge on the enemy center were without commanding generals. Lee assigned Trimble to command Maj. Gen. Dorsey Pender's Division, a move that replaced senior Brig. Gen. James Lane, who had been in charge since Pender's wounding the previous afternoon. It was Lane who placed the troops in line that morning, and Trimble probably saw his two attacking brigades for the first time when he and Lee rode along their lines that morning. The brigades, Lanes' and Brig. Gen. Alfred Scales' (under Col. William Lowrance) had been deployed in the rear of the assaulting column behind troops from Maj. Gen. Henry Heth's Division (now commanded by Brig. Gen. Johnston Pettigrew). Pettigrew's and Trimble's brigades formed the left wing of the attack force on a line that ran from McMillan's Woods to Spangler's Woods on the west slope of Seminary Ridge. Maj. Gen. George Pickett's Division formed the right wing.

The faulty alignment of Trimble's pair of brigades became obvious rather quickly once the attackers moved out against Cemetery Ridge about 3:00 p.m. Before Trimble had taken command, Lane had placed the small and bloodied brigades (worn out from heavy fighting on July 1) behind the right flank of Pettigrew's Division. Pettigrew's line, however, extended well beyond the left flank of the brigade line organized by Lane. Thus the left flank of the attacking column had no support whatsoever. If, as Pettigrew later told one of Lee's staff officers, Trimble was to have advanced *en echelon*, Lane would (or should) have positioned the pair of brigades behind and slightly beyond Pettigrew's left flank.

Trimble rode on his mare Jinny during the attack forever after known as Pickett's Charge. By the time he approached the Emmitsburg Road, much of the left of the attacking column had melted away. A bullet smashed into his ankle and also wounded his horse. Trimble sent a message to Lane to take charge of the division, which was by then a jumbled mass of disorganized regiments, each fighting on its own hook.

The ride across the mile-wide valley was Trimble's last active participation in the Civil War. He was carried to the rear, where the lower third of his leg was amputated at a farmhouse. Surgeons warned that infection would set in if he were moved in an ambulance, so Trimble remained behind and was taken prisoner. He spent the next

year and a half in Northern hands, then was exchanged in February 1865. Lee surrendered before he could return to the field.

For further reading:

Freeman, Douglas S. *Lee's Lieutenants: A Study in Command*, vol. 3. New York, 1944.

Grace, William M. "Isaac Trimble, the Indefatigable and Courageous." MA Thesis, VA Polytechnic Inst., 1984.

Long, Roger "Gen. Isaac Trimble in Captivity." *Gettysburg Magazine*, #1, 1989.

Pohanka, Brian, ed., "Gettysburg: Fight Enough in Old Man Trimble to Satisfy a Herd of Tigers: Diary of Isaac Ridgeway Trimble, Division Commander, A. P. Hill's Corps." *Civil War Magazine*, 46, Aug. 1994.

PERRIN'S BRIGADE:
(1,882 MEN)

COLONEL
ABNER MONROE PERRIN

Colonel Perrin was one of many lawyers with military experience leading a brigade in Gen. Robert E. Lee's army at Gettysburg. A native of South Carolina, he enlisted in the regular army at the age of nineteen when the Mexican War began. Like many Southern men, it is likely Perrin saw the conflict as a means of career advancement.

He served there as a lieutenant of infantry, and when the war ended in 1848, went home, studied law, and was admitted to the bar in 1854.

Perrin practiced until the Civil War broke out, when he was made captain of a company in the 14th South Carolina regiment in the summer of 1861. Ordered to the Peninsula in the spring of 1862, the 14th saw heavy fighting with Brig. Gen. Maxey Gregg's Brigade in the Seven Days' Battles at Gaines' Mill and Glendale. Cedar Mountain, Second Manassas, Sharpsburg, and Fredericksburg followed, and Perrin and his 14th South Carolina often found themselves in the thickest of the fighting.

At Fredericksburg, Union bullets killed the fearless, scimitar-wielding brigade leader Gregg, and the 14th South Carolina's energetic colonel, Samuel McGowan, took over the brigade, leaving Perrin in command of the regiment. He was promoted to colonel in January 1863, and led his regiment officially for the first time in battle during the Chancellorsville Campaign in May. McGowan was severely wounded in his debut as brigadier at Chancellorsville, leaving Perrin to lead the brigade through the rest of the engagement. At the end of that month, the thirty-six year old Colonel Perrin was placed in command of the brigade. The remarkable thing about Perrin's succession to brigade command was that he had yet to be mentioned or commended by any of his superior officers. His ascension to this leadership position may be seen as another sign of the lack of available quality brigade leaders in Lee's army after the attrition of a full year of nearly constant combat.

The brigade of South Carolinians Perrin inherited was one of the proudest in the Army of Northern Virginia, and among the most striking of the brigades in Maj. Gen. A. P. Hill's vaunted Light Division. These troops fought under a Palmetto banner, the emblem of the state that saw itself as "The Cradle of the Rebellion." Their original roster contained twenty-seven physicians, thirty attorneys, plus a number of landed gentry (cotton and rice planters), all full of dash and spirit. By the summer of 1863, the brigade's leadership had been decimated. Their leadership had devolved to lieutenant colonels, majors, and even captains. Perrin himself had not led a regiment until Chancellorsville. General Lee was relying on the veteran quality of the men in the ranks to make up for the inexperienced leadership.

Whether Perrin's Brigade's would live up to its proud reputation under the command of inexperienced leaders remained an open question as the South Carolinians tramped across the rolling Pennsylvania farmland toward Gettysburg.

GETTYSBURG: Perrin's Brigade led Maj. Gen. W. Dorsey Pender's Division through the Cashtown Gap on the morning of July 1, following in the wake of Maj. Gen. Henry Heth's Division as it tramped down the Chambersburg Pike toward Gettysburg. About 9:30 a.m., when Perrin's men had passed Marsh Creek, about 3 miles east of Gettysburg, the sounds of Heth's battle were clearly audible ahead, and the South Carolinians were sent south of the road to form the right of the division's battle line. Pender advanced his division slowly and reached Herr Ridge some time before noon. However, it was not called upon to attack until about 4:00 p.m., following the afternoon attack of Heth's Division, which had driven the Union First Corps off of McPherson's Ridge and back to Seminary Ridge. Perrin's Brigade, which was now in the center of Pender's line, was made up of four South Carolina regiments deployed from left to right as follows: 14th, 1st Provisional Army, 12th, and 13th; the 1st SC Rifles were on detached duty. Brig. Gen. Alfred Scales' Brigade was on Perrin's left, and Brig. Gen. James Lane's was on his right. Perrin advanced east toward Seminary Ridge below the Chambersburg Pike with his right flank just north of the Fairfield Road.

As Perrin's troops advanced across the 600 yards of clear ground in front of Seminary Ridge, Scales' men on the left were blasted by Federal gunners and torn to pieces, while Lane's soldiers on the right had become distracted by Union cavalrymen firing into their ranks with carbines. The sudden strength of Pender's Division was melting away brigade by brigade. By the time the South Carolinians had passed a swale about 200 yards short of the bristling Federal line built under the eaves of the Lutheran Seminary, they were largely on their own. Suffering from a storm of canister on the left (from the same guns that had shredded Scales' command), and musketry in their faces from Colonel Biddle's Federals, Perrin's men moved forward without stopping to fire. "There was no giving back on our part," wrote the brigade's historian, "the line pressed on, many men throwing away their knapsacks and blankets to keep up." When the charge wavered under the murderous fire, Colonel Perrin noticed a small gap in the Union line, where Biddle's left did not connect with the right flank of Colonel Gamble's dismounted cavalry. He boldly rode his horse through his faltering line and rallied his brigade for a final push, leading the assault in person. "Filled with an admiration for such courage as defied the whole fire of the enemy (naturally drawn to his horse, his uniform, and his slashing sword)," wrote one soldier, "the brigade followed, with a shout that was itself half a victory."

Initially only some from the 1st South Carolina followed Perrin. These troops, with vigor renewed, drove up and into the Seminary grounds, driving back the cavalry and overlapping the left end of the Federal line of infantry. With General Ewell's Second Corps turning and breaking the far right flank of the Union defensive line at about the same time, it was more than the exhausted Union First Corps men could stand. Biddle ordered his men to withdraw toward Gettysburg, and the Seminary Ridge line began to unravel. It was only 4:20 p.m., and Pender's attack was only 20 minutes old. Many of the Federals did not stop until they reached the hills south and east of town. Perrin's men captured hundreds of enemy soldiers, a cannon, and at least four battle flags; some accounts credit them as being the first Rebels to reach the streets of Gettysburg.

Perrin's South Carolina Brigade suffered heavily. All four of the attacking regiments lost more than a third of their men, and they were so torn apart and disorganized after their costly victory that Perrin was forced to halt his mass of soldiers and organize before they could continue pursuit. Perrin's tired men spent the night on Seminary Ridge south of the Fairfield Road with the rest of the division.

Perrin's men were not asked to assault the enemy for the remainder of the battle, though heavy skirmishing continued with the Union defenders on Cemetery Hill for the next two days. On the evening of July 2, Perrin's men, along with Brig. Gen. Edward Thomas', advanced to the Long Lane in support of an attack by Maj. Gen. Robert Rodes' Division, which was aborted at the last moment. Perrin remained near Long Lane with Thomas and two of Rodes' brigades until the army was pulled back on the night of July 3.

The South Carolinian's performance at the head of his veteran brigade was one of the few truly bright lights of the campaign. His tactics and brilliant (and timely) display of courage on the first day of battle won him a brigadier general's wreath two months later on September 10. Perrin continued to lead the brigade until the return of General McGowan in early 1864, when Lee transferred Perrin to take charge of Maj. Gen. Cadmus Wilcox's Brigade, since that general had just been given a division. Perrin led his men in a daring counterattack on the Bloody Angle at the Battle of Spotsylvania on May 12, 1864. Just before the battle he had vowed to emerge a live major general or a dead brigadier. The law of averages, which he had defied at the Lutheran Seminary, caught up with him when he fell from his horse pierced by no fewer than seven bullets.

For further reading:

Capers, Ellison. "South Carolina," vol. 5 of *Confederate Military History*. Ed. by Clement A. Evans. Atlanta, 1899 [vol. 6 of the extended edition. Wilmington, 1987].

Freeman, Douglas Southall. *Lee's Lieutenants: A Study in Command*, vol. 3. New York, 1944.

Miller, J. Michael. "Perrin's Brigade on July 1, 1863." *Gettysburg Magazine*, #13, 1995.

Schenck, Martin. *Up Came Hill: The Story of the Light Division and of Its Leaders.* Harrisburg, PA, 1958.

LANE'S BRIGADE:
(1,730 MEN)

BRIGADIER GENERAL
JAMES HENRY LANE

"Little Jim" Lane was one of the Confederate army's "intellectual" soldiers. Along with Lt. Gen. Thomas "Stonewall" Jackson, he taught at the Virginia Military Institute. Born on a Virginia plantation and educated by tutors, Lane graduated second in his class from VMI in 1854, and went on to receive another degree in science from the University of Virginia three years later. He stayed in academia, returning to VMI to become assistant professor of mathematics and tactics. Twenty-seven years old at the outbreak of the Civil War, he was professor of natural philosophy and instructor in military tactics at the North Carolina Military Institute.

Lane, a Virginian, decided to personally lead his North Carolina cadets, a difficult task because of a longstanding rivalry between the two states over a variety of economic matters. He was commissioned major of a group of 1,100 young men, who by reason of their early enlistment, zeal in drill, and tight discipline, were awarded the proud title of the 1st North Carolina Volunteers. Their colonel was Daniel H. Hill. The 1st North Carolina fought and won the first engagement in the East on June 10, 1861, at Big Bethel.

Three months later, in September 1861, Lane became a colonel and took command of the 28th North Carolina. His first action came in the late spring of 1862 on the Peninsula at Hanover Court House, where his brigade commander, Brig. Gen. Lawrence O'Bryan Branch, rashly attacked a Federal force three times his size and lost about 1,000 men (mostly taken prisoner). In June, Branch's Brigade was merged into Maj. Gen. A. P. Hill's newly created "Light Division,"

which in the Seven Days' Battles earned a reputation as one of the hardest-fighting divisions in the army. Lane led his men well and received a slight head wound on June 27 at Gaines' Mill, and was again wounded three days later in the right cheek at Frayser's Farm; he refused to leave the field. Lane was the first officer Branch mentioned in his commendation of his regimental commanders after the conclusion of the campaign.

After his regiment helped drive the enemy at Cedar Mountain, Lane and the 28th North Carolina fought along the Railroad Cut at Second Manassas. In September, Lane took command of the brigade at Sharpsburg when Branch was killed leading the Light Division's famous countercharge late in the day. The brigade's soldiers petitioned to have "Little Jim" named as their permanent commander and promoted to brigadier general. Lee agreed, and Lane was given his brigadier's wreath on November 1, 1862.

At Fredericksburg, however, Lane's first real combat experience leading a brigade, the Federals broke the Confederate line by crashing through a gap left between Lane's right flank and Brig. Gen. James Archer's left flank. The breach was finally mended with the help of reinforcements rushed over from Maj. Gen. Jubal Early's Division. Despite this near-calamity, Lane had shown poise by staying cool and in complete command of his brigade throughout the ordeal. At Chancellorsville in May 1863, Lane's Brigade was in the front line of Stonewall's famous flank attack. He lost a horrifying 909 men—more soldiers than any other brigade in either army. In addition, Lane's North Carolinians bore the stigma of mortally wounding the most revered man in the Confederacy when a volley fired by them in the confusion of the evening of May 2 felled Jackson.

After Jackson's death, it was a sorrowful brigade that Lane led on the road north into Pennsylvania in the summer of 1863. Also, there was renewed hostility between Carolinians and Virginians as the Gettysburg Campaign began. The politically insensitive President Davis had recently appointed a Virginian as Confederate tax collector in North Carolina, a move that disgusted Lane's men. Lane, however, had long had the strong affections of his North Carolinians. He and his men could be counted on to do the right thing when the bullets started to fly.

GETTYSBURG: Lane's Brigade arrived on Herr Ridge a little before noon on July 1 with the rest of Maj. Gen. W. Dorsey Pender's Division, and was posted on the left center of the four-brigade battle line, with its right resting on the Chambersburg Pike. The division did not become engaged at that time, and instead was halted to witness the end of Maj. Gen. Henry Heth's morning attack. Not long afterward, Lane was moved to the far right to guard against Union cavalry. Two other brigades from the division under Brig. Gen. Alfred Scales and Col. Abner Perrin moved slowly forward from Herr Ridge at about 2:30 p.m. in support of Heth's afternoon attack, but waited until 4:00 p.m. before getting the order to go in.

Lane's Brigade, composed of five North Carolina regiments, was deployed facing east from left to right as follows: 33rd, 18th, 28th, 37th; the 7th regiment was deployed in skirmish order at nearly a right angle to the brigade line facing generally south. The left flank of the brigade rested on the Fairfield Road.

By this time, Heth had driven the Union defenders back to Seminary Ridge, but his division was fought out. A lone Federal cavalry regiment under Colonel Gamble menaced the division's flank and distracted Lane's Brigade as it went slowly forward. Lane had reason to be wary in his advance, for his brigade at that moment represented the army's far right, and thus his flank was very vulnerable. Unfortunately, Lane's battle report says virtually nothing about his engagement of July 1. His men drifted somewhat to the right in their advance and eventually scattered the Union cavalrymen. The move, however, separated his brigade from those of Col. Abner Perrin's and Brig. Gen. Alfred Scales', both of which were assaulting Seminary Ridge in desperate and bloody attempt to pry the Union First Corps infantry from their position around the Lutheran Seminary. Several sources say that Lane's troops additionally became delayed when they stopped to form squares—Napoleonic-era formations used against cavalry charges. As his fitful advance continued, Perrin's South Carolinians broke through at the Seminary and the Union defense of the ridge collapsed in a chaotic retreat through Gettysburg and beyond. Lane stopped his regiments behind a stone wall at McMillan's Woods and waited for an order to advance on the Federals rallying on Cemetery Hill. The order was never issued, and his Tarheels spent the night in that location.

Other than skirmishing, Pender's Division was not engaged on July 2 and remained on Seminary Ridge while James Longstreet's men assaulted the Union left, and Richard Ewell's battled on Culp's Hill. Pender asked Lane "to take possession of a road in my front [probably Long Lane] with my skirmishers," Lane later wrote. He advanced some men, probably just the 37th North Carolina, which "executed the order very handsomely." Although Lane later wrote that "nothing of interest occurred in my command on the 2d," an event about sunset was to have a dramatic effect upon the morrow's events. At the height of Longstreet's attack, Lane was notified that he was in charge of the division, since a shell fragment had wounded General Pender. Although he was instructed to advance the division if there was "a good opportunity for doing so," he did not.

Shortly thereafter, an awkward situation arose for Lane. Second Corps chief Lt. Gen. Richard Ewell called upon him to provide support for an attack which would stretch from Culp's Hill on the far left to the northwest face of Cemetery Hill, where Maj. Gen. Robert Rodes' Division was preparing to attack. Lane was to advance and support Rodes. Thinking that Third Corps commander A. P. Hill did not yet know of Pender's fall, however, Lane had dispatched a message informing him of the command change and seeking direction. Should he wait or advance? Rather boldly, Lane decided to "act without awaiting instructions from General Hill" and advanced the brigades of Brig. Gen. Edward Thomas and Col. Abner Perrin to the Long Lane to form an obtuse angle with the right flank of Brig. Gen. Dodson Ramseur's [Rodes'] line. Lane was working to support these two brigades with two others "when the night attack was abandoned."

On July 3, the skirmishing before Long Lane was very heavy, and Lane was engaged for hours there. Before noon he was called with the two brigades that formed his second line at that time (his own and Scales' under Col. William Lowrance) to support the attack General Lee was planning to launch against the Union right center on Cemetery Ridge. Why these two were selected is unknown; Scales' men had been decimated on July 1. With Maj. Gen. George Pickett's Division on the right, supported by two Third Corps brigades, and Henry Heth's Division on the left (now under Brig. Gen. Johnston Pettigrew), Lee hoped to crack through the enemy line and win a decisive victory. Lane claims Longstreet personally ordered him to deploy his two brigades behind the right rear of Pettigrew's Division in the staging area of Seminary Ridge. His small line was formed with his own brigade on the left, and Lowrance's men on the right. As soon as this was complete, Lane was relieved of the command of the division and returned to his brigade, replaced by Maj. Gen. Isaac Trimble. The formation was fatally flawed, however. "Heth's division was much larger than Lowrance's brigade and my own,

which were its only support" reported Lane after the battle, "and there was consequently no second line in rear of its left." In other words, the left flank of the attacking column was unprotected. Whether Lane brought this to anyone's attention is not known. It is difficult to believe that Dorsey Pender would have allowed such an obviously flawed tactical arrangement advance into battle.

When the attack went forward around 3:00 p.m. the left two brigades of Pettigrew's Division (Mayo's and Davis') were quickly driven away by enfilading fire, and Lane swerved his brigade to the left to bolster the endangered flank. "My command never moved forward more handsomely," wrote the proud brigadier. As his men approached the Emmitsburg Road, Lane received a message from Trimble that he was again in charge of the division—Trimble had just been shot. By this time there was not a division worthy of the name to command, for the regiments were simply masses of men following their flags toward the blazing enemy line, and effective control was virtually impossible. Lane's horse was shot out from under him, and he continued on foot.

His North Carolinians advanced to within a few yards of the stone wall under a horrendous barrage of artillery and small arms fire when they were flanked by Federals, who had crowded forward on their left. The aggressive Lane ordered his left two regiments to continue the advance, even though most of Pettigrew's Division had already fallen back and his own right was retreating. The colonel of the 33rd North Carolina could not accept the order. "My God General!" he shouted in disbelief. "Do you intend rushing your men into such a place unsupported?" Lane wisely rescinded the order and his men fell back to Seminary Ridge. His brigade suffered almost 50% casualties, or some 600 killed, wounded and missing in the half-hour advance. Lane's men were the last Confederates to leave that part of the field, and Lane himself was one of only three of the eight generals in the attack to return unhurt.

In mid-July Brig. Gen. Cadmus Wilcox was named permanent commander of the division after Dorsey Pender died, and "Little Jim" Lane went back to command of his brigade. He served well in the Wilderness and Spotsylvania, but was badly wounded at Cold Harbor and missed the rest of the year (and perhaps his only opportunity for advancement). Lane returned and fought at Petersburg and served until the end of the war.

The capable brigadier found his family plantation ruined when he returned home. He returned to academics after the war and was a professor of civil engineering at the Alabama Polytechnic Institute when he died in 1907.

For further reading:

Freeman, Douglas S. *Lee's Lieutenants: A Study in Command*, vol. 3. New York, 1944.

Hill, D.H., Jr. "North Carolina," vol. 4 of *Confederate Military History*. Ed. by Clement A. Evans. Atlanta, 1899 [vol. 5 of the extended edition. Wilmington, 1987].

Lee, Charles C. "The First North Carolina Volunteers." *Southern Historical Society Papers*, 19, 1891.

Schenck, Martin. *Up Came Hill: The Story of the Light Division and of Its Leaders*. Harrisburg, PA, 1958.

THOMAS' BRIGADE:
(1,322 MEN)

BRIGADIER GENERAL
EDWARD LLOYD THOMAS

While Edward Thomas was a plantation owner from Georgia, he did have some military experience prior to the Civil War. After graduating from Emory College in 1846, he joined the army fighting in Mexico, which was the proper thing for a young Southern gentleman landowner to do at the time. He served there as a 2nd Lieutenant of Georgia mounted volunteers in a unit called the "Newton County Independent Horse." After Mexico had been defeated, however,

he declined a commission in the Regular Army, hung up his sword, and went back to his plantation, where he remained until the South voted for secession.

When the conflict began, his social prominence and Mexican War experience garnered him authorization from President Davis to raise a regiment, and he became colonel of the 35th Georgia infantry in October 1861. Sent to defend the Peninsula in the spring of 1862, Thomas' regiment was placed in Brig. Gen. Johnston Pettigrew's Brigade, part of the Confederate army at Yorktown. When Pettigrew was wounded and captured at the Battle of Seven Pines, Thomas took temporary command of the brigade. In the following days, however, the brigade was disbanded, Thomas reverted back to the command of his regiment, and the 35th Georgia was placed in Brig. Gen. Joseph R. Anderson's Brigade, part of Maj. Gen. A. P. Hill's newly formed "Light Division."

At Mechanicsville, the first large-scale battle of the Seven Days, the 35th Georgia was the only Confederate regiment to actually fight its way across heavily defended Beaver Dam Creek. Thomas and his men had to fall back, however, and he was wounded during the retreat. Thomas ignored his injury and after Anderson fell wounded at Frayser's Farm with a shot in the forehead, assumed command of the brigade. In his report of the campaign, Anderson commended Thomas, whom he said, "evinced fearlessness and

good judgment...throughout the expedition." Anderson soon retired to manage Richmond's Tredegar Iron Works, and his brigade of Georgians became Thomas' for the rest of the war.

The Second Manassas Campaign marked his debut as brigade commander. At the Battle of Cedar Mountain, Thomas' troops fought well, and Maj. Gen. A. P. Hill reported that, "Much credit is due Thomas' Brigade for the admirable manner in which they acted under very discouraging circumstances." At the Battle of Second Manassas, Thomas' Georgians were in the thick of the hand-to-hand fighting along the Railroad Cut. His brigade missed the Battle of Sharpsburg when it was left behind at Harpers Ferry to parole Federal prisoners after the town's capture. At Fredericksburg, when Maj. Gen. George Meade's Pennsylvanians drove through a gap in Hill's Division, Thomas' men rushed into the crumbling Confederate line. "General Thomas, responding to the call of [Brig.] General [James] Lane, rapidly threw forward his brigade of Georgians by the flank," wrote Hill, "deploying by successive formations, squarely met the enemy, charged them, and . . . drove them back, with tremendous loss, to their original position." Thomas' role was less crucial at Chancellorsville, where his brigade suffered the lightest losses of any in the division.

For a year before the Gettysburg Campaign, Thomas had led a brigade in every battle except Sharpsburg, and had shepherded his men through heavy fighting. The thirty-eight year old brigadier, however, was not the sort of soldier around whom colorful stories proliferated, and the official reports were full of references to "Thomas' Brigade," but rarely to Thomas himself. Nevertheless, the Georgians had never been "driven," and Thomas could be depended on to turn in a solid, if unspectacular, performance.

GETTYSBURG: Thomas' Brigade led a kind of charmed life at Gettysburg. On July 1, Thomas and the rest of Maj. Gen. W. Dorsey Pender's Division made a stately advance to Herr Ridge a little before noon, but the division was halted and held out of the early fighting stirred up by Maj. Gen.

Henry Heth's Division. Only that afternoon did Pender's Division attack, and then corps commander A. P. Hill held back Thomas' Brigade in reserve. The Georgians were thus spared the bloodletting in front of the Union lines at the Lutheran Seminary. The fighting ended with Thomas still in the rear, apparently forgotten by Pender. Thomas came forward that evening and spent the night on Seminary Ridge with Pender's three other brigades.

On July 2, the day passed with nothing expected of Pender's Division (largely because of its fortuitous placement on Seminary Ridge) except some skirmishing along Long Lane, which ran southwest out of Gettysburg. Early in the evening, Thomas and Col. Abner Perrin were ordered forward at the last minute to support an attack by Maj. Gen. Robert Rodes' Division on Cemetery Hill. The two brigades advanced into Long Lane, but Rodes' men moved only a short distance in the dark before the night attack was called off. Thomas and Perrin remained there that night, and therefore were not on hand when Gen. Robert E. Lee marked the two brigades of Pender's Division remaining on Seminary Ridge for the task of supporting General Heth's four brigades (now under Brig. Gen. Johnston Pettigrew) in the forthcoming assault later known as Pickett's Charge. With Lee searching for fresh units, it is unknown why Thomas' Brigade was not selected as part of the attacking column. His losses for the entire campaign were only 152 men.

Thomas continued to serve, ably but inconspicuously, at the head of his brigade through all of Lee's battles until the surrender at Appomattox. He returned to his plantation after the war and later served with the Indian Bureau in Indian Territory (Oklahoma). He died there in 1898.

For further reading:

Derry, Joseph T. "Georgia," vol. 6 of *Confederate Military History.* Ed. by Clement A. Evans. Atlanta, 1899 [vol. 7 of the extended edition. Wilmington, 1987.]

Freeman, Douglas S. *Lee's Lieutenants: A Study in Command*, vol. 3. New York, 1944.

N. A. "Gen. Edward Thomas." *Confederate Veteran*, 6, 1889.

Schenck, Martin. *Up Came Hill: The Story of the Light Division and of Its Leaders*. Harrisburg, PA, 1958.

SCALE'S BRIGADE:
(1,347 MEN)

BRIGADIER GENERAL
ALFRED MOORE SCALES

Alfred Scales was a forty-five year old, stern and humorless politician, with iron-gray hair and curly gray chin- whiskers. In many ways he embodied the Southern image of a duty-driven public official-turned-warrior. Born in Rockingham County, North Carolina, he studied law in Greensboro at the University of North Carolina and went back to Rockingham County to practice. There, he served in a number of positions of public trust, including county solicitor, and was elected four times to the state legislature. His political career continued to rise, and Scales was elected to the U.S. House of Representatives in 1857, and was a Presidential Elector for the John C. Breckenridge ticket in the 1860 presidential election.

When the war came, Scales did not angle for an officer's commission like so many of his prominent fellow politicians. Instead, he enlisted in the Confederate army as a private. Almost immediately he was elected to the captaincy of his company in the 3rd North Carolina Volunteers, a regiment led by Col. W. Dorsey Pender. When Pender was transferred to another regiment in the fall of 1861, Scales succeeded him as colonel of the 3rd (later designated the 13th North Carolina). The regiment marched to the Peninsula in time for the Battle of Williamsburg, after which Scales was commended for his conduct by division chief Maj. Gen. James Longstreet. In the Seven Days' Battles, Scales led his men in fighting at Mechanicsville, Gaines' Mill, and Malvern Hill, then collapsed from exhaustion and lay near death. Brigade leader Brig. Gen. Samuel Garland described one exploit of Scales in his report: "Colonel Scales. . .was conspicuous for his fine bearing. Seizing the colors of his regiment at a critical moment at [Gaines' Mill], and advancing to the front, he called upon the Thirteenth to stand to them, thus restoring confidence and keeping his men in position."

During the Maryland Campaign Scales was absent from his regiment, still described as "dangerously ill" by his second-in-command, and finally returned to duty in November. In the reorganization of the army in the fall of 1862, the 13th was transferred to Pender's Brigade. Pender was wounded at the Battle of Fredericksburg in December, and Scale's took command of the brigade. He was again mentioned by his division commander, now Maj. Gen. A. P. Hill, who afterward commended the ex-Congressman for "handsome action." At Chancellorsville, Scales' 13th North Carolina advanced farthest in the maelstrom of combat on May 3, and captured Union Brig. Gen. William Hays. Scales was shot through the thigh but continued fighting until loss of blood forced him to leave the field on a litter. He went home to recover but returned to duty before the Gettysburg Campaign. When now-Maj. Gen. Dorsey Pender rose to take Hill's place at the head of the division at the end of May, it was a foregone conclusion that his replacement in brigade command would be Scales.

On June 13, Scales was promoted to brigadier general and placed in permanent command of Pender's North Carolina men, a brigade which Hill had called "the best drilled and disciplined Brigade in the Division." Even with his meager experience at the brigade level, there was every confidence that the brigade had been placed in the right hands.

GETTYSBURG: In his first battle as brigadier, Scales paid dearly for a rash decision. Scales' Brigade was second in the division column as it approached Gettysburg on July 1. Pender put his soldiers into a line of battle at 9:30 in the morning, placing Scales south of the Chambersburg Pike with Col. Abner Perrin on his right and the other two brigades (Brig. Gens. Lane and Thomas) north of the road. Scales moved slowly forward with this formation through the fields to Herr Ridge.

Though they arrived on the ridge just before noon, the entire division waited until 4:00 p.m. to attack the Union First Corps, and by that time, Heth's men had driven the Northerners back to Seminary Ridge. With Thomas in reserve, the division went forward with a three-brigade front. Scales held the left, Perrin the center and Lane the right. Scales' left was touching the Chambersburg Pike, and his North Carolinians were deployed, from left to right as follows: 13th, 34th, 22nd, and 16th. Scales topped McPherson's Ridge and descended into the shallow valley in front of the Union defenders without halting. In a lapse similar to the one Brig. Gen. Alfred Iverson had committed earlier in the day, the new brigadier failed to reconnoiter the ground over which he would advance. He was thus unaware that his men were bearing down on the gaping muzzles of the First Corps' twenty-one gun artillery brigade. Scales thus led his North Carolinians impetuously into one of the most devastating storms of canister and shell fire witnessed during the Civil War.

The result was a fifteen-minute bloodbath that shredded Scales' regiments. "Here the brigade encountered a most terrific fire of grape and shell fire on our flank, and grape and musketry in our front," wrote Scales after the battle. "Every discharge made sad havoc in our line." The field officers suffered hideously, with fifty-five out of fifty-six falling in the attack. Scales himself collapsed painfully wounded in the leg by a shell fragment. "Our line had been broken up," remembered Scales, "and now only a squad here and there marked the place where regiments had rested." One of Scale's soldiers sadly noted that it was the first time that the brigade had been repulsed, and the shocked remnants of the command saved themselves as best they could. That night, only 500 men in the entire brigade answered roll call.

The next day on July 3, Col. William Lowrance, who inherited command after the bloodletting, called the brigade "depressed, dilapidated, and almost unorganized." Unbelievably, Lee called upon this remnant to participate in Pickett's Charge, which it did with great gallantry. Scores more were killed and wounded in the attempt.

Alfred Scales, who rode to Virginia in the same ambulance that carried the mortally wounded Dorsey Pender, eventually healed and returned to duty at the head of the brigade in August. He led his North Carolina regiments well until February 1865, when he left Lee's doomed army on sick leave and did not return before the surrender.

After the war, Scales resumed his North Carolina law practice and reentered politics, serving in the state legislature and in Congress before being elected governor in 1884. He died in 1892.

For further reading:

Freeman, Douglas S. *Lee's Lieutenants: A Study in Command*, vol. 3. New York, 1944.

Hill, D. H., Jr. "North Carolina," vol. 4 of *Confederate Military History*, ed. by Clement A. Evans. Atlanta, 1899 [vol. 5 of the extended edition. Wilmington, 1987].

HETH'S DIVISION:
(7,423 MEN / 15 GUNS)

MAJOR GENERAL
HENRY "HARRY" HETH

Henry "Harry" Heth was likely the only officer in the Army of Northern Virginia to benefit from the personal patronage of Gen. Robert E. Lee. Undoubtedly Lee felt a certain kinship with Heth (pronounced to rhyme with "teeth") because both men shared common social backgrounds and were West Point and Old Army. Thirty-seven years old, Heth was personally attractive and socially charming. He possessed medium height, with brown hair and a mustache, high cheekbones, strong chin and deep-set eyes. Strongly opinionated, Heth could see his own weaknesses and did not take himself too seriously. That Lee had a strong affection for the handsome officer was obvious to everyone: Heth was the only officer Lee ever called by his first name.

Heth, a cousin of Maj. Gen. George Pickett, was born near Richmond of good "Old Dominion" stock. His grandfather had been an officer in the Revolution, and his father an officer in the navy in the War of 1812. Heth was educated in private schools until he accepted an appointment to West Point from President Tyler. There he disappointed, graduating dead last in the class of 1847 (the same class as his boyhood friend

A. P. Hill). Heth went on to be a dutiful soldier, spending the next fourteen years in frontier outposts, slowly compiling a creditable record and rising to the rank of captain of infantry. He was married in 1857, and Hill served as his groomsman.

Heth resigned his commission when Fort Sumter was bombarded, and was immediately employed by General Lee as Acting Quartermaster General for the Virginia army. Heth only served in this capacity for about a month during the hectic early days of the nascent conflict, but did well in this post and attracted the attention of Lee. Thereafter, Lee interested himself in Heth's advancement as he seems to have done for no other soldier.

After his quartermaster assignment, Heth was made colonel of the 45th Virginia regiment and assigned to Western Virginia, where he would labor for the next year. He was first put under Brig. Gen. John B. Floyd, serving as that commander's inspector general in addition to leading his own regiment. In January 1862 he was promoted to brigadier general and assigned to the defense of Lewisburg in Western Virginia, gateway to the Kanawha Road through the Allegheny Mountains. There, in a small action on May 23, 1862, his entire command was routed from the field. Surprisingly, Heth freely admitted the disgraceful panic and flight of his command in his report of the battle, an unusual occurrence in any war.

The embarrassing affair did not affect his reputation. In the summer of 1862, at the same time the Virginia army was fighting on the Peninsula, Heth was assigned to Maj. Gen. Kirby Smith's army in East Tennessee. He commanded a division in the Perryville Campaign in the late summer and fall of 1862, although Heth was not engaged because Gen. Braxton Bragg fought the Perryville battle before Kirby Smith's force arrived. In January 1863, Heth became commander of the Department of East Tennessee.

A month later, Lee requested that Heth join the Army of Northern Virginia. Lee evidently lobbied hard for Heth's assignment to Lt. Gen. Thomas "Stonewall"

Jackson's corps, for Jackson wrote to Lee at one point, "From what you have said respecting General Heth, I have been desirous that he should report for duty." On March 5, 1863 Heth was given command of a brigade which had been languishing under the lackluster command of Col. John Brockenbrough since Second Manassas the summer before. Newcomer Heth was now the senior brigadier in the Light Division of his old friend, Maj. Gen. A. P. Hill—a development that must have rankled Brig. Gen. W. Dorsey Pender, the division's previous senior brigadier. Heth had never fought in a full-scale pitched battle, whereas Pender had fought hard and was wounded many times while serving with the Light Division throughout the previous year.

Heth commanded his new brigade for the first time at Chancellorsville in May 1863. Determined to show dashing qualities in his first action with the Army of Northern Virginia, he attempted an unsupported counterattack of the Federal Regular Division on the battle's first day. He was saved from a nasty repulse by a quick-witted captain who volunteered to lead a probe with two regiments. When ferocious fire from long lines of hidden Yankees greeted this reconnaissance, Heth wisely called off his attack. The next evening, Heth inherited temporary command of the division when Hill was wounded. Heth himself was slightly wounded later in the battle, but he retained command to the end of the fight, prompting a commendation for "heroic conduct" from the acting corps commander, Maj. Gen. "Jeb" Stuart. His performance standing in for Hill had not been brilliant, but he had at least proven himself steady and reliable while fighting on a scale he had never before experienced.

On May 24, Hill was promoted to the leadership of the new Third Corps. After he left Lee's tent, Hill sat down and wrote a letter concerning the leadership of the three divisions in his new command. He was especially concerned that the right man be promoted to the head of his beloved Light Division. "Of General Heth," he wrote, "I have but to say that I consider him a most excellent officer, and gallant soldier, and had he been with the Division through all its hardships, and acquired the confidence of the men, there is no man I had rather see promoted than he." Having said that, Hill went on to recommend Pender (and properly so) for the post. Hill then suggested what Lee had in fact already decided to do: unite two existing brigades from the Light Division with two other brigades brought up from the Carolinas to form a new division for Heth to lead.

Heth had so many old friends and had made new ones so quickly that there was no complaint when he was made major general after such a brief time with the Army of Northern Virginia. After the march of Lee's army into Pennsylvania in June, the inexperienced Heth led Hill's Third Corps toward Gettysburg to look for shoes on July 1. Though Pender and his division were the proper spearhead division of Hill's corps, Heth's brand-new outfit was encamped closest to the objective, and Heth specifically asked for the assignment, expecting little fighting. Whatever should happen, he was undoubtedly anxious to justify Lee's hopes for him as a major general.

GETTYSBURG: Heth's troops were on the Chambersburg Pike marching toward Gettysburg by 5:00 a.m. on the morning of July 1. The entire division was marching there to reconnoiter the town, a move better suited to either cavalry or a small handful of men. The day before, on June 30, Brig. Gen. Johnston Pettigrew had marched with his brigade to Gettysburg and discovered regular army troops in his front. The inexperienced but sage general backed off and reported the presence of the enemy to Heth, but he brushed aside the report and refused to believe it; neither did Hill. When Heth asked to take his entire division into Gettysburg the next morning to scout the area and secure supplies, Hill agreed to the move. It was a careless and fatal mistake.

Heth's column approached Gettysburg with an artillery battalion in the lead, a careless choice that showed Heth expected no serious trouble. Brig. Gen. James Archer's Brigade followed behind, with the commands of Brig. Gens. Joseph Davis,

Johnston Pettigrew, and John M. Brocken-brough brining up the rear. At 7:30 a.m., cavalry outposts were spotted about three miles east of Gettysburg and the first shots of the battle were fired. The cavalry were slowly pushed back about a mile to Herr Ridge, and when that eminence was secured, Heth deployed Archer on the south side of the Pike and Davis on the north side, both facing east. The artillery unlimbered on the crest. It was 9:30 a.m.

Not knowing what was before him, Heth ordered an advance without bringing up the rest of the division—a costly tactical blunder. His two brigades worked their way across the shallow valley in their front and began ascending McPherson's Ridge. Unknown to them or their division commander, two freshly-arrived brigades of the First Division, First Corps of the Army of the Potomac, were rushing to meet them. In this initial confrontation, which lasted until about 11:30 a.m., both of Heth's brigades were shattered and routed. Archer lost about 600 men, many of whom were captured (among them General Archer himself). Davis' Brigade fared no better and was thrown back with similar losses, including large numbers captured in the Railroad Cut. Heth's shoe expedition had stumbled into a disaster. His poor judgment and recklessness ultimately committed Lee to the battle he expressly wished to avoid until his army was concentrated.

There was a noontime lull in the fighting while Heth sent back the news to Hill and reformed his lines on Herr Ridge, bringing up Pettigrew and Brockenbrough and sending his two damaged brigades to the flanks—Archer to the right and Davis to the left. While the battle could have been stopped at this point, other events were now taking place beyond Heth's control. Maj. Gen. Robert Rodes' Division from Richard Ewell's Third Corps had come up on Oak Hill, on the right flank of the Union First Corps, and attacked the defenders on McPherson's Ridge from the north; Lee and Hill arrived to survey the situation with Heth.

At 2:30 p.m., while watching Rodes' attack and seeing that Pender's Division was available to support Heth's men, Lee ordered Heth to renew his attack, and "Harry" dutifully threw his division forward in a head-on assault. Brockenbrough's Virginians struck the Federal "Bucktail Brigade" near the Pike, and further south, Pettigrew's regiments met the Iron Brigade and another Union brigade. Both sides suffered horribly in the desperate fighting which raged on McPherson's Ridge over the next hour, with the opponents often fighting and dying only yards from one another. (One of Pettigrew's regiments alone lost 687 men.) Although Heth's men needed support, he apparently neglected to ask for it even though Pender was readily available.

During the height of the fight, Heth became the victim of a bullet that struck him in the head and cracked open his skull. His life was saved by a new felt hat he had earlier "acquired" in Cashtown. Since the hat was too large, his quartermaster had doubled up a dozen or so sheets of foolscap paper and stuffed them inside the hat, insuring a snug fit. "I am confidently of the belief that my life was saved by this paper in my hat," Heth wrote later. As it was, the bullet knocked him senseless for a nearly 24 hours. Although he insisted in sitting in on Lee's consultations with his officers the next day, Heth's part in the battle was over. General Pettigrew assumed command of the division.

Heth's clumsy and rash leadership decisions had shattered his division and cost him nearly half of his men, who rested on July 2 in reserve. Despite the disorganized and demoralized state of affairs within the division, Lee called upon the men to participate in Pickett's Charge on July 3. Why he would even consider using these troops has never been fully explained. Lining up as the left-front of the attacking column, the men advanced into history with great gallantry, and hundreds more were killed, wounded, and captured in the assault.

Henry Heth was not publicly criticized for his reckless behavior on July 1, perhaps because so many others (Lee included) experienced so many similar lapses during the battle; or perhaps because of his special relationship with Lee. Heth was back in command by July 7, although yet another defeat awaited him. On July 14, he directed the rearguard fight at Falling Waters as Lee's army recrossed the Potomac. Although Heth's role in the matter is unclear, someone issued an order that resulted in hundreds of men getting cut off and captured. Backing away from his previously straightforward style of admitting his mistakes, Heth claimed instead only stragglers had been taken prisoner. He commanded his division with steadfastness and some competence until the final surrender, and briefly took command of the corps during the final winter while Hill was on sick leave.

Heth had a hard time after the war and found it difficult to make a good living. He was involved in the insurance business in Richmond, mining, and other activities. He died several months after a severe stroke in 1899.

For further reading:

Freeman, Douglas S. *Lee's Lieutenants: A Study in Command*, vol. 3. New York, 1944.

Martin, David. *Gettysburg. July 1, 1863*. Conshohocken, 1996.

Morrison, James L., Jr., ed. *The Memoirs of Henry Heth*. Westport, 1974.

Schenck, Martin. *Up Came Hill: The Story of the Light Division and Its Leaders*. Harrisburg, 1958.

PETTIGREW'S BRIGADE:
(2,577 MEN)

BRIGADIER GENERAL
JAMES JOHNSTON PETTIGREW

Johnston Pettigrew—he dropped his first name for most purposes—was more scholar than soldier, and his intellectual accomplishments were probably the highest of any man on the field at Gettysburg. He was also slender and handsome, with shining black hair, meticulously pointed mustache, fastidiously groomed beard, dark eyes, and a high intelligent forehead; his dark complexion indicated his French Huguenot ancestry. July 4th would be his thirty-fifth birthday, and he had already achieved recognition as an author, lawyer, diplomat, linguist, and legislator. Bright to the point of genius, Pettigrew was a renaissance man whose capacity to learn new things and acquire new abilities was inexhaustible. It therefore surprised no one that he developed into a competent military officer.

Born into a wealthy North Carolina family, Pettigrew grew up on a Tyrell County plantation named "Bonarva," that stretched along the Scuppernong River. His early education was by private tutors, and he later attended the University of North Carolina, where he made the best grades ever recorded at that institution. Besides excelling in mathematics, the classical languages, and the liberal arts, he was graceful and athletic, and led his class in fencing and boxing. After graduating at the age of nineteen, no less than President James K. Polk appointed him to an assistant professorship at the Naval Observatory in Washington. When later he decided to take up law, he studied in Baltimore, and then entered the firm of his uncle, who was dean of the bar in Charleston, South Carolina.

His uncle proved hard to get along with, and young Johnston left to study civil law in Germany. He traveled extensively in Europe and became proficient in French, German, Italian and Spanish, with a reading knowledge of Greek, Hebrew, and Arabic. He spent seven years abroad, writing a travel book entitled *Notes on Spain and the*

Spaniards, and spending some time in diplomatic service.

After his sojourn in Europe, Pettigrew returned to his practice in Charleston, entered politics and was elected to the state legislature in 1856. Many goals seemed to be within his reach—perhaps even a run at the presidency—but the winds of war were blowing. Pettigrew sensed the coming hostilities and was named colonel of the 1st Regiment of Rifles, a Charleston militia outfit. The regiment occupied the harbor forts, and in April 1861 took part in the bombardment of Fort Sumter. With civil hostility an accomplished fact, the militia unit was disbanded. Pettigrew, eager to fight at any rank, enlisted as a private in Hampton's Legion as it headed for Virginia. Word got around among his North Carolina friends, however, that he had been seen at a railroad station traveling to Virginia with the Legion without so much as a corporal's stripes, and soon he was elected colonel of the 12th North Carolina Regiment (later redesignated the 22nd North Carolina).

During the inactivity of the next few months in the East, Pettigrew was offered a brigadier generalship, which he declined, protesting that he lacked combat experience. Both President Davis and Gen. Joseph E. Johnston had noticed him, however, and when the offer was renewed in February 1862, Pettigrew accepted. He was given command of a brigade, and he fought with it on the Peninsula at Yorktown, then at Seven Pines, where he was hit by a bullet which entered the lower part of his throat, struck his windpipe, passed under his collarbone, and tore the bones of his shoulder. The bullet cut an artery, and Pettigrew nearly bled to death. While he lay helpless, he received another bullet wound in the arm and was bayoneted in the right leg. Believing his wounds mortal, the young general did not permit any man to leave the ranks to carry him to the rear. Left for dead on the field, he recovered consciousness as a prisoner of war and survived his wounds. He was exchanged in August to find that his brigade had been given to Brig. Gen. Dorsey Pender. That fall and winter, he commanded a brigade in Southern Virginia and North Carolina, but saw little action.

On May 30, 1863, Pettigrew's Brigade and Brig. Gen. Joseph Davis' Mississippi Brigade were traded to the Army of Northern Virginia for two of Gen. Robert E. Lee's brigades depleted at the Battle of Chancellorsville. (This took place after a period of negotiation and "bargaining" between President Davis and the governor of North Carolina.) It was Pettigrew's first opportunity to serve under Lee (Pettigrew had been wounded on the Peninsula the day before Lee took command of the Virginia army nearly one year before). The two brigades were assigned to Maj. Gen. Harry Heth's recently constituted division. Pettigrew was by far the most dynamic, though one of the least experienced, of Heth's four brigade commanders. He was also the senior brigadier, and would take Heth's place if anything happened to him, although he was entirely unacquainted with the division.

Those who remembered Pettigrew from the Peninsula were glad to have him back in the army for the Gettysburg Campaign. "Pettigrew seemed to have every attribute of a great soldier," wrote one who knew him well, "uniting with the brightest mind and an active body a disposition which had him the idol of his men, and a courage which nothing could daunt. He was so full of theoretical knowledge that I think it really impaired his usefulness, but experience, which he was getting fast, would soon have corrected that . . .." Another who tented near him for several months described him in similar laudatory terms, calling him "quick in his movements and quick in his perception and in his decision . . . His habit was to pace restlessly up and down in front of his tent with a cigar in his mouth which he never lighted . . . As gentle and modest as a woman, there was [about him] an undoubted capacity to command, which obtained for Pettigrew instant obedience." He was "courteous, kindly and chivalric [and] unfailingly a gentleman."

GETTYSBURG: After being the first brigade in the army to make contact with Union cavalry outposts east of Gettysburg the previous day, Pettigrew's men were third in Heth's Division's column of march along the Chambersburg Pike on July 1. Pettigrew had warned Heth and A. P. Hill that regular army troops had confronted him the day before, but both superiors had discounted his report—perhaps because neither viewed Pettigrew as an experienced officer. His place in the column on July 1 caused him to miss the disastrous morning battle, during which Heth's two lead brigades under Brig. Gens. James Archer and Joseph Davis unexpectedly met the crack Federal infantry on McPherson's Ridge. When Heth reformed his division on Herr Ridge around noon, Pettigrew was put into line on the right of Col. John M. Brockenbrough's Brigade, whose left touched the Chambersburg Pike. Guarding Pettigrew's right were the dazed regiments of Brig. Gen. James Archer's Brigade, so roughly handled that morning. At 2:30 p.m., Pettigrew received the order to attack the Federals on McPherson's ridge a few hundred yards to the east, and his large 2,500-man brigade sprang forward with Brockenbrough's men. His regiments were aligned, from left to right, as follows: 26th, 11th, 47th, and 52nd.

Pettigrew drove his men across the same land where Archer's men had earlier come to grief, over Willoughby Run, and east up the wooded slope of McPherson's Ridge. The legendary Iron Brigade waited for his left front, and other Federal reinforcements hurried to confront his right. The two lines tore at each other for an hour, at times the muzzles of their guns almost touching. The fighting was frantic, intense and bloody. Hundreds of casualties piled up on both sides. It was here that the 26th North Carolina and Col. Henry Burgwyn had their famous stand-up fight with the Iron Brigade and lost hundreds of men in the process. The weight of numbers eventually told, however, and Pettigrew's men finally pried the Federals off the ridge, too fought out to organize an effective pursuit.

Pettigrew received word during the fight that General Heth had been wounded and that he, the senior yet least experienced brigadier, was now in command of the division. There was little he could do until 3:30

p.m., when the Union men had retreated sullenly east to Seminary Ridge. Pettigrew recalled his bloodied brigade and let Pender's Division take up the attack. The "division" Pettigrew inherited had been bled white by the day's head-on attacks—it had lost more than 40% of its strength, Archer was in Federal hands, and its field officers had been decimated. Pettigrew moved the remnants of his four stricken brigades back to Herr Ridge to bivouac for the night. There, the division spent the entire day of July 2 reorganizing, recovering stragglers, mending the wounded, and burying the dead. That evening the division was moved forward to the western slope of Seminary Ridge, where it waited for the dawn.

On July 3, the Pettigrew's battered division was ordered back into the battle. Lee was looking for a division he could employ alongside Maj. Gen. George Pickett's Division in an all-or-nothing assault on the enemy center. Pettigrew's brigades were chosen because they were already near the position whence the attack would be launched, and they had not fought the previous day. This was a grievous error; Lee had no idea how terribly the division had been shattered on July 1, or he undoubtedly would have chosen a fitter group. It is unknown whether Pettigrew protested the assignment. His brigades were moved forward to Seminary Ridge, just north of Spangler's Woods, a few hundred yards to the left and slightly to the rear of Pickett's Division. From left to right (north to south), they were positioned as follows: Brockenbrough (under Col. Robert Mayo), Davis, Pettigrew (under Col. James Marshall), and Archer (under Col. Birkett D. Fry). The brigades were deployed in one long line of two ranks each, with about one hundred yards separating them; half the men of each regiment were in front and the other half behind, so that when the lines inevitably crushed together, regimental integrity would be preserved. Unfortunately, the left flank of the long division line was wholly unsupported, for the two brigades selected to support Pettigrew had been aligned in his right rear. The problem was further compounded because Pettigrew's poorest and most demoralized brigade was on the exposed flank.

At 3:00 p.m., when the two-hour bombardment of the Union line went silent, Pettigrew stepped over to Colonel Marshall, now commanding his brigade, and cried out, "Now, colonel, for the honor of the good old North State, forward!" The division, numbering at the time around 4,500 men, moved out through woods before breaking into the open. As the division emerged from the trees, Pettigrew saw to his horror that Brockenbrough's and Davis' Brigades were missing on the left, though they soon broke from the woods and hurried forward to their places in line. It was an ominous omen; so were the artillery shells which immediately began tearing apart the gray ranks.

Brockenbrough's (Mayo's) men, however, had been steadily leaking out of the ranks from the beginning of the charge, and halfway across the deadly field came under fire from the left front. The most important brigade of the attack soon broke completely and ran back for the shelter of Seminary Ridge. The Federal fire was afterward concentrated on Davis' Mississippians, who now comprised the left flank of Pettigrew's Division. Still, the three remaining brigades strode forward under Pettigrew's active guidance until they got within enemy canister and musket range, when, one colonel wrote, "everything was a wild kaleidoscopic whirl." Pettigrew's horse was shot, and he continued forward on foot. As the Confederates approached the thundering Union line, Pettigrew was a hundred yards or so from the stone wall when the bones of his right hand were crushed by a canister shot. Despite the pain, he remained on the field exhorting his thinning survivors to press onward. It was a brave effort, and many men from the tattered remnants of Pettigrew's regiments managed to approach within a few feet of the wall, only to surrender or be shot down. Men in blue crowded forward on the left and leveled a crossfire at the Confederates huddled in front. Too weak to drive the enemy back, there was no where left to go but rearward. After a few minutes of this slaughter Petti-

grew's survivors turned and staggered back across the Emmitsburg Road to Seminary Ridge. The Battle of Gettysburg was over.

Johnston Pettigrew had led a charmed life in Gettysburg. He had somehow escaped the deadly fire that had felled so many in his brigade on July 1, and again survived, albeit with a painful hand wound, the desperate attack of July 3. Although almost all of the fighting for the campaign was over, the North Carolina scholar would live only a few days more. On July 14 at Falling Waters, as the Confederate army was recrossing the Potomac River, he was in command of a portion of the rearguard when Union cavalry attacked. His horse plunged, and hampered by his Gettysburg injury, he fell. Although sources conflict somewhat on exactly how he was fatally wounded, Pettigrew was probably hit with a pistol shot while pursuing an enemy cavalryman through a garden. The shot hit him in the left side of his abdomen just above the hip, passed downward, and came out his back.

Refusing to be captured even though it meant more immediate care and a painful transfer, Pettigrew was taken across the river in a litter, where he lingered for several days before dying.

For further reading:

Freeman, Douglas S. *Lee's Lieutenants: A Study in Command*, vol. 3. New York, 1944.

Martin, David. *Gettysburg. July 1, 1863*. Conshohocken, 1996.

Wilson, Clyde N., Jr. *Carolina Cavalier: The Life and Mind of James Johnston Pettigrew*. Athens, GA, 1990.

BROCKENBROUGH'S BRIGADE:
(967 MEN)

COLONEL JOHN MERCER BROCKENBROUGH

Though John Brockenbrough became a colonel early days of the Civil War and led a brigade in several battles, he was never

promoted to general and his leadership never won high esteem in the Army of Northern Virginia. Thirty-three years old at Gettysburg, Brockenbrough was a Virginia farmer who had been educated at the Virginia Military Institute. In 1861, he was made colonel of the 40th Virginia Infantry, which saw action during the Peninsula Campaign as part of Brig. Gen. Charles Field's Brigade. Brockenbrough led his regiment at Mechanicsville, Gaines' Mill, and Glendale in the Seven Days' Battles; his regiment lost 180 men, or half its strength.

Field was severely wounded at the Battle of Second Manassas in August, and Brockenbrough, as senior colonel, inherited command of the brigade. He fought his first battle two days later at Chantilly (Ox Hill), where the Federal forces repulsed his men. He continued in command through the Maryland Campaign in September. His men took part in the capture of Harpers Ferry, then marched with the rest of the "Light Division" to the rescue of the rest of Lee's army at Sharpsburg. Brockenbrough's regiments, however, were deployed on the far right of the division and were not engaged during the late-afternoon attack. At Fredericksburg in December 1862, Brockenbrough's men were ordered to help plug a hole in the Confederate line that Union troops were pouring through. Although some of his men managed to reach the threatened sector, Brockenbrough lost control of his brigade; two of his regiments (and the colonel himself) split off and never

reached the fighting. It was obvious that Field's excellent brigade of Virginians was suffering under Brockenbrough's uninspired leadership. The brigade was still called Field's Brigade even though it had been without him since the previous August, and Brockenbrough was still considered its "temporary" commander; Lee evidently did not consider him worthy of promotion.

In the spring of 1863, Brig. Gen. Henry Heth was brought in from outside the army to restore the brigade's fighting trim. Although Heth led the brigade (now "Heth's Brigade") into the Battle of Chancellorsville, he took over command of the division when Maj. Gen. A. P. Hill was wounded on May 2. Heth's ascension meant Brockenbrough was back in command during the bloody fighting of May 3, where the brigade lost around 300 men storming enemy entrenchments. After the battle General Heth gave Col. Brockenbrough a rare commendation for leading the attack. Perhaps the colonel was learning his trade?

When Heth took command of a newly-created division in the army's reorganization after Chancellorsville, Brockenbrough remained at the head of the brigade in the absence of an available qualified brigadier to replace Heth. By the time the brigade marched down the Chambersburg Pike toward Gettysburg, it had been under temporary commanders for nearly a year, and its morale was shaky. It was widely acknowledged that the brigade was unlikely to regain its élan under the uninspiring leadership of Colonel Brockenbrough.

GETTYSBURG: Brockenbrough's small brigade brought up the rear of Heth's divisional column as it marched toward Gettysburg on the Chambersburg Pike on July 1. Its position in the line of march caused it to miss the morning engagement between the leading brigades of Brig. Gens. James Archer and Joseph Davis and the Union infantrymen on McPherson's Ridge. When Heth reformed his four brigades on Herr Ridge around noon, Brockenbrough's men were put in line on the left center, with their left touching the Chambersburg Pike. Davis' battered brigade was on their left, and Brig. Gen. James Pettigrew's large brigade on their right.

About 2:30 p.m., the command came to move forward, and Brockenbrough's men advanced in tandem with Pettigrew's. The Virginians crossed a shallow valley and ascended McPherson's Ridge in front of Col. Roy Stone's Pennsylvanians and the rightmost regiments of the Iron Brigade. The attack was not aggressively made and Brockenbrough's men gave the Union defenders valuable time to adjust and prepare for the attack. After combat was joined, moreover, the Virginians were apparently content to stand and blast ineffectually at their foe from behind protective rises in the ground and stands of trees. The Federal commands incurred little danger from this generally ineffective fire, and expected to hang on indefinitely against Brockenbrough's feeble effort. The entire Union position was turned on the other flank by Pettigrew's North Carolinians, however, and the stubborn defenders withdrew about 3:30 p.m. to Seminary Ridge. At this point the attack passed to Pender's Division. The tale told by the casualty reports is a damning indictment of Brockenbrough's attack. Pettigrew's Brigade lost more than a 1,000 men in the bitter struggle for possession of McPherson's Ridge; Brockenbrough's lost about 100. The entire division rested on the slopes of Herr Ridge that night and all the next day (July 2).

For a reason that is still unexplained today, Brockenbrough was not with the brigade on July 3 when it prepared to advance against Cemetery Ridge that afternoon; neither was he on a list of wounded colonels. The change in leaders may simply have been because of his weak and ineffective performance of July 1. There may be another reason that is more credible and is often overlooked: the colonel's brother had been killed on July 1, and Brockenbrough had the body buried along the Cashtown Road. He very well may have been distraught over this fact (which may also explain his lethargic leadership on that day). Regardless, in his place was Col. Joseph Mayo of the 47th Virginia, yet another temporary commander for the brigade, which was positioned on the far left flank of Pettigrew's divisional line. The placement of the division's worst (and weakest) brigade in the place of greatest importance to the success of the attack was inexplicable—and no one seemed to notice.

After starting late and having to run to catch up with the rest of the division, the brigade took a cruel shelling from Union artillery on Cemetery Hill. A few minutes later, after an audacious Ohio regiment came up on their left, the Virginians quit the field and ran shamefully to the rear.

Even though Brockenbrough was not present during the attack, his lackluster command over much of the previous year had reduced the brigade's effectiveness and thus contributed to the poor showing of his regiments. At Gettysburg, his once-proud command escaped with a total of 171 casualties in what was probably the most timorous display by any brigade on either side during that crucial battle. Brockenbrough did not leave a report, and although General Heth implied that Colonel Mayo wrote one, it has never been published.

On July 14 at Falling Waters, as Lee's army passed once more over the Potomac into Virginia, Brockenbrough was back in command of the brigade (which lends credence to the theory that he was unable to command for just a short time, possibly because of the death of his brother). Once again, though, Brockenbrough bungled an assignment. Perhaps he was cognizant of his weak performance of July 1; certainly he was aware of the brigade's disastrous exhibition on July 3. For whatever reason, he recklessly advanced his men (Heth may have been to blame) while they formed part of the rearguard. Many were captured along with their regimental flags. Five days later, Brockenbrough's own former lieutenant colonel, Brig. Gen. Henry Walker, was given command of the brigade and Brockenbrough returned to the 40th Virginia. Disgusted with this embarrassing arrangement, Brockenbrough resigned from the army in January 1864.

Brockenbrough continued to serve as a colonel in the 2nd Reserves in late 1864. After the war he lived in Norfolk and Richmond. He died in 1892.

For further reading:

Brooks, Thomas. "Many a Hard Fought Field: The 22nd Battalion Virginia Infantry." *Civil War Regiments: A Journal of the American Civil War*, Vol. 1, No. 3 (1991).

Krick, Robert K. *40th Virginia Infantry.* Lynchburg, 1985

Schenck, Martin. Up Came Hill: *The Story of the Light Division and Its Leaders.* Harrisburg, 1958.

ARCHER'S BRIGADE
"THE TENNESSEE BRIGADE":
(1,193 MEN)

BRIGADIER GENERAL
JAMES JAY ARCHER

Archer, a native of the northern Maryland town of Bel air, was forty-five years old at Gettysburg. He attended Princeton University, where he was tagged with the rather unusual nickname: "Sally." There is some conjecture about Archer's sexual orientation. While some writers point to his feminine nickname as an indication that he was homosexual, Confederate diarist Mary Chesnut mentioned that Archer was a class-mate of her husband's, and according to Mr. Chesnut, "in Princeton College they called him Sally Archer, he was so pretty when he entered." Evidently Archer's smooth, delicate features and slight build accounted for the moniker. Others cite the fact that after his capture at Gettysburg, he played female rolls in the skits put on by the prisoners at Johnson's Island prison camp; Archer though, was slight of build, even frail, and those parts probably fell to him solely for that reason. There is also the testimony of one North Carolinian that at Johnson's Island, after a dinner party, "Capt. Taylor got some whiskey. . .& he had Gen. Archer down & they all got drink together & got to hugging each other & saying that they had slept together many a time." The observer is probably describing nothing more than drunken reminiscing by old army buddies, and it was common for soldiers to huddle together at night, or "spoon," for warmth during cold-weather campaigns. Archer never married, and was not comfortable in the presence of single women. A friend once described the general as "timid and retiring" socially. The only women known to be in his life were his sister and mother.

After graduating in 1835, Archer studied law at the University of Maryland and was admitted to the bar. He practiced until the Mexican War began in 1846, when he joined the Regular Army as a captain of infantry and received a brevet for gallantry at the Battle of Chapultepec. His only wound was suffered in a duel with a fellow officer. (Archer's "second" in the duel was his friend Thomas J. Jackson.) After the war with Mexico was over, he went back to his law practice, then reentered the Regular Army in 1855, again as an infantry captain.

On March 14, 1861, he resigned his commission and received a captaincy in the new Confederate army. He was stationed in Fort Walla Walla in Washington Territory, and had to travel overland to reach the Confederacy. In October he was appointed colonel of the 5th Texas regiment, which was organized in Richmond from independent companies that had made their way to the Southern capital from the Lone Star State.

Archer's regiment was brigaded with other Texas regiments under the leadership of Col. John B. Hood and sent to the Peninsula the following spring. With no real battle experience, Archer was plucked from his regiment—where he had not endeared himself to the Texans, who thought him a tyrant—and promoted to brigadier general on June 3, 1861, and placed in command of three Tennessee regiments after their brigadier was killed in the Battle of Seven Pines. The men of the Tennessee Brigade didn't initially take to Archer, whom they dubbed "The Little Game Cock," any more than the Texans had. ". . .His temper was irascible, and so cold was his manner that we thought him at first a Martinet," wrote one of his men. Archer was "very non-communicative, the bearing and extreme reserve of the old army officer made him, for a time, one of the most hated of men."

Archer's Brigade was combined with five others later in the month to form a new division, the "Light Division," under the command of Maj. Gen. A. P. Hill His first combat at the head of his brigade came with this division in the Seven Days' Battles. After the frustration and bloodshed at Mechanicsville, where the brigade was repulsed while assaulting a strong Union position, Archer's men plunged to within twenty paces of the Union line at Gaines' Mill before being driven back by heavy fire with severe losses. Those actions completely changed the way in which he was viewed by his men. "While in battle he seemed the very God of war and every inch a soldier according to its strictest rules," remembered one of his men, "but when the humblest private approached his quarters he was courteous. There was no deception in him and he spoke his mind freely, but always with the severest dignity." Archer had "won the hearts of his men by his wonderful judgment and conduct on the field, and they had the most implicit confidence in him."

Shifted to Jackson's command in front of Maj. Gen. John Pope's Union army, Archer and his men performed competently at the Battle of Cedar Mountain. At the climactic defeat of Pope at Second Manassas, Archer's men saw heavy fighting in defense

of the Railroad Cut, and Archer's horse was shot out from under him. In the Maryland Campaign in September, Archer participated in the capture of Harpers Ferry, then, on the march to rejoin the main army at Sharpsburg, became too ill to continue on duty, and turned the brigade over to a subordinate. As the Light Division arrived at Sharpsburg and deployed to attack, Archer got out of his ambulance and resumed command, though he could barely stay in the saddle. "My troops were not a minute too soon," remembered a grateful A. P. Hill in his after-action report. "With a yell of defiance, Archer charged [the enemy] ...and drove them back pell-mell." Spearheading the attack that saved Lee's Army proved to be the high point of Archer's Civil War. The next morning, his remaining strength completely exhausted by the previous day's effort, he relinquished command again and went back to his sickbed.

At Fredericksburg, Archer was a principal in another drama, this time one which nearly cost the Confederate army its right flank. As Hill laid out the defensive deployments there, a 500-yard gap was left between the right flank of Brig. Gen. James Lane's Brigade and the left of Archer's Brigade. The area was a marshy wood that Hill evidently thought was impenetrable. When the Pennsylvanians of Maj. Gen. George Meade's division attacked, they exploited this opening and threatened to rupture the Confederate front. Archer, again coming off sick leave on the day of the battle, proved himself equal to the crisis, bending back his line so that it remained firing at the Yankees storming through the gap. He was in the thick of the action, cutting at enemy soldiers with his heavy saber, and for a moment was engaged in a violent struggle with a Federal who held the bridle of his rearing black mare. Brig. Gen. Jubal Early, whose men came to Archer's aid, praised Archer after the fight, writing, "I feel it incumbent upon me to state that to Brigadier-General Archer . . . is due the credit of having held the enemy in check, with a small portion of his men, after his flank and rear had been gained. . .But for the gallant stand made by

General Archer the enemy would have gained an advantage which it would have required a greater sacrifice of life to wrest from him than was made."

Archer and his men were near the end of Maj. Gen. Thomas "Stonewall" Jackson's long flanking column at Chancellorsville. When the rear of the column was attacked by men from Maj. Gen. Dan Sickles' Third Corps, Archer took it upon himself to turn his and Brig. Gen. Ed Thomas' Brigade around and leave the column to repulse the Federals. In so doing, he missed the assault that evening which drove in and routed the Federal Eleventh Corps. Though he didn't clear his decision with Hill, much less with Jackson, there is no evidence that Archer was reprimanded. The morning of the next day, Archer was placed on the right of the front line, and going forward, seized the strategically crucial high ground at Hazel Grove. Artillery was quickly wheeled into position, enfilading the Union lines near the Chancellor House. Hazel Grove was also the "joint" between the separated wings of the Confederate army, and at 10:00 a.m. Robert E. Lee rode up to Archer's Brigade at the grove, signaling the reunification of the Army of Northern Virginia. So many of the high command of Jackson's force had been wounded in the desperate fighting on May 1 and 2 that Archer was actually in command of the Light Division in the latter stages of the battle.

From his writings and the testimony of men who knew him it is evident that Archer was not an especially clever man despite his Princeton education. As he approached Gettysburg in the vanguard of Lee's army on July 1, he had the self-assurance that came with the knowledge that there was very little the enemy could show him that he had not already seen over the last year of warfare.

GETTYSBURG: Archer's was the lead brigade of Maj. Gen. Henry Heth's Division as it marched toward Gettysburg along the Chambersburg Pike on July 1. The brigadier knew enough to expect an enemy cavalry outpost on the road, and thus was not unprepared when, around 7:30 that morning, enemy troopers were spotted and the first shots rang out. After the Confederate skirmishers slowly pushed the blue troopers past Herr Ridge over the next hour and a half, Heth finally deployed Archer's Brigade on the right , or south, of the pike, and Brig. Gen. Joseph Davis' Brigade left, or north, of the roadway.

About 9:30 a.m., Heth ordered Archer and Davis forward to drive the pesky cavalry away once and for all. Archer presciently protested, suggesting that his brigade should not be pushed so far forward of any support, but Heth insisted, and Archer's regiments started across the shallow valley. There is some confusion as to how Archer aligned his brigade, although it was probably deployed from left to right as follows: 7th, 14th, and 1st Tennessee, and 13th Alabama; the 5th Alabama Battalion was not in the line of battle. Archer himself decided to enter the action on foot, largely because of the difficult terrain. When his men slowly ascended the wooded ridge to the east, however, they were surprised by the appearance of the black-hatted veterans of the Iron Brigade, who were just arriving and swarming over the ridge crest. This was just the sort of thing Archer had warned against.

Within minutes the lines of muskets were roaring and Archer lost control of his brigade. His four regiments had broken into two halves, and Archer was with the right wing. Unfortunately, he could not see much if anything of the rest of his brigade, which from that moment on was leaderless. Surprised, tired from a long hot march, and probably somewhat demoralized (several regiments had taken a pounding from artillery during the advance), the right side of Archer's line buckled, followed soon thereafter by the left. The regiments fell back in confusion to Willoughby Run in their rear. Although a stand was made there, the advancing enemy quickly overran Archer's men. The right collapsed completely, then the left, and soon the entire brigade was running for the rear: Archer's veteran brigade was disintegrating before his very eyes. Those not quick enough were taken captive. General Archer, who was sick with fever for the third time in his last four battles and too weak to run, was trapped on the west bank of the ravine and taken prisoner—the first of Lee's generals to suffer such a fate in combat. When taken to the rear, Archer was greeted warmly by his former friend Abner Doubleday, who was now a Union general. Archer refused his hand and rebuffed Doubleday, who had the general sent to the rear. For Archer, both the battle and the war were over.

The sickly general was eventually confined on Johnson's Island in Ohio for about a year. He was exchanged in August 1864 and assigned to command a brigade with the Army of Tennessee, but a few days later was transferred back to Lee's army. With his health completely broken, the sickly general died of simple exhaustion two months later.

For further reading:

Freeman, Douglas S. *Lee's Lieutenants: A Study in Command*, vol. 3. New York, 1944.

Martin, David. *Gettysburg. July 1, 1863.* Conshohocken, 1996.

N.A. "Brigadier General James T. Archer." *Confederate Veteran*, 8, no. 2, 1900.

Schenck, Martin. *Up Came Hill: The Story of the Light Division and Its Leaders*. Harrisburg, PA, 1958.

Storch, Marc & Beth. "'What a Deadly Trap We Were In': Archer's Brigade on July 1, 1863." *Gettysburg Magazine*, #6, 1992.

DAVIS' BRIGADE:
(2,299 MEN)

BRIGADIER GENERAL
JOSEPH ROBERT DAVIS

As he led his brigade into Pennsylvania in the summer of 1863, "Joe" Davis had yet to experience combat. Nor had he been educated in the military arts at any military school. In fact, it is likely the main reason he was a brigadier general stemmed from the fact he was President Jefferson Davis' nephew.

One observer described Davis, who was thirty-eight years old at Gettysburg, as "a very pleasant and unpretending gentleman." He had grown up in Wilkinson County in far southwest Mississippi, with all the advantages of an only child in one of the state's finest families. He traveled north to be educated in Nashville, studied law at Miami University in Oxford, Ohio, then returned to Mississippi to practice in centrally located Madison County. As the nation moved toward war he drifted toward politics as a States' Rights advocate, and was elected to the Mississippi state senate in 1860.

Mississippi seceded on January 9, 1861, and Davis immediately joined the Confederate army, quickly becoming captain of a company from his adopted Madison County. His rise in rank was swift. He was promoted to lieutenant colonel of the 10th Mississippi in April, and four months after was promoted to full colonel and transferred to his uncle's staff in Richmond, where he served for about a year and a half. Without having ever led troops in action, Davis was commissioned brigadier general in September 1862, but the Confederate Senate showed some backbone—they voted eleven to six to reject the commission, and even dared to level the obvious charge of nepotism at President Davis. The affair proceeded to the proverbial "smoke-filled room," where the president promised political plums to the opposing senators in return for their reconsideration of their votes. Two days later, the senators convened to vote again, and this time they agreed to give Davis his general's wreath by a vote of thirteen to six.

In January 1863, Joe Davis was put at the head of a large brigade of Mississippians stationed in North Carolina. Davis was no doubt considerably assisted in his transition from staffer to brigade commander by the fact that two of his three Mississippi regiments were veterans of General Lee's Army of Northern Virginia (one North Carolina regiment was added later.) Davis and his brigade were attached to Lt. Gen. James Longstreet's command for his sluggish Suffolk Campaign in the spring of 1863, in which they saw little fighting, and they joined the Army of Northern Virginia for the first time at the end of May as Lee was assembling the troops for a raid north of the Potomac River.

GETTYSBURG: Davis' Brigade was second in Maj. Gen. Henry Heth's column as it approached Gettysburg on the Chambersburg Pike on the morning of July 1. After his lead elements pushed back Union cavalry skirmishers and secured the high ground where the pike crossed Herr Ridge, Heth deployed Davis' three regiments on the left of the road (one veteran regiment, the 11th Mississippi, was absent in the rear guarding the division's trains). Brig. Gen. James Archer's Brigade was deployed on the right. About 9:30 a.m., Heth gave his two brigadiers the order to advance. He intended to push the Federal cavalry out of the way with one firm shove.

Moving forward quickly but swerving to the left to outflank the Federals near the pike, Davis' Brigade soon became separated from Archer's, which was advancing south of the roadway. The widening of the gap between Heth's two lead brigades became critically important a few minutes later. As Davis ascended a slight rise and prepared to drive the troopers from their perch on the crest of McPherson's Ridge, his men spotted the lead elements of the crack First Division, First Corps, of the Army of the Potomac crossing the Chambersburg Pike and heading toward them on the run. At first everything went Davis' way, and two Union regiments were quickly sent retreating. With more Union men

approaching from the south of the Chambersburg Pike, Davis ordered his regiments into an unfinished railroad cut which was parallel to the road and looked like a protective trench. Unfortunately for Davis and his men, the cut was too deep and its sides too steep to be a good defensive position. Before long, hundreds of men were trapped inside, and only a handful of rifles could be pointed toward the advancing enemy. The 2nd Mississippi had the misfortune of occupying the deepest (western-most) part of the cut, with the 42nd Mississippi extending the line west, followed by the 55th North Carolina. What Davis had thought would be a good rifle trench had suddenly turned into a potential death trap.

The onrushing Federals lined the top of the Railroad Cut and proceeded to slaughter the men trapped within it. "Throw down your muskets!" they yelled, and hundreds of Mississippians complied. Davis and the remainder of his shattered command squeezed out of the cut and retreated back to Herr Ridge, leaving behind about 600 casualties. The brigade had lost all but two of its nine field officers in the mid-morning disaster, and Heth declined to ask anything more of Davis and his men for the remainder of the day. That afternoon, they accompanied the attack of the rest of Heth's Division against McPherson's Ridge, but remained on the north side of the Pike, out of the fighting. They bivouacked on Herr Ridge that evening.

The next day Heth's Division was allowed to rest and reorganize behind the army. On the evening of July 2, all four brigades were moved forward to the western slope of Seminary Ridge.

When Lee decided to assault the Union right center on Cemetery Ridge on July 3 (known thereafter as Pickett's Charge), he selected Heth's bloodied and still disorganized division as part of the attacking column. The choice was a bad one, and likely Lee did not appreciate the full extent of the damage it had suffered on July 1 (although he should have known). Davis was positioned in the left-center of Heth's line (now commanded by Brig. Gen. Johnston Pettigrew). At 3:00 p.m., when the attack commenced, Davis for some reason got a late start, and his men had to run to catch up with the rest of the advancing brigades. Unfortunately for Davis and the rest of the attackers, Col. John M. Brockenbrough's small and demoralized Virginia brigade (led by Col. Robert Mayo) held the far left, on Davis' left flank, where it suffered from an enfilading fire and quickly fell back.

The repulse of the Virginians left Davis' men with an exposed left flank, which was raked by musketry and artillery. The gallant attackers pressed onward despite heavy losses. Many in the brigade viewed the charge as an opportunity to redeem the unit's lost prestige from its actions of July 1. As a result, they drove relentlessly forward and over the Emmitsburg Road directly into the teeth of the Union defense. Canister and small arms fire from the defenders of the Second Corps, many of whom were ensconced behind stone walls or light works, disintegrated what was left of the brigade. The Mississippians fell back and the attack—and the battle—were over.

Davis was one of only three generals to emerge unhurt from Pickett's Charge. The entire battle had cost him all of his field officers along with 897 of his rank and file. Later that month, when Davis contracted typhoid fever and faced a long convalescence, Gen. Robert E. Lee considered consolidating his shattered command with another, but decided against it—perhaps out of a highly developed sensitivity in matters where the President's nephew was concerned. By October Davis was back with his brigade. Despite his poor performance at Gettysburg, he served solidly, though unspectacularly, until the end of the war with Lee's army.

Davis resumed his law practice in Biloxi, Mississippi, after the war. He died in 1896.

For further reading:

Hooker, Charles E. "Mississippi," vol. 7 of Confederate Military History. Ed. by Clement A. Evans. Atlanta, 1899 [vol. 9 of the extended edition. Wilmington, 1987].

Freeman, Douglas S. Lee's Lieutenants: A Study in Command. vol. 3. New York, 1944.

Krick, Robert K. "Failures of Brigade Leadership." in Gary Gallagher, ed., The First Day at Gettysburg, Kent, 1992.

Martin, David. Gettysburg. July 1, 1863. Conshohocken, 1996.

N.A. "General Joseph R. Davis." Confederate Veteran, 5, 1897.

Winschel, Terrence J. "Heavy Was Their Loss: Joe Davis' Brigade at Gettysburg." Gettysburg Magazine, #2 & 3, 1990.

CAVALRY DIVISION:

(6,629 MEN / 17 GUNS)

MAJOR GENERAL
JAMES EWELL BROWN STUART

In 1865, the *Army and Navy Journal*, the nation's leading military journal, examined the phenomenon of cavalry leadership and concluded that "the nature of cavalry service makes their commanders' presence a necessity, as in all formations for attack they lead their columns. They are supposed to possess those rare personal qualities that impart inspiration of invincibility to the squadrons they lead, and magnetize with individual daring each trooper." The South found such a man early on in the person of James Ewell Brown "Jeb" Stuart, the most famous cavalryman of the Civil War.

By mid-1863, Stuart was only thirty years old, and he had already performed two years of heroics with the spirit of a character out of a Sir Walter Scott novel. For him more than any Confederate general, notions of knightly chivalry influenced his approach to leadership. His eagerness to project himself as a Knight of the Round Table transcended the typical mid-nineteenth century Southern infatuation with

such images, and may have been fueled by Stuart's belief that he descended from the warlike Stuart kings of Scotland.

The "Beau Sabreur of the Confederacy," as he was called, was square-built and of average height, with an aggressive physical nature. He had china-blue eyes, and rough-hewn features which prompted his West Point classmates to jokingly call him "Beauty." He attempted to hide his receding chin with a bushy cinnamon beard. The flamboyant trooper often wore a scarlet-lined cape that covered his tunic, a soft hat with the brim pinned up on one side by a gold star supporting a foot-long ostrich plume, elbow-length gauntlets and thigh-high boots, flowers and ribbons in his lapels, yellow sash, and golden spurs. Along with the banjo pickers and fiddlers which provided his headquarters music, Stuart's affectations incurred ridicule from some (mostly infantrymen), while others wrote them off as tasteless frivolities.

The same cavalier spirit that informed his taste in apparel applied to his combat style, for he was a reckless adventurist who loved attention and played shamelessly to the newsmen and image makers. There was a shrewd rationale behind the whole business, however, for as Stuart observed, "if we oppose force to force we cannot win, for their resources are greater than ours. We must substitute esprit for numbers. Therefore I strive to inculcate in my men the spirit of the chase."

Friendly and approachable, Stuart's horsemen gladly followed him on forays and raids. One trooper remarked that "a franker, more transparent nature, it is impossible to conceive." Artillerist Maj. James Dearing regarded Stuart as "decidedly one of the very best officers we have. . .and is generally looked upon with much confidence." As to Stuart's personal habits, Dearing observed: "he neither drinks nor smokes and is the plainest, most straightforward, best humored man in the world."

Stuart's aide John Cooke wrote that he was "ardent, impetuous, brimming over with the wine of life and of rippling flags, of martial music, and the clash of sabres." Another described Stuart as "a remarkable mixture of a green, boyish, undeveloped man, and a shrewd man of business and a strong leader."

Son of a prominent Virginia politician who had been an officer in the War of 1812, Stuart inherited his love of the limelight from his father. His mother's most obvious legacy was his lifelong religious devoutness. When he attended West Point, he was known as a "Bible class man." After graduating in the top third of the Academy's Class of 1854, he campaigned against the Comanches (where he survived an Indian bullet fired into his chest at point blank range) and served in Bloody Kansas. In 1859, Stuart accompanied the force led by Robert E. Lee to crush the John Brown's raid on Harpers Ferry. Stuart wed the daughter of prominent cavalryman Philip St. George Cooke in 1855, but in April 1861 resigned from the army to join the Confederacy; his father-in-law stayed with the Union.

Stuart's served in the first months of the Civil War with the 1st Virginia Cavalry, containing the advance of a Union army in the lower Shenandoah Valley. The regiment then helped pursue and panic the Union army after First Manassas, and Stuart gained a promotion to brigadier general in September 1861. He received command of the army's Cavalry Brigade the next month, and during the winter of 1861-62, acquired a reputation as the finest reconnaissance leader in Virginia (he performed most of his scouting either alone or with a few select troopers). In mid-June 1862, as the Confederate army dug in around Richmond against Maj. Gen. George McClellan's Army of the Potomac, Stuart set out with some 1,000 cavalrymen and for the next three days made a complete circuit of McClellan's army, gathering facts about Union dispositions—especially those along the Chickahominy River. More than any other exploit, this "Chickahominy Raid" made Stuart's reputation. Even the North marveled at this accomplishment, the *New York Times* observing that it "excites as much admiration in the Union army as it does in Richmond. . . . we regard it as a feather of the very tallest sort in the rebel cap." Stuart was quickly promoted to major general and given command of the newly formed two brigade Cavalry Division.

Less than two months later in the Second Manassas Campaign, Stuart crept around Maj. Gen. John Pope's northern flank and struck his supply base at Catlett's Station on the Orange & Alexandria Railroad, capturing 300 men and such rare booty as Pope's dress uniform. In the September Maryland Campaign, the cavalier rode around McClellan a second time, and after the Battle of Fredericksburg in December, raided to within a few miles of Washington, where he tweaked the nose of Union Quartermaster Montgomery Meigs, wiring him on his own telegraph to complain about the "bad quality of the mules lately furnished, which interfered seriously with our moving the captured wagons."

During the Chancellorsville Campaign in May 1863, Stuart stealthily located the exposed Union right flank, then screened Lt. Gen. Thomas "Stonewall" Jackson's attacking column while it marched into position to crush the Federal Eleventh Corps. When Jackson was mortally wounded following the attack, Stuart stepped in and competently directed Stonewall's infantry, consolidating gains and helping to ensure victory. His actions at the head of Jackson's men received elaborate praise from Gen. Robert E. Lee and Maj. Gen. A. P. Hill. By the summer of 1863, Stuart had earned a reputation built not only on extravagance but on effective leadership. The myths that surrounded Jeb and his legion of cavaliers further increased the odds in their favor by tearing at the psyche of the Union cavalrymen.

A blot was placed on Stuart's record, however, in the June 9, 1863, fight at Brandy Station. There, Stuart and his cavalrymen were surprised by a large-scale Federal cavalry offensive and spent much of the day scramblingto hold the field. The battle was the largest cavalry fight ever conducted on the American continent, and ended as a tactical draw. The engagement signaled the rise of the Union cavalry, which from that moment on was recognized as a potent force deserving of respect. Stuart was derided in all the Richmond papers. The story went around that the surprise had occurred because Stuart and his officers were "rollicking, frolicking and running after girls" at a ball the night before.

Stuart was mortified by the press coverage and negative whispers about his performance. With the Gettysburg Campaign already underway he resolved to vindicate himself—a circumstance which may have multiplied his natural impetuosity. As the army snaked northward, Stuart fought a series of engagements at Aldie, Middleburg and Upperville (June 19-21) while screening and holding back prying enemy cavalry. The next day, June 22, Lee issued orders to Stuart to probe and harass the enemy infantry, guard the army's right flank, gather supplies, and remain in communication. On June 25, Stuart moved out with three brigades in an attempt to restore luster to his reputation by once more circling the enemy army altogether. While Lee intended that Stuart find and screen Richard Ewell's Second Corps flank in Pennsylvania and send reconnaissance information to army headquarters, his cavalier found this impossible to do during the last week of June through much of July 2. His ride behind the Union army, which was pushing north ahead of Stuart, cut him off from Lee. Stuart's absence left the commander strapped for horsemen—although Lee still had cavalry other than Stuart to call upon. Stuart's ride, however, was based upon discretionary orders from Lee himself, which allowed him to undertake it. As historian Edwin Cottington wrote, "if orders or suggestions are conditional, the conditions upon which they are based, should be made clear. Lee's orders to Stuart did not meet this standard." Jeb Stuart's role in the campaign is one of the most contentious issues surrounding the entire event.

GETTYSBURG: After crossing the Potomac on June 28, Stuart's Division headed northward, keeping to the east of the Army of the Potomac. Near Rockville, Maryland, Stuart captured 125 wagons, which ultimately slowed him even more. His troopers rode all night toward Pennsylvania, strapped now with wheeled vehicles and captives.

Early on July 1, as A. P. Hill's leading division was moving toward its confrontation with John Reynolds' First Corps at Gettysburg, Stuart's troopers cantered north into Dover, about 23 air miles northeast of Gettysburg. There, he let his exhausted men climb off their horses and get some sleep—their first rest since the Potomac crossing. Scouts fanned out in the hope that one would locate the army. After about four hours, Stuart roused his men and headed northwest toward Carlisle, where he expected to find provisions and perhaps part of Ewell's Corps. After an exhausting ride, Stuart's men found the town occupied by stubborn Pennsylvania militia. Stuart stood by the rest of that day while Brig. Gen. Fitz Lee's horse artillery tried vainly to shell the garrison into submission. About 1:00 a.m. on July 2, one of Stuart's couriers galloped up with the stunning information that the Army of Northern Virginia was heavily engaged at Gettysburg, 25 miles to the south. With that critical information finally in hand, Stuart gave the command, and the cavalry—Fitz Lee's, then Col. John Chambliss', and Brig. Gen. Wade Hampton's brigades—headed toward the fight.

About noon on July 2, Stuart finally found Lee's headquarters on the Chambersburg Pike about a mile west of town. He dismounted, saluted his commander and reported the arrival of his raiding party—over sixty hours late. There are no lack of stories as to exactly what transpired when the two generals came face to face during the middle of the battle. With Stuart standing in front of him, Lee at first rebuked him with a cold silence. According to one credible account, the general greeted him with a question: "General Stuart, where have you been?" When Stuart attempted a reply, Lee cut him short: "I have not heard a word from you for days, and you the eyes and ears of my army!" Stuart must have grimaced at the stinging remark. Lee almost never criticized his subordinates, and when he did he needed few words to produce stinging shame.

Lee regained his calm demeanor, and began to work out a new plan for Stuart's men. Earlier that morning, Hampton had driven off Brig. Gen. Judson Kilpatrick's troopers near Hunterstown, five miles northeast of Gettysburg. Lee saw an opportunity for his horsemen to move toward this locale and then sweep down on the rear of the Union army. On the morning of July 3, Stuart rode quietly out the York Pike with his three brigades, plus that of Brig. Gen. Albert Jenkins. At about 10:00 a.m., the column reached a point on the Pike two and one-half miles northeast of Gettysburg, then turned south onto a farm road. Their progress had been spotted by enemy scouts, and two brigades of Federal troopers were marched out the Hanover Road to block any attempt against the Union army's rear. Another setback occurred when it was found that Jenkins' brigade had not brought enough ammunition and it had to retire from the field earlier than desired.

At about 3:00 p.m., as Pickett's men were stepping off to assault Cemetery Ridge, another sizeable cavalry action began. There were charges and countercharges, and both sides claimed a victory. One Confederate sergeant probably came closest to the truth when he declared it a "draw." The engagement resulted in nothing worthwhile for the Confederates and succeeded only in producing a substantial number of casualties.

Stuart wrote the longest Southern report of the Gettysburg Campaign, arguing that the havoc caused to enemy communications and supply by his raid validated the delay in joining Lee. Stuart further argued pointlessly (and gracelessly) that Lee's army, in particular Maj. Gen. Jubal Early's Division, was not where it was supposed to be. He pointed disingenuously to the fact that Lee had Jenkins' Brigade on hand for reconnaissance, but everyone was aware of Jenkins' shortcomings in that regard. Over the years Stuart's late arrival became one of the accepted explanations for Lee's defeat in Pennsylvania. With Stuart on hand, say critics, General Heth would have known the composition of the Federal force in his path on the morning of July 1, and pushed boldly into the town. Or, Lee would have known of the enemy's concentration and been less eager to engage in frontal attacks and more disposed to slip nimbly around the Union left. One thing seems clear: Stuart made extravagant use of the discretion afforded him by Lee, and Lee's orders allowed him that discretion.

Stuart's status at the head of Confederate cavalry was never threatened. He supervised a reorganization of the mounted arm into a corps in September 1863 (but was never promoted to lieutenant general, an appropriate corps rank). The next spring, as Stuart battled Federal cavalry at Yellow Tavern outside Richmond, a pistol shot struck him in the abdomen. The mortally wounded Confederate horseman died twenty-seven hours later, on May 12, 1864.

For further reading:

Blackford, William W. *War Years With Jeb Stuart*. New York, 1945.

Brennan, Patrick. *Jeb Stuart*. Gettysburg, 1998.

Freeman, Douglas S. *Lee's Lieutenants: A Study in Command*. vol. 3. New York, 1944.

Gorman, Paul R. *"J.E.B. Stuart and Gettysburg,"* Gettysburg Magazine, #1, 1989.

Krolick, Marhsall D. *"Forgotten Field: The Cavalry Battle East of Gettysburg on July 3, 1863,"* Gettysburg Magazine, #4, 1991.

Longacre, Edward. *The Cavalry at Gettysburg*. Rutherford, 1986.

McClellan, H. B. *The Life and Campaigns of Major-General J.E.B. Stuart*. Boston, 1885.

Thomas, Emory. Bold *Dragoon: The Life of J.E.B. Stuart*. New York, 1986.

Trout, Robert J. *They Followed the Plume: The Story of J. E. B. Stuart and his Staff*. Harrisburg, 1993.

Wellman, Manly W. Gray *Riders: Jeb Stuart and his Men*. New York, 1954.

HAMPTON'S BRIGADE
(1,746 MEN)

BRIGADIER GENERAL WADE HAMPTON

Wade Hampton, the senior brigadier in Stuart's cavalry division, was one of the wealthiest men in the nation. He owned thousands of slaves on cotton plantations stretching over huge tracts in South Carolina and Mississippi, more than anyone else in the South. Older than the other officers in the Confederate cavalry, he was the antithesis of the banjo-screnaded "gay cavaliers" who were his peers. For Hampton, war was not a frolic or glorious adventure but a grim business to be discharged as efficiently as possible and without much relish. He conducted his affairs with a courteous reserve befitting the gentleman he was; with his friends he was candid, cordial, and completely free of lordly affectations.

The general was the last of three successive generations of Wade Hamptons. The first had served as an officer in the Revolutionary War and the War of 1812, and when he died in 1835 was the already the richest planter in the United States with 3,000 slaves. His son, the second Wade Hampton, made the family home, "Millwood," almost as much the political capital of South Carolina as was nearby Columbia. He amassed a library of over 10,000 vol-

umes, one of the largest private collections in the country. In this milieu, the ideal of Southern society, the future Confederate Wade Hampton was raised.

Just under six feet in height, Hampton was remarkable for his tremendous physical strength, combined with the fine balance of an expert horseman. "Six feet in height, broad-shouldered, deep-chested. . . with legs which, if he chose to close them in a grip, could make a horse groan with pain," was how a friend described him. He spent his youth hunting, fishing and climbing mountains, which developed his reputation as a sportsman and athlete. He was educated at South Carolina College, and after he graduated he studied law in order to better handle his business affairs. He was in his mid-thirties when the national debate over slavery came to a head in the decade before the Civil War, and by that time he had developed doubts about the economy of slave labor.

Hampton entered South Carolina politics as a dissenter from the "fire-eating" secessionists that held sway in that most militant Southern state, and served as a moderating influence in both houses of the South Carolina legislature from 1852 to 1861. Meanwhile, his father died in 1858. Hampton in his turn administrated the family holdings brilliantly—in 1861, his plantations were producing 5,000 bales of cotton a year, with each crop worth upwards of a million dollars.

Though Hampton argued against secession, once it became a fact he put all his former doubts behind him and placed his wealth and his talents at the service of the Confederacy. He allowed his cotton crop to be used as collateral for government credit, and received permission from President Davis to raise a small private army, or "legion," consisting of infantry, cavalry and artillery. Hampton clothed and equipped his force, called "Hampton's Legion," entirely out of his own pocket. He enlisted some of the best-born young men in the state to fill its roster, and its officers were recruited from the state's elite. Every step of its organization was reported in the newspapers, and its arrival in Richmond in the first weeks of the rebellion was publicly hailed. One of its officers wrote his mother, "It is by all odds the finest looking and best drilled body of men that has left the State." President Davis himself complimented the force on its personnel and appearance.

Hampton's Legion arrived on the battlefield at First Manassas on July 21, 1861, just as the guns were beginning to boom. Its commander detrained his men from railroad cars and marched them directly to the heaviest fighting. Of the 657 men Hampton led onto the field, 121 fell killed and wounded, and a bullet had grazed Hampton's scalp. Even though he possessed no military education or training, Hampton had shown personal courage his first time under fire and an instinctive ability to lead men and read terrain.

Over the next few months, by his professionalism and zeal in recruiting, Hampton won the personal friendship of army commander Gen. Joseph E. Johnston, who put him in command of a full brigade in January 1862 and recommended him for promotion to brigadier general. When he took his brigade to the Peninsula in the spring, Hampton won praise for "conspicuous gallantry" in an early skirmish, and another recommendation for promotion by Johnston, citing his "high merit." Hampton received his general's wreath on May 23, hard won and well deserved. At Seven Pines, his first battle as brigadier, Hampton was again wounded but stayed on the field. He insisted that the bullet be removed from his foot while he remained on his horse, still under fire. During his convalescence in Richmond, diarist Mary Chesnut's entries mentioned the efforts of throngs of admiring women to lionize him, with the note that "to the last, he looked as if he wished they would let him alone." Hampton returned to duty within the month, in time to lead a different brigade through the last of the Seven Days' Battles, where he did not get into the fighting.

After the triumph of the Peninsula Campaign, General Lee organized his cavalry into a division of two brigades under the command of Maj. Gen. "Jeb" Stuart. Stuart's wise choice for his senior brigadier

was Hampton. Called upon to escort the army into Maryland in the invasion of September, Hampton led cavalry for the first time in a brisk fight with the advance units of the Federal army moving toward South Mountain. Later in the campaign, Hampton participated in the Chambersburg Raid, executing a circuit of McClellan's army. He continued to show exceptional talents for leadership by conducting a series of three successful winter cavalry raids behind enemy lines in December, around the time of the Battle of Fredericksburg. These forays captured 300 prisoners and much booty without losing a man; they also won the commendation of Gen. Robert E. Lee himself. Hampton's star had risen so high by this time that when Brig. Gen. Maxey Gregg was killed at Fredericksburg, Hampton was asked to serve as his replacement at the head of the army's famous South Carolina Brigade. Although moved by the request, Hampton had no intention of leaving the cavalry and declined.

The cavalier and his brigade were south of the James River recruiting during the Chancellorsville Campaign, and missed participating in one of the army's greatest victories. Thus, December's cavalry raids stood as his last engagements prior to the Gettysburg Campaign.

Hampton's reputation by mid-summer 1863 rivaled that of his superior, Jeb Stuart, and he was an officer with whom Lee was not willing to part. Perhaps partly as a result of jealousy on Stuart's part, perhaps because of the disparity in their ages (Hampton forty-five, Stuart was thirty) or their education and social backgrounds, Hampton and Stuart did not share the camaraderie that existed between Stuart and the affable Fitz Lee. Despite their lack of personal intimacy, Hampton and Stuart always maintained a high professional regard for one another. Hampton was undoubtedly one of the finest—and perhaps the finest—civilian generals in the officer corps of the Army of Northern Virginia. Despite his total lack of military experience or training before the war, he had evolved into a superb military leader. By June 1863, he had been in command of his cavalry brigade for about a year, and had led it with unexcelled success ever since. His only shortcoming was a tendency to neglect his mounts.

As the army began moving north, Hampton was with Stuart for the Battle at Brandy Station, where his brigade was in the thick of the fighting. He was lightly wounded there, but his brother Frank Hampton was mortally wounded. Hampton's trooper's rode with Jeb Stuart's column throughout the campaign, including his raid behind and around the Union army in late June and early July.

GETTYSBURG: When the fighting began at Gettysburg on the morning of July 1, Hampton was with Stuart's division in Dover, Pennsylvania, 23 miles northeast of the battlefield. All were numb with lack of sleep after three solid days in the saddle since crossing the Potomac, but after a short rest in Dover, the division pushed on toward Carlisle in search of provisions, with Hampton's tired troopers at the rear of the column.

Halting in Dillsburg with the captured wagons and prisoners taken from an engagement near Rockville, Maryland, Hampton received word from Stuart before daybreak on July 2 that the army had been found at Gettysburg, and he headed south that morning. By 2:00 p.m., the brigade had halted a few miles northeast of Gettysburg with the tail of the column a mile south of Hunterstown. Waiting on his horse beside the road, Hampton came under fire from a Federal cavalryman about 300 yards away. Charging the rifleman alone, Hampton with his pistol became involved in a strange duel with the blue trooper at close range. Hampton's chest was grazed by a bullet, and at one point, he chivalrously stopped to let his enemy clean his carbine before resuming the fight. Hampton at last wounded his assailant in the wrist and he fled, but just then another enemy soldier wielding a sword rushed forward and blind-sided Hampton with a saber cut to the back of the head before making his escape. The general's hat and thick hair, and the angle of the blow, saved him from a death wound. He returned to his brigade with a bloody four-inch gash on his scalp as well as a shallow chest wound. Later that afternoon, Hampton's men turned back to Hunterstown and thwarted a drive on the Confederate rear by Kilpatrick's Union cavalrymen. Hampton held the ground until the next morning.

On the morning of July 3, Hampton and his men rode about two and one half miles out of Gettysburg on the York Pike, then turned south with Stuart's other cavalry brigades. Their goal was to get in the rear of the Union army when the end of the cannonade at Gettysburg signaled the beginning the main Confederate effort against Cemetery Ridge. The cavalry fighting began about 3:00 p.m. with the brigades drawn up in line; Fitz Lee held the left, Hampton deployed next to him, John Chambliss' troopers extended the line, and Albert Jenkins' men held the right Hampton's Brigade consisted of the 1st North Carolina, 1st and 2nd South Carolina, Cobb's Georgia Legion, the Jeff Davis Legion, and Phillips' Georgia Legion.

In the swirling hand-to-hand melee with the Union cavalrymen who had met their approach, Hampton received two more saber cuts to the front of his head, one of which cut through the table of his skull. The indomitable South Carolinian continued fighting until he was hit by a piece of shrapnel in the right hip, which finally put him out of action. He was carried back to Virginia in the same ambulance with the wounded Maj. Gen. John Bell Hood. Although his opportunities had been limited in the campaign, Hampton's reputation was enhanced by his performance in Pennsylvania (especially because of his personal bravery).

In September, while Hampton convalesced, the cavalry was reorganized and Lee made Hampton a major general. With his new rank he was placed him at the head of one of two cavalry divisions, with Hampton's rival "Fitz" Lee in command of the other; Stuart retained overall command. Hampton's hip wound was slow in healing, though, and he took a full four months to recover. When Stuart fell mortally wounded at Yellow Tavern on May 11, 1864,

General Lee was unable to immediately name a successor. With Lee himself acting as his own cavalry commander, Hampton continued to perform wonderfully with his division. His exploits at Trevilian Station in June and elsewhere over the course of the next three months prompted Lee to place Hampton in charge of the army's cavalry on August 11. Hampton lost a son in October at Burgess' Mill, where another, Wade IV, fell seriously wounded. In January 1865, Hampton was detached from the Army of Northern Virginia to bolster morale in the state and assist Joseph E. Johnston. He was made lieutenant general the next month and is largely responsible for getting Johnston to fight at Bentonville. Hampton surrendered in April with Johnston in North Carolina.

Hampton returned to his destroyed plantations and proceeded to once again build a prosperous life. He was a two-term governor and senator, and dabbled in railroading as well. He died in 1902.

For further reading:

Cauthen, Charles E., ed., *Family Letters of the Three Wade Hamptons, 1782-1901.* Columbia, 1953.

Freeman, Douglas S. *Lee's Lieutenants: A Study in Command.* vol. 3. New York, 1944.

Gorman, Paul R. "J.E.B. Stuart and Gettysburg," *Gettysburg Magazine,* #1, 1989.

Krolick, Marhsall D. "Forgotten Field: The Cavalry Battle East of Gettysburg on July 3, 1863," *Gettysburg Magazine,* #4, 1991.

Longacre, Edward. *The Cavalry at Gettysburg.* Rutherford, 1986.

Wellman, Manly W. *Giant in Gray: A Biography of Wade Hampton of South Carolina.* New York, 1949.

FITZHUGH LEE'S BRIGADE
(1,909 MEN)

BRIGADIER GENERAL
FITZHUGH LEE

Often called the "laughing cavalier" of the Confederate army, "Fitz" Lee was described by a contemporary as having "a square head and short neck upon broad shoulders, a merry eye, and a joyous voice of great power; ruddy, full-bearded, and overflowing with animal spirits." In his boisterously convivial manner he was a perfect match for his plumed superior and Old Army friend, Maj. Gen. "Jeb" Stuart. An acquaintance of Lee's wrote of "the strain of jollity pervading him. . . .he had hosts of friends, and no end of enjoyment." Another remarked: "he had a prevailing habit of irrepressible good humor which made any occasion of seriousness in him seem like affectation." As a military leader, he was no scholar or strategist, but a man whose strengths were physical—he was a fine horseman, with abundant athletic gifts.

Fitz Lee was only twenty-eight in the summer of 1863, though he disguised his youth behind an enormous shovel beard. A nephew of Robert E. Lee's, he was born at "Clermont," the family plantation in Fairfax County, Virginia. Sent to West Point, he was distinguished mostly for his comradeship and horsemanship, narrowly escaping dismissal for his pranks. A miserable student, he graduated 45th out of 49 cadets in the Class of 1856. Assigned to the cavalry in Texas, he was shot through the lungs with an arrow in an Indian fight in 1859 but managed to survive. He had transferred to safer duty as an assistant instructor of tactics at West Point by the time the Civil War broke out.

Resigning his U.S. Army commission in May 1861 to serve in the army of his native Virginia at the rank of lieutenant, Lee served first as a staff officer to Brig. Gen. "Dick" Ewell and as such was present at First Manassas. The month after that battle he was made lieutenant colonel of Jeb Stuart's 1st Virginia Cavalry regiment. When Stuart rose in the cavalry reorganization in the spring of 1862, Lee was elected colonel by his admiring regiment. Stuart chose him for his famous ride around McClellan on the Peninsula in June, and afterward named Fitz Lee first on the list of men deserving special recognition. "In my estimation," Stuart wrote, "no one in the Confederacy possesses more of the elements of what a brigadier of cavalry ought to be." On the basis of Stuart's report, Fitz Lee was promoted to brigadier general on July 24, 1862, and given a brigade of cavalry four days later, crowning a spectacular rise from lieutenant to brigadier general in the war's first year. "I suppose in a few days we shall see the balance of the Lees promoted also," grumbled Georgian Col Thomas R. R. Cobb, who was annoyed by the Virginian aristocracy the Lees represented.

The next month, Fitz Lee incurred Stuart's wrath by arriving late for the concentration of the cavalry before the Second Manassas Campaign, a gaffe which resulted in the embarrassing capture of Stuart's plumed hat and cape by a Federal raid. Lee vindicated himself in a particularly appropriate way only days later in a Confederate raid on Catlett's Station, where he captured Union General John Pope's headquarters tent, replete with Pope's dress uniform. "[Fitz] slipped behind a big oak-tree," wrote a major who arrived soon afterward, "and, in a moment or two, emerged. . .in the long blue cloak of a Federal general that reached nearly to his feet, and wearing a

Federal general's hat with its big plume. This masquerade was accompanied by a burst of jolly laughter that might have been heard for a hundred yards." The uniform coat was given to Stuart as partial payment for the hat he had lost.

In the Maryland Campaign of September 1862, Fitz Lee expertly covered the infantry's withdrawal from South Mountain, delayed the advance of the Federal army to Sharpsburg, and held the enemy in check the morning after the infantry recrossed the Potomac into Virginia. Uncle Robert, who was careful not to overpraise members of his family in his official reports, had to mention nephew Fitz approvingly three times in his report of the Maryland offensive. Jeb Stuart was not jealous of the rise of his close friend—he also had glowing words for the junior Lee.

After a spectacular February 1863 raid on Kelly's Ford where Fitz Lee, with 400 troopers, captured 150 men and horses with a loss of only fourteen men, Robert E. Lee wrote with obvious satisfaction, "I do not know how I can spare him upon the resumption of active operations, as I feel at liberty to call upon him . . .on all occasions."

In the Battle of Chancellorsville in May, Lee proved his worth to the army as never before. On the first evening of the battle, as General Lee and "Stonewall" Jackson deliberated earnestly on the best way to get at the Union army, Stuart rode up with the news that Fitz Lee had reconnoitered to the west and had found the Federal right flank "in the air." With the receipt of that invaluable intelligence, the two commanders resolved to attempt a desperate flank march and attack with Jackson's whole corps. The next day Fitz Lee's troopers screened and led Jackson's column around the Union right. As the Confederates approached their expected place of deployment, Fitz Lee found Jackson and led him to the crest of a hill from which he could see the enemy: Jackson had not marched him men far enough. Jackson merely muttered new orders to a courier and he and Lee returned silently to the Rebel column as it resumed its march. "I expected to be told I had made a valuable personal reconnaissance—saving the lives of many soldiers—and that Jackson was indebted to me to that amount at least," Fitz wrote later. He would never receive that thanks from Jackson, but the entire Army of Northern Virginia remained in Fitz' debt.

Late in May, Fitz Lee was incapacitated by inflammatory rheumatism, and activity was too painful for him to remain in command. For an entire month he remained out of action, missing the Battle of Brandy Station. He traveled with his brigade in an ambulance in the early stages of the campaign to Gettysburg, and on June 24, when Stuart determined to ride east around the Union army yet again, Lee had recovered from his infirmity. Fitz Lee had been at the head of his brigade for the past year through every kind of duty. West Point and Old Army, a gifted horseman, his only weakness was his lack of strategic skill—he needed to be directed.

GETTYSBURG: When the fighting began west of town on July 1, Fitz Lee was in Dover, 23 miles northeast of Gettysburg with the rest of Stuart's division-sized raiding party. The day was spent riding northwest to Carlisle in search of provisions. In the van of the column when it arrived in Carlisle about 7:00 p.m., it fell to Fitz Lee to expel the two brigades of Pennsylvania militia who garrisoned the town. He shelled the place in vain until the early hours of the morning, when Stuart sent word that the Confederate army had been found at Gettysburg. About 2:00 a.m., Lee's men turned and led the way toward Gettysburg, 25 miles to the south.

July 2 was uneventful for Fitz Lee and his men, who arrived north of town in the early hours of the afternoon, where they halted and rested until the next morning. His brigade was one regiment short, for the 1st Maryland Battalion was serving with Richard Ewell's Second Corps. The balance of his unit, Virginians to a man, consisted of the 1st, 2nd, 3rd, 4th, and 5th regiments. Moving out around 6:00 a.m. on July 3, Lee's brigade brought up the rear of Stuart's cavalry column, four brigades which moved stealthily northeast from Gettysburg on the York Pike, then turned south into

the broad fields east of town. Stuart's goal was to get in the rear of the Union army at the same time the main infantry effort was hurtling toward the Union center on Cemetery Ridge. The cavalry alignment was arranged with Fitz Lee's men holding the left end of the line. When the charges and countercharges started churning the fields that afternoon about 3:00 p.m., Fitz Lee led not only his own brigade, but, for a time, gave orders to some of Brig. Gen. Wade Hampton's men—a liberty which Hampton did not appreciate. Little came of the cavalry battle other than casualties, and both sides retired to their starting positions when the combat died out.

In his long report of the campaign, Stuart singled no one out for praise except Fitz Lee, whose many fine qualities he listed and who, he said, was "one of the first cavalry leaders on the continent, and richly [entitled] to promotion."

Two months later, when the cavalry was reorganized, Fitz Lee was made major general and given command of one of the two new divisions. His rival, Wade Hampton, was given the other. In August 1864, three months after the death of Jeb Stuart, it was Hampton—by reason of his seniority and the fact that he was a better commander—who inherited Stuart's mantle as head of cavalry. In March 1865, however, after Hampton was detached from the Army of Northern Virginia, Fitz Lee took command of the army's cavalry arm and ended the war at its head.

After the war, Lee spent two decades farming Virginia's soil and won the governor's house in 1885. He was consul general to Cuba at the outbreak of the Spanish-American War in 1898, and was given the rank of major general (although he saw no fighting). One of the leading proponents of the Lost Cause myth, Lee died in Washington, D. C., in 1905.

For further reading:

Bond, Frank. *"Fitz Lee in the Army of Northern Virginia."* Confederate Veteran, 6, no. 9, 1898.

Freeman, Douglas S. *Lee's Lieutenants: a Study in Command. vol. 3.* New York, 1944.

Gorman, Paul R. *"J.E.B. Stuart and Gettysburg,"* Gettysburg Magazine, #1, 1989.

Krolick, Marhsall D. *"Forgotten Field: The Cavalry Battle East of Gettysburg on July 3, 1863,"* Gettysburg Magazine, #4, 1991.

Longacre, Edward. *The Cavalry at Gettysburg.* Rutherford, 1986.

Nichols, James L. *General Fitzhugh Lee: a Biography.* Lynchburg, 1989.

Readnor, Harry W. *"General Fitzhugh Lee, 1835-1915."* Thesis, Univ. of VA, 1971.

"ROONEY" LEE'S BRIGADE
(1,169 MEN)

COLONEL JOHN RANDOLPH CHAMBLISS, JR.

In the frantic melee of the cavalry battle at Brandy Station about three weeks before Gettysburg, brigade leader Brig. Gen. "Rooney" Lee fell with a severe gunshot wound to the leg, and his senior colonel was killed. The attrition elevated Col. John Chambliss, who had previously led only three squadrons, to command of the brigade. His first experience at that level would be in the Gettysburg Campaign.

Dark and handsome, with a spade beard and mustache, Chambliss was a thirty-year-old native of southeast Virginia, the son of a landowner who in the summer of 1863 was serving a term in the Confederate congress. Chambliss had been educated at West Point, where he turned in an indifferent performance and graduated 31st out of 52 cadets in the Class of 1853. He was posted with the Regular Army mounted rifles, but lasted only a year as a peacetime soldier before he resigned and returned to the family plantation. Back in Virginia he was active in the militia and served as an aide to the governor. When Fort Sumter fell and Virginia seceded, Chambliss' state militia unit was taken over by the Confederacy. In July 1861 he was commissioned colonel of an infantry regiment, the 41st Virginia, which was placed in Col. William Mahone's Brigade. Chambliss was absent from his regiment during the Seven Days' Battles on the Virginia Peninsula.

Chambliss transferred to the mounted arm and was given command of the newly formed 13th Virginia cavalry regiment. After months of mundane service, on November 10, 1862, the 13th Virginia was placed in a new cavalry brigade under Robert E. Lee's second son, Brig. Gen. W. H. F. "Rooney" Lee. A week later, when the other regiments of the brigade were ordered to Fredericksburg to participate in the campaign of the same name, Chambliss' regiment was left to picket the upper Rappahannock. In April 1863, Chambliss and about fifty troopers fought at Beverly's Ford under the watchful eye of brigadier Lee, who reported, "I cannot speak too highly of Colonel Chambliss and his command." Orders thwarted the possibility of an active role in the Chancellorsville Campaign, where Chambliss was again detached from the main body of the army and posted in and around Culpeper to protect the Orange & Alexandria and Virginia Central railroads against Stoneman's cavalry raid. As a result, he and his men did little more than ride and skirmish.

Although he had enjoyed little chance to distinguish himself thus far in the war, Chambliss was known by the time of Gettysburg to be a competent West Pointer and cavalry tactician. At the Battle of Brandy Station on June 9, he had led a group of dismounted troopers against the Federal advance and had fought well. There was no perceptible anxiety by any of the high command when "Rooney" Lee's brigade came under Chambliss' command.

GETTYSBURG: Chambliss' men rode with Jeb Stuart's column throughout the campaign, including his raid behind and around the Union army in late June and early July. On June 30, Chambliss attacked Judson Kilpatrick's brigade of cavalry at Hanover and captured some prisoners. On July 1, the opening day of the battle, Chambliss' Brigade shared the fate of the rest of Stuart's 4,500-man raiding party—they rode, stupefied from lack of sleep, from Dover, 23 miles northeast of Gettysburg, to Carlisle, 25 miles to the north, looking for provisions and searching for word of the army's location. Stuart finally received a courier with news of Lee's army's whereabouts that night about 1:00 a.m., and Chambliss, along with Fitz Lee and Hampton, moved toward the battle on the morning of July 2. They spent that afternoon and evening resting north of town, broken down and worn out.

On July 3, Chambliss' Brigade was second in the cavalry column that Stuart led out of Gettysburg to the northeast along the York Pike. When they were about two and one half miles from town, Stuart turned south in preparation for a cavalry attack that would, hopefully, put them in the Union rear about the time the main infantry attack on Cemetery Ridge was commencing. Stuart's four brigades were drawn up in line, with Fitz Lee holding the left, Hampton deployed next to him, Chambliss' troopers extended the line left, and Albert Jenkins' men on the right. Chambliss' Brigade consisted of the 2nd North Carolina, and the 9th, 10th and 13th Virginia regiments.

About 3:00 p.m., the same time the cannonade ended south of town, the gray troopers trotted forward in the first attack, and for some time the fields east of Gettysburg were pounded by charge and counter-charge. Chambliss handled his men well in his first large pitched engagement, but the fighting ended in nothing more than a bloody tactical draw. Chambliss finished the campaign escorting and protecting the army's trains as they rolled back to Virginia.

Colonel Chambliss continued in command the brigade and in January 1864 was made brigadier general and given permanent command of the unit (Rooney Lee was still a prisoner of war). When Lee returned and was given command of a division, Chambliss served as one of his brigadiers. He was often mentioned by superiors for his gallantry and ability. On August 16, 1864, he was shot through the body and killed in a cavalry battle on the Charles City Road near Richmond. "His fall will be felt throughout the Army," Lee wrote to Hampton, "in which by his courage, energy and skill, he had won for himself an honorable name."

For further reading:

Balfour, Daniel T. *13th Virginia Cavalry*. Lynchburg, 1986.

Freeman, Douglas S. *Lee's Lieutenants: a Study in Command. vol. 3.* New York, 1944.

Gorman, Paul R. "J.E.B. Stuart and Gettysburg," *Gettysburg Magazine*, #1, 1989.

Krolick, Marhsall D. "Forgotten Field: The Cavalry Battle East of Gettysburg on July 3, 1863," *Gettysburg Magazine*, #4, 1991.

Longacre, Edward. *The Cavalry at Gettysburg.* Rutherford, 1986.

JENKINS' BRIGADE
(1,175 MEN / 2 GUNS)

BRIGADIER GENERAL ALBERT GALLATIN JENKINS

When Robert E. Lee received permission from President Davis to reinforce his army for the march into Pennsylvania, one of his requests was for the services of Brig. Gen. Albert Gallatin Jenkins' Brigade, a cavalry troop of independent "raiders" from western Virginia. Jenkins was thirty-two years old,

"about 5 foot 10 inches high, well-formed and of good physique. The blue-eyed cavalryman, who sported a long heavy brown beard and a pleasing countenance, possessed affable manners and was a fluent conversationalist. He was, "quick, subtle, and argumentative in debate," according to a Southern newspaper correspondent in 1863.

Jenkins was a Southern aristocrat—a slave owner, planter, and politician before the war—whose way of life embodied the spirit of the Old South. His father, already rich from a career operating a fleet of sailing vessels on the James River, had moved in 1825 to farthest west Virginia in Cabell County, along the Ohio River. He acquired an estate of 4,441 acres extending seven miles along the river front and up into the neighboring hills. "Green Bottom" grew into the finest plantation in the county. Albert, born in 1830, received a privileged country gentleman's upbringing at Green Bottom, leaving to study at a series of schools which culminated in a two-year course of law at Harvard. After completing his education in 1850, he opened a law practice in Charleston, Virginia.

During the following decade of intense national debate over slavery, Jenkins developed an active interest in politics. He was chosen as a delegate to the National Democratic Convention in 1856, and that same year was elected to Congress. He served until the outbreak of the Civil War, when he resigned his seat and offered his services to the Confederacy. Although he had no military training or experience, he was among those whose social standing and habits of leadership alone were enough to recommend them for an officer's commission in the Confederacy. He was elected captain of the "Border Rangers," the first company of cavalry formed in Cabell County.

After skirmishing and raiding with his company in the backwater theater of western Virginia during the first few months of the war, he was made lieutenant colonel of the 8th Virginia Cavalry in early 1862, but left the regiment in February to go to Richmond as a representative in the First Regular Confederate Congress. He quickly tired of the committees and bureaucracy in the capital, so he got himself commissioned brigadier general on August 5, 1862, and headed back to western Virginia to lead a brigade of cavalry. Within two weeks of his return, he led his men on a 500-mile raid through Western Virginia and Ohio, an exploit that made him wildly popular back home.

In the summer of 1863, after President Davis approved the Pennsylvania Campaign, Lee attached Jenkins and his men to Lt. Gen. Richard Ewell's Second Corps, which led the advance of the army north of the Potomac. Jenkins and his mountain horsemen had been good enough at guerrilla tactics in their home counties, but were outside their element working in cooperation with infantry in Lee's large and well-organized army; problems arose immediately.

Ewell attached Jenkins to Maj. Gen. Robert Rodes' Division, which engaged an unsuspecting enemy garrison at Martinsburg, Virginia, at the start of the campaign. Somehow Jenkins either misinterpreted his instructions or simply ignored them, for he neglected to occupy key river crossings and allowed the enemy to slip away. Rodes was frustrated and angry at Jenkins' failure at Martinsburg, and matters did not improve as the army moved north. In the advance into Pennsylvania, "irregularities"—horse-stealing, violence to property, and fraud—in Jenkins' Brigade were mentioned in Rodes' reports. The last straw occurred when Jenkins and his men rode into Chambersburg, Pennsylvania, on June 15, a few miles in advance of Rodes' infantry division. Before he could confiscate any property, Jenkins was startled by a bugle signaling the approach of an enemy force from the north. Without even trying to determine the enemy's strength, Jenkins galloped away with his men to the safety provided by Rodes' infantry. As it turned out, the Union force approaching from the north had been a 13-man detachment of Federal troopers scouting the approach of the Confederate army. "The result," wrote Rodes with barely concealed anger, "was that most of the property in that place which would have been of service to the troops, such as boots, hats, leather, etc., was removed or concealed before it was occupied." Ewell wisely recognized the strain that the unreliable Jenkins was putting on Rodes and agreed to give orders to Jenkins himself.

Two weeks later as Ewell's Second Corps was approaching Gettysburg, Jenkins' Brigade was fanned out ahead of the infantry, scouting and probing for the enemy. Unfortunately, Jenkins' men were also straggling badly and melting away from the main army. They preferred the life of "home guards" and guerrillas over the organized warfare practiced by Lee. In addition, Jenkins was a poor disciplinarian and lacked administrative abilities, two key talents that further crippled the usefulness of his command. It was becoming apparent that Jenkins was more of a liability to the Army of Northern Virginia than an asset.

GETTYSBURG: As the Second Corps approached Gettysburg from the north on July 1, Jenkins' men were not in their proper place scouting in the vanguard of the infantry column. Instead, the horsemen brought up the rear, apparently because Ewell forgot to notify them of the corps' move. They were thus among the last in the Second Corps to know that battle had been joined with the Army of the Potomac that day. About 5:00 p.m., just as the fight was winding down for the day, Jenkins crossed Rock Creek ahead of his men and surveyed the debris of the battlefield north of town. Jenkins ordered his men to dismount and

rest, and they spent the night in the fields along the Harrisburg Road two miles north of town. Jenkins' Virginia Brigade consisted of the 14th, 16th and 17th regiments, the 34th and 36th battalions, and Jackson's Virginia battery.

During the morning hours of July 2, Jenkins was summoned to Lee's tent on Seminary Ridge. His task would be the important one of guarding Ewell's (and the army's) open left flank east of town. At that time two infantry brigades, Brig. Gens. John Gordon's and William Smith's, were performing the duty; when Jenkins relieved them, both could take part in Ewell's planned assault against Culp's Hill. Jenkins guided his 1,200-man brigade only for about one mile on the Harrisburg Road before stopping the column. He moved the brigade off the road and into a patch of timber known as Blocher's Woods along the north side of Rock Creek. There his men huddled in the trees for hours, miles from their destination on Ewell's left flank, waiting to play their role in the day's attack (which had, unbeknownst to Jenkins been postponed until late afternoon). This curious behavior leads one to believe that either Jenkins badly misinterpreted his orders, or perhaps he was waiting for a signal or a staff officer to lead him to his place of deployment.

When some time passed and no attack was forthcoming, Jenkins rode forward a short way to Blocher's Knoll, where Brig. Gen. Francis Barlow's Federal division had been crushed by the Confederates the day before. On the treeless mound he took out his field glasses and began to survey the Union positions on the hills south of town, about two and one half miles away. An army staff officer rode up with a map and began to trace for Jenkins the route to the position he was meant to occupy, when puffs of white smoke appeared on the enemy-held hills, followed by the whine of shells. A blinding light and deafening explosion rocked the knoll and knocked Jenkins and his horse to the ground. The animal was killed by the explosion and the general's head and face were covered with blood from a shrapnel wound. The metal fragments effectively ended his small role in the campaign, and Jenkins was carried to the rear.

With Jenkins gone, his brigade never reached its assigned position, and thus Ewell's left flank remained guarded by infantry. Had Jenkins not been wounded and if his brigade had made it to the army's far left, Smith's infantry brigade would have been available for either the evening attack against Culp's Hill, or more likely, the later thrust against East Cemetery Hill. An additional brigade, properly placed in either assault, might have been significant.

On July 3 Jenkins was replaced by his senior officer, Col. M. J. Ferguson, and the brigade's performance immediately improved. However, a final gaffe awaited the men when they were forced to withdraw prematurely from the cavalry battle east of Gettysburg that afternoon because they had only been issued ten bullets each.

Jenkins was taken back to western Virginia, where he recovered and took up command of his irregular raiders again that fall. The next May, his arm was shattered by a musket ball at the Battle of Cloyd's Mountain, and Jenkins died after his arm was amputated, on May 21, 1864.

For further reading:

Dickinson, Jack L. *Eighth Virginia Cavalry.* Lynchburg, 1986

──────. *Jenkins of Greenbottom: a Civil War Saga.* Charleston, 1988.

Freeman, Douglas S. *Lee's Lieutenants: a Study in Command. vol. 3.* New York, 1944.

Gorman, Paul R. *"J.E.B. Stuart and Gettysburg,"* Gettysburg Magazine, #1, 1989.

Krolick, Marhsall D. *"Forgotten Field: The Cavalry Battle East of Gettysburg on July 3, 1863,"* Gettysburg Magazine, #4, 1991.

Longacre, Edward. *The Cavalry at Gettysburg.* Rutherford, 1986.

Shevchuck, Paul M. *"The Wounding of Albert Jenkins, July 2, 1863,"* Gettysburg Magazine, #3, 1990.

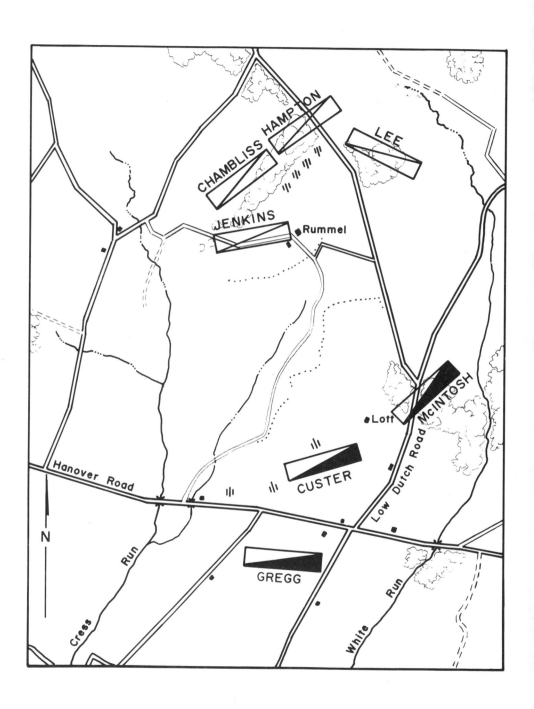

ARTILLERY

BRIGADIER GENERAL WILLIAM NELSON PENDLETON

Though he looked remarkably like Robert E. Lee with his white hair and beard, Pendleton had none of the Army of Northern Virginia commander's military prowess. In fact, Pendleton was one of the weakest links in the Southern army's chain of command.

A Richmond native, Pendleton graduated from West Point in 1830 and served in the U.S. artillery for three years. He spent much of this time, however, lying in hospitals with fever, nausea, and paralyzed limbs from an illness that may have been yellow fever. The ill gunner resigned his commission in 1833 to teach at Delaware College in Pennsylvania. Experiencing fits of depression and neurotic physical symptoms that tormented him throughout his life, he switched careers again in 1837 and became an Episcopal minister in order to heal his "depraved and unsanctified heart." He later assumed the rectorship at Grace Episcopal church in Lexington, Virginia.

Radical abolitionist John Brown's 1859 raid on Harpers Ferry inspired a revival of the Southern militia system. Some of the local Lexington youths formed a battery in 1860 and asked the aging fifty-year old ex-artilleryman to instruct them in the science of gunnery. When the war began the next year, they named themselves the Rockbridge Artillery and elected Pendleton their captain on May 1. He accepted the command, then spent the rest of the day writing a memorandum to himself in which he attempted to rectify his military position with his sacred calling. In keeping with the religious theme of their battery, the artillerists nicknamed their four pieces "Matthew," "Mark," "Luke," and "John." From the beginning of the conflict, the Rockbridge Artillery was a conspicuous presence in the Confederate army, as a press hungry for picturesque heroes picked up Captain Pendleton's story. By early July, the reading public was already familiar with the warrior-minister who, so the story went, had loaded and aimed his gun at Federals in the Shenandoah Valley and then raised his hand in a blessing: "May the Lord have mercy on their misguided souls—fire!"

At First Manassas on July 21, 1861, Pendleton had his horse shot out from under him and was grazed by bullets in the ear and back. He received "great praise" from Brig. Gen. Thomas "Stonewall" Jackson, as well as a mention in Gen. Joe Johnston's report. He was promoted to colonel without delay and, being the first artillerist to distinguish himself, acted as Johnston's Chief of Artillery that fall—a position for which he was wholly unsuited. During this service Pendleton continued to preach, delivering sermons when not drilling, fitting, and organizing the army's artillery. In so doing, he kept himself in the public eye, and was soon rewarded for his efforts: on

March 26, 1862, he was promoted to brigadier general.

Pendleton's deficiencies, however, showed up as soon as active campaigning resumed. While he had dedicated substantial thought to the theory and organization of artillery, he showed no aptitude for actually directing guns in action. At the Battle of Malvern Hill on July 1, Pendleton had charge of the Reserve Artillery, more than fourteen batteries totaling about ninety guns. The Confederate infantry desperately need artillery support during that engagement, yet Pendleton never managed to reach army headquarters and employed only one of his fourteen batteries. He began to be held in contempt by many of his junior officers. One remarked on "the great superabundance of artillery and the scanty use that was made of it" during Malvern Hill, but General Lee was silent on this issue.

Pendleton's Reserve was next used when the army crossed the Potomac into Maryland in September 1862. The parson's moment in the campaign came after the Battle of Sharpsburg on September 17, when Lee counted on Pendleton and forty-four of his guns to guard the rear of the army as it limped across the Potomac River. Not long after midnight a panicked Pendleton wakened Lee in his tent. The Federals had suddenly thrown a corps across the Potomac, he gasped, driving off the cannoneers and their infantry supports; even worse, all the guns of the Confederate Reserve Artillery had been captured. "All?," said Lee with mounting concern. "Yes, General, I fear all," Pendleton ominously rejoined.

When Jackson heard the story, he put a division in motion at once and drove the Federals back across the river. In so doing, he found that an artillery major had actually withdrawn the "captured" fieldpieces the previous evening. Pendleton had been unaware of this, and had given them up for lost, and his prestige plummeted after this embarrassing affair. "Pendleton is Lee's weakness," one lieutenant wrote. "He is like the elephant, we have him and we don't know what on earth to do with him, and it costs a devil of a sight to feed him."

Pendleton's reputation rebounded somewhat with his competent reorganization of the Rebel "long arm" during the fall of 1862 and the first part of 1863. Any meager gains in this area, however, were forfeited by his performance at Chancellorsville in May. When called upon to help defend the Fredericksburg heights with his batteries against the Union Sixth Corps, he bungled the operation by sending most of his guns away prematurely; eight cannons were lost to the Federals before he withdrew. (Some observers said Pendleton retreated in a panic.) Lee carefully praised "the batteries under" Pendleton after the battle—but not the man himself. Hearing that Lee was dissatisfied with his handling of the artillery in the Chancellorsville battle, the Reverend became disconsolate.

In the reorganization of the Army of Northern Virginia after Chancellorsville, Pendleton lost his direct command of the Reserve Artillery. He reverted to his earlier status as General in Chief of Artillery, but the new arrangement was actually a demotion, for he now simply functioned as an advisor.

GETTYSBURG: Pendleton rode toward Gettysburg on the Chambersburg Pike on July 1, arriving at Cashtown and hearing the sound of guns to the east about the same time as Lee. When Lee rode rapidly toward the battlefield in the early afternoon, Pendleton stayed near him for instructions. When they reached the scene of the fighting on McPherson's Ridge, Lee sent Pendleton to the right with some artillery, but the Reverend declined to open fire without infantry support. He moved the guns forward to Seminary Ridge after the Federals had been sent flying back to Cemetery Hill late that afternoon, but failed to open fire on the new Union stronghold, not being aggressive enough to renew the battle on his own initiative (a problem pandemic among Confederate commanders that evening).

Pendleton's most significant contribution on July 2 was as a member of a scouting party that Lee dispatched to the Round Tops soon after sunrise. Although Pendleton probably rode no farther than Spangler's Woods, the rest of the riders continued to a point they later claimed was in the rear of the Round Tops. They later reported that Union troops were not stationed there at that time—a strange finding since several Federal organizations were in the area. Pendleton's report that an attack in that direction "might succeed" may have had some influence on Lee's decision to strike there that afternoon. Pendleton stayed on the right during the afternoon, but the artillery pieces engaged during Lt. Gen. James Longstreet's onslaught were handled by Col. Edward Porter Alexander, the able First Corps artillery chief; Pendleton had little chance to contribute.

Alexander was again employed to do the lion's share of the work preparing for Longstreet's assault on the Union center on July 3. Although Pendleton "reviewed" Alexander's work, he raised no objections to any of the gun emplacements. Pendleton was far too complacent in his judgments, for many of the guns were posted too far away from the enemy on Cemetery Ridge to strike the crushing blow needed to disorganize the enemy line. Pendleton did make one valuable contribution when he rounded up nine short-range howitzers from Lt. Gen. A.P. Hill's corps and collected them into a mobile battery that could be rushed forward to blast away at the enemy during the infantry assault. With the Rebel bombardment at hand, however, Alexander could not find them because Pendleton had reconsidered and withdrawn four of them, while another nervous officer had withdrawn the remaining five—both without informing Alexander. Pendleton created a bigger problem later when, at the height of the cannonade, he moved the ammunition wagons farther to the rear—again without informing the gunners. As a result, artillery fire slackened while gun crews frantically searched for ammunition. Since Alexander wrote one of the best accounts of the Battle of Gettysburg, these blunders by Pendleton became well entrenched in the lore of the engagement.

Despite his gross inabilities, Lee never removed the parson. He remained Chief of Artillery for the remainder of the war,

though it became more and more an administrative and organizational position; Pendleton was seldom consulted when the armies clashed, although he performed good service on the final retreat to Appomattox.

After the war, Pendleton returned to Lexington and his Episcopal Church. He died in January 1883 and was buried there beside his only son, Sandie Pendleton, who had been killed during the war.

For further reading:

Alexander, Edward Porter, *Fighting for the Confederacy: The Personal Recollections of*, Gary Gallagher, ed. Chapel Hill, 1989.

Freeman, Douglas S. *Lee's Lieutenants: A Study in Command*. vol. 3. New York, 1944.

Lee, Susan D. *Memoirs of William Nelson Pendleton, D. D.* Harrisonburg, 1991.

Wert, Jeffrey C. "'Old Artillery': William Nelson Pendleton." *Civil War Times Illustrated*, 13, June ,1974.